THE NEW INTERNATIONAL COMMENTARY ON
THE NEW TESTAMENT

F. F. BRUCE, *General Editor*

THE BOOK OF
REVELATION

by

ROBERT H. MOUNCE

WILLIAM B. EERDMANS PUBLISHING COMPANY

Library of Congress Cataloging in Publication Data

Mounce, Robert H.
  The Book of Revelation.

  (The New International Commentary on the New Testament; 17)
  Bibliography: p. 49.
  Includes indexes.
    1. Bible. N. T. Revelation—Commentaries.
I. Bible. N. T. Revelation. English. American
revised. 1977. II. Title.
BS2825.3.M69   228'.06   77-7664
ISBN 0-8028-2348-3

TO
MRS. GEORGE D. MOUNCE, SR.,
in grateful appreciation for the
profound impact of her godly life.

CONTENTS

Contents

EDITOR'S FOREWORD

The volume on Revelation in the New International Commentary on the New Testament was one which the former General Editor, the late Ned Bernard Stonehouse, had reserved for himself. His interest in this book was of long standing: his doctorate from the Free University of Amsterdam was awarded in 1929 for a dissertation on *The Apocalypse in the Ancient Church,* and a sample of his exegetical study appeared in the article on "The elders and the living-beings in the Apocalypse" which he contributed to the Festschrift for his former teacher, Professor F. W. Grosheide, *Arcana Revelata* (1951). But when he died in 1962 the projected commentary had not taken shape, and it became necessary to find someone else to undertake the task. Happily, Dr. Robert H. Mounce was willing to undertake it, and he has devoted nearly all his spare time to it in the intervening years. The finished product now lies before us.

Dr. Mounce received the Ph.D. degree from the University of Aberdeen in 1958 for a thesis on "The New Testament herald: his mission and message." (A somewhat less technical version of this was published by Eerdmans in 1960 under the title *The Essential Nature of New Testament Preaching.*) Shortly after that he was appointed to the teaching staff of the Department of Religion in Western Kentucky University, where he is now Dean of the Potter College of Arts and Humanities. To the non-academic reading public he is known, among other things, as the contributor of a regular feature, "Here's my answer," in *Eternity* magazine.

Dr. Mounce has thought long and deeply about the problems of the Apocalypse, and his conclusions deserve careful consideration. The Seer, he judges, should be identified with the apostle John. There is certainly no question about the authority with which the Seer speaks. He writes as a prophet—one who, like the great prophets of Old Testament times, has been admitted to the inner council of heaven, and has seen things there which no previous prophet had seen. If his book is entitled "The revelation of Jesus Christ, which God gave to him," this is because John has

9

actually seen God handing over the revelation, recorded in the seven-sealed scroll, to the Messiah who has won the victory of the ages by submission to violent death. The denouement which John sees unfolded before his eyes belongs to the end-time, but from his perspective the end-time is at hand. The return of the Lamb from the place of sacrifice to the heavenly glory and his enthronement alongside the Father have inaugurated the process; the consummation will not be long delayed.

The message of the Apocalypse was well calculated to instill resolution in hard-pressed Christians under the Roman Empire. Their Savior had been invested as Lord of history, and the destiny of the world was firmly secured in his hands. As he won his victory, so they were encouraged to win theirs "by the blood of the Lamb and the word of their testimony." Since the future was his, it was also theirs, for they were on his side: "our Lamb has conquered; let us follow him." With but little modification, the same message speaks a word of encouragement to all those in any age who suffer for their Christian faith.

As in all first editions of this series of commentaries, the English text adopted as a basis is that of the American Standard Version of 1901. Despite its archaisms, this version with its extremely literal rendering (which no doubt makes it unsuitable for many other purposes) is admirably designed to serve as the basis of a commentary which endeavors to pay close attention to the details of the text.

F. F. BRUCE

AUTHOR'S PREFACE

The commentary on Revelation in the New International Commentary on the New Testament was to have been written by the late Dr. Ned B. Stonehouse, who was also General Editor of the series. His death in 1962 was a serious loss to New Testament scholarship. A year later Professor F. F. Bruce, who took over the task of editing the volumes still in preparation, invited me to write on Revelation. Unfortunately, the only access I had to Dr. Stonehouse's thinking was a set of class notes supplied by Dr. William Lane, formerly of Gordon-Conwell Theological Seminary and now my colleague at Western Kentucky University.

For the first several years I occupied myself with reading as much of the literature as I could lay my hands on. Discovering in depth the world of apocalyptic was an exciting experience. Primary literature has an appeal all its own, especially for those whose professional responsibilities require that they spend much of their time and energy reading one another. Considerable attention was given to the development of a detailed syntactical outline of the Greek text. I wanted the book to disclose to me from within whatever organizational structure it might possess. All too often it has been thrust into a predetermined outline. Commentaries tend to begin with an openness to the text which before many chapters have passed narrows into a rigidity which allows the text to say only that which the developing schema allows. Statements which in the early chapters would have been qualified by such adverbs as ''perhaps'' or ''probably'' attain a degree of certainty out of all proportion to the evidence.

During the early period of study I was discouraged to learn that R. H. Charles had spent twenty-five years in preparing his two-volume classic on Revelation for the International Critical Commentary. As I more fully realized the magnitude of the task, the same bit of information was a constant encouragement. Several geographic relocations, a determination not to leave five growing children fatherless, and a vocational shift into administration in higher education have not hastened the completion of the commentary.

A critical problem facing every writer on the book of Revelation grows out of the literary genre in which the book is cast. It is difficult to say what anything means until one has decided in a sense what everything means. What kind of literature are we dealing with is the essential question. An informed sensitivity to the thought forms and vocabulary of apocalyptic is the *sine qua non* of satisfactory exegesis. The vivid and often bizarre symbolism of Revelation has led many contemporary writers into either an indefensible literalism or a highly imaginative subjectivism. I have attempted to steer a middle course because that is the way I believe the ancient text fell upon the ears of the seven first-century churches in Asia to whom it was written. How well this course has been navigated the reader will need to determine.

My indebtedness to critical scholarship in apocalyptic is amply footnoted throughout the commentary. Of the many helpful commentaries on Revelation, those of Swete, Hort (alas, he writes only on chaps. 1–3), Charles, and Beckwith have supplied the most helpful observations on the Greek text. Among recent writers Austin Farrer and G. B. Caird have most often challenged my thinking. The excellent, although relatively brief, commentaries of F. F. Bruce, Leon Morris, and George Ladd represent a common interpretive approach to which I have been drawn through my own study of the text. At times their works gave me pause to wonder whether anything else needed to be said.

A note on my method of reference to the standard works on Revelation is in order. Rather than footnoting each commentary I have simply used the author's name and the appropriate page number. All names used in this way are found in the list of abbreviations, and full publication information is supplied in section A of the bibliography. My intention has been to keep the text and footnotes as clean as possible while not depriving the reader of the additional information necessary for further study.

While the printed text upon which the commentary is based is the American Standard Version (1901), I have used the Revised Standard Version for all biblical quotations apart from the book of Revelation (except where otherwise noted). The third edition of the United Bible Societies Greek text has been followed, although the somewhat simplified apparatus of G. D. Kilpatrick in the second edition of the British and Foreign Bible Society text (1958) is normally cited. Bruce M. Metzger's *Textual Commentary on the Greek New Testament* (1971) has been especially helpful.

I am deeply appreciative of the many individuals who have helped in many different ways. Professor Bruce read an early chapter and made important suggestions. Later he carefully edited the entire manuscript. My wife Jean has read extensively in the literature and time and again has forced me to support a position on firmer ground than I had at that time provided. Two excellent secretaries, Phyllis Rzeszowski and Nelda Steen, have typed and retyped many portions of the manuscript. Drs. Dorothy and Bill McMahon have graciously given of their time to read and correct galley proofs.

I am also profoundly thankful for the opportunity of having lived in the world of John the Seer for the past decade or so. While the specific meaning of every detail may not be clear, the great central truths of Revelation emerge with tremendous force to those who prayerfully open themselves to its pages. Evil has over-extended itself, persecution will come, but God who is sovereign over all will step into human history to vindicate the faithful and forever defeat the forces of evil. To the promise, "Surely I am coming soon" the church responds with confidence and anticipation, "Amen. Come, Lord Jesus" (Rev 22:20).

Bowling Green, Kentucky   ROBERT H. MOUNCE

ABBREVIATIONS

I. COMMENTARIES

Alford	Henry Alford: "Apocalypse of John" *(The Greek Testament)*
D'Aragon	J. L. D'Aragon: "The Apocalypse" *(Jerome Biblical Commentary)*
Barclay	William Barclay: *The Revelation of John*
Beasley-Murray	G. R. Beasley-Murray: *The Book of Revelation*
Beckwith	I. T. Beckwith: *The Apocalypse of John*
Bengel	J. A. Bengel: "Word Studies in Revelation" *(New Testament Word Studies)*
Blaney	H. J. S. Blaney: "Revelation" *(The Wesleyan Bible Commentary)*
Bousset	Wilhelm Bousset: *Die Offenbarung Johannis*
Bowman	J. W. Bowman: *The Drama of the Book of Revelation*
Bruce	F. F. Bruce: "The Revelation of John" *(A New Testament Commentary)*
Caird	G. B. Caird: *A Commentary on the Revelation of St. John the Divine* (Harper's New Testament Commentaries)
Carrington	P. Carrington: *The Meaning of Revelation*
Charles	R. H. Charles: *The Revelation of St. John*
Dana	H. E. Dana: *The Epistles and Apocalypse of John*
Erdman	Charles R. Erdman: *The Revelation of John*
Farrer	Austin Farrer: *The Revelation of St. John the Divine*
Ford	J. Massyngberde Ford: *Revelation* (The Anchor Bible)
Glasson	Thomas F. Glasson: *The Revelation of John* (The Cambridge Bible Commentary)
Hendriksen	William Hendriksen: *More Than Conquerors*
Hengstenberg	E. W. Hengstenberg: *The Revelation of St. John*
Hort	F. J. A. Hort: *The Apocalypse of St. John*
Kelly	William Kelly: *Lectures on the Book of Revelation*
Kiddle	Martin Kiddle: *The Revelation of St. John* (The Moffatt New Testament Commentary)

14

Kraft	Heinrich Kraft: *Die Offenbarung des Johannes* (Handbuch zum Neuen Testament)
Kuyper	Abraham Kuyper: *The Revelation of St. John*
Ladd	George E. Ladd: *A Commentary on the Revelation*
Lenski	R. C. H. Lenski: *The Interpretation of St. John's Revelation*
Lilje	Hanns Lilje: *The Last Book of the Bible*
Lohmeyer	E. Lohmeyer: *Die Offenbarung des Johannes*
Love	J. P. Love: *The Revelation to John* (The Layman's Bible Commentary)
L7C	William Barclay: *Letters to the Seven Churches*
L7CA	W. M. Ramsay: *The Letters to the Seven Churches of Asia*
Milligan	William Milligan: *The Book of Revelation*
Moffatt	James Moffatt: *The Revelation of St. John the Divine* (The Expositor's Greek Testament)
Morris	Leon Morris: *The Revelation of St. John* (The Tyndale New Testament Commentaries)
Niles	D. T. Niles: *As Seeing the Invisible*
Preston and Hanson	R. H. Preston and A. T. Hanson: *The Revelation of Saint John the Divine* (Torch Bible Commentaries)
Richardson	Donald W. Richardson: *The Revelation of Jesus Christ*
Rist	Martin Rist: *The Revelation of St. John the Divine* (The Interpreter's Bible)
Robertson	A. T. Robertson: "The Revelation of John" (*Word Pictures in the New Testament*)
Scott	E. F. Scott: *The Book of Revelation*
Seiss	Joseph A. Seiss: *The Apocalypse*
7C	E. M. Blaiklock: *The Seven Churches*
7CA	C. J. Hemer: *A Study of the Letters to the Seven Churches of Asia with Special Reference to their Local Background*
Summers	Ray Summers: *Worthy is the Lamb*
Swete	H. B. Swete: *The Apocalypse of St. John*
Torrance	Thomas F. Torrance: *The Apocalypse Today*
Walvoord	John F. Walvoord: *The Revelation of Jesus Christ*

II. OTHER

ASV	*American Standard Version*
AV	*Authorized Version*
BAG	Bauer-Arndt-Gingrich: *A Greek-English Lexicon of the New Testament*
Beck	W. F. Beck: *The New Testament in the Language of Today*
BSac	*Bibliotheca Sacra*
CBQ	*Catholic Biblical Quarterly*
comm.	commentary

DNTT	*Dictionary of New Testament Theology*
Epigr. Graec.	*Epigrammata Graeca ex lapidibus conlecta.* G. Kaibel, ed.
ET	*Expository Times*
EvQ	*Evangelical Quarterly*
Feine-Behm-Kümmel	*Introduction to the New Testament,* 14th ed.
Grammar	Dana and Mantey: *A Manual Grammar of the Greek New Testament*
HDB rev.	Hastings' *Dictionary of the Bible.* Rev. ed. by F. C. Grant and H. H. Rowley
HDB	Hastings' *Dictionary of the Bible*
IB	*The Interpreter's Bible*
IDB	*The Interpreter's Dictionary of the Bible*
Idiom Book	C. F. D. Moule: *An Idiom Book of New Testament Greek*
Int	*Interpretation*
JBL	*Journal of Biblical Literature*
JTC	*Journal for Theology and the Church*
JTS	*Journal of Theological Studies*
LAE	A. Deissmann: *Light from the Ancient East*
LSJ	Liddell-Scott-Jones: *Greek-English Lexicon*
LXX	Septuagint
Moods and Tenses	E. deW. Burton: *Syntax of the Moods and Tenses in New Testament Greek*
Moult. *Grammar*	J. H. Moulton: *A Grammar of New Testament Greek,* Vol. 1
MM	J. H. Moulton and G. Milligan: *The Vocabulary of the Greek Testament*
MS(S)	manuscript(s)
NBD	*The New Bible Dictionary*
NEB	*New English Bible*
NovT	*Novum Testamentum*
NT	New Testament
NTS	*New Testament Studies*
OT	Old Testament
Phillips	J. B. Phillips: *The New Testament in Modern English*
RSV	*Revised Standard Version*
SE	*Studia Evangelica*
Strack-Billerbeck	H. L. Strack and P. Billerbeck: *Kommentar zum Neuen Testament aus Talmud und Midrasch*
TCGNT	Bruce Metzger: *A Textual Commentary on the Greek New Testament*
TCNT	*The Twentieth Century New Testament*
TDNT	*Theological Dictionary of the New Testament.* G. Kittel and G. Friedrich, eds.
Tg. Jer.	*Jerusalem Targum*
tgs.	targums
TR	Textus Receptus

UBS	United Bible Societies
WTJ	*Westminster Theological Journal*
Weymouth	R. F. Weymouth: *The New Testament in Modern Speech*
Williams	Charles B. Williams: *The New Testament: A Translation in the Language of the People*
Word Pictures	A. T. Robertson: *Word Pictures in the New Testament*
ZNW	*Zeitschrift für die neutestamentliche Wissenschaft*

INTRODUCTION

I. REVELATION AND APOCALYPTIC
LITERATURE

The book of Revelation is normally considered as belonging to a class of literature referred to as apocalyptic. The term "apocalypse" used to denote a literary genre is derived from Revelation 1:1 where it designates the supernatural unveiling of that which is about to take place. In contemporary discussion "apocalyptic" applies more broadly to a group of writings which flourished in the Biblical world between 200 BC and AD 100 and to the basic concepts contained in those writings. While it is not possible to establish with any precision the exact boundaries of apocalyptic (it often verges off into other literary styles and conceptual modes), it is generally true that an apocalypse normally purports to be a divine disclosure, usually through a celestial intermediary to some prominent figure in the past, in which God promises to intervene in human history to bring times of trouble to an end and destroy all wickedness.[1] The writers were normally pessimistic about man's ability to cope with the evil world. The great cosmic forces which lie behind the turmoil of history are portrayed by vivid and often bizarre symbols. Visions abound. The apocalyptists followed a common practice of rewriting history as prophecy so as to lend credence to their predictions about that which still lay in the future.

The problem of the origin of apocalyptic is far too complex a subject for adequate discussion at this point. Some scholars, such as Betz,

---

[1]Rist defines apocalypticism as "the eschatological belief that the power of evil (Satan), who is now in control of this temporal and hopelessly evil age of human history in which the righteous are afflicted by his demonic and human agents, is soon to be overcome and his evil rule ended by the direct intervention of God, who is the power of good, and who thereupon will create an entirely new, perfect, and eternal age under his immediate control for the everlasting enjoyment of his righteous followers from among the living and the resurrected dead" (p. 347). Cf. introductory paragraphs of Ladd's article, "Why Not Prophetic-Apocalyptic?" *JBL,* 76 (1957), pp. 192–200.

who understands apocalyptic as a Hellenistic phenomenon,[2] and Conzelmann, who takes it as a development from Iranian religion,[3] argue for a non-Jewish origin. While various influences were undoubtedly at work in shaping apocalyptic, the stubborn fact remains that it is essentially a Jewish and Christian phenomenon.[4] Rowley is correct in his judgment that "apocalyptic is the child of prophecy."[5] D. S. Russell acknowledges that while apocalyptic drew nourishment from many sources, "there can be no doubt that the tap root, as it were, went deep down into Hebrew prophecy."[6] Later he writes that apocalyptic is not a substitute for prophecy but a readaptation and development of the same message for a new historical situation—"prophecy in a new idiom" is the phrase he borrows from B. W. Anderson (*op. cit.,* p. 92). Paul Hanson, in a recent and important work entitled *The Dawn of Apocalyptic,* holds that "the rise of apocalyptic eschatology is neither sudden nor anomalous, but follows the pattern of an unbroken development from pre-exilic and exilic prophecy" (pp. 7–8).

George Ladd holds that apocalyptic rose out of a historical milieu which involved a historical-theological problem consisting of three elements: (1) the emergence of a "righteous remnant" who maintained loyalty to the law over against the prevailing mood of compromise; (2) the problem of evil in the sense that even when Israel was apparently keeping the law she was undergoing suffering and national abuse; and (3) the cessation of prophecy at the very time when the people needed a divine explanation for their historical plight.[7] A major role of the apocalypse was to explain why the righteous suffered and why the kingdom of God delayed. Prophecy had dealt primarily with the nation's ethical obligations at the time when the prophet wrote. Apocalyptic focused on a period of time yet future when God would intervene to judge the world and establish righteousness.

The genre apocalyptic may be distinguished by the presence of certain basic elements which combine to form an overall religious or philosophical perspective. In the first place, it is always eschatological. It treats a period of time yet future when God will break into this world of time and space to bring the entire system to a final reckoning. While prophecy was also predictive (contrary to the opinion that the prophets

[2]*JTC,* 6 (1969), p. 155.
[3]*An Outline of the Theology of the New Testament,* p. 23.
[4]Leon Morris, *Apocalyptic,* pp. 30–33.
[5]*The Relevance of Apocalyptic,* p. 15.
[6]*The Method and Message of Jewish Apocalyptic,* p. 88.
[7]"Apocalyptic, Apocalypse" in *Baker's Dictionary of Theology,* pp. 50–51.

were preachers only), a distinction remains. Rowley put it this way: "Speaking generally, the prophets foretold the future that should arise out of the present, while the apocalyptists foretold the future that should break into the present" (*op. cit.*, p. 38).

Secondly, apocalyptic is dualistic. This dualism is not metaphysical but historical and temporal. There exist two opposing supernatural powers, God and Satan. There are also two distinct ages: the present one which is temporal and evil, and the one to come which is timeless and perfectly righteous. The first is under the control of Satan and the second under the immediate supervision of God. Closely related to the teaching of two ages is the idea of two worlds, the present visible universe and the perfect world which has existed from before time in heaven. While some are of the opinion that this dualism betrays the influence of Persian thought, it should be observed that it may also be accounted for by ideas contained in the OT prophets.[8]

Apocalyptic is also characterized by a rigid determinism in which everything moves forward as divinely preordained according to a definite time schedule and toward a predetermined end. While this led to a rather complete pessimism about man's ability to combat the evils he encountered,[9] it nevertheless bred confidence that God would emerge victorious even in the apocalyptist's own lifetime. It also shed some light on the problem of suffering. Concern about why the righteous suffer abated with the growing conviction that all of life had been determined by God and that what he did or allowed was by definition good. Other features that went to make up the apocalyptic outlook include the willingness to abandon the historical process in favor of the all-important consummation,[10] an interest in consoling the righteous rather than rebuking them for their failures, and the conviction that they were living in the last days.

Not only may apocalyptic be distinguished by certain motifs which combine to form its general outlook, but also by several distinctive literary characteristics. Russell identifies apocalyptic as "esoteric in character, literary in form, symbolic in language and pseudonymous in authorship."[11] Beckwith writes that "the highly elaborated vision, or similar

---

[8]Ladd mentions the prophetic expectation of the future kingdom including a redeemed earth, the transformation being accomplished by a divine visitation which will cause a new order to emerge from the old (*op. cit.*, p. 52).

[9]Schmithals writes, "The apocalyptist meets this present age with radical pessimism. The world is on a downward course and cannot be halted" (*The Apocalyptic Movement*, p. 21).

[10]Hanson says that in apocalyptic, history becomes no more than a "timetable of cosmic events" which indicates how close men are to the end (*Int*, 25 [1971], pp. 478 f).

[11]*Op. cit.*, p. 106. These four features are discussed at length in his chapter, "Characteristics of the Apocalyptic Writings" (pp. 104–39).

mode of revelation, is the most distinctive feature in the *form* of apocalyptic literature" (p. 169). The content of apocalyptic normally comes to the author by means of a dream or vision in which he is translated into heavenly realms where he is privileged to see revealed the eternal secrets of God's purpose. Often an angelic interpreter is present to guide him on his heavenly journey and disclose the meaning of the extraordinary things he is seeing (*eg.*, many-headed monsters, cosmic catastrophes, etc.). Such visions are held to have been given to ancient seers and handed down for generations by means of a secret tradition which now in the last days is being revealed to the people of God. The apocalyptist was a "wise man uncovering the mysteries of God's purpose" (Russell, *op. cit.*, p. 117).

While the prophets were primarily preachers whose messages were written down at a later time, the apocalyptists were literary men who put their confidence in the written word as a method of propagating their point of view. The prophet spoke out of an immediate relationship with God. His message was properly prefaced with the open declaration, "Thus saith the Lord." The apocalyptist, on the other hand, adopted a conventional literary style and adapted his message accordingly. Much of his basic material was drawn from a common tradition.

Symbolism plays a major role in apocalyptic. In giving free rein to the imagination, symbols of the most bizarre sort became the norm.[12] Over the years a common stock of remarkable symbols developed. The origin of a specific image is difficult if not impossible to determine with any degree of certainty. While much of it stems from the OT, some of it extends back into ancient mythology. Russell discusses the Babylonian account of a combat between the Creator and a great sea-monster as an example of the influence of primitive mythology on both the canonical and apocalyptic writings (*op. cit.*, pp. 123–25). The extensive use of symbolism in apocalyptic literature may be accounted for in part by its subject matter (the close of this age and the dawning of a new age to come) and by the temperament of its spokesmen. It comes as no surprise that visionaries who specialize in the world to come feel compelled to resort almost completely to symbol.

With only a few exceptions,[13] the apocalypses are pseudonymous. The apocalyptist did not write in his own name but projected his work back

---

[12]*I Enoch* 86:1–4 tells of stars falling from heaven, becoming bulls who "let out their privy members" and "cover the cows of the oxen." These then "bare elephants, camels, and asses" (the three classes of giants, according to R. H. Charles, *Apocrypha and Pseudepigrapha of the Old Testament*, II, p. 250).

[13]Revelation is the outstanding exception: Beckwith refers to the *Shepherd of Hermas* (p. 172), and Rist mentions the apocalyptic treatise by Hippolytus, *On Christ and Antichrist*, as well as Isaiah 24–27, which he regards as "an anonymous interpolation into Isaiah" (p. 350).

into the past by assigning its authorship to some outstanding person of antiquity. As a result, past history is rewritten as prophecy. Although symbolically portrayed, this march of events is usually quite clear up until the time of the actual writer (who understood himself to be standing at or near the end of time). From this point on "prediction" loses its clarity. Pseudonymity is usually explained as an excusable method of gaining a hearing in a time when prophecy had ceased and the law had been elevated to such prominence that there remained no other way for a new voice to be heard.[14] Some have explained it as a precautionary measure taken in times of danger. Others, that it resulted from a sort of fascination with antiquity. Rowley holds that the phenomenon grew out of the genesis of the book of Daniel. The stories in the first part were circulated separately and secured immediate popularity. They were mainly about Daniel. Later, the second part of the book containing visions was written under the guise of Daniel, "not in order to deceive his readers, but in order to reveal his identity with the author of the Daniel stories." Thus the purpose of pseudonymity was "the precise opposite of deceit" and became artificial only when woodenly copied by imitators (*op. cit.*, pp. 40–41).

A more satisfying explanation is suggested by Russell, who brings to bear on the discussion the idea of corporate personality (which stresses the identity of the person and the group to which he belongs), the peculiar time-consciousness of the Hebrews (which could telescope the past into the present and establish such a strong sense of contemporaneity that the Seer became in a sense a spiritual reproduction of the ancient worthy), and the significance of the proper name in Hebrew thought (to take the name of an ancient would be to think of oneself as an extension of his personality).[15] Although these perspectives are relatively unfamiliar to the modern reader, they played a significant role in the world-and-life view of the Hebrew. While we may remain unconvinced that pseudonymity involved no element

---

[14]Cf. R. H. Charles, *Religious Development Between the Old and the New Testaments,* pp. 38–46; cf. S. B. Frost, *Old Testament Apocalyptic,* pp. 11 f, 166 f. Russell says this view of the "autocracy" of the law "cannot find any substantiation in fact" (*op. cit.,* p. 131). Morris thinks Charles may be claiming too much and that "the closed canon was probably one factor in the situation" (*op. cit.,* p. 52).

[15]*Op. cit.,* pp. 132–38. Bruce Jones acknowledges some truth in explanations such as Russell's but notes that "Noah's daughter-in-law was not a person with whom a later writer might easily feel 'corporate solidarity,' nor would her name give authority to any writing" ("More About the Apocalypse as Apocalyptic," *JBL,* 86 [1968], p. 326). Jones writes that pseudonymity (whose function is simply to identify the books as "old") along with *vaticinium ex eventu* prophecy says in effect, "Now is the decisive time. Even the ancient heroes were talking about us" (*loc. cit.*).

of deception, there is no reason to doubt that it was the accepted standard of apocalypticism.

The book of Revelation is regularly regarded as belonging to that literary genre we have described as apocalyptic. It is the NT counterpart to the OT apocalyptic book of Daniel. There are good reasons to support this classification. The extensive use of symbolism, the vision as a major instrument of revelation, concentration on the close of this age and the dramatic inauguration of the age to come, the unveiling of the spiritual order lying behind and determining the course of events in history, the use of common apocalyptic motifs—all combine to justify the application of the term apocalyptic to the book of Revelation. These similarities account for the ease with which the first word of the Greek text (*apokalypsis*) came to serve as a technical designation for all the other literature of the same general class. What is sometimes overlooked, however, are the dissimilarities between Revelation and the rest of apocalyptic literature. Consider, for example, the fundamental fact that the author himself considers his work to be prophecy (1:3, "the words of this[16] prophecy"; cf. 22:7, 10, 18, 19). Ladd notes that although apocalyptic literature had lost its prophetic self-consciousness, the entire NT is the product of the revival of the prophetic spirit (*op. cit.,* p. 53).[17] We have already indicated that while apocalypses were regularly pseudonymous, the author of Revelation identifies himself clearly as "John" (1:4, 9; 22:8; cf. 1:1). He does not search out some notable person in history in an attempt to gain a hearing or to heighten the significance of the present, but writes in his own name with the conviction that he himself speaks the word of God and that therefore his message is both authoritative and binding upon his readers. Bruce Jones emphasizes that John's direct communication with his contemporaries in his own name is too deliberate to be accidental: "We are forced to the conclusion that John wants to stress the difference between his book and previous apocalyptic writing."[18]

While the apocalyptists are generally pessimistic about the present age, John maintains the balance expressed in the gospel logion, "In the world you have tribulation; but be of good cheer, I have overcome the world" (John 16:33). Although there will be an outbreak of Satanic activity in the last days, history remains under the sovereign control of God. Redemption has already been won by the Lamb, who conquered through

---

[16]1611 *pc* vg sy co add ταύτης, making the designation even more specific.
[17]Cf. J. Comblin, *Le Christ dans l'Apocalypse,* pp. 5 f, 85.
[18]*Op. cit.,* p. 327.

death (5:9) and whose great act in history provides victory over Satan for the faithful (12:10–11). While the prospect of suffering is realistically set forth, a genuine optimism permeates the entire work.

Revelation differs from standard apocalyptic in its view of history. G. von Rad stresses that apocalyptic and prophecy have distinctly different views of history.[19] For the apocalyptists the present age is evil and without meaning. It is only a passing interlude on the way to that all-important final period preceding the end. In contrast, the book of Revelation takes as its starting point the redemptive activity of God in history. John does not present a survey of world history as a prelude to God's eschatological intervention, but interprets the period bounded by the two advents of the Lamb in which all the forces opposing righteousness will be destroyed. It is from the perspective of a prophetic *Heilsgeschichte* that the author is able to comfort and challenge a church about to enter into severe persecution.[20]

Other differences between Revelation and apocalyptic could be cited, such as the moral urgency of the Biblical book (cf. the call for repentance in 2:5, 16, 22; 3:3, 19), its practice of simply narrating visions and leaving the interpretive task to the reader instead of supplying a heavenly tutor (17:7 ff and a few other passages are exceptions), its open declaration of eschatological truth rather than transmitting esoteric knowledge secretly preserved from antiquity (cf. Dan 12:9; II Esdr 12:35–38), and the remarkable inclusion of seven pastoral letters to churches in Asia. While there can be no doubt that Revelation shares certain characteristics common to the apocalyptic genre, it would be wrong to overlook all the ways in which it resists being placed without qualification in that category.[21] After surveying a number of features in Revelation that are prophetic rather than apocalyptic, David Hill concludes that the author of the book considered himself a prophet and that although he employed much of the traditional apparatus of apocalyptic his work lacked many of the most characteristic

---

[19]*Theology of the Old Testament*, II, pp. 303 ff.

[20]Feine-Behm-Kümmel write, "The conception of salvation history, in whose center Jesus stands, lies at the basis of the Apocalypse's philosophy of history, gives to it the tone which comes from the certainty of salvation" (*Introduction to the New Testament*, p. 323).

[21]James Kallas argues on the basis of its attitude toward suffering that Revelation is not an apocalyptic book ("The Apocalypse—An Apocalyptic Book?" *JBL*, 86 [1967], pp. 69–80). He holds that in apocalyptic thought suffering comes from the forces that oppose God, while the regular OT view is that it comes from God and should not be resisted. "The nonapocalyptic nature of Revelation is seen most markedly . . . in its total reinterpretation of suffering" (*op. cit.*, p. 78). While it has subsequently been pointed out that the attitude toward suffering in Revelation is not as consistent as Kallas holds (cf. Jones, *op. cit.*, pp. 325–26), it nevertheless adds support to the more general argument that in a number of ways the book diverges from standard apocalyptic.

features of that genre. It "may justifiably, and probably correctly, be regarded as prophetic in intention and character."[22]

II. AUTHORSHIP

The author of the Apocalypse identifies himself simply as John. The epistolary introduction of 1:4 reads, "John to the seven churches that are in Asia." Apparently it could be assumed that there could be no possibility of mistaken identity. The author's matter-of-fact approach and his extensive knowledge of the precise conditions which existed in each of the seven churches indicate that he wrote as a person of authority to Christian communities which were in some sense under his jurisdiction. The name John occurs four times in Revelation. In 1:1 he designates himself as a "servant" who serves as a vital link in making known "what must soon take place." In 22:8 he is the one "who heard and saw these things." His role as Seer is joined with that of faithful witness in 1:9 where he writes, "I John, your brother, who share with you in Jesus the tribulation and the kingdom and the patient endurance, was on the island called Patmos on account of the word of God and the testimony of Jesus."

Within the book itself, however, there is no specific indication as to who exactly this John was. Some suggestions need not detain us long. Dionysius of Alexandria speculates that it may have been John Mark, the young man who accompanied Paul and Barnabas on the first missionary journey (Acts 13:5), but then appears to dismiss the idea on the historical grounds that John returned to Jerusalem instead of going with them into Asia (Eusebius, *Hist. Eccl.* vii.25). There exist no significant linguistic similarities between Mark's gospel and the Apocalypse, nor does the Evangelist display characteristics of a visionary possessed of a strong prophetic consciousness.

That the work is not pseudonymous has been argued convincingly by Charles (I, pp. xxxviii–xxxix). The reasons for Jewish apocalyptists resorting to using the name of an ancient worthy (the centrality of law in post-exilic Judaism and the formation of the canon) were no longer valid

---

[22]"Prophecy and Prophets in the Revelation of St. John," *NTS*, 18 (1971–2), p. 406. Newman has a good bibliography of works discussing the similarities and differences between prophecy and apocalyptic in *NTS*, 10 (1963), p. 134, n. 4. Kenneth Strand reviews the commentaries of Minear, Morris, and Ladd and concludes that they all slight the apocalyptic nature of Rev ("The Book of Revelation," *Andrews University Seminary Studies*, 11 [1973], pp. 181–93).

with the advent of Christianity. Furthermore, there is nothing in the book itself that in any way suggests pseudonymity. Charles concludes that there is not "a shred of evidence" or even "the shadow of a probability for such a hypothesis" (I, p. xxxix). His own position is that the author was "John the prophet—a Palestinian Jew, who late in life migrated to Asia Minor" (I, p. xxxviii). The argument rests on the basis that the author distinctly claims to be a prophet (never an apostle) and his awkward use of the Greek language (it is "unlike any Greek that was ever penned by mortal man"; I, p. xliv). Charles' solution to the problem of authorship has won few advocates. Actually, it does not go much beyond what the book itself teaches, that is, that the author was John and that he was a prophet. It is worth noting that the author of the Apocalypse exercised an authority over the Asian churches that went beyond that normally associated with NT prophets. This leads to the conclusion that although he wrote as a prophet, he functioned among his churches as an apostle. Other variations of an "unidentifiable John" have been offered, but these as well fail to move us toward a solution.[23]

A goodly number of modern writers favor the ancient conjecture of Eusebius that the author of the Apocalypse was probably John the Elder, who is mentioned by Papias as distinct from John the disciple of the Lord (*Hist. Eccl.* iii.39). There is some doubt, however, that Papias intended to distinguish between two separate Johns.[24] But even if Papias spoke of two Johns, and if the report mentioned by Dionysius that there were two monuments in Ephesus each bearing the name of John (Eusebius, *Hist. Eccl.* vii.25) were accurate, it does not follow necessarily that the Elder John was the author of the Apocalypse. It is difficult to see how a single reference in an obscure fragment can supply any convincing basis for establishing authorship. Guthrie brings up the problem of the confusion which would result from the author's failure to identify himself if in fact two authoritative leaders with the same name resided at Ephesus. He writes, "The Elder theory seems tenable only on the supposition that John the apostle had never lived at Ephesus, and that from the early second century the whole Church mistakenly assumed that he had."[25]

In her recent commentary on Revelation in the Anchor Bible, J. Massyngberde Ford argues that the Apocalypse is a composite work emanating from the circle of John the Baptist and his later followers (pp.

---

[23]J. N. Sanders suggests as a "substantial hypothesis" the view that John, the Seer of the Apocalypse, was a Sadducean aristocrat who also edited the Fourth Gospel ("St John on Patmos," *NTS*, 9 [1962–3], pp. 75–85).

[24]Cf. Zahn, *Introduction to the New Testament*, II, p. 452.

[25]*New Testament Introduction: Hebrews to Revelation*, p. 267.

28–46, 50–56). Her hypothesis is that chapters 4–11 originated with revelations given to John the Baptist before the public ministry of Jesus; chapters 12–22 (except for a few passages in the last chapter) were written before AD 70 by a disciple of the Baptist who knew about Jesus but was only partially informed; and chapters 1–3 (plus 22:16–17a, 20–21) were added still later by a Jewish-Christian redactor. Revelation is neither a Christian apocalypse nor a Jewish apocalypse with Christian additions (p. 26). It is a "composite work from the 'Baptist School' which represented a primitive form of Christianity and inherited the Baptist's prophetic, apocalyptic and 'fiery' (boanergic) tendencies" (p. 56). Professor Ford acknowledges that she has advanced a "bold hypothesis" and hopes, not necessarily that it will be accepted, but that it will stimulate further discussion (p. xi). A major question that Ford does not answer is how an essentially Jewish apocalypse ever found its way into the Christian canon. How did it happen that during the same period of time a number of Christian apocalypses were excluded from the canon and a decidedly Jewish apocalypse was included? Until this question is answered, many will suspect that Revelation is more Christian than the author's hypothesis will allow.

Early tradition is unanimous in its opinion that the Apocalypse was written by John the apostle. Justin Martyr, who lived for some time at Ephesus during the first part of the second century,[26] was familiar with the Revelation and held that the apostle John was its author (*Dial. with Trypho* lxxxi.15). This is corroborated by a remark in Eusebius (who himself did not accept the apostolic authorship of Rev), who says that Justin mentioned the Revelation of John, "plainly calling it the work of the apostle" (*Hist. Eccl.* iv.18). In his work against heresies Irenaeus frequently cites from the Apocalypse and holds it to be the work of "John the disciple of the Lord" (*Adv. Haer.* iv.14.1; v.26.1), by which title few would deny that he means the apostle. This witness is of special interest because as a boy Irenaeus had known Polycarp, who in turn sustained a close relationship with John (Eusebius, *Hist. Eccl.* v.20). Clement of Alexandria cited the Apocalypse in several places and accepted it as the work of John the apostle (*Paed.* ii.119; *Quis Div. Salv.* 42; *Strom.* vi.106–7). Writing from Carthage Tertullian quotes from all but four chapters of Revelation (mostly in his Montanist works), holding it to be the work of the apostle John (*Adv. Marc.* iii.14, 24).[27]

---

[26]Charles dates the testimony about AD 135 (I, p. xxxvii, n. 2).

[27]Other ancient witnesses to the apostolic authorship often listed are Papias (according to Andreas of Caesarea), Melito of Sardis (Eusebius, *Hist. Eccl.* iv.26), Origen (*Com. in Joh.* ii.5), Hippolytus (*Antichr.* 36, 50), and the *Antimarcionite Prologue to Luke*.

An important witness for the apostolic authorship of Revelation has more recently come from the Gnostic materials discovered in 1945 at Chenoboskion in Upper Egypt. One of the documents is the *Apocryphon of John,* which cites Revelation 1:19 and claims to be written by "John, the brother of James, these who are the sons of Zebedee." Helmbold cites authorities who date the *Apocryphon* as early as the end of the first century and notes that in any event it cannot be given a date much later than about AD 150.[28] He concludes, "Either date establishes the Apocryphon as an early witness, alongside the secondary testimony of Papias and Justin Martyr in Eusebius, for the Apostolic authorship of the Apocalypse" (*op. cit.,* p. 79).

Although there was some hesitation in the East after the time of Dionysius (mid-third century), it cannot be disputed that the Apocalypse was widely accepted by the second-century church as the work of John the apostle. Morris cites B. W. Bacon (who himself did not accept the view) as saying, "There is no book of the entire New Testament whose external attestation can compare with that of Revelation, in nearness, clearness, definiteness, and positiveness of statement."[29] Opposition to the apostolic authorship apparently began with Marcion, the second-century heretic, who, in promulgating a "gospel of love," ruled the Evangelists blinded by Jewish influence and thus rejected all non-Pauline writing (except an edited recension of Luke). Slightly later the Apocalypse was attacked by a group of heretics in Asia Minor who in their opposition to Montanism rejected both the Gospel of John and Revelation. According to Epiphanius they attributed the Apocalypse to the Gnostic Cerinthus (*Haer.* li.33). Apparently this same ascription was made by Gaius of Rome in the early third century (Eusebius, *Hist. Eccl.* iii.28.1–2).[30]

In spite of the strong external evidence for apostolic authorship the majority of modern writers are unwilling to assign the work to John the apostle. A number of reasons are set forth. (1) The author of Revelation calls himself John (1:1), a servant of God (1:1), a brother of his readers (1:9), and a prophet (22:8), but nowhere calls himself an apostle. In answer to this objection it only needs to be noted that the authority with which he writes reveals an implicit assumption of apostolicity and in no way would be materially strengthened by insisting on a title. To the contrary, that he does not feel obliged to remind his readers of apostolic rank strengthens the

---

[28]"A Note on the Authorship of the Apocalypse," *NTS,* 8 [1961–2], pp. 77–79.
[29]Morris, p. 27; Bacon, *The Making of the New Testament,* pp. 190–91.
[30]Disputed by Westcott, *On the Canon of the New Testament,* p. 275, n. 2. Charles calls authorship by Cerinthus "an utterly baseless and gratuitous hypothesis" (I, p. xxxix, n. 2).

authority with which he writes. (2) There is nothing in the Apocalypse that indicates the author knew the historical Jesus nor are there any indications that he was present at those events depicted in the gospels which involved the disciple John. This, of course, is an argument from silence and fails to consider the specific purpose of the Apocalypse. While the gospels dealt specifically with the ministry of the historic Jesus, the Revelation looks forward to the consummation of history. (3) There exists a tradition that John the apostle suffered an early martyrdom which would preclude the possibility that he wrote any of the "Johannine" material. Charles reviews the testimony and concludes that "John the Apostle was never in Asia Minor, and that he died a martyr's death" between about AD 64 and 70 (I, pp. xlv–1; conclusion on p. 1). Beckwith, on the other hand, writes an excursus of some 15,000 words on "The Tradition of John the Apostle at Ephesus" (pp. 366–93) and concludes that "in every instance there appear good grounds for questioning the validity of the inference drawn against the tradition (that John was martyred and never lived in Asia)" (p. 393). The weakness of the tradition and the compelling evidence to the contrary have led most writers to avoid arriving at a conclusion about authorship on the basis that the apostle could conceivably have been martyred at an early date. (4) Another argument against apostolic authorship was first advanced by Dionysius, bishop of Alexandria, about the middle of the third century. Disturbed by the excessive chiliasm in his diocese, Dionysius attempted to remove the Apocalypse from the arsenal of his theological opponents by comparing it with the Gospel and the Epistle, concluding that it could not have been written by the same author (Eusebius, *Hist. Eccl.* vii.25). Assuming that the other works were apostolic in origin led to the conclusion that the Apocalypse must necessarily have been the work of some other John. He mentions a report that in Ephesus there were two monuments each bearing the name of John and leaves the impression that the other John was perhaps the author of Revelation. In dwelling on the distinctions in language, style, and thought, Dionysius set the pattern for much modern Biblical criticism. He notes the many similarities between the Gospel and the Epistle and then declares that the Apocalypse contains "not . . . a syllable in common with them." While the former are "most elegant in diction," the latter includes "barbarous idioms, and in some places solecisms." Charles concludes that "the theory of Dionysius as to diversity of authorship has passed out of the region of hypothesis and may now be safely regarded as an established conclusion" (I, p. xl).

While dissimilarity with the Gospel neither proves nor disproves the apostolic authorship of the Apocalypse (since more often than not the Gospel is held by modern critics to be the work of someone other than John the apostle),[31] it inevitably enters the discussion. The linguistic evidence which would indicate separate authorship has been assembled by Charles.[32] A comparison of the two works reveals a number of differences. While the Greek of the Gospel is relatively simple and normally correct, the Apocalypse seems to pay little attention to the basic laws of concord. There are differences in vocabulary, style, and thought. For instance, the verb "to believe" is found ninety-eight times in the Gospel, but is absent from the Apocalypse. Words with one meaning in the Gospel have a somewhat different meaning in the Apocalypse.[33] Swete notes that one out of every eight words in the Apocalypse is not found elsewhere in the NT (p. cxxi). While the eschatological focus of the Apocalypse is on a time yet future in which God will bring salvation, the Gospel is concerned with an eschatology that has already been "realized" in the present age. Other theological differences are thought to exist in such areas as the doctrine of God (creatorship and majesty vs. love), Christology (conquering Messiah vs. revealer of God), and the doctrine of the Spirit (the seven spirits of Rev 1:4 vs. the Paraclete).

The dissimilarities just mentioned are widely acknowledged. They have been discussed at great lengths in the literature. What is less often stressed is the significant number of similarities that exist between the books. The Gospel and Revelation share a number of characteristic words and phrases. Certain words are used with the same special meaning. For example, *logos* is used in a personal sense in Revelation 19:13 and elsewhere in the NT only in John 1:1, 14 and I John 1:1 in the same way. The prophecy of Zechariah 12:10 regarding Jerusalem looking on the one they have pierced is quoted in both Revelation 1:7 and John 19:37 using the same Greek verb (*ekkenteō*), which in turn is not used by the LXX nor is it found elsewhere in the NT. At the close of a substantive discussion of the vocabulary, grammar, and style of the Apocalypse, Swete concludes that the evidence "creates a strong presumption of affinity between the Fourth Gospel and the Apocalypse" (p. cxxx).

Guthrie argues that there are internal considerations which pose serious difficulties if authorship is denied to the apostle John.[34] Unless the

---

[31]After surveying the question, F. C. Grant concludes that it is "impossible to ascribe it [the Gospel of John] to the son of Zebedee without a full explanation of serious difficulties and discrepancies" (*HDB rev.*, p. 515).

[32]I, pp. xxix–xxxii; cf. also the forty-two-page "Short Grammar of the Apocalypse," I, pp. cxvii–clix, for all the grammatical peculiarities of the Apocalypse.

[33]*Eg.*, ἀληθινός is said by Charles to mean "genuine" as opposed to unreal in the Gospel, while it means "true in word as opposed to false" in the Apocalypse (I, p. xxxi; cf. other examples *in loco.*).

[34]This point is convincingly made on pp. 256–58 (*op. cit.*).

writer John were the apostle and his authority therefore recognized, how can we account for such a bold departure from the apocalyptic tradition in which he dispenses with the device of pseudonymity and writes in his own name under the conviction that the spirit of prophecy had once again become active? If we remember that in the Synoptics John and James are called "Boanerges . . . sons of thunder" (Mk 3:17) and that they wanted the Lord to call down fire from heaven upon a Samaritan village (Lk 9:54), it does not appear out of character for this same John to be the one who in the Apocalypse describes the plagues which are about to fall upon the enemies of God in the final days.

Who then was the John who wrote the Revelation? Internal evidence has convinced the majority of writers that whoever he was, there is little possibility that he was also the author of the Fourth Gospel.[35] Apart from the possibility that in some way the apostle may have given rise in Asia to a tradition which later found expression in the Apocalypse, John the son of Zebedee is held to have had no part in the last book of the Bible. On the other hand, the unusually strong and early external evidence supporting apostolic authorship should cause us to hesitate before accepting a conclusion based on subjective appraisal of internal considerations. Since internal evidence is not entirely unfavorable to apostolic authorship and since external evidence is unanimous in its support, the wisest course of action is either to leave the question open or to accept in a tentative way that the Apocalypse was written by John the apostle, son of Zebedee and disciple of Jesus.

III. DATE

The book of Revelation has been dated as early as Claudius (AD 41–54) and as late as Trajan (AD 98–117). The early date[36] interprets certain statements and allusions as best understood in light of the political, cultural, and religious milieu of the middle of the first century. The late date is found only in authorities many centuries removed from the events. Dorotheus, a sixth-century ascetic, and Theophylact, an eleventh-century Byzantine exegete, place John's exile in the time of Trajan.[37] The majority of scholars

[35]Caird acknowledges the possibility of mounting a case for common authorship but adds that "the balance of probability is still against it" (p. 5).

[36]Maintained by Epiphanius, fourth-century bishop of Salamis (*Haer*. li.12), although Guthrie notes that "this was no doubt an error for Nero Claudius" (*op. cit.*, p. 277).

[37]*Synopsis de vita et morte prophetarum* is attributed to Dorotheus; cf. Theophylact on Mt 20:22 (it is interesting to note that he wrote commentaries on all the books of the NT except Revelation!). Swete (p. c) notes that the reference to Trajan was perhaps suggested by Irenaeus, *Adv. Haer*. ii.22.5.

place the composition of the Apocalypse either during the reign of Domitian (AD 81–96) or toward the end or immediately after the reign of Nero (AD 54–68). Since the Domitian date is accepted by most writers, it will be examined first.

The earliest external reference placing Revelation in the reign of Domitian is that of Irenaeus.[38] Speaking of the Apocalypse he says, "For it was seen, not long ago, but almost in our generation, near the end of Domitian's reign" (*Adv. Haer.* v.30.3; cf. ii.22.5; iii.4.4). Although Hort, along with Westcott and Lightfoot at Cambridge, regarded the work as originating during the reign of Nero or shortly thereafter, he admitted that "if external evidence alone could decide, there would be a clear preponderance for Domitian" (p. xx).[39] The words of Irenaeus are later quoted by Eusebius (*Hist. Eccl.* iii.18.3). While Clement of Alexandria (*Quis Div. Salv.* 42) and Origen (*In Mt.* xvi.6), early third century, do not actually use the name of Domitian, there is little doubt that he is the emperor they have in mind. Later references quite explicitly place the Apocalypse in the time of Domitian: Victorinus (*In Apoc.* x.11; xvii.10), Eusebius (*Hist. Eccl.* iii.18.1; iii.20.9; iii.23.1), and Jerome (*De Vir. Illus.* ix).

When one turns to Revelation itself, it is evident that the background is one of conflict between the demands of a totalitarian secular power and allegiance to the Christian faith.[40] The Roman Empire is personified as a beast who demands universal worship (13:4, 15–17; 14:9; 16:2; 19:20), insisting that all men bear his "mark" or be put to death (13:15–17; 14:9; 16:2; 19:20; 20:4). These references can be reasonably interpreted only in terms of the development of the imperial cult, specifically in Asia Minor. The concept of emperor worship had a natural evolution in the ancient Gentile world, aided by polytheism, ancestor-worship, and the subsequent deification of legendary heroes. In the Roman Empire an earlier deification of the state among the provinces provided the rationale for emperors to strengthen their authority by making certain claims to divine status. Julius Caesar accepted worship as a god during his lifetime.[41] Augustus was more

---

[38]There is the possibility that Melito of Sardis in the second century understood the book to have come from that period (Eusebius, *Hist. Eccl.* iv.26.9).

[39]The argument that the subject of ἑωράθη in Irenaeus is not ἡ ἀποκάλυψις but ὁ τὴν ἀποκάλυψιν ἑωρακώς, that is, ὁ Ἰωάννης, was not employed by Hort (cf. Swete, pp. cv–cvi).

[40]Barclay Newman rejects the idea that Rev originated amidst a persecution of a political-religious nature and supports the idea that the work is to be understood against an anti-gnostic polemical background ("The Fallacy of the Domitian Hypothesis," *NTS,* 10 [1963–4], pp. 133–39). Cf. his later book, *Rediscovering the Book of Revelation* (1968).

[41]In Ephesus a temple was erected to him bearing the inscription, "To the goddess Roma and the divine Julius."

cautious in the city of Rome but sanctioned temples to himself in the provinces. Following his death he was worshipped widely in Asia and the western provinces. Caligula was not content with voluntary worship. He demanded that his subjects everywhere do homage to his statue. By the time of Nero the imperial cult was firmly established as a religious institution, although the persecution of Christians under Nero resulted not from the emperor's claims of deity but because he needed some group on which to lay the blame for the great fire in Rome. It was not until the reign of Domitian that failure to honor the emperor as a god became a political offense and punishable. Kümmel notes that under Domitian "persecution of Christians by the state on religious grounds took place for the first time."[42] While the picture of universal enforcement of the imperial cult given in Revelation 13 is a forecast rather than a descriptive account of the conditions under Domitian, all the elements were present in the final decade of the first century from which a reasonable projection could be made.[43] The imminent conflict of loyalties between Christ and Caesar indicates that the Apocalypse should probably be placed no earlier than the reign of Domitian. Kümmel writes, "The picture of the time which the Apocalypse sketches coincides with no epoch of the primitive history so well as with the period of Domitian's persecution" (*op. cit.*, p. 328).

Within the book itself are indications that the storm of persecution is about to break. The author has been banished to the island of Patmos "on account of the word of God and the testimony of Jesus" (1:9). Even if this exile resulted from the action taken by a local authority, it is not unreasonable to assume that behind the decision was a general policy emanating from Rome. In the letter to Pergamum we learn of Antipas, God's faithful witness, who was put to death, presumably for not denying his faith (2:13). Believers at Smyrna are warned of impending suffering and imprisonment in which some may be called upon to sacrifice their lives (2:10). The Philadelphians are promised that as a result of their faithfulness, they will be kept "from the hour of trial which is coming on the whole world" (3:10). When the fifth seal is removed, there appear those "who had been slain for the word of God and for the witness they had borne" (6:19). While this description could be interpreted broadly enough to include martyrs of all times, the instruction that they "rest a little longer" until their number be complete suggests that yet more persecution awaits. Persecution

---

[42]Feine-Behm-Kümmel, *op. cit.*, p. 327. It is pointed out that in AD 96 members of the emperor's house were charged with ἀθεότης, an offense against the state religion (*loc. cit.*).
[43]Moffatt acknowledges that insufficient evidence exists to posit a general Asiatic persecution, but suggests that a few drops of rain warn of an approaching storm (*Introduction to the Literature of the New Testament*, p. 504).

is obviously implied in a number of passages about the great harlot (Rome) being drunk with the blood of the saints and martyrs (17:6; 18:24; 19:2; cf. 16:6; 20:4).

The immediate question has to do with which period of time during the first century supplies the most probable setting for this persecution. While the early church was almost from the beginning at odds with its pagan environment (they disapproved of the Gentiles' manner of life, I Pet 4:3; recognized an authority greater than the emperor; and held frequent meetings which were misunderstood by the rulers), the first outbreak of persecution by the Roman government was under Nero in AD 64 (Tacitus, *Ann.* xv.44). This organized retaliation was apparently confined to the city of Rome and therefore distinct from the universal persecution envisioned in Revelation. It was not until the time of Domitian that active persecution again broke out. Behind many of Domitian's religious charges lay the desire to get rid of those he thought to be politically dangerous. Dio Cassius reports that Domitian had his cousin Flavius Clemens executed and his niece Domitilla banished to the island of Pontia on the charge of "atheism."[44] Clement of Rome, a contemporary of Domitian, speaks of "the sudden and repeated calamities and adversities which have befallen us" (i.1), which agrees with what we know of Domitian[45] from later writers who spoke of his persecution of Christians.[46] Although the evidence for widespread persecution under Domitian is not especially strong, there is no other period in the first century in which it would be more likely. Beckwith notes that the book reflects a stage in the development of emperor worship which had not been reached at an earlier date and concludes that "the place then which the persecutions occupy in the motives and prophecies of the apocalyptist seems clearly to point to the time of Domitian" (pp. 206–7).

Other arguments that may be marshalled to support a Domitianic date include: (1) the particular form of the Nero myth which underlies chapters 13 and 17 could not have developed and been generally accepted until near the end of the century, (2) the spiritual decline at Ephesus, Sardis, and Laodicea would require an extended period of time, (3) the existence of a distinct heretical sect with the well-known title, the Nicolaitans, presupposes some distance in time from the apostolic epistles (in which they are not even hinted at), (4) the absence of any reference to

---

[44]ἀθεότης (Dio Cassius, *Hist. Rom.* lxvii.14). Domitilla is thought from inscriptions in the Cemetery of Domitilla to have been a Christian.

[45]"Arrogant to the point of megalomania" is Rist's description of the emperor (p. 355).

[46]Eusebius, *Hist. Eccl.* iii.18.4; Sulpicius Severus (an early fifth-century historian, one of whose works summarized sacred history from creation up until his own day), *Chronicle* ii.31.

the pioneer work of Paul in Asia Minor, (5) the probable use of Matthew (and perhaps Lk) would argue a date later than 80 to 85, if the common dating is accepted, (6) the church at Smyrna may not have existed until after AD 60–64,[47] and (7) Revelation 3:17 describes the church at Laodicea as rich although the city was almost completely destroyed by an earthquake in AD 60–61.

The only other major claim for the date of origin of Revelation is during the close or slightly after the reign of Nero. Evidence in support of an early date is less than persuasive. It is argued, for instance, that the instructions in 11:1–2 to measure the temple assume that the literal temple in Jerusalem was still standing and therefore must have been given prior to AD 70. The reference, however, is symbolic. Zahn holds that by designating Jerusalem "Sodom" (in 11:8) the author indicates that the city had already fallen.[48] Some who choose to interpret the unit non-allegorically resort to a theory of sources to evade the implications for an early date. Guthrie mentions that Clement of Rome speaks of the temple in the present tense, and no one would conclude from this that his writing must be dated before AD 70.[49]

A second argument for the early date comes from the interpretation of 666 (13:18) as a cryptic reference to Nero (cf. comm. on 13:18 for a discussion of this problem). When Nero(n) Caesar is transcribed in Hebrew letters (rather than Latin or Greek), the numerical value comes to 666. This identification, according to Zahn, was first suggested by Fritzsche in 1831 (*op. cit.*, III, p. 447, n. 4). At least Irenaeus in the third century, when discussing the various conjectures known to him, did not even mention Nero as a possibility (*Adv. Haer.* v.28–30). The tentative nature of this interpretation offers no substantial ground for determining date of composition.

The interpretation of the seven heads of the beast set forth in 17:10–11 is also presented as favoring the early date. Here again the divergence of opinion regarding this figure precludes the advisability of attempting to build a chronology on it. The five kings who "have fallen" (if they are to be taken literally; cf. comm. on 17:10) would probably be Augustus (27 BC–AD 14) through Nero (AD 54–68). But who is the one who is? If the three minor claimants who ruled in 68 and 69 are to be counted, Galba becomes the ruler at the time of composition of Revelation. But this would make Vitellius the dreaded eighth who "belongs to the seven" (vs. 11), the beast of the Apocalypse! On the other hand, if the

---

[47]Cf. the argument for this in Charles, I, p. xciv.
[48]*Op. cit.*, III, p. 438.
[49]*Op. cit.*, p. 280.

three are skipped and Vespasian is counted as the sixth, then Domitian would be the eighth. Since the seven heads are also seven hills (17:9) and the eighth is one of the seven (17:11), it is probably unwise to base a literal computation on what appears to be a highly symbolic figure.

Swete draws attention to the fact that the Cambridge trio (Westcott, Lightfoot, and Hort) were unanimous in assigning the Apocalypse to the reign of Nero or the years immediately following (pp. cii–cvi). Westcott argued an early date on the basis of the Greek, which is rather uncouth in comparison with the Fourth Gospel and displays an earlier point in the development of the author's thought (*St. John,* pp. lxxxvi f). Hort holds that the language about Rome, the empire, and the beast fits the last days of Nero and the time immediately following. "The book breathes the atmosphere of a time of wild commotion" which fits only the anarchy of the earlier time (pp. xxvi f). Swete notes that in the partition of the NT between the three, the Apocalypse was "not finally assigned" and thus their published works contain only incidental references to the question of its date (p. ciii). Acknowledging that "such a threefold cord of scholarly opinion is not quickly broken" (p. ciii), he concludes that he is "unable to see that the historical situation presupposed by the Apocalypse contradicts the testimony of Irenaeus which assigns the vision to the end of the reign of Domitian" (p. cvi). Very few contemporary writers would argue against his conclusion.

IV. CIRCULATION AND RECEPTION IN THE EARLY CHURCH

Perhaps more than any other book in the NT, the Apocalypse enjoyed wide distribution and early recognition.[50] Addressed to seven specific churches in Asia Minor, each of which may have served as a circulation center for the surrounding area, it would within a brief period of time have been read throughout the entire province. Since its message centered on that difficult period into which the church universal was about to enter, it would quickly spread beyond the borders of proconsular Asia and be read by believers in every part of the empire.

Opinion differs as to whether traces of the Apocalypse are to be found in the Apostolic Fathers. A number of apparent parallels may be cited from the *Shepherd of Hermas,* such as reference to the coming great

---

[50]For a complete and thorough treatment of the external evidence cf. Ned Stonehouse, *The Apocalypse in the Ancient Church.*

tribulation (*Vis*. ii.2.7; iv.2.5; iv.3.6; cf. Rev 7:14 and 3:10) and the author being transported by the Spirit (*Vis*. i.1.3 with Rev 17:3). There are also a number of common images in the two works (the church as a woman, her enemy as a beast, the apostles as part of a spiritual building, etc.).[51] While such parallels may indicate nothing more than that both books drew from a common apocalyptic tradition, the possibility that Hermas may have known the Apocalypse is by no means precluded. The parallels in *Barnabas* (xxi.3 with Rev 22:10, 12; vii.9 with Rev 1:7, 13; and vi.13 with Rev 21:5) and Ignatius (*Ad Eph*. xv.3 with Rev 21:3; *Ad Phil*. vi.1 with Rev 3:12) are incidental rather than substantive and offer no solid base for literary dependence.

According to Andreas in the prologue to his commentary on Revelation (sixth century), Papias, bishop of Hierapolis in the early years of the second century, knew the book and accepted it as inspired.[52] Justin Martyr, who lived and taught at Ephesus shortly after his conversion about AD 130, wrote that "a certain man among us, whose name was John, one of the apostles of Christ, prophesied in a revelation made to him, that those who believed in our Christ would spend a thousand years in Jerusalem" (*Dial*. lxxxi.15). Another witness from the geographical area to which the Apocalypse was first sent was Melito, bishop of Sardis, who in about AD 175 wrote a work on Revelation, the title of which is preserved by Eusebius (*Hist. Eccl*. iv.26.2).

Irenaeus (born in Asia Minor, probably at Smyrna), bishop of Lyons in South Gaul, quotes frequently from the Apocalypse in his major work, *Against Heresies* (written in the last decade of the second century). He speaks of "all the genuine and ancient copies" of the Revelation of John (Eusebius, *Hist. Eccl*. v.8), thus indicating its early circulation. In an epistle to the believers in Asia and Phrygia, the churches of Lyons and Vienne (AD 177) make several references to the Apocalypse (14:4; 12:1; 19:9; 22:11), one of which is introduced by the NT formula for citing Scripture (Eusebius, *Hist. Eccl*. v.1.58).

That the Apocalypse was included in the Muratorian Canon (the earliest extant list of NT writings) indicates its circulation and acceptance as canonical in Rome by the end of the second century. Hippolytus, the most important third-century theologian of the Roman church, quotes it repeatedly, considering its author to be "the apostle and disciple of the

---

[51]Cf. Charles, I, p. xcvii, n. 2 for a full listing with appropriate references.

[52]Although Eusebius does not list Rev among the NT books known to Papias (*Hist. Eccl*. iii.39), the statements attributed to him concerning a "millennium after the resurrection" and "a corporeal reign of Christ on this very earth" (iii.39.12) seem to echo a personal knowledge of the book.

Lord." In Carthage (the "daughter of the Roman church") the Apocalypse was accepted as authoritative by the end of the second century. Tertullian, the great Carthaginian apologist for Christianity, quotes extensively from Revelation (citations from eighteen of its twenty-two chapters) in the first years of the third century (*eg., Adv. Marc.* iii.14.24; *De Pud.* 12 ff). About the same time, Clement of Alexandria accepted the book as apostolic scripture (*Paed.* ii.119; *Quis Div. Salv.* 42; *Strom.* vi.106–7), as did his younger contemporary Origen (*Comm. in Joh.* v.3). In western Syria, Theophilus, bishop of Antioch, made use of "testimony from the Revelation of John" in his treatise "Against the Heresy of Hermogenes" (Eusebius, *Hist. Eccl.* iv.24). Additional references are available, but these will demonstrate that by the close of the second century the Apocalypse had circulated throughout the empire and was widely accepted both as Scripture and as the product of the apostle John.

Some attention, however, should be given to the opposition which arose against Revelation. Marcion rejected it on the grounds of its Jewish character. Later in the second century, the Alogi, a group of anti-Montanists in Asia Minor, rejected the Apocalypse on the basis of its unedifying symbolism and because they held it to contain errors of fact (*eg.,* no church existed at Thyatira at that time). Gaius, a zealous anti-Montanist in Rome, rejected the book, holding it to be the work of a certain heretic Cerinthus who conceived of the millennium in terms of sensual gratification (Eusebius, *Hist. Eccl.* iii.28). The writing of Gaius was convincingly countered by the great Hippolytus and from the early years of the third century the Apocalypse was uniformly accepted in the West. Only Jerome seems to have expressed certain doubts (*Ad Dard.* cxxix; however, cf. *In Ps.* cxlix). It was in the East that the Apocalypse encountered sustained opposition. In order to refute the millennial position of Nepos (an Egyptian bishop), Dionysius of Alexandria examined the book critically and came to the conclusion that, although inspired, the Apocalypse could not have been written by the apostle John (Eusebius, *Hist. Eccl.* vii.24–25). Rejection of apostolic authorship led to severe questions about canonicity. Eusebius, bishop of Caesarea in the early fourth century, was apparently influenced by the work of Dionysius and suggested that the book was written by a John the Elder of whom Papias spoke (*Hist. Eccl.* iii.39). Others in the East who questioned the work include Cyril of Jerusalem (315–386), Chrysostom (347–407), and Theodoret (386–457). It was not included among the canonical books at the Council of Laodicea (c. 360)[53] and was subsequently omitted from the Peshitta, the official Bible in Syriac-speaking Christian lands in the fifth century.

[53]Beckwith, however, notes that "that part of the decree as now extant is not generally regarded genuine" (p. 342).

In evaluating the opposition to Revelation, one should keep in mind the rise of Montanism, which found in the work support for its apocalyptic extremism. Prior to any universally accepted and authoritative canon individual scholars felt free to undermine the heretical movement by denying to it the one NT book which seemed to lend it some legitimacy. The age of persecution had passed without the major prophecies of Revelation being fulfilled, so questions naturally arose in the popular mind concerning the validity of the book. It is worth noting that those who opposed Revelation did not appeal to the testimony of early history.

In the West from the second century on the Apocalypse had won wide acceptance. In time the East began to reverse its earlier negative position. In the fourth century Athanasius in Alexandria endorsed it without hesitation. The Third Council of Carthage (397) listed the Apocalypse as canonical and appropriate for public reading in services. When the decrees of Laodicea and Carthage were ratified at the Third Council of Constantinople (680) the Apocalypse received formal acceptance as NT scripture in the eastern church. This favorable opinion was due in part to the first Greek commentaries on Revelation, which appeared about the sixth century.[54]

V. APPROACHES TO INTERPRETATION

It is not surprising that Revelation with its visions and elaborate symbolism has been interpreted in widely differing ways. We may assume that its original readers understood its central message without undue difficulty. However, with the passing of that generation and the apparent failure of the book's eschatological promises to find fulfillment, confusion began to set in. Early writers such as Justin, Irenaeus, and Hippolytus were chiliasts.[55] They held that the Apocalypse foretold a literal millennial kingdom on earth to be followed by a general resurrection, judgment, and a renewal of heaven and earth. Late in the third century Victorinus introduced both the Nero Redivivus theory and the idea of recapitulation in which the bowls parallel the trumpets instead of following in a continuous series.

In the Alexandrian church a spiritualizing approach was developing due in part to the influence of Greek thought, the fact that centuries had

---

[54]Oecumenius is the author of the oldest extant Greek commentary on Revelation. He held it to be divinely inspired and canonical, relevant for his day as well as important for an understanding of both past and future. The other two Greek commentaries of the first millennium were by Andreas (bishop of Caesarea in Cappadocia, fifth or sixth century) and Arethas (tenth century).

[55]This brief historical survey draws heavily upon Beckwith's essay, "History of Interpretation" (pp. 318–34).

passed without the establishment of the awaited kingdom, and in reaction to the excessive chiliasm of the Montanist movement. Origen played a major role in the rise of an allegorical method of exegesis. The mysteries of the Apocalypse can be learned only by going beyond the literal and historical to the spiritual. The spiritualizing method was greatly advanced by the work of Tyconius, who interpreted nothing by the historical setting or events of the first century. Augustine followed Tyconius in his capitulation to a totally mystical exegesis. For the next thousand years this allegorical approach was normative for the interpretation of Revelation. Andreas followed Origen in finding a threefold sense in Scripture (ie., literal, figurative, spiritual) and making the spiritual predominant. Primasius, a sixth-century North African bishop, wrote a commentary on Revelation in which he drew heavily upon Tyconius and Augustine. His general method was to discover the abstract or universal which was represented by the particulars in the text.

A new departure was taken in the twelfth century by Joachim of Floris. Since the rise of the allegorical approach it had been generally thought that the millennial reign had begun with the historic Christ. Joachim divided world history into three periods and held that the millennium (which corresponded to the third period, that of the Holy Spirit) was still in the future. He viewed the coming age as one of perfected monasticism which would restore the corrupt Church to its primitive purity. Joachim was loyal to the Church and its hierarchy, but his followers were quick to identify the Pope as the beast and papal Rome as the woman astride the scarlet beast. This antipapal interpretation was later taken over by the Reformation movement and continued for several centuries.

A new approach to the predictions of Revelation appeared with the writings of Nicolas of Lyra (Parisian theologian, died 1340). Abandoning the theory of recapitulation, he held that Revelation contained the prediction of a continuous series of events from the apostolic age all the way to the consummation. This approach was destined to be followed by many in the following years.

Over against these last two approaches a method of interpretation was developing in which renewed attention was given to the circumstances of the writer's own day in an attempt to arrive at a proper understanding of the book. Late in the sixteenth century the Spanish Jesuit, Ribeira, proposed that the Apocalyptist foresaw only the near future and the last things, the intervening period not being in view. While it is not incorrect to call Ribeira a futurist, the title should not be allowed to obscure the fact that he paid a great deal of attention to the historical basis of Revelation. Another Spanish Jesuit, Alcasar (died 1614), was the first to interpret the entire premillennial part of Revelation (chaps. 4–19) as falling totally within the age of the Apocalyptist and the centuries immediately following. Chapters 4–11 and 12–19 refer respectively to the church's conflict with Judaism and with paganism;[56] chapters 20–22 describe her present triumph which began with Constantine. Alcasar was a thoroughgoing "preterist."

This return to the age of the author for a proper understanding of the book of Revelation is characteristic of most contemporary interpreters. Late in the eighteenth century Eichhorn suggested that the Apocalypse should be taken as a great dramatic poem portraying the progress of the Christian faith. In Germany special attention has been given to the identification of sources. Revelation is seen as a composite made up primarily of Jewish apocalyptic literature and adapted for reading in Christian congregations.

In this brief summary we have already touched upon what have become in our day four basic interpretive approaches to Revelation. Almost all expositors of the book may be placed without significant reservations into one of the four categories. The essential lines of interpretation are as follows.

The preterist, or contemporary-historical (*zeitgeschichtlich*), interpretation understands the Apocalypse from the standpoint of its first-century historical setting. The church, threatened by the growing demands of emperor worship, is entering into a period in which its faith is to be severely tested. Persecution will increase, but those who endure will share in the final victory of God over the demonic powers which control and direct the totalitarian state. The great merit of the preterist approach is that it understands and interprets the plight of the first-century church in terms of the crisis which had developed at that particular time. By not relegating the book to some future period the encouragements to the church as well as the warnings to "those who dwell upon the earth" are taken with immediate seriousness. Preterists hold that the major prophecies of the book were fulfilled either in the fall of Jerusalem (AD 70) or the fall of Rome (AD 476).

Charles notes that although the "real historical horizons of the book were early lost," the approach was not driven from the field until the rise of the spiritualizing method in Alexandria. It remained lost to use until its revival by scholars in the seventeenth century (I, p. clxxxiii). The major problem with the preterist position is that the decisive victory portrayed in

---

[56]M. Hopkins ("The Historical Perspective of Apocalypse 1–11," *CBQ*, 27 [1965], pp. 42–47) is a contemporary exponent of the view that Rev 1–11 recalls Christianity's triumph over Judaism in order to encourage their encounter with Rome (chaps. 12–20).

the latter chapters of the Apocalypse was never achieved. It is difficult to believe that John envisioned anything less than the complete overthrow of Satan, the final destruction of evil, and the eternal reign of God. If this is not to be, then either the Seer was essentially wrong in the major thrust of his message or his work was so hopelessly ambiguous that its first recipients were all led astray.

A second approach is commonly called the historicist view. While the preterist placed the book entirely within the period in which it was written, the historicist interpreted it as a forecast of the course of history leading up to his own time. Of little significance to its initial readers, the Apocalypse was held to sketch the history of western Europe through the various popes, the Protestant Reformation, the French revolution, and individual leaders such as Charlemagne and Mussolini. The subjectivity of this approach is underscored by the fact that no essential agreement can be found between the major proponents of the system. Harrison adds that "It is antecedently doubtful that the Spirit of God would be concerned to inform the apostolic church with a rather detailed picture of events lying beyond their own time and having only a remote bearing on the consummation of the age."[57]

The futurist, or eschatological, view is prominent among writers who find in Revelation a major emphasis on the final victory of God over the forces of evil. Many futurists (especially dispensationalists) regard everything from Revelation 4:1 on as belonging to a period of time yet future. Kuyper insists that Revelation has nothing to do with the history of the world prior to the eve of the parousia. He writes that "the only proper conclusion is . . . that we are still in the normal period of history, and that the events which form the prophetic content of the Apocalypse shall only come to pass, when the end of the world is at hand" (p. 22).[58] The letters to the seven churches are often held to represent the successive ages of church history which lead up to the rapture of the church in 4:1 (symbolized by the transport of the Seer which follows the heavenly summons, "Come up hither, and I will show you what must take place after this."[59] The major weakness with this position is that it leaves the book without any particular significance for those to whom it is addressed. It would be little comfort for

---

[57]*Introduction to the New Testament*, p. 436.
[58]Later he writes that chap. four "makes a giant leap across what in no case could be less than twenty centuries" (p. 49).
[59]This is said to correspond with a tripartite division of 1:19: "Now write what you see [the vision of 1:12–16], what is [seven periods of church history symbolized by the seven letters of chaps. 2 and 3], and what is to take place hereafter [the final events following the rapture of the church: chaps. 4–22]." For a more satisfactory interpretation cf. comm. on 1:19.

a first-century believer facing persecution to learn that after seven long church ages Christ would return and punish the enemy. There are, of course, many futurists who do not hold to this interpretation of the early chapters of the book. Revelation 4:1 represents no more than a change in the Seer's perspective from earth to a position within the throne room of heaven. The seals represent events which are characteristic of all of history, and until they are removed the scroll of destiny (revealing the consummation) is not opened. This approach is still futurist because the central focus of the book is eschatological and belongs to the final period of history. It avoids the excessive literalism that often accompanies the dispensational approach.

A fourth method of interpretation is the idealist or timeless symbolic. Its proponents hold that Revelation is not to be taken in reference to any specific events at all but as an expression of those basic principles on which God acts throughout history. Almost a century ago Milligan wrote, "We are not to look in the Apocalypse for special events, but for an exhibition of the principles which govern the history both of the world and the Church" (pp. 154 f). The Apocalypse is thus a theological poem setting forth the ageless struggle between the kingdom of light and the kingdom of darkness. It is a "philosophy of history wherein Christian forces are continuously meeting and conquering the demonic forces of evil."[60] The idealist approach continues the allegorical interpretation which dominated exegesis throughout the medieval period and still finds favor with those inclined to minimize the historical character of the coming consummation. It is supported by the obvious fact that Revelation employs symbol as its major literary device. Its weakness lies in the fact that it denies to the book any specific historical fulfillment. From the idealist's point of view the symbols portray an ever present conflict: there exists no necessary consummation of the historical process.[61]

From this brief survey it is readily apparent that each approach has some important contribution to a full understanding of Revelation and that no single approach is sufficient in itself. It is vitally important to see with the preterist that the book must be interpreted in light of the immediate historical crisis in which the first-century church found itself. The author employs a literary genre that grew out of his own cultural and linguistic milieu. His figures of speech and imagery are to be interpreted in the context of his own historical setting. They are not esoteric and enigmatic references to some future culture totally foreign to first-century readers

---

[60]T. S. Kepler, "Revelation, Book of," *HDB rev.*, p. 850.
[61]Other approaches sometimes mentioned are the literary-critical, the philological, and the religious-historical.

(*eg.*, cobalt bombs, Telstar, the European Common Market, etc.). With the historicist it is important to notice that the philosophy of history revealed in the Apocalypse has found specific fulfillment in all the major crises of human history up to the present day. With the futurist we must agree that the central message of the book is eschatological, and to whatever extent the End has been anticipated in the course of history, it yet remains as the one great climactic point toward which all history moves. This age will come to an end. Satan and his hosts will be destroyed and the righteous will be vindicated. These are historical events which will take place in time. And they are future. With the idealist one must agree that the events of history give expression to basic underlying principles. God is at work behind the scenes to bring to pass his sovereign intention for man. To whatever extent the idealist rules out a consummation, it is difficult to see from history alone any cause for optimism. It is the end that gives meaning to the process.

It is interesting to note that these varying approaches are, to a considerable extent, an accident of history. The author himself could without contradiction be preterist, historicist, futurist, and idealist. He wrote out of his own immediate situation, his prophecies would have a historical fulfillment, he anticipated a future consummation, and he revealed principles which operated beneath the course of history. The interpretive problem grows out of the fact that the End did not arrive on schedule. Beckwith raises the question of how to deal with the many predictions of the book which were not fulfilled. Emperor worship with its hostility to the church passed away and Christianity became the recognized religion of the state. Beckwith solves the problem by holding that while the truth of prophecy is eternal, its form is transitory. Thus he confidently believes in the final realization of the divine ideal but does not "look for anything like a literal fulfillment of predictions shaped by the facts and conditions of a transient period of history" (p. 301).[62]

The problem with this solution is that one is asked to commit himself to the essential truthfulness of a message which in its specific presentation may bear no resemblance to what actually will occur. It will be better to hold that the predictions of John, while expressed in terms reflecting his own culture, will find their final and complete fulfillment in

---

[62]Cf. the section, "Permanent and Transitory Elements in the Apocalypse Distinguished," pp. 291–310. Caird argues that Biblical eschatology is a characteristic product of the Semitic mind, and its primary concern is not with the future but the present—"it is in fact a figurative way of interpreting current history" ("On Deciphering the Book of Revelation: III. The First and the Last," *ET*, 74 [1962–3], pp. 82–84.

the last days of history. Although John saw the Roman Empire as the great beast which threatened the extinction of the church, there will be in the last days an eschatological beast which will sustain the same relationship with the church of the great tribulation. It is this eschatological beast, portrayed in type by Rome, that the Apocalypse describes. Otto Piper notes that many modern interpreters overlook the distinction between the historical fulfillment of prophecy and its eschatological fulfillment.[63] The pattern of imperceptible transition from type to antitype was already established by the Olivet Discourse in which the fall of Jerusalem becomes in its complete fulfillment the end of the age.

VI. STRUCTURE

The twenty-sixth edition of the Nestle-Aland Greek text divides the text of Revelation into 102 separate units each of which describes a scene, presents a vision, or records a statement. No particular problem exists in identifying the units and supplying a descriptive phrase for each. It is when scholars set out to organize the smaller units into larger blocks in an attempt to discover the underlying plan that widely differing schemes begin to appear. The basic structural question is whether John intended his readers to understand the visions recorded in his work in a straightforward chronological sense or whether some form of recapitulation is involved. R. H. Charles is usually cited as the major proponent of the continuous approach. He holds that apart from the Prologue and Epilogue the book falls naturally into seven parts in which the events described in the visions are in strict chronological order (I, pp. xxiii–xxv).[64]

The continuous chronological approach is not accepted by the majority of contemporary writers. Farrer, for instance, writes, "There is not a line in the book which promises us (for example) a continuous exposition of predicted events in historical order" (p. 23). Farrer's own position is that the book has the form of a half-week (corresponding to the terrible half-week of Daniel) embracing four lesser weeks, themselves also halved. The sequence is a sequence of topics (the patience of the saints, the reign of Antichrist, the victory of God) which, although not adhering to a

---

[63]*God in History*, p. 24.

[64]Three sections lie outside the orderly development of the author's theme and are proleptic. Charles finds hopeless confusion in the traditional order of 20:4–22:21, which he explains as the work of a less than intelligent editor whose interpolations can be found elsewhere in the book as well (I, pp. 1–1v).

continuous time-scheme, attach to three periods of genuine historical order (pp. 7, 23).[65] Others find in Revelation a seven-act play,[66] a poem that follows no logical plan but builds up the impression of inevitable judgment (Kiddle, pp. xxvii–xxxiii), a book of seven groups of seven visions each,[67] or a work built upon an underlying liturgical pattern.[68] This rather complete lack of consensus about the structure of Revelation should caution the reader about accepting any one approach as definitive. The outline followed in this commentary represents an attempt to organize the book on the basis of its literary structure alone. Units that seem to go together are placed together without any particular thought as to whether this agrees or not with some predetermined theory of recapitulation, the millennial question, or any other interpretive concern. Had the author intended a precise chronology of the last days, he undoubtedly would have made that plain. If he had wanted us to understand the three numbered series of plagues (to say nothing of the unnumbered ones) as parallel presentations of the messianic woes, he could have made them match more completely. At times he moves ahead quickly to the eternal state in order to encourage the redeemed with a vision of the bliss that awaits them. At other times he returns to the past to interpret the source of the hostility being experienced by the church in the present time. He is bound by neither time nor space as he moves with sovereign freedom to guarantee the final destruction of all evil and the vindication of those who follow the Lamb. The Apocalypse is a broad canvas upon which the Seer paints without restrictions the ultimate triumph of God over evil.[69]

There is progress in the book, but it is more a progress that moves the reader to a fuller experience of the divine plan for final victory than it is a progress which ticks off the minutes on an eschatological clock. Each new vision intensifies the realization of coming judgment. Like a mounting storm at sea each new crest of the wave moves history closer to its final destiny. The numbered plagues reveal this intensification. The seals allow

[65]Guthrie questions the complexities of Farrer's approach and notes that an author with a burning message to proclaim would put it in a form more readily understood than the theory supposes (*op. cit.*, p. 291). For a good summary and appreciative evaluation of Farrer's view on the structure of Rev cf. E. J. Stormon, "Austin Farrer on Image-Patterns in the Apocalypse," *Australian Biblical Review*, 10 [1962], pp. 21–31.

[66]J. W. Bowman, "The Revelation to John: Its Dramatic Structure and Message," *Int*, 9 [1955], pp. 436–53.

[67]Lohmeyer, *Die Offenbarung des Johannes*, pp. 185 f. Cf. Hendriksen, pp. 25, 47 f.

[68]M. H. Shepherd, *The Paschal Liturgy and the Apocalypse*, pp. 75–97. Cf. André Feuillet, *The Apocalypse*, pp. 23–36 for a good discussion of the structure of Revelation. Also pp. 289–94 of Guthrie's *NT Introduction*.

[69]Fiorenza builds a rather formidable case for her view that the eschatological understanding underlying the Apocalypse has determined the structure of the book ("The Eschatology and Composition of the Apocalypse," *CBQ*, 30 [1968], pp. 537–69). Cf. the review of Fiorenza's article by A. J. Bandstra in *Calvin Theological Journal*, 5 (1970), pp. 180–83.

the scroll to be opened and in the process anticipate its contents. The trumpets announce that divine retribution has arrived. The bowls are the pouring out of God's wrath.[70] The outline followed in the commentary does not claim to answer many of the questions which can be raised about exact sequence. It reflects, rather, the literary structure of the book. This is not to say that we cannot anticipate in a general way that course of events which will bring an end to history and usher in eternity. We know that the persecuted church will witness the victorious return of Christ and share in his subsequent reign. We also know that the forces of evil will be totally defeated and Satan and his hordes will forever be destroyed. This sequence, however, belongs to the interpretation of the book and has not been incorporated into the outline, which is descriptive only.

VII. ANALYSIS

I. PROLOGUE (1:1–20)
    1. Superscription (1:1–3)
    2. Salutation and Doxology (1:4–8)
    3. Inaugural Vision and Commission to Write (1:9–20)
II. LETTERS TO THE SEVEN CHURCHES (2:1–3:22)
    1. Ephesus (2:1–7)
    2. Smyrna (2:8–11)
    3. Pergamum (2:12–17)
    4. Thyatira (2:18–29)
    5. Sardis (3:1–6)
    6. Philadelphia (3:7–13)
    7. Laodicea (3:14–22)
III. ADORATION IN THE COURT OF HEAVEN (4:1–5:14)
    1. Worship of God as Creator (4:1–11)
    2. Worship of the Lamb Who Alone Is Worthy to Open the Scroll (5:1–14)
IV. THE SEVEN SEALS (6:1–8:1)
    1. First Four Seals: The Four Horsemen (6:1–8)
    2. Fifth Seal: Cry of the Martyrs (6:9–11)
    3. Sixth Seal: The Great Earthquake (6:12–17)

        INTERLUDE: VISIONS OF SECURITY AND SALVATION (7:1–17)
        A. Sealing of God's Servants (7:1–8)
        B. Bliss of the Redeemed in Heaven (7:9–17)

    4. Seventh Seal: A Dramatic Pause (8:1)

---

[70]Morris writes, "It seems to be part of the method of our author to repeat his themes, not exactly, it is true, but on another level like a spiral staircase. In this way the same ground is traversed, but other perspectives are revealed and fresh facts of the revelation are brought out" (p. 41).

V. THE SEVEN TRUMPETS (8:2–11:19)
1. Preparation (8:2–5)
2. First Four Trumpets (8:6–12)
3. Eagle's Warning (8:13)
4. Fifth Trumpet (First Woe): Demonic Locusts (9:1–12)
5. Sixth Trumpet (Second Woe): Fiendish Cavalry (9:13–21)

INTERLUDE: VISIONS OF THE PROPHETIC ROLE (10:1–11:14)
A. The Mighty Angel and the Little Scroll (10:1–11)
B. Measuring the Temple (11:1–2)
C. The Two Witnesses (11:3–14)

6. Seventh Trumpet (11:15–19)

VI. CONFLICT BETWEEN THE CHURCH AND THE POWERS OF EVIL (12:1–14:5)
1. The Woman, Dragon, and Male Child (12:1–6)
2. War in Heaven (12:7–12)
3. War on Earth (12:13–17)
4. The Beast from the Sea (13:1–10)
5. The Beast from the Earth (13:11–18)
6. The Redeemed and the Lamb on Mt. Zion (14:1–5)

INTERLUDE: VISIONS OF FINAL JUDGMENT (14:6–20)
A. Impending Judgment Announced (14:6–13)
B. Harvest of the Earth (14:14–16)
C. Vintage of the Earth (14:17–20)

VII. THE SEVEN LAST PLAGUES (15:1–16:21)
1. Preparation for the Bowl-Plagues (15:1–8)
2. Plagues Poured Out (16:1–21)

VIII. THE FALL OF BABYLON (17:1–19:5)
1. The Harlot and the Scarlet Beast (17:1–6)
2. Interpretation of the Harlot's Destruction (17:7–18)
3. Babylon Declared Desolate (18:1–8)
4. Lament of Kings, Merchants, and Seamen (18:9–20)
5. Babylon Destroyed (18:21–24)
6. Hymn of Vindication (19:1–5)

IX. THE FINAL VICTORY (19:6–20:15)
1. Marriage of the Lamb Announced (19:6–10)
2. Warrior-Messiah Appears (19:11–16)
3. Antichrist and Allies Destroyed (19:17–21)
4. Satan Bound (20:1–3)
5. Millennial Reign (20:4–6)
6. Satan Destroyed (20:7–10)
7. Final Judgment (20:11–15)

VIII. SELECT BIBLIOGRAPHY

A. COMMENTARIES ON REVELATION

Alford, Henry. "Apocalypse of John" in *The Greek Testament,* IV, 544–750. Chicago: Moody, 1958.

Allo, E. B. *Saint Jean, l'Apocalypse,* 3rd ed. Paris: Gabalda, 1933.

D'Aragon, J. L. "The Apocalypse" in *The Jerome Biblical Commentary,* XII, 467–93. Englewood Cliffs, NJ: Prentice Hall, 1968.

Barclay, William. *The Revelation of John,* 2 vols., 2nd ed. Philadelphia: Westminster, 1960.

Beasley-Murray, G. R. *The Book of Revelation* (New Century Bible). London: Oliphants, 1974.

Beckwith, I. T. *The Apocalypse of John.* New York: Macmillan, 1922.

Bengel, J. A. "Word Studies in Revelation" in *New Testament Word Studies,* II, 831–933, new trans. by C. T. Lewis and M. R. Vincent. Grand Rapids: Kregel, 1971 (*Gnomon Novi Testamenti,* 1742).

Blaney, Harvey J. S. "Revelation" in *The Wesleyan Bible Commentary,* VI, 399–520. Grand Rapids: Eerdmans, 1966.

Bousset, Wilhelm. *Die Offenbarung Johannis.* Göttingen: Vandenhoeck & Ruprecht, 1906.

Bowman, J. W. *The Drama of the Book of Revelation.* Philadelphia: Westminster, 1955.

Bruce, F. F. "The Revelation to John" in *A New Testament Commentary,* ed. G. C. D. Howley, pp. 629–66. London: Pickering & Inglis, 1969.

Caird, G. B. *A Commentary on the Revelation of St. John the Divine* (Harper's New Testament Commentaries). New York: Harper and Row, 1966.

Carrington, P. *The Meaning of Revelation.* London: SPCK, 1931.

Case, Shirley Jackson. *The Revelation of John.* Chicago: University of Chicago, 1919.

Charles, R. H. *The Revelation of St. John,* 2 vols. (The International Critical Commentary). Edinburgh: T. & T. Clark, 1920.

Dana, H. E. *The Epistles and Apocalypse of John.* Dallas: Baptist Book Store, 1937.

Elliott, E. B. *Horae Apocalypticae,* 4 vols. St. Louis: Christian Publishing Company, 1898.

Erdman, Charles R. *The Revelation of John*. Philadelphia: Westminster, 1936.

Farrer, Austin M. *The Revelation of St. John the Divine*. Oxford: Clarendon, 1964.

Ford, J. Massyngberde. *Revelation* (The Anchor Bible). Garden City, NY: Doubleday, 1975.

Franzmann, Martin H. *The Revelation to John*. St. Louis: Concordia, 1976.

Gilmour, S. MacLean. "The Revelation to John" in *The Interpreter's One Volume Commentary on the Bible*, pp. 945-68. New York: Abingdon, 1971.

Glasson, Thomas F. *The Revelation of John* (The Cambridge Bible Commentary). Cambridge: University Press, 1965.

Harrington, Wilfrid J. *The Apocalypse of St John*. London: Geoffrey Chapman, 1969.

Hendriksen, William. *More Than Conquerors*. Grand Rapids: Baker, 1944.

Hengstenberg, E. W. *The Revelation of St John,* trans. by P. Fairbairn, 2 vols. Edinburgh: T. & T. Clark, 1852.

Hort, F. J. A. *The Apocalypse of St John I-III*. London: Macmillan, 1908.

Hoste, William. *The Visions of John the Divine*. Kilmarnock, Scotland: John Ritchie, 1932.

Hough, L. H. "The Revelation of St. John the Divine," Exposition, in *The Interpreter's Bible*, XII, 345-613. New York: Abingdon, 1957.

Kelly, William. *The Revelation*. London: Thomas Weston, 1904.

Kepler, Thomas J. *The Book of Revelation*. New York: Oxford University Press, 1957.

Kiddle, Martin. *The Revelation of St. John* (The Moffatt New Testament Commentary). London: Hodder and Stoughton, 1940.

Kraft, Heinrich. *Die Offenbarung des Johannes* (Handbuch zum Neuen Testament). Tübingen: J. C. B. Mohr, 1974.

Kuyper, Abraham. *The Revelation of St. John,* trans. by John Hendrik de Vries. Grand Rapids: Eerdmans, 1935.

Ladd, George E. *A Commentary on the Revelation of John*. Grand Rapids: Eerdmans, 1972.

Laymon, Charles M. *The Book of Revelation*. New York: Abingdon, 1960.

Lenski, R. C. H. *The Interpretation of St. John's Revelation*. Minneapolis: Augsburg, 1943.

Lilje, Hanns. *The Last Book of the Bible,* trans. by Olive Wyon. Philadelphia: Muhlenberg, 1957.

Lohmeyer, E. *Die Offenbarung des Johannes,* 2nd ed. (Handbuch zum Neuen Testament). Tübingen: J. C. B. Mohr, 1953.

Lohse, E. *Die Offenbarung des Johannes* (Das Neue Testament Deutsch). Göttingen: Vandenhoeck & Ruprecht, 1960.

Love, Julian Price. *The Revelation to John* (The Layman's Bible Commentary). Richmond, VA: John Knox, 1960.

McDowell, E. A. *The Meaning and Message of the Book of Revelation*. Nashville: Broadman, 1951.

Milligan, William. *The Book of Revelation* (The Expositor's Bible). New York: George H. Doran, 1889.

Minear, Paul S. *I Saw a New Earth*. Washington: Corpus Books, 1968.

Moffatt, James. "The Revelation of St. John the Divine" in *The Expositor's Greek Testament*, V, 279–494. Grand Rapids: Eerdmans, 1951.

Morris, Leon. *The Revelation of St. John* (The Tyndale New Testament Commentaries). Grand Rapids: Eerdmans, 1969.

Newman, Barclay M., Jr. *Rediscovering the Book of Revelation*. Valley Forge: Judson Press, 1968.

Niles, D. T. *As Seeing the Invisible*. New York: Harper & Brothers, 1961.

Oman, J. *The Book of Revelation*. Cambridge: University Press, 1923.

Peake, Arthur S. *The Revelation of John*. London: Holborn, 1920.

Preston, R. H. and Hanson, A. T. *The Revelation of Saint John the Divine* (Torch Bible Commentaries). London: SCM, 1949.

Richardson, Donald W. *The Revelation of Jesus Christ*. Richmond, VA: John Knox, 1964.

Rist, Martin. "The Revelation of St. John the Divine," Introduction and Exegesis, in *The Interpreter's Bible*, XII, 345–613. New York: Abingdon, 1957.

Scott, C. Anderson. *Revelation* (The Century Bible). Edinburgh: T. C. & E. C. Jack, 1902.

Scott, E. F. *The Book of Revelation*. New York: Scribner, 1940.

Scott, Walter. *Exposition of the Revelation of Jesus Christ*. London: Pickering and Inglis, 1920.

Seiss, Joseph A. *The Apocalypse*. Grand Rapids: Zondervan, 1957.

Simcox, William H. *The Revelation of St. John the Divine* (Cambridge Greek Testament). Cambridge: University Press, 1893.

Smith, J. B. *A Revelation of Jesus Christ*. Scottdale, PA: Herald Press, 1961.

Summers, Ray. *Worthy is the Lamb*. Nashville: Broadman, 1951.

Swete, Henry B. *The Apocalypse of St. John*. Grand Rapids: Eerdmans, 1951 (orig. pub. 1906).

Tenney, Merrill C. *Interpreting Revelation*. Grand Rapids: Eerdmans, 1957.

Torrance, Thomas F. *The Apocalypse Today*. Grand Rapids: Eerdmans, 1959.

Walvoord, John F. *The Revelation of Jesus Christ*. Chicago: Moody, 1966.

Wilcock, Michael. *I Saw Heaven Opened*. Downers Grove: Inter-Varsity, 1975.

Zahn, Theodor. *Die Offenbarung des Johannes*, 2 vols. Leipzig: Deichert, 1924–26.

B. JOURNAL ARTICLES

Aldrich, R. L. "Divisions of the First Resurrection." *Bibliotheca Sacra*, 128 (1971), 117–19.

Baines, W. G. "The Number of the Beast in Revelation 13:18." *Heythrop Journal*, 16 (1975), 195–96.

Bandstra, A. J. "History and Eschatology in the Apocalypse." *Calvin Theological Journal*, 5 (1970), 180–83.

Barclay, W. "Great Themes of the New Testament: V. Revelation xiii." *Expository Times*, 70 (1958-9), 260–64, 292–96.

Barrett, C. K. "The Lamb of God." *New Testament Studies,* 1 (1954–5), 210–18.

———. "Things Sacrificed to Idols." *New Testament Studies,* 11 (1964–5), 138–53.

Beardslee, W. A. "New Testament Apocalyptic in Recent Interpretation." *Interpretation,* 25 (1971), 419–35.

Beasley-Murray, G. R. "Commentaries on the Book of Revelation." *Theology,* 66 (1963), 52–56.

———. "The Contribution of the Book of Revelation to the Christian Belief in Immortality." *Scottish Journal of Theology,* 27 (1974), 76–93.

———. "The Rise and Fall of the Little Apocalypse Theory." *Expository Times,* 64 (1952), 346–49.

Betz, H. D. "On the Problem of the Religio-Historical Understanding of Apocalypticism." *Journal for Theology and the Church,* 6 (1969), 134–56.

Bissonette, G. "The Twelfth Chapter of the Apocalypse and Our Lady's Assumption." *Marian Studies,* 2 (1951), 170–92.

Boyd, W. J. P. "I am Alpha and Omega: Rev 1:8; 21:6; 22:13." *Studia Evangelica,* 2 (1964), 526–31.

Bowman, J. W. "The Revelation to John: Its Dramatic Structure and Message." *Interpretation,* 9 (1955), 436–53.

Braaten, C. E. "The Significance of Apocalypticism for Systematic Theology." *Interpretation,* 25 (1971), 480–99.

Brewer, R. R. "The Influence of Greek Drama on the Apocalypse of John." *Anglican Theological Review,* 18 (1936), 74–92.

———. "Revelation 4, 6 and the Translations Thereof." *Journal of Biblical Literature,* 71 (1952), 227–31.

Brown, S. "The Hour of Trial: Rev 3,10." *Journal of Biblical Literature,* 85 (1966), 308–14.

Brownlee, W. H. "The Priestly Character of the Church in the Apocalypse." *New Testament Studies,* 5 (1958), 224–25.

Bruins, E. M. "The Number of the Beast." *Nederlands Theologisch Tijdschrift,* 23 (1969), 401–7.

Brunk, M. J. "The Seven Churches of Revelation Two and Three." *Bibliotheca Sacra,* 126 (1969), 240–46.

Bruns, J. E. "The Contrasted Women of Apocalypse 12 and 17." *Catholic Biblical Quarterly,* 26 (1964), 459–63.

Burrows, E. "The Pearl in the Apocalypse." *Journal of Theological Studies,* 43 (1942), 177–79.

Caird, G. B. "On Deciphering the Book of Revelation." *Expository Times,* 74 (1962–3), 13–15, 51–53, 82–84, 103–5.

Considine, J. S. "The Rider on the White Horse, Apoc 6:1–8." *Catholic Biblical Quarterly,* 6 (1944), 406–22.

———. "The Two Witnesses, Apoc 11:3–31." *Catholic Biblical Quarterly,* 8 (1946), 377–92.

Cross, F. M. "New Directions in the Study of Apocalyptic." *Journal for Theology and the Church,* 6 (1969), 157–65.

Davis, D. R. "The Relationship Between the Seals, Trumpets, and Bowls in the

Book of Revelation." *Journal of the Evangelical Theological Society*, 16 (1973), 149–58.

Fiorenza, E. S. "Apocalyptic and Gnosis in the Book of Revelation." *Journal of Biblical Literature*, 92 (1973), 565–81.

―――. "The Eschatology and Composition of the Apocalypse." *Catholic Biblical Quarterly*, 30 (1968), 537–69.

―――. "Redemption as Liberation: Apoc 1:5f. and 5:9f." *Catholic Biblical Quarterly*, 36 (1974), 220–32.

Ford, J. Massyngberde. "The Divorce Bill of the Lamb and the Scroll of the Suspected Adulteress. A Note on Apoc. 5,1 and 10,8–11." *Journal for the Study of Judaism*, 2 (1971), 136–43.

―――. "'For the Testimony of Jesus is the Spirit of Prophecy' (Rev 19:10)." *Irish Theological Quarterly*, 42 (1975), 284–91.

―――. "'He that Cometh' and the Divine Name (Apocalypse 1, 4.8; 4, 8)." *Journal for the Study of Judaism*, 1 (1970), 144–47.

Freedman, D. N. "The Flowering of Apocalyptic." *Journal for Theology and the Church*, 6 (1969), 166–74.

Gaechter, P. "The Original Sequence of Apocalypse 20–22." *Theological Studies*, 10 (1949), 485–521.

Giblin, C. H. "Structural and Thematic Correlations in the Theology of Revelation 16–22." *Biblica*, 55 (1974), 487–504.

Glasson, T. F. "The Order of Jewels in Revelation xxi.19–20: A Theory Eliminated." *Journal of Theological Studies*, new series 26 (1975), 95–100.

Hamerton-Kelly, R. G. "The Temple and the Origins of Jewish Apocalyptic." *Vetus Testamentum*, 20 (1970), 1–15.

Hanson, P. D. "Old Testament Apocalyptic Reexamined." *Interpretation*, 25 (1971), 454–79.

Helmbold, A. "A Note on the Authorship of the Apocalypse." *New Testament Studies*, 8 (1961–2), 77–79.

Hill, D. "Prophecy and Prophets in the Revelation of St John." *New Testament Studies*, 18 (1971–2), 401–18.

Hillyer, N. "'The Lamb' in the Apocalypse." *Evangelical Quarterly*, 39 (1967), 228–36.

Hodges, Z. C. "The First Horseman of the Apocalypse." *Bibliotheca Sacra*, 119 (1962), 324–34.

Hopkins, M. "The Historical Perspective of Apocalypse 1–11." *Catholic Biblical Quarterly*, 27 (1965), 42–47.

―――. "History in the Apocalypse." *Bible Today*, 1 (1965), 340–44.

Hughes, J. A. "Revelation 20:4–6 and the Question of the Millennium." *Westminster Theological Journal*, 35 (1973), 281–302.

Jart, U. "The Precious Stones in the Revelation of St. John xxi.18–21." *Studia Theologica*, 24 (1970), 150–81.

Johnson, S. E. "Early Christianity in Asia Minor." *Journal of Biblical Literature*, 77 (1958), 1–17.

―――. "Laodicea and Its Neighbors." *Biblical Archaeologist*, 13 (1950), 1–18.

Jones, B. W. "More about the Apocalypse as Apocalyptic." *Journal of Biblical Literature*, 87 (1968), 325-27.

Kallas, J. "The Apocalypse—an Apocalyptic Book?" *Journal of Biblical Literature*, 86 (1967), 69-80.

Klassen, W. "Vengeance in the Apocalypse of John." *Catholic Biblical Quarterly*, 28 (1966), 300-11.

Kline, M. G. "The First Resurrection." *Westminster Theological Journal*, 37 (1975), 366-75.

Ladd, G. E. "Revelation 20 and the Millennium." *Review and Expositor*, 57 (1960), 167-75.

―――. "The Theology of the Apocalypse." *Gordon Review*, 7 (1963), 73-86.

―――. "Why Not Prophetic-Apocalyptic?" *Journal of Biblical Literature*, 76 (1957), 192-200.

Mackay, W. M. "Another Look at the Nicolaitans." *Evangelical Quarterly*, 45 (1973), 111-15.

Michael, J. H. "A Slight Misplacement in Revelation 1,13-14." *Expository Times*, 42 (1930-1), 380-81.

Miller, P. D. "God the Warrior." *Interpretation*, 19 (1965), 39-46.

Minear, Paul S. "The Wounded Beast." *Journal of Biblical Literature*, 72 (1953), 93-101.

Mitten, D. G. "A New Look at Ancient Sardis." *Biblical Archaeologist*, 29 (1966), 55.

Mounce, R. H. "The Christology of the Apocalypse." *Foundations*, 11 (1969), 42-45.

Mowry, L. "Revelation IV-V and Early Christian Liturgical Usage." *Journal of Biblical Literature*, 71 (1952), 75-84.

Murdock, W. R. "History and Revelation in Jewish Apocalypticism." *Interpretation*, 21 (1967), 167-87.

Newman, B. M. "The Fallacy of the Domitian Hypothesis." *New Testament Studies*, 10 (1963), 133-39.

Oke, C. C. "The Misplacement in Revelation 1, 13-14." *Expository Times*, 43 (1931), 237.

O'Rourke, J. J. "The Hymns of the Apocalypse." *Catholic Biblical Quarterly*, 30 (1968), 399-409.

Ostella, R. A. "The Significance of Deception in Revelation 20:3." *Westminster Theological Journal*, 37 (1974-5), 236-38.

Peterson, E. H. "Apocalypse: The Medium is the Message." *Theology Today*, 26 (1969), 133-41.

Repp, A. C. "Ministry and Life in the Seven Churches." *Concordia Theological Monthly*, 25 (1964), 133-47.

Rife, J. M. "The Literary Background of Revelation II-III." *Journal of Biblical Literature*, 60 (1941), 179-82.

Rissi, M. "The Rider on the White Horse: A Study of Revelation 6, 1-8." *Interpretation*, 18 (1964), 407-18.

Robb, J. D. "*Ho Erchomenos* Apoc 1, 4." *Expository Times*, 73 (1961-2), 338-39.

Roberts, J. W. "The Interpretation of the Apocalypse." *Restoration Quarterly*, 8 (1965), 154-62.

————. "The Meaning of the Eschatology in the Book of Revelation." *Restoration Quarterly*, 15 (1972), 95-110.

Rollins, W. G. "The New Testament and Apocalyptic." *New Testament Studies*, 17 (1970-1), 454-76.

Rudwick, M. J. S. and Green, E. M. B. "The Laodicean Lukewarmness." *Expository Times*, 69 (1957-8), 176-78.

Russell, E. "A Roman Law Parallel to Revelation Five." *Bibliotheca Sacra*, 115 (1958), 258-64.

Sanders, H. A. "The Number of the Beast in Revelation 13:18." *Journal of Biblical Literature*, 37 (1918), 95-99.

Sanders, J. N. "St. John on Patmos." *New Testament Studies*, 9 (1962-3), 75-85.

Scott, R. B. Y. "Behold He Cometh with Clouds." *New Testament Studies*, 5 (1958-9), 127-32.

Shepherd, N. "The Resurrections of Revelation 20." *Westminster Theological Journal*, 37 (1974-5), 34-43.

Silberman, L. H. "Farewell to O AMHN. A Note on Rev 3, 14." *Journal of Biblical Literature*, 82 (1963), 212-15.

Skehan, P. W. "King of Kings, Lord of Lords (Apoc 19, 16)." *Catholic Biblical Quarterly*, 10 (1948), 398.

Smith, D. C. "The Millennial Reign of Jesus Christ. Some Observations on Rev. 20:1-10." *Restoration Quarterly*, 16 (1973), 219-30.

Stagg, F. "Interpreting the Book of Revelation." *Review and Expositor*, 72 (1975), 331-43.

Staples, P. "Rev. XVI 4-6 and its vindication formula." *Novum Testamentum*, 14 (1972), 280-93.

Stormon, E. J. "Austin Farrer on Image-Patterns in the Apocalypse." *Australian Biblical Review*, 10 (1962), 21-23.

Stott, W. "A Note on the Word KYRIAKH in Rev. I.10." *New Testament Studies*, 12 (1965-6), 70-75.

Strand, K. A. "Another Look at 'Lord's Day' in the Early Church and in Rev. 1.10." *New Testament Studies*, 13 (1966-7), 174-81.

————. "The Book of Revelation: A Review Article on Some Recent Literature." *Andrews University Seminary Studies*, 11 (1973), 181-93.

Summers, R. "Revelation 20: An Interpretation." *Review and Expositor*, 57 (1960), 176-83.

Thomas, R. L. "The Glorified Christ on Patmos." *Bibliotheca Sacra*, 122 (1965), 241-47.

————. "John's Apocalyptic Outline." *Bibliotheca Sacra*, 123 (1966), 334-41.

Thompson, L. "Cult and Eschatology in the Apocalypse of John." *Journal of Religion*, 49 (1969), 330-50.

Trites, A. A. "*Martys* and Martyrdom in the Apocalypse: A Semantic Study." *Novum Testamentum*, 15 (1973), 72-80.

Trudinger, P. "*Ho Amēn* (Rev. III: 14), and the Case for a Semitic Original of the Apocalypse." *Novum Testamentum*, 14 (1972), 277–79.

————. "Some Observations Concerning the Text of the Old Testament in the Book of Revelation." *Journal of Theological Studies*, new series 17 (1966), 82–88.

Unnik, W. C. van. "A Formula Describing Prophecy." *New Testament Studies*, 9 (1962–3), 86–94.

————. "Le nombre des élus dans la première de Clément." *Revue d'Histoire et de Philosophie Religieuses*, 42 (1962), 237–46.

Walker, N. "The Origin of the 'Thrice-Holy'." *New Testament Studies*, 5 (1958–9), 132–33.

Walvoord, J. F. "Revival of Rome." *Bibliotheca Sacra*, 126 (1969), 317–28.

Wilder, A. N. "The Rhetoric of Ancient and Modern Apocalyptic." *Interpretation*, 25 (1971), 436–53.

Wood, P. "Local Knowledge in the Letters of the Apocalypse." *Expository Times*, 73 (1961–2), 263–64.

C. OTHER WORKS CITED

The Apocrypha and Pseudepigrapha of the Old Testament, 2 vols., ed. R. H. Charles. Oxford: Clarendon, 1913.

Arndt, W. F. and Gingrich, F. *A Greek-English Lexicon of the New Testament*, 4th rev. and augmented ed. of Walter Bauer's *Griechisch-Deutsches Wörterbuch zu den Schriften des Neuen Testaments*. Cambridge: University Press, 1957.

Bacon, B. W. *The Making of the New Testament*. Folcroft, PA: Folcroft Library Editions, 1900.

Baker's Dictionary of Theology, ed. E. F. Harrison. Grand Rapids: Baker, 1960.

Barclay, William. *Letters to the Seven Churches*. New York: Abingdon, 1957.

Beck, W. F. *The New Testament in the Language of Today*. St. Louis: Concordia, 1963.

Blaiklock, E. M. *The Seven Churches*. London: Marshall, Morgan & Scott, 1951.

Boll, Franz J. *Auf der Offenbarung Johannis: Hellenistische Studien zum Weltbild der Apokalypse*. Berlin: B. G. Teubner, 1914.

Burrows, M. *Dead Sea Scrolls*. New York: Viking, 1955.

Bruce, F. F. "The Spirit in the Apocalypse" in *Christ and Spirit in the New Testament*, ed. B. Lindars and S. S. Smalley. Cambridge: University Press, 1974.

Burton, Ernest de Witt. *Syntax of the Moods and Tenses in New Testament Greek*, 3rd ed. Edinburgh: T. & T. Clark, 1898.

Caird, G. B. *The Apostolic Age*. London: Duckworth, 1955.

Chapot, V. *La Province Romaine Proconsulaire d'Asie*. Paris: E. Bouillon, 1904.

Charles, R. H. *Religious Development Between the Old and the New Testaments*. New York: Holt, 1914.

SELECT BIBLIOGRAPHY

Comblin, J. Le Christ dans l'Apocalypse. Paris: Desclée, 1965.

Conzelmann, H. An Outline of the Theology of the New Testament. New York: Harper and Row, 1969.

Cullmann, O. Christ and Time, rev. ed., trans. by Floyd V. Filson. Philadelphia: Westminster, 1964.

———. The State in the New Testament. New York: Scribner, 1956.

Dana, H. E. and Mantey, J. R. A Manual Grammar of the Greek New Testament. New York: Macmillan, 1927.

Deissmann, G. A. Bible Studies, Eng. ed. by A. Grieve. New York: Harper and Brothers, 1901.

———. Light from the Ancient East, new ed., trans. by L. R. M. Strachan. Grand Rapids: Baker, 1965.

A Dictionary of the Bible, 5 vols., ed. James Hastings. Edinburgh: T. & T. Clark, 1898-1904.

Dictionary of the Bible, rev. ed. F. C. Grant and H. H. Rowley (orig. ed. James Hastings). New York: Scribner, 1963.

Driver, S. R. Joel (The Cambridge Bible for Schools and Colleges). Cambridge: University Press, 1907.

Encyclopedia Biblica, 4 vols., ed. T. K. Cheyne and J. S. Black. New York: Macmillan, 1899-1903.

Epigrammata Graeca ex lapidibus conlecta, ed. G. Kaibel. Berlin: G. Reimer, 1878.

Farrer, Austin M. A Rebirth of Images. Boston: Beacon, 1949.

Feine, P., Behm, J. and Kümmel, W. G. Introduction to the New Testament, 14th rev. ed. (founded by Feine-Behm, reedited by Kümmel), trans. by A. J. Mattill, Jr. New York: Abingdon, 1966.

Feuillet, A. The Apocalypse, trans. by Thomas E. Crane. Staten Island, NY: Alba House, 1965.

———. Johannine Studies, trans. by Thomas E. Crane. Staten Island, NY: Alba House, 1965.

Frost, S. B. Old Testament Apocalyptic: Its Origins and Growth. London: Epworth, 1952.

Giet, S. L'Apocalypse et l'Histoire. Paris: University of Paris, 1957.

Goodspeed, Edgar J. The New Testament: An American Translation. Chicago: University of Chicago Press, 1923.

The Greek New Testament, 3rd ed. by Aland, Black, Martini, Metzger, Wikgren. New York: United Bible Societies, 1975.

Guthrie, Donald. New Testament Introduction: Hebrews to Revelation. Chicago: Inter-Varsity, 1962.

Hanson, A. T. The Wrath of the Lamb. London: SPCK, 1957.

Hanson, Paul D. The Dawn of Apocalyptic. Philadelphia: Fortress, 1975.

Harrison, E. F. Introduction to the New Testament. Grand Rapids: Eerdmans, 1964.

Hemer, C. J. A Study of the Letters to the Seven Churches of Asia with Special

57

Reference to their Local Background. Unpublished Ph.D. thesis at the University of Manchester, 1969.

Holtz, Traugott. *Die Christologie der Apokalypse des Johannes,* 2nd ed. Berlin: Akademie-Verlag, 1971.

Hunter, A. M. *Probing the New Testament.* Richmond, VA: John Knox, 1971.

The Interpreter's Bible, 12 vols., ed. G. A. Buttrick. New York: Abingdon, 1957.

The Interpreter's Dictionary of the Bible, 4 vols., ed. G. A. Buttrick (supplementary vol., 1976, ed. K. Crim). New York: Abingdon, 1962.

Jeremias, J. *Jesus' Promise to the Nations* (Studies in Biblical Theology, No. 24). London: SCM, 1970.

Jewett, Paul K. *The Lord's Day.* Grand Rapids: Eerdmans, 1971.

The Jewish Encyclopedia, 12 vols. New York: Funk and Wagnalls, 1901-6.

Jung, C. G. *Answer to Job.* Princeton: University Press, 1972.

Kassing, A. T. *Die Kirche und Maria; Ihr Verhältnis im 12 Kapitel der Apokalypse.* Düsseldorf: Patmos, 1958.

Kircher, A. *Oedipus Aegyptiacus.* Rome: V. Mascardi, 1652-54.

Liddell, H. C. and Scott, R. *Greek-English Lexicon,* new ed. by H. S. Jones. Oxford: Clarendon, 1940.

Lightfoot, J. B. *Notes on the Epistles of St. Paul.* Grand Rapids: Zondervan, 1957.

————. *Saint Paul's Epistles to the Colossians and to Philemon.* London: Macmillan, 1904.

————. *St. Paul's Epistle to the Galatians,* 6th ed. London: Macmillan, 1880.

Lohse, Eduard. *Die Offenbarung des Johannes (Das Neue Testament deutsch).* Göttingen: Vandenhoeck & Ruprecht, 1960.

Marshall, I. Howard. "Martyrdom and the Parousia in the Revelation of John" in *Studia Evangelica,* IV, ed. F. L. Cross, pp. 333-39. Berlin: Akademie-Verlag, 1968.

Martin, R. P. *Worship in the Early Church.* Westwood, NJ: Revell, 1964.

McIlvaine, J. H. *The Wisdom of the Apocalypse.* New York: Anson D. F. Randolph, 1886.

Metzger, Bruce M. *A Textual Commentary on the Greek New Testament.* New York: United Bible Societies, 1971.

Milligan, W. *St. Paul's Epistles to the Thessalonians.* London: Macmillan, 1908.

Moffatt, J. *An Introduction to the Literature of the New Testament.* New York: Scribner, 1927.

————. *The New Testament: A New Translation.* New York: Harper and Row, 1964.

Morris, Leon. *Apocalyptic.* Grand Rapids: Eerdmans, 1972.

————. *The Gospel According to John* (New International Commentary on the New Testament). Grand Rapids: Eerdmans, 1971.

Moule, C. F. D. *An Idiom Book of New Testament Greek.* Cambridge: University Press, 1953.

Moulton, J. H. *A Grammar of New Testament Greek,* Vol. I, Prolegomena, 3rd ed. Edinburgh: T. & T. Clark, 1908.

Moulton, J. H. and Milligan, G. *The Vocabulary of the Greek Testament*. Grand Rapids: Eerdmans, 1974 (one-vol. ed. first issued in 1930).

The New Bible Dictionary, ed. J. D. Douglas. London: The Inter-Varsity Fellowship, 1962.

The New English Bible: New Testament. London: Oxford University Press, 1961.

The New International Dictionary of New Testament Theology, Vols. I, II, ed. Colin Brown, trans. with additions and revisions from *Theologisches Begriffslexikon zum Neuen Testament* (ed. L. Coenen). Grand Rapids: Zondervan, 1975, 1976.

H KAINH ΔIAΘHKH, 2nd ed. G. D. Kilpatrick. London: The British Foreign Bible Society, 1958.

Newton, John. *Voice of the Heart*. Chicago: Moody, 1950 (author's intro. 1780).

Novum Testamentum Graece, 25th ed. E. Nestle and K. Aland. New York: American Bible Society, 1963.

Oman, J. *The Text of Revelation: A Revised Theory*. Cambridge: University Press, 1928.

The Oxford Dictionary of the Christian Church, 2nd ed. by F. L. Cross. London: Oxford University Press, 1958.

Phillips, J. B. *The New Testament in Modern English*. New York: Macmillan, 1958.

Piper, Otto. *God in History*. New York: Macmillan, 1939.

Prigent, Pierre. *Apocalypse 12, Histoire de l'Exégèse*. Tübingen: Mohr, 1959.

Rad, G. von. *Old Testament Theology*, II, trans. by D. M. G. Stalker. New York: Harper and Row, 1962.

Ramsay, W. M. *The Letters to the Seven Churches of Asia*. Grand Rapids: Baker, 1963 (1st pub. 1904).

Rissi, M. *The Future of the World* (Studies in Biblical Theology, 2nd series, No. 25). Naperville, IL: Allenson, 1972.

————. *Time and History*, trans. by G. C. Winsor. Richmond, VA: John Knox, 1966.

Robertson, A. T. "The Revelation of John" in *Word Pictures in the New Testament*, VI, 267–488. New York: Harper and Brothers, 1933.

Rowley, H. H. *The Relevance of Apocalyptic*. New York: Association Press, 1963.

Russell, D. S. *The Method and Message of Jewish Apocalyptic*. Philadelphia: Westminster, 1964.

Schlatter, A. *The Church in the New Testament Period*, trans. by Paul P. Levertoff. London: SPCK, 1955.

Schmithals, Walter. *The Apocalyptic Movement*, trans. by John E. Steely. Nashville: Abingdon, 1975.

Schnackenburg, R. *God's Rule and Kingdom*, 2nd ed., trans. by John Murray. New York: Herder and Herder, 1968.

Schürer, E. "Die Prophetin Isabel in Thyatira, Offenb. Joh. 2, 20" in *Theologische Abhandlungen*, pp. 39–58. Freiburg, 1892.

Shepherd, M. H. *The Paschal Liturgy and the Apocalypse*. London: Lutterworth, 1960.

Stauffer, E. *Christ and the Caesars*. London: SCM, 1965.

———. "666 (Apoc. 13,18)" in *Coniectanea Neotestamentica*, 1947, pp. 237–41. Lund: Gleerup, 1947.

Stonehouse, N. B. *The Apocalypse in the Ancient Church*. Goes, Holland: Oosterbaan & Le Cointre, 1929.

———. *Paul Before the Areopagus*. London: Tyndale, 1957.

Strack, H. L. and Billerbeck, P. *Kommentar zum Neuen Testament aus Talmud und Midrasch*. Munich: Beck, 1922–61.

Tarn, W. W. and Griffith, G. T. *Hellenistic Civilization*, 3rd ed. London: E. Arnold, 1952.

Tasker, R. V. G. *The Biblical Doctrine of the Wrath of God*. London: Tyndale, 1951.

Theological Dictionary of the New Testament, ed. Gerhard Kittel and Gerhard Friedrich, trans. by G. W. Bromiley, 10 vols. Grand Rapids: Eerdmans, 1964–76.

Trench, R. C. *Commentary on the Epistles to the Seven Churches in Asia*, 3rd ed. London: Macmillan, 1867.

———. *Synonyms of the New Testament*, 11th ed. London: Kegan, Trench, Trubner, 1890.

The Twentieth Century New Testament. Chicago: Moody Press, 1961 (original edition, 1898–1901).

Underhill, Evelyn. *Worship*. New York: Harper, 1957.

Westcott, B. F. *On the Canon of the New Testament*. London: Macmillan, 1875.

———. *St. John* (Speaker's Bible). London: John Murray, 1882.

Weymouth, R. F. *The New Testament in Modern Speech*. New York: Harper & Brothers, 1943.

Williams, Charles B. *The New Testament: A Translation in the Language of the People*. Chicago: Moody, 1937.

Yadin, Y. *The Art of Warfare in Biblical Lands*. London: Weidenfeld and Nicolson, 1963.

Zahn, T. *Introduction to the New Testament*, 3 vols., trans. by M. W. Jacobus and others. New York: Scribner, 1909.

Text, Exposition,
and Notes

CHAPTER 1

I. PROLOGUE (1:1–20)

1. SUPERSCRIPTION (1:1–3)

1 *The Revelation of Jesus Christ, which God gave him to show unto his servants, even the things which must shortly come to pass: and he sent and signified it by his angel unto his servant John;*

2 *who bare witness of the word of God, and of the testimony of Jesus Christ, even of all things that he saw.*

3 *Blessed is he that readeth, and they that hear the words of the prophecy, and keep the things that are written therein: for the time is at hand.*

1 In the earliest manuscripts the book was given the simple title "The Apocalypse of John." Later manuscripts modified and expanded the title in various ways. The Textus Receptus has, "The Apocalypse of John the theologian."[1]

Verses 1–3 form an introduction or prologue to the book. They tell how and for what purpose the revelation was given, and pronounce a blessing on both reader and obedient listener. There is no reason to believe that the prologue is the work of some later redactor.[2] It appears to have been added by the author himself after completing the book.

The work designates itself as "The Revelation of Jesus Christ." It is an apocalypse[3] or unveiling. The term as used here is not a literary

---

[1]Τοῦ θεολόγου (also added in **046** 2329 *al;* see Metzger, *TCGNT,* p. 731, for the twenty-seven-word title on a manuscript of Rev at Mount Athos). BAG define θεολόγος (only here in the NT) as one who speaks of God or divine things, God's herald (p. 356).

[2]Ford conjectures that this first prologue (Rev 1:1–3) may have been written by a disciple of the Baptist (p. 375) while the second prologue (Rev 1:4–8) may have been the work of a Jewish Christian who expected the imminent return of Jesus (p. 380).

[3]See Milligan, *St. Paul's Epistles to the Thessalonians,* pp. 149–51, for a concise treatment of ἀποκάλυψις. In relation to παρουσία and ἐπιφάνεια it reminds us that the second advent is "a 'revelation' of the Divine plan and purpose which has run through all the ages, to find its consummation at length in the 'one far-off divine event,' to which the whole Creation is slowly moving" (Milligan, p. 151).

classification but an indication of the nature and purpose of the book. Modern scholarship has appropriated the term to describe a body of literature widely diffused in Judaism from about 200 BC until AD 100. It is pseudonymous, pseudo-predictive (the writer places himself at some point in the past and by means of symbols rewrites history under the guise of prophecy), and pessimistic (Ladd, p. 20). It deals with the final catastrophic period of world history when God, after mortal combat with the powers of evil, emerges victorious. It is clear that Revelation has much in common with such Jewish apocalypses as *I Enoch* and II Esdras. However, that it is not apocalyptic as opposed to prophetic is established by verse 3, which promises a blessing to those who hear "the words of the prophecy" (cf. Rev 22:7, 10, 18, 19).

The work is a revelation mediated by Jesus Christ rather than a revelation of Christ himself. The following clauses indicate that God gave it to him for the purpose of showing to his servants "the things which must shortly come to pass." Although Hort argues that in the NT both verb and noun are used for "the unveiling of the hidden Christ to man" (p. 4), he goes on to say that "the revealing of Jesus Christ would be at the same time and for that reason a revealing of things shortly to come to pass" (p. 6). Christ is the revealer, not in the sense that he accompanies John on his visionary experiences (angels play this role), but in that he alone is worthy to open the scroll of destiny (Rev 5:5, 7) and disclose its contents (Rev 6:1, 3, 5, 7, 9, 12; 8:1).

The full designation, "Jesus Christ," is found three times in Revelation 1:1–5 but not elsewhere in the book. It is appropriate in the elevated style of the prologue. Throughout the text, the single term "Jesus" is used.

God is the source of all revelation. He is, as Daniel declared to Nebuchadnezzar, the one who reveals secrets and makes known what shall come to pass (Dan 2:28, 29, 45). In Revelation this disclosure is mediated by Jesus Christ. (In the Fourth Gospel the role of taking the things of God and showing them to man is often assigned to Christ: Jn 1:18; 5:19–23; 12:49; 17:8; cf. Mt 11:27.) The express purpose of God in giving the revelation is to show to his servants the things which must shortly come to pass. History is not a haphazard sequence of unrelated events but a divinely decreed ordering of that which must come to pass. It is a logical necessity arising from the nature of God and the revelation of his purpose in creation and redemption.

John writes that these events which constitute the revelation must take place shortly.[4] That more than 1900 years of church history have

---

[4] ἐν τάχει; also in Rev 22:6; cf. ταχύ, Rev 22:7, 12, 20; also ὁ γὰρ καιρὸς ἐγγύς in Rev 1:3 and 22:10.

passed and the end is not yet poses a problem for some. One solution is to understand "shortly" in the sense of suddenly, or without delay once the appointed time arrives. Another approach is to interpret it in terms of the certainty of the events in question. Of little help is the suggestion that John may be employing the formula of II Peter 3:8 ("with the Lord one day is as a thousand years"). Caird believes that the coming crisis was not the consummation of history but the persecution of the church (p. 12). Indeed, that did take place shortly. The most satisfying solution is to take the word in a straightforward sense, remembering that in the prophetic outlook the end is always imminent. This perspective is common to the entire NT. Jesus taught that God would vindicate his elect without delay (Lk 18:8), and Paul wrote to the Romans that God would soon crush Satan under their feet (Rom 16:20).[5]

The servants who are to receive the revelation are primarily the Christian prophets (in the sense of Amos 3:7, "Surely the Lord God does nothing, without revealing his secret to his servants the prophets"; cf. Rev 10:7; 11:18), although the term as used elsewhere in the book includes all believers (Rev 7:3; 19:5; 22:3).

The revelation is said to be signified by an angel sent to John. If the subject of the verb "signified" is Christ, then an angel acts as an intermediary between Christ and John. It would be the angel who appears again in chapter 22 to rebuke John for falling at his feet to worship (Rev 22:8). In Revelation 22:16 Jesus says, "I Jesus have sent my angel to you with this testimony for the churches." On the other hand, it is possible that "signified" is parallel to "gave" and God is the subject of both. In this case, angel would have the general meaning of messenger (as in 1:20; 2:1, 8; etc.) and refer to Christ himself. As mediator of the revelation, Christ performs the function of an angel in the general sense of messenger.[6]

The revelation is said to be signified to John. The Greek verb carries the idea of figurative representation. Strictly speaking it means to make known by some sort of sign (Hort, p. 6). Thus it is admirably suited to the symbolic character of the book. This should warn the reader not to expect a literal presentation of future history, but a symbolic portrayal of that which must yet come to pass.

2 John is further designated as one "who bare witness of the word of God, and of the testimony of Jesus."[7] The reference is to the revelation

---

[5]Both verses use ἐν τάχει, as does Rev 1:1.
[6]Note the many and various angels that are mentioned in the book: the strong angel, 5:2; the angel ascending from the east, 7:2; the angel astride sea and land, 10:1–2; the angel with the sickle, 14:19; etc.
[7]2036 *pc* omit τοῦ θεοῦ with the result that John is said to have borne witness to the word and the testimony of Jesus Christ. 2060 *al* add a variation of 1:19 after εἶδεν.

given by God and testified to by Christ.[8] Beckwith (p. 421) suggests that
the writer is following his customary mode of making a general term (in
this case, "word of God") more specific by adding another phrase for
clarification ("testimony of Jesus Christ"). In either case, the final clause
of the verse is appositional and limits the scope of both. In this context, the
message of God attested by Jesus consists of "all things that he [John]
saw." If the prologue were composed after John wrote down the visionary
experiences described in the book, it would be natural for him to use the
past tense (Gk. aorist), "bare witness." It is unnecessary to conjecture
some prior incident when John may have witnessed to the word of God
with the result that he was banished to Patmos.

3 A blessing is pronounced upon the one who reads the revelation
to the church and upon those who hear the prophecy and obey it. This is the
first of seven beatitudes in the book. (The others are found in 14:13; 16:15;
19:9; 20:6; 22:7, 14.) It virtually reproduces the words of Jesus in Luke
11:28, "Blessed . . . are those who hear the word of God and keep it!" The
public reading of Scripture was taken over from Jewish practice (Neh 8:2;
Lk 4:16; Acts 13:15; cf. Col 4:16; I Thess 5:27). At first the reader was
probably someone chosen from the congregation who had acquired some
proficiency in the art. The ability to read well was not widespread in
antiquity. Later the office of reader became an official position in the
church.[9]

That the congregation was to keep the things written in the
prophecy indicates that the work was considered as moral instruction and
not mere prediction. John viewed his work as prophetic literature on a par
with the prophetic books of the OT and possessing an authority which
required the obedient response of all believers. Although the beatitude is
certainly true in a general sense, here it takes on special significance in
view of the fact that "the time is at hand." The Greek *kairos* (translated
"time") was commonly used in an eschatological sense to indicate the
time of crisis or the decisive moment. The statement seems to have come
from the standard Jewish messianic expectations of the day. For instance,
Jesus warned his disciples that many would come in his name claiming,
"The time is at hand."[10] The critical moment for the fulfillment of all that
John had seen in his visions had drawn near. Hence the urgency of hearing
and keeping the words of the prophecy.

---

[8]Both genitives are subjective, as they are in 1:9 as well. Cf. 6:9; 12:17; 19:10.
[9]Tertullian, *Praescr. Haer.* 41.
[10]Cf. καιρός in Mt 8:29; Mk 13:33; I Cor 4:5.

2. SALUTATION AND DOXOLOGY (1:4–8)

4 *John to the seven churches that are in Asia: Grace to you and peace, from him who is and who was and who is to come; and from the seven Spirits that are before his throne;*

5 *and from Jesus Christ,* who is *the faithful witness, the firstborn of the dead, and the ruler of the kings of the earth. Unto him that loveth us, and loosed us from our sins by his blood;*

6 *and he made us* to be *a kingdom,* to be *priests unto his God and Father; to him* be *the glory and the dominion for ever and ever. Amen.*

7 *Behold, he cometh with the clouds; and every eye shall see him, and they that pierced him; and all the tribes of the earth shall mourn over him. Even so, Amen.*

8 *I am the Alpha and the Omega, saith the Lord God, who is and who was and who is to come, the Almighty.*

4 The book of Revelation takes the form of a letter which begins with a normal salutation in 1:4 and continues through the benediction of 22:21. It differs only in that the initial vision is followed by seven rather stylized letters to specific churches in the Roman province of Asia. That each of these seven "letters" is intended for the moral and spiritual progress of all, follows from the repeated exhortation of each, "He that hath an ear, let him hear what the Spirit saith to the churches" (2:7, 11, 17, 29; 3:6, 13, 22: note the plural, "churches"). Since apart from the prologue (1:1–3) Revelation is an epistle, the usual format (From A To B—Greetings) is followed.

The author refers to himself simply as John. His close relationship with the seven churches and his intimate knowledge of their affairs make it unnecessary to add any identifying phrase. The authority with which he writes indicates his role as a leader in the Asian church.

The letter is addressed to "the seven churches that are in Asia." In the NT, Asia normally refers to the Roman province which occupied the entire western portion of Asia Minor stretching inland to the Anatolian plateau. It is the area represented by the ancient kingdom of Pergamum, which in 133 BC fell to the Romans. It is not quite certain why Revelation was addressed to seven churches, and, more specifically, to these seven churches. There were other churches in Asia (Troas, Acts 20:5 ff; Colossae, Col 1:2; Hierapolis, Col 4:13) which were of equal importance. Ramsay has argued that the Asian church had gradually evolved into an organization of seven groups and that at the center of each stood one of the seven churches to which John writes.[11] Furthermore, the seven cities were located "on the great

---

[11]Ramsay, *The Letters to the Seven Churches of Asia,* p. 178; referred to in the body of the text hereafter as *L7CA.*

circular road that bound together the most populous, wealthy, and influential part of the Province'' (Ramsay, *L7CA*, p. 183). Others feel that the number seven was chosen intentionally because it represented completeness or perfection. In Judaism seven had special significance because of the Sabbath (the seventh day), the sabbatical year (Ex 23:10–11), and the Year of Jubilee (the year of release after seven sabbatical years; cf. Lev 25:8–17, 29–31). It is possible that these particular seven were chosen because of some special relationship to emperor worship.

The salutation combines a religious variation of the normal Hellenistic greeting[12] and the customary Hebrew *shālôm*. This dual salutation is found in all the Pauline letters (with ''mercy'' added in I Tim 1:2 and II Tim 1:2). Grace is the divine favor showed to man, and peace is that state of spiritual well-being which follows as a result. More than a casual greeting, it bestows what it proclaims.

Grace and peace proceed from a threefold source. First mentioned is the one ''who is and who was and who is to come.'' This paraphrase of the divine name stems from Exodus 3:14–15 and calls attention to the fact that all time is embraced within God's eternal presence. While it contains grammatical difficulties,[13] it does not merit Farrer's verdict of being ''the most tortured piece of Greek [the] book contains'' (p. 61). In the Greek world, similar titles for the gods are found. In the song of the doves at Dodona we read of ''Zeus who was, Zeus who is, and Zeus who will be.''[14] Since the finite cannot conceive of the eternal in other than temporal terms, John paraphrases the divine name in such a way as to remind his readers that God is eternally existent, without beginning or end. Such a reminder would be especially appropriate at a time when the church stood under the shadow of impending persecution. An uncertain future calls for One who by virtue of his eternal existence exercises sovereign control over the course of history.

[12]χάρις (grace) in place of χαῖρε (hail, welcome; cf. LSJ, p. 1970).
[13]Usually mentioned are: (1) the name stands in the nominative where we would expect the genitive after ἀπό, and (2) the finite ἦν is placed in parallel with the two participial clauses. The use of the nominative after ἀπό indicates that John considers the paraphrase of the divine name as an indeclinable noun. ''He perhaps regards the unchangeable form more appropriate to the majesty of God and to the grandioseness of the apocalyptic style'' (Beckwith, p. 424). That it is not due to ignorance of the language is obvious from the fact that the second ἀπό is immediately followed by the genitive τῶν ἑπτὰ πνευμάτων. The use of the finite is usually explained by the lack of a past participle for εἰμί. Charles suggests that we are dealing with the exact reproduction of a Hebrewism, הַהֹוֶה וְהָיָה (I, p. 10). ὁ γενόμενος would have been unacceptable because γίνομαι means ''to become'' as well as serving as a substitute for εἰμί, and John would use no word which could imply change in God.
[14]Pausanias x.12. The shrine of Minerva at Sais provides the inscription, ''I am all that hath been and is and shall be'' (Plutarch, *De Isid.* 9).

The invocation of grace and peace also comes from "the seven Spirits that are before his [God's] throne." From the perspective of a fully developed trinitarian theology it is tempting to interpret the seven spirits as the one Holy Spirit represented under the symbolism of a sevenfold or complete manifestation of his being. The source would be the LXX rendering of Isaiah 11:2.[15] This interpretation goes back at least to Victorinus of Pettau in the late third century, and is still widely accepted today. Morris, for example, says that the phrase is probably "an unusual way of designating the Holy Spirit" (p. 48). It is argued that it would be improper to bracket anyone less than deity with the Father (vs. 4a) and the Son (vs. 5), especially since in this context all three are given as the source of grace and peace. The argument loses its force, however, in view of such verses as Luke 9:26, which speaks of the return of the Son "when he comes in his glory and the glory of the Father and of the holy angels," and I Timothy 5:21, in which Paul charges obedience "in the presence of God and of Christ Jesus and of the elect angels."

Other interpreters understand the designation as a reference to the seven archangels of Jewish tradition. In *I Enoch* 20:1–8 they are listed as Uriel, Raphael, Raguel, Michael, Saraqâêl, Gabriel, and Remiel (cf. Tob 12:15; II Esdr 4:1; Dan 10:13). But this would represent a strange intrusion of Jewish tradition into Christian thought (cf. also Rev 8:2).

Reference to the seven spirits of God is found in three other places in Revelation. To the angel of the church in Sardis John is told to write, "The words of him who has the seven spirits of God and the seven stars" (3:1). Since in the address of each of the seven letters the exalted Christ is designated in terms taken from the initial vision to John (1:12–16), we should expect to find some help by turning to that vision. In 1:16 we learn that there are seven stars which are held in the hand of the "one like a son of man" and in 1:20 that these are interpreted as the angels of the seven churches. There is no mention in the initial vision of the seven spirits of God. Only if the "and" in 3:1b is taken as epexegetic rather than copulative would the seven spirits be identified with the seven angels.

The other two references to the seven spirits of God are found in the throne-room vision of chapters 4 and 5. In 4:5 they are identified as seven torches of fire which burn before the throne and in 5:6 as seven eyes of the Lamb. The background for this imagery seems to be Zechariah 4:2b, 10b where seven lamps (the LXX uses the diminutive of the same word used in Rev 4:5) are "the eyes of the Lord, which range throughout the whole

---

[15]The MT lists three couplets of two virtues each, for a total of six. The LXX breaks the poetic parallelism and inserts εὐσεβείας, "godliness" (plus a verb and direct object) for a total of seven.

earth'' (cf. ''sent out into all the earth'' in Rev 5:6). But since John is never in bondage to the source of his symbolism but ''with sovereign freedom he bends and reshapes it to serve his special purpose,''[16] little help would come from a careful exegesis of the OT passage.

Thus a survey of the four places in Revelation where the seven spirits of God are mentioned fails to provide sufficient information to arrive at a certain understanding of this enigmatic phrase. Although only a conjecture, it would seem that they are perhaps part of a heavenly entourage that has a special ministry in connection with the Lamb.[17]

5 Grace and peace proceed from the eternal God, the seven spirits before the throne, and from Jesus Christ, who is designated by the threefold title ''faithful witness,'' ''firstborn of the dead,'' and ''ruler of the kings of the earth.''[18] The doxology that immediately follows (vss. 5b–6) indicates that the order of mention in no way subordinates the Son to the seven spirits.

The first element in the title assigned to Jesus indicates that he is ''the faithful witness.''[19] This designation should not be limited to his role in mediating the revelation which comprises the book itself (''this testimony for the churches'' as mentioned in 22:16). It refers to the larger purpose of his life as the one who bore witness to the truth from God (Jn 3:32 f; 18:37) with special emphasis on his death that followed as a result. The Greek word for witness (*martys*) has come over into English as martyr, one who suffers death for allegiance to a cause. Throughout Revelation the word is associated with the penalty of death which results from a firm and constant witness (cf. 2:13; 11:3; 17:6).[20] To the Asian Christians about to enter into a time of persecution, Jesus is presented as the faithful witness. He is the model of how to stand firm and never compromise the truth of God (cf. I Tim 6:13).

Secondly, Jesus is ''the firstborn of the dead.'' The title is also found in Colossians 1:18, where Christ is declared sovereign over the

---

[16]F. F. Bruce, ''The Spirit in the Apocalypse'' in *Christ and Spirit in the New Testament*, p. 336.

[17]Bruce, in the article just mentioned (p. 336), favors Beckwith's interpretation that they represent the one Spirit symbolized by the seven torches (4:5) and the seven eyes (5:6).

[18]Fiorenza concludes that in Rev 1:5 f John quotes from a traditional baptismal formula (''Redemption as Liberation: Apoc 1:5f and 5:9f,'' *CBQ*, 36 [1974], pp. 220–22). In the latter hymn John changes his anthropological understanding of redemption by expressing it in socio-political images (p. 231).

[19]Charles explains the anomaly of the title in the nominative standing in apposition with the genitive as a Hebraism (the Hebrew noun in the indirect cases is not inflected) and notes similar instances (2:20; 3:12; 9:14; etc.; I, p. 13).

[20]The noun μαρτυρία carries the same connotations (cf. 1:9; 6:9; 11:9; 12:11, 17; 20:4). Allison Trites argues that μάρτυς in Rev is moving toward but still does not have the meaning of martyr (''Μάρτυς and Martyrdom in the Apocalypse,'' *NovT*, 15 [1973], pp. 72–80).

church by virtue of his resurrection from the dead. Lightfoot points out that the two main ideas are priority and sovereignty and that in messianic contexts the latter predominates.[21] The messianic interpretation stems from Psalm 89:27, which says of David (and extends to his descendants culminating in Jesus the Messiah), "I will make him the firstborn, the highest of the kings of the earth." If faithful witness should result in a martyr's death, the believer is to remember that Jesus, the ideal martyr, is also the firstborn from the dead. As the risen Christ now exercises sovereign control, so also will the faithful share in his reign (20:4–6).

Psalm 89:27 is the source of the third element in the title as well. As firstborn of the dead, Jesus becomes "the ruler of the kings of the earth." The expression looks forward to his open manifestation as King of kings (17:14; 19:16). What the devil offered in return for worship ("all the kingdoms of the world and the glory of them," Mt 4:8–10) Jesus has achieved through faithful obedience that led to death. Vindicated by the resurrection, he is, at the consummation, to be universally acknowledged as supreme ruler (cf. Phil 2:10–11). The threefold title is intended to encourage and sustain believers about to enter severe persecution for their faith in Jesus. It reminds them that he has gone before and opened the way through death to victory.

The reference to Christ gives rise to the first of a number of doxologies (4:11; 5:9, 12 f; 7:10; etc.). He is the one "that loveth us, and loosed[22] us from our sins." The change of tense between the two participles (present, aorist) is instructive, although it should not be pressed. The love of Christ is a continuing relationship which in point of time expressed itself in the redemptive act of Calvary. This release was purchased by the blood of Christ. Translations which follow the TR and read "washed" rather than "loosed" were probably affected by the Greek preposition normally translated "in." Here, however, it is used in the Hebraic sense of denoting a price. The ransom paid to redeem the faithful was the sacrificial death of Jesus Christ (cf. 5:9).

6 By means of his death Jesus constituted his followers a kingdom.[23] On Mt. Sinai God had promised that if the emerging Jewish nation would obey his voice and keep his commandments, he would establish them "a kingdom of priests and a holy nation" (Ex 19:5–6; cf. Isa 61:6). The early church understood itself to be the true Israel and the inheritors of

---

[21]J. B. Lightfoot, *Saint Paul's Epistles to the Colossians and to Philemon,* pp. 144–48; cf. pp. 155–56.

[22]The TR (following **P 046** 82 2059 *al g* vg co) reads λούσαντι rather than λύσαντι. Cf. Metzger, *TCGNT,* p. 731 for arguments in favor of the more difficult λύσαντι.

[23]Charles calls the change from participle to finite verb in parallel clauses "a pure Hebraism" (I, p. 15).

all the blessings promised to their spiritual predecessors (I Pet 2:5, 9). Corporately they are a kingdom (which stresses their royal standing in connection with the exaltation of Christ as ruler of all earthly kings), and individually they are priests[24] of God (which emphasizes their immediate access to God as a result of Christ's sacrificial death).

The doxology concludes with the ascription to Christ of glory and dominion forever and ever. Lenski notes that "the Greek takes its greatest term for time, the eon, pluralizes this, and then multiplies it by its own plural" (p. 48). In this context, "glory" is praise and honor, and "dominion" connotes power and might. The two are likewise joined in the doxology to God and the Lamb found in 5:13. The statement is both a confident assertion about the exalted Christ and an exhortation to regard him correspondingly.

7 In Daniel's vision of the four beasts, the prophet saw one like a son of man coming "with the clouds of heaven" (Dan 7:13). Zechariah prophesied that in the day of the Lord the inhabitants of Jerusalem would "look on him whom they have pierced" and "mourn for him" (Zech 12:10). These two prophetic motifs are joined by John and adapted to describe the impending advent of the victorious Christ and the response of a hostile world to the revelation of his universal sovereignty. The event is so immediate and certain that John can announce, "Behold, he cometh" (cf. 3:11; 22:7, 12, 20). Note that, like the man-figure of Daniel 7:13, he comes *with* the clouds rather than on or in them.[25] Hort suggests that the rather unusual phrase means that "he compels all the clouds into his retinue" (p. 12). In any case, the cloud in Hebrew thought is commonly associated with the divine presence (Ex 13:21; 16:10; Mt 17:5; Acts 1:9).

When he comes, his sovereignty will be openly manifested to all, for "every eye shall see him." The following clause ("even such as pierced him") is parenthetical. The Fourth Gospel indicates that the piercing of Jesus' side by the Roman soldier fulfilled the scripture, "They shall look on him whom they have pierced" (Jn 19:37 quoting Zech 12:10).[26] The reference in Revelation should not be limited to that incident or, as in Zechariah 12:10, to the tribes of Israel, but extends to all those of every age whose careless indifference to Jesus is typified in the act of piercing. At his

---

[24]ἱερεῖς stands in apposition with βασιλείαν and stresses the mediating role of believers in their consecration to the service of God.

[25]Rev 1:7 reads μετὰ τῶν νεφελῶν; Mt 24:30 has ἐπί and Mk 13:26/Lk 21:27 has ἐν. R. B. Y. Scott holds that νεφέλαι are not the ordinary clouds of nature, but clouds *in heaven* seen in the vision around the throne of God ("Behold, He Cometh with Clouds," *NTS*, 5 [1958–9], pp. 127–32).

[26]In the NT ἐκκεντέω is found only in Jn 19:37 and Rev 1:7. The LXX of Zech 12:10 uses κατορχέομαι, "to mock."

coming all the tribes of earth (not the twelve tribes of Israel but the non-Christian world represented in terms of ethnic divisions) will mourn for him. The mourning of Zechariah 12:10–12 was that of repentance, but the mourning of Revelation is the remorse accompanying the disclosure of divine judgment at the coming of Christ (cf. 16:9, 11, 21).

The thrust of the verse is that upon the imminent return of Christ unbelievers will mourn the judgment which follows from their rejection. The final "Even so, Amen" combines the Greek and Hebrew forms of affirmation (cf. "grace and peace" in 1:4). It is an expression of vigorous approval.

8 Only here and in 21:5 ff does God himself speak. He declares that he is "the Alpha and the Omega" (the first and last letters of the Greek alphabet). In 21:6 the title is expanded and interpreted by the parallel expression, "the beginning and the end."[27] Alpha and Omega represent the Hebrew *Aleph Tau,* which was regarded not simply as the first and last letters of the alphabet, but as including all the letters in between. Hence, God is the sovereign Lord of all that takes place in the entire course of human history. He is the beginning and he is the end. In the immediate context God is not revealing his eternality for the theological edification of believers, but for the encouragement of Asian Christians about to suffer persecution for their faith.

As sovereign Lord he is "the Almighty."[28] Although the title occurs extensively throughout the Greek OT, it is found only ten times in the NT, and nine of these occurrences are in Revelation (1:8; 4:8; 11:17; 15:3; 16:7, 14; 19:6, 15; 21:22; in II Cor 6:18 it is used in a quotation from the OT). Like the other titles in the verse it is intended to encourage and support believers in a time of crisis. The reference is more to God's supremacy over all things (cf. Michaelis in *TDNT,* III, p. 915) than to the related idea of divine omnipotence. The latter half of the verse is not spoken by God but about him. The use of the threefold title in 1:4 and the third person in "and [he] was" supports this position.

3. INAUGURAL VISION AND COMMISSION TO WRITE (1:9–20)

> 9 *I John, your brother and partaker with you in the tribulation and kingdom and patience* which are *in Jesus, was in the isle that is called Patmos, for the word of God and the testimony of Jesus.*

[27]In 22:13 Jesus applies the same title to himself and adds yet another interpretive phrase, "the first and the last." W. J. P. Boyd calls the title "a brilliant translation of the Hebrew logion found in Isaiah 44,6" ("I am Alpha and Omega," *SE,* IV [1964], p. 526).

[28]παντοκράτωρ was used at times in secular literature to describe an attribute of the gods (*eg., Epigr. Graec.* 815, of Hermes).

10 *I was in the Spirit on the Lord's day, and I heard behind me a great voice, as of a trumpet*

11 *saying, What thou seest, write in a book and send* it *to the seven churches: unto Ephesus, and unto Smyrna, and unto Pergamum, and unto Thyatira, and unto Sardis, and unto Philadelphia, and unto Laodicea.*

12 *And I turned to see the voice that spake with me. And having turned I saw seven golden candlesticks;*

13 *and in the midst of the candlesticks one like unto a son of man, clothed with a garment down to the foot, and girt about at the breasts with a golden girdle.*

14 *And his head and his hair were white as white wool,* white *as snow; and his eyes were as a flame of fire;*

15 *and his feet like unto burnished brass, as if it had been refined in a furnace; and his voice as the voice of many waters.*

16 *And he had in his right hand seven stars: and out of his mouth proceeded a sharp two-edged sword: and his countenance was as the sun shineth in his strength.*

17 *And when I saw him, I fell at his feet as one dead. And he laid his right hand upon me, saying, Fear not; I am the first and the last,*

18 *and the Living one; and I was dead, and behold, I am alive for evermore, and I have the keys of death and of Hades.*

19 *Write therefore the things which thou sawest, and the things which are, and the things which shall come to pass hereafter;*

20 *the mystery of the seven stars which thou sawest in my right hand, and the seven golden candlesticks. The seven stars are the angels of the seven churches: and the seven candlesticks are seven churches.*

9 Verses 9–20 record John's vision of the exalted Christ and his commission to write to the seven churches what he is about to see. Both Isaiah and Ezekiel began their ministry with a great vision of the glory of God (Isa 6; Ezek 1). After the direct statement from God in the preceding verse, John once again identifies himself.[29] He writes to the churches as one who has paid the price of exile for his faithfulness in proclaiming the word of God. He can fully understand the difficulty in which they find themselves in that he is a partaker with them (a "fellow sharer") in the tribulation that accompanies the Christian faith. "Brother" was a common designation among believers and reflects the close relationship they experienced as members of the same religious body.

Their common lot is described as "tribulation," "kingdom," and "patience in Jesus."[30] "Tribulation" refers to the suffering which accom-

---

[29]The personality of the writer is kept to the fore in apocalyptic literature (cf. Dan 8:1; 10:2; *I Enoch* 12:3).

[30]Other MSS read ἐν Χριστῷ (A), ἐν Ἰησοῦ Χριστῷ (ℵᶜ sy), Ἰησοῦ Χριστοῦ (1 2329 *al*).

panies faithfulness to Christian principles (Jn 16:33, "In the world you have tribulation"; cf. Acts 14:22; II Tim 3:12) but extends to include the final period of intensified affliction which precedes the establishment of the millennial kingdom. Ladd notes that the great tribulation at the end of time "will be only the intensification of what the church has suffered throughout all history" (p. 30). With tribulation, John joins kingdom and patience. "Kingdom" refers to the coming period of messianic blessedness, and "patience" is the active endurance required of the faithful. The order of the three is instructive. Since the present is a time of tribulation and the kingdom a period of future blessedness, believers must during the interim period exercise that kind of patient endurance which was exemplified by Jesus.[31]

The place of John's exile was Patmos, a small (about sixteen square miles), rocky island in the Aegean Sea some forty miles west-southwest of Miletus. Its rugged terrain enters the imagery of the Apocalypse in its emphasis on rocks and mountains. In addition to its significance for navigation between Ephesus and Rome, it was a penal settlement to which the Roman authorities sent offenders.[32] John says that he was on the isle of Patmos "for the word of God and the testimony of Jesus." Apparently the Asian authorities had interpreted his preaching as seditious and removed him from the mainland in an attempt to inhibit the growth of the early church. The suggestion that he went to Patmos for the purpose of preaching is unlikely. In Revelation 1:2 "the word of God and the testimony of Jesus" described the content of the Apocalypse. Here the phrase refers more broadly to the content of John's preaching. The message originated with God and was testified to by Jesus.

10 John records that he was "in the Spirit" on the day of his revelation. This expression refers to a state of spiritual exaltation best described as a trance. Peter at Joppa (Acts 10:10; 11:5) and Paul at Jerusalem (Acts 22:17; cf. II Cor 12:2–4) had similar ecstatic experiences. Caird suggests as a stimulus for John's vision Domitian's edict which insisted on the worship of the reigning emperor. He saw in it "the emergence of a new totalitarianism which Christians were bound to resist, and which would therefore result in war to the death between church and state" (p. 23). Or perhaps it was simply that the messianic era had dawned in which it was to be expected that "young men shall see visions" and

---

[31]ἐν Ἰησοῦ is equivalent to the Pauline ἐν Χριστῷ and is joined more closely to ὑπομονῇ than to the two other nouns.

[32]Pliny, *Hist. Nat.* iv.69, is frequently invoked in this connection, but all that Pliny says about Patmos is that it was thirty miles in circumference. Eusebius reports that John was released by the emperor Nerva (AD 96–98) and returned to Ephesus (*Hist. Eccl.* iii.20.9).

"old men shall dream dreams" (Acts 2:17). Following the letters to the seven churches in chapters 2 and 3 John continues "in the Spirit" for subsequent visions.

The vision takes place "on the Lord's day." Some have interpreted this as a reference to "the day of Yahweh." That is, John is carried forward by the Spirit to the day of consummation when Christ is unveiled and the judgment of God falls on mankind. It is more probable that this is the first mention in Christian literature of the Lord's day as a technical term for the first day of the week.[33] It is the Lord's day because on the first day of the week Christ rose victorious from the grave. As paganism had set aside a day on which to honor their emperor, so also Christians chose the first day of each week to honor Christ. The Lord's day should be understood over against the emperor's day.

In this state of existential openness to the Spirit of God, John hears a great voice behind him. There is no possibility of misunderstanding the command because the voice is as clear and unmistakable as the sound of a trumpet.[34] Since Christ's voice is later described as "the voice of many waters" (1:15), some have held that the voice must have been that of an angel. In the verses that follow (vss. 17–19), however, it is Christ who commands John to write, and it is therefore natural to assume that it is also he who speaks in verses 10 and 11.

11 The voice like a trumpet instructs John to commit to writing what he is about to see.[35] The scroll is then to be sent to the seven churches. Ramsay's suggestion that the seven cities named by John were chosen because they were the distribution centers for the seven postal districts of west-central Asia Minor (*L7CA,* p. 191) is attractive and quite plausible. The cities were located roughly thirty to fifty miles apart along a circular

---

[33]If the reference were to the eschatological day of the Lord, we would have expected the more usual ἡμέρα κυρίου of I Thess 5:2; II Pet 3:10 rather than ἡ κυριακή, which apart from our text occurs in the NT only in I Cor 11:20. Cf. *Didache* 14:1; Ignatius, *Magn.* 9.1; *Gospel of Peter* 9; Melito of Sardis (Eusebius, *Hist. Eccl.* iv.26). W. Stott summarizes his study saying, "κυριακὴ ἡμέρα in Rev. i.10 may be taken to refer to the first day of the week, the Christian Sunday, and not to the Last Day, or to Easter" ("A Note on the Word **KYPIAKH** in Rev. I.10," *NTS,* 12 [1965–6], p. 75). Strand criticizes Stott for not giving adequate attention to the view of C. W. Dugmore (that the earliest Christian 'Lord's Day' references are to Easter), and argues that while the thesis is plausible for early Christianity in general, it cannot be applied to Rev 1:10 ("Another Look at 'Lord's Day' in the Early Church and in Rev. I.10," *NTS,* 13 [1966–7], pp. 174–81). Cf. the discussion in Paul K. Jewett, *The Lord's Day,* pp. 58–60.

[34]The voice of God as a trumpet goes back to the theophany at Sinai (Ex 19:16, 19; cf. Heb 12:19). It had acquired eschatological significance for the early church (Mt 24:31; I Cor 15:52; I Thess 4:16).

[35]Note that the participle λεγούσης agrees with the dependent genitive σάλπιγγος, rather than the noun φωνή. Cf. 4:1 and 6:7. Similar commands to write are found in Tob 12:20 and II Esdr 12:37.

road that went north to Pergamum, turned southeast to Laodicea, and returned full circle to Ephesus through the valley of the Maeander. The seven letters written to the seven churches (chaps. 2 and 3) should not be taken as a group of covering letters, each one to be read only at the appropriate location. The entire scroll was to be read at each church. That there were seven letters (rather than six or eight) may stem from the fact that that was the number of postal districts on the circular route. It is at the same time, however, a decidedly symbolic number, standing for completeness and especially appropriate for the Apocalypse. The order in which the churches are addressed is strictly geographical. They do not portray seven successive periods of church history. Although the letters are written to real churches of the first century, they are relevant to the church universal, for the strengths and weaknesses of the seven are characteristic of individual churches throughout history.

12–13 Upon hearing the great voice, John turned to see the one who had instructed him to write. There in the midst of seven golden lampstands[36] was one like a son of man. Exodus 25:31–37 records the instructions given to Moses for making the seven-branched lampstand of pure gold. In John's vision, however, there are seven separate lampstands, perhaps like those placed before the inner sanctuary by Solomon when he dedicated the temple (I Kgs 8:49). From Revelation 1:20 we learn that the lampstands signify the seven churches to whom the letters are addressed. The purpose of the church is to bear the light of the divine presence in a darkened world (Mt 5:14–16). Failing this, its reason for existence has disappeared (cf. Rev 2:5).

In the midst of the lampstands was "one like unto a son of man." The background of the phrase is Daniel 7:13, which describes the presentation to the Ancient of Days of "one like a son of man" who had come with the clouds of heaven. Commentators differ on the significance of the designation. Swete holds that it means "a human being" (p. 15), while Charles takes it as a technical term in apocalyptic for "like an angel" (I, p. 27).[37] In either case, the One who speaks is none other than the exalted Christ, for in subsequent verses (17–18) he identifies himself in terms of pre-existence, death, and resurrection.

Some writers hold that in the introductory verses of Revelation Jesus is presented in his threefold office of prophet, priest, and king. Bruce

---

[36]λυχνία was a lampstand, not a candlestick. λύχνος was the portable lamp which was placed upon the stand. Candles as we now know them were not in use.

[37]Charles maintains that "ὡς υἱὸς ἀνθρώπου in the Apocalypse is the exact equivalent of ὁ υἱὸς τοῦ ἀνθρώπου in the Gospels and Acts vii.56" and the one who appears to the Seer is not "like the Son of Man" but is "the Son of Man" (p. 27).

notes that in verse 1 he is the recipient of God's revelation, in verse 5 he is "ruler of kings on earth," and in verse 13 he wears the high-priestly vestments (p. 636).[38] This interpretation is supported by the fact that he wears the full-length robe of the high priest (Ex 28:4; 29:5). The Greek word translated "a garment down to the foot" in the *ASV* occurs only here in the NT, while in all but one of its seven occurrences in the LXX it is used in connection with the attire of the high priest. The girdle of the priest was made of fine twined linen and embroidered with needlework (Ex 39:29), while the girdle which gathered together the long robe of the exalted Christ was of gold. Josephus, however, speaks of the priest's girdle as being interwoven with gold. This, plus the fact that high girding ("at the breasts") denotes the dignity of an important office, suggests that this part of the description as well is intended to set forth the high-priestly function of Christ.

14 The description of the celestial visitor continues with statements about his hair, eyes, feet, and voice. Caird wisely cautions against overinterpretation, noting that to track down the source of each descriptive phrase and compile a catalogue would be "to unweave the rainbow." John uses his allusions "for their evocative and emotive power. . . . His aim is to set the echoes of memory and association ringing . . . to call forth from his readers the same response of overwhelming and annihilating wonder which he experienced in his prophetic trance" (pp. 25–26).

The expression "his head and his hair" should be translated "his head, that is, his hair." [39] In Daniel 7:9 the Ancient of Days is described as having hair "like pure wool" and raiment "white as snow." With minor modification (it is the hair of Christ that is "white as white wool, as snow"; [40] cf. Isa 1:18) this description is transferred in Revelation to the exalted Christ. The ascription of the titles and attributes of God to Christ is an indication of the exalted Christology of the Apocalypse. Ancient expositors attempted to find in the reference to white hair an allusion to the eternal pre-existence of the Son. This is not intended. The hoary head was worthy of honor and conveyed the idea of wisdom and dignity (Lev 19:32; Prov 16:31). Continuing with the description, we learn that his eyes are "as a flame of fire," an item repeated in the letter to Thyatira (2:18) as well as

---

[38]Barclay finds all three offices in the dress of the risen Lord (I, pp. 57–58). Robert Thomas writes that the ten distinguishing characteristics of the risen Christ serve to prepare the apostle for the vision to follow ("The Glorified Christ on Patmos," *BSac*, 122 [1965], pp. 241–47).

[39]*I Enoch* 46:1 says of the Ancient of Days, "His head was white like wool," but it is doubtful that the description in Revelation resulted from combining the two texts in *Enoch* and Daniel.

[40]Hugh Michael would transfer λευκὸν ὡς χιών from vs. 14 and place the phrase immediately following ποδήρη in vs. 13 ("A Slight Misplacement in Revelation i. 13, 14," *ET*, 42 [1930–1], pp. 380–81). The suggestion receives additional support from C. Cave Oke (*ET*, 43 [1931–2], p. 237).

in the account of the victorious return of the conquering Messiah (19:12). It expresses the penetrating insight of the one who is sovereign, not only over the seven churches, but over the course of history itself.

15 Below the long robe John saw the feet of Christ as "burnished brass." The etymology of this Greek word (which occurs nowhere in the literature independent of Rev) is difficult[41] but best understood as an alloy of gold or fine brass. Considerable textual uncertainty exists in the companion phrase. The *ASV* follows the most commonly accepted reading and translates, "as if it had been refined in a furnace."[42] A slightly different, but reasonable, reconstruction could read, "like unto burnished brass out of a heated oven."[43] In any case, the shining, bronze-like feet portray strength and stability. The voice of Christ is described as "the voice of many waters," suggesting the awe-inspiring power of a great waterfall. It is used of the voice of God in Ezekiel 43:2 and of the great multitude in Revelation 19:6 (cf. Rev 14:2).

16 In his right hand Christ has[44] (or holds; cf. 2:1) seven stars. Four verses later we are told that "the seven stars are the angels of the seven churches" (1:20). The number of stars is determined quite simply by the number of churches to which the Apocalypse is addressed. There is no need to search for a mythological or astrological background such as Pleiades (the seven daughters of Atlas and Pleione, placed by Zeus among the stars) or the seven planets (sun, moon, Mercury, Venus, Mars, Jupiter, and Saturn). That Christ has the full complement of stars in his right hand indicates his sovereign control over the churches. It may also imply protection (Jn 10:28).

A sharp two-edged sword proceeds from the mouth of Christ.[45] In the letter to the church at Pergamum, Christ warns that unless they repent he will come and war against them with the "sword of [his] mouth" (2:16; cf. comm. on 2:12). Chapter 19 pictures the return of Christ from whose mouth issues a sharp sword (19:15, 21). The sword in these vignettes

---

[41]If the basic roots of the compound are χαλκός (copper) and κλίβανος (furnace), it could refer to bronze ore in the process of smelting. Hort takes the second root to be λίβανος, frankincense, and understands the compound to be an amber colored metal, electrum, which in the LXX is designated ἤλεκτρον (p. 17). The Syriac version takes it to be a metal from Lebanon. Cf. comm. at 2:18 and reference to Hemer's discussion.

[42]πεπυρωμένης is favored because of strong textual attestation (**A C**) and because it explains the others. πεπυρωμένῳ (**ℵ** 205 *pc g b* vg sy Ir Prim) qualifies καμίνῳ, and πεπυρωμένοι (**P 046** 1 82 2329 *pl* Tyc TR) qualifies οἱ πόδες.

[43]This meets the problem of the feminine genitive participle πεπυρωμένης by joining it with a modified ἐκ καμίνου.

[44]ἔχων continues the participial construction of vs. 13. The last finite verb was εἶδον in vs. 12. **A** omits ἔχων while the original version of **ℵ** reads εἶχεν.

[45]Outside of Rev (1:16; 2:12, 16; 6:8; 19:15, 21) ῥομφαία occurs only in Lk 2:35 in the NT. It appears to have been a large Thracian weapon, although it is not certain whether it was a sword or a spear (*HDB*, IV, p. 634). See note on 6:8.

symbolizes the irresistible power of divine judgment.[46] The authoritative word of Christ is to be understood over against the fraudulent demands of the imperial cult. It is the word of Christ which will ultimately prevail.

John's account of the vision reaches its high point by describing the countenance of the exalted Christ as the sun shining in its strength. The Greek word occurs but three times in the NT. It may mean "face" as in John 11:44, or "outward appearance" as in John 7:24. In the context of Revelation 1:13–16 its primary reference is to the face but should not be limited to that alone. There was a brillance about Christ which surrounded his entire person. Once before, on the Mount of Transfiguration, John beheld the Lord when "his face shone like the sun, and his garments became white as light" (Mt 17:2; cf. Ex 34:29; Judg 5:31; Mt 13:43).

17 John's response to the vision was to fall at the feet of Christ as though dead. Similar responses are found in Joshua 5:14; Ezekiel 1:28; Daniel 8:17; 10:15; Matthew 17:6; Acts 26:14; and *I Enoch* 14:14. But to call the response "stereotyped behaviour in such apocalyptic trances" (Moffatt, p. 345) would incorrectly imply that John was playing out a role rather than experiencing a supernatural phenomenon of such magnitude that to stand as an equal would be tantamount to blasphemy.

Christ now lays his right hand upon John and speaks a word of strong assurance. That he is described in the previous verse as having seven stars in the same right hand should cause no problem. The entire account is visionary and symbolic, and as such should not be expected to conform to literalistic requirements. The laying on of the right hand communicated power and blessing. It is a commissioning hand which restores John's confidence and prepares him to hear the words of consolation and command.

The celestial visitor speaks, and his very words remind the prostrate Seer of earlier days when as Jesus of Nazareth this one had shared his earthly ministry with the twelve. More than once John had heard the familiar "Fear not," for example, when Jesus approached the disciples walking on the water (Mt 14:27) and when they had fallen on their faces having heard the voice of God from heaven (Mt 17:7). There is no cause for fear because he who speaks is "the first and the last."[47] This title is essentially the same as the divine self-designation in 1:8, "the Alpha and the Omega." In 22:13 both titles are joined by a third, "the beginning and

---

[46]The imagery is widely attested; cf. Isa 49:2 ("He made my mouth like a sharp sword"); Wis 18:15–16 ("Thy all-powerful word leaped from heaven . . . a stern warrior carrying the sharp sword of thy authentic command"); II Esdr 13:10; Heb 4:12; etc. Some have noted the appropriateness of the imagery in that the short Roman sword was tongue-like in shape.

[47]ἐγώ εἰμι would also have a familiar ring. It is a favorite Johannine phrase (twenty-four times in the Fourth Gospel while less than a dozen times in the Synoptics).

the end." In Isaiah 44:6 God declares, "I am the first and I am the last; besides me there is no god" (cf. Isa 48:12). The title emphasizes the absolute sovereignty of God. Thus, in Revelation, the words "Fear not" come from a sovereign being. Even death holds no terror because he is the Living One who has conquered death and holds it in his power (vs. 18).

18 The idea involved in the title "the first and the last" is expanded epexegetically by, "that is, the Living one."[48] The designation is based on OT references to "the living God" (Josh 3:10; Ps 42:2; 84:3; etc.) and is used freely in the NT (Mt 16:16; Acts 14:15; Rom 9:26; etc.). It declares that in his essential nature Christ possesses life and therefore is to be understood in sharp contrast to the dead gods of paganism. Even though he experienced death in the course of his earthly ministry, he is alive forever.[49] He has in his possession the keys of death and Hades.[50] This grants him power and authority over their domain (cf. Mt 16:19). According to Jewish literature, power over these keys belongs to God alone (*Tg. Jer.* on Gen 30:22; *Sanh.* 113a). That they now are in the possession of Christ is evidence of the high Christology of the Apocalypse.

19 The initial command to write what is about to be seen (vs. 11) is repeated and expanded. Many commentators accept a threefold division of the verse interpreting "the things which thou sawest" as a reference to the vision of the Son of man (in the verses immediately preceding), "the things that are" as referring to the present condition of the church in chapters 2 and 3, and "the things which shall come to pass hereafter" in reference to the visions beginning in chapter 4 and continuing to the end of the book. Charles (I, p. 33) says they "summarize *roughly* the contents of the Book," and Swete (p. 21) accepts the division with some reservation, noting that it is "rough and superficial." Others, however, are less reserved about the threefold hypothesis. Walvoord, for example, says, "It is not too much to claim that this outline is the only one which allows the book to speak for itself without artificial manipulation" (p. 48).[51] The proper division, however, is twofold, not three.[52] The first statement

---

[48]Translating ϰαί as an explicative. That the phrase goes with what precedes is assumed by the punctuation in the *ASV* (also the *RSV, NEB,* and others). Charles, however, connects it with what follows (I, p. 31). It is omitted in the Vulgate.

[49]The *ASV* "for evermore" connotes for all future time, which, although true, fails to catch the antithesis between ἐγενόμην νεϰρός and ζῶν εἰμι. The emphasis is not on the resurrection but on the reality of Christ's continuing life.

[50]Hades is always joined with death in Rev (6:8; 20:13–14). It is the Greek equivalent of the Hebrew Sheol and stands for the abode of departed spirits. It is not Gehenna, the place of torment (Mt 5:22, 29, 30).

[51]Cf. Robert Thomas, "John's Apocalyptic Outline," *BSac,* 123 (1966), pp. 334–41.

[52]W. C. van Unnik calls attention to the three-part formula used in *Ap John* ("Now I have come to reveal to you that which is, that which has been, and that which will be") and points out examples in pagan and Christian literature where it is found ("A Formula Describing

("Write therefore the things which thou sawest") is the essential unit and parallels the earlier command in vs. 11 ("What thou seest, write in a book"). Both relative clauses are proleptic[53] and have as their referents the vision to be unfolded in the coming chapters. The "and" is epexegetical and introduces two additional clauses which make more specific what John is to write. Translate, "Write, therefore, the things you are about to see, that is, both what now is and what lies yet in the future." This relationship between present and future underlies the entire Apocalypse. It recognizes that the great throne-room drama of chapters 4 and 5, the vision of the woman giving birth to the man-child in chapter 12, and much of chapter 17 belong in the past and the present as well as the future. Moffatt is right in holding that "the contents of the vision . . . consist of what is and what is to be" (p. 347).

20 The punctuation of the *ASV* connects the first half of verse 20 with the preceding verse, making the mystery of the seven stars part of the command to write. The *RSV* (and many others) places a full stop at the end of verse 19 and begins verse 20, "As for the mystery of the seven stars." In Daniel 2:47 Nebuchadnezzar acknowledges that Daniel's God is a "revealer of mysteries." It is in this same sense of the "inner meaning of a symbolic vision" (Swete, p. 21) that Christ now supplies the interpretation of the seven stars and seven candlesticks (*ASV*, lampstands). The lampstands are the churches. In verse 13 we learned that Christ stands in the midst of his churches. Facing persecution in a hostile environment, they are to recognize his abiding presence. The seven stars are said to be the angels of the seven churches. Many explanations have been proposed for the angels. If they are human beings (Mt 11:10 and other verses would allow this), they could be prominent officials of the local congregations or delegates sent to Patmos to be entrusted with the letters. The use of "angel" in the book of Revelation (it occurs some sixty times) favors identifying the angels as heavenly beings. They could be guardian angels (cf. Dan 10:13, 20–21; Mt 18:10; Acts 12:15) or perhaps heavenly counterparts which came to be identified with the church. The most satisfactory answer, however, is that the angel of the church was a way of personifying the prevailing spirit of the church. This interpretation is strengthened by the fact that all seven letters are addressed to separate angels, a strange phenomenon if they refer to anything but the church since the contents are obviously intended for the congregation as a whole.

Prophecy," *NTS,* 9 [1962–3], pp. 86–94). He holds that by using this apocalyptic formula the authors are indicating the prophetic-revelation character of their works.

[53]ὃ βλέπεις in vs. 11 and ἃ εἶδες in vs. 19.

CHAPTER 2

II. LETTERS TO THE SEVEN CHURCHES (2:1–3:22)

The letters to the seven churches of Asia (chaps. 2 and 3) form a distinct unit in the book of Revelation. That they are integrally related to the vision in chapter 1 follows from the fact that in the introduction to each letter the writer (Christ) identifies himself by means of a descriptive phrase taken from the vision and appropriate for the specific church. To the angel of the church in Ephesus the message comes from the one who "holdeth the seven stars in his right hand" and "walketh in the midst of the seven golden candlesticks" (2:1; cf. 1:12, 16). To Smyrna he writes as "the first and the last, who was dead, and lived *again*" (2:8; cf. 1:17, 18). To Pergamum he is the one who "hath the sharp two-edged sword" (2:12; cf. 1:16).[1] Charles understands this phenomenon as the result of the author re-editing an earlier set of his letters dealing with the spiritual conditions of the churches so as to relate them to the impending crisis. Part of the process consisted in bringing the original titles into closer conformity with the divine titles of Christ in 1:13–18 (I, pp. 46–47). The plausibility of this conjecture rests on one's larger understanding of the nature and purpose of the letters themselves.

The older view is that the letters existed independently of the rest of the book. Charles maintains that they were originally sent to the various churches separately at a time prior to the fundamental antagonism which developed between Christianity and the imperial cult. The allusion in 3:10 to universal persecution, therefore, would belong to the period of later redaction (Charles, I, p. 44).

Most modern commentators understand the letters as an integral part of the Apocalypse, but differ as to their nature and purpose. Dis-

---

[1] Cf. also Thyatira (2:18 with 1:14–15), Sardis (3:1 with 1:16), Philadelphia (3:7 with 1:18), Laodicea (3:14 with 1:5).

pensational writers take them as real letters to historical churches, but also as a preview of church history in its downward course toward Laodicean lukewarmness. Walvoord says that to interpret such a remarkable progression as pure accident would be incredible. "The order of the messages to the churches seems to be divinely selected to give prophetically the main movement of history" (p. 52). Richardson, on the other hand, maintains that this idea is "based on pure fancy" but argues that God is in control of history, moving it toward ultimate victory through the agency of the church (pp. 44–45).

Both Swete and Beckwith note that what we have are not true letters, but "messages" (Swete, p. xi) or "special words" (Beckwith, pp. 446–47). They form a sequel to chapter 1 and part of a common epistle sent to all seven. Feuillet suggests that a greater emphasis should be placed on their being oracles. Christ comes to inspect his churches, and issues words of warning and notes of encouragement. The utterances, says Feuillet, resemble the prophetic oracles of the OT more than the epistles of the NT.[2] In any case, the messages are a vital part of the Apocalypse as a whole and are intended for the exhortation and edification of the church universal. Each oracle contains the challenge, "He who has an ear, let him hear what the Spirit says to the *churches*" (the plural is significant!).

The symmetry of the seven letters has long interested commentators. Each letter is prefaced by a charge to write to the angel of the specific church. This is followed by an identification of the author in descriptive phrases taken from the vision in chapter 1. The body of each letter is composed of an acknowledgment of the church's positive achievements (except in Laodicea and, perhaps, in Sardis), followed by words of encouragement, censure, counsel, or warning. Only Smyrna and Philadelphia escape some note of censure. The letters close with the exhortation to hear and a promise to those who conquer.[3] The orderliness and symmetry of the seven letters betray a purpose that goes beyond ethical instruction to seven particular churches in the Roman province of Asia. The entire sequence is a literary composition designed to impress upon the church universal the necessity of patient endurance in the period of impending persecution. It is this motif which binds the oracles to that which follows. In the final conflict between Christ and Caesar, believers will need to hold fast to their confession of faith and stand ready for whatever sacrifice may be required. Bruce writes that the letters give a vivid impres-

---

[2]*The Apocalypse*, pp. 48–49. The τάδε λέγει in 2:1, 8, 12, 18; 3:1, 7, 14, is customarily used in the LXX to announce a prophetic message.

[3]Cf. Beckwith (p. 260), Morris (p. 58), or Caird (p. 27) for the general pattern common to each of the seven letters.

sion of Christian life in Asia at a time when "pressure is being brought to bear on the Christians to be less unyielding in their negative attitude to such socially approved activities as emperor worship and the like" (p. 637).

1. EPHESUS (2:1–7)

1 *To the angel of the church in Ephesus write:*

> *These things saith he that holdeth the seven stars in his right hand, he that walketh in the midst of the seven golden candlesticks:*

2 *I know thy works, and thy toil and patience, and that thou canst not bear evil men, and didst try them that call themselves apostles, and they are not, and didst find them false;*

3 *and thou hast patience and didst bear for my name's sake, and hast not grown weary.*

4 *But I have* this *against thee, that thou didst leave thy first love.*

5 *Remember therefore whence thou art fallen, and repent and do the first works; or else I come to thee, and will move thy candlestick out of its place, except thou repent.*

6 *But this thou hast, that thou hatest the works of the Nicolaitans, which I also hate.*

7 *He that hath an ear, let him hear what the Spirit saith to the churches. To him that overcometh, to him will I give to eat of the tree of life, which is in the Paradise of God.*

1 The first letter is directed to the angel of the church in Ephesus. The reference is to the prevailing spirit of the church rather than to the guardian angel or ruling official of the congregation.[4] It is appropriate that Ephesus receive the first letter: it was the most important city of proconsular Asia. Situated at the mouth of the Cayster River on a gulf of the Aegean Sea,[5] it flourished as an important commercial and export center for Asia. The traveler from Rome landing at Ephesus would proceed up a magnificent avenue thirty-five feet wide and lined with columns which led from the harbor to the center of the city. Ephesus was part of the kingdom of Pergamum which Attalus III bequeathed to Rome in 133 BC. By NT times it had grown to better than a quarter of a million in population. Its commercial importance was heightened by the fact that three great trade routes converged at the city (from the Euphrates by way of Colossae, from Galatia through Sardis, and from the Maeander valley[6] to the south and east).

---

[4]Brownlee notes that while previously having interpreted the angel as a spiritualized personification of the church, he now takes the term as referring to the priestly role of the bishop ("The Priestly Character of the Church in the Apocalypse," *NTS*, 5 [1958-9], pp. 224–25).
[5]Pliny (*Hist. Nat.* ii.201) wrote that "once the sea used to wash up to the temple of Diana."
[6]Kraeling writes that the route up the Maeander to the Lycus and on toward Apamea was "the most important avenue of civilization in Asia Minor under the Roman Empire" (*HDB rev.*, p. 262).

Although Ephesus was not the titular capital of Asia (Pergamum retained this honor), it was a city of great political importance. As a free city it had been granted by Rome the right of self-government. It also served as an assize city in which the Roman governor on a regular schedule tried important cases and dispensed justice. It boasted a major stadium, marketplace, and theater. The latter was built on the west slope of Mt. Pion overlooking the harbor, and seated some 25,000 persons.

The imperial cult was not neglected in Ephesus. Temples were built to Claudius, Hadrian, and Severus. The major religious attraction, however, was the Temple of Artemis (Diana in Latin), one of the seven wonders of the ancient world. About four times the size of the Parthenon, it was adorned by the work of many great artists. After a great fire in 356 BC destroyed the first temple, it was rebuilt, with Dinocrates (who later built Alexandria) as architect. Pliny the elder (*Hist. Nat.* xxxvi.95 ff) gives the dimensions of the temple as 425 feet long, 220 feet wide, and sixty feet high. He also notes that the 127 pillars were of Parian marble, with thirty-six of them overlaid with gold and jewels (Barclay, *L7C,* pp. 14–15). Artemis herself was originally an Anatolian fertility goddess, but under the influence of Greek culture had become the focus of an extensive religious cult.

The Christian faith came to Ephesus perhaps with Aquila and Priscilla about AD 52 when Paul left them there en route from Corinth to Antioch (Acts 18:18–22). On his next missionary journey the apostle remained in Ephesus more than two years (Acts 18:8, 10), and some time later Timothy ministered there (I Tim 1:3). It was the apostle John, however, who is most closely associated with the city.

The letter to Ephesus comes from the One who holds the seven stars in his right hand and who walks among the seven lampstands. From 1:20 we learned that the lampstands are churches and the stars their angels (personifications of the prevailing spirit). The two participles are instructive: Christ *holds* the angels (they are in his control) and *walks* among the lampstands (he is present in their midst and aware of their activities). In the context of the seven letters his presence is better interpreted in terms of inspection and resulting knowledge than in relationship to the fundamental theme of the Holiness Code, "I will walk among you, and will be your God, and you shall be my people" (Lev 26:12).

2 As one who walks in the midst of the churches, Christ is able to say, "I know thy works" (cf. 2:9; 3:1, 8, 15).[7] The works which Christ

---

[7]Lightfoot's opinion that οἶδα refers to knowledge of facts absolutely and γινώσκω to the attainment or manifestation of knowledge (*St. Paul's Epistle to the Galatians,* p. 171; also *Notes on the Epistles of St. Paul,* pp. 178 f) is not generally accepted (cf. MM, p. 439; Morris, *Commentary on the Gospel of John,* pp. 206–7, n. 96).

knows are not so much separate acts as they are an overall manner of life. The two nouns which follow (toil and patience)[8] give the active and passive sides of this lifestyle. The Ephesians had toiled to the point of exhaustion and borne patiently the hostility of a society at odds with their goals and efforts (cf. the problems of Paul in Ephesus with disbelieving Jews, the seven sons of Sceva, and the mob aroused by Demetrius the silversmith; Acts 19:8–40). Much of the church's trouble, however, stemmed from men who tried to place themselves within the believing community. These Christ labels as "evil men," men who called themselves apostles but were found to be false.[9] The importance of Ephesus in the ancient world and its crucial location on the trade route between Rome and the East made it susceptible to itinerant frauds. The problem was especially acute in predominantly Gentile areas, where recent converts were not schooled in OT backgrounds and could easily misunderstand Christian terminology. The false apostles mentioned have been variously identified as Judaizers from Jerusalem (as in II Cor 11:13–23), Nicolaitans (vs. 6), or any self-styled apostles who claimed a position over that of the local elders. Jesus warned his own followers of false prophets who come in sheep's clothing but inwardly are ravenous wolves (Mt 7:15). Paul had told the Ephesian elders in his farewell, "After my departure fierce wolves will come in among you, not sparing the flock" (Acts 20:29), and the message to the Ephesian church in Revelation confirms the accuracy of his prediction. The context suggests that the self-appointed apostles were antinomians rather than legalists. The necessity of testing doctrine and advice was widely recognized in the early church (I Thess 5:21; I Cor 14:29; I Jn 4:1). Jesus provided the very simple and pragmatic, "You will know them by their fruits" (Mt 7:20). In the *Didache* the test for a true prophet is that "he have the behavior of the Lord" (11:8; cf. *Herm. Mand.* xi.16). The Ephesians heeded this advice, tested those who called themselves apostles, and found them not simply self-deceived, but deceivers. They were liars because when tested they could not measure up to their pretensions.

3 Verse 3 brings to a close the sentence which began with verse 1. Its content is somewhat repetitive. The church is again commended for its patience, its willingness to put up with difficulty,[10] and its dedicated labor (the Greek perfect may suggest some specific work in the recent history of the church).

---

[8]They are linked by one pronoun, σου (Sinaiticus and the Byzantine text, however, add σου after κόπον).

[9]We need not distinguish between two separate groups (evil men and false apostles), although the latter may be only one kind included in the more general term mentioned first.

[10]1 2059 *pc* read ἐβάπτισας rather than ἐβάστασας.

4 Every virtue carries within itself the seeds of its own destruction. It seems probable that desire for sound teaching and the resulting forthright action taken to exclude all imposters had created a climate of suspicion in which brotherly love could no longer exist. Barclay conjectures that "the eagerness to root out all mistaken men had ended in a sour and rigid orthodoxy" (I, p. 77). Good works and pure doctrine are not adequate substitutes for that rich relationship of mutual love shared by persons who have just experienced the redemptive love of God. The Ephesian church had left its first love. The expression includes both love of God and love of mankind at large, but seems to refer mainly to their love for one another (as in II Jn 5).[11] Jeremiah 2:2 is instructive. God speaks through the prophet to apostate Israel, "I remember the devotion of your youth, your love as a bride, how you followed me in the wilderness" (cf. Judg 2:7, 10–11; Hos 2:14–16). A cooling of personal love for God inevitably results in the loss of harmonious relationships within the body of believers. Jesus had made it clear that "by this all men will know that you are my disciples, if you have love for one another" (Jn 13:35). Brotherly love was the distinctive badge of Christian discipleship,[12] but at Ephesus hatred of heresy and extensive involvement in the works appropriate to faith had allowed the first fresh glow of love to God and one another to fade.[13]

5 The church is called upon to remember the earlier days in which love abounded in the congregation. Memory can be a powerful force in effecting a return to a more satisfying relationship (cf. the prodigal son in Lk 15:17–18). First love is pictured as a height from which the church had fallen. The present imperative, "remember," stands in contrast to the aorist imperative, "repent," and suggests a continuing attitude over against a decisive break. Bear in mind the loving relationships you once enjoyed and make a clean break with your present manner of life! The "first works" they are to do are the works that spring from the first love. The love that John requires is not an "undiscriminating amiability" (Kiddle, p. 24), but an attitude toward the brethren which expresses itself in loving acts. Moffatt remarks that "the way to regain this warmth of affection is neither by working up spasmodic emotion nor by theorising about it . . . but by doing its duties" (p. 351). Repentance is an active step.[14] If

---

[11]Moffatt translates, "You have given up loving one another as you did at first" (*The NT: A New Translation*).

[12]Tertullian records the heathens' observation on the Christians, "See, they say, how they love one another" (*Apol.* 39).

[13]In "Letters to a Nobleman" John Newton acknowledges that there is something very beautiful in the "honest vehemence of a young convert" but also finds it attended with considerable defects (*Voice of the Heart*, pp. 25–28).

[14]Note the role of repentance in the letters to Pergamum (2:16), Thyatira (2:22), Sardis (3:3), and Laodicea (3:19).

the church does not repent, Christ will come and move its lampstand out of its place. The reference is not so much to the parousia as it is to an immediate visitation[15] for preliminary judgment. Remember that Christ walks in the midst of his churches (2:1). Without love the congregation ceases to be a church. Its lampstand is removed. From the prologue to Ignatius' *Epistle to the Ephesians* (also i.1) we learn that the church heeded the warning. One ought not to soften the warning out of theological concern for doctrines appropriate to other settings.

6 The reprimand for having left their first love is followed by commendation for hating, as Christ does, the works of the Nicolaitans. This heretical group is mentioned in both the letter to Ephesus (2:6) and the letter to Pergamum (2:15). The mention of eating food sacrificed to idols and practicing immorality in the letter to Thyatira (2:20–21) as well as in the letter to Pergamum (2:14, where this is connected with the teaching of Balaam and closely related to the teaching of the Nicolaitans)[16] indicates that all three of the churches were in some way affected by the sect.[17] D. M. Beck takes the Nicolaitans to be "a heretical sect, who retained pagan practices like idolatry and immorality contrary to the thought and the conduct required in Christian churches" (*IDB*, III, p. 548). Broadly speaking, they had worked out a compromise with the pagan society in which they lived.[18] But this compromise violated the requirements of the apostolic decree in which Gentiles entering the fellowship should abstain from "what has been sacrificed to idols . . . and from unchastity" (Acts 15:29; cf. vs. 20).

Early tradition identifies the Nicolaitans with Nicolaus, the proselyte of Antioch who was appointed one of the first seven deacons in the church (Acts 6:5).[19] There is no particular reason, however, why this connection needs to be made. If Eusebius is correct that the sect lasted only "a very short time" (*Hist. Eccl.* iii.29.1), it may be that the only informa-

---

[15]The present tense, ἔρχομαι, emphasizes the nearness of the time. ταχύ is added in **046** 82 1006 *pl* vg^s; τάχει in 1 *pc* TR.

[16]The name combines νῖκος (victory) and λαός (people), and is held by some to be roughly the Greek equivalent of Balaam (according to *Sanh*. 105a Balaam is derived from בלע עם, meaning "he has consumed the people").

[17]W. M. Mackay finds three separate sects in Rev 2 which represent the three great obstacles to the witness of the church in all ages; each is connected with a personal name—Balaam, worldliness; Jezebel, false doctrine; Nicolas, ritualism ("Another Look at the Nicolaitans," *EvQ*, 45 [1973], pp. 111–15).

[18]Fiorenza identifies the Nicolaitans as a Christian group within the churches of Asia Minor whose professed insight into the divine allowed them freedom to become part of their syncretistic pagan society ("Apocalyptic and Gnosis in the Book of Revelation and Paul," *JBL*, 92 [1973], pp. 565–81; esp. p. 579).

[19]Irenaeus, *Haer*. i.26.3; iii.11.1; Hippolytus, *Philos*. vii.36; Tertullian, *Adv. Marc*. i.29, *Praescr. Haer*. 33, *De Pud*. 19; Clement of Alexandria, *Strom*. ii.20, iii.24.

tion the patristic writers had was the book of Revelation itself. In any case, their claim to practice idolatry and immorality under the banner of spiritual liberty was soundly rejected by the Ephesian congregation. The church shared Christ's own hatred of evil when it refused to tolerate any compromise with paganism.

7 The exhortation to hear[20] what the Spirit says introduces a promise in the first three letters and follows a promise in the last four. There is no apparent reason for this variation in format. Charles thinks the call to hear was added to each of the seven letters when they were incorporated in an edition of his visions (I, p. 53), but this judgment stems from a critical methodology which need not be accepted. The Spirit which speaks to the churches is probably "the prophetic Spirit sent by Christ to illumine His followers" (Kiddle, p. 25), or Christ's own spirit (Beckwith, p. 451). He promises to the overcomer the privilege of eating of the tree of life in the Paradise of God. The overcomer in Revelation is not one who has conquered an earthly foe by force, but one who has remained faithful to Christ to the very end. The victory he achieves is analogous to the victory of Christ on the cross. Lilje says that "all the promises about 'victory' point beyond this world to another" and the entire Apocalypse is an exposition of this concept (p. 72). Genesis speaks of a tree of life in the garden of Eden (2:9) which, following the sin of Adam and Eve, was guarded by a flaming sword lest man eat of its fruit and acquire immortality (3:22–24). It is appropriate that at the end of time the faithful be allowed access to this symbolic source of eternal life. In apocalyptic thought the tree of life exists as a reward for the righteous following judgment.[21] Proverbs 3:18 says that wisdom is "a tree of life to those who lay hold of her." In Revelation 22:2 the tree of life produces its perennial fruit in the heavenly Jerusalem. Paradise was originally a Persian word for pleasure garden. In later Judaism it was used to portray the abode of the righteous dead. The Paradise of God in Revelation symbolizes the eschatological state in which God and man are restored to that perfect fellowship which existed before the entrance of sin into the world.

2. SMYRNA (2:8–11)

8 *And to the angel of the church in Smyrna write:*
   These things saith the first and the last, who was dead, and lived again:

---

[20]Cf. Mt 11:15; 13:9, 43; Mk 4:23; etc.
[21]*I Enoch* 24:4–25:6; *Test. Levi* 18:11; cf. also II Esdr 8:52; *II Enoch* 8:3.

9 *I know thy tribulation, and thy poverty (but thou art rich), and the blas-phemy of them that say they are Jews, and they are not, but are a synagogue of Satan.*

10 *Fear not the things which thou art about to suffer: behold, the devil is about to cast some of you into prison, that ye may be tried; and ye shall have tribulation ten days. Be thou faithful unto death, and I will give thee the crown of life.*

11 *He that hath an ear, let him hear what the Spirit saith to the churches. He that overcometh shall not be hurt of the second death.*

8 The second letter is addressed to the church in Smyrna, the only one of the seven cities still in existence (modern Izmir). It lay about thirty-five miles north of Ephesus on the west shore of the Aegean Sea. Its excellent harbor was sufficiently narrow at the mouth that it could be closed for protection in time of war. Eastward from Smyrna extended an important road over which the produce of the rich valley of the Hermus moved. In exports, Smyrna was second only to Ephesus.

Smyrna was a proud and beautiful city. Three to four hundred years after it had been destroyed by Alyattes, king of Lydia, it was rebuilt in 290 BC by Lysimachus and Antigonus as a model city. It boasted a famous stadium, library, and public theater (the largest in Asia). It claimed to be the birthplace of the great epic poet Homer. A famous thoroughfare called the Street of Gold curved around Mt. Pagus (which rose over 500 feet from the harbor) like a necklace on the statue of a goddess. At either end was a temple, one to a local variety of Cybele, known as Sipylene Mother (a patron divinity), and the other to Zeus. The acropolis on Mt. Pagus was called the crown or garland of Smyrna. In NT times the population may have been about 200,000. Coins describe the city as "First of Asia in beauty and size."

Smyrna sustained a special relationship to Rome and the imperial cult. During the period when Rome was engaged in a struggle for suprem-acy against the Carthaginian empire (roughly 265–146 BC) Smyrna had placed itself on the side of the Romans, and in 195 BC it became the first city in the ancient world to build a temple in honor of *Dea Roma*. Later, in 23 BC, Smyrna won permission (over ten other Asian cities) to build a temple to the emperor Tiberius (Tacitus, *Ann.* iv.55–56). This strong al-legiance to Rome plus a large Jewish population which was actively hostile to the Christians made it exceptionally difficult to live as a Christian in Smyrna. The most famous martyrdom of the early church fathers was that of the elderly Polycarp, the "twelfth martyr in Smyrna," who, upon his refusal to acknowledge Caesar as Lord, was placed upon a pyre to be burned.

We do not know when the church was first founded at Smyrna, but it is reasonable to suppose that it could have been during the time Paul lived in Ephesus on his third missionary journey (cf. Acts 19:26).[22] From Ignatius' letter to Smyrna (early second century AD) we learn that the church was already well organized, with a bishop (Polycarp), elders, and deacons (xii.2).

In the salutation of each of the seven letters, Christ identifies himself by means of some part of the description in the initial vision (1:13–16). There is normally a certain appropriateness between the identifying characteristic and the church which is addressed. The church at Smyrna was a persecuted church, so the letter comes from the sovereign One ("the first and the last"; cf. discussion on 1:17), who died and came to life again (BAG, p. 336, 1.β). As he was victorious over death, so they too can face martyrdom knowing that faithfulness is rewarded with eternal life.

9 The church at Smyrna is reminded that its tribulation (Morris calls this "the burden that crushes, p. 63) and stark poverty[23] have not gone unnoticed by the Lord of the church universal. He is fully aware of the pressures brought upon the faithful. The linking of tribulation and poverty suggests a close connection between the two. In an antagonistic environment it would be difficult for the Christian to make a living, and thus many were economically destitute. They may also have been the victims of mob violence and looting (cf. Heb 10:34). Their poverty, however, was a material poverty: spiritually they were rich (note the contrast with the Laodicean church which claimed to be rich but was poor; 3:17). James wrote to a similar group, indicating that "God has chosen the poor in the world to be rich in faith" (Jas 2:5; cf. Mt 6:20; II Cor 6:10).

Christ is also aware of the slanderous accusations directed against the believers by the Jewish population at Smyrna. The *Martyrdom of Polycarp* documents this hostility most clearly. After the venerable Polycarp confessed that he was a Christian, "the multitude of heathen and *Jews living in Smyrna* cried out with uncontrollable wrath" (*Mart. Pol.* xii.2; italics added). They then joined (although it was the Sabbath) with the mob in gathering wood to burn Polycarp alive (*Mart. Pol.* xiii.1).[24] Jewish hostility to Christians seems to have stemmed both from their conviction that to worship a Galilean peasant who had died a criminal's

---

[22]According to Pionius, *Life of Polycarp* 1 f, Paul visited Smyrna on his way to Ephesus.

[23]Trench's oft-quoted distinction between the two Greek words for "poor" is, "The *penēs* has nothing superfluous, the *ptōchos* nothing at all" (*Synonyms of the NT*, p. 129).

[24]Jewish agitation against Paul and others is well attested in Acts (13:50 at Antioch; 14:2, 5 at Iconium; 14:19 at Lystra; 17:5 at Thessalonica). Barclay lists six kinds of slander leveled against the Christians: cannibalism, lust and immorality, breaking up homes, atheism, political disloyalty, and incendiarism (I, p. 98).

death would be blasphemy and the apparent success of the Christians in evangelizing God-fearers and even some from within Judaism (cf. Ignatius, *Smyrn.* i.2).[25] Antagonism against believers would lead Jews to become informers for the Roman overlords. In a city like Smyrna with its strong ties to Rome it would be a fairly simple matter to incite the authorities to action.

The Jews who blasphemed, however, were not real Jews. This should be taken in the sense of Romans 2:28–29, where Paul says that "he is not a real Jew who is one outwardly . . . [but] . . . he is a Jew who is one inwardly."[26] Farrer remarks, "Whereas the Ephesian angel is troubled by self-styled apostles, the Smyrnaean is troubled by self-styled Israelites" (p. 72). Like the Jews of John 8:31–47 who claimed to be descendants of Abraham, they were, instead, of their father the devil. The hostile Jews of Smyrna were, in fact, a synagogue of Satan (the term is Hebrew and means "adversary"; its Greek equivalent means "slanderer" or "false accuser"). Regardless of their national descent, they had become by their bitter opposition to the church and its message, a synagogue carrying out the activities of God's supreme adversary, Satan.

10 The church is told not to fear the things they are about to suffer.[27] Jesus had counseled his disciples not to fear those who could kill the body but not the soul (Mt 10:28), and Paul had warned that the godly would be persecuted (II Tim 3:12). Yet as the time approached, believers needed to be admonished lest the threat of martyrdom would cause the fainthearted to relinquish their hold on Christ. They must recognize that while the persecution would be carried out by Roman authorities, it was in reality the devil himself who was responsible for their plight. He is the one who would try their faith through imprisonment and tribulation. Most commentators note that in the ancient world prison was a place where the accused awaited execution. Acts 16:23 and II Corinthians 11:23 would suggest that it also served as a place of temporary confinement and punishment.

Believers at Smyrna (or at least some of them) are to have tribulation ten days (or "within ten days," Robertson, p. 302).[28] Opinions vary

---

[25]Charles gives additional sources (Justin, Tertullian, Ignatius, etc.) which indicate strong Jewish opposition to the Christian church (II, pp. 56–57).

[26]For a different view cf. Tarn, who believes that since Zeus was worshipped in synagogues in Mysia and at Delos, the reference in 2:9 to those who claimed to be Jews but were not genuine may indicate some sort of syncretistic worship (Tarn and Griffith, *Hellenistic Civilization,* 3rd ed., p. 225).

[27]The present imperative φοβοῦ with μή may indicate "stop being afraid" and betray an existing atmosphere of fear.

[28]Lenski translates ἡμερῶν δέκα "during ten days," genitive of time within; for extent of time the accusative would be used (pp. 99–100). TR *al* read ἡμέρας.

about the time intended. Most view the ten days as a round number indicating a short period of time (Charles, I, p. 58; Kiddle remarks, "As we should say, 'a week or so,'" p. 28), but others hold it to be a prolonged but definitely limited period (Summers defines it as "a number symbolizing extreme, complete tribulation," p. 113). The latter interpretation is more in keeping with the seriousness of the impending crisis.[29] The church is to continue faithful even though it may lead to death (cf. Rev 12:11; Heb 12:4). The reward for faithfulness is the crown of life. It is not the royal crown (the *diadēma*) which is promised, but the wreath or garland (the *stephanos*) which was awarded to the victor at the games. According to Pausanias, Smyrna was famous for its games (vi.14.3). With others, Bruce thinks that the imagery is suggested by the circle of colonnaded buildings on the crest of Mt. Pagos called the crown of Smyrna (p. 638).

11 The call to hear what the Spirit says to the churches is repeated (cf. comm. on 2:7). The overcomer is promised that he shall not in any way (strong double negative in Greek) be hurt by the second death. The second death is a rabbinic term for the death of the wicked in the next world (*Tg. Jer.* on Deut 33:6; cf. *tgs.* on Jer 51:39, 57 and Isa 52:14; 65:6, 15). In Revelation 20:14 it is identified as the lake of fire, and in 21:8 as the final lot of "the cowardly, the faithless, the polluted," etc. Over the faithful, who share in the first resurrection, it has no power (20:6).

3. PERGAMUM (2:12–17)

12 *And to the angel of the church in Pergamum write:*
   These things saith he that hath the sharp two-edged sword:
13 *I know where thou dwellest, even where Satan's throne is; and thou holdest fast my name, and didst not deny my faith, even in the days of Antipas my witness, my faithful one, who was killed among you, where Satan dwelleth.*
14 *But I have a few things against thee, because thou hast there some that hold the teaching of Balaam, who taught Balak to cast a stumblingblock before the children of Israel, to eat things sacrificed to idols, and to commit fornication.*
15 *So hast thou also some that hold the teaching of the Nicolaitans in like manner.*
16 *Repent therefore; or else I come to thee quickly, and I will make war against them with the sword of my mouth.*
17 *He that hath an ear, let him hear what the Spirit saith to the churches. To him that overcometh, to him will I give of the hidden manna, and I will*

---

[29]Moffatt says the "ten days" is originally due to the rough Semitic division of a month into "decades" (p. 354).

*give him a white stone, and upon the stone a new name written, which no
one knoweth but he that receiveth it.*

12 The road north from Smyrna follows the coastline some forty miles
and then turns inland in a northeasterly direction up the valley of the Caicus
River. About ten miles inland from the Aegean Sea stands the impressive
capital city of Pergamum.[30] Pliny called it "by far the most distinguished
city in Asia" (*Hist. Nat.* v.30). Built on a cone-shaped hill a thousand feet
in height, it dominated the surrounding valley of the Caicus. Its very name
in Greek (*Pergamon*) means "citadel." Although the site appears to have
been inhabited from prehistoric times, its rise to prominence came in the
third century BC when it became the capital of the Attalids. Under
Eumenes II (197–159 BC) Pergamum became "the finest flower of Hel-
lenic civilization" (Hough, *IB,* XII, p. 385). It boasted a library of more
than 200,000 volumes. Legend has it that parchment was invented there
when the supply of papyrus from Egypt was cut off in reprisal for
Eumenes' attempt to lure a famous librarian by the name of Aristophanes
away from Alexandria.[31] Until Attalus III bequeathed his kingdom to
Rome in 133 BC the Pergamene kings continued as enthusiastic patrons of
Hellenistic culture.

The most spectacular aspect of this remarkable city was the upper
terrace of the citadel with its sacred and royal buildings. Of these, the most
remarkable was the great altar of Zeus which jutted out near the top of the
mountain. A famous frieze around the base of the altar[32] depicts the gods of
Greece in victorious combat against the giants of earth (symbolizing the
triumph of civilization over barbarism). It commemorates the victory of
Attalus I (the first ruler in Asia to refuse tribute to the plundering Gauls)
over the Galatians. Religion flourished in Pergamum. It was a center of
worship for four of the most important pagan cults of the day—Zeus,
Athene (the patron goddess), Dionysos, and Asklepios (who was designated *Sōtēr,* Savior).[33] The shrine of Asklepios, the god of healing (also
known as "the Pergamene god"), attracted people from all over the world.
Charles calls it "the Lourdes of the Province of Asia" (I, p. 60). Galen,

---

[30]Ramsay's argument that Pergamum continued as the capital city until about AD 130 (*HDB,*
III, pp. 750–51) is contested by V. Chapot, who holds that Ephesus had become the capital
early in the Roman period (*La Province Romaine Proconsulaire d'Asie,* pp. 138–39).
[31]The word "parchment" is derived from περγαμηνή. Wiseman notes that parchment is
attested from c. 1288 BC in Egypt (*NBD,* p. 1343), a thousand years earlier.
[32]It may now be seen in the Pergamon Museum in East Germany.
[33]The emblem of Asklepios was a serpent. Pausanias (ii.26.8) says the cult was introduced
from Epidaurus.

one of the most famous physicians of the ancient world, was a native of Pergamum and studied there.

Of greatest import for the Christians living in Pergamum was the fact that it was the official center in Asia for the imperial cult. It was the first city of Asia to receive permission to build a temple dedicated to the worship of a living ruler. In 29 BC Augustus granted permission that a temple be erected in Pergamum to "the divine Augustus and the goddess Roma" (Tacitus, *Ann.* iii.37). Of all the seven cities, Pergamum was the one in which the church was most liable to clash with the imperial cult. To the church Christ writes as the one who has "the sharp two-edged sword." In the context of life in a provincial capital where the proconsul was granted the "right of the sword" (*ius gladii*), the power to execute at will, the sovereign Christ with the two-edged sword would remind the threatened congregation that ultimate power over life and death belongs to God.[34]

13 The letter to Pergamum begins with an acknowledgment of the difficulty of living in an environment so distinctly pagan and a commendation for the church's faithful witness in the face of severe opposition. The risen Christ *knows*[35] where they live (the Greek word suggests permanent residence): it is "where Satan sits enthroned" (Moffatt, *The NT: A New Translation*). Many suggestions have been put forward to explain the phrase, "Satan's throne." Frequent mention is made of the great throne-like altar to Zeus which overlooked the city from the citadel (Deissmann, *LAE*, p. 281, n. 3). Others take the phrase in reference to the cult of Asklepios, who was designated Savior and whose symbol was the serpent (this would obviously remind Christians of Satan; cf. 12:9; 20:2).[36] Wood notes that as the traveler approached Pergamum by the ancient road from the south, the actual shape of the city-hill would appear as a giant throne towering above the plain.[37] The expression is best understood, however, in connection with the prominence of Pergamum as the official cult center of emperor worship in Asia. In addition to the erection of a temple to Augustus in 29 BC, a second temple was built in the time of Trajan when the city acquired the title "twice *neōkoros* (temple warden)." It was here that Satan had established his official seat or chair of state.[38] As Rome had

---

[34]Some think that the two-edged sword is mentioned in view of the impending visitation threatened in vs. 16.

[35]**046** 1 82 2059s *pl* TR add τὰ ἔργα σου καί (from 2:2).

[36]Zahn notes that under Diocletian, Christian stone cutters from Rome working in the quarries of Pannonia refused to carve an image of Aesculapius (Latin designation of Asklepios) and consequently were put to death for being followers of Antipas of Pergamum (Zahn, *Introduction to the NT*, III, p. 421).

[37]"Local Knowledge in the Letters of the Apocalypse," *ET*, 73 (1961–2), pp. 263–64.

[38]MM, p. 293. Swete notes that θρόνος is always used in this sense in the NT (cf. Mt 19:28; Lk 1:32, 52; Mt 5:34; 25:31) and occurs forty-five times as such in the Apocalypse (p. 34).

become the center of Satan's activity in the West (cf. 13:2; 16:10), so
Pergamum had become his "throne" in the East.

In these adverse conditions the church at Pergamum had held fast to
the name of Christ. They had not denied their faith by yielding to the
pressure of burning incense to the emperor and declaring "Caesar is
Lord." Not even in the days of Antipas,[39] who was put to death in their
midst, did they deny their faith. Little is known of this early martyr[40] apart
from the reference in Revelation. The name is found in a third-century
inscription of Pergamum (Deissmann, *Bible Studies*, p. 187), and he is mentioned by Tertullian (*Scapul.* 12). The legend appears in later hagiographers
(Simon Metaphrastes, the Bollandists) that he was slowly roasted to death in
a brazen bull during the reign of Domitian. His name (abridged from
Antipater) has mistakenly been taken to mean "against all," and the idea
that he gained the name by his heroic stand against the forces of evil
is unfounded.[41] What *is* noteworthy is that he is given the Lord's own
title from Revelation 1:5—"faithful witness." Later martyrs in Pergamum
are identified as Carpus, Papylus, and Agathonike (Eusebius, *Hist. Eccl.*
iv.15). The verse concludes with a repeated emphasis on Pergamum as
the place "where Satan dwelleth." A contrast is intended with the first
clause—both the believers and their ultimate adversary live in the same
locality. Little wonder that martyrdom begins in Pergamum.

14 Although the church at Pergamum had remained faithful in the
midst of severe opposition (even when Antipas was martyred), they were
guilty of allowing within their number some who held the teaching of
Balaam. It is clear from the context that this reference is not to a body of
doctrine,[42] but to Balaam's activity of advising the Midianite women how
to beguile the Israelites into acting treacherously against the Lord. Numbers 25:1 ff reports that the Israelites "began to play the harlot with the
daughters of Moab," who in turn were successful in getting them to worship their gods and take part in their sacred meals. Although there is no
mention of Balaam at this point, we learn in Numbers 31:16 of his role in
Israel's apostasy (the Midianite women acted "by the counsel of
Balaam"). Blaiklock notes that Balaam's clever notion was to break down

---

[39]Short for Ἀντίπατρος (cf. Josephus, *Ant.* xiv.10). Lachmann conjectures a genitive
Ἀντιπᾶ on the basis of an accidental doubling of the following omicron, which was then
taken as a sigma (cf. Metzger, *TCGNT,* p. 734).
[40]Bruce notes that a passage like this marks the beginning of the transition of the meaning of
the Greek μάρτυς from witness to martyr (p. 638).
[41]Alford writes, "It is hardly possible to withhold indignation at the many childish symbolic
meanings which have been imagined for the name, in defiance of philology and sobriety
alike" (p. 569).
[42]διδαχή is often used in a passive sense of what is taught; cf. Mt 16:12; Jn 7:16–17; etc.
Apparently the *ASV* understood διδαχή in this sense.

Israel's power by an indirect attack on their morale. "Pagan food and pagan women were his powerful tools against the rigidity of the Mosaic Law" (p. 39). Thus Balaam became a prototype of all corrupt teachers who betrayed believers into fatal compromise with worldly ideologies. At Pergamum, where Satan sat enthroned, some within the church had decided that accommodation was the wisest policy. Caird explains the action of this group by saying that "the sum total of the Nicolaitans' offence, then, is that they took a laxer attitude than John to pagan society and religion" (p. 39). He conjectures that they may have been a group who honestly believed that it was possible without disloyalty to maintain a peaceful co-existence with Rome. "The very plausibility of the case explains the violent and abusive language John uses to refute it" (p. 41). While not denying that the compromisers were able to rationalize their position (perhaps along the lines Caird suggests), it is doubtful that the risen Christ (not John) would need to resort to "violent and abusive language" to refute heresy.

"Things sacrificed to idols" probably refers to meat which was eaten at pagan feasts rather than that sold in the open market after having been offered to idols. "Fornication" should also be understood literally as part of the pagan festivities. Some writers take both expressions metaphorically as referring to idolatrous practice in general and religious infidelity.

15 The construction of verse 15 is not altogether clear. "So" refers to the preceding verse and indicates a comparison between the situation at Pergamum and that of Israel being led astray by the cunning of Balaam. "Thou also" emphasizes this comparison.[43] If the first four words are to be taken as a unit, it follows that the Nicolaitans are essentially the same group as the Balaamites. Both describe an antinomian group which had accommodated itself to the religious and social requirements of the pagan society in which they lived.[44] The final "in like manner" is repetitive and further strengthens the earlier "so."[45]

16 The indifference of the church at Pergamum to the presence of Nicolaitans is a matter of considerable concern. Unless they repent Christ will come and war against them with the sword of his mouth. Only a portion of the church has fallen prey to the pernicious doctrine of the Balaamites, but all are guilty of not taking action against their presence.

---

[43]Charles, however, takes καὶ σύ as a reference to the Ephesian church; cf. 2:6 (I, p. 64).

[44]Kiddle remarks that the church's path lay between two deadly giants—legalism with its exaltation of trivialities and Pharisaical insistence on codes of rules, and antinomianism which in its reliance upon the strength of a devoted spirit insisted upon freedom from the tyranny of legal precepts and prohibitions (pp. 33–34).

[45]Copyists sensed this awkwardness and some altered ὁμοίως to ὃ μισῶ (1 al), or added ὃ μισῶ (**P** al).

The fault of Pergamum is the opposite of Ephesus where the heretics were rooted out but love was missing (2:2, 4). The "coming" of Christ should be understood as a coming in judgment. From the perspective of the first century it would also be the second or final coming of Christ (cf. 3:11; 22:7, 12, 20).

17 To the faithful at Pergamum the risen Lord promises the hidden manna and a white stone inscribed with a new name known only to the recipient. Manna was the food supernaturally supplied to the Israelites during their sojourn from Egypt to Canaan. The idea of hidden manna reflects a Jewish tradition that the pot of manna which was placed in the ark for a memorial to future generations (Ex 16:32–34; cf. Heb 9:4) was taken by Jeremiah at the time of the destruction of Solomon's temple (sixth century BC) and hidden underground in Mt. Nebo (II Macc 2:4–7). There it was to remain until the coming of the Messiah when Jeremiah would reappear and return the ark and its contents to the new messianic temple in Jerusalem. Charles (I, p. 65) takes a different view: that the reference is to a treasury of manna (cf. Ps 78:25, "bread of the angels") which was to descend from heaven during the messianic kingdom to feed the blessed (cf. *II Bar.* 29:8; *Sib. Or.* 7:149). Since John is never limited by his sources, there is no reason to exclude either as a possible source. In the context of the letter to Pergamum it alludes to the proper and heavenly food of spiritual Israel in contrast to the unclean food supplied by the Balaamites. While the promise is primarily eschatological, it is not without immediate application for a persecuted people.[46]

There are perhaps a dozen or more plausible interpretations of the "white stone."[47] Ancient jurors signified innocence by casting a white pebble into an urn. There existed a Thracian custom of marking every good day by a white stone (Pliny, *Hist. Nat.* vii.40.131). It could have been an amulet or charm to ward off evil. According to popular superstition mysterious powers were associated with the name of a god. According to rabbinic lore precious stones fell from heaven with the manna. Reference could be to a stone in the breastplate of the high priest (or perhaps to the Urim, Ex 28:30). In the context of a messianic feast (the "hidden manna") it seems best to take the white stone as a *tessera* which served as a token for admission to the banquet. These little tablets of wood, metal, or stone were used in ancient times for many purposes. They were distributed to the poor

---

[46]Walvoord calls it "the present spiritual food of the saints as well as a part of their future heritage" (p. 70).

[47]See the extended discussion in Hemer, *A Study of the Letters to the Seven Churches of Asia with Special Reference to their Local Background,* unpublished Ph.D. thesis, Manchester, 1969 (referred to subsequently in the text as *7CA*).

in Rome by the emperors to insure a regular supply of corn (Suetonius, *Aug.* 40.2; 42.3), given to the victor at games, and to gladiators who had won the admiration of the public and had been allowed to retire from further combat.

The stone awarded to the overcomer at Pergamum was white in that it symbolized the triumph of his faith. Commentators are divided on the identity of the "new name." It is normally held to be the name of Christ by those who interpret the white stone as a magical charm. It is thought that secret knowledge of a god's name (note: "which no one knoweth but he that receiveth it") gave special power over the deity. Exactly in what sense the name of Christ could be considered secret, or "new," for that matter, is not explained. The new name is more likely the name of the victor himself. No one else can know the transforming experience of fidelity in trial and the joy of entrance to the great marriage supper of the Lamb.

4. THYATIRA (2:18–29)

18 *And to the angel of the church in Thyatira write:*
> *These things saith the Son of God who hath his eyes like a flame of fire, and his feet are like unto burnished brass:*

19 *I know thy works, and thy love and faith and ministry and patience, and that thy last works are more than the first.*

20 *But I have this against thee, that thou sufferest the woman Jezebel, who calleth herself a prophetess; and she teacheth and seduceth my servants to commit fornication, and to eat things sacrificed to idols.*

21 *And I gave her time that she should repent; and she willeth not to repent of her fornication.*

22 *Behold, I cast her into a bed, and them that commit adultery with her into great tribulation, except they repent of her works.*

23 *And I will kill her children with death; and all the churches shall know that I am he that searcheth the reins and hearts: and I will give unto each one of you according to your works.*

24 *But to you I say, to the rest that are in Thyatira, as many as have not this teaching, who know not the deep things of Satan, as they are wont to say; I cast upon you none other burden.*

25 *Nevertheless that which ye have, hold fast till I come.*

26 *And he that overcometh, and he that keepeth my works unto the end, to him will I give authority over the nations:*

27 *and he shall rule them with a rod of iron, as the vessels of the potter are broken to shivers; as I also have received of my Father:*

28 *and I will give him the morning star.*

29 *He that hath an ear, let him hear what the Spirit saith to the churches.*

18 Concerning the letter to Thyatira, Hemer writes, "The longest and most difficult of the seven letters is addressed to the least known, least important, and least remarkable of the cities" (*7CA*, p. 235). The difficulty in interpreting the letter grows out of its numerous references to the details of daily life which have become obscured with the passing of time and the lack of archaeological evidence which would reveal its past.

Following the overland route from Pergamum to Sardis, the traveler would head eastward along the south bank of the Caicus River, turn southward over a low-lying range of hills, and descend into the broad and fertile valley of the Lycus. His journey of about forty miles would take him just across the Mysian border to the city of Thyatira situated on the south bank of the Lycus in the long north-south valley which connected the Caicus and Hermus valleys. Thyatira was founded[48] by Seleucus I as a military outpost to guard one of the approaches to his empire. Since it possessed no natural fortifications, it would draw heavily upon the spirit of its soldier-citizens to make up for its vulnerability. In 190 BC the city fell to the Romans and became part first of the kingdom of Pergamum and then of the Province of Asia.

With the coming of stable conditions under Roman rule, Thyatira was destined for growth and prosperity as a center for manufacturing and marketing. An outstanding characteristic of Thyatira was the large number of trade guilds that flourished there. Ramsay notes that inscriptions, although not especially numerous, mention "woolworkers, linen-workers, makers of outer garments, dyers, leather-workers, tanners, potters, bakers, slave-dealers and bronze-smiths."[49] In Acts 16:14 ff we meet "a woman named Lydia, from the city of Thyatira, a seller of purple goods"[50] who also had a house at Philippi. It would appear that Thyatira's market extended across the Aegean Sea into Macedonia. Since the trade-guilds were inseparably intertwined with local religious observances, they posed a special problem for the economic well-being of Christians. The divine guardian of the city was the god Tyrimnos[51] (identified with the Greek sun-god Apollo), who would be conceived of as the patron of the guilds and therefore honored in their festivities.

The writer of the letter to Thyatira describes himself as "the Son of God." Only here in the book of Revelation is this title found (although it is

---

[48]An earlier settlement probably existed there as indicated by the fact that the name seems to be old Lydian in origin and means "the citadel/castle of Thya."

[49]*The Letters to the Seven Churches of Asia*, p. 325 (hereafter designated *L7CA* and noted in the body of the text).

[50]The purple dye of Thyatira was not taken from shellfish, but was a "turkey red" brewed from the madder root which grew in abundance in the valley.

[51]On coins he is portrayed astride a horse with a battle-axe on his shoulder.

implied in many other places; *eg.*, 2:27; 3:5). Since Psalm 2:9 is quoted later in the letter (vs. 27), it may be that Psalm 2:7 ("the Lord... said to me, 'You are my son'") suggested its use here. In any case, it stands in strong contrast to the local cultic worship of Apollo Tyrimnos, which was merged with that of the emperor (identified as Apollo incarnate) so that both were acclaimed as sons of Zeus. Thus it is not the emperor or the guardian deity of Thyatira, but the resurrected Christ, who is the true son of God. He is described as having eyes like flames of fire and feet like burnished brass. Both descriptions are taken from the initial vision of chapter 1 (cf. vss. 14–15). In Daniel's great vision of the last days (chaps. 10–12) the celestial being appearing to him has "eyes like flaming torches" and "legs like the gleam of burnished bronze" (Dan 10:6). The flaming eyes suggest the penetrating power of Christ's ability to see through the seductive arguments of Jezebel and those who were being led astray by her pernicious teaching. Feet (or legs; cf. on 1:15) like burnished brass [52] convey the idea of strength and splendor.

19 The glorified Christ is not unmindful of the works which characterize the Thyatiran church. They are listed as love, faith, ministry, and patience.[53] The first two identify the motive forces of Christian activity, and the other two, the results that follow. While the love of the Ephesian church had been lost (2:4), the practical expression of love at Thyatira had grown ("thy last works are more than the first"). This rather liberal praise is explained by Swete as a preface for the blame which is to follow (p. 42).

20 Major attention is given to the self-styled prophetess Jezebel (vss. 20–24), whose seductive teachings had led some of the believers at Thyatira into fatal compromise with the secular environment. The choice of the epithet, Jezebel, and references to fornication and eating things sacrificed to idols indicate a first-century parallel with the wicked queen of Ahab who fostered in Israel the idolatrous worship of the Canaanite Baal (I Kgs 16:29 ff; II Kgs 9:30 ff). Blaiklock describes the NT Jezebel as "a clever woman with a gift of speech, who professed to interpret God's will, offered prosperity at the price of compromise with heathendom" (p. 49).[54]

---

[52]In a careful fifteen-page study of χαλκολίβανος Hemer concludes that this *hapax legomenon* probably refers to a refined alloy of copper or bronze with metallic zinc (*7CA*, pp. 247–62, cf. p. 291).

[53]The single σου following the grouping of four nouns suggests they be taken together as an expansion of the preceding σου τὰ ἔργα.

[54]Bruce explains the choice of the epithet saying, "She is described here as 'that Jezebel of a woman' because her relaxation of the terms of the apostolic decree or further compromise with paganism (cf. verse 14) placed her in the succession of the OT Jezebel, whose Baal-cult was marked by idolatry and ritual prostitution" (p. 639).

In a city whose economic life was dominated by trade guilds in which pagan religious practices had become criteria for membership, the Christian convert would be faced with the problem of compromising his stand at least enough to allow participation in a common meal dedicated to some pagan deity. To reject this accommodation could mean social isolation and economic hardship. With her Nicolaitan orientation the prophetess could suggest that since "an idol has no real existence" (I Cor 8:4), believers need not undergo the privation which would follow from unwillingness to go along with the simple requirements of the trade guild. Christ, however, speaks with great severity about any such compromise. Since they did not repent, Jezebel and her adulterous associates are to be cast into great tribulation (vs. 22) and her children are to be struck dead (vs. 23).

Several identifications for Jezebel have been proposed. Some have suggested Lydia, the seller of purple from Thyatira, who was converted to the Christian faith at Philippi (Acts 16:14–15). While as a business woman she may have faced some of the same problems to which Jezebel encouraged an antinomian response, there is no substantial reason why we should identify the two. Schürer advanced the view that she may have been the Sibyl Sambathe, whose sanctuary was outside the walls of the city[55] and apparently in existence at the time of Revelation. This view is unlikely in that it is doubtful that the religious syncretism of the day could have infected the church to the point that a Sibylline priestess could also function so effectively within the church itself. The opportunity for repentance (vs. 21) suggests someone from within the church who had gone astray rather than a female fortune teller from the pagan world.

One variant reading translates "your wife Jezebel,"[56] which would make her the wife of the bishop or leader of the church at Thyatira. As the variant is improbable, so also is the identification. The Thyatiran Jezebel is probably some prominent woman within the church who, like her OT counterpart, was influencing the people of God to forsake loyalty to God by promoting a tolerance toward and involvement in pagan practices. This extended to fornication and participation in the religious feasts connected with membership in trade guilds.

It is questionable whether her teaching was in any sense formal. It may only have taken the form of popular persuasion built upon unexamined assumptions. In any case, it had seduced a considerable number of believers into a fatal compromise with paganism. While at Pergamum antinomianism had made its way into the church and affected some (2:14), at Thyatira it was aggressively promoted by a prominent woman

---

[55]*Theologische Abhandlungen*, pp. 39 f; cf. discussion in Hemer, *7CA*, pp. 263 ff.
[56]σου is added after γυναῖκα, **A 046** 82 1006 *al* sy Prim.

claiming the gift of divine prophecy. Since the eating of "things sacrificed to idols" is undoubtedly intended in a literal sense, it is best to take "commit fornication" in the same way.[57] Pagan feasts often led to sexual promiscuity.

21 Participation in the guild-feast with its penchant for licentiousness would involve the believer in yet another kind of fornication. The concept of religious infidelity under the figure of harlotry is common in the OT. "Rejoice not, O Israel! . . . for you have played the harlot, forsaking your God" (Hos 9:1; cf. Jer 3:6; Ezek 23:19; etc.). The fornication of which Jezebel was not willing to repent was her adulterous alliance with the pagan environment. She had been given time (perhaps by the Seer) to repent, but had refused.

22 Severe punishment is about to be meted out[58] to Jezebel and her adulterous associates. She is to be cast into a bed, and they into great tribulation. The bed is not a "funeral-bier" (Hort, p. 30) or a "dining-couch" of the guild-feasts (Ramsay, *L7CA,* pp. 351–52), but a bed of sickness or pain. Disease as a punishment for sin was an accepted view. Paul wrote that participation in the Lord's Supper in an unworthy manner was the reason why many of the Corinthians were weak and ill and some had died (I Cor 11:27–29). The parallel structure of the two main clauses sets "bed"[59] over against "great tribulation." Jezebel's associates in adultery were all those she had led astray within the church. It appears that her time for repentance had passed (vs. 21) but that "*they* [still had the opportunity to] repent of *her* works" (italics added).[60]

23 The promise of certain punishment continues. Jezebel's "children" are not the literal offspring of her adulteries (so Beckwith, p. 467) or a second generation of heretics (Lenski, p. 118), but those who have so unreservedly embraced the antionomian doctrines of their spiritual mother that they are best described as younger members of her family. No particular distinction should be drawn between the children of Jezebel and "them that commit adultery with her" (vs. 22), although the reference to the killing of her children may reflect the bloody occasion when the rulers of

[57]Some take the reference in a metaphorical sense as referring to religious infidelity; cf. Hos 9:1; Jer 3:6; Ezek 23:19; etc.

[58]Βάλλω is futuristic present, stressing the imminence and certainty of the act.

[59]The scribal conjectures (φυλακήν, prison; κλίβανον, an oven or furnace; and ἀσθένειαν, weakness or illness) indicate the uncertainty felt with the somewhat unusual κλίνην. Metzger (*TCGNT,* p. 735) suggests that the glosses were introduced out of a desire to increase the threatened punishment.

[60]Other manuscripts read αὐτῶν (A 1 2059s *pm* vg[s,cl] sy[ph] TR), which understands the followers of Jezebel repenting of their own works, while the Bohairic version omits everything after μετανοήσωσιν.

Samaria slew the seventy sons of Ahab and sent their heads to Jezreel in baskets (II Kgs 10:1–11). To "kill with death" is a Hebraism that means "to slay utterly" (cf. Moffatt, p. 361) or (preferably) "to kill by pestilence" (cf. *ASV* margin).

The persuasive logic of the compromisers had confused many in the church at Thyatira, but imminent punishment would demonstrate that the one who searches the "inner reaches"[61] of men had found them guilty. Each is to receive "according to [his] works." Through the prophet Jeremiah, God expressed in the clearest of terms the principle of divine judgment: "I the Lord search the mind and try the heart, to give to every man according to his ways, according to the fruit of his doing" (Jer 17:10). It is restated both by Jesus ("the Son of man . . . will repay every man for what he has done," Mt 16:27) and by Paul ("He will render to every man according to his works," Rom 2:6).[62]

24–25 Upon those in Thyatira who have not been led astray by the Jezebel party, Christ lays no additional burden[63] "except that you hold on to what you have until I come" (Phillips). To combine the two verses in this way answers the question, What burden? which would go unanswered if verse 25 is separated and introduces a new idea (cf. Beckwith, p. 470). Those who have remained faithful at Thyatira are described as not knowing "the deep things of Satan." This phrase is normally taken in one of two ways. On the one hand it may be no more than "a sarcastic reversal of their main slogan" (Lilje, p. 86). Claiming to know the deep things of God, they are told that the "deep things" they claim to know are really the deep things of Satan. Moffatt (p. 362) notes that to know "the depths" of a divine being was commonly claimed by Ophites, an early Gnostic sect whose opposition to the God of the OT led them to worship the serpent (Gk., *ophis*) as the great liberator of mankind.[64] To tamper with truth often leads to a position of complete reversal.

On the other hand, "the deep things of Satan" may be a reference to the view that in order to appreciate fully the grace of God one must first plumb the depths of evil. Later gnosticism boasted that it was precisely by entering into the stronghold of Satan that believers could learn the limits of

[61]νεφροί are the kidneys, and commonly used metaphorically of the will and the affections. καρδία, the heart, may designate the center of man's rational life, although physiological distinctions should not be pressed in theological contexts.
[62]See also Rev 18:6; 20:12–13; 22:12.
[63]It is possible that the apostolic decree (Acts 15:28–29) is in mind, although apart from βάρος there are no linguistic parallels: the verb is βάλλω rather than ἐπιτίθημι, and is followed by ἐφ᾽ ὑμᾶς rather than ὑμῖν.
[64]*Oxford Dictionary of the Christian Church,* 2nd ed., p. 984.

his power and emerge victorious. On the basis that a believer's spirituality is unaffected by what he does with his body, Jezebel could argue that the Thyatiran Christians ought to take part in the pagan guild-feasts (even if they were connected with the deep things of Satan) and thus prove how powerless is evil to alter the nature of grace.

26-27 In the first three letters the exhortation "He that hath an ear . . ." preceded the concluding promise. Beginning with the Thyatiran letter the order is changed and the exhortation follows the promise. Hemer notes two additional changes in the form of the letter: (1) only here is the final promise made dependent on a double condition, and (2) only here and at Pergamum (2:17) are two apparently distinct promises made to the victor, each separately introduced by "I will give" (*7CA*, p. 281). Authority over the nations and "the morning star" are promised to the overcomer, that is,[65] the one who continues in the works of Christ until the end. It is by faithful allegiance to the cause of Christ that believers overcome in the hostile environment of pagan values and practices. Morris notes that "unto the end" reminds us that "the Christian life is not a battle but a campaign" (p. 74).

Verses 26b–27 are a free rendering of Psalm 2:8–9, which had been interpreted messianically as early as the first century BC. *The Psalms of Solomon* (written probably between 70 and 40 BC) say of the son of David who is to rule over Israel, "He shall destroy the pride of the sinners as a potter's vessel. With a rod of iron he shall break in pieces all their substance" (17:23–24). It was a regular feature of Jewish eschatology that the followers of the Messiah would share in his final rule. This feature carried over into Christian thought (Mt 11:28; I Cor 6:3; Rev 5:10).

Christ promises the overcomer that he will rule the nations with a rod of iron. The verb means "to shepherd"[66] and should be taken in the sense of wielding the shepherd's staff or club (the "rod of iron" may have been an oak club capped with iron) to ward off the attacks of marauding beasts. In Revelation 12:5 and 19:15 the prerogative of ruling (shepherding) the nations belongs to the conquering Christ. A share in this rule is promised to the overcomers in Thyatira. The description of this rule as the shattering of the potter's vessel speaks of the absolute power of the victorious Christ and his followers over the rebellious nations. The concluding

---

[65]Taking καί as introducing the explanatory phrase ὁ τηρῶν, etc.

[66]ποιμαίνω in the LXX translates the Hebrew רָעַע, which means "to break, or destroy." In Ps 2:9, the LXX, using a difficult vocalization of the original, derived it from the verb רָעָה, meaning "to tend, or pasture." While the former meaning would seem preferable in that it parallels συντρίβεται here and πατάξῃ in 19:15, Hemer concludes that the context is against the idea of destroying (*7CA*, pp. 282–83).

clause of the verse picks up from verse 26. Christ will give authority to the overcomer as he has received it from his Father.[67] It reflects the messianic "You are my son, today I have begotten you" of Psalm 2:7.

28 In addition to authority over the nations the overcomer is promised the morning star. No completely satisfactory answer for this symbol has been offered. Among the many suggestions one finds (1) an allusion to Lucifer of Isaiah 14:12, (2) Christ himself (cf. 22:16), (3) a reference to Daniel 12:3 and the immortality of the righteous, (4) the dawn of eternal life, (5) a literal reference to the planet Venus, and (6) the Holy Spirit. Hemer suggests rather tentatively that the author's mind may have passed from Psalm 2:7–9 to Numbers 24:17 (the rod or scepter in each passage symbolizes authority) with its mention of a star which then suggested the "morning star," a local concept whose significance has now been forgotten (*7CA*, p. 288; cf. complete discussion on pp. 284–88).

29 Once again the exhortation to hear what the Spirit says to the churches is repeated (cf. 2:7, 11, 17). This same emphasis on hearing and doing marks the conclusion of Jesus' Sermon on the Mount. Wise men build against the coming storm of judgment by hearing and doing (Mt 7:24–25).

---

[67]God is called the Father of Christ in 1:6; 3:5, 21; and 14:1.

CHAPTER 3

5. SARDIS (3:1-6)

1 *And to the angel of the church in Sardis write:*
These things saith he that hath the seven Spirits of God, and the
seven stars: I know thy works, that thou hast a name that thou livest, and
thou art dead.
2 *Be thou watchful, and establish the things that remain, which were ready*
to die: for I have found no works of thine perfected before my God.
3 *Remember therefore how thou hast received and didst hear; and keep it,*
and repent. If therefore thou shalt not watch, I will come as a thief, and
thou shalt not know what hour I will come upon thee.
4 *But thou hast a few names in Sardis that did not defile their garments: and*
they shall walk with me in white; for they are worthy.
5 *He that overcometh shall thus be arrayed in white garments; and I will in*
no wise blot his name out of the book of life, and I will confess his name
before my Father, and before his angels.
6 *He that hath an ear, let him hear what the Spirit saith to the churches.*

1 In the sixth century BC Sardis was one of the most powerful cities of
the ancient world. Yet by the Roman period it had declined to the point that
Ramsay could appropriately describe it as "a relic of the period of barbaric
warfare, which lived rather on its ancient prestige than on its suitability to
present conditions."[1] It was located some fifty miles east of Ephesus on a
northern spur of Mt. Tmolus overlooking the broad and fertile plain of the
Hermus. The acropolis, with its nearly perpendicular rock walls rising
1500 feet above the lower valley (on all but the south side), was essentially

---

[1]*The Letters to the Seven Churches*, p. 354 (hereafter designated *L7CA* and noted in the body
of the text). Hemer concludes that Ramsay's picture of Sardis as a city in decay in NT times is
overdrawn (*Seven Churches of Asia,* unpublished doctoral dissertation, pp. 328, 342; referred
to subsequently in text as *7CA*).

inaccessible and provided a natural citadel.[2] As Sardis grew, it became necessary to develop a lower city to the north and west of the acropolis on the banks of the Pactolus, a southern tributary of the Hermus. Excavations in the lower city have unearthed a Roman theater and stadium as well as an exceptionally large (160 by 300 feet) temple dedicated to Artemis. Its seventy-eight Ionic columns (of which two are still standing) are each fifty-eight feet in height. Built on the sixth-century-BC foundations of an ancient temple constructed by Croesus, it was destroyed in 499 BC and reconstructed but never completely finished in the time of Alexander the Great. It was dedicated to a local Asiatic goddess usually referred to as Cybele, who was identified with the Greek Artemis. This patron deity was believed to possess the special power of restoring the dead to life.

Sardis was the capital of the ancient kingdom of Lydia, the most obstinate of the foreign powers encountered by the Greeks during their early colonization in Asia Minor. In 546 BC it fell to Cyrus and became the seat of the Persian governor. Later it became part of the Seleucid kingdom, then passed to Pergamum and subsequently to Rome (133 BC). In AD 17 Sardis suffered a catastrophic earthquake,[3] but it was rebuilt with considerable help from the emperor Tiberius (10,000,000 *sesterces*—about a million dollars—and five years of tax remission; Tacitus, *Ann.* ii.47). Nine years later (in AD 26) it competed with ten other Asian cities for the privilege of building an imperial temple but lost out to Smyrna, which stressed its practical services to Rome (Tacitus, *Ann.* iv.55–56). Situated at the western end of a famous highway from Susa through Asia Minor, Sardis was a city of wealth and fame. Under Croesus gold was taken from the Pactolus. Jewelry found in the local cemeteries indicates great prosperity. It was at Sardis that gold and silver coins were first struck. It claimed to be the first to discover the art of dyeing wool.

The church at Sardis comes under the most severe denunciation of the seven. Apparently untroubled by heresy and free from outside opposition, it had so completely come to terms with its pagan environment that although it retained the outward appearance of life, it was spiritually dead. Moffatt writes that the church at Sardis "had lapsed from its pristine vitality, just as the township of S. had by this time declined from its old historical prestige" (p. 364). Like the fig tree of Matthew 21:19 it had

---

[2]Due to erosion the present summit is perhaps one-third of its size in the period of the city's prime under Cyrus (D. G. Mitten, "A New Look at Ancient Sardis," *The Biblical Archaeologist*, 29 [1966], p. 55).

[3]Pliny calls it the greatest disaster in human memory (*Hist. Nat.* ii.86.200).

leaves but no fruit. Caird calls Sardis "a perfect model of inoffensive Christianity" (p. 48).

The letter to Sardis comes from the one who has "the seven Spirits of God, and the seven stars." We are reminded that the letter to Ephesus came from the one who "holds the seven stars in his right hand" (2:1).[4] The seven stars are identified in 1:20 as the angels of the seven churches, but the seven spirits of God are enigmatic at best. Perhaps Ramsay is right in his opinion that they "must certainly be taken as a symbolic or allegorical way of expressing the full range of exercise of the Divine power in the Seven Churches" (L7CA, p. 370), although from 1:4 it would seem that the figure represents some part of a heavenly entourage that has a special ministry in connection with the Lamb.[5]

Christ knows their works, and there is little to commend. Although they have the reputation of being alive, they are, in fact, dead. Subsequent verses indicate that while the entire church had not fallen into a state of complete spiritual death (vss. 4–5), the majority had so fully compromised with the pagan environment that the church was Christian in name only (ie., "nominally" Christian). Like the prodigal son of whom the father said, "This my son was dead" (Lk 15:22), only by repentance and return could life be restored (cf. Eph 5:14).

2 The first of five imperatives in verses 2 and 3[6] is joined to a participle and should be translated "show yourself watchful" rather than "wake up" (as in the translations by Moffatt and Beck, the TCNT, and others). The exhortations to watchfulness would carry special weight in Sardis because twice in its history the acropolis had fallen to the enemy due to a lack of vigilance on the part of the defenders. In 549 BC Cyrus captured the acropolis by deploying a climber to work his way up a crevice on one of the nearly perpendicular walls of the mountain fortress.[7] Late in

[4]Similarities between the letters to Ephesus and Sardis have often been noticed: both are censured for a fall from a former position (2:5 with 3:3), both are called upon to remember and repent (2:5 with 3:3), and both promise the victor ζωή under appropriate figures (cf. Hemer, 7CA, p. 325).

[5]Cf. discussion on 1:4. Most commentators hold them to be planetary deities (Bousset, pp. 184–87) or the sevenfold operation of the Spirit from Isa 11:2 (first found in Justin, Dial. 87). Beckwith understands the Holy Spirit represented by symbols taken directly from Zech 4:1–10 (pp. 424–27).

[6]γίνου, στήρισον, μνημόνευε, τήρει, μετανόησον.

[7]Hemer notes that although the accounts of this extraordinary physical achievement differ, they all postulate a lack of vigilance on the part of the defenders (7CA, p. 304). Most commentators rely on Herodotus, the Greek historian (cf. Barclay, I, pp. 142–144), but Hemer indicates that "much of the familiar Herodotean account of Croesus may safely be pronounced unhistorical" (p. 301).

the third century the city was again captured in the same way. A Cretan by the name of Lagoras discovered a vulnerable point and with a band of fifteen men made a daring ascent, opened the gates from within, and allowed the armies of Antiochus the Great to overpower the rebel Archaeus (216 BC). As in history, so in life, to consider oneself secure and fail to remain alert is to court disaster.

Although the church at Sardis was dead (vs. 1), some things still remained (although on the verge of dying). Rather than attempting to distinguish what was in fact dead and what could still be saved, it is better to take the two statements as paradoxical. Although Sardis could be pronounced dead, it still had the possibility of restoration to life. It is to "strengthen[8] what still remains though it is at the point of death" (Weymouth). Christ, who knows their works (vs. 1), has not found any of them[9] carried out fully. Like the unfinished temple of Artemis, the works of the church constantly fell short of completion. They lacked the appropriate motivation and spiritual orientation without which all external activity is morally impotent. The believers at Sardis had established a name for themselves in the eyes of the community, but "before God" their works had not measured up.

3 The church is called upon to bear in mind (present imperative) what[10] they had received and heard and to keep it. The change in tense between "hast received" (perfect) and "didst hear" (aorist) is instructive. Members of the church had received the faith as an abiding trust at the moment faith came by hearing (cf. Swete, p. 50). Like the churches at Ephesus, Pergamum, and (later) Laodicea, Sardis is told to repent (cf. 2:5, 16; 3:19). Behm writes that "the urgent call for conversion in the epistles of Rev . . . is based on the prospect of the imminent end" and summons the churches "from sin and weakness, to the renewal of their former state of life" (*TDNT*, IV, p. 1004). If the church does not wake up to its perilous position, Christ will unexpectedly (*ie.*, as a thief) visit them in judgment. In other NT passages where the coming of Christ (or the day of the Lord) is said to be like a thief in the night (Mt 24:42–44; I Thess 5:2; II Pet 3:10), the second advent is in view. Here, however, some historical visitation must be in mind since the eschatological coming is not dependent on

---

[8]Swete notes that στηρίζειν was a technical word in primitive *pastoralia* (p. 49).

[9]Following **A C** 1^mg arm, which omit τά. The argument that σου τὰ ἔργα corresponds with the author's normal pattern (2:2, 19; 3:1, 8, 15) and makes better sense in context violates the canon of choosing the more difficult reading.

[10]Although πῶς regularly indicates manner ("how"), the connection with τήρει, which needs an object, suggests it should be translated "what" (cf. Beckwith, p. 474).

repentance in Sardis.[11] When it happens, it will be swift and unexpected (they will not know "what hour" he comes).[12]

4 Although the majority of the church had become thoroughly secularized, there were a few names (persons)[13] who had not defiled their garments. Without citing references, Moffatt writes that in the votive inscriptions in Asia Minor soiled clothes disqualified the worshipper and dishonored the god (p. 364). It is often noted as well that since the manufacture and dyeing of woolen goods was a principal trade in Sardis, an allusion to defiled garments would be immediately recognized. It is unlikely, however, that anything more than a general reference to the danger of contaminating the Christian witness by accommodation to the prevailing standards of a pagan city is in mind.[14]

The promise to the undefiled minority is that they shall walk with Christ in white. While there could be a reference to Enoch who "walked with God" (Gen 5:22, 24), it is more likely an allusion to the itinerant ministry of Jesus in Galilee (cf. Jn 6:66). In Revelation 17 the great multitude robed in white (vss. 9–10) is guided by the Lamb to springs of living water (vs. 17), and in chapter 14 the 144,000 "follow the Lamb wherever he goes" (vs. 4). In the context of the following verse, where those arrayed in white garments do not have their names blotted out of the book of life, it would seem that walking "in white" is a way of describing those who are justified. Other possible references are to purity, festivity, resurrection bodies, or the Roman custom of wearing white on the day of triumph (Ramsay, *L7CA,* p. 386). Ford says that the speaker "is probably thinking of triumphal (perhaps messianic) procession in the Roman style" (p. 413). Here, as elsewhere, the author is not limited to our knowledge of possible sources. While background is helpful, it does not determine how a figure must be used or what it may subsequently mean. The faithful at Sardis walk with Christ in white, "for they are worthy." They themselves have done nothing to merit their exalted position, but are worthy in the

---

[11]Charles (I, p. 80) and others insert the parenthetic Rev 16:5 ("Lo, I am coming like a thief!" etc.) before 3:3c. Cf. Hemer (*7CA,* pp. 332–33) for arguments against this transposition.

[12]The accusative ποίαν ὥραν ("a rare classical idiom," Robertson, p. 314) refers to a point of time. Ford notes that the members of Qumran studied and prayed throughout the night (1QS 6:6–8), apparently because "the messianic hour of judgment could not be known in advance" (p. 409).

[13]Cf. 11:13; Acts 1:15. Deissmann (*Bible Studies,* pp. 196 f) shows that in the second century AD ὄνομα was used in the sense of "person."

[14]Blaiklock says the cult of Cybele was "one of the so-called 'enthusiastic' religions, whose votaries worshipped by wild dancing, revel, and self-mutilation" (*The Seven Churches,* p. 60; hereafter in the text this will be designated *7C*).

sense that they have withstood the pressure to apostatize and hence have done nothing which would result in forfeiting their position.

5   To the overcomer a threefold promise is given: (1) he will be arrayed in white garments, (2) his name will not be blotted out of the book of life, and (3) Christ will confess his name before God and the angels. The white garments, according to Charles, are "the spiritual bodies in which the faithful are to be clothed in the resurrection life" (I, p. 82).[15] White garments (or robes)[16] are mentioned seven times in Revelation, but no distinctive pattern is established. The Laodiceans are counseled to buy them to hide the shame of their nakedness (3:18). The martyrs awaiting vindication are given white robes (6:11). In the heavenly throne room the twenty-four elders are clad in white garments (4:4), and before the Lamb stands a great multitude clothed in white robes who have washed them in his blood (7:9, 13). The armies of heaven who appear with the warrior Messiah are "arrayed in fine linen, white and pure" (19:14). It would seem, therefore, that the white garments promised to the overcomer in 3:5 represent an attire appropriate to the heavenly state. Since they are made white by washing in the blood of the Lamb (7:13), the figure is highly appropriate to portray justification.

The second promise is that the overcomer's name will not be blotted out of the book of life. The idea of a divine ledger is first mentioned in the OT in Exodus 32:32–33 where Moses prays that if God will not forgive the sin of his people, he wishes to be blotted out "of the book which thou hast written" (cf. Ps 69:28; Dan 12:1). Thus, in the OT, the book of life was a register of all those who held citizenship in the theocratic community of Israel. The idea was common in the secular world as well. Kiddle writes that "when a criminal's name was removed from the civic register of an Asiatic town, he lost his citizenship" (p. 47; cf. Hemer, 7CA, pp. 338–39). Walvoord is troubled lest someone interpret the concept of being blotted out of the book of life as indicating the possibility of a person losing his salvation. Consequently, he suggests that (1) there is no explicit statement that anybody will, in fact, have his name blotted out, or (2) the book of life lists all mankind and those who do not accept Christ are blotted out (p. 82). Caird, on the other hand, suggests that John believes in a "conditional predestination" in which the decrees of God wait on the acceptance or rejection of man (pp. 49–50). It is hermeneutically unsound to base

---

[15]He finds this idea expressed in II Cor 5:1, 4; Mt 13:43; Phil 3:21; Asc. Isa. 4:16; II Enoch 22:8; and elsewhere (cf. I, pp. 82–83).

[16]ἱμάτιον in 3:5, 18; 4:4; στολή in 6:11; 7:9, 13; and βύσσινος in 19:14.

theological doctrine solely on either parables or apocalyptic imagery. Better to allow the text, even when difficult, to present its own picture.

Finally, to the overcomer Christ promises that he will confess his name before his Father and the angels. This is a clear reminiscence of Matthew 10:32 (cf. Lk 12:8; Mk 8:38/Lk 9:26), "Everyone who acknowledges me before men, I also will acknowledge before my Father who is in heaven." Faithfulness in trial now is to be rewarded beyond measure in the life to come.

6 See commentary on 2:7.

6. PHILADELPHIA (3:7–13)

7 *And to the angel of the church in Philadelphia write:*
    These things saith he that is holy, he that is true, he that hath the key of David, he that openeth and none shall shut, and that shutteth and none openeth:
8 *I know thy works (behold, I have set before thee a door opened, which none can shut), that thou hast a little power, and didst keep my word, and didst not deny my name.*
9 *Behold, I give of the synagogue of Satan, of them that say they are Jews, and they are not, but do lie; behold, I will make them to come and worship before thy feet, and to know that I have loved thee.*
10 *Because thou didst keep the word of my patience, I also will keep thee* • *from the hour of trial, that hour which is to come upon the whole world, to try them that dwell upon the earth.*
11 *I come quickly: hold fast that which thou hast, that no one take thy crown.*
12 *He that overcometh, I will make him a pillar in the temple of my God, and he shall go out thence no more: and I will write upon him the name of my God, and the name of the city of my God, the new Jerusalem, which cometh down out of heaven from my God, and mine own new name.*
13 *He that hath an ear, let him hear what the Spirit saith to the churches.*

7 Philadelphia (modern Alashehir)[17] lies at the eastern end of a broad valley which, passing through Sardis (some thirty miles west-northwest), leads down to the Aegean Sea near Smyrna. Its location commanded high ground on the south side of the river Cogamis, a tributary of the Hermus. This strategic location at the juncture of trade routes leading to Mysia, Lydia, and Phrygia (the imperial post route from Rome via Troas passed through Philadelphia and continued eastward to the high central plateau)

---

[17]Ramsay says the modern name means "the reddish city" (*HDB*, III, p. 832), while Swete calls it "the white city" (p. 52).

had helped it earn the title "gateway to the East" and made it a city of commercial importance. The great volcanic plain to the north (*katakekaumenē*, the burnt land) was fertile and well suited to growing grapes. With an economy based on agriculture and industry, Philadelphia enjoyed considerable prosperity. Its one major drawback was that it was subject to earthquakes. The devastating earthquake of AD 17 which leveled twelve cities of Asia overnight (Pliny, *Hist. Nat.* ii.86.200; Tacitus, *Ann.* ii.47; Strabo, xii.579; xiii.628) had been particularly severe on Philadelphia, perhaps because it was nearer the fault line and also suffered a long series of tremors which followed. With the defeat of Antiochus IV at Magnesia in 190 BC Lydia passed to Pergamene control. Although Philadelphia is the most recently established of the seven cities of the Apocalypse, there is some confusion as to whether Eumenes II, king of Pergamum, or his younger brother Attalus II Philadelphus, who reigned from 159 to 138 BC, founded the city (cf. Hemer, *7CA*, p. 351, esp. n. 1, for other possibilities). What is certain is that its name commemorates the loyalty and devotion of Attalus II to his brother (this is what earned him the epithet Philadelphus, "lover of his brother"). Hemer calls attention to two incidents of special note: (1) a false rumor of Eumenes' assassination led Attalus to accept the crown, which he then relinquished when his brother returned from Greece, and (2) Attalus' resistance to Roman encouragement to overthrow his brother and become king (*7CA*, p. 354). The city was probably founded between 189 BC when the region came under the control of Eumenes and 138 BC when Attalus died, although without doubt it was built on the site of some earlier settlement. In its development under Pergamene rule Philadelphia was intended to serve as a "missionary city" to bring Greek culture to the recently annexed area of Lydia and Phrygia. Ramsay indicates the success achieved by noting that before AD 19 the Lydian tongue had been replaced by Greek as the only language of the country (*L7CA*, p. 392).

Following the great earthquake of AD 17 it took the name of Neocaesarea for a time in appreciation for the imperial help received for rebuilding. At a later date, under Vespasian (AD 69–79), the name Flavia began to appear on coins. Philadelphia was remarkable for its many temples and religious festivals. For this reason, in the fifth century AD it was called "little Athens." Because it was located in a vine-growing district, the worship of Dionysus was its chief pagan cult. After Tiberius' help it founded a cult of Germanicus, the adopted son and heir of the emperor. Between AD 211 and 217 a provincial temple to the imperial cult was built and Philadelphia was honored with the title Neocoros, warden of the temple.

Attention has often been called to the similarities between the letters to Smyrna and Philadelphia. Kiddle, for example, points out that both
are designed to strengthen the faithful and, in fact, point by point cover the
same ground (p. 48; cf. Ramsay, *L7CA,* pp. 402–3). They are the two
churches that receive unqualified praise from the Lord.

Apparently all suitable phrases from the vision of chapter 1 have
been used up,[18] so from other sources the speaker identifies himself as the
true Messiah who controls access to the eternal kingdom. In Jewish culture
the Holy One was a familiar title for God (*eg.,* Isa 40:25; Hab 3:3; Mk
1:24; Jn 6:69; *I Clem.* 23:5). Here it is joined with "the True One" and
applied to Christ. In Revelation 6:10 they are combined to further describe
God just addressed as "Sovereign Lord." If "true" is taken in the classical
sense of "genuine," it may be used here to refute those Jews of Philadelphia who would claim that Christ was a false Messiah.[19] If it is taken
in the OT sense of "faithful" (Hort, p. 34; Charles, I, p. 85), it could
serve to remind the believers at Philadelphia that not only has Christ been
set apart (the root meaning of *hagios*) to carry out his messianic task, but
that he can be counted on to carry it to completion.

Christ is next described as having "the key[20] of David,"[21] a
metaphorical expression indicating complete control over the royal household. Specifically, in view of the following clauses, it means the undis-
puted authority to admit or exclude from the New Jerusalem. The background is the oracle against Shebna, Hezekiah's major-domo (Isa 22:15–
25), who was to be removed from office and replaced with Eliakim. Concerning the new chief steward the text says, "I will place on his shoulder
the key of the house of David; he shall open, and none shall shut; he shall
shut, and none shall open" (Isa 22:22; cf. Job 12:14b). The language of
Isaiah is used to present Christ as the Davidic Messiah with absolute power
to control entrance to the heavenly kingdom. It may be an intentional
contrast with the practice of the local synagogue in excommunicating
Christian Jews.

[18]Although there remain the long robe, the golden girdle, white hair, voice as many waters,
and face like the shining sun (vss. 13–16).
[19]Farrer interprets the title in terms of the Isaianic reference which lies behind the rest of the
verse. He writes, "In Isaiah's text an unfaithful key-bearer is deposed and a worthy minister
put in his place; so Christ here names himself the holy, the true, in contrast to the elders of the
synagogue, who are false pretenders to the authority of David's house" (p. 80).
[20]Blaiklock notes that a key in ancient times would be "a considerable piece of wood designed
to thrust in and lift the bar which held the two leaves of a door in position" (*7C,* p. 68).
[21]Probably due to 1:18 (τὰς κλεῖς τοῦ θανάτου καὶ τοῦ ᾅδου) some manuscripts instead of
Δαυίδ read ᾅδου or the fuller τοῦ θανάτου καὶ τοῦ ᾅδου. The Armenian reads τοῦ
παραδείσου (cf. Metzger, *TCGNT,* p. 736).

8 A preliminary problem in verse 8 is the punctuation of the first clauses. The *ASV* takes "behold, I have set before thee a door opened, which none can shut" as parenthetical (the UBS Greek text accomplishes the same end by the use of dashes). Commentators who follow this punctuation take the following "that" as declarative and the remainder of the verse as detailing the "works" that Christ knows. If a major stop occurs after "works," then the word "that" (Gk., *hoti*) is better translated "because" and supplies the reason for the open door being placed before the church. The *RSV* takes the first four words as a complete sentence and after the somewhat parenthetical statement repeats the "I know" from the first sentence and carries on "that you have but little power." This is the most satisfying solution to the syntactical problem.

Most of the discussion centers on the meaning of the open door. The more common interpretation is that it denotes a great opportunity for missionary activity. Paul uses the metaphor in this way. He writes to the Corinthians of his plans to stay in Ephesus until Pentecost, "for a wide door for effective work has opened to me" (I Cor 16:9; cf. II Cor 2:12; Col 4:3). Ramsay explains the expression in terms of Philadelphia's geographic position at the eastern end of the valley leading up onto the great central plain. As the "keeper of the gateway to the plateau" it had been given a unique opportunity to carry the gospel to the cities of Phrygia (*L7CA,* pp. 404–5).[22]

A different interpretation, however, fits the context better. The preceding verse spoke of a messianic kingdom whose access was under the absolute control of Christ. He is the one who possesses the key and can open and shut at will. Now in verse 8 he reminds the Christians at Philadelphia who may have been excommunicated from the local synagogue (vs. 9) that he has placed before them an open door into the eternal kingdom, and no one can shut it. No matter if the door to the synagogue has been closed, the door into the messianic kingdom remains open (cf. Beckwith for a good presentation of this position, p. 480). Others have suggested that the door is Christ (Moffatt, p. 366), or perhaps a door of prayer, or immediate access to God by way of martyrdom (Kiddle, p. 50); but the eschatological interpretation is to be preferred.

Christ recognizes that although they have but little power (it was probably a fairly small congregation and they had not made a major impact upon the city), they have faithfully kept his word and not denied his name.

---

[22]For the same interpretation of the open door see Trench, *Commentary on the Epistles to the Seven Churches in Asia,* pp. 180–81; Charles, II, p. 87; Swete, p. 54; Hort, p. 35; etc. Glasson cites the translation, "a great opportunity has opened up for effective work" (p. 34).

The two aorist verbs point to a particular period of trial in the past. In the remainder of the letter we will learn the threefold reward for faithfulness: vindication before their foes (vs. 9), deliverance in the final period of testing (vs. 10), and security in the coming age (vs. 11).

9 Verse 9 takes us into the heart of a serious conflict between church and synagogue in Philadelphia. The Jewish population was convinced that by national identity and religious heritage it was the people of God. Not so, claimed the Christians. Had not Paul taught that "he is not a real Jew who is one outwardly. . . . He is a Jew who is one inwardly, and real circumcision is a matter of the heart" (Rom 2:28–29)? It was the church that could now be called "the Israel of God" (Gal 6:16), for the Jewish nation had forfeited that privilege by disbelief. Members of the local synagogue may claim to be Jews, but the very claim constitutes them liars. By their slander and persecution of Christians they have shown themselves to be the "synagogue of Satan" (cf. Ignatius, *Ad Phil.* 6). Jesus had said to hostile and unbelieving Jews, "You are of your father the devil" (Jn 8:44), and later in Revelation Satan is labeled "the accuser of our brethren" (12:10). Little wonder that their synagogue was called "the synagogue of Satan" (cf. Rev 2:9; also II Cor 11:14–15).

As in the preceding verse, the syntax of verse 9 is somewhat awkward. The initial clause should perhaps be expanded to read, "Behold I give [to you those] of the synagogue of Satan" so as to parallel the later "behold, I will make them to come and worship before thy feet." The intervening phrases describe these persons as falsely claiming to be Jews. The major question is whether they are given in the sense of becoming converts to the Christian faith or given in the sense that they will finally come to understand that "you [the church] are my beloved people" (*NEB*). The first alternative supports the interpretation of the open door (vs. 8) as a missionary opportunity, but we have already shown that to be less probable. Once again, an eschatological interpretation is to be preferred. Isaiah 60:14 represents the post-exilic confidence that with the restoration of Israel the nations would come to honor and serve the people of God ("the sons of those who oppressed you shall bow at your feet"). The nations will bring their wealth to Israel, become their servants, and acknowledge their God (Isa 45:14; cf. Isa 2:3; 49:23; Zech 8:20 ff). Now, in what Moffatt calls "the grim irony of providence" (p. 367), what the Jews fondly expected from the Gentiles, they themselves will be forced to render to the Christians. They will play the role of the heathen and acknowledge that the church is the true Israel of God.

Caird takes issue with commentators who hold that John envisages here, not the conversion, but the ultimate humiliation of the Jews. He reasons that "we should not submit to this gloomier interpretation" because (1) post-exilic Judaism looked for a reversal in world affairs which would include the redemption of Gentile nations, and (2) John had boundless confidence in the power of Christ (pp. 51–53). But Christ's words in verse 9 certainly do not demand a cringing response from conquered foes. To come and worship is simply an Oriental metaphor that in this context involves no more than the acknowledgment that the church is the object of Christ's love and that with his return their faith in him will be vindicated.

10 Because the believers at Philadelphia had kept "Christ's command to endure patiently for His sake" (Bruce, p. 640),[23] he will keep them from the hour of trial which is about to come[24] upon the whole world. The major question is whether Christ is promising deliverance from the period of trial or safekeeping through the trial. The preposition "from" (Gk., ἐχ) is inconclusive. Walvoord holds that "if this promise has any bearing on the question of pretribulationism, however, what is said emphasizes deliverance *from* rather than deliverance *through*" and "implies the rapture of the church before the time of trouble referred to as the great tribulation" (p. 87). The thrust of the verse is against this interpretation. It is precisely because the church was faithful to Christ in time of trial that he in turn will be faithful to them in the time of their great trial. The promise is consistent with the high-priestly prayer of Jesus, "I do not pray that thou shouldest take them out of the world, but that thou shouldest keep them from the evil one" (Jn 17:15). It is their preservation in trial that is taught. That the martyrs of 6:9–11 are told to wait for vindication until their full number would be killed indicates that the issue is not physical protection. The spiritual protection of the church is presented elsewhere in Revelation under such figures as sealing (7:1 ff) and flight to the wilderness (12:6).

The hour of trial is that period of testing and tribulation that precedes the establishment of the eternal kingdom. It is mentioned in such passages as Daniel 12:2, Mark 13:14, and II Thessalonians 2:1–12. It is the three and a half years of rule by Antichrist in Revelation 13:5–10. In fact, all the judgments from 6:1 onward relate to this final hour of trial. It is during this period that Christ will reward the faithfulness of the Philadelphian church by standing by to ward off all the demonic assaults of Satan. The text indicates that the hour of trial comes upon the "whole world" to try "them that dwell upon the earth." In the other places in Revelation

---

[23]It is regularly noted that μου governs ὑπομονῆς rather than the entire phrase (Moffatt, p. 367), which stresses that the patience enjoined is that exemplified by Christ himself.
[24]μέλλω with the present infinitive in the eschatological context of this letter (and especially the ἔρχομαι ταχύ which follows) points to what is about to happen rather than what is destined to be.

where the latter phrase occurs (6:10; 8:13; 11:10 [twice]; 13:8, 14; 17:8) the enemies of the church are always in mind.[25] The hour of trial is directed toward the entire non-Christian world, but the believer will be kept from it, not by some previous appearance of Christ to remove the church bodily from the world, but by the spiritual protection he provides against the forces of evil. Ladd writes, "Although the church will be on earth in these final terrible days and will suffer fierce persecution and martyrdom at the hands of the beast, she will be kept from the hour of trial which is coming upon the pagan world. God's wrath, poured out on the kingdom of Antichrist, will not afflict his people" (p. 62).

11 The "coming" of Christ to Ephesus (2:5), Pergamum (2:16), and Sardis (3:3) posed a threat to each church. At Ephesus the lampstand would be removed unless they repented; at Pergamum Christ would war against them with the sword of his mouth; at Sardis he would come like a thief in the night. The "coming" to Philadelphia, however, would end their time of trial and establish them as permanent citizens of the eschatological kingdom. Verse 11 presupposes the continuance of the church until the second advent (Charles, I, p. 90). The promise is not that Christ's coming will take place quickly whenever it happens, but that it will take place without delay. It is to be taken in the sense of 1:1, "what must soon take place" (cf. 2:16; 22:7, 12, 20). Since the end is not far off, they are to hold fast what they have (faith in Christ and obedience to his word; cf. vs. 8) so that no one will take their crown. The crown was the wreath awarded to the winner of an athletic contest (cf. I Cor 9:25; II Tim 4:8). The metaphor would be especially appropriate in this letter in that Philadelphia was known for its games and festivals.[26]

12 To the overcomer (the one who holds fast, vs. 11) is given the promise of being made a pillar in the temple of God. The metaphor is found elsewhere in the NT (James, Cephas, and John were "reputed to be pillars," Gal 2:9; the church is "the pillar and bulwark of truth," I Tim 3:15) and is current in most languages. It conveys the idea of stability and permanence. This latter aspect is emphasized in the following clause, "and he shall go out thence no more." To a city that had experienced devastating earthquakes which caused people to flee into the countryside and establish

---

[25]See the helpful article, "The Hour of Trial, Rev 3:10," by Schuyler Brown in *JBL*, 85 (1966), pp. 308–14. Brown summarizes his position by stating that "as a reward for its faithful perseverance Christ promises the church of Philadelphia (and all faithful Christians) his special protection in the hour of universal tribulation which is to precede his return" (p. 314).

[26]Inscriptional evidence is cited by Hemer, *7CA*, p. 379. In a note on the same page he suggests that the depressions between the three summits of the acropolis may have been the location of a theater and a stadium.

temporary dwellings there, the promise of permanence within the New Jerusalem would have a special meaning. Various sources for the figure of the pillar have been suggested. Some refer to the custom in which the provincial priest of the imperial cult erected in the temple area at the close of his tenure of office his statue inscribed with his name (cf. Charles, I, pp. 91–92; Moffatt, p. 369; Kiddle, pp. 53–54; and others). Hemer, while acknowledging this as plausible, notes that no provincial temple of the cult existed in Philadelphia until its neocorate was conferred about AD 213 (p. 381). Others suggest the two pillars in Solomon's temple that bore personal names (Jachin and Boaz, I Kgs 7:21), the colonnades of the Artemisium at Ephesus, or the occasional sculpturing of pillars in human shapes. Probably no single allusion is intended. If the Isaiah passage (22:15–25) is still in mind (from vs. 7), the stability of the pillar may be in contrast to Eliakim, who was fastened like a peg in a sure place (vs. 23) to bear the whole weight of his father's house (vs. 24) yet in time would give way (vs. 25). Rist's comment that in Revelation 21:22 "John forgets this prophecy," this being an example of his "indifference to consistency in details" (p. 395), is unnecessary. Apocalyptic imagery is sufficiently fluid to allow the figure of a temple in one vision and dismiss it in another. It is not a matter of forgetfulness or inconsistency.

A further promise to the overcomer is that Christ will write on him[27] the name of his God, the name of God's city, and his own new name. The impact of the threefold inscription is to show that the faithful belong to God, hold citizenship in the New Jerusalem, and are in a special way related to Christ. Aaron, the high priest, wore on his forehead a golden plate with the engraving "Holy to the Lord" (Ex 28:36–38). In Revelation 7:3 the servants of God are sealed upon their foreheads, which according to 14:1 takes the form of the name of the Lamb and of his Father written on their foreheads (cf. 22:4). The name of the city of God indicates citizenship in the heavenly commonwealth (cf. Gal 4:26; Phil 3:20). Christ's own new name symbolizes the full revelation of his character, which awaits the second advent (cf. 19:12). It is not hidden at the present time because of some primitive superstition that if known could be used to his disadvantage (Moffatt, p. 369), but reflects man's current inability to grasp the full theological significance of the incarnation. While it is interesting that Philadelphia twice adopted a new name (Neocaesarea, out of gratitude to Tiberius for his help in rebuilding after the great earthquake, and, later, Flavia, the family name of Vespasian), it adds little to our understanding of the verse.

[27]The antecedent of the second αὐτόν could be στῦλον but is the unexpressed subject of ἐξέλθῃ, that is, ὁ νικῶν ("I will write upon *him* . . .").

13 Once again we hear the exhortation, "He that hath an ear, let him hear what the Spirit saith to the churches." The message to each church is at the same time a message to all churches.

7. LAODICEA (3:14–22)

14 *And to the angel of the church in Laodicea write:*
   These things saith the Amen, the faithful and true witness, the beginning of the creation of God:
15 *I know thy works, that thou art neither cold nor hot: I would thou wert cold or hot.*
16 *So because thou art lukewarm, and neither hot nor cold, I will spew thee out of my mouth.*
17 *Because thou sayest, I am rich, and have gotten riches, and have need of nothing; and knowest not that thou art the wretched one and miserable and poor and blind and naked:*
18 *I counsel thee to buy of me gold refined by fire, that thou mayest become rich; and white garments, that thou mayest clothe thyself, and that the shame of thy nakedness be not made manifest; and eyesalve to anoint thine eyes, that thou mayest see.*
19 *As many as I love, I reprove and chasten: be zealous therefore, and repent.*
20 *Behold, I stand at the door and knock: if any man hear my voice and open the door, I will come in to him, and will sup with him, and he with me.*
21 *He that overcometh, I will give to him to sit down with me in my throne, as I also overcame, and sat down with my Father in his throne.*
22 *He that hath an ear, let him hear what the Spirit saith to the churches.*

14 Laodicea (modern Eski-hisar, "the old fortress") was located in the Lycus valley in southwest Phrygia at the juncture of two important imperial trade routes[28]—one leading east from Ephesus and the Aegean coast following the Maeander and then via the gentle ascent of the Lycus to the Anatolian plateau, and the other from the provincial capital at Pergamum south to the Mediterranean at Attaleia. Five of the seven cities to which John wrote lay in order along this latter road (Pergamum, Thyatira, Sardis, Philadelphia, and, some forty miles on to the southeast, Laodicea). Its sister cities were Hierapolis, six miles to the north across the Lycus River, and Colossae, ten miles on up the Lycus glen.[29] To the south lay mountains that rise to over 8,000 feet. The city occupied an almost square plateau several hundred feet high some two miles south of the river. It was founded

---

[28]Ramsay calls it "a knot on the road system" and mentions additional roads that met there (*L7CA*, p. 416).
[29]Laodicea is mentioned in Col 2:1; 4:13, 15, 16, and Hierapolis in Col 4:13. One of Paul's four prison epistles was addressed to the church at Colossae (Col 1:2).

about the middle of the third century BC by Antiochus II to command the
gateway to Phrygia and settled with Syrians and Jews brought from
Babylonia.[30] Antiochus named the city after his wife (and sister?) Laodice.

In Roman times Laodicea became the wealthiest city in Phrygia.
The fertile ground of the Lycus valley provided good grazing for sheep. By
careful breeding a soft, glossy black wool had been produced which was
much in demand and brought fame to the region (Strabo xii.578). Among
the various garments woven in Laodicea was a tunic called the *trimita*. So
widely known was this tunic that at the Council of Chalcedon in AD 451
Laodicea was called *Trimitaria* (Ramsay, *L7CA*, p. 416). Agricultural and
commercial prosperity brought banking industry to Laodicea. Cicero, the
Roman statesman and philosopher of the last days of the Republic, wrote of
cashing his treasury bills of exchange there (*Fam.* iii.5.4; *Att.* v.15.2). The
most striking indication of the city's wealth is that following the devastating earthquake of AD 60[31] the city was rebuilt without financial aid from
Rome. Tacitus wrote, "Laodicea arose from the ruins by the strength of her
own resources, and with no help from us" (*Ann.* xiv.27).

Laodicea was widely known for its medical school, established in
connection with the temple of Mēn Carou[32] thirteen miles to the north and
west. It boasted such famous teachers as Zeuxis and Alexander Philalethes
(who appear on coinage). Ramsay notes that the Laodicean physicians
followed the teaching of Herophilos (330–250 BC) who, on the principle
that compound diseases require compound medicines, began a strange
system of heterogeneous mixtures (*L7CA*, p. 419). Two of the most famous were an ointment from spice nard for the ears, and an eye-salve made
from "Phrygian powder" mixed with oil (Galen vi.439).

Laodicea's major weakness was its lack of an adequate and convenient source for water. Its location had been determined by the road system
rather than natural resources. Thus water had to be brought in from springs
near Denizli (six miles to the south) through a system of stone pipes
approximately three feet across and hollowed through the middle. Such an
aqueduct could easily be cut off, leaving the city helpless, especially in the
dry season when the Lycus could dry up. Blaiklock writes, "Such vulnerable communities must learn the arts of appeasement and conciliation" (*7C*,
p. 75).

A large number of Jews had emigrated to the area, so many, in fact,
that the Rabbis spoke bitterly of those who sought the wines and baths of

---

[30]Josephus reports that Antiochus III brought 2,000 Jewish families to Lydia and Phrygia from
Mesopotamia (*Ant.* xii.3.4).
[31]Tacitus' dating; Eusebius and Orosius place it after the fire of Rome (cf. Hemer, *7CA*, p.
417, esp. n. 3).
[32]Mēn was an ancient Carian god, a god of healing who was later identified with Asklepios.

Phrygia. From the amount of gold seized as contraband following an embargo on the export of currency by Flaccus, governor of Asia (62 BC), Barclay estimated that there were at least 7,500 adult male Jews in Laodicea and the surrounding district (I, pp. 175–76). Laodicea was the center of the imperial cult and later received the Temple-Wardenship under Commodus (AD 180–191). The church was probably founded during the time Paul spent at Ephesus on his third missionary journey (Acts 19:10), perhaps by Epaphras (Col 4:12). There is no evidence that Paul visited the church, although he wrote them a letter (Col 4:16) which was subsequently lost.

The One who writes to the angel of the church in Laodicea identifies himself as "the Amen." The title is unique and perhaps reflects Isaiah 65:16, which speaks of "the God of Amen."[33] In the OT and Judaism "amen" is primarily the acknowledgment of that which is valid and binding (*TDNT,* I, 335–36). As a personal designation it would indicate the one in whom perfect conformity to reality is exemplified.[34] The suggestion that Amen is appropriate as a liturgical conclusion to the seven letters is beside the point. What the title means is further expressed by the following appositional phrase, "the faithful and true witness." Ford suggests that it was added to clarify for the non-Hebrew-speaking audience the meaning of "amen" (p. 418). It presents the trustworthiness of Christ in sharp contrast to the unfaithfulness of the Laodicean church. The final designation, "the beginning of the creation of God," is undoubtedly linked to Paul's great christological passage in Colossians 1:15 ff, where Christ is designated "the beginning" (vs. 18) and "the firstborn of all creation" (vs. 15). The close geographical proximity of the two cities and Paul's instructions to Colossae that they exchange letters make it all but certain that the writer of Revelation knew the Colossian epistle.[35] Although Wisdom's declaration in Proverbs 8:22, "The Lord created me at the beginning of his work, the first of his acts of old," is often mentioned as a back-

---

[33]LXX: τὸν θεὸν τὸν ἀληθινόν, which implies אָמֵן rather than אָמָן (followed by *RSV*). Silberman, in an article with the optimistic title "Farewell to O AMHN" (*JBL,* 82 [1963], pp. 213–15), argues on the basis of a midrash on Prov 8:22 that ὁ ἀμήν should be rendered "master workman" and that Christ is being presented as God's adviser in creation. Trudinger accepts Silberman's suggestions as essentially correct but does not feel they imply a Semitic original document ("O AMHN (Rev. III:14), and the Case for a Semitic Original of the Apocalypse," *JTS,* n.s. 17 [1966], pp. 277–79).

[34]The *TCNT* translation, "These are the words of the Unchanging One."

[35]Charles (I, pp. 94–95) calls attention to other verbal parallels (Rev 3:17 with Col 1:27 and Rev 3:21 with Col 3:1), and Hemer goes on to point out that the similarity in christological content reflects a common response to similar tendencies of thought in the local situations (*7CA,* p. 426).

ground for the NT use of the expression, as applied to Christ it carries the idea of "the uncreated principle of creation, from whom it took its origin" (Swete, p. 59). The Arian meaning, "the first thing created," is at variance with the Colossian passage that declares that "in . . . through . . . and for him" *all* things were created (Col 1:16). Moffatt calls this "the most explicit allusion to the pre-existence of Jesus in the Apocalypse" (p. 370).

15–16   Once again we hear the familiar "I know thy works" (cf. 2:2, 19; 3:1, 8). Their "works" show them to be neither hot nor cold, but lukewarm. Consequently Christ is about to spew (Spanish, *vomitar*) them out of his mouth. This rather vivid portrayal has long been interpreted against the local background. Six miles north across the Lycus was the city of Hierapolis, famous for its hot springs which, rising within the city, flowed across a wide plateau and spilled over a broad escarpment directly opposite Laodicea. The cliff was some 300 feet high and about a mile wide. Covered with a white incrustation of calcium carbonate, it formed a spectacular natural phenomenon. As the hot, mineral-laden water traveled across the plateau, it gradually became lukewarm before cascading over the edge. Blaiklock is representative of those who see this as the background for picturing the lukewarmness of the Laodicean church and Christ's reaction to it. Expecting an affirmative response, he asks, "Did the eyes of listeners seek through door and window the distant view of the lime and sulphur encrusted cliffs under Hierapolis, where the plumes of steam told of hot pools and sickly insipid water seeping over the slimy rock, water rough with alum which the unsuspecting visitor drank only to spit upon the ground?" and adds, "Such was their Christianity" (*7C*, pp. 77–78).[36] Others speak of the "moral nausea roused by tepid religion" (Moffatt, p. 370), and that the Laodicean Christians were "*lukewarm* toward the call to vigorous spiritual activity" (Beckwith, p. 490).

In an important article, Rudwick and Green argue that the adjectives "hot," "cold," and "lukewarm" are not to be taken as describing the spiritual fervor (or lack of it) of people.[37] The contrast is between the hot medicinal waters of Hierapolis and the cold, pure waters of Colossae. Thus the church in Laodicea "was providing neither refreshment for the spiritually weary, nor healing for the spiritually sick. It was totally ineffective, and thus distasteful to its Lord" (p. 178). On this interpretation the church is not being called to task for its spiritual temperature but for the

---

[36]The remains of a remarkable aqueduct leading from Denizli (not Hierapolis as some hold; *eg.*, Ford, pp. 418–19) are well known. Water flowing through these stone pipes would arrive at Laodicea tepid and nausea provoking.

[37]"The Laodicean Lukewarmness," *ET*, 69 (1957–8), pp. 176–78.

barrenness of its works.[38] Among the several advantages of this interpretation is the fact that it is no longer necessary to wonder why Christ would
prefer the church to be "cold" rather than "lukewarm." It should be noted
that although the Lord was about to spew[39] them out of his mouth, there
was yet opportunity to repent (vss. 18–20).

17 Verse 17 explains why their works were offensive to God.
Secure in their affluence, they were unaware that in reality they were
wretched, miserable, poor, blind, and naked. Lilje notes that "the inevitable result of spiritual complacency and self-satisfaction is the loss of all true
self-knowledge" (p. 101). The material wealth of Laodicea is well established. The huge sums taken from Asian cities by Roman officials during
the Mithridatic period and following indicate enormous wealth.[40] The
Zenonid family (private citizens of Laodicea) is a remarkable example of
the power of individual wealth (cf. Hemer, *7CA,* pp. 443, 471 ff). The
"wealth" claimed by the Laodicean church, however, was not material but
spiritual. Their pretentious claim was not only that they were rich but that
they had achieved it on their own. And even beyond that, they had need of
nothing. Like the farmer in Jesus' parable who counseled his soul to eat,
drink, and be merry for ample goods had been laid in store for many years
(Lk 12:19), the Laodiceans felt they were secure in their spiritual attainment. But the truth was that *they* (the Greek pronoun is emphatic) were the
ones who were poor, blind, and naked. It is frequently noted that Laodicea
prided itself on three things: financial wealth, an extensive textile industry,
and a popular eye-salve which was exported around the world. It is hard
not to see here and in the following verse a direct allusion to Laodicea's
banking establishments, medical school, and textile industry. The adjectives "wretched" and "miserable" are coordinate with the other three (one
article governs all five) and present five aspects of one and the same
condition. And saddest of all, they did not realize their wretched condition.
Philo remarked, "The witless are all paupers" (quoted by Moffatt, p.
371).

18 A tone of "sustained irony" (Blaiklock, *7C,* p. 77) runs
through verses 17 and 18. The smug satisfaction of the Laodiceans is
countered with the counsel that they make some purchases in those specific
areas in which they are confident that no need exists. Since they are in fact

---

[38]Hemer accepts the exegesis of Rudwick and Green and supplements the position with a
discussion of the water supply of the district (*7CA,* pp. 432–40). He concludes that "judgment is passed upon the 'works' of the Laodiceans, not their enthusiasm: the following verses
detail the symptoms" (p. 440).
[39]2329 reads ἐλέγχω σε ἐκ ("I refute thee out of...") instead of μέλλω σε ἐμέσαι ἐκ,
undoubtedly to soften the expression.
[40]Cf. Tarn and Griffith, *Hellenistic Civilization,* 3rd ed., p. 113.

"poor" (vs. 17), they need to buy from Christ (the prepositional phrase "from me" is emphatic) "gold refined by fire" so that they may become genuinely rich. The gold is spiritual wealth that has passed through the refiner's fire and has been found to be totally trustworthy.[41] The Laodiceans need white garments as well to cover the shame of their nakedness. A contrast with the black woolen fabric for which the city was famous could be intended, but the figure of white garments as symbolic of righteousness is so widely used in Revelation (3:4, 5; 4:4; 6:11; 7:9, 13–14; 19:14) that no local allusion is necessary. In the Biblical world nakedness was a symbol of judgment and humiliation. Isaiah walked naked for three and a half years as a sign that Assyria would lead captive the Egyptian and Ethiopian exiles, "naked and barefoot, with buttocks uncovered, to the shame of Egypt" (Isa 20:1–4; cf. II Sam 10:4; Ezek 16:37–39). At the same time, to receive fine clothing was an indication of honor (cf. Joseph being honored by Pharaoh in Gen 41:42 and Mordecai by Ahasuerus in Esth 6:6–11). Thus in God's sight (certainly not their own!) the Laodiceans were walking about spiritually naked, not understanding their humiliation and needing the white robes of righteousness which could be purchased at no cost (cf. Isa 55:1) except the acknowledgment of their shameful condition. The immediate cause of their problem was spiritual blindness. Laodicea was known for its famous medical school (established, according to the Greek geographer Strabo, in his own time, in connection with the temple of Mēn Carou; xii.8.20) and exported a "Phrygian powder" widely used as an eye-salve.[42] Confident of their clear vision into spiritual matters, the Laodiceans needed, as it were, their own eye-salve to restore sight. We are reminded of Jesus' dictum, "For judgment I came into this world, that those who do not see may see, and that those who see may become blind" (Jn 9:39). Jesus now says, Recognize your blindness or there is no hope of healing.

19 Ramsay considers 3:19–22 as an epilogue to all seven letters rather than the concluding portion of the letter to Laodicea. He argues that (1) since the seven letters are a single literary unit they call for an epilogue, (2) it would be inconsistent to join Laodicea (sharply condemned) with courageous Philadelphia as the two churches singled out as loved by Christ, and (3) at this point clear references to Laodicea cease (*L7CA*, pp. 431–33). Hemer answers the first two points almost in passing and then spends considerable time showing that both verse 20 and verse 21 are to be

---

[41]In I Pet 1:7 the same figure is used to portray the genuineness of faith.

[42]κολλύριον (Latin, *collyrium*) is the diminutive of κολλύρα, a long roll of coarse bread. The Phrygian powder was apparently applied to the eyes in the form of a doughy paste. Horace, in the first century BC, reports using *collyrium* en route to Brundisium (*Sat.* 1.5).

understood against the local background of Laodicea (*7CA*, pp. 446–78).[43] Few have followed Ramsay in separating verses 19–22 from the Laodicean letter. The rather stereotyped and continually repeated pattern of the seven letters calls for the promise (cf. 2:7b, 11b, 17b, 26; 3:5, 12) and the exhortation (cf. 2:7, 11, 17, 29; 3:6, 13) in Laodicea as well.

The syntax of the sentence places emphasis both on "I" and "as many as" (inclusive, without exception; cf. BAG, p. 590). One might loosely paraphrase, "Now *my* practice is that all those I love, I also correct and discipline." The principle of reproof and discipline as an expression of love is found in Proverbs 3:11–12, "My son, do not despise the Lord's discipline or be weary of his reproof, for the Lord reproves him whom he loves, as a father the son in whom he delights" (cf. also *Ps. Sol.* 10:1–3; 14:1; Heb 12:5–6). Of note is the fact that the LXX word for love (*agapan*) has been changed in the Laodicean letter (to *philein*). The "unconquerable attitude of benevolence and good will" has become the "warmest and most tender affection" (Barclay, I, p. 183). This unexpected show of personal affection has seemed strange to some but not to those who recognize that God's stern hatred of evil is a necessary part of his love for man. Charles mentions that "love is never cruel, but it can be severe" (II, p. 100). It takes the form of reproof[44] and discipline.[45] The idea of divine discipline runs throughout Scripture (Ps 94:12; Job 5:17; I Cor 11:32; Heb 12:7–8). "It is the fact of life that the best athlete and the finest scholar receive the hardest and the most demanding training" (Barclay, I, p. 184).

The advice to the Laodiceans, therefore, is that they repent (in one decisive act: aorist imperative) and make it the practice of their lives to continue zealously (present imperative).[46] This is the fourth direct call to repentance in the seven letters (cf. 2:5, 16; 3:3; reference to repentance at Thyatira is indirect, 2:21–22).

20 Verse 20 is often quoted as an invitation and promise to the person outside the community of faith. That it can be pressed into the

---

[43]Vs. 20 shows Christ pleading for willing hospitality in contrast to the enforced hospitality of the corrupt Roman officials who exploited the wealth of the local citizens (*7CA*, pp. 465–70). Vss. 20 and 21 are tied together by a reference to a historical incident in which Polemo shut out an invader and received a throne in reward for his resolute action (*7CA*, pp. 470–73, 480).

[44]Barclay writes that ἐλέγχω is "the kind of rebuke which compels a man to see the error of his ways" and adds that "the rebuke of God is not so much punishment as it is illumination" (I, p. 183). Büchsel says that "it implies educative discipline" and means "to show someone his sin and to summon him to repentance" (*TDNT*, II, p. 474).

[45]Bertram says that in the context of the admonitory letters of Rev, παιδεύω has as a main emphasis the idea of rousing or stirring (*TDNT*, V, p. 623).

[46]There may be some intended comparison between ζήλευε here and ζεστός of vss. 15–16 (the words begin similarly but are not cognate).

service of evangelism in this way seems evident. Compared with other world religions the seeking God of the Judaeo-Christian heritage is perhaps its major uniqueness. In the context of the Laodicean letter, however, it is self-deluded members of the church who are being addressed. To the *church* Christ says, "Behold, I stand at the door and knock." In their blind self-sufficiency they had, as it were, excommunicated the risen Lord from their congregation. In an act of unbelievable condescension he requests permission to enter and re-establish fellowship.

Two principal interpretations of verse 20 exist: (1) that it represents a call to the individual for present fellowship, and (2) that it is eschatological and speaks of the imminent return of Christ. The latter interprets the verse in conjunction with the reward promised the overcomer in verse 21 (an eschatological scene to be sure), while the former ties it in with the call to repentance in verse 19.[47] In that the phrase "he that overcometh" elsewhere in the letters serves as a semi-technical term that opens a new subsection of the letter (cf. 2:7, 11b, 17b, 26; 3:5, 12) and because verse 20 provides a strong positive motivation for the repentance demanded in the previous verse, it seems best to interpret the saying as personal and present rather than ecclesiastical and eschatological.

As in Holman Hunt's famous picture (*The Light of the World*), Christ is outside the door and knocking. There is no particular reason why we should agree with Caird's idea that Christ is knocking "with the imperious hammering of the divine initiative, loud enough to penetrate even the deaf ears of Laodicea" (p. 57). It has never been the practice of God to storm the ramparts of the human heart.[48] The invitation is addressed to each individual in the congregation: "if any man" hear and open. The response of Christ to the opened door is that he enters and joins in table fellowship. In Oriental lands the sharing of a common meal indicated a strong bond of affection and companionship. As such it became a common symbol of the intimacy to be enjoyed in the coming messianic kingdom. Enoch portrays the future blessedness of the elect saying, "And with that Son of Man shall they eat and lie down and rise up for ever and ever" (*I Enoch* 62:14). In Luke 22:30 Jesus tells his disciples that they are to eat and drink at his table

---

[47]The eschatological view is followed by Moffatt (p. 373), Swete (pp. 63–64), Beckwith (p. 491), Kiddle (p. 60), and others. Beasley-Murray says that taking the words as applying to the church's part in the future kingdom "is not a natural interpretation" (p. 107). Cf. Charles, I, p. 101.

[48]Attention is often drawn to Cant 5:2–6 as a possible background, but apart from the knock (in vs. 2) the settings are distinct. In Cant the maiden's lover has gone before she can answer the knock; in Rev Christ has taken his stand (ἕστηκα) outside the door and knocks for decidedly less sensual reasons.

in the kingdom (cf. Mt 26:29; Rev 19:9). Whether eucharistic associations are intended or not,[49] it is hard not to see in the picture at least an anticipation of the future messianic kingdom. All present fellowship with God is a foretaste of eternal felicity.

21 The promise of sitting with Christ on his throne is wholly eschatological. Jesus had promised his disciples that in the coming age when the Son of man would sit on his glorious throne, they also (those who had followed him) would sit on twelve thrones judging the tribes of Israel (Mt 19:28). But now the faithful are promised that they will sit with him on *his throne* (which is also the Father's throne, 22:1). The martyrs in 6:10 cried out for vindication. It is to be fully realized when the overcomers take their place beside the Lamb on his throne. Their victory and consequent exaltation follow the pattern of the victory of Christ, who also overcame and sat down with his Father on the heavenly throne.[50] Paul, as well, had promised, "If we endure, we shall also reign with him" (II Tim 2:12).

22 Here for the seventh and last time we hear the exhortation to hear what the Spirit is saying to the churches. We are reminded that the messages to the seven historic churches in Asia are at the same time a composite word to the church universal throughout time. Walvoord calls it a "comprehensive warning" in which the dangers of losing our first love (Ephesus), fear of suffering (Smyrna), doctrinal compromise (Pergamum), moral compromise (Thyatira), spiritual deadness (Sardis), failure to hold fast (Philadelphia), and lukewarmness (Laodicea) are brought home with amazing relevance for the contemporary church (pp. 99–100).

[49]Caird, p. 58; Beckwith holds, "The symbol is altogether eschatological; there is no reference to the eucharist" (p. 491).
[50]In a number of places in *I Enoch* it is said that the elect one (the Messiah) is to sit on the throne of glory (*I Enoch* 45:3; 51:3; 55:4; etc.).

CHAPTER 4

III. ADORATION IN THE COURT OF HEAVEN
(4:1–5:14)

The letters to the seven churches are now complete. Christians of Asia Minor are to receive personal correspondence from the risen and glorified Lord of the church. While correction and commendation have varied with the different congregations, the challenge to overcome goes out to all (2:7, 11, 17, 27; 3:5, 12, 21), for all are about to enter that period of intensified conflict which immediately precedes the return of Christ. It is announced by the angel in 12:12 with the grim words, "Woe for the earth and for the sea: because the devil is gone down unto you, having great wrath, knowing that he hath but a short time." For consolation and courage in the coming tribulation (cf. 2:10; 3:10; 7:13) John is now swept up in the Spirit to the very door of heaven. There he beholds a vision of a sovereign God in full command of the course of human affairs as they move swiftly to their denouement. On the plane of history the church appears unable to resist the might of hostile worldly powers, but the course of history is not determined by political power but by God enthroned and active. At his appointed time the scroll of destiny is to be handed to the Lamb, who himself will open the seals, bring history to a close, and usher in the eternal state. The great throne-room vision of chapters 4 and 5 serves to remind believers living in the shadow of impending persecution that an omnipotent and omniscient God is still in control.

1. WORSHIP OF GOD AS CREATOR (4:1–11)

1 *After these things I saw, and behold, a door opened in heaven, and the first voice that I heard,* a voice *as of a trumpet speaking with me, one saying, Come up hither, and I will show thee the things which must come to pass hereafter.*

2 *Straightway I was in the Spirit: and behold, there was a throne set in heaven, and one sitting upon the throne;*

3 *and he that sat was to look upon like a jasper stone and a sardius: and there was a rainbow round about the throne, like an emerald to look upon.*

4 *And round about the throne were four and twenty thrones: and upon the thrones I saw four and twenty elders sitting, arrayed in white garments; and on their heads crowns of gold.*

5 *And out of the throne proceed lightnings and voices and thunders. And there were seven lamps of fire burning before the throne, which are the seven Spirits of God;*

6 *and before the throne, as it were a sea of glass like unto crystal; and in the midst of the throne, and round about the throne, four living creatures full of eyes before and behind.*

7 *And the first creature was like a lion, and the second creature like a calf, and the third creature had a face as of a man, and the fourth creature was like a flying eagle.*

8 *And the four living creatures, having each one of them six wings, are full of eyes round about and within: and they have no rest day and night, saying,*

Holy, holy, holy, is the Lord God, the Almighty, who was and who is and who is to come.

9 *And when the living creatures shall give glory and honor and thanks to him that sitteth on the throne, to him that liveth for ever and ever,*

10 *the four and twenty elders shall fall down before him that sitteth on the throne, and shall worship him that liveth for ever and ever, and shall cast their crowns before the throne, saying,*

11 *Worthy art thou, our Lord and our God, to receive the glory and the honor and the power: for thou didst create all things, and because of thy will they were, and were created.*

1   The throne-room vision (chaps. 4 and 5) follows the earlier vision (1:12 ff) apparently without delay.[1] There is no way of knowing for sure just when and how John recorded his visionary experiences. Since the vision moves on naturally to the breaking of the seals and ultimately to the unveiling of the close of history, it is best to understand it as referring essentially to a time yet future. While God is eternally adored in heaven, the book of Revelation reveals those specific events with which history is brought to a close.

---

[1]Most commentators note that μετὰ ταῦτα εἶδον introduces a new division of special importance while other phrases mark subordinate sections.

John sees a door standing[2] open in the vault of heaven.[3] In Ezekiel the prophet reports, "The heavens were opened, and I saw visions of God" (Ezek 1:1). Whether John goes through the door into heaven or only to the door to look within is not certain. The door may suggest that the vision was limited to John alone. In any case, we must remember that we are dealing with symbolism and guard against the tendency to read into the text more than is there. The voice, which in chapter 1 commanded John to write (1:10), now bids him to come to the door of heaven.[4] That Christ would invite John to a scene in which he as the Lamb is an integral part is a problem only for those who approach the Apocalypse without a sympathetic imagination. John is about to see "the things which must come to pass hereafter." This definitely assigns the content of the following chapters to a period of time yet future. In 1:19 Christ had commanded John to write of "the things which shall come to pass hereafter"; now he will show him those things. Since events on earth have their origin in heaven, the heavenly ascent is not unexpected. A true insight into history is gained only when we view all things from the vantage point of the heavenly throne.

2 It would appear that the Seer had returned to a normal state of consciousness (since "Straightway I was in the Spirit" suggests a new departure), yet the preceding verse, with its open door in heaven and voice like a trumpet, is most certainly part of a visionary experience. What we have, then, is a continuation of the ecstatic state. Ezekiel 11:1, 5 is parallel: the prophet is first carried away to the east gate by the Spirit, and then the Spirit of the Lord falls upon him to prophesy. Moffatt speaks of a "fresh wave of ecstasy" that catches up the Seer (p. 376).[5]

The idea of prophetic rapture is widespread in Jewish literature. Micaiah told the king of Israel, "I saw the Lord sitting on his throne, and all the host of heaven standing beside him on his right hand and on his left" (I Kgs 22:19). Amos reports that God does nothing "without revealing his

---

[2]The perfect participle, ἠνεῳγμένη, could suggest that the door had been opened and left that way for John's arrival. Cf. *I Enoch* 19:9 ff; *Test. Levi* 5:1; *As. Mos.* 4:2.

[3]John uses the singular, οὐρανός, some fifty times in Rev. Only in 12:12 (perhaps influenced by Isa 44:23) is the plural found. John's view of a single heaven is in contrast with the fairly widespread concept in antiquity of a plurality of heavens (cf. Rist, p. 401, for references in the literature of Judaism).

[4]While many dispensationalists see in the ascent of John the rapture of the church, one prominent spokesman, Walvoord, writes that "it is clear from the context that this is not an explicit reference to the rapture of the church" (p. 103). He does hold, however, that the rapture may be viewed as having taken place before the events of chap. 4 and following.

[5]Swete (p. 67) writes, "The state of spiritual exaltation which preceded the first vision . . . has returned, but in greater force." Charles (I, p. 110) takes the two visions as coming at different times and says that 1b–2a is a link supplied by the Seer.

secret to his servants the prophets'' (Amos 3:7). John views himself as a prophet (1:3), and being ''in the Spirit'' (the Holy Spirit, not his human spirit) is an appropriate state for what he is about to experience. That John does not record a physical relocation from earth to heaven suggests that we are to understand the heavenly ascent in a spiritual sense. There is no basis for discovering a rapture of the church at this point.

The first thing that John sees in heaven is a throne. This symbol occurs more than forty times in Revelation. It symbolizes the absolute sovereignty of God. The one upon the throne is ''the Lord God, the Almighty'' (4:8), before whom the twenty-four elders fall down and worship (4:10) and all creation joins in a doxology of praise and honor (5:13). The throne of God is often referred to in Jewish literature. ''I saw the Lord sitting upon a throne, high and lifted up'' is the testimony of Isaiah (6:1), and the Psalmist sings, ''God reigns over the nations; God sits on his holy throne'' (Ps 47:8). This scene of heaven opened and God upon the throne is said to have been the inspiration for Handel's *Messiah*.

3 The one seated upon the throne of heaven does not appear in human form but is portrayed as the brilliance of light reflected from precious stones. The Psalmist spoke of God as one who covered himself ''with light as with a garment'' (Ps 104:2), and Paul described the Lord as dwelling ''in unapproachable light, whom no man has ever seen or can see'' (I Tim 6:16). The source of the description is the vision of Ezekiel 1 in which the throne appears like sapphire surrounded by a rainbow (1:26–28).

Identification of the three stones (jasper, sardius, and emerald) is somewhat uncertain. Since modern jasper is opaque, many interpret the ancient stone as a translucent rock crystal (in 21:11 it is said to be ''clear as crystal''), perhaps a diamond. The sardius was a blood-red stone named after Sardis near where it was found. If the rainbow which surrounded the throne was a halo, then the emerald is usually pictured as green; otherwise it is a colorless crystal which would refract a rainbow of prismatic colors. These three stones held an honorable place in antiquity. They are mentioned by Plato as representative of precious stones (*Phaed.* 110e). Of the king of Tyre it is written, ''Every precious stone was your covering, carnelian [sardius: *ASV*] . . . jasper . . . and emerald'' (Ezek 28:13). They are among the twelve precious stones which adorned the breastplate of the high priest (Ex 28:17).[6]

---

[6]Ex 28:17–21 lists the twelve stones, each inscribed and representing a tribe in Israel. Note that the jasper and carnelian (sardius) are the last and the first (Benjamin and Reuben; cf. Gen 49:3–27). On this basis the emerald (no. 4) would stand for the tribe of Judah.

Various meanings have been attached to the different stones. Jasper suggests such qualities as majesty, holiness, or purity. Sardius is often interpreted as wrath or judgment, and the emerald as mercy. The rainbow reminds us of God's covenant with Noah (Gen 9:16–17). Caird writes that the rainbow tells us that "there is to be no triumph for God's sovereignty at the expense of his mercy"—a warning not to interpret the following visions of disaster as if God had forgotten his promise to Noah (p. 63). It is probably wise, however, to see the gems as part of an overall description. They portray in symbolic form the majesty of God, resplendent and clothed in unapproachable light. As in the parables of Jesus, many of the details are merely descriptive and not intended to carry a special significance of their own.

4 Around the throne of God are twenty-four thrones occupied by twenty-four elders dressed in white and wearing crowns of gold. Throughout the book they are pictured as falling down before God in worship (5:14; 11:16; 19:4). Twice one of their number acts as a spokesman or interpreter (5:5; 7:13). On one occasion they join the four living creatures in presenting the prayers of the saints to God (5:8). Adoration and praise are continually on their lips (4:11; 5:9–10; 11:17–18; 19:4).

The identity of the twenty-four elders has been widely discussed. Commentators who tend to find the source of John's imagery in the astromythological tradition of Eastern polytheism take the elders to be a Judaic counterpart of the twenty-four star-gods of the Babylonian pantheon.[7] Others interpret them as symbolic of the twenty-four courses of Aaronic priests (I Chron 24:5), who in heaven render to God that perfect worship of which the priestly worship on earth is but an imperfect copy. A great many writers interpret the twenty-four elders as symbolic of the church in its totality—a combination of the twelve patriarchs and the twelve apostles[8]—but this seems unlikely in that their song of praise (5:9–10) definitely sets them apart from those who were purchased by the blood of Christ (most certainly the church!). Since no exact counterparts are to be located in Jewish literature, it seems best to take the twenty-four elders as an exalted angelic order who serve and adore God as the heavenly counterpart to the twenty-four priestly and twenty-four Levitical orders (I Chron

[7]Beasley-Murray rejects the theory that the twenty-four elders have come from Babylonian astrological religion via Jewish apocalyptic (as proposed by Zimmern and Gunkel) on the basis that "there is no evidence at all that Jewish apocalyptic knew of an angelic order of twenty-four in heaven" (p. 115, n.).

[8]In 21:12–14 the names of the twelve tribes of Israel are inscribed on the twelve gates of the New Jerusalem and the names of the twelve apostles on the twelve foundations.

24:4; 25:9–13).[9] Their function is both royal and sacerdotal, and may be judicial as well (cf. 20:4). Their white garments speak of holiness, and their golden crowns of royalty.[10]

5 The lightnings and thunders that proceed out of the throne (the "voices" are essentially the same as the "thunders") are symbolic of the awesome power and majesty of God. They remind the reader of the great theophany of Sinai when God descended in fire and smoke heralded by thunder and lightning (Ex 19:16 ff). Frequently in the OT God disclosed himself in the dramatic activity of nature (cf. Ps 18:12 ff). "The crash of thy thunder was in the whirlwind; the lightnings lighted up the world" (Ps 77:18). In Revelation the symbols of thunder and lightning are always connected with a temple scene and mark an event of unusual import. In 8:5 they follow the breaking of the seventh seal, in 11:19, the blowing of the seventh trumpet, and in 16:18, the pouring out of the seventh bowl of wrath. The seven lamps of fire which burn before the throne are interpreted by the Seer as the seven Spirits of God. In 1:4 we tentatively identified the seven Spirits as angelic beings rather than the Holy Spirit in his sevenfold activity (cf. Isa 11:2).

6 Stretching out before the throne was, as it were, a sea of glass. Unlike the semi-opaque glass of antiquity, it was clear as crystal. Many connect this with the Jewish idea of a celestial sea. In Genesis 1:7 God divided the waters which were under the firmament (the heavenly expanse) from the waters which were above the firmament. In *II Enoch* 3:3 the prophet sees in the first heaven "a very great sea, greater than the earthly sea." Apparently God's throne rested on these waters: Ps 104:3 speaks of God laying the beams of his chambers thereon. Some writers compare the idea with the Assyrian myth of the creation of the gods by the union of the celestial waters (masculine) and the earthly waters (feminine). The text, however, speaks only of "something like a sea of glass." We are intended to understand it as a visual phenomenon which adds to the awesome splendor of the throne-room scene. Its crystal surface stretches out before the throne, reflecting the flashing, many-colored light from the throne, furnishing a surface for the activity around the throne, and creating for the Seer an unspeakably heightened sense of the transcendence and majesty of God.

If we are to find a source for the "sea of glass," we should probably turn to the great throne-chariot vision of Ezekiel 1 (a primary source for Rev 4–5). Over the heads of the cherubim spread out "the likeness of a

---

[9]Stonehouse discusses the issue at length in *Paul Before the Areopagus*, chap. 4. For the view that the elders are glorified saints rather than angels, cf. Feuillet, "The Twenty-Four Elders of the Apocalypse," *Johannine Studies*, pp. 183–214.
[10]In 14:14 Christ himself is crowned with a στέφανος χρυσοῦς.

firmament, shining like crystal" (vs. 22). Above this shining firmament was the throne. In Job 37:18 the sky is pictured as "hard as a molten mirror."[11] The sea of glass is part of the larger scene and, apart from heightening the sense of God's separateness from his creatures, has no special significance such as the cleansing blood of Christ (Hendriksen, p. 105), divine providence (Lenski, p. 178), or everything that is recalcitrant to the will of God (Caird, p. 65).

In addition to the twenty-four elders there were "in the midst . . . and round about the throne" four living creatures.[12] The exact location is a bit uncertain, but "in the midst" apparently means "in the immediate vicinity." Thus they surround the throne as an inner circle.[13] This position is appropriate to their function as leaders in worship (cf. 4:9–10; 5:14). The four living creatures of John's vision are related to the cherubim of Ezekiel 1, although several differences should be noted. In Ezekiel each of the four has four faces (vss. 6, 10), four wings (vs. 6) instead of six as in Rev 4:8, and the rims of the wheels with which they are associated, not their bodies as in Rev 4:6, are full of eyes (Ezek 1:18). The four living creatures of Revelation also suggest the seraphim of Isaiah 6:2–3 who lifted up their voices in praise singing, "Holy, holy, holy, is the Lord of hosts" (cf. the *six* wings of vs. 2 with Rev 4:8).

Like the twenty-four elders, the four living creatures have been variously interpreted. Lenski (p. 179) says that one writer lists twenty-one efforts at solution, to which he then adds another equally unacceptable. In a five-page discussion Charles traces three stages of development from Babylonian mythology through the OT to Jewish apocalyptic. But in that our author was "wholly unacquainted" with the earliest stage (I, p. 122), it seems fruitless to conjecture about any relationship between John's images and the four principal signs of the zodiac (Taurus, Leo, Scorpio, and Aquarius).[14] Beckwith is undoubtedly right in his judgment that "the figures which throng the court of heaven are the traditional orders of heavenly beings" (p. 501). A consistent interpretation of the entire throne-room

---

[11]Moffatt says the sea of glass portrays "the ether, clear and calm, shimmering and motionless" (p. 379). Others associate it with the molten sea in Solomon's temple (I Kgs 7:23–26).

[12]The *AV*'s translation, "beasts," is unfortunate in that ζῷον is used in Rev exclusively for the four living creatures, while θηρίον ("wild beast") depicts the hideous figures of chaps. 13 and 17.

[13]Brewer explains the arrangement in terms of the Greek amphitheater with its circular orchestral area containing a speaking place for the gods, an altar, and a semicircular row of carved seats ("thrones") for dignitaries ("Revelation 4, 6 and the Translations Thereof," *JBL*, 71 [1952], pp. 227–31). Although John may well have seen such marble thrones in the theater in Ephesus, his imagery is profoundly Jewish in this and other visions of Revelation.

[14]Just how Aquarius became an eagle in John's account has never been satisfactorily explained!

vision requires us to understand the living creatures as an exalted order of angelic beings who as the immediate guardians of the throne lead the heavenly hosts in worship and adoration of God. It is possible that they also represent the entire animate creation. That they are full of eyes before and behind (cf. vs. 8: "round about and within") speaks of alertness and knowledge. Nothing escapes their notice.

7 While each of Ezekiel's cherubim had four faces (lion on the right, ox on the left, human in front, and eagle behind; cf. Ezek 1:6, 10), only one of John's creatures has a face[15]—the other three have the form of a lion, a calf, and an eagle. Swete writes that "the four forms suggest whatever is noblest, strongest, wisest, and swiftest in animate Nature" (p. 71). It does not follow, however, that the living creatures are a personification of divine immanence in nature. We are dealing with angelic beings. Hendriksen (p. 107) interprets them as having the strength of a lion (cf. Ps 103:20), the ability to serve of an ox (cf. Heb 1:14), the intelligence of a man (cf. Lk 15:10), and the swiftness (to serve) of an eagle (cf. Dan 9:21). All attempts to equate the living creatures with the four gospels (eg., Jn the lion, Lk the calf (ox), Mt the man, Mk the eagle; cf. Irenaeus about AD 170) are groundless.[16]

8 Like the seraphim of Isaiah 6:2 each of the four living creatures had six wings. The wings may suggest swiftness to carry out the will of God. In Psalm 18:10 God is pictured as riding upon a cherub, and the parallel clause adds, "He came swiftly upon the wings of the wind." In Ezekiel 10 the chariot-throne of God is carried by the cherubim, who "lifted up their wings to mount up from the earth" (vs. 16). The description of the eyes "round about and within" is awkward. It probably means that the living creatures had eyes all around their bodies and on the underside of their wings.[17] Here as elsewhere we are dealing with visions which were meant to stir the imagination, not yield to the drawing board.

Night and day without ceasing the four living creatures lift their praise to God. Continuous adoration is a common feature in apocalyptic descriptions of heaven. *I Enoch* 39:12 pictures sleepless angels standing before God and extolling his greatness (cf. *Test. Levi* 3:8; *II Enoch* 21:1).

---

[15]**P** 1 2059s *pm* sy[h] TR read the nominative ἄνθρωπος, which would suggest that the third creature had the form of a man rather than simply a human face.

[16]Irenaeus, *Adv. Haer.* iii.11.11. Cf. Barclay, I, p. 203 for three other arrangements. Lenski's identification with the four places where God's providence is carried out (lion, the wild places; ox, the cultivated spots; man, cities and towns; eagle, the air) grows out of his prior identification of the sea of glass as the providence of God (p. 183).

[17]It is of no help to read κυκλόθεν with the previous clause even when ἔξωθεν καί (**046** 69 *pc*) is added before ἔσωθεν. Eyes "within" still poses a problem.

Like the seraphim of Isaiah 6 they sing "Holy, holy, holy,"[18] but their praise is here directed to those attributes of God which are central to the Apocalypse—his holiness, power, and eternity.[19] To acknowledge God as holy is to declare his complete separateness from all created beings.

Praise of his holiness leads to an affirmation of his omnipotence: he is the Almighty.[20] To churches about to enter a period of severe testing and persecution a declaration of God's unlimited might would bring strength and encouragement. During his earthly ministry Jesus had said, "In the world you have tribulation: but be of good cheer; I have overcome the world" (Jn 16:33). The protection Christ offers is not physical but spiritual (cf. Mt 10:28). Nothing lies beyond his control, for he is *all*-mighty.

Beyond this, his holiness and omnipotence stretch from eternity to eternity: he is the One "who was and who is and who is to come" (cf. comm. on 1:4). The truth which finds expression in this phrase—an expansion of God's "I AM WHO I AM" in Exodus 3:14—is repeated in the following verses where God is twice designated the one "that liveth for ever and ever" (vss. 9–10).

9–10   As often as the living creatures give glory and honor to God (cf. 5:8, 14; 11:16; 19:4), the twenty-four elders prostrate themselves before the throne, casting down their crowns and joining in adoration of the One who lives forever and ever. To fall down is a proper response to the majesty of God: to worship is appropriate for his eternal being. The suggestion that these spontaneous outbursts of praise contradict the continuous worship of verse 8 represents that kind of unimaginative criticism which looks for "strict logic in the poetry of adoration" (Barclay, I, p. 206). The word "worship" originally involved the idea of prostrating oneself before deity to kiss his feet or the hem of his garment. As an act of reverence and respect it was not uncommon in the East. In casting down their crowns before the throne the elders acknowledge that their authority is a delegated authority. The honor given them is freely returned to the One who alone is worthy of universal honor.

11   The praise of the elders differs from that of the living creatures

---

[18]Norman Walker suggests that "Thrice-Holy" of Isa 6:3 was a conflate reading signifying "HOLY, EXCEEDING HOLY" ("The Origin of the 'Thrice-Holy,'" *NTS*, 5 [1958–9], pp. 132–33).

[19]Ralph Martin cites Rev 4:8 as the most illustrious example of material in Rev which was borrowed directly from the synagogues of the Greek-speaking Jewish world. The entire group of Jewish-Christian fragments offers praise to the "holy and righteous God of Judaism who is extolled . . . in the synagogue Liturgy as Creator and Sustainer of the world, and Judge of all" (*Worship in the Early Church*, p. 45).

[20]In Jewish and Christian writers, παντοκράτωρ is used only of God.

in that it is addressed directly to God[21] and is based on his work in creation rather than his divine attributes. Here is direct refutation of the dualistic idea that God as spirit would not himself be involved in a material creation. Lilje notes that the first words of the hymn[22] are taken from the political language of the day: "Worthy art thou" greeted the entrance of the emperor in triumphal procession, and "our Lord and God" was introduced into the cult of emperor worship by Domitian (p. 108; cf. Suetonius, *Dom.* 13). For the Christian only the One upon the heavenly throne is worthy: the claims of all others are blasphemous. The earlier doxology (4:8) ascribed might and power to God. To this the elders now add "glory" and "honor." He is worthy because in accordance with his will all things "were, and were created." This unusual phrase suggests that all things which are, existed first in the eternal will of God and through his will came into actual being at his appointed time.[23]

---

[21]Ἄξιος εἶ; note as well the emphatic σύ.

[22]J. J. O'Rourke holds that John borrowed from liturgical sources when he composed certain sections of the book: the doxologies in 1:6; 5:13; 7:12; the acclamations of worthiness in 4:11; 5:9, 12; and the trisagion, 4:8b ("The Hymns of the Apocalypse," *CBQ*, 30 [1968], pp. 399–409). His criteria are "parallelism similar to that found in Pss, solemn tone of expression apt for use in worship, and grammatical inconcinnity" (p. 400). Cf. L. Mowry, "Revelation IV-V and Early Christian Liturgical Usage," *JBL*, 71 (1952), pp. 75–84.

[23]Some manuscripts solve the apparent problem of existence before creation by reading εἰσίν for ἦσαν (**P** 1 *al* TR). Others (**046** 2020 *pc*) place οὐκ before ἦσαν (an "ingenious correction" according to Swete; p. 75).

CHAPTER 5

2. WORSHIP OF THE LAMB WHO ALONE IS WORTHY TO OPEN THE SCROLL (5:1–14)

1 *And I saw in the right hand of him that sat on the throne a book written within and on the back, close sealed with seven seals.*

2 *And I saw a strong angel proclaiming with a great voice, Who is worthy to open the book, and to loose the seals thereof?*

3 *And no one in the heaven, or on the earth, or under the earth, was able to open the book, or to look thereon.*

4 *And I wept much, because no one was found worthy to open the book, or to look thereon:*

5 *and one of the elders saith unto me, Weep not; behold, the Lion that is of the tribe of Judah, the Root of David, hath overcome to open the book and the seven seals thereof.*

6 *And I saw in the midst of the throne and of the four living creatures, and in the midst of the elders, a Lamb standing, as though it had been slain, having seven horns, and seven eyes, which are the seven Spirits of God, sent forth into all the earth.*

7 *And he came, and he taketh* it *out of the right hand of him that sat on the throne.*

8 *And when he had taken the book, the four living creatures and the four and twenty elders fell down before the Lamb, having each one a harp, and golden bowls full of incense, which are the prayers of the saints.*

9 *And they sing a new song, saying,*
Worthy art thou to take the book, and to open the seals thereof: for thou wast slain, and didst purchase unto God with thy blood men *of every tribe, and tongue, and people, and nation,*

10 *and madest them* to be *unto our God a kingdom and priests; and they reign upon the earth.*

11 *And I saw, and I heard a voice of many angels round about the throne and the living creatures and the elders; and the number of them was ten thousand times ten thousand, and thousands of thousands;*

12 *saying with a great voice,*

Worthy is the Lamb that hath been slain to receive the power, and riches,
and wisdom, and might, and honor, and glory, and blessing.

13 *And every created thing which is in the heaven, and on the earth, and*
under the earth, and on the sea, and all things that are in them, heard I
saying,

Unto him that sitteth on the throne, and unto the Lamb, be the blessing,
and the honor, and the glory, and the dominion, for ever and ever.

14 *And the four living creatures said, Amen. And the elders fell down and*
worshipped.

1 On the right hand of the One seated on the throne is a book of unparalleled significance. Filled to overflowing and sealed with seven seals to insure the secrecy of its decrees, it contains the full account of what God in his sovereign will has determined as the destiny of the world.[1] Once again the background is Ezekiel where in chapter 2 a book of lamentations "written within and without" is handed to the prophet (vs. 10). The idea of a heavenly book containing the future course of history is reflected in such passages as Psalm 139:16, "In thy book were written every one of them, the days that were formed for me, when as yet there was none of them." In Jewish apocalyptic we read of "heavenly tablets" which contain "all the deeds of men . . . that will be upon the earth to the remotest generations" (*I Enoch* 81:1–2; cf. also 47:3; 106:19; 107:1).[2] According to Roman law certain documents were required to be sealed by seven witnesses,[3] although the idea of seven seals as used here is undoubtedly governed by the symbolic use of the number seven in Revelation and signifies the absolute inviolability of the scroll. In Daniel 8:26 the prophet is told, "Seal up the vision, for it pertains to many days hence" (cf. Isa 29:11). When the time has fully come, the seals will be removed and history will move swiftly to its consummation.

Some have suggested that the scroll of destiny was in the form of a book rather than a papyrus roll. The argument is based primarily on the fact that it was held "*upon* the right hand" of God rather than *in* his hand. That the expression is no more than an idiom is seen in 20:1 where an angel

---

[1]Other suggestions are (1) the Lamb's book of life (3:5; 13:8; 17:8; 20:12, 15; 21:27), (2) the OT, (3) a testament which insures inheritance for the saints, and (4) a doubly inscribed contract deed (cf. Beasley-Murray, pp. 120–22, for a discussion of this interpretation). Cf. Emmet Russell, "A Roman Law Parallel to Revelation Five," *BSac*, 115 (1958), pp. 258–64.

[2]The related concept of a heavenly pattern for things on earth is seen in the instructions given to Moses concerning the tabernacle and its furniture (Ex 25:9–10; 26:30). Cf. Eph 2:10.

[3]Stauffer, *Christ and the Caesars*, pp. 182–83.

comes down from heaven with a key and a great chain "upon his hand." By altering the punctuation and following an inferior text, some read "a book written within, and sealed without with seven seals,"[4] but this amounts to saying the obvious; where else would a book be written, or sealed, for that matter? Admittedly the scroll is arranged in an unusual way, because as each seal is broken a portion of its content is enacted. We would not expect, however, that all the details of a vision conform to normal expectations. That the scroll is also written on the back indicates how extensive and comprehensive are the decrees of God.[5]

2 There now appears upon the scene a strong angel (Gabriel?) who calls for someone who is worthy to open the book and loose its seals. A great voice is needed because the challenge is sent out to the far reaches of creation. We will meet this angelic herald again in 10:1, where he stands astride the sea and cries out as a lion roaring, and in 18:21, where he casts a great millstone into the sea—symbolic of the overthrow of Roman might. Since these are the great proclamations of God, the voice of a strong angel is required. The call is for someone who is worthy[6] to perform the supreme service of bringing history to its foreordained consummation. God himself does not perform this task but calls for a mediator. Opening the book is mentioned before loosening the seals not because the seals are placed at intervals within the scroll but because the content of the book is of first importance.[7]

3 The challenge has gone out to all those dwelling throughout the entire creation and no one is able to accept it. The tripartite division of the universe (heaven, earth, under the earth) is also found in Philippians 2:10—incidentally, in a scene of universal adoration of Christ—and probably stems from the second commandment which forbids making any likeness of that which is in "heaven above, or . . . in the earth beneath, or . . . in the water under the earth" (Ex 20:4). As used here it stresses the universality of the proclamation rather than some particular cosmology. It seems somewhat forced to make the phrases refer systematically to angels, living men, and departed spirits as if when each declines the challenge, hope gradually vanishes (Swete, p. 76). In any case, no one is found able to open the book or to look into its contents.

4 It appears that the promise of 4:1 ("Come up hither, and I will

---

[4]**P 046** 82 1006 *pm* lat bo read ἔξωθεν rather than ὄπισθεν.

[5]Writing on the side of a papyrus scroll where the fibers run horizontally (the *recto*) was much easier than the reverse side (the *verso*) where they were vertical.

[6]Morris comments, "His concern is with worthiness, not naked power" (p. 94).

[7]Grammarians call this *hysteron proteron*.

show thee the things which must come to pass hereafter'') is about to be thwarted. Unless the seals are broken and the scroll of destiny unrolled, God's plan for the universe will be frustrated. Hence the Seer[8] breaks out in unrestrained weeping.[9] All suggestions that John wept out of disappointment for his own sake are unworthy of the Seer. He wept at the prospect of an indefinite postponement of God's final and decisive action. The universe itself was morally incapable of effecting its own destiny.

5 One of the elders steps forward and tells the Seer to cease weeping. The scroll will not remain unopened, for there is One who has conquered and is therefore worthy to break the seals. He is the Lion of the tribe of Judah, the Root of David. Preston and Hanson judge the next two verses to be among the most profound in the entire Apocalypse in that "they relate Jewish Messianic hopes to the distinctively Christian good news of the advent of the Messiah in the person of Jesus of Nazareth'' (p. 75). Both of the titles ascribed to Jesus are taken from the common stock of Jewish messianism. The first is from Genesis 49:9–10 where in Jacob's final blessing on his twelve sons Judah is called a "lion's whelp'' and is promised that the scepter shall not depart from him "until Shiloh come'' (*ASV*). That these verses were interpreted messianically in the first century BC is seen in the *Testament of Judah* 24:5.[10] The second title is an allusion to Isaiah 11:1 ("There shall come forth a shoot out of the stock of Jesse''; cf. also vs. 10), which looks forward to an ideal king of the line of David who will judge with righteousness and usher in an era of peace. Isaiah 11:1 is quoted as messianic in Romans 15:12.

That it is "one of the elders'' who addresses John is of no particular significance. He appears again, as an interpreter, in 7:13. John is to cease weeping, for Christ has conquered once and for all.[11] Paradoxically, this decisive victory over Satan and death was accomplished on the cross. He conquered by an act of total self-sacrifice. The result is that he alone is worthy to open the scroll of destiny both to reveal and to carry out the final dissolution of all forces set in opposition to the eternal kingdom of God.

6 John now looks to the center of the celestial scene and beholds, not a Lion, but a Lamb! A Lamb with seven horns and seven eyes, bearing the wounds of sacrificial slaughter, yet standing in readiness for action. In one brilliant stroke John portrays the central theme of NT revelation—victory through sacrifice.

---

[8]TR *al* vg add ἐγώ to identify the subject. Since ἔκλαιον is third person plural as well as first person singular, the subject could be those surveyed in vs. 3.

[9]Cf. Lk 19:41 for a similar use of κλαίω.

[10]Cf. II Esdr 12:31 for the Messiah as a lion.

[11]The aorist ἐνίκησεν stands unqualified and in an emphatic position.

Only in the writings of John is Jesus called the Lamb (cf., however, I Pet 1:19). In John 1:29 the Baptist declares, "Behold, the Lamb of God, who takes away the sin of the world." In Revelation the title is used of Jesus twenty-eight times.[12] It is common to trace the source of John's imagery to Isaiah 53:7, "Like a lamb that is led to the slaughter, and like a sheep that before its shearers is dumb, so he opened not his mouth." Others find the background in the theme of the paschal Lamb which plays such an important part in John's passion narrative. While it is true that a slaughtered lamb obviously connoted sacrifice, the lamb in John's vision is now standing upright, "having seven horns and seven eyes"—symbols of perfect power and wisdom. The Lamb of Revelation is the "Lord of lords, and King of kings" who wages a victorious warfare against the beast and his confederates (17:12–14) and before whose wrath the men of earth call upon the rocks and mountains to fall on them (6:15–17). Charles is undoubtedly right in holding that the concept of a lamb with seven horns comes directly from the apocalyptic tradition (I, p. 141).[13] In *I Enoch* 90:9 the Maccabees are symbolized as "horned lambs." It is a *lamb* in the *Testament of Joseph* that destroys the enemies of Israel (19:8 f). In *I Enoch* 90:37 this military leader is portrayed as a "white bull . . . with large horns." Rather than symbolizing innocent submission, the Lamb in Revelation is a "mystic, apocalyptic designation (or title) of the glorified Christ, enthroned with God and destined to be victorious over all the opposing forces in the universe, both human and demonic."[14]

Any attempt to visualize a seven-horned, seven-eyed lamb in a totally literal fashion should remind us of the symbolic nature of John's visions. The throne-room scene is not a graphic description of heaven but a symbolic representation of the decrees of God concerning the final stages of human history. The seven horns of the Lamb symbolize his irresistible

---

[12]It should be noted that ἀρνίον is consistently used instead of ἀμνός, the word used of Christ in Jn 1:29, 36 (also in I Pet 1:19). Of its thirty occurrences, only once is it found outside the Apocalypse (in Jn 21:15). Apart from Rev 13:11 (where the beast out of the earth has two horns "like a lamb"), ἀρνίον is used exclusively of the resurrected and victorious Christ. For a discussion of the data see Mounce, "The Christology of the Apocalypse," *Foundations*, 11 (1969), pp. 42–45; also " 'The Lamb' in the Apocalypse" by Norman Hillyer, *EvQ*, 39 (1967), pp. 228–36. Cf. C. K. Barrett, "The Lamb of God," *NTS*, 1 (1954–5), pp. 210–18.

[13]Beasley-Murray writes, "Despite protestations to the contrary (notably by Traugott Holtz, *Die Christologie der Apokalypse des Johannes*, 1971, p. 41) there seems to be no doubt that this figure is derived from Jewish apocalyptic imagery, which represented the people of God as the flock of God out of which arises a deliverer who rescues them from their foes" (pp. 124–25).

[14]F. C. Grant, "Lamb of God," *HDB rev.*, p. 562.

might.[15] His seven eyes speak of that completeness of vision which leads to perfect knowledge.[16] The eyes are further identified as "the seven Spirits of God, sent forth into all the earth."[17] In 4:5 the seven Spirits of God were seven lamps of fire burning before the throne, but here, as the eyes of the Lamb, they have a mission to carry out on earth.

The Lamb is standing in the center of the angelic beings which surround the throne. This interpretation of "in the midst of the throne" is supported by the use of the same phrase in 4:6, which places the four living creatures there as well. Some take the expression to represent a Hebrew idiom and accordingly place the Lamb between the living creatures and the elders. The use of the Greek perfects ("having taken his stand and in appearance as having been slain") emphasizes the lasting benefits of his sacrificial death and resurrection.

7 The verb tenses serve to dramatize the action of the Lamb as he steps forward and receives the scroll: "He went (aorist) and now he has taken (perfect) the book from the right hand of the One upon the throne." The advance of the Lamb is no argument for placing him between the living creatures and the elders in the preceding verse. He could step to the throne from its immediate vicinity as well. This is not to be taken as the coronation of the risen Christ (as in Heb 2:8–9; cf. Hendriksen, p. 110), but as an event yet to take place at the end of time.

8 With the handing of the scroll to the Lamb we enter into one of the greatest scenes of universal adoration anywhere recorded. The living creatures and the twenty-four elders prostrate themselves before the Lamb with harps and bowls of incense, ready to sing of his infinite worth as revealed in his great act of redemptive self-sacrifice. It is assumed that he has taken his place upon the throne of God. Since the function of the living creatures is not priestly, it may be best to take the harps and bowls as applying only to the elders. The harp (or lyre) was the traditional instrument used in the singing of the Psalms. "Praise the Lord with the lyre, make melody to him with the harp of ten strings" (Ps 33:2). The golden bowls[18] are full of incense symbolizing the prayers of the saints. Despised

---

[15]The horn is an ancient Jewish symbol for strength or power (cf. Deut 33:17) and is so used in Rev (12:3; 13:1, 11; 17:3 ff). In Dan 7:7, 20 the powerful fourth beast had ten horns, and the ram of Dan 8:3 had two great horns. In Dan 8:5 the one large horn of the he-goat is replaced by four smaller ones. The portrayal of Moses having two horns stems from a confusion between the Hebrew *qāran* (to shine) and *qeren* (horn). Seven horns would indicate perfect might.

[16]Zech 4:10 ("These seven are the eyes of the Lord, which range through the whole earth") is the probable source for this image.

[17]Although ἀπεσταλμένοι agrees in gender with ὀφθαλμούς, it is the πνεύματα which are sent out.

[18]φιάλη was a flat, shallow cup or bowl for drinking or libations (LSJ); cf. Josephus, *Ant.* iii.6.6.

on earth, the prayers of the saints are now brought before God in golden bowls. Ladd suggests that their prayer was the age-long prayer of the church, "Thy Kingdom come, thy will be done on earth as it is in heaven" (p. 89).[19] The use of incense was a normal feature in Hebrew ritual (Deut 33:10). Because of the prominent role played by incense in pagan worship, it is unlikely that the image is taken from that source. Lilje sees here a reference to the use of incense as symbolic of the prayers of the saints (cf. Ps 141:2, "let my prayer be counted as incense before thee").[20]

The idea of angels acting as intermediaries and presenting the prayers of saints to God is common in later Jewish thought. In Tobit 12:15 an angel says, "I am Raphael, one of the seven holy angels, who present the prayers of the saints, and who go in and out before the glory of the Holy One." In *III Baruch* 11 it is Michael the Archangel who descends to the fifth heaven to receive the prayers of men. It was the increasing emphasis in Jewish thought on the transcendence of God that made such intermediaries appropriate. In Revelation the twenty-four elders perform this function.

9 In chapter 4 the twenty-four elders praised the worthiness of God for his work in creation (vs. 11). In chapter 5 they direct their praise to the Lamb for his work of redemption.[21] In both cases the "Worthy art thou!" is the *vere dignus* with which the emperor's arrival was celebrated. The idea of a *new* song grows out of the use of the expression in the Psalms; *eg.*, 98:1, "Oh sing to the Lord a new song, for he has done marvelous things!" (cf. 33:3; 40:3; 96:1; etc.). Every new act of mercy calls forth a new song of gratitude and praise. In the midst of a prophetic passage (Isa 42:5-17) which extols the glorious victory of the One who "created the heavens and stretched them out" (vs. 5; cf. Rev 4:11), we find the admonition, "Sing to the Lord a new song, his praise from the end of the earth!" (vs. 10). The song to the Lamb is a new song because the covenant established through his death is a new covenant. It is not simply new in point of time, but more important, it is new and distinctive in quality.[22]

---

[19]*I Enoch* 47:1 ff speaks of the prayers of the righteous and their blood ascending unto the Lord of Spirits urging their vindication. This would be a more appropriate parallel to the cry of the martyrs in 6:10 than here.

[20]αἵ has as its antecedent θυμιαμάτων rather than φιάλας—the gender determined by attraction to προσευχαί (Sinaiticus **046** *pc* made an understandable change to ἅ). Beckwith (p. 512) says the entire phrase is probably a gloss from 8:3 because the scene is heavenly, its theme is precise, and the utterances of the saints would be among those mentioned in vs. 13.

[21]The elders are probably joined in song by the cherubim. Even if the action of 8b (involving the harps and the bowls of incense) is limited to the elders, vs. 9 could continue quite naturally the adoration of 8a.

[22]The word is καινός rather than νέος. Behm distinguishes the adjectives, noting that νέος is new in time or origin while καινός is "what is new in nature, different from the usual,

The Lamb is worthy to open the book for a threefold reason: he was slain (a historical fact), he purchased men unto God (the interpretation of that fact), and he made them a kingdom and priests (the result of the fact). That the same ascription of worth is directed both to the One upon the throne (4:11) and to the Lamb (5:9) indicates the exalted Christology of the Apocalypse.

The worthiness of the Lamb does not at this point stem from his essential being, but from his great act of redemption. He is worthy precisely because he was slain.[23] His sacrificial death was the means whereby he purchased men unto God. This interpretation is one with that of the other writers of the NT. During his earthly ministry Jesus taught that the Son of man had come to give his life a *ransom* for many (Mk 10:45). In I Corinthians 6:20 Paul reminds the believers that they were "bought with a price."[24] In our verse "with [at the cost of] thy blood" denotes the price.

The idea that the *elders* were the ones purchased by Christ's death stems from inferior variants which make the text read, "Thou wast slain, and hast redeemed *us* to God . . . and hast made us unto our God kings and priests: and *we* shall reign on the earth" (*AV,* italics added).[25] The *Revised Version* is correct in omitting the first pronoun and reading "them" and "they" for the other two.

Those who are redeemed are from every tribe, tongue, people, and nation. It is fruitless to attempt a distinction between these terms as ethnic, linguistic, political, etc. The Seer is stressing the universal nature of the church and for this purpose piles up phrases for their rhetorical value.[26] In contrast with the exclusivism of Judaism which prided itself in having been chosen out from among the nations, the church was genuinely ecumenical, recognizing no national, political, cultural, or racial boundaries.

10 What was promised to the Israelites at Sinai ("You shall be to me a kingdom of priests, and a holy nation," Ex 19:6) is fulfilled in the establishment of the church through the death of Christ. Corporately be-

---

impressive, better than the old, superior in value or attraction" (*TDNT,* III, p. 447). Theologically "καινός is the epitome of the wholly different and miraculous thing which is brought about by the time of salvation" (p. 449).

[23]σφάζω, to slaughter, is used only in Rev to describe the death of Christ. Its use in this connection probably derives from Isa 53:7 (ὡς πρόβατον ἐπὶ σφαγὴν ἤχθη).

[24]ἀγοράζω as in Rev 5:9.

[25]א P 046 82 2059s 2329 *pm* TR (also 104 *al* lat in a different order) add ἡμᾶς after τῷ θεῷ. In vs. 10, א A 046 and others have αὐτούς, while the TR accepts ἡμᾶς. The TR carries out its identification between the elders and those for whom Christ died by reading βασιλεύσομεν instead of the βασιλεύσουσιν of א P 1 82 2036 2059 *al* g vg^w or the βασιλεύουσιν of A 046 2060 2329 *al*.

[26]The same four occur (but always in a different order) in 5:9; 7:9; 11:9; 13:7; and 14:6.

lievers are a kingdom, and individually they are priests to God (cf. comm. on 1:6). This motif occurs three times in Revelation (1:6; 5:10; 20:6) and suggests to Swete that it may have been derived from a primitive hymn (p. 82). Both of the terms are active in meaning: as a *kingdom* "they shall reign," and as *priests* they serve. By his death Jesus established his church "a Kingdom of Priests in the service of our God" (*TCNT*).

Textual evidence is rather evenly divided between "they reign" (*ASV*) and "they shall reign" (*RSV*), although the latter is favored both by the Nestle text (25th ed.) and the UBS text (3rd ed.). It seems unlikely that John is here referring to a present spiritual reign of believers.[27] The hymn of praise is not a cryptic reference to Christians as the true kings in spite of the apparent rule of the Caesars. The promise is that the church is to share in the eschatological reign of Christ and all that it will involve (2:26–27; 20:4; 22:5).

The adoration of the Lamb moves out in ever widening circles. Now it is the innumerable host of angels who lift their voices in a great doxology of praise.[28] Their number ("myriads of myriads and thousands of thousands") is not to be taken arithmetically but as an apocalyptic symbol for countless thousands. Angels were held to be so numerous as to be beyond human calculation. The second part of the expression is neither an anti-climax nor what remained even after the greatest number in antiquity was multiplied by itself (as in Lenski, p. 210). The background is Daniel 7:10, which speaks of "a thousand thousands and ten thousand times ten thousand" who stood before the Ancient of Days to minister unto him.[29]

11–12 The adoration of the angels may be more of a chanted response than a hymn that is sung.[30] Corresponding to their position outside the inner circles of the cherubim and the elders, the angels do not address the Lamb directly. Their sevenfold ascription of praise is in the third person and antiphonal to the elders' hymn of redemption.[31] One is reminded of the opening verses of David's farewell prayer in I Chronicles 29:10–19. Power, riches, wisdom, and might are not benefits which the

---

[27]Even if βασιλεύουσιν is read instead of βασιλεύσουσιν the reference is probably future, the verb serving as a futuristic present and imparting a tone of assurance (Moulton, *Grammar*, 3rd ed., I, p. 120).

[28]The voice is that of angels only. The genitives τῶν ζῴων and τῶν πρεσβυτέρων are parallel to τοῦ θρόνου and are determined by κύκλῳ used as a preposition (BAG, p. 458). It is unnecessary for Charles to bracket the phrase as a gloss (I, p. 148).

[29]In *I Enoch* 40:1; 60:1; and 71:8 the more natural order is found. Cf. the "innumerable angels" in Heb 12:22.

[30]λέγοντες; although in 5:9 the elders ᾄδουσιν . . . λέγοντες.

[31]The increase from three attributes in 4:9–11 to four in 5:13 and to seven in 5:12; 7:12 is stylistic and reflects the tendency of the Apocalypse toward progressive expansion. That all seven are governed by one article indicates that they are to be taken together as a unit.

Lamb is about to receive but qualities he possesses and for which he is worthy to be praised. The last three (honor, glory, and blessing) are more closely related to the response of men and angels. Elsewhere in the NT each of the qualities mentioned is ascribed to Christ: power and wisdom, I Corinthians 1:24; riches, II Corinthians 8:9; Ephesians 3:8; might, Luke 11:22; honor, Philippians 2:11; glory, John 1:14; blessing, Romans 15:29. Of the last term, which he calls "the inevitable climax of it all," Barclay says it is "the one gift that we who have nothing can give to Him who possesses all" (I, p. 227).

13 In verses 9 and 10 the four living creatures and the twenty-four elders raised their voices in praise of the redemptive work of the Lamb. This is followed (in vss. 11 and 12) by an innumerable host of angels praising the worthiness of the Lamb. The climax of the scene is reached in verse 13 where all creation gives blessing, honor, glory, and dominion to God and to the Lamb. John hears the "roar of the great acclamation as it rises to heaven" (Swete, p. 83). It is the adoration of the entire created world. Caird notes that the universality of Christ's achievement calls for a universal response (p. 77). The created order is specified as that which is in heaven, on earth, under the earth, and on the sea.[32] The added phrase "and all things that are in them" stresses that no living creature failed to join in the great and final hymn of praise (cf. Phil 2:9–11). The doxology is fourfold, repeating three elements of the previous seven (vs. 12), but exchanging "might" for "power."[33] It may be that the fourfold ascription corresponds to the fourfold division of creation. The praise of the entire created order is addressed to the One who sits upon the throne and to the Lamb. Throughout the Apocalypse the two are regularly joined. In 22:1 the water of life flows "from the throne of God and of the Lamb" (cf. 6:16; 17:10).

14 The four living creatures were the first to offer praise in the throne-room vision of chapters 4 and 5; it is fitting that they should also bring it to a close (Morris, p. 102). If the verb "said" is taken as an iterative imperfect, it may be that the four living creatures cry "Amen" after each of the seven attributes of verse 12 and the four of verse 13. As the cherubim say "Amen," the elders fall down in worship.[34]

[32]Charles reads ἐν τῇ θαλάσσῃ with Sinaiticus and various versions, noting that ἐπί *cum gen.* would be impossible here (I, p. 150). Moffatt interprets the ἐπὶ τῆς θαλάσσης as a reference to sea-monsters, rather than sea-faring men (p. 387).

[33]Michaelis notes the use of κράτος in doxologies (I Tim 6:16; I Pet 4:11; 5:11; Jude 25; Rev 1:6; 5:13) and says "it denotes the superior power of God to which the final victory will belong" (*TDNT*, III, p. 908).

[34]Evelyn Underhill (*Worship*, pp. 91–92) and others are of the opinion that the scenes of worship in Rev reflect the liturgical practices of first-century churches in Asia Minor.

CHAPTER 6

IV. THE SEVEN SEALS (6:1–8:1)

The vision of the glorified Son of man in chapter 1 led to the writing of the seven letters to the churches (chaps. 2–3). Similarly the throne-room vision of chapters 4 and 5 sets the stage for the opening of the scroll with its sequence of seals, trumpets, and bowls (chaps. 6–16). The dramatic portrayal of God's righteous judgment is now under way. It should be noted that the scroll is not actually opened until all seven seals are removed. Thus the content of the scroll begins with chapter 8 and the sounding of the seven trumpets. As each seal is removed we are introduced to a series of preliminary judgments representing forces operative throughout history by means of which the redemptive and judicial purposes of God are being carried out prior to the end.

1. FIRST FOUR SEALS: THE FOUR HORSEMEN (6:1–8)

1 *And I saw when the Lamb opened one of the seven seals, and I heard one of the four living creatures saying as with a voice of thunder, Come.*
2 *And I saw, and behold, a white horse, and he that sat thereon had a bow; and there was given unto him a crown: and he came forth conquering, and to conquer.*
3 *And when he opened the second seal, I heard the second living creature saying, Come.*
4 *And another* horse *came forth, a red horse: and to him that sat thereon it was given to take peace from the earth, and that they should slay one another: and there was given unto him a great sword.*
5 *And when he opened the third seal, I heard the third living creature*

saying, Come. And I saw, and behold, a black horse; and he that sat thereon had a balance in his hand.

6 *And I heard as it were a voice in the midst of the four living creatures saying, A measure of wheat for a shilling, and three measures of barley for a shilling; and the oil and the wine hurt thou not.*

7 *And when he opened the fourth seal, I heard the voice of the fourth living creature saying, Come.*

8 *And I saw, and behold, a pale horse: and he that sat upon him, his name was Death; and Hades followed with him. And there was given unto them authority over the fourth part of the earth, to kill with sword, and with famine, and with death, and by the wild beasts of the earth.*

1   It is the Lamb himself who opens the first seal. He alone is worthy to set into motion those events which will bring about the culmination of human history. One of the living creatures calls out with a voice of thunder for the first of the four apocalyptic horsemen to ride forth. Translations which read "Come and see" are the result of copyists who understood the command as an invitation to the Seer.[1]

2   John looks, and behold, a white horse! Mounted on the horse is a rider with a bow and a crown who comes forth conquering and to conquer. The "Four Horsemen of the Apocalypse" are among the more widely recognized symbols of the book of Revelation. The imagery comes from Zechariah's visions of the variously colored horses in 1:8–17 and 6:1–8. As usual, John modifies his sources with great freedom. In Zechariah the colors (red, sorrel, white, black, dappled gray) appear to have no special significance. In Revelation they correspond to the character of the rider and symbolize conquest (white), bloodshed (red), scarcity (black), and death (pale, livid). In Zechariah they are sent out to patrol the earth, while in Revelation their release brings disasters to the earth.[2]

It should be noted that although the form of John's vision is related to Zechariah, the subject matter corresponds to the eschatological discourse of Jesus in the synoptic gospels. Luke records wars and tumults, nation rising against nation, great earthquakes, famines, pestilences, great signs from heaven, and persecution (Lk 21:9 ff; cf. Mk 13:7 ff and Mt 24:6 ff). By combining earthquakes and the cosmic disturbances, the seven woes of Luke are included within the six seals of Revelation (Charles, I, pp. 158–

---

[1]Ἔρχου καὶ ἴδε, ℵ **046** 82 2028 2329 *al* g vg^{s,cl} (TR reads βλέπε). The suggestion that ἔρχου is *nature's* prayer for the return of Christ and the final redemption of creation stems from a misunderstanding of the four living creatures.

[2]Lilje notes the chariot races with the colors symbolizing the four winds which accompanied the official opening of an emperor's reign (pp. 123–24). Cf. the description of the "apocalyptic death race" in Stauffer, *Christ and the Caesars*, p. 184.

60). In Jewish thought the "age to come" would be preceded by a period of unprecedented woe. "This is but the beginning of sufferings," Jesus said, "the end is not yet" (Mk 13:7–8).

The scenes depicted by the seals (except the fifth, vss. 9–11) are seen as taking place upon the earth. They are not a kind of heavenly counterpart.

The question of the identity of the white horse and rider has been extensively discussed by commentators. One of two answers is usually given. First, that the rider on the white horse is Christ, and the white horse, the victorious progress of the gospel. In 19:11 we again meet a white horse and rider. That this rider is the Christ follows from verse 13 where he is named "The Word of God" and from verse 16 where on his garment and thigh is written "KINGS OF KINGS, AND LORD OF LORDS." The argument runs as follows: should not the Apocalypse be allowed to explain its own symbolism? He rides upon a white horse (the color of righteousness) and goes forth to conquer (cf. 5:5, "Lo, the Lion of the tribe of Judah . . . has conquered").[3] In Mark 13:10 the universal proclamation of the gospel seems to precede the beginning of travail—at least it is one of the events which take place before the end (cf. Mt 24:14). Hence its appearance as one of the seals is not at all unexpected. Furthermore, no calamities follow after the white horse as in the three other cases.[4]

The arguments against Christ as the rider of the white horse, however, are of sufficient strength to make the identification unlikely. A comparison of chapters 6 and 19 shows that the two riders have little in common beyond the fact that they both are mounted on white horses. In 6:2 the rider wears a victor's wreath and carries a bow; in 19:11 ff he is crowned with "many diadems"[5] and armed with a sharp sword proceeding from his mouth. The context of 6:2 is one of conquest while that of 19:11 ff is righteous retribution.

A second difficulty is that the identification brackets the proclamation of the gospel with a series of devastating calamities following one another as the inevitable results of human sinfulness (war, scarcity, death). Some point out the confusion involved in the Lamb opening the seals while at the same time being the one who rides forth when the first seal is broken.

[3]ἐνίκησεν as in 6:2 (νικῶν καὶ ἵνα νικήσῃ). Cf. also Jn 16:33; Rev 3:21.
[4]Hendriksen (pp. 113–17) lists seven reasons for understanding the white horse as symbolizing the Christ. Zane Hodges identifies the first horseman as Christ and writes that the first of his many triumphs is the rapture of the church ("The First Horseman of the Apocalypse," *BSac*, 119 [1962], pp. 324–34). S. J. Considine ("The Rider on the White Horse," *CBQ*, 6 [1944], pp. 406–22) concludes that the rider signified Christ or the victorious course of the gospel (p. 421).
[5]διαδήματα rather than στέφανος as in 6:2.

Caird lists as "the final and fatal objection" the repeated use of "there was given," which normally in Revelation refers to "the divine permission granted to evil powers to carry out their nefarious work—the denizens of the abyss (ix.1, 3, 5), the monster (xiii.5, 7), and the false prophet (xiii.14, 15)" (p. 81).

The other prominent interpretation of the white horse and rider is that they symbolize the spirit of conquest and militarism.[6] In the OT the bow was a symbol of military power. God told the prophet Hosea that he would "break the bow of Israel in the valley of Jezreel" (Hos 1:5). The mighty men of Babylon were taken and "their bows are broken in pieces" (Jer 51:56). The crown is a symbol of victory. D. T. Niles notes, "When men wage war they always pretend to be fighting for righteousness" (p. 58).[7]

Some writers see in the bow a veiled reference to a much-feared invasion from beyond the eastern boundaries of the Roman Empire. The Parthians were the most famous archers of antiquity, and in AD 62 Vologeses had won an unprecedented victory over a Roman army. This had unnerved the West and led them to fear an all-out invasion. While this may be a secondary reference, John has in mind military conquest in general.[8]

3–4 When the second seal is removed, John sees a red horse whose rider is given a great sword and the authority to take peace from the earth, allowing men to slay one another. The color of the second horse[9] corresponds to the mission of its rider and symbolizes slaughter and bloodshed. If the first seal suggested invasion from without, the second seal may refer to internal strife.[10] The sword which was given to the rider was the Roman short sword appropriate to this sort of internecine warfare.[11] His mission is to remove peace from the earth and allow men to turn

[6]Rissi argues that the rider on the white horse is the Antichrist, whose form is depicted in Rev in various fashions (11:7; 13:17) and is seen in action throughout the eschatological period ("The Rider on the White Horse," *Int*, 18 [1964], pp. 405–18).

[7]Kraft writes, "Der Reiter symbolisiert den Sieg eines barbarischen, beritten vorzustellenden Volkes" (p. 116).

[8]Others interpret the first seal as a Roman emperor, the prince of Dan 9:26 who will head up the revived Roman Empire, periods of peace granted in the providence of God, the proclamation of the gospel, etc.

[9]πυρρός, red (as fire—πῦρ); **A P 046** 1 2059 2329 *pm* read πυρός, wheat (perhaps because of its flame color when ripe).

[10]Barclay notes that in the thirty-year period before the reign of Herod the Great (67–37 BC), 100,000 men died in revolutions and rebellions in Palestine alone. John wrote in a time "when internecine strife was tearing the world apart" (II, p. 6).

[11]Hendriksen (pp. 120–22) takes μάχαιρα as the sacrificial knife in order to support his interpretation of the red horse as "religious persecution." The use of the word in the NT fails to substantiate this meaning.

their destructive instincts upon one another.[12] It recalls Paul's words in II Thessalonians 2:6 ff concerning the removal of that which restrains and the resultant lawlessness. Typical of the Jewish view of the end times is Zechariah 14, which pictures the final warfare leading to the universal reign of God. Verse 13 reads, "And on that day a great panic from the Lord shall fall on them, so that each will lay hold on the hand of his fellow, and the hand of the one will be raised against the hand of the other." Isaiah says that God will stir up the Egyptians "and they will fight, every man against his brother and every man against his neighbor" (19:2).[13]

The mission of the red horse would be quickly understood in John's day, which was well acquainted with rebellion and civil disorder. In the one year, AD 68–69, Rome had been ruled by four different emperors. Anarchy and bloodshed are harbingers of the end.

5–6 With the opening of the third seal and at the command of the third living creature, there comes forth a black horse whose rider holds a balance in his hand. A voice from the center of the throne room announces famine prices for wheat and barley, and warns against hurting the oil and wine. The balance indicates a time of scarcity when the basic commodities of life are measured out at greatly inflated prices. In portraying the siege of Jerusalem, God told Ezekiel that its inhabitants would "eat bread by weight [and] drink water by measure" (Ezek 4:16; cf. Lev 26:26). The denarius was a Roman silver coin equivalent to the daily wage of a working man (cf. Mt 20:2). For a day's work a man could buy only enough wheat for himself or enough of the less nutritious barley for three. The price appears to be ten to twelve times what it should have been (cf. Cicero, *Verr.* iii.81).

The most common interpretation of the black horse and rider is that they symbolize famine. Famine is implied by the balance and the exorbitant prices. It was a normal result of warfare in ancient times when invading armies lived off the lands they were conquering. The warning against hurting the oil and wine sets limits to the destruction about to be carried out by the horseman. Since the roots of the olive and vine go deeper, they would not be affected by a limited drought which would all but destroy the grain. This interpretation is in harmony with the increasing intensity of the three cycles of judgment. The fourth seal affects "the fourth part of the earth" (6:8), the trumpets destroy a third (8:7, 8, 10, 12), and the destruction by the bowls is complete and final (16:1 ff).

---

[12]σφάζω means to slaughter or to murder by violence. The king of Babylon slew (ἔσφαξε) the sons of Zedekiah before his eyes (Jer 52:10). It is not the normal word for death in battle.
[13]Cf. also *I Enoch* 100:12; II Esdr 5:9; 6:24; *II Bar.* 70:2–8; 48:37 for the Jewish view.

The warning about the oil and wine has been variously interpreted. Some feel it was added to underscore the social inequity existing in a time of scarcity. It is the poor, not the rich, who suffer. Oil and wine, however, were not luxuries, but part of the basic commodities of life.[14] It would also be difficult to understand why the Lamb—the voice "in the midst of the four living creatures" (vs. 6; cf. 5:6)—would issue an order favoring the rich and aggravating the plight of the poor. Lilje sees in the oil and wine a reference to the sacrament (cf. Jas 5:14) and understands the clause as a promise that believers will not suffer from the famine (p. 126). It is simpler to take it as a natural limitation to the famine.

Commentators who hold that much of John's imagery grows out of his contemporary culture usually mention the decree of Domitian in AD 92 to destroy half the vineyards throughout the provinces. The order met such resistance that it was rescinded. John is portrayed as an ascetic, who was displeased and therefore predicted an evil time when men would have oil and wine in abundance but lack bread.[15]

7–8 When the fourth seal is opened, there comes forth a horse the color of a corpse.[16] His rider is Death, and following along behind is his inseparable companion Hades (cf. 1:18, 20; 13:14). Authority is given to them over a fourth part of the earth. This expression does not indicate a geographical area but is qualitative and expresses the limitations placed upon their murderous activity. They bring about the death of one-fourth of mankind. The four specific ways in which they kill are based on the "four sore acts of judgment" of Ezekiel 14:21—the sword, the famine, the evil beasts, and the pestilence.[17] No significance should be attached to the fact that John here chooses a different sword than he does in 6:4. The two are frequently used as synonyms in the Septuagint.[18] It may be that this fourfold plague represents an intensification of that which is represented by the first three seals. Death by wild beasts (the "evil beasts" of Ezek) would be expected in a land decimated by war and famine.

---

[14]Grain, new wine, and oil was a standard formula for the staples of life. Cf. Deut 7:13; 11:14; Hos 2:8, 22.

[15]Moffatt (p. 390) says this recent event "provided the seer with a bit of colour for his palette as he painted the final terrors." Cf. the discussion in Beckwith (p. 522) and Charles (I, pp. 167–68).

[16]χλωρός is used elsewhere in Rev to describe the yellow green of vegetation (8:7; 9:4; cf. Mk 6:39 and Gen 1:30, χόρτον χλωρόν), but here describes the pallor of death or the blanched appearance of a person struck with terror.

[17]θάνατος in Rev 6:8b as well as Ezek 14:21 refers to pestilence, a particular form of death (cf. also Rev 2:23a).

[18]Strictly speaking the ῥομφαία (cf. 1:16) is a large blade, perhaps of Thracian origin, and μάχαιρα is a short sword. Cf. note on 6:4.

The overlapping of verse 8 with the judgments of the first three seals leads Charles to judge the text corrupt. He shortens it considerably by dropping the clauses which refer to Hades and the four instrumentalities of death (I, pp. 169–71). One writer takes the second sentence of verse 8 as a separate paragraph which refers to all four seals. In this way it becomes the Seer's own interpretation of the riders.[19]

2. FIFTH SEAL: CRY OF THE MARTYRS (6:9–11)

9 *And when he opened the fifth seal, I saw underneath the altar the souls of them that had been slain for the word of God, and for the testimony which they held:*

10 *and they cried with a great voice, saying, How long, O Master, the holy and true, dost thou not judge and avenge our blood on them that dwell on the earth?*

11 *And there was given them to each one a white robe; and it was said unto them, that they should rest yet for a little time, until their fellow-servants also and their brethren, who should be killed even as they were, should have fulfilled* their course.

9 The seven seals divide into two groups of four and three. Now that the four horsemen have ridden forth, the scene changes. The opening of the fifth seal reveals an altar in heaven beneath which are the souls of the faithful martyrs. If the first four seals portrayed the troubled times of the approaching consummation, the fifth supplies an interpretation of Christian martyrdom.

The idea of heaven as the temple of God is common in Jewish thought. "The Lord is in his holy temple; let all the earth keep silence before him" (Hab 2:20; cf. Ps 18:6; *Test. Levi* 18:6). It is probably unimportant to conjecture whether the altar is the altar of burnt offering or the altar of incense. The theme of sacrifice would suggest the former, and the prayers which rise (vs. 10) seem to indicate the latter. There is no reason why in John's vision the two should not blend together as one.

In OT ritual sacrifice the blood of the bullock was poured out at the base of the altar of burnt offering (Lev 4:7; Ex 29:12). This blood contained the life, or soul, of the flesh (Lev 17:11). That the souls of the martyrs were underneath the altar is a way of saying that their untimely deaths on earth are from God's perspective a sacrifice on the altar of heaven. Paul viewed

---

[19]McIlvaine, *The Wisdom of the Apocalypse*, pp. 133–35. It is difficult, however, to equate wild beasts with the rider on the white horse.

his coming death as an offering to be poured out (II Tim 4:6; cf. Phil 2:17). A somewhat parallel idea in rabbinic writing—that "the souls of the righteous are kept under the throne of glory" (*Shabb.* 152b)—may suggest the idea of martyrs as having reached a place of safety.

The martyrs had given up their lives because of the word of God and the testimony they were holding. Morris writes that "John's words are a reminder that throughout history there has been a persistent hostility towards deeply-committed Christians on the part of those wielding power" (p. 108). Ladd adds that the church is called to be a martyr-people and that Jesus' teaching that to be a disciple a man must "take up his cross" (Mt 10:38; 16:24) meant that he must be willing to suffer martyrdom (p. 104). The martyrs' testimony was not primarily their witness about Jesus but the witness that they had received from him (cf. 12:17; 20:4).[20] Instead of being coordinate, the second phrase ("the testimony which they held") may serve to make the first ("the word of God") more specific. Caird translates "because of the word spoken by God and attested by Jesus" (p. 84). Those who died, therefore, are those who gave their lives in faithfulness to God as revealed in and through Jesus Christ.

10 From beneath the altar there rises a plea for vindication. With a great voice the martyrs cry out, "How long, O Master,[21] until you avenge our deaths?" Some writers emphasize what appears to be a marked contrast between this prayer and that of Stephen the first martyr, whose last words were a request that those who were stoning him be not held responsible for their act (Acts 7:60). Had not Jesus himself prayed at Calvary, "Father, forgive them; for they know not what they do" (Lk 23:24)? Glasson concludes, "It should be frankly recognized that this is not a Christian prayer" (p. 49).

Before we arrive at this conclusion, certain other considerations should be taken into account. The idea of divine vindication of the people of God is common throughout the OT. Psalm 79:10 reads, "Why should the nations say, 'Where is their God?' Let the avenging of the outpoured blood of thy servants be known among the nations before our eyes." This request does not rise from a personal desire for revenge, but out of concern for the reputation of God. It is unlike the attitude of the Jewish writer of the *Assumption of Moses* who promised the saints that they would look down

---

[20]Obviously holding this testimony would involve their own testimony as well. The two could hardly be separated. **046** 82 205 2028 *al* sy[h] add τοῦ ἀρνίου after μαρτυρία.

[21]ὁ δεσπότης is a term used for the master of slaves and emphasizes the absolute power of God. In the LXX κύριος is more commonly used for God. δεσπότης is found twenty-five times. Josephus notes that the Zealots endured torture and death rather than acknowledge the Roman emperor as δεσπότης (*Bell.* vii.418–19).

from on high and rejoice that their enemies were in Gehenna (10:10). It certainly has none of the vindictiveness of Tertullian (the early third-century apologist), who writes of how he will laugh and exult at the last judgment as he sees the proud monarchs groaning in the lowest abyss of darkness, and the magistrates liquefying in fiercer flames than they ever kindled against the Christians (*De Spec.* 30).[22]

Caird makes the interesting suggestion that the martyrs' cry should be interpreted against the background of Hebrew jurisprudence in which a plaintiff must plead his own case. Condemned in a human court, the decision stands unless reversed by a higher court. The real point at issue is not the relation of the martyrs to their accusers, but the validity of their faith (p. 85).

God is appealed to as "holy and true." Totally separate from all evil, he will vindicate with integrity those who have given their lives for the cause of righteousness.[23] Through centuries of oppression the cry, How long? has constantly risen to heaven. "How long shall the wicked exult?" asks the Psalmist (94:3). "How long shall I cry for help," asks the prophet, "and thou wilt not hear?" (Hab 1:2). Vindication, not bitter revenge, is the theme.

"Them that dwell on the earth" is a semi-technical designation for mankind in its hostility to God.[24] In 11:10 they are those who rejoice over the death of the two witnesses. In chapter 13 they are pictured as worshipping the beast (vss. 8, 12), and in chapter 17 as drunk with the wine of fornication of the great harlot (vs. 2). Their names are not written in the book of life (17:8), and they are subject to the coming hour of trial (3:10; 8:13).

11 To each of the martyrs was given a white robe. Some writers understand this as a reference to spiritual or glorified bodies which are given to the martyrs ahead of time as a token of special honor.[25] It is thought to have developed from God's clothing himself with garments of light (cf. Ps 104:2). Apocalyptists spoke of the resurrection bodies of the righteous as "garments of glory" (*I Enoch* 62:16; *II Enoch* 22:8), which were "stored up on high in the seventh heaven" (*Asc. Isa.* 4:16). Paul's

---

[22]Ford writes, "Retribution in the sense of punishing the wicked does enter into the picture but the idea of vengeance in the sense of personal satisfaction does not" (p. 100).

[23]Since the prayer comes from under the altar, it may be that we are to understand that it is the blood of the martyrs (rather than the martyrs themselves) that cries out for vindication—not personal vengeance (Ladd, pp. 105–6).

[24]In 1QH 8:19–36 the "dwellers on earth" are set over against the army of the holy ones (cf. Burrows, *Dead Sea Scrolls,* pp. 404 f).

[25]Cf. Charles, I, p. 176 and the additional note, pp. 184–88. Also Caird, p. 86, and Preston and Hanson, p. 81.

reference to "a building from God, a house not made with hands, eternal in the heavens" which will clothe the believer at death (II Cor 5:1 ff) is thought to be analogous (cf. also I Cor 15:35 ff; Phil 3:21).

In the book of Revelation, however, white robes are symbols of blessedness and purity. The redeemed throng before the throne in 7:11 are arrayed in white robes. They have come out of the great tribulation and washed their robes white in the blood of the Lamb (7:13–14; cf. 22:14). The church at Laodicea is counseled to buy gold, white robes,[26] and eye-salve (3:18), a strange suggestion if white robes are glorified bodies.

The martyrs are bidden to rest yet a little while until their number is complete. The victims of Nero's persecution are about to be joined by those who will give their lives rather than pay homage to Domitian as divine. The charge is not to control their impatience but to rest in the enjoyment of their blessedness. There are others who are yet to join their number. Jewish thought portrayed God as governing the world according to a predetermined time schedule (cf. *II Bar.* 23:4–5; II Esdr 4:35–37) in which the end will not come until the full number of the righteous are offered (*I Enoch* 47:4; II Esdr 2:41).[27] Those to be killed are their fellow servants, even their brethren. The verse does not distinguish two separate groups.

3. SIXTH SEAL: THE GREAT EARTHQUAKE (6:12–17)

12 *And I saw when he opened the sixth seal, and there was a great earth-quake; and the sun became black as sackcloth of hair, and the whole moon became as blood;*

13 *and the stars of the heaven fell unto the earth, as a fig tree casteth her unripe figs when she is shaken of a great wind.*

14 *And the heaven was removed as a scroll when it is rolled up; and every mountain and island were moved out of their places.*

15 *And the kings of the earth, and the princes, and the chief captains, and the rich, and the strong, and every bondman and freeman, hid themselves in the caves and in the rocks of the mountains;*

16 *and they say to the mountains and to the rocks, Fall on us, and hide us from the face of him that sitteth on the throne, and from the wrath of the Lamb;*

17 *for the great day of their wrath is come; and who is able to stand?*

---

[26]ἱμάτια λευκά, synonymous with στολαὶ λευκαί.

[27]Cf. van Unnik, "Le nombre des élus dans la première de Clément," *Revue d'histoire et de philosophie religieuses,* 42 (1962), pp. 237–46.

12–14 With the opening of the sixth seal the great cosmic disturbances which are to herald the last days begin. For a people who held that the well-ordered movements of heavenly bodies were a token of God's providential control, the breakdown of this order would be a grim announcement that the end of the world was at hand. The details in this dramatic description of a universe in turmoil are drawn from the common stock of current apocalypticism.[28] They are not to be taken with complete literalness.[29] Those who first read John's description would not have bothered to debate whether or not the details were to be taken literally. They were part of a well-established tradition that went back through contemporary apocalyptic literature to the earlier prophetic portrayals of the day of the Lord.[30]

The earthquake was a regular feature of divine visitation. When God descended on Sinai, "the whole mountain quaked greatly" (Ex 19:18). Isaiah prophesies that men will hide in caves from the terror of the Lord "when he ariseth to shake mightily the earth" (Isa 2:19, *ASV*). "Once again, in a little while, I will shake the heavens and the earth," writes Haggai (2:6).[31] This great earthquake is to be accompanied by the sun turning black as sackcloth of hair[32] and the moon becoming as blood.[33] In a passage quoted by Peter on the day of Pentecost as partially fulfilled at that time (Acts 2:20), the prophet Joel says of the coming great and terrible day of the Lord, "The sun shall be turned to darkness, and the moon into blood."[34] The stars of heaven are pictured as falling to the earth like unripe figs in a winter gale.[35] Isaiah spoke of the host of heaven fading away as a leaf falling from the fig tree (Isa 34:4). It is one of the signs which

---

[28]Some MSS (A *c* vg(6) Prim TR) add ἰδού before σεισμός ("typical of the apocalyptic style," Metzger, *TCGNT*, p. 741), but external support is inadequate.

[29]Eugene Peterson calls upon the insights of Marshall McLuhan to help the literary-oriented individual to grasp the impact of Rev ("Apocalypse: The Medium is the Message," *Theology Today*, 26 [1969], pp. 133–41). Although it will probably take another two generations before the Christian church will overcome the "Gutenberg distortion," the future, he thinks, looks good (p. 141).

[30]Beasley-Murray notes that only in fairly recent times have we come to appreciate that John's symbolism constituted a language drawn from an ancient tradition yet spoke eloquently to his contemporaries ("The Contribution of the Book of Revelation to the Christian Belief in Immortality," *Scottish Journal of Theology*, 27 [1974], pp. 76–93).

[31]Cf. *As. Mos.* 10:4; II Esdr 5:8; *II Bar.* 70:8.

[32]The reference is to the rough cloth made from the hair of a black goat and worn in times of mourning.

[33]The deep blood-red color of the moon would result from whatever in the atmosphere caused the sun to be darkened.

[34]Cf. Isa 13:10; Ezek 32:7; Amos 8:8; *As. Mos.* 10:4–5; Mk 13:24.

[35]ὄλυνθοι are the green figs which appear in winter before the leaves and are easily blown from the tree.

immediately precede the coming of the Son of man (Mt 13:25–26). The falling of stars upon the earth could mean but one thing to the ancient—the end had come. The heavens are removed like an unrolled papyrus scroll which, should it break in the middle, would roll quickly back on either side.[36] The moving of every mountain and island out of its place has no parallel in apocalyptic writing. It may have been suggested by Nahum 1:5 ("the earth is upheaved at his presence," *ASV*) or Jeremiah 4:24 ("the mountains . . . were quaking, and all the hills moved to and fro").

We need not expect that these cataclysmic events will take place in a completely literal sense, although whatever they depict is sufficient to drive men in terror to the mountains where they plead for death rather than face the wrath of the Lamb (vss. 15–17)—an unlikely consequence if they symbolize no more than social and political upheavals. Elsewhere in Revelation man is pictured as so adamant in pursuing his own goals that neither demonic plague (9:20) nor scorching heat is sufficient to make him repent. Nothing short of the awesome dissolution of the world itself will strike terror to the heart of man in the last days.

15–17 For the enemies of righteousness the day of the Lord will be a day of terror. Isaiah writes that "every man's heart shall melt . . . they will be in anguish like a woman in travail" (Isa 13:7–8). "Who can endure the day of his coming?" asks Malachi; "for he is like a refiner's fire" (Mal 3:2). John pictures the men of earth fleeing to the mountains and crying for death rather than standing before the judgment of God and the wrath of the Lamb. "What sinners dread most is not death, but the revealed Presence of God," is Swete's oft-quoted comment (p. 94).

In listing the various groups which seek refuge in that great day of wrath, it is not John's intention to cover the entire range of human society but to emphasize that those who might normally have reason to feel secure will be utterly undone.[37] The kings of the earth are those in positions of ultimate governmental authority. The princes are next in rank. The chief captains are military authorities at whose word the Roman armies advanced into battle.[38] In that day the proud monarchs as well as the hardened military will flee in terror. The security of the rich and the strong will be shattered, and all alike will panic in wild confusion.

John's graphic portrayal reflects Isaiah's description of the day of the Lord as a time when men will seek refuge in the caves of the rocks before the terror of the Lord (Isa 2:10, 19, 21). From the day when Adam

---

[36]Cf. Isa 34:4; *Sib. Or.* 3:83. II Pet 3:12 explains that the heavens shall be dissolved by fire.
[37]Only the last group ("every bondman and freeman") fails to fit this category. It was probably added to stress the idea of completeness.

and Eve hid themselves from the presence of God (Gen 3:8), the guilty
conscience has made man a fugitive from God. But now there is no longer
a place to hide. God will confront in judgment all those who have rebelled
against his sovereign authority. Men's terrified appeal for the mountains
and rocks to fall on them comes from Hosea 10:8, a verse applied by Jesus
to the coming destruction of Jerusalem (Lk 22:30). Better death by a
crushing avalanche than face the wrath of the Lamb. Caird refers to this
phrase as "a deliberate paradox, by which John intends to goad his readers
into theological alertness" (p. 90). Others reject it entirely on the basis that
wrath would be incongruous with a slain lamb.

The wrath of God is a fundamental theme in NT teaching. It is both
a present reality (Rom 1:18) and an eschatological event (Rev 19:15). It is
neither personal vindictiveness nor an impersonal process of retribution
which works itself out in the course of history.[39] It is rather the "response
of [God's] holiness to persistent and impenitent wickedness."[40] The wrath
of the *Lamb,* however, is an unusual and dramatic expression. Only once in
the gospels is the word for wrath used of Jesus (Mk 3:5). Yet if Christ as
the Lamb in Revelation is primarily messianic rather than sacrificial (cf.
comm. on 5:6), the element of paradox is not as pronounced as it is usually
thought to be.

The prophet Joel described the day of the Lord as "great and very
terrible" (Joel 2:11; cf. vs. 31). It is a day of wrath and retribution (Zeph
1:14–18). According to those attempting to escape the presence of God and
the Lamb, this day of wrath has come.[41] Their rhetorical question "Who is
able to stand?" echoes Nahum 1:6 ("Who can stand before his indignation? Who can endure the heat of his anger?"—cf. Mal 3:2). The announcement of the end need not be understood as the mistaken opinion of
terrified mankind. The beginning of the end has arrived, and the plagues of
8:7–9:21 and 16:2–21 follow upon the actual opening of the seven-sealed
scroll.

---

[38]A χιλίαρχος at that time was the commander of a cohort (about 600 men).

[39]As in A. T. Hanson, *The Wrath of the Lamb,* pp. 159–80.

[40]F. F. Bruce, p. 645. Torrance calls the wrath of God's Lamb "the consuming passion of His
holy love that wills to destroy all that is unloving and untrue" (p. 49). Cf. R. V. G. Tasker,
The Biblical Doctrine of the Wrath of God, for a general treatment of the subject.

[41]Some manuscripts read αὐτοῦ (**A P 046** 1 82 2059s *pl* sa^pl bo^pt Prim TR), an understandable
scribal alteration, since ὀργή in vs. 16 is used in connection with ἀρνίον only.

CHAPTER 7

INTERLUDE: VISIONS OF SECURITY AND SALVATION (7:1–17)

Chapter 7 comes as a parenthesis between the sixth and seventh seals—a stylistic feature repeated in the trumpet sequence (10:1–11:13) but not with the bowls (cf. 16:12–21). It is not intended to take the reader back to a time before the Four Horsemen are released in order to parallel the trumpets with the seals. It contrasts the security and blessedness which await the faithful with the panic of a pagan world fleeing from judgment. In a sense it answers the question just posed, ''Who is able to stand?'' (6:17).

Chapter 7 also serves as a dramatic interlude. It delays for a brief moment the disclosure of that which is to take place when the seventh and final seal is removed from the scroll of destiny. The chapter consists of two visions—one, the sealing of the 144,000, and the other, the blessedness of the great multitude before the heavenly throne. A great deal has been written about the identity of the 144,000 as well as the relationship between the two visions. The position taken in the following pages is that in both visions it is the church which is in view, but from two vantage points. Prior to the trumpet judgments the last generation of believers is sealed so as to be saved from the destruction coming upon the earth and to be brought safely into the heavenly kingdom. The second vision is anticipatory of the eternal blessedness of all believers when in the presence of God they realize the rewards of faithful endurance.

A. SEALING OF GOD'S SERVANTS (7:1-8)

1 *After this I saw four angels standing at the four corners of the earth, holding the four winds of the earth, that no wind should blow on the earth, or on the sea, or upon any tree.*

2 *And I saw another angel ascend from the sunrising, having the seal of the living God: and he cried with a great voice to the four angels to whom it was given to hurt the earth and the sea,*

3 *saying, Hurt not the earth, neither the sea, nor the trees, till we shall have sealed the servants of our God on their foreheads.*

4 *And I heard the number of them that were sealed, a hundred and forty and four thousand, sealed out of every tribe of the children of Israel:*

5 *Of the tribe of Judah were sealed twelve thousand;*
Of the tribe of Reuben twelve thousand;
Of the tribe of Gad twelve thousand;

6 *Of the tribe of Asher twelve thousand;*
Of the tribe of Naphtali twelve thousand;
Of the tribe of Manasseh twelve thousand;

7 *Of the tribe of Simeon twelve thousand;*
Of the tribe of Levi twelve thousand;
Of the tribe of Issachar twelve thousand;

8 *Of the tribe of Zebulun twelve thousand;*
Of the tribe of Joseph twelve thousand;
Of the tribe of Benjamin were sealed twelve thousand.

1   John sees four angels standing at the four corners of the earth, holding back the four winds of destruction.[1] In apocalyptic thought the forces of nature are often pictured as under the charge of angels. Later in Revelation we are introduced to "the angel of the waters" (16:5) and the angel who "hath power over fire" (14:18). On the basis that the four angels are not able to keep the Sabbath (cf. *Jub.* 2:18 ff), some writers classify them as a lower order. They are pictured as standing at the four corners of the earth. This does not demand that we interpret first-century cosmology as believing in a square (or rectangular?) world. It is quite possible that the ancients conceived of the earth as a round disk. When Isaiah foretells the return of the remnant from "the four corners of the earth" (Isa 11:12), he uses the expression in much the same way as we would today.

[1]Some commentators, noting that in Zech 6:5 (*ASV*) the four horses are said to be "the four winds of heaven," suggest that the four winds of Rev 7:1 may be another way of referring to the four horsemen of chap. 6 (Morris, p. 113; Beasley-Murray, p. 142). Thus Rev 7:1-3 would be retrospective and relate to the earlier events. The *RSV* rightly translates Zech 6:5 as saying that the four chariots "are going forth to the four winds of heaven"—no identification between horses and winds is made.

The four winds as destructive agents of God are a regular feature in apocalyptic. The harmful winds were not those which blew straight from the four quarters (N S E W) but those that blew diagonally (cf. *I Enoch* 76; cf. 34:3).[2] In Daniel 7:2 the four winds of heaven blow upon the sea and four great and terrible beasts come forth on their mission of destruction. In Jeremiah 49:36 ff the four winds carry out the fierce anger of Jehovah upon Elam. According to the *Apocalypse of Pseudo-John* 15, four great winds will sweep the face of the earth and cleanse it from sin. In our text the winds are held in check by the four angels until the servants of God are sealed. They are not to blow *upon* the earth or sea or *against* any tree.[3] Trees are especially vulnerable to high winds and are pictured here in a representative role rather than as a specific target.[4] The Greek text may be translated "lest a wind keep on blowing," indicating that the winds of destruction have already begun to mount.[5] In a semi-arid land where vegetation withered easily, the sirocco—a hot wind from the southeast—came to play a part in the presentation of final destruction. Hosea speaks of the hot east wind as the "wind of the Lord . . . rising from the wilderness," drying up springs and fountains (13:15; cf. Zech 9:14; Isa 40:7, 24).

That these winds are never referred to subsequently in Revelation is one argument for the position that 7:1–8 represents an earlier source which John incorporated into his apocalypse. It is supported by the fact that a Christian writer in identifying the church as the true Israel would probably not bother to list a detailed division of the twelve tribes (as in vss. 5–8). Hence some writers hold that John has borrowed a Jewish apocalyptic source in which the people of Israel are protected from some calamity by receiving the seal of God upon their foreheads, and has reapplied the material to the church as it enters the period of final turmoil upon the earth.[6]

---

[2] *I Enoch* 76 pictures twelve portals at the ends of the earth open to the four quarters of heaven. Through the center portal on each side blew the winds of blessing and through the outside portals blew (diagonally) the hurtful winds.

[3] This seems to be the significance of the change from the genitive γῆς and θαλάσσης to the accusative δένδρον.

[4] OT verses such as Isa 2:13; 14:8; and 61:3, in which trees are interpreted as people in the targums, have suggested to some that "tree" in Rev 7:1 may be taken metaphorically for those who dwell upon the earth (cf. Ford, p. 115).

[5] ἵνα μὴ πνέῃ, a negative purpose clause with the present subjective; cf. Robertson, *Word Pictures*, VI, p. 348.

[6] Charles, I, pp. 191–201, suggests two independent traditions behind 7:1–8: the first (vss. 1–3) brought in without essential alteration to introduce the second (vss. 4–8) which originally referred to literal Israel but is modified by the Seer to represent spiritual Israel. Beasley-Murray favors the view that vss. 1–8 constituted a single Jewish apocalyptic prophecy which John adopted and reapplied to fit his own purpose (p. 141).

2–3   Another angel enters the vision, rising from the east and calling to the four restraining angels to hold back destruction until the servants of God are sealed. This reference to the east is probably no more than a picturesque detail, although some see in it a reminiscence of Ezekiel 43:4 where the glory of the Lord enters by the east gate. Others see an indirect reference to the Nativity story and the Wise Men who came from the east (Mt 2:1).[7] In any case it is appropriate that the angel who seals the 144,000 from the tribes of Israel should come from the direction of Palestine.

The seal which the angel bears is probably a signet ring like that used by Oriental kings to authenticate and protect official documents.[8] From 14:1 we learn that the mark it leaves on the forehead is "his name [the Lamb's], and the name of his Father" (cf. 22:4). The followers of the beast also have a mark (16:2; 19:20)—the beast's name (14:11) or the number of his name (13:17)—on their right hand or on their forehead (13:16; 14:9; 20:4 say forehead *and* hand). The sealing of God's servants is based on Ezekiel 9 where God instructs a man with an inkhorn to place an X[9] on the forehead of all those who are deeply troubled over the sins of Jerusalem in order to protect them from the judgment coming upon the city. The seal should not be interpreted in a sacramental sense as referring to baptism.[10] Its primary purpose is to insure protection for the believers in the coming judgments.[11] The seal of God in II Timothy 2:19 is "the Lord knoweth them that are his." Ownership entails protection.

It is the seal of the *living* God that the angel bears. This designation is frequent in the OT. Upon crossing the Jordan, Joshua tells the people that "the living God" is among them (Josh 3:10). Hezekiah calls upon God to deliver Israel out of the hands of Sennacherib, who sent his messenger "to defy the living God" (II Kgs 19:4, 16). The title is appropriate wherever God is about to intervene on behalf of his people. It contrasts the one true and eternal God with all the false and idolatrous gods of heathendom.

The servants of God are not a select group singled out from among the rest to receive the seal of God. They are the full number of faithful

---

[7]Cf. Gen 2:8 where the garden of Eden is planted "in the east"; also *Sib. Or.* 3:652, "from the sunrise God shall send a king." There is a natural connection between the place where light originates and the source of divine blessing.

[8]Ford lists six things that a seal would connote to the prophet's contemporaries (pp. 116–17).

[9]The mark of Ezek 9:4 was the Hebrew *tau*, made like an X or +.

[10]In passages such as II Cor 1:22; Eph 1:13; 4:30 it is not baptism which is the seal of the Holy Spirit, but the Spirit himself.

[11]Charles holds that the sealing is "to secure the servants of God against the attacks of demonic powers coming into open manifestation" (I, p. 205).

believers alive when that event takes place. The angel's reference to them as servants of our God implies that men and angels are fellow servants in the service of God (cf. 19:10; 22:9).

4–8 No description of the sealing follows. John does not see but hears the number of those who have been sealed—144,000 out of every tribe of Israel. The identity of this group has been extensively discussed. A few commentators interpret the 144,000 as a literal reference to the nation Israel. Walvoord accepts this passage as proving that the twelve tribes are still in existence.[12] This interpretation seriously complicates the book of Revelation by bringing in racial distinctions which no longer exist in the NT purview. It disregards the historical fact that ten of the twelve tribes disappeared in Assyria and the remaining two lost their separate identity when Jerusalem fell in AD 70. Glasson holds that John has adopted the common apocalyptic view that the lost tribes were in some unknown hiding place and would return before the end (p. 52).

The number is obviously symbolic. Twelve (the number of tribes) is both squared and multiplied by a thousand—a twofold way of emphasizing completeness. It refers to that generation of faithful believers who are about to enter the final turbulent period which marks the end of human history. In this scene we have "a picture of all the Christians who will remain faithful during the coming trial when the Beast appears" (Preston and Hanson, p. 84). Their being sealed does not protect them from physical death but insures entrance into the heavenly kingdom. It indicates that they will remain faithful in the coming persecution.

The idea of the church as the new Israel appears to have grown out of Jesus' promise to his disciples that they would one day "sit on twelve thrones, judging the twelve tribes of Israel" (Mt 19:28; cf. Lk 22:30). Paul writes that the believer in Christ is the true Jew (Rom 2:29), and refers to the church as "the Israel of God" (Gal 6:16). James addresses his letter to "the twelve tribes in the Dispersion" (1:1) when writing to the Christians scattered throughout the Roman world. Peter speaks of believers as "a chosen race, a royal priesthood, a holy nation" (I Pet 2:9), phrases taken directly from the OT (Isa 43:20; Ex 19:6) and reapplied to the NT church.

Some commentators would restrict the 144,000 to that portion of the entire church which in the last days is marked out for martyrdom. The martyrs under the fifth seal cried out for vindication, and it was said to

---

[12]Walvoord, p. 141. He notes that although genealogies are lost, the modern Jew can be assured that God knows in which tribe he should be classified (p. 143). Kraft takes the 144,000 as "der heilige Rest Israels" (p. 126) and the multitude as "die Erlösten aus den Heiden" (p. 128).

them to rest a little while until the full number of their fellow servants should be killed (6:9–11). Kiddle represents this position when he writes that the 12,000 from each tribe "represents that proportion of Christians who in the book of destiny are inscribed as martyrs" (p. 136). This interpretation is supported by reference to the prophetic role of the two witnesses in chapter 11 and the 144,000 in chapter 14 who are "purchased from among men, to be the first-fruits unto God" (14:4). Caird (p. 97) holds that John envisaged the great martyrdom which lay ahead as a new Exodus (15:2–4) in which the martyrs were marked with the name of the Lamb if not with his blood (cf. Ex 12:23).

The arguments for identifying the 144,000 with a select group of martyrs is not conclusive. The detailed listing of the twelve tribes as well as the symbolism of the number emphasizes the idea of completeness. Twelve times 1,000 come from each tribe: no one is excluded. Further, there seems to be no place in Revelation for any believer who will not face martyrdom in the last days (cf. 13:15, "as many as should not worship the image of the beast should be killed").[13]

Several irregularities appear in the listing of the twelve tribes. The first is that Judah rather than Reuben (Jacob's oldest son) heads the list. The reason for this change is obvious. Christ belonged to the tribe of Judah (Heb 7:14; cf. Gen 49:10). Giving this priority to Judah would be perfectly natural for a Christian writer. The second is the inclusion of both Manasseh and Joseph, since Manasseh (as well as his brother Ephraim, who does not occur in this list) is included in Joseph. The answer to this peculiarity is perhaps bound up with yet another—the omission of Dan.

Some have suggested that *Dan* was inadvertently copied as *Man,* which was later taken as an abbreviation for Manasseh.[14] This would solve both problems. Unfortunately it is only conjecture unsupported by any solid evidence. Apparently Dan was omitted because of an early connection with idolatry. When the tribe of Dan migrated to the north and settled in Laish, they set up for themselves the graven image (Judg 18:30). Later Dan became one of the two great shrines in the northern kingdom (I Kgs 12:29). In the *Testament of Dan* (5:6) Satan is said to be the prince of the tribe. Irenaeus, writing in the latter part of the second century, noted that the omission of Dan was due to a tradition that the Antichrist was to come

---

[13]Kiddle (pp. 135–36) pictures the church as dwelling in the desert and thus protected from the plagues which fall on the great city where the martyrs carry out their testimony and eventually die (11:8). Yet in 12:13–17 the dragon, when unable to overtake the woman who has been taken away to the safety of the wilderness, goes away "to make war with the rest of her seed, that keep the commandments of God, and hold the testimony of Jesus"—most certainly a reference to the church.

[14]In 7:6 the Bohairic reads Δάν rather than Μανασσῆ. In 7:5, 42 1854 *pc* have Δάν for Γάδ.

from that tribe (*Adv. Haer.* v.30.2).[15] This apparently rested on rabbinic interpretations of such passages as Genesis 49:17 and Jeremiah 8:16. Whatever the precise reason for omitting Dan, the inclusion of Manasseh was undoubtedly to bring the total number back to twelve.

There seems to be no particular reason for the order in which the tribes are given. This should not be surprising in that the tribes are listed in some eighteen different orders in the OT, none of which agrees with the order in Revelation. By placing verses 5c–6 after verse 8, Buchanan Gray (*Encyclopedia Biblica,* IV, pp. 5208 f) organized the list into the sons of Leah, Rachel, Zilpah (Leah's maid), and Bilhah (Rachel's maid). However that may be, the various irregularities of the list do not affect the interpretation of the passage. The 144,000 are faithful believers about to enter the period of final testing.

B. BLISS OF THE REDEEMED IN HEAVEN (7:9–17)

9 *After these things I saw, and behold, a great multitude, which no man could number, out of every nation and of all tribes and peoples and tongues, standing before the throne and before the Lamb, arrayed in white robes, and palms in their hands;*

10 *and they cry with a great voice, saying,*
Salvation unto our God who sitteth on the throne, and unto the Lamb.

11 *And all the angels were standing round about the throne, and about the elders and the four living creatures; and they fell before the throne on their faces, and worshipped God,*

12 *saying,*
Amen: Blessing, and glory, and wisdom, and thanksgiving, and honor, and power, and might, be unto our God for ever and ever. Amen.

13 *And one of the elders answered, saying unto me, These that are arrayed in the white robes, who are they, and whence came they?*

14 *And I say unto him, My lord, thou knowest. And he said to me, These are they that come out of the great tribulation, and they washed their robes, and made them white in the blood of the Lamb.*

15 *Therefore are they before the throne of God; and they serve him day and night in his temple: and he that sitteth on the throne shall spread his tabernacle over them.*

16 *They shall hunger no more, neither thirst any more; neither shall the sun strike upon them, nor any heat:*

17 *for the Lamb that is in the midst of the throne shall be their shepherd, and shall guide them unto fountains of waters of life: and God shall wipe away every tear from their eyes.*

---

[15]Hippolytus, writing a few years later, says, "As the Christ was born from the tribe of Judah, so will the Antichrist be born from the tribe of Dan" (*De Ant.* 14).

9-10   The second vision of chapter 7 stands in marked contrast to the first. Instead of 144,000 there appears a great multitude which no man can number. Rather than being sealed for the impending persecution, they are said to have "come out of the great tribulation" (vs. 14). No longer on earth, they crowd the throne room of heaven clad in victors' robes and bearing the emblem of festive joy. The new vision anticipates a glorious day yet future when those who are to pass through the final persecution will enter the blessedness of the eternal state. The innumerable multitude includes far more than the 144,000 of the previous vision. All the faithful of every age are there. Some have been called upon to give their lives as martyrs. All have been prepared to pay the price of fidelity.

The purpose of the vision is to grant a glimpse of eternal blessedness to those about to enter the world's darkest hour. For a brief period John is privileged to look beyond this age to the hour of ultimate triumph. The entire scene is not unlike the Transfiguration in which Jesus revealed his coming glory to disciples who had recently learned of the suffering which lay ahead for the Son of man (Mk 8:32; 9:2–8). Without doubt it is one of the most exalted portrayals of the heavenly state to be found anywhere in Scripture. The lyric prose of verses 15–17 is charged with a spiritual excitement that has caused the faithful of all ages to yearn for that final redemption.

The great throng is pictured as standing before the throne and the Lamb. The elders, living creatures, and angels of chapters 4 and 5 are now joined with so vast a multitude of redeemed that to number them would be impossible. In every direction they stretch out as far as the eye can see. As God promised Abraham, they are in number as the stars of heaven (Gen 15:5) and the sand of the sea (Gen 32:12). The universality of the multitude is stressed by the fourfold division into nations, tribes, peoples, and tongues.[16] Their robes of white symbolize not only the victory of faith but the righteousness of Christ. Verse 14 specifically says that the robes are white by virtue of being washed in the blood of the Lamb. Victory by sacrifice is a recurring motif in Revelation (cf. 5:9, 12). The palms are appropriate in this scene of festive joy. Those who went out to meet Jesus as he rode toward Jerusalem on the day of the triumphal entry carried palm branches and cried out "Hosanna! Blessed is he who comes in the name of the Lord" (Jn 12:13).[17]

---

[16]These four designations occur together in Rev 5:9; 7:9; 11:9; 13:7; and 14:6 (also with the modification of one member in 10:11 and 17:15). It is interesting that the order differs in each case.

[17]For similar use of palms cf. I Macc 13:51; II Macc 10:7.

With a single voice the great multitude cries out, "Salvation to our God and to the Lamb." This salvation is more than the triumphant passage of the martyrs through persecution (Caird, p. 100). It is deliverance from everything which stands over against the blessedness portrayed in verses 15–17. It is salvation from sin and all its dire consequences. The great multitude joyfully acknowledges that their deliverance rests on the sovereign will of God and the redemptive activity of the Lamb. Weymouth translates, "To our God . . . and to the Lamb, we owe our salvation!"

11–12 The thousands upon thousands of angels which surround the throne (5:11) respond to the jubilant cry of the saints by falling prostrate before God and offering to him a sevenfold doxology of praise. The redemption of man, that ultimate purpose of God in creation, has at last been realized. If there is "joy before the angels of God over one sinner who repents" (Lk 15:10), how unbelievably great will be the joyful adoration of the heavenly host when *all* the redeemed stand before their God! We need not inquire into the relative positions of the angels and the saints around the throne. Visions are not for diagramming but for insight into truths which lie beyond the ken of human intelligence.

The two "Amens" are liturgical, prefacing and concluding the angelic doxology.[18] The repetition of the article before each attribute (as in 4:11) tends to heighten its meaning. For instance, it is not a blessing which the angelic hosts have in mind, but *the* blessing—"the blessing above all others" (Morris, p. 117). Six of the seven attributes occur in an earlier doxology (5:12) but in a totally different order.[19] Preston and Hanson define blessing as "that spontaneous act of thanks which men utter when they realize more vividly than ever before their happiness" (p. 47). Glory is the radiance of the divine Person. In this context wisdom is the divine knowledge God exhibited in his plan of redemption (cf. Eph 3:10). Thanksgiving is the appropriate response for salvation, and honor its public acknowledgment. If power is God's ability to act, might is his redemptive presence in the events of history. This ascription of praise is apparently directed both to God and the Lamb, although the latter is not specifically mentioned here (cf. vss. 12, 14, 17).

13–14 One of the elders, anticipating the question which John is about to ask, inquires rhetorically, "Who are the white-robed throng, and where have they come from?" Prompted by the Seer, he answers that they

---

[18] The first Amen may be in response to the praise of the great multitude. The omission of ἀμήν at the close of the verse (C and a few other MSS) seems to suggest it may have been a liturgical addition (Metzger, *TCGNT,* p. 742).
[19] "Thanksgiving" in 7:12 replaces "riches" in 5:12.

are the ones who have come out of the great tribulation and washed their robes in the blood of the Lamb.

The question and answer format is often used in prophetic literature for introducing the explanation of a vision. Following Zechariah's vision of the golden lampstand and the two olive trees, an angel poses the question, "Do you know what these are?" (4:5). When the prophet admits his lack of understanding, the angel proceeds to explain the visions.[20] John's mode of address to the angel ("My lord")[21] is in keeping with the reverence he shows for angelic beings elsewhere in the book (cf. 19:10; 22:8–9). In itself it does not necessarily imply a supernatural person. It may be only an expression of courtesy such as Mary used to the gardener on Easter morning (Jn 20:15). *"Thou* knowest" (the personal pronoun is emphatic) expresses John's lack of understanding and his confidence in the ability of his interpreter.

The white-robed multitude are those who have come out of the great tribulation. Charles interprets the scene as one in which martyrs are *still* arriving from the great persecution.[22] The larger context favors a point in time when the complete number of the redeemed stand before God and the blessings of the eternal state are about to be realized.

The use of the definite article in the phrase "the great tribulation" indicates that the angel is referring primarily to that final series of woes which will immediately precede the end. It is the hour of trial which is to come upon the whole world (3:10). Prophesied by Daniel (12:1) and reflected on the screen of history at the fall of Jerusalem (Mk 13:19 and parallels), it finds its fulfillment in that final persecution which supplies the full complement of Christian martyrs (6:11). John views the entire company of faithful believers in the light of the 144,000 who have just come through the final period of testing. Not all are martyrs. There is no mention here of being slain (as in 6:9) or beheaded (as in 20:4) for the testimony they bore. Their robes are white by virtue of the redemptive death of the Lamb. Their rewards are those of all the faithful. Persecution has always been the lot of those who follow the Lamb (Jn 16:33; II Tim 3:12). The intensity of the final conflict of righteousness and evil will rise to such a pitch as to become *the great tribulation.*

---

[20]Cf. Jer 1:11, 13; 24:3; Amos 7:8; 8:2; *Asc. Isa.* 9:25–26.

[21]μου is omitted by **A,** a few minuscules, versions, and the TR.

[22]Taking οἱ ἐρχόμενοι as an imperfect participle (Charles, I, p. 213). The participle should be understood in a general sense to mean "such as come" (cf. Burton, *Moods and Tenses,* p. 56) or perhaps as a more vivid way of saying "they that have just come." The aorist ἦλθον of vs. 13 makes unlikely the idea that οἱ ἐρχόμενοι refers to some who are still arriving.

The multitude before the throne have washed their robes and made them white in the blood of the Lamb. The tense of both verbs (aorist) indicates once-for-all actions which took place in the past.[23] The cleansing effect of the blood of Christ is also pictured in such verses as Hebrews 9:24 ("the blood of Christ... [shall] cleanse your conscience from dead works," *ASV*) and I John 1:7 ("the blood of Jesus his Son cleanses us from all sin"). The background may be Exodus 19 where the children of Israel wash their garments in readiness for the descent of Jehovah upon Mt. Sinai (Ex 19:10, 14). The prophet Isaiah compares the righteous deeds of Israel to a "polluted garment" (64:6; cf. Zech 3:3–5), but elsewhere promises that "though your sins are like scarlet, they shall be as white as snow" (1:18). The idea of making robes white by washing them in blood[24] is a striking paradox. It is the sacrifice of the Lamb upon the cross which supplies white garments for the saints. Their act of washing the robes is not a meritorious work but a way of portraying faith.

15 It is because they are clothed in the righteousness of Christ that the multitude is able to stand before the throne of God. There they serve him day and night. The suggestion that John later corrects himself on this point (Swete, p. 104)—21:25 says "there shall be no night there" (cf. 22:5)—is unnecessary.[25] "Day and night" is an idiom meaning unceasingly or without pause.[26] The temple in which the faithful serve is not to be thought of as a building in heaven. In John's vision heaven itself is the sanctuary: within, all God's children are worshipping priests (1:6; 5:10).[27] Their service is not the ritual performance of Levitical priests but a spiritual worship of adoration and praise (cf. 22:3–5). The same verb is used of Anna the prophetess, who "did not depart from the temple, *worshipping* with fasting and prayer."[28] The shift to the future tense in verses 15c–17 does not intend to separate in time the arrival of the redeemed and their heavenly reward. Once clothed in white and before the throne, the bless-

---

[23] In 22:14 the present tense πλύνοντες may refer to a continuing practice.

[24] (1) 82 1854 2329 *al* read ἐπλάτυναν, enlarged or made broad (cf. Mt 23:5), perhaps because the figure of washing garments in blood seemed unacceptable.

[25] Another point said to be corrected later is the existence of a temple in the New Jerusalem: 21:22 says there is "no temple therein" (Swete, p. 104). But the New Jerusalem is not identical with the heavenly presence of God.

[26] 20:10 speaks of the devil and his cohorts tormented in the lake of fire "day and night for ever and ever," hardly a reference to successive periods of light and darkness.

[27] When distinguished from the ἱερόν (the entire temple enclosure), the ναός refers to the inner shrine (cf. Mt 23:35).

[28] λατρεύουσα (Lk 2:37). Paul speaks of the true circumcision "who worship (λατρεύοντες) by the Spirit of God" (Phil 3:3). Cf. also Rom 12:1, λογικὴν λατρείαν. In the LXX priestly service in the temple is usually indicated by λειτουργέω.

ings of heaven are theirs without delay. Both time and space are finite categories which blend together in the visionary experience. From the throne room in heaven is projected a description of life upon the new earth (21:3).

The promise that God shall spread his tabernacle over them would evoke memories of the tabernacle in the wilderness (Lev 26, etc.), the pillar of cloud and of fire (Ex 13:21–22), and the Shekinah glory (the radiance of God's presence in the midst of his people; cf. Ex 40:34–38; also II Chron 7:1–3). For the tabernacle to be *over* his people is a way of saying that the immediate presence of God will shelter and protect them from all that would harm (Isa 4:5–6). It is the fulfillment of the OT promise that God will dwell in the midst of his people (Ezek 37:27; Zech 2:10). The *RSV* translates, "He who sits upon the throne will shelter them with his presence," that is, "will make his Shekinah to dwell with them" (Morris, p. 118).

16–17 The eternal blessedness of the redeemed is pictured in phrases drawn for the most part from Isaiah's description of the exiles returning from Babylon (Isa 49:10). The promise that they will neither hunger nor thirst would be especially meaningful in an ancient land where both were constant threats. Yet the promise goes beyond physical privation. It points to that ultimate satisfaction of the soul's deepest longing for spiritual wholeness. "Blessed are those who hunger and thirst for righteousness," said Jesus, "for they shall be satisfied" (Mt 5:6). And again, "He who comes to me shall not hunger, and he who believes in me shall never thirst" (Jn 6:35; cf. 4:14; 7:37). In the age to come neither sun nor scorching east wind will strike the redeemed.[29] They are sheltered from all discomfort by the presence of God.

The idea of the Lamb as the shepherd of God's flock is an intriguing exchange of roles.[30] Elsewhere in the writings of John, Christ is pictured as the good shepherd (Jn 10:1–30; 21:15–17; cf. I Jn 3:16 with Jn 10:11).[31] The metaphor builds on the OT picture of God as the shepherd of Israel. Such passages as Psalm 23:1 ("The Lord is my shepherd; I shall not want") and Isaiah 40:11 ("He will feed his flock like a shepherd") speak of the gentle care and daily provision of the ancient shepherd. God through

---

[29]Taking καῦμα in the sense of ὁ καύσων in Isa 49:10. John's choice of καῦμα suggests a contrast with 16:9 where, as the result of the fourth bowl being poured upon the earth, ἐκαυματίσθησαν . . . καῦμα μέγα. οὐδὲ μή with the aorist subjunctive is a strong double negative.

[30]The paradoxical quality mentioned by so many writers is less striking if ἀρνίον in Rev carries the idea of messianic leadership. Cf. comm. on 5:6.

[31]The figure is used by other NT writers as well; Heb 13:20; I Pet 2:25; 5:4.

Ezekiel tells of a coming shepherd—"my servant David"—who is to tend his flock (Ezek 34:23). Christ is this promised good shepherd.

Elsewhere in Revelation, the shepherding activity of the Lamb is of a radically different sort. He is to rule (shepherd)[32] the nations with a rod of iron (12:5; 19:15). In 2:27 the overcomers at Thyatira are promised a share in this rule. With a rod of iron they will shepherd the nations "as the vessels of the potter are broken to shivers."[33]

The Lamb as heavenly shepherd leads his flock to the wellspring of life and wipes away the last trace of earthly sorrow. "Thou hast led in thy steadfast love the people whom thou hast redeemed," sang Moses and the children of Israel (Ex 15:13). "Lead me, O Lord, in thy righteousness," prayed the Psalmist (Ps 5:8). As God has led in the past, so will he lead in the future. He directs the heavenly multitude to the fountain and source of life—that is, to the immediate presence of God. The inverted syntax of the expression in Greek lays emphasis on the word life.[34] The Psalmist says that the children of men will drink of the river of God's pleasures, for with him is the fountain of life (Ps 36:8–9). The same concept lies behind Jesus' promise that "whoever drinks of the water that I shall give him will never thirst; the water that I shall give him will become in him a spring of water welling up to eternal life" (Jn 4:14; cf. 7:38; and the "inexhaustible fountain of righteousness" in I Enoch 48:1). As in the preceding verse, the figure points beyond itself to that ultimate satisfaction of man's spiritual longings. As a fresh-water spring in a semi-arid land would be to a shepherd and his thirsty flock, so will be the eternal presence of God to redeemed man in his longing for spiritual wholeness.

The tears which God wipes away are not the tears of grief over a wasted life. Rather, like the tears of a child brought suddenly from sorrow to delight they linger rather ridiculously on the faces of the redeemed.[35]

Rist suggests that John is here indoctrinating prospective martyrs by the use of a hymn which would prepare them for their coming ordeal (p. 424). A glimpse into the bliss of heaven would certainly encourage Christians caught in a hostile world, but to interpret the vision as premeditated indoctrination scarcely does credit to the integrity of the Seer.

---

[32]ποιμαίνω normally means to tend or lead to pasture, but in these verses it pictures the shepherd's action against preying beasts.

[33]Cf. Ps 2:9, LXX, ποιμανεῖς αὐτοὺς ἐν ῥάβδῳ σιδηρᾷ.

[34]Swete translates, "to Life's water-springs" (p. 105). The normal order is found in 21:6; cf. 22:1, 17.

[35]Cf. Isa 25:8 as a probable source. The phrase is repeated in 21:4.

CHAPTER 8

Following the two parenthetical visions of chapter 7 the Lamb opens the seventh and final seal. There follows a dramatic pause during which the prayers of the saints rise to God as incense from the golden altar. An angel casts fire upon the earth and the seven trumpet-angels raise their instruments in preparation to sound another series of seven judgments (8:7–11:19; with 10:1–11:13 a parenthesis between the sixth and seventh elements as in the seals).

Many suggestions have been offered to explain the relationship between the three major series of judgments (seals, trumpets, and bowls). One solution would be a strictly chronological arrangement with each new series evolving from the seventh element of the previous series. Charles and Oman are prominent exponents of this approach, but both find it necessary to posit considerable textual rearrangement. For Charles the culprit was a "shallow-brained fanatic and celibate" who took unwarranted liberties with the text (I, p. lv).[1] Oman holds that the confusion resulted primarily from an incorrect arrangement of the papyrus sheets.[2]

Most of the other solutions involve some sort of recapitulation, an approach that goes back to Victorinus of Pettau in the third century. Hendriksen finds seven parallel sections each of which spans the entire dispensation from the first to the second coming of Christ (p. 25). For Kiddle the book is the work of a creative artist and must not be pressed into a

---

[1] Charles holds that the Apocalypse proper (excluding the Prologue and Epilogue) consists of seven parts. "The events in these seven parts are described in visions *in strict chronological order*, save in the case of certain proleptic visions which are inserted for purposes of encouragement and lie outside the orderly development of the theme of the Seer" (I, p. xxiii).

[2] J. Oman, *The Book of Revelation* (1923); also *The Text of Revelation: A Revised Theory* (1928).

clearly defined plan (pp. xxvii–xxxiii). Bowman sees it as a drama in seven acts separated by passages which he likens to "stage props."[3] Farrer holds to a sequence of three topics which, without adhering to a continuous time sequence, yet attach to three periods which are in genuine historical sequence (pp. 22–23). One of the more helpful suggestions is that of Caird, who compares John to a guide in an art gallery who has his students stand back to absorb a general impression (the sevenfold visions) and then move up to study the details (the unnumbered visions). He holds that the unity of the book "is neither chronological nor arithmetical, but artistic" (p. 106).[4]

The position maintained in the following discussion is that the visions of John neither follow in a strict chronological sequence nor do they systematically recapitulate one another. While there is a rather clearly discernible *literary* development,[5] it is not intended to represent a corresponding *historical* development. Obviously there is progression, but not without considerable restatement and development of detail. The further one moves toward the consummation the greater is this enlargement. All attempts to press the material into well-defined patterns[6] leave the impression that John was more interested in producing a work of literary subtlety than sharing with his fellow believers the awe-inspiring visions that God had dramatically revealed to him. E. F. Scott wisely remarks that a perfectly logical apocalypse would be a contradiction in terms (p. 26).

4. SEVENTH SEAL: A DRAMATIC PAUSE (8:1)

1 *And when he opened the seventh seal, there followed a silence in heaven about the space of half an hour.*

1 When the seventh seal is opened, a great hush settles over the worshipping hosts of heaven. For a period of about half an hour there is breathless silence as all await the judgments of the scroll now unsealed. Kiddle judges it a "brilliant device for deepening the suspense" (p. 144). It is similar to

---

[3]J. W. Bowman, "The Revelation to John: Its Dramatic Structure and Message," *Int*, 9 (1955), pp. 436–53.

[4]For surveys of the many approaches to the structure of Revelation cf. Guthrie, *NT Introduction: Hebrews to Revelation*, pp. 289–94 and André Feuillet, *The Apocalypse*, pp. 23–36.

[5]The seven trumpets are an expansion of the seventh seal; and the seven bowls, after some intervening visions, follow the seventh trumpet.

[6]Lohmeyer (*Die Offenbarung des Johannes*) allows the number seven to control his analysis of the entire book, as does Farrer, especially in his earlier work, *A Rebirth of Images*. Commenting on Farrer's ability to fit all the complexities of the Apocalypse into his scheme, Guthrie notes that this should cause no surprise, "for the pursuer of symbols can see them wherever he chooses" (*op. cit.*, p. 291).

the restraining of the four winds of destruction (7:1–3) and the sealing up of the utterance of the seven thunders (10:4).

The silence is neither a symbol of eternal rest[7] nor a necessary precaution so God can hear the prayers of the suffering saints (Charles, I, pp. 223–24).[8] It is a dramatic pause which makes even more impressive the judgments about to fall upon the earth. D'Aragon calls the silence "a striking contrast between the hymns that go before and the crash that follows" (p. 478). It is reminiscent of the prophetic injunction, "The Lord is in his holy temple; let all the earth keep silence before him" (Hab 2:20; cf. Zeph 1:7–8; Zech 2:13).[9] Although a thirty-minute period is a relatively short period, it would form an impressive break in such a rapidly moving drama. Apparently the angelic activity of verses 2–5 takes place during this interval of silence. Trumpets are given to the seven angels before the throne. An angel standing over the altar mingles incense with the prayers of the saints,[10] and taking fire from the golden altar fills his censer and casts it upon the earth. The intensity of the scene is incredibly heightened by the complete absence of any sound.

V. THE SEVEN TRUMPETS (8:2–11:19)

1. PREPARATION (8:2–5)

2 *And I saw the seven angels that stand before God; and there were given unto them seven trumpets.*

3 *And another angel came and stood over the altar, having a golden censer; and there was given unto him much incense, that he should add it unto the prayers of all the saints upon the golden altar which was before the throne.*

4 *And the smoke of the incense, with the prayers of the saints, went up before God out of the angel's hand.*

5 *And the angel taketh the censer; and he filled it with the fire of the altar, and cast it upon the earth: and there followed thunders, and voices, and lightnings, and an earthquake.*

---

[7]Victorinus, a third-century exegete, wrote *"significatur initium quietis aeternae"* (cited by Swete, p. 107).

[8]There is reference in the Talmud to angels refraining from singing during the day so that the praises of Israel may be heard in heaven (*Chag.* 12b), but this should probably be taken metaphorically.

[9]II Esdr 7:30 speaks of a seven-day period of primeval silence between this age and the age to come. In reporting the siege of Jerusalem Josephus tells of a great light which appeared as a sign in the sanctuary for half an hour (*Bell.* vi.5.3).

[10]Following the *RSV*. However, cf. comm. on vs. 4.

2 The use of the definite article indicates that the seven angels to whom the seven trumpets were given constitute a specific group. Raphael identifies himself to Tobit as "one of the seven holy angels who present the prayers of the saints and enter into the presence of the glory of the Holy One" (Tob 12:15). In *I Enoch* 20:2–8 the names of these seven archangels are listed as Uriel, Raphael, Raguel, Michael, Saraqâêl, Gabriel, and Remiel.[11] The Angels of the Presence (a designation that goes back to Isa 63:9) are mentioned repeatedly in the book of *Jubilees* (1:27, 29; 2:1–2, 18; 15:27; 31:14). "I am Gabriel, who stand in the presence of God," avows the angel to Zacharias (Lk 1:19).

Whatever the connection may be between the seven trumpet-angels of John's vision and the seven archangels of Jewish apocalyptic, their role in the book of Revelation is to announce a series of plagues which is to fall upon the earth and its inhabitants. It is possible that they are also the seven angels who later pour out the seven bowls of the wrath of God (15:1, 6–8; 16:1; 17:1; 21:9).

That this is the first mention of the seven angels does not mean that they have only recently entered the throne room to take their place among the other groups already there. As the drama continues, details which were earlier passed by are gradually brought to light. To stand before God is to maintain oneself in readiness for service.[12]

The action begins with the giving of seven trumpets to the seven angels standing before God. In the OT the trumpet was used extensively for a variety of purposes. In Numbers 10 Moses was instructed to make two trumpets of silver. They were used to call the people together (vs. 3), to move the tribes on their journey (vss. 5–6), to sound the alarm in time of war (vs. 9), and to celebrate days of sacred feasts (vs. 10). Seven priests with trumpets led the armies of Israel around the city of Jericho (Josh 6).[13] The Jewish New Year (Tishri 1) is called "a day for you to blow the trumpets" (Num 29:1; also Lev 23:24). The trumpet was regularly used at the coronation of kings (I Kgs 1:34, 39; II Kgs 9:13).

The trumpets in Revelation, however, are eschatological trumpets. They herald the day of God's wrath. Zephaniah 1:14–16 describes the great day of Jehovah as "a day of wrath . . . a day of distress and anguish . . . a day of trumpet blast and battle cry." In II Esdras 6:23 the sounding of a trumpet announces the day of judgment, striking sudden terror to the hearts

---

[11]Vs. 7 calls them archangels. Cf. also Rev 1:4; *I Enoch* 81:5; 90:21–22; *Test. Levi* 3:5.

[12]Cf. the phrase, "As Jehovah liveth, before whom I stand" (*ASV*) in II Kgs 5:16 and, with minor modification, in I Kgs 17:1; 18:15; and II Kgs 3:14.

[13]Caird (p. 108) says that John must have had this story in mind because of the appearance of the ark in 11:19 (cf. Josh 6:4, 6, 8, etc.).

of people. In the *Apocalypse of Abraham* (31) the trumpet heralds the coming of the Elect One to burn the wicked (cf. *Sib. Or.* 4:174). John's trumpet-angels call forth four great calamities upon the physical universe (8:7–12), two demonic plagues upon unrepentant man (9:1–21), and the great proclamation that this world has fallen to the sovereignty of God (11:15 ff).

3 The scene depicted in verses 3–5 as a prelude to the seven trumpet-plagues is somewhat similar to the earlier vision of the twenty-four elders with golden bowls of incense (5:8) which preceded the opening of the seven seals. The angel who performs the priestly functions is not identified. He is called "another angel" in order to distinguish him from the seven angels of verse 2 who are about to sound their trumpets and initiate the next series of plagues. It is unlikely that the angel is to be taken as representative of Christ in his intercessory work as high priest.[14] Would the central figure of Revelation be introduced into the text with such an indefinite title? In 7:2 it is "another angel" who seals the servants of God against the coming persecution.

The angel comes and stands before the altar.[15] A few commentators hold that this altar is to be distinguished from the golden altar mentioned later in the verse. The angel is pictured as offering the prayers of the saints in much the same way as the priests in the temple at Jerusalem would daily take hot coals from the altar of sacrifice and carry them into the holy place to the golden altar of incense (cf. Lk 1:9). It is more likely that only one altar is in view, the golden altar of incense (Ex 30:1–10; II Kgs 6:22; Heb 9:4).[16]

In the angel's hand is a golden censer or fire-pan. The censers of the tabernacle were made of brass (Ex 27:3), while those of Solomon's temple were of gold (I Kgs 7:50).[17] Although the word John uses for censer elsewhere means frankincense,[18] the adjective "golden" indicates that he had the implement in mind rather than that which was placed into it.

To the angel is given much incense "that he should add it unto the prayers of all the saints" (*ASV*). The clause has been variously understood,

---

[14]This position is apparently accepted by Walvoord (p. 152). Cf. Bede, Elliott, and other early commentators. Accordingly, the incense would be, as Hendriksen says, "our Savior's intercession in heaven" (p. 142).

[15]ἐπί may indicate that he is leaning *over* the altar. Acts 5:23 speaks of the keeper of the prison standing ἐπὶ τῶν θυρῶν (at or before the doors).

[16]Charles says there is no evidence in either Jewish or Christian apocalyptic of two altars in heaven (I, p. 227).

[17]The reference in I Kgs 7:50 and II Chron 4:22 may be to golden snuff-dishes (*NBD*, p. 203). I Esdr 2:13 speaks of "silver censers" which Nebuchadnezzar had carried away from Jerusalem (cf. II Kgs 25:15).

[18]λιβανωτός, I Chron 9:29; *Mart. Pol.* 15:2.

but the major options are two. Either the incense is mingled with the prayers of the saints or the incense is the prayers. The majority of commentators and English translations favor the former alternative. The *RSV* translates, "and [the angel] was given much incense to mingle with the prayers of all the saints . . . and the smoke of the incense rose with the prayers of the saints."[19] F. F. Bruce follows the second option, taking the dative case in both verses 3 and 4 ("unto the prayers," "with the prayers") as equivalent to the Hebrew *le* of definition and translating, "he was given much incense to offer, consisting of the prayers of all the saints" (p. 646). This interpretation harmonizes with 5:8 where the bowls of incense are definitely identified with the prayers of the saints.

In either case the role of the angel does not consist in making the prayers of the saints acceptable to God. The mediatorial role of angels which is so prevalent in Jewish apocalyptic (Tob 12:15; *I Enoch* 9:3; *Test. Levi* 3:5–6; etc.) does not find a place in NT theology.[20] At best the angel of 8:3–5 is a heavenly priest who presents the prayers of all the saints (not only those of the martyrs in 6:10) before God. That the altar is before the throne is another example of the ease with which otherwise separate elements may be conjoined in a vision.

4 When incense is added to the hot coals, a cloud of fragrant smoke rises from the altar as a symbol of divine acceptance. Paul writes to the Ephesians that Christ loved them and gave himself for them as "a fragrant offering and sacrifice to God" (Eph 5:2). The scene in heaven suggests that there is something sacrificial about genuine prayer. Both the believer and his prayer enter the presence of God by way of the altar.

5 The scene of intercession now becomes one of judgment. The angel priest takes[21] the censer, fills it with fire from the altar, and casts it upon the earth.[22] The action is somewhat parallel to that of Ezekiel's vision in which a man clothed in linen fills his hands with coals of fire from between the cherubim and scatters them over the city (Ezek 10:2–7). The prayers of the saints play an essential part in bringing the judgment of God upon the earth and its inhabitants. The martyrs' plea in 6:10 ("How long, O Master, the holy and true, dost thou not judge and avenge our blood on them that dwell on the earth?") is here answered in part.

That God is about to answer the prayers of the saints is indicated by

---

[19]Swete thinks that the prayers of the saints are the live coals on which the grains of incense fall (p. 108).

[20]In Dan 9:20 ff Gabriel plays a mediatorial role; cf. Dan 10:12–14.

[21]εἴληφεν is a dramatic perfect which heightens the vividness of the scene.

[22]There is no way of knowing whether it is fire or burning incense which the angel casts to the earth. Since ἔβαλεν stands without an object, it may be that the censer is thrown down as well.

the thunders, voices, lightnings, and earthquake which follow.[23] Like the theophany at Sinai the world trembles before the presence of God (Ex 19:16 ff).

2. FIRST FOUR TRUMPETS (8:6–12)

6 *And the seven angels that had the seven trumpets prepared themselves to sound.*

7 *And the first sounded, and there followed hail and fire, mingled with blood, and they were cast upon the earth: and the third part of the earth was burnt up, and the third part of the trees was burnt up, and all green grass was burnt up.*

8 *And the second angel sounded, and as it were a great mountain burning with fire was cast into the sea: and the third part of the sea became blood;*

9 *and there died the third part of the creatures which were in the sea, even they that had life; and the third part of the ships was destroyed.*

10 *And the third angel sounded, and there fell from heaven a great star, burning as a torch, and it fell upon the third part of the rivers, and upon the fountains of the waters;*

11 *and the name of the star is called Wormwood: and the third part of the waters became wormwood; and many men died of the waters, because they were made bitter.*

12 *And the fourth angel sounded, and the third part of the sun was smitten, and the third part of the moon, and the third part of the stars; that the third part of them should be darkened, and the day should not shine for the third part of it, and the night in like manner.*

6 Verse 6 returns to the action of verse 2 and leads on to the seven trumpet-plagues which follow. The intervening verses (3–5) suggest that the plagues result in part from the prayers of the saints.[24] We do not know what is involved in the angels preparing themselves to sound, but it probably means no more than that they raised their instruments in readiness to sound. This action would heighten the sense of expectancy.

7 With the sounding of the first trumpet[25] the second major series of calamities begins. They neither recapitulate the seal judgments nor do they follow in a strictly chronological sense. The sixth seal found men fleeing to the mountains and calling for sanctuary against the wrath of the Lamb (6:15–17). The tribulation of this period is considerably more ad-

---

[23]Kiddle calls this John's formula for the world's dissolution (p. 147). Cf. comm. on 4:5.
[24]Charles places vs. 6 after vs. 2 (which in turn should follow vss. 3–5) and removes vss. 7–12 as a later addition which has necessitated a change to seven angels and trumpets from the original three (I, pp. 218–23). He holds that the sealing in 7:4–8 is not against cosmic phenomena, but against the demonic woes of 8:13–9:21; 11:14 ff (I, p. 218).
[25]Josephus describes the trumpet as a narrow tube about a cubit in length with a mouthpiece wide enough to admit the breath and a bell-shaped extremity (*Ant.* iii.291).

vanced than that portrayed by the initial trumpets. While the first four seals depicted judgments which are the inevitable consequences of human sinfulness, the trumpets reveal the active involvement of God in bringing punishment upon a wicked world.

The church is not in view in the judgments which follow. Its lot in this turbulent period is dealt with in chapters 11–13. While it cannot but be affected by the first four plagues, it is kept from the demonic assaults which follow.[26]

The trumpet-plagues are directed against a world adamant in its hostility toward God. As the intensity of the judgments increases, so also does the vehemence with which man refuses to repent (9:20–21; 16:9, 11, 21). But the trumpet judgments are not final. They affect a significant proportion but not all of the earth (one-third occurs twelve times in vss. 7–12). Their purpose is not so much retribution as to lead men to repentance. Like the watchman and his trumpet in Ezekiel 33, they warn the people of impending danger.

The division of the seven trumpets into groups of four and three (or 4, 2, and 1) is like that of the seals. The four plagues directed toward the world of nature (8:7–13) correspond to the four horsemen (6:1–9). The fifth and sixth of each series is separated from the last by a parenthesis (chap. 7 and 10:1–11:13). Within each sequence there is an increasing severity, with the trumpets going beyond the seals in their more detailed portrayal of the essential conflict between God and evil. It would be unwise to force the scenes which follow into a perfectly consistent pattern. John writes in the exalted idiom of an ecstatic experience. Morris says that it would be a "great mistake to read this fiery, passionate and poetic spirit as though he were composing a pedantic piece of scientific prose" (p. 123). To worry about the prohibition in 9:4 against hurting the grass, when in 8:7 the green grass was already burned up, or about the question of how a great star could fall from heaven in 8:10 when the stars had already fallen in 6:12, is to misunderstand the literary genre in which the Apocalypse is written. As plagues preceded the release of the children of Israel from their Egyptian masters, so also will plagues precede the Exodus of the church from hostile political powers.[27] We are dealing here with that montage of divine judgments upon a recalcitrant world which leads to the return of Jesus Christ as sovereign Lord.

The first angel sounds his trumpet and there follow hail and fire mingled with blood. The imagery comes primarily from the seventh Egyp-

---

[26]9:4 specifically exempts the faithful from the locust plague and 9:20–21 implies they are not under consideration in the second Woe (9:13–21).

[27]Cf. Moffatt (p. 404) for references to the Jewish tradition concerning the disasters which were to preface the second great redemption.

tian plague (Ex 9:13–35). Moses stretched forth his rod toward heaven and God sent down thunder, hail, and "fire flashing continually in the midst of the hail" (Ex 9:24). The reference to blood probably comes from Joel's prophecy of the last days (Joel 2:31; cf. Acts 2:19).[28] The fire which accompanied the violent thunderstorm would be lightning. The blood refers to the awesome color of the storm rather than the fire and destruction which the lightning would cause. The syntax of the verse suggests that the blood-red storm appeared in heaven before it was cast upon the earth. In *Chagigah* 12b the sixth heaven is pictured as a storehouse of hail, storm, and noxious vapors, maintained within gates of fire. The *Sibylline Oracles* speak of a rain of fire and blood as one of the signs of the end (5:377 f).

John's constant use of Jewish material makes it unlikely that his imagery here would arise from the volcanic activity of the Aegean islands. Swete refers to a blood-red rain which fell in Southern Europe in 1901, said to be the result of fine red sand from the Sahara (p. 110).

Great devastation follows in the wake of the storm. A third of the surface of the earth is consumed by fire. In Zechariah 13:8–9 two-thirds of the people of the land are to die and one-third are to be brought through the refiner's fire. In our text it is one-third of the land and its vegetation that is devastated by fire.[29] The fraction would indicate that although God is bringing punishment upon the earth, it is not as yet complete and final.[30] The purpose of the visitation is to warn men of the full wrath of God yet to fall, and in so doing to bring them to repentance. It is the fulfillment of Jesus' prophecy that in the last days there will be signs in the heavens, distress upon the earth, and men fainting for fear of what is about to come upon the world (Lk 21:25–26).

The added references to a third part of the trees and all green grass serve to make more specific the burning of the land.[31] The trees that are destroyed are probably to be taken as fruit trees,[32] which were so important to the maintenance of life in Palestine. Although the plague is directed primarily against nature, it seriously affects mankind as well. The trees and green grass which are burned are within the third of the land surface

---

[28]That this passage may have been in his mind is supported by references to other eschatological features also mentioned by Joel (fire, cf. Rev 8:7, 8, 10 with Joel 2:30, and the darkening of the sun, Rev 8:12 with Joel 2:31).

[29]The thrice-repeated κατεκάη lends to the verse the aura of a prophetic oracle; cf. "For three transgressions . . . and for four" of Amos 1:3, 6, 9, 11, etc.

[30]Ford notes that the predictions of fractions of land being affected were not unknown among the prophets (Ezek 5:12; Zech 13:8–9), the unaffected part being the remnant (pp. 132–40).

[31]In this context γῆ means the land in contrast to the sea (vss. 8–9) and inland waters (vss. 10–11).

[32]δένδρον refers quite normally to fruit trees; cf. Mt 7:17 ("every sound tree bears good fruit") and Jude 12 ("fruitless trees in late autumn").

devastated by fire. The verse is not at variance with 9:4, which prohibits hurting the grass.

8-9 As the first plague scorched a third of the land, the second brings destruction to a third of the sea. With the sounding of the second trumpet something like a great mountain on fire is cast out of heaven and into the sea. A third of the sea becomes blood, with the result that a third of the marine life dies and a third of the shipping is destroyed. This death and destruction take place within the third part of the sea affected by the fiery mass.

In many cases it is difficult, if not impossible, to identify the source of John's imagery. Some find the raw material for this plague in the volcanic action of the area. Less than twenty years before John wrote the Apocalypse, Vesuvius had erupted and destroyed Pompeii and Herculaneum. This catastrophe was widely known and variously interpreted. According to Lilje, Jewish writers regarded it as a divine judgment on Rome for having destroyed Jerusalem (p. 143). Among the volcanic islands of the Aegean, Thera was especially notable. The Greek geographer Strabo reports the formation of a new island as the result of an eruption in 196 BC (i.3.16).

Others look to Jewish apocalyptic for the source of the imagery. *I Enoch* 18:13 speaks of "seven stars like great burning mountains," and the *Sibylline Oracles* (5:158) of a "great star from heaven" which fell into the divine sea.[33] It is well to remember that the visionary experience may take elements from several sources and blend them together into a totally new figure. Although the visions are in essential continuity with the totality of John's experiences (physical, psychic, and spiritual), their ultimate cause is God and not the decision of the Seer to compose a dramatic presentation of the last days. They are visions which he saw.

The mention of fire in each of the first three trumpet-plagues corresponds to the action of the angel-priest of verse 5 who filled his censer with fire from the altar and cast it upon the earth. First there is a violent electrical storm which sets the earth ablaze (vs. 7), then a great fiery mass is cast into the sea (vs. 8), and finally a burning star falls on the inland waters (vs. 10). In the second plague the blazing mountain turns the waters of the sea into blood. Here we are reminded of the first Egyptian plague, in which the rivers were turned to blood, killing the fish and making the water undrinkable (Ex 7:20–21). The plague in Revelation is not to be understood as widespread pollution from volcanic action. Not only did creatures of the

---

[33]Cf. also *I Enoch* 21:3 ff; 108:3–6. On the basis of these verses Rist suggests that the burning mountain of Rev may represent a fallen angel expelled from heaven to wreak destruction on the world (pp. 428–29).

sea die, but shipping was destroyed as well. It represents an eschatological judgment which goes beyond any explanation in terms of natural phenomena. Again the judgment is partial. It affects but one-third of the sea, its life and commerce. The purpose is to warn and lead to repentance.

10–11 The third plague consists of a burning star which falls from heaven upon the inland waters, turning them bitter and causing the death of many men. This contamination of the fresh water supply recalls the first Egyptian plague in which the water was turned to blood (Ex 7:20). That the star which pollutes the waters falls from heaven is a way of saying that God is the active agent in bringing the plague. The figure is that of a great meteorite set afire as it plunges through the earth's atmosphere.[34] Like the blood-red storm and the burning mountain, it is a symbol of divine visitation. God is beginning to move in judgment, and man must repent or bear the full fury of his coming wrath. Some writers note a similar phenomenon in Persian eschatology, but Charles is right in denying any real parallel (I, p. 235).[35]

The star falls upon a third part of the rivers and the fountains of water.[36] It is possible that John may be revealing divine displeasure against the rather widespread worship of supernatural spirits thought to be associated with rivers and springs.[37] Like the other plagues, however, it is directed primarily against the world of nature. Only indirectly does it affect man or the spirit world.

The star is named for the effect it has on the water. It is called Wormwood after the strong bitter taste of the plant of that name. In the OT wormwood was used as a symbol of bitterness and sorrow. Proverbs warns against the strange woman whose lips drop honey but in the end is "bitter as wormwood" (Prov. 5:3–4). The writer of Lamentations prays, "Remember my affliction and my bitterness, the wormwood and the gall!" (Lam 3:19). Because Israel has forsaken God, he will "feed [them] with wormwood, and give them poisonous water to drink" (Jer 9:15; cf. Jer 23:15).[38]

Although the text says "the waters became wormwood," we are to understand that they became as bitter as wormwood. It is the reverse of the miracle at Marah where Moses cast a tree into the bitter waters and they

---

[34]Shooting stars and meteorites were considered omens of destruction in the ancient world.
[35]Cf. Beckwith (p. 557) and Moffatt (p. 405) for references to the secondary literature.
[36]Vs. 11 indicates that it was *one-third* rather than *all* of the waters (which could be inferred from the final clause of vs. 10) which was affected by the plague.
[37]Moffatt notes that springs would appear somewhat mysterious to the ancient mind and, rising from the subterranean abyss, could have demonic associations (p. 405).
[38]Caird's suggestion that "Wormwood is the star of the new Babylon which has poisoned by its idolatry the springs of its own life" (p. 115) is ingenious but overly subtle.

were made sweet (Ex 15:25). Although wormwood itself is not poisonous, its bitter taste suggests death.[39] What John is saying is that a portion of the inland waters were contaminated by a spectacular act of God and many men died as a result of drinking the water. Repetition of the fractional one-third indicates as before the restricted scope of the judgment. "Many men" rather than "the third part of men" is no more than a stylistic alteration.

12 When the fourth angel sounded his trumpet, a third of the sun, moon, and stars were struck with a blow[40] that darkened them for a third of the day and the night. The first part of the verse, when interpreted in parallel with the other plagues, seems to indicate a decrease in the intensity of available light as a result of a third of the luminaries being darkened. The last two phrases, however, indicate the total absence of light for a third part of both day and night. This absolute darkness would be far more terrifying than a partial eclipse. The scene recalls the ninth Egyptian plague with its thick darkness that spread over the land for a period of three days (Ex 10:21–23). Constant allusion to the Egyptian plagues is a way of saying that in the last days God will again bring punishment upon those hostile powers which oppress his people. They are the prelude to that great and final Exodus in which the church is taken out of the world and enters into the eternal presence of God.

Darkness as a symbol of judgment runs throughout the OT. The prophet Amos spoke of the day of the Lord as a day of darkness rather than light (Amos 5:18). For Joel it will be a "day of darkness and gloom, a day of clouds and thick darkness!" (Joel 2:2). Jesus, quoting Isaiah, says that in the day of the Lord "the sun will be darkened, and the moon will not give its light" (Mk 13:24; cf. Isa 13:10). The fourth trumpet-plague is a fulfillment of these prophecies.

In the NT darkness is often connected with the demonic. Unbelieving Israel is to be cast into outer darkness where there is weeping and gnashing of teeth (Mt 8:12). In II Corinthians 6:14–15 light and darkness stand parallel to Christ and Belial. According to Colossians 1:13 the saints are those who have been delivered out of the power of darkness (cf. Col 2:13–15). The darkness of the fourth plague anticipates the transition from divine warnings to demonic woes. It previews that ultimate excommunica-

---

[39]Fresh water was of prime importance in times of ancient warfare. The poisoning of water had military significance; cf. Y. Yadin, *The Art of Warfare in Biblical Lands,* II, pp. 320–22.
[40]πλήσσω (only here in the NT) is used in Ex 9:31–32 (LXX) of the devastating effects of hail upon crops standing in the field. Cf. Ps 102:4 (101:4, LXX), "My heart is smitten (ἐπλήγην), like grass, and withered."

tion of unrepentant man to the punishment prepared for the devil and his angels (Mt 25:41).

3. EAGLE'S WARNING (8:13)

13 *And I saw, and I heard an eagle, flying in mid heaven, saying with a great voice, Woe, woe, woe, for them that dwell on the earth, by reason of the other voices of the trumpet of the three angels, who are yet to sound.*

13 Verse 13 serves as a transition between the four plagues brought by God upon nature to lead man to repentance and the subsequent demonic woes in which man will be directly subjected to the forces of the abyss. Previous plagues have been called forth by angelic beings, but those which follow are announced quite appropriately by a bird of prey[41] hovering overhead. The majority of commentators understand the bird to be an eagle, which figure suggests such qualities as strength and swiftness. In *II Baruch* an eagle is commissioned to fly without tarrying to the Jews exiled in Babylon and deliver an account of the author's vision (*II Bar.* 77:17–26). II Esdras records a vision of a three-headed eagle with twelve wings that reigned over all the earth (II Esdr 11–12). Others understand the bird to be a vulture,[42] which in this context would symbolize impending doom. Habakkuk described the invading Chaldeans as vultures which hasten to devour (Hab 1:8). In either case it is the predatory nature of the bird that is in view. In 19:17–18 the birds of prey (those that "fly in mid heaven"; cf. 8:13) are gathered to eat the flesh of kings and men.

The vulture hovers in mid-heaven so as to be seen by all, and cries out in a great voice[43] so none will fail to hear, "Woe, woe, woe, for them that dwell on the earth." While in chapter 18 the exclamation "Woe" is twice repeated for emphasis on each of three occasions (18:10, 16, 19), here it occurs three times to correspond to the three last trumpets. These final plagues are not to fall upon the church but upon a pagan and wicked world.[44]

---

[41]The *AV* follows **P** 1 2059s *al* TR, which read ἀγγέλου rather than ἀετοῦ (perhaps suggested by ἀγγελον πετόμενον in 14:6) and translate "an angel." 42 Prim read ἀγγέλου ὡς ἀετοῦ.
[42]ἀετός may be used for the vulture as well as the eagle. Goodspeed translates Lk 17:37, "Wherever there is a dead body the vultures (ἀετοί) will flock."
[43]104 2037 *al* add τρίς after λέγοντος φωνῇ μεγάλῃ ("shrieking loudly three times," Ford, p. 134).
[44]Cf. comm. on 6:10 for "them that dwell on the earth" as a semi-technical designation of man in his wickedness. 9:4 indicates that the locusts are to torment only those who have not been sealed by God. 9:20 implies the same for the second Woe.

The first two Woes follow immediately in chapter 9. They are the fifth and sixth trumpet-plagues. The third Woe is postponed by two major visions in 19:1–11:13. But even then when the last trumpet sounds (11:14–15), we do not immediately learn of the nature of the third Woe. Instead there is a scene of heavenly adulation (11:15–19). For this reason some think that the third Woe is the descent of Satan in 12:7 ff. In 12:12 a great voice from heaven says, "Woe to you, O earth and sea, for the devil has come down to you in great wrath, because he knows that his time is short!" Others take the bowl judgments of chapter 16 to be the third Woe. This, however, would separate in kind the first two (demonic assaults) from the third (judgments of God).

CHAPTER 9

John required but six verses to set forth the first four trumpet-plagues (8:7–12). But now he is about to devote an entire chapter to the first two Woes. This additional attention corresponds to the seriousness of the calamities which follow. Men who were earlier discomforted by judgments upon the world of nature are now directly subjected to torments which arise from the underworld.

4. FIFTH TRUMPET (FIRST WOE): DEMONIC LOCUSTS (9:1–12)

1 *And the fifth angel sounded, and I saw a star from heaven fallen unto the earth: and there was given to him the key of the pit of the abyss.*

2 *And he opened the pit of the abyss; and there went up a smoke out of the pit, as the smoke of a great furnace; and the sun and the air were darkened by reason of the smoke of the pit.*

3 *And out of the smoke came forth locusts upon the earth; and power was given them, as the scorpions of the earth have power.*

4 *And it was said unto them that they should not hurt the grass of the earth, neither any green thing, neither any tree, but only such men as have not the seal of God on their foreheads.*

5 *And it was given them that they should not kill them, but that they should be tormented five months: and their torment was as the torment of a scorpion, when it striketh a man.*

6 *And in those days men shall seek death, and shall in no wise find it; and they shall desire to die, and death fleeth from them.*

7 *And the shapes of the locusts were like unto horses prepared for war; and upon their heads as it were crowns like unto gold, and their faces were as men's faces.*

8 *And they had hair as the hair of women, and their teeth were as the teeth of lions.*

9 *And they had breastplates, as it were breastplates of iron; and the sound*

of their wings was as the sound of chariots, of many horses rushing to war.

10 *And they have tails like unto scorpions, and stings; and in their tails is their power to hurt men five months.*

11 *They have over them as king the angel of the abyss: his name in Hebrew is Abaddon, and in the Greek tongue he hath the name Apollyon.*

12 *The first Woe is past: behold, there come yet two Woes hereafter.*

1 When the fifth angel sounded his trumpet, John saw a star which had just fallen[1] from heaven to earth. The star in 8:10 which fell from heaven and contaminated the waters was a mass of molten material. This star, however, is a person, for he receives a key (vs. 1) and with it opens the pit of the abyss (vs. 2). In Isaiah 14:12 the king of Babylon is portrayed as a day-star fallen from heaven. *I Enoch* 21:6 depicts the fallen angels as "stars of heaven which have transgressed the commandment of the Lord." In the NT Jesus told the seventy as they returned from their preaching mission that he had seen "Satan fall like lightning [a blazing comet?] from heaven" (Lk 10:18). Jewish thought readily symbolized living beings as stars. Many expositors take the next step and concede that in Jewish thought the stars were held to be celestial spirits possessing conscious personalities. The usual passages cited in support of this position are Judges 5:20 ("From heaven fought the stars, from their courses they fought against Sisera") and Job 38:7 ("When the morning stars sang together"). In that both verses occur in poetic sections it would seem unwise to press upon them such a literal interpretation. Elsewhere Israel is sternly warned against worshipping stellar deities (Deut 4:19; Jer 7:18).

The one symbolized by the star has been variously identified.[2] Some, interpreting the phrase "from heaven *fallen*" in a theological sense, take the star to be a fallen angel. This is strengthened by reference to the nefarious nature of his activity (unlocking the shaft of the abyss and releasing its demonic hordes). Perhaps he is one of the stars of heaven swept down to earth by the tail of the great red dragon (12:4).[3] It is more likely, however, that the star-angel is simply one of the many divine agents who throughout the book of Revelation are pictured as carrying out the will of God. Charles shows that when applied to stars symbolizing angels, "to fall" means no more than "to descend" (I, pp. 238–39). Furthermore, his role is not essentially different from that of the fifth trumpet-angel at whose

---

[1]Taking πεπτωκότα as a dramatic perfect; cf. Dana and Mantey, *Grammar*, pp. 204–5.
[2]Cf. Morris, p. 127, for a convenient summary.
[3]Some identify him more closely as Abaddon, the angel of the abyss (9:11). Others suggest Satan.

call the action begins. He is probably the same angel who in 20:1 comes down out of heaven with the key of the abyss.[4]

2 The key which is given to the angel unlocks the shaft leading down into a subterranean chasm called the abyss. When the shaft is opened, out pour great clouds of smoke. Then from the smoke come evil spirits who have been imprisoned in the abyss. Their mission is to torment all mankind who have not the seal of God on their foreheads. While there is no specific indication in Revelation that the abyss is a place of torment, the rising smoke would normally be thought of as coming from fires below. According to Enoch the final prison of the fallen angels was the abyss, a horrible place with "great descending columns of fire" (*I Enoch* 21:7; cf. 18:11).[5] Of the nine NT references to the abyss, seven are found in Revelation. It is inhabited by the "scorpion centaurs" of chapter 9, their demonic prince (9:11), and the beast of the abyss (11:7; 17:8). It is also the place of Satan's imprisonment during the thousand-year period (20:1–3). Luke 8:31 reflects the fear of the evil spirits lest they be sent to this terrible place. In Romans 10:7 it appears to be the place of the dead, although in the NT this is usually designated as Hades (Acts 2:27).

The dense clouds of smoke which rise up out of the abyss recall the scene of God's descent upon Mt. Sinai. Exodus 19:18 says that the smoke of the mountain rose "as the smoke of a furnace" (*ASV*).[6] As the smoke rises, it blots out the sun and darkens the atmosphere of the earth.[7] Joel 2:10 tells of a plague of locusts which darkened the sun and the moon. In Revelation 8:12 the luminaries were darkened as a direct act of God; here it is effected by the tremendous quantity of smoke which pours up out of the abyss.[8]

3 Out of the billowing smoke come locusts upon the earth. Back of this picture are two scenes from the OT. Exodus 10:1–20 tells of the plague of locusts which devoured all vegetation throughout the land of Egypt. Joel 1:2–2:11 interprets the devastation of Israel by locusts as a portent of the destruction which will come with the day of the Lord (Joel 1:15; 2:1, 11). Throughout the OT the locust is a symbol of destruction

---

[4]In *I Enoch* 19:1; 20:2 it is the archangel Uriel who is in charge of the abyss.

[5]Cf. Charles (I, pp. 240–41) for a discussion of the abyss in *Enoch*. The background for this figure could be the volcano belching forth smoke and fire from below.

[6]The LXX reads ὡσεὶ καπνὸς καμίνου.

[7]ὁ ἀήρ in this context has no meaningful connection with Eph 2:2, which speaks of a spirit being who has control over τοῦ ἀέρος.

[8]The omission of two six-word clauses, καὶ ἤνοιξεν ... ἀβύσσου (ℵ **046** 82 205 1611 2053 *al* vg^pc sy^ph sa(2) bo) and ἐκ τοῦ καπνοῦ τοῦ φρέατος. καὶ (ℵ* *pc* Prim), seems to have resulted from attempts to prevent redundancy. The substitution of καιομένης for μεγάλης (**046** 82 104 *pm*) is understandable.

(Deut 28:42; I Kgs 8:37; Ps 78:46). Bred in the desert, they invade cultivated areas in search of food. They may travel in a column a hundred feet
deep and up to four miles in length, leaving the land stripped bare of all
vegetation.[9] The cloud of smoke is not the swarm of locusts. The locusts
come out of the smoke. Moffatt envisions a shifting vision in which "the
dense smoke resolves itself into a swarm of infernal demons in the form of
locusts" (p. 406).

To the locusts is given a scorpion-like power to torment those who
dwell upon the earth. Their poisonous strike does not kill but causes men
such torment that they seek death (vss. 5–6). The scorpion was well known
in Palestine. A lobster-like vermin some four or five inches long, it had a
claw on the end of the tail that secreted a poison when it struck.[10] Hiding
under stones or in the chinks of a wall by day, it would move out at night to
feed on small living animals. It should be noted that the demonic locusts of
the first Woe have the power rather than the appearance of scorpions.

4 The locusts are told not to injure the vegetation of earth but
only[11] those who do not bear the seal of God. We are not told who it is that
issues the prohibition. The use of the passive voice in speaking of the
release (vs. 1, "there was given"), the empowering (vs. 3, "power was
given them"), and the limiting (vs. 5, "it was given them that they should
not kill") of the locusts suggests that this plague, even though demonic, is
under the sovereign control of God. Throughout the Apocalypse he is the
"Lord God Almighty" (4:8; 11:17; 15:3; 16:7; 21:22).

In the Egyptian plague (as well as in Joel) the fields and trees were
laid bare by the swarming locusts (Ex 10:15; Joel 2:3). The locusts of
John's vision have a different mission. Their destructive power is not
directed against the grass, the green herbs, or the leaves of trees, but
against wicked men. Of all those upon the earth during this perilous time
only the Christians will escape the demonic assault, for they alone have
"the seal of God on their foreheads" (cf. 7:1–8).[12] As the children of Israel
were protected from the plagues which fell upon the Egyptians,[13] so also
will the new Israel escape the torments which are to arise from the abyss.

---

[9]Barclay notes that in 1866 there were 200,000 people who perished of famine following a
plague of locusts invading Algiers (II, p. 60). Cf. the excursus on Palestinian locusts in S. R.
Driver's commentary on Joel in *Cambridge Bible for Schools and Colleges*, pp. 82 ff.

[10]Ladd (p. 131) notes that "the scorpion, like the snake, was a creature hostile to man and so
became a symbol of the forces of spiritual evil (Lk 10:19; *Sirach* 39:29)."

[11]2053 *pc* vg arm TR add μόνους after ἀνθρώπους.

[12]That this fifth trumpet is necessarily subsequent to the sealing which follows the sixth seal
makes any precise recapitulation impossible.

[13]Specifically mentioned in Ex 8:22; 9:4, 26: 10:23; and 11:7 ("that you may know that the
Lord makes a distinction between the Egyptians and Israel").

5   The mission of the demonic locusts is to inflict suffering upon the wicked. They are not to kill but to torment.[14] Their torment is limited to a period of five months.[15] This period has been variously explained. It may have been determined by the life cycle of the locust, which is of five months' duration. It corresponds as well to the dry season (spring through late summer) in which the danger of a locust invasion is always present.[16] Whatever the source of the number, it represents a limited period of time during which men in torment may yet turn from their wickedness and repent (cf. vss. 20-21). The plague is not an act of wanton cruelty but a stark indication that wickedness cannot continue indefinitely without divine retribution.

6   Speaking as a prophet, John foretells that in those days men will actively seek release from torment through death yet find that it is impossible to die.[17] Job's remarks about the miserable and bitter longing for death that seems never to come (Job 3:20-22) are rhetorical rather than descriptive of a scene such as here portrayed. In the eschatological plague it will not be despondency but actual pain which drives men earnestly to desire death.[18] It is ironic that in that day death, which the wicked inflicted upon Christian martyrs, will be eagerly desired, yet men will find that it "keeps running from them" (Morris, p. 129).[19] What a dramatic contrast to Paul's desire "to depart and be with Christ" (Phil 1:23)! For one, death leads to eternal blessing; for the other, it is an "escape" from torment on earth to torture in the lake of fire.

7   Up to this point we have learned of the origin and mission of the demonic locusts. Now John describes them. Long-haired, horse-shaped, flying locusts with scorpion tails and golden crowns above human faces marred by lion's teeth, they have to be reckoned among the more bizarre creatures in the Apocalypse. The total impact is one of unnatural and awesome cruelty. It will be well to exercise considerable reserve in treating

---

[14]Here as elsewhere in Rev βασανίζω carries the idea of punishment: 11:10; 14:10; 20:10 (12:2 is an exception). The cognate noun βασανισμός has the same connotation (14:11; 18:7, 10, 15).

[15]Prim reads ἕξ.

[16]Ford cites an "interesting interpretation" by S. Giet in which the first four seals point to troubles preceding the Jewish War and the five months' period of torment by the monstrous locusts reflects "the five months during which the troops of Gessius Florus cast terror over Palestine" (p. 149).

[17]Jer 8:3 is not relevant. Death there refers to corpses that have been unearthed, not the desire to die.

[18]For the idea of death as preferable to life in the writings of Greek and Roman poets cf. Swete, p. 117. Barclay (II, p. 62) quotes Cornelius Gallus as saying, "Worse than any wound is the wish to die and yet not be able to do so."

[19]Robertson (*Word Pictures*, VI, p. 363) calls φεύγει a "vivid futuristic present." Alford (p. 641) says the present tense indicates the *habitual* avoidance of death in those days.

the details which make up the larger picture. Kiddle is probably right in saying that "John's account is so straightforward and vivid that comment is superfluous" (p. 158).

The locusts appear to be shaped like horses.[20] John apparently would have us understand the locusts to be of considerable size. Otherwise the description of hair, face, teeth, etc. would tend toward the comic. The Seer draws from Joel's account of swarming locusts who appear as horses (Joel 2:4) and whose sound is like the noise of chariots in battle or the raging fury of a prairie fire (Joel 2:5). The details of the description, however, are largely his own. Most commentators note the similarity between the head of the locust and that of the horse. An Arabian proverb is often quoted to the effect that the locust has a head like a horse, a breast like a lion, feet like a camel, body like a serpent, and antennae like the hair of a maiden. This likeness accounts for the word for locust in German (*Heupferd,* hay-horse) and in Italian (*cavalletta,* little horse). That they were prepared for war may indicate either the eagerness with which they sprang forth to inflict punishment or the protective armament described in verse 9. It does not specifically say they were wearing golden crowns, but the symbolism is the same—they possessed the power to carry through their mission to a victorious end.[21] The faces of the locusts were as men's faces. When John looked directly into the face of the advancing horde, he did not see the rather torpid expression of the animal world but the highly intelligent cunning and cruelty of demonic beings. Man and beast are combined in a figure both unnatural and diabolical.

8 The locusts were covered with long, flowing hair. When they opened their jaws they revealed the teeth of lions. It is doubtful that the mention of hair has any reference to the two relatively short organs of sensation which protrude from the head of the locust (called antennae). Less likely is any reference to the long hair of the Parthian warriors, which would stream out behind them as they rode into battle. If we need a point of contact it would probably be the hair on the legs or bodies of the locusts, which in flight would emphasize the speed with which they carry forth their mission. The idea that it symbolizes seductiveness ignores the overall grotesque appearance of the locust. That both Samson (Judg 16:13, 19) and

---

[20]This point is softened somewhat in the *RSV* translation of τὰ ὁμοιώματα by "in appearance."

[21]The golden crowns may have been suggested by the yellowish color of their breasts. Ford thinks the image may have come from the bronze helmets of the Roman legionnaires, which were burnished with gold (p. 151). The plural, χρυσοῖ (read by **046 0207** 82 94 *pm*), is rare and less strongly supported than ὅμοιοι χρυσῷ (Metzger, *TCGNT,* p. 743).

Absalom (II Sam 14:25–26) wore their hair long should show that long hair may be a symbol of vitality rather than femininity.

In Joel 1:6 the invading nation is pictured as having the teeth of a lion and the jaw-teeth of a lioness. In John's vision the teeth emphasize the fierceness of the locusts. Yet they do not tear apart their victims as would the lion. Their torment was inflicted by scorpion-like tails (vs. 10).

9 The locusts were protected with breastplates of iron, indicating that there was no possible way of striking back in a vulnerable spot. The scaly exterior of the locust resembled a coat of mail.[22] In flight they sounded like a great phalanx of horses and chariots rushing into war.[23]

10 Once again John points out the scorpion-like tails of the locusts and their ability to inflict pain for five months (cf. vss. 3, 5). More significant than the awesome appearance of the horde is their power to punish. The shift to the present tense ("they have"; cf. verbs in vss. 7–9) adds to the vividness of the description. Tails "like unto scorpions" means tails like those of scorpions. The description is not parallel with 9:19 where the horses' tails are like serpents and have heads. As the scorpion holds its prey with its claws and kills with a venomous tail, so the apocalyptic locusts possess an agonizing sting.[24] They do not kill but torment. Their purpose is to bring men to repentance (vss. 20–21).

Many commentators interpret the plague as a condition of sinful life rather than an eschatological event. Hendriksen sees the description as "the operation of the powers of darkness in the soul of the wicked during this present age" (p. 147). For Hengstenberg it is the hellish spirit that penetrates the earth (I, pp. 429 ff), and for Dana, the forces of decay and corruption which God will use to undermine the Roman Empire (pp. 126 ff). While the major motifs of the consummation are reflected many times throughout history, the visions of John have as their primary focus the ultimate conflict of God and Satan which brings history to its close.

11 The advancing army of locusts have as their king the angel of the abyss. This angel is not the fallen star of verse 1 who unlocks the abyss. Nor is he the archangel Uriel, who according to *I Enoch* 20:2 has authority

---

[22]Goliath wore a θώρακα ἀλυσιδωτόν, a breastplate of chain-mail (I Sam 17:5).

[23]The genitives ἁρμάτων and ἵππων are not coordinate; cf. the *RSV*, "the noise of many chariots with horses." ἵππων is omitted by 325 2031 *pc*. For reference to large chariot forces cf. I Sam 13:5 (30,000) and I Chron 19:7 (32,000). In I Macc 6:43 war elephants were protected by wearing coats of mail. A charge by elephants equipped in this way would make a terrible din.

[24]κέντρον is used in Acts 26:14 for the goad used in directing oxen and in I Cor 15:55 for the sting of death. The whip in I Kgs 12:11 was called a scorpion because of the severe pain of the animal's bite.

over Tartarus.[25] These are messengers of God, not leaders of the opposition. Since he is nowhere specifically identified, we should probably understand the designation "king" as no more than a detail in the larger scene of organized assault. It is unlikely that Satan would be introduced into the visions at this point in such an indefinite manner (cf. chap. 12).

The name of the king of the abyss is in Hebrew, Abaddon. In the OT Abaddon refers to destruction (Job 31:12) or the place of destruction.[26] The personification of destruction in Job 28:22 could give rise quite naturally to the idea of a prince of the underworld, appropriately named Abaddon.[27] In case the reader did not grasp the significance of the Hebrew name, John adds its Greek equivalent—Apollyon, Destroyer. Farrer notes the John used *Apollyōn* (Destroyer) rather than *Apōleia* (Destruction) because he wanted a concrete masculine rather than a feminine abstract (p. 119). Many commentators feel that the verse contains a derogatory reference to the Greek god Apollo and those emperors who claimed a special relationship to him. To name the king of the underworld Apollyon would be a cryptic way of saying that an emperor such as Domitian who liked to be regarded as Apollo incarnate was in reality a manifestation of the powers of the underworld. As early as the fifth century BC, the Greeks had derived the name of Apollo from the same Greek verb which is the root of Apollyon.[28] The allusion is strengthened by the observation that the locust was one of the symbols of the god Apollo. Beasley-Murray says that if John had in mind the fact that both Caligula and Nero aped the deity of Apollo and Domitian claimed to be his incarnation, "His last word about the fifth trumpet was a master stroke of irony: the destructive host of hell had as its king the emperor of Rome!" (pp. 162–63).

12 Lest the reader think that with the release of the demonic locusts the plagues have somehow been exhausted, John now announces that only the first Woe is past. There are yet two to come. Phillips' translation catches the vividness of the scene, "The first disaster is now past, but I see two more approaching." As the end draws near, there is a marked increase in the intensity and severity of the trumpet-plagues.

There can be no specific answer to the question of exactly who or what is symbolized by the plague of locusts. All we can know for sure is that in the period immediately before the end the wicked will be subjected

---

[25]Uriel, whose name means "Fire of God," is "the archangel of fire and of Gehenna, where flame is the chief element" (*Jewish Encyclopedia*, XII, p. 383).

[26]It is parallel with Sheol in Job 26:6; Prov 15:11; 27:20; with Death in Job 28:22; and with the grave in Ps 88:11.

[27]Cf. Jeremias on Ἀβαδδών in *TDNT*, I, p. 4. P⁴⁷ reads βάττων (βάττος, the stammerer, was a king of Cyrene), and the Bohairic reads Μακεδών, a Macedonian.

[28]ἀπόλλυμι, (Aeschylus, *Agam.* 1082).

198

to a time of unprecedented demonic torment. Exactly how this will take place will remain unknown until disclosed by history itself.[29]

5. SIXTH TRUMPET (SECOND WOE): FIENDISH CAVALRY (9:13–21)

13 *And the sixth angel sounded, and I heard a voice from the horns of the golden altar which is before God,*

14 *one saying to the sixth angel that had the trumpet, Loose the four angels that are bound at the great river Euphrates.*

15 *And the four angels were loosed, that had been prepared for the hour and day and month and year, that they should kill the third part of men.*

16 *And the number of the armies of the horsemen was twice ten thousand times ten thousand: I heard the number of them.*

17 *And thus I saw the horses in the vision, and them that sat on them, having breastplates as of fire and of hyacinth and of brimstone: and the heads of the horses are as the heads of lions; and out of their mouths proceedeth fire and smoke and brimstone.*

18 *By these three plagues was the third part of men killed, by the fire and the smoke and the brimstone, which proceeded out of their mouths.*

19 *For the power of the horses is in their mouth, and in their tails: for their tails are like unto serpents, and have heads; and with them they hurt.*

20 *And the rest of mankind, who were not killed with these plagues, repented not of the works of their hands, that they should not worship demons, and the idols of gold, and of silver, and of brass, and of stone, and of wood; which can neither see, nor hear, nor walk:*

21 *and they repented not of their murders, nor of their sorceries, nor of their fornication, nor of their thefts.*

13–14   When the sixth angel sounds his trumpet, a voice is heard from the golden altar which commands the release of the four angels of destruction who have been temporarily restrained at the eastern boundary of the empire. The voice could be that of the angel-priest of 8:3–5 who presented the prayers of the saints to God upon the golden altar. Or it could be the prayers themselves with their unified concern[30] for vindication (cf. 6:9). In either case John is recalling the fundamental truth that the prayers of God's

---

[29]That vs. 12 ends with μετὰ ταῦτα has caused considerable textual alteration. A number of MSS read the words with the following vs., either moving the initial καί or omitting it (cf. Metzger, *TCGNT*, p. 743).

[30]φωνὴν μίαν means a "single or solitary voice." Here it is appropriately used of the universal desire of the church. Textual variants indicate confusion as to the identity of the voice. λέγοντα (vs. 14), read by ℵ* **A,** is the preferred reading; λέγουσαν (**P**[47] **P 0207** 1 *pm* TR) would take φωνήν as an antecedent, while λέγοντος (**046** 82 1006 2329 *al*) would take θυσιαστηρίου.

people play an active role in the eschatological drama. The voice does not proceed out of the horns or corners of the altar but from the altar itself.[31] This same personification occurs in 16:7 where the altar declares the judgments of God to be true and righteous. That it is "before God" is a reminder that divine retribution is a personal act of the One whose sovereignty and love have been rejected by man.

Only here does one of the trumpet-angels become involved in the event which he heralds. Having sounded the trumpet, the sixth angel is now to unleash the four angels of destruction. Attempts to identify the four angels[32] with any definiteness have not been successful. Apparently they are not mentioned elsewhere in apocalyptic writings. A few commentators suggest a connection with the four restraining angels of 7:1. This earlier group, however, was stationed at the four corners of the world (rather than being bound at the Euphrates, 9:14), and held back the winds of destruction (rather than being released to bring about destruction, 9:15).[33] Beckwith suggests as a probable source a familiar apocalyptic tradition in which four destructive powers are connected with the four quarters of the earth (p. 567).[34] In our immediate text the four angels appear to be in charge of the limitless horde of demonic horsemen who ride across the pagan world spreading terror and death. They correspond to the king of the locusts in 9:11 and like him seem to disappear into the demonic forces they release.

When God made a covenant with Abram, he promised him and his seed the land which stretched from the Nile to the Euphrates[35] (Gen 15:18; cf. Deut 11:24; Josh 1:4). The Euphrates marked the boundary (the "ideal limit," Driver) between Israel and her chief enemies. In Isaiah 8:5–8 the invading armies of Assyria are pictured as a mighty flood in which the great river overflows its banks and sweeps over Judah. The Euphrates was also the eastern boundary of the Roman Empire, and the mention of invading horsemen from that quarter would immediately suggest the much feared Parthian warriors. Caird speaks of the "Roman neurosis about Parthia" which began with the defeat of Crassus in 53 BC and deepened with the disgraceful capitulation of Vologeses in AD 62 (p. 122). But John

[31]Understanding ἐκ [μέσου] τῶν τεσσάρων κεράτων; cf. Mt 17:45. For the horns of the altar of incense, cf. Ex 30:2, 10. External evidence is evenly divided for the inclusion or omission of τεσσάρων. The UBS committee included it in square brackets. Metzger notes that it may have been added to make an antithesis with φωνὴν μίαν or a parallel with τοὺς τέσσαρας ἀγγέλους (of vs. 14) or accidentally omitted because of similarity with the following κεράτων (TCGNT, p. 744).

[32]P47 omits τέσσαρας.

[33]Cf. Kiddle (pp. 161–63) for arguments supporting the identification.

[34]Cf. the "four winds of heaven" in Zech 6:5; Dan 7:2; and the four angels with torches in II Bar. 6:4.

[35]The Euphrates is the longest river in western Asia, some 1700 miles.

is not describing a Parthian invasion. While his imagery is freely drawn from sources both secular and sacred, he weaves it into an eschatological tapestry uniquely his own. The 200,000,000 demonic horsemen and their plague of death is an eschatological event of fantastic proportions. To restrict John to his sources is to misunderstand the nature of apocalyptic.

15 The four angels are loosed for the purpose of killing a third of the world's population. The torment of the first Woe gives way to the widespread massacre of the second. Under the fourth seal a fourth part of mankind was put to death (6:8). Now a third more are to be killed by the demonic cavalry as they sweep across the earth. As in the previous Woe, so also here, believers are to be spared (9:4, 20–21). The assault is directed against "them that dwell on the earth," a standard designation of man in his hostility to God.[36] Ladd draws attention to an important distinction between John's version and similar expectations of prophets and apocalyptists: "The latter always envision the foreign invasion as an attack against the people of God by pagan hosts while John sees it as a divine judgment upon a corrupt civilization" (p. 135).

The four angels are said to have been prepared for this specific moment. The use of the perfect tense[37] strengthens the idea of their existing in a state of readiness. In apocalyptic thought God has fixed the exact time for every event (cf. *I Enoch* 92:2). The use of a single article for all four time designations tends to focus attention upon the specific moment of God's appointment. The ascending order (hour, day, month, year) is of no particular significance. At the exact moment decreed by God the angels of destruction and their demonic horde will be released upon mankind. All the forces of history are under the sovereign control of God. He is the Almighty One (1:8; 4:8; 11:7; 19:15; etc.).

16 Quite abruptly we learn of an unbelievably large cavalry force about to invade the land. The number which John *hears*—who could count such a throng!— is twice $10,000 \times 10,000$. Attempts to reduce this expression to arithmetic miss the point. A "double myriad of myriads" is an indefinite number of incalculable immensity.[38] Reference to a *Time* article which reports the People's Republic of China as having a militia of 200,000,000 men and women is interesting but no special help (Walvoord, p. 166, n. 13). John's eschatological steeds breathe out fire and brim-

---

[36]Cf. comm. on 6:10 and 8:13.

[37]ἡτοιμασμένοι. Cf. Mt 25:34 where the king invites the sheep to inherit the kingdom prepared (ἡτοιμασμένην) for them, and the reference a few verses later to the eternal fire prepared (ἡτοιμασμένον) for the devil and his angels (vs. 41).

[38]BAG, p. 198 under δισμυριάς. The source of the number seems to be Ps 68:17 where the chariots of God are said to be "thousands upon thousands" (cf. Dan 7:10; Rev 5:11).

stone and have serpent-like tails with lethal heads (vss. 18-19). They spread out as far as the eye can see. Who could escape the onslaught of such a gigantic force! The specter of a huge hostile cavalry had always been a source of terror for the Jewish people. In the *Assumption of Moses* we read of a king from the east (Nebuchadnezzar) who comes against them and whose "cavalry shall cover their land" (3:2). The Parthian threat would intensify this fear. Thus the figure of a great army of horsemen riding in from beyond their boundaries supplies the vivid imagery for John's second Woe.

17 Only here in the book of Revelation does John specifically indicate that his revelations are being mediated to him in a vision.[39] The remark is not a "superfluous addition" (Beckwith, p. 568) but an indication that his descriptions are apt to be highly symbolic in nature.

While it is possible to interpret the verse as indicating that both the riders and their mounts wore breastplates,[40] it is better to limit the armor to the riders alone. The breastplates were of red, blue, and yellow to match the fire, smoke, and brimstone that was coming out of the mouths of the horses. It is difficult to determine whether the breastplates were of three colors each or whether each breastplate was of a single color (some red, some blue, some yellow). In either case the overall impression would be the same. Swete apparently feels that the breastplates were actually made of fire (p. 123).[41] While the Greek text would allow this, it seems unnecessarily literal. Hyacinth normally referred to the deep blue color of the jacinth, but here it probably indicates the "dusky blue colour as of sulphurous smoke" (MM, p. 647). Brimstone is what is known today as sulphur, hence yellow.

It should be noted that the riders play no active part in carrying out the plague. This is accomplished by the horses. Their description in the following verses is grotesque to say the least. Beasley-Murray says, "The picture is meant to be inconceivable, horrifying, and even revolting" (p. 165). Perhaps the most terrifying aspect of the horses is their lion's head (cf. the lion's teeth of the locusts in the preceding vision, 9:8), which symbolizes cruelty and destruction. From their mouths proceed fire, smoke, and brimstone. This feature argues their demonic origin. It does not symbolize the tanks, cannons, and battleships of modern warfare (Hendrik-

---

[39] ὅρασις in 4:3 refers to the appearance of what is seen.

[40] Moffatt (p. 409) notes that in the Persian heavy cavalry both horses and horsemen were clad in bright plate. Cf. also Alford (p. 646) and Beckwith (p. 568). The horse-shaped locusts of 9:9 had θώρακας σιδηροῦς.

[41] Swete notes that πύρινος is properly "of fire" while πυρρός is "flame-coloured." Ps 103:4 is quoted in support.

sen, p. 148; cf. Walvoord, p. 167). The plague anticipates the eternal torment which awaits the devil (20:10), his demonic cohorts (19:20), and all who bear the mark of the beast (14:10). Fire-breathing monsters were common in mythology.[42] John's source is probably Leviathan, the sea-monster, of Job 41 ("out of his mouth go flaming torches ... out of his nostrils comes forth smoke," vss. 19–20). The cavalry as a whole recalls Habakkuk's description of the Chaldeans who were to invade Judah with horses swifter than leopards and fiercer than wolves (Hab 1:8).

18 The fire, smoke, and brimstone are intended to be taken as three separate plagues. The result is that a third part of mankind is killed. The scene is reminiscent of the fire and brimstone which fell upon Sodom and Gomorrah in divine judgment (Gen 19:24; cf. Jude 7). The first Woe brought torment; the second brings death.

19 The power of the horses to kill lies entirely in their mouths. Like the locusts, however, they have the power to hurt,[43] and this power is in their tails. The tails are like serpents and have heads. Many suggestions have been offered for this unusual feature. In the great altar of Zeus at Pergamum the legs of the giants were in the form of snakes. In ancient myth the *amphisbaena* had a serpent's head at either end (Pliny, *Hist. Nat.* viii.35). Some see a reference to the Parthian practice of shooting arrows behind them in flight. Others refer to the horsetails formerly carried by the Turkish pashas as symbols of authority.[44]

It is impossible to say what prompted this particular feature in John's vision. Even if the source could be isolated, it would not necessarily throw much light on the interpretation, for John develops his imagery along lines uniquely his own. That the horses had tails like serpents is perhaps another way of emphasizing the demonic origin of the horses. In 12:9 the devil is designated "the old serpent," and throughout antiquity snakes and demons were closely associated.

Caird links this vision with Ezekiel's prophecy of the invasion of Israel by Gog (Ezek 38–39). Coming after Israel had been punished and restored, the invasion symbolized the immense reserve power of evil in view of which there can be no security until the final victory of God. John adapts the Gog tradition to show that the demonic army from beyond the Euphrates is necessary precisely because the Roman world has tried to find security in that which is not God (Caird, pp. 122–23). Whatever inference may be drawn from the description, John's concern at the moment is to

---

[42]Moffatt refers us to Ovid's bulls and Diomede's horses (p. 409).
[43]ἀδικοῦσιν; cf. the same verb in 9:4.
[44]For other suggestions cf. Beckwith, p. 569.

203

relate an eschatological vision which portrays a plague of death brought upon man by fire-breathing monsters from the underworld.

20 Those who were not killed by the plagues of fire, smoke, and brimstone repented not[45] of their idolatry (vs. 20) or the conduct that accompanied it (vs. 21).[46] Once the heart is set in its hostility toward God not even the scourge of death will lead men to repentance. The "works of their hands" which man chooses to worship rather than God are the idols of gold, silver, brass, stone, and wood. The folly of idolatry is a common theme in Jewish literature. Gods of wood and stone "neither see, nor hear, nor eat, nor smell" (Deut 4:28). They have eyes but do not see, ears but do not hear, and feet but do not walk (Ps 115:5–7; cf. Ps 135:15 ff; Dan 5:23). At the same time heathen idolatry was considered as worship rendered to demons. *Jubilees* speaks of the people of Ur being assisted by malignant spirits in making graven images and unclean *simulacra* (*Jub.* 11:4). In following after strange gods the Israelites had "sacrificed unto demons" (Deut 32:17). In the NT Paul writes that the Gentiles sacrifice "to demons and not to God" (I Cor 10:20). Although one-third of mankind is massacred by the demonic cavalry, those that remain continue to worship the very malignant forces which are bringing about their destruction. Such is the delusion of sin.

21 Closely associated with idolatry are the heathen practices of murder, sorcery, fornication, and theft. Three of the four are fundamental vices prohibited in the ten commandments (sixth, seventh, and eighth; Ex 20:3–17). They occur elsewhere in the NT in various orders (Rom 13:9; Lk 18:20). Sorcery[47] refers to witchcraft and the use of magic potions which were a part of heathen idolatry. It is listed by Paul as one of the works of the flesh (Gal 5:20), and later in Revelation it proves to be the method by which Rome deceives the nations (18:23). In Revelation 22:15 the sorcerers are included with fornicators, murderers, idolaters, and liars as having no part in the New Jerusalem (cf. 21:8). When men turn from the knowledge of God, the path leads downward to idolatry and immorality (cf. Rom 1:18–32). Although clearly and unmistakably warned by God, men persist in their error and sin.

---

[45]A number of MSS read οὐ (C 82 104 *al*) or καὶ οὐ (2329 *al* Tyc) because of the difficulty of construing οὐδέ without a corresponding clause (cf. Metzger, *TCGNT,* p. 744).

[46]ℵ* A *pc* read πονηρίας ("wickedness") rather than πορνείας ("fornication"); BAG say "of every kind of unlawful sexual intercourse," p. 699).

[47]φάρμακον occurs only here in the NT. Moffatt (p. 410) says it is used of the prevalent Asiatic vice of magic spells inciting to illicit lust.

CHAPTER 10

INTERLUDE: VISIONS OF THE PROPHETIC ROLE (10:1–11:14)

The three sevenfold visions of Revelation are the seals (chap. 6), the trumpets (chaps. 8–9) and the bowls (chap. 16). Between the sixth and seventh seal there was an interlude consisting of two visions—the sealing of the 144,000 (7:1–8) and the heavenly multitude (7:9–17). The seventh seal is followed by a second sevenfold vision, that of the trumpets. With the close of chapter 9 six of the seven trumpets have sounded. Once again we encounter an interlude of two related visions—the angel with the little book (10:1–11) and the two witnesses (11:1–13). These interludes are not so much pauses in the actual sequence of events as they are literary devices by which the church is instructed concerning its role and destiny during the final period of world history.[1] There will be no corresponding interlude between the sixth and seventh bowl judgments (the final series yet to come) because at that time all warning and preliminary judgment will be over. When the bowls of divine wrath are poured out, the consummation will have been irrevocably set into motion.

Each numbered series moves us closer to the end; not so much because it follows the preceding series in sequence but because it heightens and intensifies the final and climactic confrontation of God and the forces of evil. Detailed outlines of Revelation sacrifice the existential heartbeat of the Apocalypse in an unfortunate attempt to intellectualize that which belongs primarily to the realm of experience.[2]

---

[1]Beasley-Murray (p. 168) notes that by means of the interlude John wishes to make two points unambiguously plain: the first answers the perennial question "How long?" (cf. 10:7), and the second answers a question not yet raised in the visions, "What is the task of the Church in these troublous times?" (11:1–13).

[2]Cf. the introductory notes on chap. 8.

A. THE MIGHTY ANGEL AND THE LITTLE SCROLL
(10:1–11)

1 *And I saw another strong angel coming down out of heaven, arrayed with a cloud; and the rainbow was upon his head, and his face was as the sun, and his feet as pillars of fire;*

2 *and he had in his hand a little book open: and he set his right foot upon the sea, and his left upon the earth;*

3 *and he cried with a great voice, as a lion roareth: and when he cried, the seven thunders uttered their voices.*

4 *And when the seven thunders uttered* their voices, *I was about to write: and I heard a voice from heaven saying, Seal up the things which the seven thunders uttered, and write them not.*

5 *And the angel that I saw standing upon the sea and upon the earth lifted up his right hand to heaven,*

6 *and sware by him that liveth for ever and ever, who created the heaven and the things that are therein, and the earth and the things that are therein, and the sea and the things that are therein, that there shall be delay no longer:*

7 *but in the days of the voice of the seventh angel, when he is about to sound, then is finished the mystery of God, according to the good tidings which he declared to his servants the prophets.*

8 *And the voice which I heard from heaven, I heard it again speaking with me, and saying, Go, take the book which is open in the hand of the angel that standeth upon the sea and upon the earth.*

9 *And I went unto the angel, saying unto him that he should give me the little book. And he saith unto me, Take it, and eat it up; and it shall make thy belly bitter, but in thy mouth it shall be sweet as honey.*

10 *And I took the little book out of the angel's hand, and ate it up; and it was in my mouth sweet as honey: and when I had eaten it, my belly was made bitter.*

11 *And they say unto me, Thou must prophesy again over many peoples and nations and tongues and kings.*

1 From the beginning of chapter 4 through the end of chapter 9 John has seen the visions unfold from his position in heaven. Now, apparently, he is on earth, for the angel of light descends from heaven (vs. 1) and it is from heaven that the voice is heard (vss. 4, 8). The angel is called "another strong angel." The expression does not intend to compare this angel with the trumpet-angel of 9:13. It means simply "another angel, a strong one" (cf. 6:4). Three of the angels we meet in Revelation are called strong angels. Because the strong angel of 5:2 speaks with a great voice (cf. 10:3) and is connected with the opening of the book of destiny (cf. 10:2), it is quite possible that he is also the one who appears here in chapter 10.[3]

Some commentators have taken the strong angel to be Christ.[4] The phrases by which he is described are elsewhere used of deity. He is dressed in a cloud (cf. Ps 104:3), there is a rainbow upon his head (Rev 4:3), his face is as the sun (cf. Rev 1:16), and his feet are as pillars of fire (cf. Ex 13:21 f). This identification is rejected by most because in the Apocalypse Christ never appears as an angel. His use of an oath in verse 6 would be inappropriate for Christ. Others, arguing on the basis of a rather clear parallel with Daniel 12:7, take the angel to be Gabriel (cf. Dan 8:16).[5]

John views the angel as he descends from heaven to earth.[6] Coming directly from the presence of God, he arrives on a mission of crucial significance for the persecuted church. Like the son of man in Daniel 7:13, he is arrayed in a cloud. This feature has eschatological significance in Scripture. In Matthew 24:30, for example, the Son of man is to come "on the clouds of heaven."[7] There is a rainbow upon the angel's head. One cannot help but notice the similarities between John's description of the angel and that of Yahweh in Ezekiel 1:26–28. However, there the brightness like a rainbow was round the throne (Ezek 1:28), while in Revelation the bow rests upon the head of the angel like a many-colored turban.[8] Some interpret the rainbow as the natural result of light from the angel's face refracted by the cloud in which he was arrayed. Like the face of Jesus on the Mount of Transfiguration (Mt 17:2) the face of the angel shone as the sun.

His legs appeared as pillars of fire.[9] Since the theme of the Exodus is always in the background of this central section of Revelation, it is quite possible that the angel's legs would recall the pillar of fire and cloud that gave both protection (Ex 14:19, 24) and guidance (Ex 13:21–22) to the children of Israel in their wilderness journey. Farrer notes that the description of the angel fits his message—the affirming of God's fidelity to his covenants (10:7): the bow reminding of God's promise through Noah, the

---

[3]The strong angel of 18:21 has a different function, yet one which would also require strength.
[4]Walter Scott, *Exposition on the Revelation of Jesus Christ,* p. 219; Seiss, p. 223; Richardson, p. 101.
[5]Charles (I, pp. 258–59) suggests that the Hebrew equivalent of ἰσχυρός (גִּבּוֹר) may be a play on the name of Gabriel (גַּבְרִיאֵל).
[6]Note the present participle, καταβαίνοντα.
[7]Also Jesus' statement before Pilate, Mk 14:62; cf. Rev 1:7.
[8]Cf. the description of Jaoel in the *Apocalypse of Abraham* 11.
[9]As χείρ may refer to the arm (Lk 4:11), so may πούς indicate the leg. BAG (p. 703) cite Lucian, *Pseudomant.* 59, ποὺς μέχρι τοῦ βουβῶνος (groin).

pillar of fire God's presence in the wilderness, and the scroll the tablets of stone (p. 123).

2 In the hand of the angel is a little book (or scroll).[10] Unlike the great scroll of chapter 5 which was fastened with seven seals, this scroll lies open in the hand of the angel.[11] The scene which follows recalls Ezekiel 2:8–3:3 in which the scroll of lamentations was spread out before the prophet with the command that he should eat it. Although related to the Ezekiel passage, John's vision nevertheless develops along its own lines. The contents of the little scroll will be discussed at verse 8.

As the angel descends to earth he places his right foot upon the sea and his left foot upon the land. Such a stance is most appropriate in view of the colossal size of the angel. It could also symbolize his authority over the earth in its entirety.[12] Less likely is the suggestion that the stance symbolizes the universality of the message (Morris, p. 137), or that one foot is placed upon the sea to defy its instability (Swete, p. 127). The visual impact is that of an enormous and resplendent angel descending from heaven and standing astride both sea and land. This dramatic appearance of an authoritative figure from heaven stands in marked contrast to the immediately preceding tableau of man's rebellious idolatry and immorality (9:20–21).

3 The voice of the angel is commensurate with his gigantic size. He cries out with a great voice as the roar of a lion. Hosea 11:10 speaks of Yahweh roaring like a lion (cf. Amos 3:8), and II Esdras of the lion "roused from the wood and roaring" who is identified as the Messiah (12:31–32). That the Greek verb translated "roareth" is commonly used to denote the mooing of cattle[13] suggests that the angel's voice had a deep resonance which would demand the attention of those who heard. The voice of the angel calls forth a response from the seven thunders.[14] They too utter their voices. According to Beckwith they are "premonitions of God's anger about to burst forth in judgment" (p. 578; cf. p. 574). Elsewhere in Revelation thunder is associated with divine retribution. In 8:5 it follows the casting of fire upon the earth. In 11:19 it is associated with the

---

[10]βιβλαρίδιον is a diminutive of βιβλίον. 2329 reads βιβλάριον, and **C*** 69 *al* have βιβλιδάριον; cf. the same variants in vss. 8, 9, and 10 (also βιβλίδιον by **P**⁴⁷ and 2065 in vs. 10).

[11]The perfect participle ἠνεῳγμένον conveys the idea that the scroll, having been opened, is to remain that way.

[12]For the idea of earth and sea in this comprehensive sense cf. Ex 20:11; Ps 68:22; Rev 7:2.

[13]μυκάομαι is an onomatopoetic word for the mooing of cattle. The cognate noun is used for the roar of a lion by Theocritus (BAG, p. 531).

[14]ἑπτά is omitted by **P**⁴⁷ 1876 *pc*.

seventh trumpet-plague, and in 16:18 with the final bowl of God's wrath. Here as well it forebodes the coming peril of divine retribution.

The use of the definite article (*"the* seven thunders")[15] indicates that the image was familiar to John's readers. Many commentators see a connection with Psalm 29 in which the thunderstorm is interpreted as "the voice of the Lord," the phrase being repeated seven times as the idea is developed. Less likely is the suggestion that they represent "the thunderous echoes of ancient prophecy" (Farrer, p. 124) or the thunder which comes from the seven planetary spheres.[16] Note that the thunders speak articulately. John is about to write down what they said when he is prevented by a voice from heaven. Charles interprets verses 3 and 4 in the light of II Corinthians 12:4 and understands the content of the seven thunders to be a vision which John is forbidden to disclose (I, pp. 261–62). Actually, there is no way of knowing what the thunders said. We have no indication of an additional vision, and John is immediately ordered to seal up what they *uttered.*[17]

4 John is about to write what the seven thunders said when a voice from heaven tells him not to. In his initial encounter with the exalted Christ of the Apocalypse the Seer was to write his visions in a book and send them to the seven churches (1:11). It appears that he had been keeping some sort of record of all that had happened and at this point was about to record the utterances of the seven thunders. The voice from heaven could be that of God or Christ (cf. 14:13; 18:4). In any case a voice from heaven would be a voice of authority (cf. II Esdr 6:17).

The instructions to John are that he should seal up what the thunders said and write them not. This prohibition contrasts with 1:19 (Write what you saw, what is, and what will be) and 22:10 (Do not seal up the prophecy). Some think that John brings in the voice from heaven to justify his omission of some traditional eschatological material.[18] If that were the case, it is difficult to see why he would mention the thunders at all. Others appeal to II Corinthians 12:4 and contest that what the thunders said was too sacred to be shared. It is more plausible that the seven thunders, like the seals and trumpets, formed another series of warning plagues. Man's adamant decision not to repent (9:20–21) would render another series use-

---

[15]Note, however, that αἱ is omitted by ℵ* 1 1611 1876 2059 *al.*

[16]Boll, *Auf der Offenbarung Johannis,* p. 22.

[17]In Jn 12:28–29 the voice from heaven is interpreted both as thunder and as the voice of an angel.

[18]Moffatt, p. 412. Farrer (p. 125) says that John seems to be skipping a part of the prefigured scheme and moving on to the climax.

less. Possibly it is too late to record any further warnings (Erdman, p. 98). In the verses which immediately follow, an angel under oath will declare that there shall be no further delay (vss. 5-7).

In this context, to seal up means not to disclose. John seals up what the thunders said by not writing them down. What was said is not to be made known to the churches. In Daniel 12:4 the prophet is told to "shut up the words, and seal[19] the book, until the time of the end" (cf. Dan 12:9). In contrast, what the thunders said is never to be revealed.[20]

5-6 After the brief reference to the seven thunders John's attention returns to the strong angel standing over sea and earth. The angel raises his right hand to heaven (the place of God's abode, Isa 57:15) and solemnly swears that the period of delay is over. With the sounding of the seventh trumpet God's great purpose in creation and redemption is to be brought to completion.

In the OT the lifting of the hand was a part of oath-taking. Abram declined the spoils of battle saying, "I have lifted up my hand ["I have sworn," *RSV*] unto Jehovah, God Most High, possessor of heaven and earth, that I will not take a thread nor a shoe-latchet nor aught that is thine" (Gen 14:22-23, *ASV*). In the Song of Moses God himself lifts up his hand to heaven in solemn oath to carry out vengeance upon his adversaries (Deut 32:40). It is Daniel 12:7, however, that supplies the interpretive background for this section. There the man clothed in linen who is above the waters of the stream raises up both hands toward heaven and swears by him who lives forever that the end shall come in a "time, two times, and half a time" (three and a half years) when the power of the holy people will be shattered. Apocalyptic thought has always been concerned with the question, How long until the End? In Daniel one of the angels addresses the man clothed in linen with the query, "How long shall it be till the end of these wonders?" (Dan 12:6). The martyrs in Revelation 6:11 asked, "How long ... dost thou not judge and avenge our blood?" The answer of the strong angel is, "There shall be delay no longer." Most early writers interpret this statement as a metaphysical assertion about the end of time as a sequence of events. The translation in the *AV* ("There shall be time no longer") reflects this interpretation.[21] This is not the meaning of "time"

---

[19]σφραγίζω commonly connotes ownership or authenticity, but here and in 22:10 it is used in the sense of to conceal or keep hidden (as the sealing of a scroll prevents its contents from being read).

[20]There are a number of textual variants for vs. 4, but none affects the interpretation of the vs. to any significant degree. Metzger calls ὅσα (read by P^{47} ℵ several minuscules cop^{sa,bo} *al*) for ὅτε an "exegetical modification" (*TCGNT*, pp. 744-45).

[21]Bede (the famous eighth-century Benedictine monk and theologian) wrote "*mutabilis saecularium temporum varietas in novissima tuba cessabit.*" This point of view is still

(Gk., *chronos*)[22] here. It would hardly be necessary for an angel to put himself under oath just to make an assertion about the timeless nature of eternity.

The announcement of no further delay would come as welcome news. The martyrs under the altar (6:9–12) had been told to rest a while until the full number of their fellow servants should be put to death. The seven thunders would have involved yet another delay had they not been cancelled. Now nothing stands in the way of the final dramatic period of human history. From this point forward God will not intervene to give man further opportunity to repent. Restraint is to be removed and the Antichrist is to be revealed (cf. II Thess 2:3 ff). The forces of God and Satan will meet in final confrontation. This is the "time of trouble, such as never has been," foretold by Daniel (12:1) and repeated in the synoptic apocalypse (Mk 13:19 and parallels). It is the darkness before the dawn—the awesome period of Satan's wrath (12:12, 17). The appointed delay is over, and the period of the end is irrevocably set into motion.

It is worth noting that the angel describes God as the One who lives forever and ever. This designation is frequent in the Apocalypse (1:18; 4:9–10; 15:7). It is especially appropriate in the context of impending martyrdom. Soon many believers in the Asian churches will be called upon to sacrifice their lives out of faithfulness to the Christian faith. Only a God who lives beyond the threat of death can promise them life after the sword has taken its toll. God is not only eternal; he is creator of heaven, earth, and sea, and everything therein (cf. Ex 20:11; Neh 9:6; Ps 146:6).[23] To speak of God as creator underscores his power to accomplish that which he set out to do. For the Seer it means that the One who brought all things into being can carry them through in fulfillment of his redemptive purpose. The end of history, as was the beginning, is under the sovereign control of God.

7 The proclamation of the strong angel is that there shall be no further delay but[24] with the sounding of the seventh trumpet the hidden purpose of God will be fulfilled. The *ASV* translation, "when he is about to sound," could be taken to mean that the mystery of God will be completed

---

maintained by a few contemporary interpreters, *eg.* Lenski, who says that the clause means "one thing and only one, namely what we call 'time' shall be at an end" (p. 317).

[22]Cullmann (*Christ and Time*, p. 49) takes χρόνος in Revelation 10:6 not as a reference to an era of timelessness, but in the sense of delay. The contrast between time and eternity is a philosophical notion and has no support in Biblical theology.

[23]The omission of καὶ τὴν θάλασσαν καὶ τὰ ἐν αὐτῇ by ℵ* A 205 (1611) *al* g syᵖʰ Tyc was probably accidental, arising from homoeoarcton and homoeoteleuton (Metzger, *TCGNT*, p. 745).

[24]ἀλλά denotes a strong contrast.

211

before the sounding of the seventh trumpet.[25] What the angel is saying, however, is that within that period of time to be introduced by the seventh trumpet blast the mystery of God will be brought to completion.[26]

A great deal of attention has been given to the meaning of "the mystery of God." In Colossians 2:2 the exact phrase is used to refer to Christ, in whom are hidden the treasures of wisdom and knowledge.[27] The idea of mystery was important in apocalyptic thought. Mysteries were secrets preserved in heaven and revealed to the enraptured apocalyptist (*I Enoch* 71:3 ff; also 40:2; 46:2). Bornkamm writes of the essence of mystery in apocalyptic as "God's counsels destined finally to be disclosed" (*TDNT*, IV, p. 816). It is this eschatological orientation which is always present in the NT use of the word. In Romans 11:25 the final destiny of Israel is a "mystery." The "mystery" of I Corinthians 15:55 is the change which will overtake the believer at Christ's return. In II Thessalonians 2:7 the "mystery of lawlessness" which is at present restrained will soon be fully revealed and at the coming of Christ will be destroyed. The mystery of God in Revelation 10:7 shares this apocalyptic coloring and refers to the purpose of God as revealed in the consummation of human history.[28] In the NT this divine purpose in history is a mystery "not because it is something entirely unknown, but because it would have remained unknown if God had not revealed it" (Hendriksen, p. 150). John is saying that with the sounding of the seventh trumpet that which God purposed in creation and made possible through the blood of the Lamb (5:9–10) will be brought to its fulfillment. That this purpose is in fact the kingdom of God is clearly seen in Revelation 11:15 where following the seventh trumpet the heavenly voices proclaim, "The kingdom of this world has become the kingdom of our Lord, and of his Christ; and he shall reign for ever and ever." Down through the centuries the church has prayed, "Thy kingdom come... on earth as it is in heaven" (Mt 6:10). Taking his stand between the sixth and seventh trumpets John declares, There will be no more delay: the time is now!

---

[25]μέλλω with the infinitive may be used with the force of a future indicative, especially in the case of an action which is certain to take place (Burton, *Moods and Tenses*, p. 36). The *NEB* translates, "When the time comes for the seventh angel to sound his trumpet...."

[26]ἐτελέσθη may be taken as an "aorist of anticipation" or a Hebraism for τελεσθήσεται. In either case it is proleptic, as is the aorist ἥμαρτεν in I Cor 7:28.

[27]The preferred reading in I Cor 2:1 is μαρτύριον, supported by אᶜ B D G *pm* lat syʰ sa TR. The alternate reading (μυστήριον) has considerable support with P⁴⁶ א* A *al* syᵖ bo Ambr Ambst Aug.

[28]Cf. Swete, p. 130; Charles, I, p. 265; etc. Niles' suggestion that it is the "mystery of God's delays" is too narrow (p. 70), as is Kelly's idea that it is "the wonder of evil prospering and good being trodden underfoot" (p. 206).

Only by insisting on a strict chronological sequence can the objection be raised that the material which comes before the seventh trumpet (10:8–11:14) constitutes another delay. The drama has now moved to that moment immediately preceding the final scene. From this point on the Apocalypse becomes a multi-dimensional presentation of the final triumph of God over evil. Any attempt to arrange the material in a strictly sequential pattern is doomed to failure. From his vantage point on the brink of eternity John unveils the evil forces which operate behind the scenes of history and in the last days will mount a final and furious assault upon the faithful (12:12, 17). As persecution and martyrdom precede the seventh trumpet, the overthrow and destruction of the persecutors (demonic powers as well as their earthly agents) will follow it. The bowls of God's wrath (16:1–16) are a prelude to the final destruction of all evil and the inauguration of the eternal state.

That God has from the beginning willed the complete and final defeat of evil should come as no surprise. Although the details have not been revealed, the substance has been made known to God's servants the prophets. There is no reason why this designation should be limited to either OT or NT prophets.[29] Seven hundred years before Christ the prophet Amos asserted, "Surely the Lord God does nothing without revealing his secret to his servants the prophets" (3:7).[30] One purpose has run throughout history, and wherever God has revealed his intentions to man it has touched upon the divine promise of ultimate blessing. This is why the hidden purpose of God is said to have been "gospeled"[31] to the prophets.

8 The voice from heaven which in verse 4 had told John to seal up the utterances of the seven thunders speaks once again. This time it tells him to go and take the little book which lies open on the hand of the strong angel. Although the syntax of verse 8 is awkward, the meaning is quite apparent.[32] That the voice is a voice from heaven emphasizes the authoritative nature of the command. The Seer would be reluctant to approach a great and glorious angel without specific instructions from One even

---

[29]The addition of καί after δούλους (P[47] ℵ 2329 and the Sahidic version) would divide the two groups.

[30]Cf. II Kgs 17:13, 23; Jer 7:25; 25:4; Ezek 38:17; Dan 9:10 for this well-known OT designation.

[31]εὐηγγέλισεν; *TCNT* translates, "he told the good news."

[32]The subject (φωνή) stands without a verb, and the two participles (λαλοῦσαν and λέγουσαν) which modify the subject are accusative, not nominative. The *ASV* takes φωνή as a nominative absolute and adds "I heard it." Another possibility is that the participles are attracted from the nominative into agreement with ἥν and an original linking verb (ἥν) was omitted. λαλοῦσαν and λέγουσαν are translated as finite verbs in the *AV*.

greater. The book on the hand of the angel is an open book. In contrast to the seven-sealed scroll of chapter 5 which remained securely fastened until the Lamb broke its seals, the little scroll lay permanently opened[33] on the hand of the angel. Once again the angel is described as standing on sea and earth. It is not certain whether this thrice-repeated description (vss. 2, 5, 8) indicates some special importance which the Seer attaches to the fact or whether it is no more than rhetorical repetition. The latter is probably the case.

9-10 In obedience to the heavenly voice John goes to the angel and asks for the little book. He is told to take it and eat it. It will be sweet as honey in his mouth but will make his belly bitter. John has now returned to earth, the arena of final conflict.[34] Upon asking the angel to give him the little book, he is told once again to take it. Some commentators see in the specific command to take the scroll the truth that God's revelation must be actively appropriated rather than passively received.[35] The command, however, is not to snatch the little scroll out of the angel's hand. Asking the angel to give it to him[36] does not violate his instructions.

The angel repeats the command of the voice from heaven (Take the little book) and supplies the additional instruction, Eat it. The account of the commissioning of the prophet Ezekiel (Ezek 2:8-3:3) is an obvious parallel. Ezekiel is told to open his mouth and eat what is given to him. A hand appears with a scroll with words of lamentation and mourning written on the front and on the back. Upon eating the scroll Ezekiel found it to be as sweet as honey in his mouth. We are reminded of the Psalmist's words, "How sweet are thy words to my taste, sweeter than honey to my mouth!" (Ps 119:103). A well-known passage in Jeremiah is similar, "Thy words were found, and I ate them, and thy words became to me a joy and the delight of my heart" (Jer 15:16). The command to devour[37] the book is not simply a figurative way of saying, Digest it mentally. In John's case it led to a real act (although within a visionary experience), which in turn symbolizes the complete appropriation of prophetic revelation. John is to assimilate the content of the scroll before communicating it to others. Every

[33]Cf. ἠνεῳγμένον in vs. 2. That John uses βιβλίον here but βιβλαρίδιον in vss. 2, 9, 10 indicates that the two are relatively interchangeable.
[34]Alford notes that from this point on John's principal spot of observation is the earth (p. 653).
[35]Cf. Barclay, II, pp. 68-69; Morris, p. 143. Swete, referring back to 5:2 ff, says that by taking the book John shows his fitness for the task (p. 130).
[36]**P** 1 2059s 2329 *pm* place John's words in direct discourse, using the imperative Δός (rather than δοῦναι and indirect discourse).
[37]The compound κατεσθίω has this stronger connotation.

true prophet of God knows the absolute necessity of this crucial require-
ment.

The identity of the little scroll has been extensively discussed.
Hendriksen is representative of those who take it to be "the Word of God,
his Gospel in which the mystery of salvation is set forth."[38] Morris holds it
to be "the Word of God to John" but goes on to caution the reader that
since John did not specify what it referred to with any precision, we would
be on dubious ground if we were to attempt to improve on him (p. 141).
That the scroll or its contents is not specifically mentioned again in Revelation supports this reticence. Summers sees in the book a general message of
woe—for men under the judgment of God, for Christians in the hands of
their enemies, for the church in her conflict with Rome, and for Rome
herself as she faces destruction (pp. 161–62). Ford (pp. 164–65)[39] suggests
as a key to interpretation Numbers 5:12–31 and *Soṭah,* the tractate on the
suspected adulteress. She conjectures that the scroll in Revelation 10 represents the parchment on which the priest's curse had been written and which
was then soaked in bitter water until the writing was blotted out, after
which the water was drunk by the accused woman to see if her abdomen
would swell (guilty) or her beauty and fertility would increase (innocent).

Other commentators, with varying degrees of certainty, hold that
the first thirteen verses of the following chapter (11:1–13) make up the
content of the little scroll. F. F. Bruce writes, "The contents of John's little
scroll are apparently represented by Rev 11:1–13, originally a separate and
earlier apocalypse now incorporated in John's record and reinterpreted by
him."[40]

The answer to the identity of the little scroll is to a considerable
extent tied up with the interpretation of its being sweet as honey in the
mouth but making the belly bitter.[41] It is usually held to be sweet because it
is a word from God.[42] Why it turns the stomach bitter is less certain.

[38]Hendriksen, p. 151; cf. Lenski, pp. 322–24; Walvoord, pp. 173–74.

[39]Cf. also "The Divorce Bill of the Lamb and the Scroll of the Suspected Adulteress. A Note
on Apoc. 5,1 and 10,8–11," *Journal for the Study of Judaism in the Persian, Hellenistic, and
Roman Period,* 2 (1971), pp. 136–43.

[40]Bruce, p. 649; cf. Charles, I, p. 260; Lilje, p. 158; Erdman, p. 99; Rist, p. 442.

[41]א 1854 2329 *g* Tyc read ἐγεμίσθη ("was filled") for ἐπικράνθη ("was made bitter"), and
others (א^c 1854 2329 *g* arm^{pt} Tyc) follow on to add πικρίας ("bitterness") at the end of the
sentence.

[42]Cf. Barclay, II, p. 69; Morris, p. 142. Rist, however, thinks that it was sweet "because the
prophecies it contained were most agreeable to him," and unlike Ezra who was appalled by
the doom awaiting the wicked (II Esdr 7:17–25, 102 ff) John is not grieved (pp. 441–42).
Caird writes of Ezekiel (in the parallel passage) that he found the scroll sweet to taste "no
doubt because the harshness of its contents was congenial to his austere spirit" (pp. 129–30).
Both evaluations are unnecessarily severe.

Commentators who do not limit the contents of the little book to chapter 11 tend to emphasize the judgment and woe which are to fall on the unbelieving world. It seems more plausible that the little scroll is a message for the believing church and is to be found in the following verses (11:1–13). In the parallel passage in Ezekiel the message of lamentation, mourning, and woe is to be delivered to the rebellious house of Israel (Ezek 3:4 ff). The prophet is not sent to a people of strange speech and a hard language (Ezek 3:5, 6). The parallel in John's case would be the church, the new Israel. It is *after* the eating of the book that John is told he must prophesy again, this time concerning many peoples, nations, tongues, and kings (Rev 10:11). This begins with chapter 12. The sweet scroll which turns the stomach bitter is a message for the church. Before the final triumph believers are going to pass through a formidable ordeal. As the great scroll of chapter 5 outlined the destiny of all mankind, so the little scroll unveils the lot of the faithful in those last days of fierce Satanic opposition. It tells of the two witnesses who, when they have finished their testimony, are destroyed by the beast out of the abyss (11:7). Like the crucified Lord their dead bodies are exposed for public contempt (11:8). Erdman writes concerning the people of God faithfully bearing their testimony, that "they are delivered not *from* martyrdom and death, but *through* martyrdom and death to a glorious resurrection" (p. 99). The prospect of no further delay in the fulfillment of God's eternal purposes is sweet indeed. That it will involve a bitter prelude is hard to swallow.[43]

11 John is now told that he must prophesy again about many peoples, nations, tongues, and kings. If we are correct in our interpretation of the little scroll as a message to believers about to enter the final period of persecution (11:1–13), then this renewed commission relates to the prophecies following the seventh trumpet in 11:15. The seals of chapter 6 (except the fifth) and the trumpets of chapters 8 and 9 are judgments directed against an ungodly world. After the parenthesis of chapters 10 and 11 which treats the church in the last days John will turn again to prophesy against society in its hostility toward God.[44]

The fourfold classification of peoples, nations, tongues, and tribes occurs five times in Revelation (cf. comm. on 7:9). Here "tribes" is replaced by "kings" perhaps to suggest that God's word through the prophets takes precedence over the highest rank of human authority. It may

---

[43]Lilje holds the book to be sweet and bitter at the same time since the commission includes both the announcement of wrath and the promise of succor (p. 157); Beasley-Murray favors the same interpretation (p. 175). Others reverse the order and refer the sweetness to final blessedness (Kepler cited by Morris, pp. 142–43; Blaney, p. 462).

[44]Cf. A. Feuillet, *Johannine Studies*, pp. 215–31.

be that the seven kings of 17:10 and the ten kings of 17:12 are in the Seer's purview. In any case, the prophecies deal with man in general without attention to racial, geographic, ethnic, or social distinctions. The only real distinction is between man with the seal of God and man with the mark of the beast.

The commission is introduced rather curiously by the words, "they say unto me." If the reference were to the voice from heaven (vss. 4, 8) or the strong angel (vs. 9), we would have expected a singular verb.[45] It is probably best to take the expression as an indefinite plural or the equivalent of the passive "it was said."

There is a sense of divine compulsion in the charge given to John. He *must*[46] prophesy again. The prophecy relates to many peoples and nations.[47] It is the final act in the great drama of God's creative and redemptive activity. The meaning of history comes into sharp focus at the end point in time. John's mission is to lay bare the forces of the supernatural world which are at work behind the activities of men and nations. His prophecy is the culmination of all previous prophecies in that it leads on to the final destruction of evil and the inauguration of the eternal state.

---

[45]The reading λέγει in **P** and a number of the minuscules and versions is undoubtedly a scribal attempt to relieve the problem.

[46]δεῖ always involves some sort of compulsion, whether of inner necessity, the demands of society, or divine decree.

[47]ἐπί with the dative here does not mean against in a hostile sense (as in Lk 12:52-53) but about, or concerning (as in Jn 12:16; Rev 22:16).

CHAPTER 11

Most commentators note that chapter 11 is especially difficult to interpret. Part of the difficulty stems from the necessity of having to take a rather clear-cut position on the interpretation of apocalyptic language. Walvoord represents a school of thought which approaches the material in a straightforward and literal manner: the temple will actually exist during the tribulation, the two witnesses are two individuals, and the altar will be a place where ancient sacrifices are renewed (pp. 175-76). A distinctly different approach is represented by Kiddle, who interprets the chapter in a highly symbolic sense: the temple is the church, the two witnesses are that part of the church which must suffer martyrdom, and the great city represents civilization utterly alien to the will of God (pp. 174-88).

The notes which follow understand the entire section to be symbolic of the fate of the witnessing church during its final period of opposition and persecution. It forms the contents of the "little book" of chapter 10 which was sweet to the taste but made the belly bitter (10:9-10). That the language of prophecy is highly figurative has nothing to do with the reality of the events predicted. Symbolism is not a denial of historicity but a matter of literary genre. Apocalyptic language has as one of its basic characteristics the cryptic and symbolic use of words and phrases.

Many writers believe that the first thirteen verses of chapter 11 have been taken over from a previous source (or sources). Charles follows Wellhausen in accepting the first fragment (11:1-2) as an oracle written before AD 70 by a Zealot prophet in Jerusalem (I, pp. 270-73), a theory that Caird judges "improbable, useless, and absurd" (p. 131). Beckwith acknowledges the plausibility of an original Jewish source but understands the present author as using it to predict the repentance of the people of Israel in the last days (pp. 586-90).[1] Since we have seen that John makes

[1]See pp. 604-6 for a listing of various possible origins. Ladd lists as four plausible interpretations of the chapter, (1) an earlier Jewish apocalypse written before the destruction of the

use of his sources with a sort of sovereign freedom, it is far more important to understand what he is saying than to reconstruct the originals.

B. MEASURING THE TEMPLE (11:1–2)

1 *And there was given me a reed like unto a rod: and one said, Rise, and measure the temple of God, and the altar, and them that worship therein.*

2 *And the court which is without the temple leave without, and measure it not; for it hath been given unto the nations: and the holy city shall they tread under foot forty and two months.*

1 In the preceding section (10:8–11) John's role as passive spectator gave way to active involvement in his own vision. He took the book from the hand of the angel and ate it. In the opening verses of chapter 11 his participation continues. He receives a reed like a rod and the command to measure the temple of God, its altar, and those that worship therein. Biblical prophets commonly employed symbolic action to dramatize their message. Isaiah walked about naked and barefoot as a sign of Egypt's impending captivity to Assyria (Isa 20:2–5). Ezekiel dug through the wall and carried out his luggage in the sight of Israel as a symbol of the coming exile (Ezek 12:1–7). In the NT the prophet Agabus bound his feet and hands with Paul's girdle to show that the apostle would be bound by the Jews at Jerusalem (Acts 21:10–11). The measuring of the temple is a symbolic way of declaring its preservation.[2] The background is probably Ezekiel 40–42 where the prophet in a vision watches every part of the temple measured with painstaking care.[3] This would be a necessary prerequisite to the restoration of the real temple in Jerusalem.

For John, the preservation symbolized by the measuring was not security against physical suffering and death but against spiritual danger. It corresponds to the sealing of 7:1–8, which did not protect from physical death but insured entrance into the heavenly kingdom (cf. comm. on 7:4–8). This interpretation understands the temple to stand for the church, the

---

temple and to be taken historically in that sense, (2) a prophecy of the restoration of the Jewish temple and the eschatological struggle between restored Jews and the Antichrist, (3) a prophecy of the fate of the church in a hostile world, and (4) a prophecy of the preservation and ultimate salvation of the Jewish people (pp. 149–51). Ladd opts for the fourth alternative (p. 151).

[2]Ford lists four explanations of the measuring in Rev 11:1–2: (1) rebuilding or restoring, (2) destruction, (3) preservation from physical harm, and (4) preservation from spiritual harm (p. 176).

[3]Zech 2:1–5 is often cited as an example of measuring for the purpose of protection. What it implies, however, is that it need not be measured in order to erect walls because of the adequate protection provided by God's presence.

people of God (as in I Cor 3:16–17; II Cor 6:16; Eph 2:19–22).[4] Whatever the imagery may have intended if it originally belonged to a Jewish apocalypse, there is little doubt that for John it means that God will give spiritual sanctuary to the faithful believers against the demonic assault of the Antichrist. As the altar is linked so closely with those worshipping in the holy place, it should probably be taken as the altar of incense (cf. 8:3). The objection that only the priests were permitted to enter the inner sanctuary, hence those worshipping could not represent the entire body of the faithful, is countered by the NT teaching that all believers are in fact part of a royal priesthood (I Pet 2:5, 9; Rev 1:6; 5:10).

The instrument for measurement was a "reed like unto a rod." In the Jordan valley grew certain bamboo-like canes which were both sufficiently long and rigid (cf. Lk 7:24) to be used for measuring.

2 The court which is outside[5] the temple would be the court of the Gentiles. While Solomon's temple had two courtyards (I Kgs 6:36), the inner court of Herod's temple was divided into three courts (the court of the women, of the Israelites, and of the priests). Separating these three from the court of the Gentiles was a barrier with inscriptions threatening death to any Gentile who would pass beyond (Josephus, *Bell.* v.5.2; cf. Eph 2:14). Opinion is divided as to what the outer court stands for. One common answer is that it is symbolic of those members of the professing church who, like the followers of Balaam (2:14) and Jezebel (2:20), have compromised with the world.[6] It is the true church, however—those who refuse the mark of the beast (13:7, 16–17)—who are about to suffer; and not those who have compromised their faith.

It is more probable that the outer court refers to the church viewed from a different perspective. It is to be cast out[7] and measured not; that is, it is to be given over to persecution in the last days. Thus, the distinction between the sanctuary and the outer court is a way of pointing up the limitations placed upon pagan hostility (cf. Morris, pp. 146–47). It may physically decimate the witnessing church (in 11:7 the two witnesses are killed), but it cannot touch its real source of life (the witnesses are raised and ascend to heaven; 11:11–12).

---

[4]See Hendriksen, pp. 154–55, for six supporting arguments.

[5]א 1 2059 2329 *al* TR read ἔσωθεν, which makes ἔκβαλε more understandable but helps little in the interpretation of the vs.

[6]They are "those who although outwardly belonging to the church are not true believers," according to Hendriksen (p. 154); cf. Kiddle (p. 189).

[7]ἔκβαλε ἔξωθεν. Most translations adopt a more metaphorical interpretation of this phrase (*NEB*, "have nothing to do with").

In John's imagery the holy city is yet another designation for the church.[8] The faithful are to be trodden under foot[9] by paganism for a period of forty-two months. The background for this is the prophecy concerning Antiochus Epiphanes in Daniel 8:9–14. The sanctuary is to be trodden under foot by the little horn for 2300 days. Then it is to be cleansed (Dan 8:14). Likewise the church is to be oppressed and profaned by the beast out of the abyss (Rev 11:7), but it will not be destroyed. To what extent its victory will be triumph through death or continued existence on earth is not clear. In either case the promise of Jesus in Matthew 16:18 that "the powers of the underworld shall never overthrow [the church]" (Williams) is carried through.

The temporal designation of forty-two months (11:2; 13:5) is also given in Revelation as 1260 days (11:3; 12:6) and "a time, and times, and half a time" (12:14). Its primary reference is to the period of Jewish suffering under the Syrian despot Antiochus Epiphanes in 167–164 BC.[10] It became a conventional symbol for a limited period of time during which evil would be allowed free rein. In Luke 21:24 it is called "the times of the Gentiles." The repeated use of the various designations in Revelation and the contexts in which they appear may serve to point out that the periods of final witness, divine protection, and pagan antagonism are simultaneous.

C. THE TWO WITNESSES (11:3–14)

3 *And I will give unto my two witnesses, and they shall prophesy a thousand two hundred and threescore days, clothed in sackcloth.*

4 *These are the two olive trees and the two candlesticks, standing before the Lord of the earth.*

5 *And if any man desireth to hurt them, fire proceedeth out of their mouth and devoureth their enemies; and if any man shall desire to hurt them, in this manner must he be killed.*

6 *These have the power to shut the heaven, that it rain not during the days of their prophecy: and they have power over the waters to turn them into blood, and to smite the earth with every plague, as often as they shall desire.*

---

[8]The designation of Jerusalem as the holy city is common in Jewish writing (Neh 11:1; Isa 48:2; *Ps. Sol.* 8:4; Mt 4:5).

[9]The concept of trampling to overthrow and defile is seen in vss. such as Ps 79:1 and Isa 63:18 (cf. Lk 21:24).

[10]The drought in the days of Elijah lasted three and a half years (Lk 4:25; Jas 5:17). Moffatt (p. 416) notes that originally the period reflected the Babylonian three and a half months of winter. See the helpful excursus in Glasson, pp. 67–70.

7 *And when they shall have finished their testimony, the beast that cometh up out of the abyss shall make war with them, and overcome them, and kill them.*

8 *And their dead bodies lie in the street of the great city, which spiritually is called Sodom and Egypt, where also their Lord was crucified.*

9 *And from among the peoples and tribes and tongues and nations do* men *look upon their dead bodies three days and a half, and suffer not their dead bodies to be laid in a tomb.*

10 *And they that dwell on the earth rejoice over them, and make merry; and they shall send gifts one to another; because these two prophets tormented them that dwell on the earth.*

11 *And after the three days and a half the breath of life from God entered into them, and they stood upon their feet; and great fear fell upon them that beheld them.*

12 *And they heard a great voice from heaven saying unto them, Come up hither. And they went up into heaven in the cloud; and their enemies beheld them.*

13 *And in that hour there was a great earthquake, and the tenth part of the city fell; and there were killed in the earthquake seven thousand persons: and the rest were affrighted, and gave glory to the God of heaven.*

14 *The second Woe is past: behold, the third Woe cometh quickly.*

3 Over a hundred years ago Henry Alford, Dean of Canterbury, wrote that "no solution has ever been given to this portion of the prophecy" (p. 658). Although a quick survey of several commentaries will reveal more than a dozen possibilities for the two witnesses, the chances for a satisfactory interpretation of the section are not hopeless.

There is little doubt that the witnesses are modeled after Moses and Elijah. In the description which follows (vss. 5–6) they have the power, like Elijah, to consume their enemies with fire (II Kgs 1:10 ff) and to shut the heavens so that it will not rain (I Kgs 17:1), and like Moses they can turn water into blood (Ex 7:14–18) and smite the earth with every plague (Ex 8:12). Further, it was a common expectation that Elijah and Moses would return before the end of the world. Malachi had prophesied, "Behold, I will send you Elijah the prophet before the great and terrible day of the Lord comes" (Mal 4:5; cf. Mk 9:11 and Mt 11:14). Apparently Deuteronomy 18:18 ("I will raise up for them a prophet like you from among their brethren") had given rise to a similar expectation regarding Moses (cf. Jn 6:14; 7:40). It was Moses and Elijah who appeared with Jesus on the Mount of Transfiguration (Mk 9:4). Furthermore, the ascension of the two witnesses into heaven (vs. 12) corresponds with II Kings

2:11 (Elijah's transport) and the tradition underlying the pseudepigraphical *Assumption of Moses*.[11]

But who are these two witnesses and what do they symbolize in John's vision? Beckwith holds that they are two great prophets of the last days who come in the spirit of Elijah and Moses to preach repentance to Israel (p. 595).[12] It seems more likely, however, that they are not two individuals but a symbol of the witnessing church in the last tumultuous days before the end of the age.[13] That the church is presented under the figure of two witnesses stems either from the well-known law in Deuteronomy 19:15 which required a second witness for adequate testimony (cf. Jn 8:17)[14] or from the Seer's desire to emphasize the church's "royal and priestly functions" as suggested by the two metaphors in verse 4 (Bruce, p. 649).[15] Some commentators would limit the witnesses to that portion of the church which suffers martyrdom.[16]

It is God, rather than Christ, who commissions his witnesses to prophesy.[17] The opening word of verse 3 ("and") ties that which follows closely to what has just been said. In spite of pagan oppression God will send forth his witnesses. The period of their ministry is the same as that allotted to the trampling of the holy city. Its designation in days rather than months is no more than literary variation (solar months are thirty days in length). It does not intend to teach that witnessing is a day-by-day activity.

---

[11]Some early writers (*eg.*, Tertullian, *De Anima*, 50) understand Enoch rather than Moses since Scripture records that he was translated to heaven without seeing death (Gen 5:24; Heb 11:5). Enoch, however, does not fit the description in Rev 11:5–6.

[12]Walvoord (p. 179), governed by a dispensational orientation, says they are two prophets raised up from those who turn to Christ after the rapture. Others holding to two distinct individuals suggest Zerubbabel and Joshua, Elijah and Elisha, James and John, Peter and Paul. Allegorically they could be the Law and the Prophets, the Law and the Gospel, the OT and the NT, Israel and the Church, Israel and the Word of God, the churches of Smyrna and Philadelphia (cf. the list of candidates in Ford, pp. 177–78).

[13]J. S. Considine concludes that they represent "the universality of Christian preachers and teachers [whose] mission is to combat the enemies of Christ and his Church" ("The Two Witnesses: Apoc. 11:3–13," *CBQ*, 10 [1948], p. 392).

[14]Jesus sent out his messengers two by two (Lk 10:1; cf. Acts 15:39–40). Kraft writes, "Das es zwei sind . . . kommt daher, das es Zeugen sind. . . . Sie müssen zwei sein, weil sie im Gericht als Zeugen Gottes gegen die Stadt auftreten werden" (p. 156).

[15]Beasley-Murray (p. 184) writes, "As prophetic witnesses they fulfil the role of kings (like Zerubbabel) and priests (as Joshua)."

[16]So Morris, p. 148. For Caird, their description in vs. 4 as "the two lamps" (cf. the seven of 1:20) provides "the clearest possible evidence that John did not expect all loyal Christians to die in the great ordeal" (p. 134).

[17]Note that Christ is spoken of in the third person in the same discourse (vs. 8, "their Lord was crucified"; however, αὐτῶν is omitted by P⁴⁷ and the original version of Sinaiticus).

As latter-day prophets the two witnesses wear the rough garb of their ancient predecessors (Zech 13:4). Their message is a call to repentance. Sackcloth was the garment of mourning and penitence. "Gird you with sackcloth, lament and wail," counseled Jeremiah (4:8). "Woe to you," said Jesus to the cities that had witnessed his miracles and repented not, "for if the mighty works done in you had been done in Tyre and Sidon, they would have repented long ago in sackcloth and ashes" (Mt 11:21).

4 John now identifies the two witnesses as the two olive trees and the two lampstands standing[18] before the Lord of the earth. The background is Zechariah's vision recorded in chapter 4 of his prophecy. There, a single golden lampstand (Israel?) supports a bowl with seven lamps ("the eyes of the Lord," vs. 10) and is flanked by two olive trees (Joshua, the high priest, and Zerubbabel, the Jewish governor under the Persian king Darius) which supply it with "golden oil" (vs. 12, *ASV*). The angelic interpretation is, "Not by might, nor by power, but by my Spirit, says the Lord of hosts" (vs. 6). As God's Spirit works through his chosen leaders, the temple will be brought to completion.

As usual, John uses his source with considerable freedom.[19] The one lampstand becomes two and these two in turn are said to be synonymous with the two olive trees. Already in chapter 1 the seven churches (symbolic of the church universal) have been symbolized by seven lampstands. They are the bearers of divine light (cf. Mt 5:15-16). These lightbearers are also olive trees in that "the oil of the Spirit . . . keeps alive the light of life" (Swete, p. 135). By these two metaphors John is emphasizing a truth concerning the church which has always been true but is especially appropriate in times of persecution—that the power and authority for effective witness lie in the Spirit of God.

5-6 The two witnesses are protected by supernatural powers for the period of their prophetic activity. The fire which proceeds out of their mouth to destroy the enemy recalls Elijah's encounters with the emissaries of King Ahaziah (II Kgs 1). The first two groups of fifty were consumed by fire from heaven at the word of the prophet (vss. 10, 12). While the fire in John's vision is often taken figuratively,[20] it would be more consistent to maintain a parallel with the literal drought and plagues which follow in the same description. Fire-breathing prophets would not seem strange in the

---

[18]The masculine ἑστῶτες goes back to μάρτυρες and seems abrupt after the feminine ἐλαῖαι and λυχνίαι.

[19]Charles calls it a "bold and independent interpretation" of Zechariah's symbols (I, p. 283).

[20]"The 'fire' of God's anger," Kiddle, p. 197; the message had a "fiery aspect," Morris, p. 148.

bizarre world of apocalyptic imagery. This of course does not deny that the words of a prophet can be like fire (as in Jer 5:14; *Ecclus.* 48:1).

The witnesses also have the power to shut the heavens so it will not rain during the time of their prophecy. The background is the drought of Elijah's day (I Kgs 17:1; *Ecclus.* 48:3) which, according to Luke 4:25 and James 5:17, lasted three and a half years.[21] They can also turn water into blood (cf. Ex 7:20) and smite the earth with whatever plague they wish (cf. Ex 8:12).[22] The purpose of John's portrayal at this point may be to express "the truth that God's servants in the new dispensation have just as great resources as did Moses and Elijah in the old" (Morris, p. 149).

7 As soon as their ministry has been fulfilled,[23] the witnesses are no longer protected from physical harm. The beast of the abyss makes war on them and emerges victorious. Here for the first time we meet a figure who represents the major antagonist of the church in the last days. In contrast to the Lamb, who bears the marks of slaughter, he is the beast.[24] His demonic origin and character are portrayed by the fact that he "cometh up out of the abyss," the haunt of demons (cf. Lk 8:31). The definite article indicates that he is a well-known figure. It may be a reference to the beast of Daniel 7:7 ff, who had become a "familiar representation of Antichrist" (Beckwith, p. 601),[25] or it may anticipate the detailed presentation in chapters 13 and 17. At the moment all that John wishes to do is to set forth the death of the witnesses at the hand of the beast. As the little horn of Daniel 7 made war with the saints (vs. 21), so the beast of the abyss overcomes and kills the two witnesses. The expression "make war" supports the interpretation of the witnesses as a large group rather than two individuals. The scene is the last epic struggle between the kingdoms of this earth and the witnessing church. The very word "witness"[26] has the grim flavor of martyrdom. What is true in this last conflict has also been true of the massacres of history "in which brute force has seemed to

---

[21]The NT writers follow a Jewish tradition which extended the period to three and a half years to coincide with the symbolic designation for a time of calamity. I Kgs 18:1 says the promise of rain came "in the third year" (cf. vss. 41–45), which could be only a little over one full year (by an inclusive count). Josephus (*Ant.* viii.13.2) cites Menander of Ephesus to this effect. The ground had already been dry for six months when Elijah made his first announcement to Ahab (I Kgs 17:1). "If the cessation lasted till the third month thereafter, the total period of drought would necessarily be about three years and nine months" (J. Orr, *The Bible Under Trial* [1907], pp. 264 f).

[22]I Sam 4:8 (LXX) reads οἱ πατάξαντες τὴν Αἴγυπτον ἐν πάσῃ πληγῇ.

[23]τελειόω is more than temporal: it carries the idea of accomplishing a goal.

[24]θηρίον, a wild animal, in contrast to ζῷον, a living thing (unfortunately translated "beast" in the *AV* of Rev 4:6–9 and elsewhere).

[25]The reading of Alexandrinus (τὸ θηρίον τὸ τέταρτον) supports this reference.

[26]μάρτυς.

triumph over truth and righteousness" (Swete, p. 137). Ladd states as a fundamental clue to the understanding of Biblical prophecy that "eschatological events are foreshadowed in historical events" (p. 156).

8 The bodies of the martyred witnesses are left unburied on the broad street of the great city.[27] From the Eastern point of view, to be deprived of burial was an act of great indignity.[28] When Tobit learned that one of his countrymen had been strangled and left dead in the marketplace, he jumped up from a ceremonial meal, went and took the body to one of the outbuildings until he could bury it after the sun went down (Tob 2:1–7; cf. Jer 8:1–2).

The majority of commentators take "the great city" to be Jerusalem in spite of the fact that in the seven other references in Revelation (16:19; 17:18; 18:10, 16, 18, 19, 21) it consistently refers to Rome.[29] The identification rests primarily on the last clause of verse 8, which seems to identify the great city as the place where "their Lord was crucified." Several Jewish references can be cited indicating that the title had been used of Jerusalem (Josephus, *Ap.* i.197; *Sib. Or.* 5:154, 226, 413). Isaiah 1:9–10 and Ezekiel 16:46–49 are usually pointed out as places where Jerusalem is called Sodom. But, as Alford has pointed out, in the Isaiah passage it is the Jewish people (not the city) who are so designated, and in Ezekiel, Jerusalem is being compared with her sisters, Samaria and Sodom (p. 661). In neither place is Jerusalem called Sodom, and in the OT it is never designated Egypt.

In view of the consistent use of the term elsewhere in the book as a reference to Rome (as well as such verses as 18:24, "In her was found the blood of prophets and of saints") it seems best to conclude that the witnesses meet their death at the hands of the Antichrist, whose universal dominion was in John's day epitomized by the power of Rome. The inclusion of a reference to the crucifixion is not to identify a geographical location but to illustrate the response of paganism to righteousness. Morris says that the great city is "every city and no city. It is civilized man in organized community."[30] Spiritually (or allegorically) it is "Sodom and Egypt."

[27]For τῆς πλατείας supply ὁδοῦ. 2036 and a few other manuscripts supply the verb ἐάσει ("he will leave") and add ἄταφα (unburied) after μεγάλης.
[28]Beasley-Murray calls it "the limit of outrage and indignity that can be accorded to the dead" (p. 186).
[29]It is also called "Babylon the great" in 14:8; 16:19; 17:5; and 18:2. Caird writes that in the Apocalypse Rome is represented by three successive symbols: (1) Vanity Fair, whose name is Sodom and Egypt, 11:8; (2) the beast, 13:1; and (3) the great harlot, chaps. 17–18 (*The Apostolic Age*, pp. 179–80).
[30]Morris, p. 150. Kiddle calls it the Earthly City as opposed to the Heavenly City, "typified once by Jerusalem, now by all civilization, where the Satanic power of Rome was dominant" (p. 199).

Sodom refers to the depths of moral degradation (cf. Gen 19:4–11), and Egypt is a symbol of oppression and slavery. The great city in which the martyred church lies dead is the world under the wicked and oppressive sway of Antichrist.

9 The dead bodies of the two witnesses are left lying on the streets of the great city, where they are viewed by men of every race and nationality.[31] The three and a half days of their public exposure correspond to the 1260 days of their prophetic activity. In comparison it is a brief period of time. We have already noted (in vs. 8) that denial of a proper burial was an act of ignominy[32] and reflected the scorn of man for the church which had called him to repentance. The dead bodies of the witnesses are not symbols of a spiritually dead church, but portray the destiny of the faithful who hold their convictions firm till the end. To Smyrna, John wrote, "Be thou faithful unto death, and I will give thee the crown of life" (Rev 2:10).

10 When the followers of the beast realize that those who have tormented their consciences are dead, they are overjoyed. In effect, a holiday is declared, with merrymaking and the exchange of gifts. Swete writes that their delight was "at once fiendish and childish" (p. 138). Their torment, consisting of denunciation (vs. 3) and physical affliction (vss. 5–6), had lasted for three and a half years, but now it was over and rejoicing was in order.

"They that dwell on the earth" is another designation for the pagan world as described in the preceding verse.[33] It supports the interpretation of the great city as the whole earth. God's truth through the testimony of faithful witnesses has always harassed the consciences of evil men. To Ahab, the prophet Elijah was a "troubler of Israel" (I Kgs 18:17). Herod feared John the Baptist, yet heard him gladly (Mk 6:20). The world has always shown hostility to the message of God—a truth which ought to give some concern to the contemporary church existing for the most part rather comfortably in a world of increasing wickedness.

The celebration of the earth's inhabitants over the death of the witnesses is a perverse counterpart to the Jewish feast of Purim—a "day for gladness and feasting . . . a day on which they send choice portions to one another . . . and gifts to the poor" (Esth 9:19, 22). Some have suggested as another parallel the period between the crucifixion and the

---

[31]While ἐκ τῶν λαῶν is probably a partitive genitive, it should not be pressed to indicate a specific representative group. Cf. Jn 16:17 for the partitive genitive used as subject.

[32]In *Ps. Sol.* (2:30–31) Pompey's decapitated body lay unburied on the shore, "with none to bury him, because God had rejected him with dishonor."

[33]Cf. comm. on 6:10. The attempt by Charles to restrict the phrase to Palestinian Jews (I, p. 289) is not successful.

resurrection. Of this time Jesus said that the disciples "will weep and lament, but the world will rejoice" (Jn 16:20).[34]

11 The merriment of the world is cut short, for after three and a half days God sends the breath of life into the dead bodies of the witnesses, who then stand again upon their feet. The language of this verse follows the vision recorded in Ezekiel 37 in which God sends the breath of life into the dry bones, which come to life and stand upon their feet.[35] The revelling is cut short, and great fear settles upon the inhabitants of the earth who have just witnessed this remarkable event. Since murder is the last resort of man, what can be done about those who rise from the dead! The resurrection of the church is a sure indication that God possesses the ultimate authority over life and death.[36]

12 The two witnesses are now summoned by a great voice from heaven and ascend in full view of their startled enemies. Charles explains the definite article (*"the* cloud") by reference to a tradition recorded by Josephus that Moses was taken from his followers by a cloud as he was talking with them (I, p. 291; Josephus, *Ant.* iv.8.48). In II Kings 2:11 Elijah is taken up into heaven in a whirlwind.[37] The voice from heaven is heard by the two witnesses (and probably everyone else), although some manuscripts read "I heard" and restrict the verb to the Seer.[38] The triumph of the witnesses is no secret rapture; it is openly visible[39] to all (cf. Mt 24:27; I Thess 4:17).

13 As the witnesses are taken up into heaven, a great earthquake levels a portion of the city, killing 7,000 and forcing the rest to acknowledge the transcendent majesty of God. Ezekiel 38:19–20 predicted a great earthquake which would precede the end. Zechariah says that the Mount of Olives will be split in two from east to west when God returns to crush his enemies (Zech 14:15). Although the earthquake may symbolize some great upheaval in the social order (cf. Hag 2:6-7), here, as in Revelation

---

[34] εὐφραίνομαι in the NT is often used for purely secular joy. In Lk 15:23 the father of the prodigal says, "Let us eat and make merry (εὐφρανθῶμεν)." The same word is used by the elder brother a few vss. later (vs. 29).

[35] πνεῦμα ζωῆς (Ezek 37:5), εἰσῆλθεν εἰς αὐτούς (a number of MSS, including P[47] and ℵ, read εἰς rather than ἐν in Rev 11:11), and ἔστησαν ἐπὶ τοὺς πόδας αὐτῶν (cf. Ezek 37:10).

[36] Ladd, who interprets the entire chapter as predicting "the preservation of the Jewish people and their final salvation" (p. 151), understands vs. 11 as indicating that "the conversion of Israel is to be accomplished by a miracle of resurrection" (p. 158).

[37] For the ascension of Moses see the reference in Clement of Alexandria (*Strom.* vi.5) to the account in a lost portion of the *As. Mos.*

[38] ἤκουσα (P[47] **046** 1 82 2059s *pl* g co arm Tyc) is in keeping with the author's usage (twenty-four times), but the plural is appropriate in this context.

[39] P[47] reads ἐμέτρησαν ("measured") instead of ἐθεώρησαν ("beheld"), a rather strange concept!

6:12, it is part of an apocalyptic vision which portrays in a literal manner the events yet to come. The tenth part of the city which fell would be a sizeable portion but not enough to disable it. The figure of 7,000 does not seem to have any particular meaning beyond serving to indicate the approximate number of individuals in one-tenth of a good-sized city in John's day.

Scholars differ in their interpretation of the response of the world to this demonstration of divine power. The text simply says that those who were not killed were filled with terror and "gave glory to the God of heaven." Some think that, unlike the survivors of 9:20–21, these turn from their apostasy in true repentance. Caird argues that John was more optimistic about the conversion of the world than he is commonly given credit for. "Where retributive punishment had failed to bring men to repentance, the death of the martyrs would succeed" (p. 140). It was not the death of the martyrs, however, but their resurrection which struck terror[40] to the hearts of their enemies and caused them to give glory to God. Revelation 13:3–4 specifically says that "the whole earth wondered after the beast; and they worshipped the dragon . . . and the beast."

Kiddle is correct in his view that in that day "the great mass of mankind will have committed the unpardonable crime of deifying evil." They give glory to God "when they are compelled by overriding terror to recognize that the true Lord is Christ and not Antichrist" (p. 206).[41] This scene does not stand in contrast to 6:15–17 but is a parallel. The term "God of heaven" occurs only here and in 16:1 in the NT, although it is frequent in Jewish writings. The source may be Daniel 2:17–19, where the title reflects the majesty and wisdom of God without any specific contrast with the gods of the Chaldeans.

14 Verse 14 stands in isolation, separated from the second Woe by the visions of 10:1–11:13, and announcing a third Woe which is then postponed until a number of subplots have been brought forward.

6. SEVENTH TRUMPET (11:15–19)

15 *And the seventh angel sounded; and there followed great voices in heaven, and they said,*
The kingdom of the world is become the kingdom *of our Lord, and of his Christ: and he shall reign for ever and ever.*
16 *And the four and twenty elders, who sit before God on their thrones, fell upon their faces and worshipped God,*

---

[40]ἔμφοβοι ἐγένοντο ; cf. Acts 24:25.
[41]Phillips translates, "and acknowledged the glory of the God of heaven."

17 *saying,*

> *We give thee thanks, O Lord God, the Almighty, who art and who wast; because thou hast taken thy great power, and didst reign.*

18 *And the nations were wroth, and thy wrath came, and the time of the dead to be judged, and the time to give their reward to thy servants the prophets, and to the saints, and to them that fear thy name, the small and the great; and to destroy them that destroy the earth.*

19 *And there was opened the temple of God that is in heaven; and there was seen in his temple the ark of his covenant; and there followed lightnings, and voices, and thunders, and an earthquake, and great hail.*

15 Barclay notes that the remainder of chapter 11 is a "summary of all that is still to come" (II, p. 89). The declaration of triumph by the heavenly hosts (vs. 15) and the anthem of praise by the worshipping elders (vss. 17–18) introduce the great themes of the following chapters. The extensive use of the aorist tense conveys a sense of absolute certainty about the events yet to come.[42] Glasson refers to the common saying, "It's all over bar the shouting," and remarks that the only difference here is that the shout of victory has already begun (p. 71).

We would expect the seventh trumpet blast to be followed by the third Woe (cf. 9:1, 13), but instead we hear voices of a great heavenly host declaring the final triumph of the kingdom of God and the establishment of his eternal reign. The voices are not those of a glorified church. The expression "Our Lord, and . . . his Christ" would not be appropriate for the church because their Lord *is* the Christ. The voices should not be limited to any particular class of angelic beings (such as the four living creatures of chaps. 4 and 5) but represent the hosts of heaven with the same sort of indefiniteness that we find in 12:10 and 19:16.

The burden of the angelic declaration is that the dominion and rule of this world have been transferred to God and his Christ, who shall reign forever and ever. This great eschatological event which establishes once and for all the universal sovereignty of God is a recurring theme in OT prophecy. Daniel predicted the day when the kingdom of God would utterly destroy the kingdoms of this world (Dan 2:31–45, esp. vs. 44). The day is coming, said Zechariah, when God will be "King over all the earth" (Zech 14:9). As the drama of the consummation moves toward the final scene, the hosts of heaven proclaim it *fait accompli*. During his earthly ministry Jesus had resisted the tempting offer of Satan to hand over the kingdoms of this world in exchange for worship (Mt 4:8–9). Now this

---

[42]*Eg.,* "Thou hast taken (εἴληφας) thy great power, and didst reign (ἐβασίλευσας)" (vs. 17).

sovereignty passes to him as a rightful possession in view of the successful completion of his messianic ministry. "Our Lord and his Christ" reflects Psalm 2:2, which was interpreted messianically by the early church (Acts 4:26–28).[43] Although the Son will ultimately be subjected to the Father (I Cor 15:28), he will nevertheless share the eternal rule of God. The singular ("he shall rule") emphasizes the unity of this joint sovereignty.

16 The twenty-four elders last appeared in 7:11, where they were kneeling before the throne of God in worship and praise. Although normally seated, they are here once again upon their faces (cf. 4:10; 5:8, 14; 19:4) and singing a hymn of anticipated victory. The elders are an angelic order—the heavenly counterpart to God's people in all ages (cf. comm. on 4:4).

17 The song of the elders is a hymn of thanksgiving to the One who with a great display of power will enter upon his eternal reign. The event is so certain that throughout this section it is repeatedly spoken of as already having taken place.[44] "Great power" does not indicate omnipotence as a divine attribute in a general sense, but points to the final conflict in which God overpowers all his enemies. As in 1:8 and 4:8, he is the Lord God, the Almighty. He is able to accomplish all that in his decrees he has determined to perform. In the same two passages, as well as in 1:4, he is the one who is, who was, and who is to come. In the present verse (and in 16:5) the third member is omitted[45] because his coming is no longer seen as future. Already he has come and entered upon his reign.

18 The reign of God is established by a great demonstration of divine wrath against the defiant anger of the world (cf. 16:9–11, 21). The eschatological crisis has arrived with its inevitable judgment. As the proclamation of the heavenly host drew upon a messianic interpretation of Psalm 2, so also does the song of the elders. Nations rage and rulers take counsel against God and his anointed (Ps 2:2), and he will answer with wrath (Ps 2:5, 12). There is an appropriateness in God's tailoring the punishment to fit the crime.[46] A final fierce assault upon the power and authority of God is a common apocalyptic theme. The triumph of God's wrath is pictured in 14:10–11; 16:15–21; and 20:8–9.

---

[43]Charles (I, p. 194) says that the first book in which ὁ Χριστός was used as a technical reference to the messianic king was *I Enoch* (cf. 48:10).

[44]Morris notes that the perfect (εἴληφας) may indicate that God has taken the power permanently, while the aorist (ἐβασίλευσας) points to the crisis in which he decisively dethroned evil and entered on his reign (p. 153). The aorist is inceptive, "has begun to reign" (cf. 19:6).

[45]The *AV*, following inferior texts (1006 2026 *al* vg[s,c1] bo TR), adds καὶ ὁ ἐρχόμενος after ἦν. Another reading to be rejected is that of P[47] (μένουσαν for μεγάλην).

[46]Lilje (p. 167) calls the indignation of the peoples met by the holy wrath of God, a "majestic antithesis."

In the schedule of God's redemptive program a decisive point has now been reached. It is a fitting time[47] for judgment, reward, and destruction. The judgment anticipated by the elders is carried out in the great white throne scene of 20:11–15. It is preceded by resurrection and followed by retribution. If the wrath of God is the judgment of the wicked, the vision of a New Jerusalem (21:9–22:5) with the presence of God its crowning joy (22:4) is the reward of the faithful. Although rewards are all of grace (Rom 4:4), they vary according to what each has done (I Cor 3:8).

The various classes of the faithful are taken in a number of ways. A reasonable translation would be, "To thy servants the prophets, and to the saints—those who fear thy name, both small and great." There are two groups (prophets and saints), who are further described as fearing the name of God. This arrangement holds intact the expression "thy servants the prophets" (which occurs again at 10:7) and joins to it a second group (the saints) as in 16:6 ("the blood of saints and prophets"), 18:24 (order reversed), and 22:9 ("the prophets and . . . them that keep the words of this book"—that is, saints). John holds the prophetic office in highest esteem. One might almost say that in Revelation the prophet has replaced the apostle.[48] By taking "them that fear thy name" as a further description of the prophets and saints, it is unnecessary to find additional distinctions such as Jewish and Gentile Christians.[49] In 19:5 all God's servants are addressed as "you that fear him, small and great." The latter phrase (perhaps from Ps 115:13) is common in Revelation and stresses the all-inclusive nature of the group involved, whether saints (11:18; 19:5) or sinners (13:16; 19:18; 20:12).

The consummation will bring not only reward to the faithful but destruction to the destroyers (cf. II Thess 1:6–7). God repays in kind, and for those who wreak havoc upon the earth, there is reserved the wrath of a righteous God (cf. Rom 2:5). Those that destroy would be for John the Roman Empire and all who serve her sinister designs. The pagan empire of his day becomes a model for the final assault which knows no limitations, national or racial.

19 Verse 19 is a response to the hymn of praise in verses 17 and 18. The ark of the covenant corresponds to the rewarding of the faithful,

---

[47]ὁ καιρός; cf. Delling's article in *TDNT*, III, pp. 460–62 (C.1.b) for other decisive points.
[48]In Rev there are eight references to the prophet (10:7; 11:10, 18; 16:6; 18:20, 24; 22:6, 9) and, apart from a reference to false teachers at Ephesus (2:2) and another to the apostolic band (21:14), the designation apostle occurs only once (18:20).
[49]Charles, I, p. 296. Beckwith says such a division (into Jewish and Gentile Christians) is "wholly foreign to our author" (p. 610).

and the cosmic disturbances to the outpouring of God's wrath.[50] The sanctuary which opens to reveal the ark of the covenant is not an earthly temple (as in 11:1) but the sanctuary of God in heaven (cf. 3:12; 7:15; 15:5–8; 21:22). From this most holy place proceed both the promise of covenant love and righteous anger (cf. 16:1). The opening of the temple is of limited duration (cf. 15:5) and serves to reveal a heavenly ark, the symbol of God's faithfulness in fulfilling his covenant promises. For the days of wrath which lie immediately ahead, believers will need the assurance that God will bring his own safely to their eternal reward. Hendriksen says the ark is "the symbol of the superlatively real, intimate, and perfect fellowship between God and his people" (p. 161).

In the OT the ark of the covenant was a symbol of the abiding presence of God. It was undoubtedly destroyed when Nebuzaradan razed Jerusalem and burned the temple (II Kgs 25:8–10). Yet II Maccabees 2:4–8 records a legend that Jeremiah took the ark (along with the Tent of Meeting and the incense-altar) and hid it in a cave on Mt. Nebo. It was to remain hidden until "God finally gathers his people together and shows mercy to them" (II Macc 2:7). This reflects the Jewish expectation of the recovery of the ark as an eschatological event with messianic significance. It is unlikely, however, that the heavenly ark of John's vision is in any sense a fulfillment of this expectation. The entire scene is a gracious reminder that God will faithfully carry out his covenant promises and destroy the enemies of his people.

[50]For thunder and lightning as symbols of divine anger see 8:5 and 16:18. Earthquakes appear at 6:12; 8:5; 11:13; 16:18; and hail at 8:7 and 16:21.

CHAPTER 12

VI. CONFLICT BETWEEN THE CHURCH AND THE POWERS OF EVIL (12:1–14:5)

Chapter 12 marks a major division in the book of Revelation. Before the seven last plagues of chapter 16, in which the wrath of God is finished (15:1), John turns aside to explain the underlying cause for the hostility about to break upon the church. During his earthly ministry Jesus had warned, "If they persecuted me, they will persecute you" (Jn 15:20). It is the age-long conflict between God and Satan which accounts for the persecution the church is to experience. Although the crucial battle was won when Christ arose victorious over death and the grave, the adversary continues his struggle. Cast down from heaven and knowing that his time is short (12:12), Satan turns in rage against the faithful who "keep the commandments of God, and hold the testimony of Jesus" (12:17). By laying bare the root cause of persecution John would encourage believers to hold fast in the coming tribulation. The death struggle of a defeated foe will bring severe tribulation, but the outcome is certain—God will come in judgment to destroy his enemies (chaps. 15-19) and reward his own (chaps. 20-22).

The stage is set for the final confrontation. Chapters 12-14 introduce the actors who play the major roles. Some writers identify the seven main characters as the radiant woman, the dragon, the man-child, Michael, the seed of the woman, and the two beasts (cf. Walvoord, p. 187). Others, organizing the chapters around the number seven, find seven oracles depicting the supernatural conflict between the forces of light and the forces of darkness (Kiddle, p. 215; cf. pp. 213-14), or seven signs connected with the troubles of the church (Morris, p. 155).[1]

---

[1]Morris' "signs" correspond only in part with Kiddle's "oracles"; perhaps the sevenfold pattern is not as clear as it could be.

234

Much has been written about the sources thought to lie behind the visions of chapter 12.[2] Charles finds two major sources: 12:7-10, 12, an original product of Judaism (even though some of its subject matter may go back to the Zend religion), and 12:1-5, 13-17, a primitive international myth applied messianically by a Pharisaic Jew about AD 67-69 and then borrowed and transformed by the Seer to give spiritual insight into the underlying cause of the final persecution of the church (I, pp. 298-314). That partial parallels can be found in the ancient folklore of many nations cannot be denied. In Greek mythology the pregnant goddess Leto, pursued by the dragon Python, is brought safely to the island of Ortygia (Delos, in a variant form of the myth) where she gives birth to Apollo, who then returns and kills the dragon. In Egyptian mythology, the red dragon Set-Typhon pursues Isis and is later killed by Horus her son. A Babylonian myth tells of the overthrow of Tiamat, the seven-headed water monster, by Marduk, the young god of light. John probably borrowed some of his imagery from the thought-world of his day, but it is very unlikely that he consciously took over a pagan myth to explain the spiritual significance of the persecution coming upon faithful Christians. Would a writer who elsewhere in the book displays such a definite antagonism toward paganism draw extensively at this point upon its mythology? As always, John is a creative apocalyptist who, although gathering his imagery from many sources, nevertheless constructs a scenario distinctly his own.

1. THE WOMAN, DRAGON, AND MALE CHILD (12:1-6)

1 *And a great sign was seen in heaven: a woman arrayed with the sun, and the moon under her feet, and upon her head a crown of twelve stars;*

2 *and she was with child; and she crieth out, travailing in birth, and in pain to be delivered.*

3 *And there was seen another sign in heaven: and behold, a great red dragon, having seven heads and ten horns, and upon his heads seven diadems.*

4 *And his tail draweth the third part of the stars of heaven, and did cast them to the earth: and the dragon standeth before the woman that is about to be delivered, that when she is delivered he may devour her child.*

5 *And she was delivered of a son, a man child, who is to rule all the nations with a rod of iron: and her child was caught up unto God, and unto his throne.*

6 *And the woman fled into the wilderness, where she hath a place prepared*

---

[2]Beasley-Murray (p. 192, n. 1) calls attention to the extensive survey of interpretation of Rev 12 by P. Prigent, *Apocalypse 12, Histoire de l'exégèse*. Cf. also A. Feuillet, *The Apocalypse*, pp. 109-17 and A. T. Kassing, *Die Kirche und Maria*.

of God, that there they may nourish her a thousand two hundred and threescore days.

1-2 The pageant opens with the display of a great marvel in the sky.[3] A woman appears who is arrayed with the sun, crowned with twelve stars, and standing upon the moon. As in 12:3 and 15:1, the word "sign" is to be understood as a great spectacle which points to the consummation (cf. Lk 21:11, 25; Acts 2:19). Elsewhere in Revelation the word is used of the deceptive miracles performed by the representatives of Satan (13:13, 14; 16:14; 19:20). The woman is not Mary the mother of Jesus but the messianic community, the ideal Israel.[4] Zion as the mother of the people of God is a common theme in Jewish writings (Isa 54:1; II Esdr 10:7; cf. Gal 4:26). It is out of faithful Israel that Messiah will come. It should cause no trouble that within the same chapter the woman comes to signify the church (vs. 17). The people of God are one throughout all redemptive history. The early church did not view itself as discontinuous with faithful Israel (cf. D'Aragon, p. 482).

As God covers himself "with light as with a garment" (Ps 104:2), so the woman is arrayed with the sun. The world may despise the true Israel and hold it in lowest esteem, but from God's point of view she is a radiant bride (cf. Jer 2:2). She stands as an obvious contrast to the scarlet whore of chapter 17. The moon beneath her feet speaks of dominion, and the crown of twelve stars[5] depicts royalty.

---

[3]The "stars of heaven" in vs. 4 places the episode in the sky rather than in heaven.

[4]On the basis that according to astral thinking everything that happens on earth has already taken place in heaven, Rist holds that John's account is not an "allegorical depiction of the earthly birth of Jesus to Mary," but relates "the birth of the heavenly Messiah to a celestial mother, possibly before creation began" (pp. 452–53). Ladd interprets chap. 12 as "a vision in highly imaginative terms of the heavenly warfare between God and Satan, which has its counterpart in history in the conflict between the church and demonic evil" (p. 166). This leads him to insist, for instance, that the birth of a male child (vs. 5) "does not refer to the birth of Jesus to Mary in Bethlehem" (p. 169; note the same position stated less absolutely on pp. 167–68). It is probably unnecessary to insist so strongly upon the nonhistorical nature of the visions since the antagonism of Satan toward the Messiah and the church (the offspring of the true Israel, vs. 17) has, in fact, been a determining factor in the course of human history. If chap. 12 is to be consistently interpreted as a celestial and nontemporal struggle between God and Satan, there should be no direct reference to "actual Christians who constitute the empirical church on earth" (Ladd, p. 174) as the explanation of "the rest of her seed" (vs. 17).

[5]The twelve stars may be an allusion to the twelve tribes of Israel (21:12) or the twelve apostles (21:14)—perhaps both. Apuleius (a second-century-AD novelist and philosopher) describes the goddess Isis in somewhat similar terms (*Met.* xi.3–4).

3 The radiant woman is about to give birth to a child. She cries out in travail and pain to be delivered.[6] The OT frequently pictured Israel as a woman in travail. Isaiah speaks of Israel in bondage as "a woman with child, who writhes and cries out in her pangs, when she is near her time" (Isa 26:17; cf. 66:7; Mic 4:10). In John's vision the woman in travail is "the true Israel in her pre-messianic agony of expectation" (Kiddle, p. 220).

A second sign now appears in the heavens—a great red dragon with seven heads. John does not leave us in doubt as to the identity of this monster: he is "the old serpent, he that is called the Devil and Satan" (vs. 9; cf. 20:2). Ancient mythology is replete with references to dragons. In Canaanitish lore the great monster of the deep was known as Leviathan. Closely associated was Rahab (alias Tiamat?), the female monster of chaos.[7] Allusions to these dragons are not uncommon in the OT. More often than not they refer metaphorically to Israel's enemies. In Psalm 74:14 Leviathan is Egypt. In Isaiah 27:1 he is Assyria and Babylon. Elsewhere we read of Pharaoh as "the great dragon that lies in the midst of his streams" (Ezek 29:3) and of Behemoth, a great beast whose "limbs are like bars of iron" (Job 40:18). Against this background the dragon of John's vision would immediately be understood as the archenemy of God and his people.

The red color of the dragon (which may be a part of tradition)[8] symbolizes the murderous character of Satan. Jesus had told the Jews, "You are of your father the devil. . . . He was a murderer from the beginning" (Jn 8:44). The several heads of Leviathan are mentioned in Psalm 74:14 and attested in Ugaritic texts.[9] John's fondness for the number seven as a symbol of completeness suggests that the seven heads of the dragon depict the universality of his power. The ten horns recall the fourth beast of Daniel 7, awesome and powerful with its great iron teeth and ten horns (Dan 7:7, 24). That the beast out of the sea has ten horns and seven heads

---

[6] ἐν γαστρὶ ἔχουσα goes with the preceding description and should be followed by a major break (Westcott and Hort). βασανίζω is not used elsewhere in the NT of childbirth, but as an expression of physical distress it is entirely appropriate (cf. Mt 8:6). Burton takes τεκεῖν as an objective infinitive "governed by the idea of desire implied in the preceding participles" (*Moods and Tenses*, p. 154, par. 389). Most often it is taken as epexegetical.

[7] F. F. Bruce, "Rahab" in *NBD*, p. 1074. Rist notes that "the Greeks had Python and the nine-headed Hydra; the Egyptians depicted Set-Typhon as a red crocodile; for the Persians, Azhi Dahaka was a three-headed monster" (pp. 453–54).

[8] Homer speaks of a δράκων δαφοινός (blood red), *Iliad* ii.308. Some manuscripts (**C 046** 1 82 1006 1611 2059* 2329 *al* sy) read πυρός, "fire," in place of πυρρός, "red."

[9] "The accursed one of seven heads"; cf. Bruce, p. 651.

(13:1; cf. 17:12) indicates that Satan's earthly emissaries are like him in their destructive power. The diadems are not wreaths of victory but *"crowns of arrogated authority"* (Hendriksen, p. 165).[10] They are Satan's presumptuous claim of royal power over against the "KING OF KINGS AND LORD OF LORDS" upon whose head are "many diadems" (19:12, 16).

4 The scene in the heavens continues as the dragon gathers a third of the stars with his great tail and hurls them down to the earth. One is reminded of Daniel 8:10 where the little horn (Antiochus Epiphanes) casts to the ground some of the stars and tramples them under foot. The cataclysmic action emphasizes the tremendous size and awesome power of the dragon. That he casts down a third part of the stars indicates no more than a very great number. John is not teaching a theology of fallen angels[11] but reporting a great pageant enacted in the heavens.

The dragon stands in readiness before the woman with child so that when the child is born he can devour it. This explains the violent antagonism with which the child of the messianic community was met during the years of his life on earth. It began with the determination of King Herod to murder the Christ-child (Mt 2), continued throughout the dangers and temptations of his earthly life, and culminated in the crucifixion. As Nebuchadrezzar devoured Israel ("He has swallowed me like a monster; he has filled his belly with my delicacies," Jer 51:34), so has Satan determined to devour the child. He has taken his position[12] and awaits the victim.

5 The radiant woman gives birth to a son, a male child,[13] who is destined to rule the nations with a rod of iron. In Psalm 2 the messianic Son is to receive the nations as an inheritance and "break ["shepherd"; cf. comm. on 7:17] them with a rod of iron" (vs. 9). As a shepherd defends his flock against the wild beasts of prey, so will Christ at his return strike the nations which oppress and persecute his church (cf. 19:15; in 2:27 the overcomers at Thyatira are promised a part in this rule).

Without mention of any intervening events John moves directly from the birth of Christ to his ascension. It is possible that this omission stems from the fact that the Seer was reshaping earlier material which

---

[10]They are not στέφανοι but διαδήματα.
[11]Although the imagery lends itself to that end; cf. II Pet 2:4; Jude 6; also comm. on 9:1.
[12]ἔστηκεν is perfect.
[13]The neuter ἄρσεν stands in apposition to the masculine υἱόν and emphasizes the sex of the child; cf. Gen 1:27 (LXX), ἄρσεν καὶ θῆλυ ἐποίησεν αὐτούς. Isa 66:7 uses the same word for Israel reborn.

included nothing which could be appropriately applied to the earthly ministry of Christ. It is much more probable that the essential truths of the vision
could be best served by brevity. The significant point is that the evil
designs of Satan were foiled by the successful completion of Christ's
messianic ministry, which culminated in his ascension and exaltation (cf.
Phil 2:5–11).[14] The child is caught up to God and his throne.

6 The woman flees into the wilderness to be nourished there by
God for 1260 days. The flight of the woman may in part reflect the escape
of the Palestinian church to Pella at the outbreak of the Jewish war in AD
66 (Eusebius, *Hist. Eccl.* iii.5; cf. Mk 13:14). God's children have often
been in flight. The nation Israel was born in the Exodus (Deut 8:2 ff).
Elijah fled into hiding by the brook Cherith and was nourished there by the
ravens (I Kgs 17:2 ff). Joseph and Mary fled to Egypt to save the life of the
Christ-child (Mt 2:13 ff). The intent of the verse, however, is not so much
the flight of the church as the provision of God for her sustenance. To the
Jewish people the wilderness spoke of divine provision and intimate fellowship. It was in the wilderness that God had rained down bread from
heaven (Ex 16:4 ff) and nourished his people for forty years. Of Israel God
said, "I will allure her, and bring her into the wilderness, and speak
tenderly to her" (Hos 2:14; cf. I Kgs 17:2–3; 19:3–4). For John's readers
the wilderness would not connote a desert waste inhabited by evil spirits
and unclean beasts, but a place of spiritual refuge. Some writers interpret
the figure in a completely symbolic sense. Kiddle says that the desert
represents "a condition of *spiritual detachment* from the affairs and fortunes of the civilized world" (p. 229). Verses such as II Corinthians 6:17
("Come out from them, and be separate") and John 17:15 ("I do not pray
that thou shouldest take them out of the world, but that thou shouldest keep
them from the evil one") are often quoted in support. The purpose of the
vision, however, is not to describe a "quality of life" (Kiddle) but to
assure those facing martyrdom that God has prepared for them a place of
spiritual refuge and will enable them to stand fast against the devil. The
duration of divine nourishment (1260 days) corresponds to the period of
persecution (cf. 11:2; 13:5). The place is one set in readiness[15] by God
himself.

---

[14]Caird (p. 149) makes the interesting suggestion that the anomaly exists only in the fancy of
the modern critics because for John "the birth of the Messiah . . . means not the Nativity but
the Cross." Following the lead of Ps 2, the birthday of a king is the day of his accession.
Beasley-Murray describes this interpretation as attractive but doubtful (pp. 199–200).
[15]ἡτοιμασμένον, a perfect passive participle.

2. WAR IN HEAVEN (12:7-12)

7 *And there was war in heaven: Michael and his angels* going forth *to war with the dragon; and the dragon warred and his angels;*

8 *and they prevailed not, neither was their place found any more in heaven.*

9 *And the great dragon was cast down, the old serpent, he that is called the Devil and Satan, the deceiver of the whole world; he was cast down to the earth, and his angels were cast down with him.*

10 *And I heard a great voice in heaven, saying,*
Now is come the salvation, and the power, and the kingdom of our God, and the authority of his Christ: for the accuser of our brethren is cast down, who accuseth them before our God day and night.

11 *And they overcame him because of the blood of the Lamb, and because of the word of their testimony; and they loved not their life even unto death.*

12 *Therefore rejoice, O heavens, and ye that dwell in them. Woe for the earth and for the sea: because the devil is gone down unto you, having great wrath, knowing that he hath but a short time.*

7 The Seer now reports a war in heaven between Michael and his angels and the dragon with his angels. This conflict is not a spectacle taking place in the sky (as in vss. 1–6), but a warfare in heaven itself. It is an all-out attempt on the part of Satan to regain his position in the presence of God. It does not refer to the original expulsion of Satan from heaven (more a product of *Paradise Lost* than Scripture), nor is it a pictorial expression of Christ's victory on the cross (cf. Jn 12:31).[16] It is the cosmic prelude to the consummation. It explains the intense hostility to be poured out upon the church in the days of final tribulation. Unless the hymn of verses 10–12 is to be taken proleptically, Satan has just been cast down to earth and in his great wrath, and knowing that his time is short (vs. 12), has turned his anger upon the church of John's day. The details of sequence and time should not be pressed in apocalyptic.[17] The final outpouring of Satanic wrath is the result of his defeat in heavenly battle.

According to Jewish thought, Satan was once an angel who attempted to achieve equality with God. Whereupon, according to Enoch, he was cast out of heaven with his angels and flies continuously in the air

---

[16]For a persuasive presentation of the contrary position cf. Caird ("On Deciphering the Book of Revelation: I. Heaven and Earth," *ET,* 74 [1962], pp. 13–15). He writes, "Michael's victory is simply the heavenly and symbolic counterpart of the earthly reality of the Cross" (p. 13).

[17]Derwood Smith finds a three-step fall of Satan in Rev: (1) from heaven to earth, 12:9; (2) from earth to the abyss, 20:2; and (3) from the abyss, after his release, into the lake of fire, 20:10 ("The Millennial Reign of Jesus Christ: Some Observations on Rev. 20:1–10," *Restoration Quarterly,* 16 [1973], p. 224, n. 10).

(*II Enoch* 29:4–5).[18] The Babylonian account of the expulsion of Ishtar, goddess of the morning star, is parallel. Allusions to this fall may occur in Isaiah 14:12 ("How you are fallen from heaven, O Day Star, son of Dawn!") and I Timothy 3:6 ("Or he may be puffed with conceit and fall into the condemnation of the devil"). Yet elsewhere Satan is depicted as having access to heaven (Job 1:6–9; 2:1–6; Zech 3:1 ff).[19] This may have led to the expectation of a final celestial battle which would precede the consummation (cf. *Sib. Or.* 3:796–808; also II Macc. 5:1–4; Josephus, *Bell.* vi.5).

It is the archangel Michael, not the Messiah, who wars against Satan in this final struggle. In Daniel 12:1 Michael is presented as the guardian of Israel who in the last days will deliver them from tribulation (cf. *I Enoch* 90:14). Somewhat later he is pictured as "a mediator between God and man" who will "stand up against the kingdom of the enemy" (*Test. Dan* 6:2). He is the angelic intercessor who contended with the devil about the body of Moses (Jude 9). It is he who will go forth in victory against Satan and his host. Satan lays claim to the rank of archangel on the basis that he has angels[20] under him who do his bidding.

There is no basis in the text for the idea that the war in heaven results from Satan's pursuit of Christ in his ascension. When a suitable verb is supplied in the second clause to govern the infinitive "to war,"[21] the idea is conveyed that the attack is launched by Michael and his angels.

8 Satan and his forces are defeated in battle and must forfeit their place in heaven. Up until this time Satan, in some sense, had a place in heaven. It is the irretrievable loss of any further opportunity to fulfill his wicked plan that sends Satan out in such great anger against the church.

9 The dragon and his angels are defeated in heavenly battle and cast down to the earth. It is the beginning of the end. Lilje notes that "what

---

[18]Cf. the later use of this tradition in *Adam and Eve* 1:6. Eph 2:2 speaks of Satan as "the prince of the power of the air."

[19]*I Enoch* 40:7 speaks of several satans. In the NT Paul writes that believers are in conflict with "the spiritual hosts of wickedness in the heavenly places" (Eph 6:12).

[20]ἄγγελος, which can mean messenger, frequently designates supernatural beings both good and evil. *Test. Asher* speaks of "the angels of the Lord and of Satan," and Mt 25:41 of eternal fire prepared for "the devil and his angels."

[21]The two grammatical problems are the articular infinitive τοῦ πολεμῆσαι and the nominative ὁ Μιχαήλ. Of the many suggestions (for which see Charles, I, pp. 321–22), the repetition of ἐγένετο before the infinitive is the simplest. Charles takes the infinitive as a Hebraism ("they had to fight") and the nominative as a literal reproduction of a Hebrew construction in which the subject before ל and the infinitive is in the nominative (I, p. 322). Moule doubts that a "less barbarous Greek than that of Revelation would have tolerated the subjects of the Infinitive in the Nominative" (*Idiom Book*, p. 129).

Jesus saw *ahead* in a vision—'I saw Satan fall like lightning from heaven!'
(Lk 10:18)—is fulfilled in these mighty conflicts at the end of history" (p.
172). The dragon is identified as the old serpent (a reference to Gen 3:1 ff),
the one who is called the devil or Satan. The word *śāṭān* was not
originally a proper name. It simply meant adversary. In Numbers 22:22 the
angel of the Lord who placed himself in Balaam's path is called a *śāṭān*, an
adversary (cf. also I Sam 29:4; I Kgs 5:4; 11:14, 23). In time, however, it
became a proper name. Satan is the Adversary, the prosecutor who accuses
men before God in the heavenly court. In the prologue to Job, when the
sons of God presented themselves before the Lord, Satan was there to
accuse Job of honoring God for personal advantage (Job 1:6–11). In the
vision of Zechariah (3:1–10) Satan stands at the right hand of Joshua the
high priest to level accusation against him. Barclay mentions the paid
informer of Roman days (the *delator*) who made a profession of accusing
people before the authorities (II, p. 102). This notorious practice would
make extremely vivid the portrayal of Satan as the Accuser.

Satan is also known as the devil, that is, the Slanderer.[22] It is a thin
line that divides accusation and slander. He is also the deceiver of the
whole world. Later in Revelation (20:8) he comes forth after the thousand
years of imprisonment to deceive the nations and lead them to destruction.
He put it into the heart of Judas to betray Christ (Jn 13:2), and was out to
undermine the faith of Peter (Lk 22:31). Paul warns of his evil devices
(II Cor 2:11) and says that he "deceived Eve by his cunning" (II Cor 11:3;
cf. I Tim 2:14). His false prophets would "lead astray, if possible, even the
elect" (Mt 24:24; cf. Rev 13:11–15). The twin evils of deception and
accusation are brought together in the book of *Jubilees* ("Let not the spirit
of Beliar rule over them to accuse them before thee, and to ensnare them,"
1:20). It is a momentous event when this prince of evil is defeated in battle
and cast forever from the court of heaven.

10 By now the reader of Revelation will be accustomed to the
sudden outbursts of praise which meet him in the book.[23] The voice from
heaven which John hears is not that of the martyrs of 6:9–11. Their cry for
vindication is distinct from the adulation of the verses here. The voice
could be that of one of the twenty-four elders (note the repeated emphasis
on power: 4:11; 7:12; 11:17; 12:10) or of some undesignated heavenly
being. The argument that the designation "our brethren" rules out an angel
overlooks 19:10 in which an angel declares himself a fellow servant with
John and his brethren.

---

[22]ὁ διάβολος translates the Hebrew הַשָּׂטָן in the LXX in Job 2:1; Zech 3:1 f, etc.
[23]4:8, 11; 5:9–10, 12, 13; 7:10, 12; 11:15, 17–18; 12:10–12; 15:3–4; 19:1–2, 4, 6–8.

It is unnecessary to determine whether or not verses 10–12 are to be taken proleptically. From John's perspective, the great tribulation about to break upon the church was a direct result of the defeat of Satan in heavenly conflict. The salvation, power, and kingdom of God are present realities. Although defeated, Satan is still a powerful foe. It is true that history has shown that "the things which must shortly come to pass" (1:1) have taken longer than John expected, but the point of the passage is not to establish a chronology but to reveal the supernatural cause behind Satan's opposition to the church whenever and wherever it occurs. It should be no surprise that as the end draws near, this hostility will increase in intensity.

The phrase "of our God" modifies all three of the preceding nouns. It is not only the sovereign reign of God which has come, but also the deliverance which he effects and the authority by which he rules. Christ the Son shares in this authority[24] because it is by his death that Satan has been defeated (5:9; 12:11).[25] The sovereign rule of God becomes a present reality in that "the accuser[26] of the brethren is cast down." Satan's role as the greater accuser, as we have seen, finds classic statement in the book of Job (1:6–12; 2:1–5; cf. *I Enoch* 40:7). His accusations against the righteous continue night and day. But by virtue of the death of Christ he is unable successfully to lodge a charge against God's elect (Rom 8:33–34). The accuser is cast down to earth. Caird offers the interesting suggestion that although John depicts the battle between Michael and Satan in military terms, it is essentially a legal battle between opposing counsel in which the loser is disbarred (p. 155).

11 Not only does Satan suffer defeat at the hands of the archangel, but he is conquered by faithful believers as well.[27] The primary cause[28] of their victory is the blood of the Lamb. The great redemptive act which loosed them from their sins (1:5) and established their right to reign (5:9) is the basis for their victory. Their share in the conquest stems from the testimony they have faithfully borne (cf. 6:9; 11:7). Their willingness to proclaim the message overcame even the natural fear of death: "In their love of life they shrank not from death" (*TCNT*).

---

[24]See comm. on 11:15; cf. Ps 2:8; Mt 28:18; Jn 17:2.
[25]Ladd writes that 12:11a "shows clearly that the victory over Satan which John has described in mythological terms actually was accomplished in history at the cross" (p. 172).
[26]κατήγωρ occurs only here in the NT (and only in Alexandrinus; but see the minority report in Metzger, *TCGNT*, pp. 747–48); elsewhere the more common κατήγορος is found (*eg.*, Acts 25:16, 18). It may be a transliteration from the Aramaic, although Deissmann finds it in a fourth-century vernacular papyrus with no indication of Jewish or Christian influence (*LAE*, pp. 93 f).
[27]Note the emphatic pronoun αὐτοί.
[28]διά here gives the ground, not the means, of their victory.

12 Verse 12 refers back to verse 10: the heavens[29] are to rejoice because the accuser is cast down. The call for rejoicing echoes such exclamations as Isaiah 49:13 ("Sing for joy, O heavens")[30] and Psalm 96:11 ("Let the heavens be glad, and let the earth rejoice"). Those that dwell in heaven are angelic beings. That they "tabernacle"[31] there does not indicate a temporary residence, but emphasizes the presence of God (cf. 7:15; 21:3). While the casting out of Satan brings rejoicing in heaven, it is cause for woe upon the earth and the sea.[32] Some writers identify this as the third Woe (see 8:13; 9:12; 11:14). In that the first two Woes are plagues unleashed upon unbelievers while the verses which follow in chapter 12 (vss. 13–17) describe the hostility of Satan toward Christians, it is unlikely that this should be considered as the final Woe. The reason for the great wrath of Satan is the relatively short period of time between his defeat in heaven and the final judgment. Morris observes that "the troubles of the persecuted righteous arise not because Satan is too strong, but because he is beaten" (p. 163). This short time is not "the whole course of human history" (Preston and Hanson, p. 94)[33] but the period of Satan's final and desperate struggle. It is the time of unprecedented peril into which the church is entering and throughout which John desires to encourage the believers faithfully to endure.

3. WAR ON EARTH (12:13–17)

13 *And when the dragon saw that he was cast down to the earth, he persecuted the woman that brought forth the man* child.

14 *And there were given to the woman the two wings of the great eagle, that she might fly into the wilderness unto her place, where she is nourished for a time, and times, and half a time, from the face of the serpent.*

15 *And the serpent cast out of his mouth after the woman water as a river, that he might cause her to be carried away by the stream.*

16 *And the earth helped the woman, and the earth opened her mouth and swallowed up the river which the dragon cast out of his mouth.*

17 *And the dragon waxed wroth with the woman, and went away to make war with the rest of her seed, that keep the commandments of God, and hold the testimony of Jesus:*

---

[29]The plural οὐρανοί is found only here in Rev; the singular occurs more than fifty times.

[30]LXX, Εὐφραίνεσθε οὐρανοί.

[31]*ASV* margin; Gk. σκηνοῦντες. κατοικοῦντες is regularly used throughout Revelation in connection with the pagan population of the earth (6:10; 8:13; 11:10; etc.).

[32]1 2026 *pc* TR add τοῖς κατοικοῦσιν after οὐαί to specify that the woe is to those who dwell upon the earth.

[33]They justify this interpretation by reference to Ps 90:4 ("A thousand years in thy sight are but as yesterday").

13 The narrative, which for a few verses gave way to a hymn of praise (vss. 10–12), is once again resumed. Failing to destroy the child and defeated in heavenly conflict, the dragon now turns with persecuting zeal[34] against the mother. Verses 13–17 expand verse 6. The woman is the true Israel. Earlier (vs. 5) she gave birth to the Messiah; now she shares in the hostility which Satan directs against her Son. On the Damascus road the young rabbi Saul was asked, "Why do you persecute me?" He learned that in persecuting the church he was persecuting Jesus (Acts 9:4–5). From the very first, Christ has been inseparably united with those who have received him by faith (cf. Mt 25:45).

Exodus typology is woven throughout this entire episode. The pursuit of the woman is similar to Pharaoh's pursuit of the children of Israel as they fled from Egypt (Ex 14:8). The two wings of the great eagle which made possible her escape echo the words of God from Sinai, "I bore you on eagles' wings and brought you to myself" (Ex 19:4). The river of water which flowed from the dragon's mouth may reflect Pharaoh's charge to drown the male children of the Israelites in the Nile (Ex 1:22). The opening of the earth is reminiscent of the destruction of the men of Korah when in the wilderness they were swallowed by the earth and went down alive into Sheol (Num 16:31–33).

The major theme of the paragraph is the persecution of the woman and her seed. It is important to note that the antagonism directed against the church has its origin in the hatred of Satan for Christ. Jesus taught his disciples that they would receive the same hostile treatment from the world that he had received. "All this they will do to you on my account" (Jn 15:21).

14 The woman is given the two wings of the great eagle,[35] symbolizing divine deliverance and enablement. In the Song of Moses we read of God finding Jacob in the wilderness and caring for him as an eagle that "fluttereth over her young." He "spread abroad his wings" and "bare them on his pinions" (Deut 32:10–11, *ASV;* cf. Ex 19:4). Elsewhere the prophet writes that those who wait upon the Lord "shall mount up with wings like eagles" (Isa 40:31). The wings enable the woman to fly into the desert, a place of spiritual refuge (cf. comm. on 12:6). In time of persecution God protects his own. Kiddle interprets the wilderness as that state of

---

[34]ἐδίωξεν may be an ingressive aorist (even though the verb is not one denoting a state or condition). One correction of the Sinaiticus supplies the more intensive ἐξεδίωξεν. P⁴⁷ (perhaps following ἀπῆλθεν ποιῆσαι πόλεμον of vs. 17) has ἀπῆλθεν ἐκδιῶξαι.

[35]The articles do not refer to some specific eagle in traditional folklore (αἱ is omitted by P⁴⁷ ℵ **046** 82 2060 *pm* TR), nor to the eagle of 8:13, but are generic. ἀετός may be a vulture (as in Lk 17:37), but not necessarily. In Mic 1:16 (LXX) the reference to baldness suggests the griffon vulture.

complete spiritual detachment from the world (the great city) which is a necessary preparation for life in the New Jerusalem (p. 238). It is there that the woman is nourished (or perhaps trained)[36] for three and a half years. This period of time corresponds to the forty-two months of Jewish oppression under the Syrian tyrant Antiochus Epiphanes (Dan 7:25).[37] "From the face of the serpent" completes the earlier clause, "that she might fly into the wilderness."

15–16 As the woman flies to the wilderness, the serpent opens its mouth and sends forth a great flood of water to overtake her. The earth comes to her rescue by opening up and swallowing the torrent. The flood is a common metaphor in the OT for overwhelming evil ("The floods of ungodliness," Ps 18:4, *ASV*) and tribulation ("When you pass through the waters, I will be with you," Isa 43:2). But Jewish literature supplies no parallels to verse 15. Bruce suggests that it may refer to some event in the war of AD 66–73 which threatened to cut off the escape of the church from Jerusalem, or, less likely, to a literal flood such as the one which prevented the Jews of Gadara from escaping across the Jordan from the Romans in March, AD 68 (p. 652).[38] Some writers think that it is part of a legend which John was using and has no particular Christian application (Glasson, p. 78). In any case, John is never restricted by the sources of his imagery. Historically the episode could refer to the attempt on the part of the Jewish authorities in Jerusalem to stamp out the early church (Acts 8:1–3; Preston and Hanson, p. 94). Or it could refer to the river of lies which will threaten even the elect (II Thess 2:9–11; Rev 13:14; Mt 24:24) in the last days. This river of deceit (cf. 2:9; 3:9) has as its counterpart the "river of water of life" which flows bright as crystal from the heavenly throne (21:1).

The opening of the earth to swallow the men of Korah (Num 16:30) may have suggested the imagery of verse 16, but sheds little light on its meaning. Commentators note various references to rivers or streams in Asia which disappear into the earth.[39] The entire scene illustrates Jesus' promise that he would build his church and that "the powers of death shall not prevail against it" (Mt 16:18). While nature is somehow involved with the consequences of man's sin (Rom 8:19–22), it is unlikely that the present verse is teaching that nature is on God's side in the moral struggle between right and wrong.

[36]τρέφω may be used of the rearing of children. In Lk 4:16 Nazareth is the place where Jesus was "brought up" (ἦν τεθραμμένος).

[37]Ford points out that where forty-two occurs in the OT it is always associated with violent death (II Kgs 2:23–24; 10:14). She concludes that "forty-two may symbolize violent useless killing" (p. 192). The coincidence is fortuitous.

[38]This slaughter by the swollen Jordan is reported in Josephus, *Bell.* iv.433–36.

[39]Herodotus had heard that the Lycus flowed underground near Colossae (Swete, p. 159).

17 Angered by his failure to harm the woman, the dragon goes off "to make war with the rest of her seed."[40] Those who understand the pursuit of the woman by the dragon as Satan's attempt to destroy the Palestinian church will interpret "the rest of her seed" to be Gentile believers throughout the empire. It is more probable that the phrase refers to believers in general as distinguished from the male child of verses 5 and 13. They are the brethren of Christ (cf. Rom 8:29; Heb 2:11). The faithful are described as those who "keep the commandments of God, and hold the testimony of Jesus." The testimony of Jesus (cf. 1:2, 9; 19:10; 20:4) is not their witness to him,[41] but the testimony that he bore. It may intend to make more explicit the "commandments of God," which could be taken in a general sense (as in I Cor 7:19).[42]

---

[40]The use of τοῦ σπέρματος αὐτῆς may echo Gen 3:15 (LXX).

[41]Swete's comment that "obedience to the Law does not constitute sonship without faith in Christ" (p. 160) understands Ἰησοῦ as an objective genitive.

[42]Schrenk notes that John never speaks of ἐντολαί without mentioning Jesus (TDNT, II, p. 555).

CHAPTER 13

In chapter 13 we are introduced to the two agents through whom Satan carries out his war against believers (see 12:17). In the language of apocalyptic they are beasts. The first comes out of the sea, a grotesque seven-headed monster (one head mutilated by the slash of a sword; 13:3, 12, 14) who combines characteristics of leopard, bear, and lion. The second beast comes out of the earth. He is less terrifying in appearance but able to deceive men by his power to work miracles. Together with the dragon the two beasts constitute an unholy trinity of malicious evil.

The last verse of chapter 12[1] pictured Satan standing by the sea as if to summon his henchmen from its troubled waters. Unable to reach the woman, he calls upon his wicked cohorts to destroy her offspring. Lilje stresses that "the figure of the beast is not simply a contemporary interpretation clothed in the garment of prophecy," but points "to the events of the last days" (p. 189). Although the vision employs references to contemporary history, its complete fulfillment is reserved for the final eschatological conflict. Charles' extended analysis of underlying sources (I, pp. 334–44) is interesting but sheds little light on the meaning of the vision.

4. THE BEAST FROM THE SEA (13:1–10)

1 *and he stood upon the sand of the sea.*
And I saw a beast coming up out of the sea, having ten horns and seven heads, and on his horns ten diadems, and upon his heads names of blasphemy.
2 *And the beast which I saw was like unto a leopard, and his feet were as the*

---

[1]Vs. 18 is sometimes left unnumbered (*eg.*, *RSV*) and is often taken as part of the following chapter. The *AV* follows the reading ἐστάθην (**P 046** 1 82 1006 1611 2059s 2329 *pm* sy^ph co Tyc TR) and understands the subject to be John. Textual evidence favors ἐστάθη (**P**47 ℵ **A** 205 1854 *al* lat sy^h), which connects the clause with the preceding verse.

feet *of a bear, and his mouth as the mouth of a lion: and the dragon gave him his power, and his throne, and great authority.*

3 *And I saw one of his heads as though it had been smitten unto death; and his death-stroke was healed: and the whole earth wondered after the beast;*

4 *and they worshipped the dragon, because he gave his authority unto the beast; and they worshipped the beast, saying, Who is like unto the beast? and who is able to war with him?*

5 *and there was given to him a mouth speaking great things and blasphemies; and there was given to him authority to continue forty and two months.*

6 *And he opened his mouth for blasphemies against God, to blaspheme his name, and his tabernacle, even them that dwell in the heaven.*

7 *And it was given unto him to make war with the saints, and to overcome them: and there was given to him authority over every tribe and people and tongue and nation.*

8 *And all that dwell on the earth shall worship him, every one whose name hath not been written from the foundation of the world in the book of life of the Lamb that hath been slain.*

9 *If any man hath an ear, let him hear.*

10 *If any man is for captivity, into captivity he goeth: if any man shall kill with the sword, with the sword must he be killed. Here is the patience and the faith of the saints.*

1   The first beast to appear rises up "out of the sea." The order in which the various parts of his body are mentioned (horns, head, body, feet) has led some to find here an eyewitness account of the beast's actual emergence from the waters.[2] The same expression, however, is used of the second beast who comes up "out of the earth." Consistent interpretation would make such literalism highly unlikely. John's figure was undoubtedly suggested by Daniel's vision of the four great beasts which came up from the sea (Dan 7:3).[3] While the sea may well be a symbol of the "disturbed and stormy social and political conditions out of which tyrannies commonly arise" (Erdman, p. 112), it is questionable whether the Seer would load the word with such theological significance. Yet the ancient world commonly associated the sea with evil, and for the last great enemy of God's people to arise from the reservoir of chaos would be entirely appro-

---

[2]Cf. Hendriksen, pp. 176 f. The mouth is mentioned last because it is the main point of the figure.

[3]D'Aragon writes, "The Seer has blended into one image various characteristics of the four beasts in Dn 7; the result is a monstrous creature that defies the imagination" (p. 483).

priate. In 11:7 and 17:8 the beast is said to come up out of the abyss. Any contradiction is only apparent: in both cases the reference is to the source of all evil.

The beast has ten horns and seven heads. On the horns are diadems, and on the heads are names[4] of blasphemy. Extended discussion of the horns and heads will be reserved for chapter 17 in which an angel of judgment supplies a detailed interpretation of the beast and his rider. The ten horns are like those of Daniel's fourth beast (Dan 7:7). There they are the ten kings which rise out of the fourth kingdom.[5] In Revelation 17 the ten horns are also ten kings (17:10), although in the present vision we learn only that they wear diadems, the insignia of royal authority (cf. 19:12). There are a number of suggestions as to why the diadems are placed on the horns rather than on the heads of the beast. The most plausible is that his claim to authority rests on brute force. It is hardly necessary in apocalyptic to shift the diadems to the horns in order to have sufficient room to stamp the heads with blasphemous names (as Moffatt suggests, p. 429). The Seer does not intend us to visualize the beast with such precision.[6] That the horns are mentioned before the heads (elsewhere the order is reversed; 17:3, 7; cf. 12:3) has no special significance. John is given to variation.

That the beast has seven heads stresses its relationship to the seven-headed dragon of chapter 12 (vs. 3). The power and authority of the beast come from the dragon (13:4). It is unlikely that John arrived at the number seven by adding the total number of heads on Daniel's four beasts (four beasts, one of which had four heads, for a total of seven). In apocalyptic the number seven carries the idea of completeness. A seven-headed beast would be an appropriate symbol for the ultimate enemy of the believing church. The names of blasphemy upon the seven heads reflect the increasing tendency of the Roman emperors to assume titles of deity. During his lifetime Augustus had allowed his eastern subjects to pay him divine honors, and at his death the Romans proclaimed him *divus* (one like the gods). On his coins Nero was referred to as Savior of the World. The Roman senate regularly declared its deceased emperors divine. Domitian

---

[4]Textual evidence is fairly evenly divided between the singular, ὄνομα (P[47] א C P 1 1006 2059s 2329 *al* TR), and the plural, ὀνόματα (A **046 051** 82 1611 *pm*). Nestle (25th ed.), Kilpatrick, and the UBS text all print the plural, but the latter brackets the ending (ὀνόμα[τα]).

[5]The four kingdoms are Babylonia, Media, Persia, and Greece. The ten horns would be ten Seleucid rulers between Alexander the Great and Antiochus Epiphanes (the "little horn," Dan 7:8, 24–26).

[6]Consider the problem of locating ten horns on only seven heads! And where would the mouth (στόμα, sing., vs. 2) be on a seven-headed beast?

was addressed as *Dominus et Deus noster,* Our Lord and God.[7] To all who held a high view of God and his sovereignty such pretentious claims were sheer blasphemy. "You shall worship the Lord your God, and him only shall you serve" (Lk 4:8). For man to assume the titles of divinity was arrogant blasphemy.

But who is the beast of John's vision? From the verses which follow we learn that he possessed the authority of Satan (vs. 4), blasphemed the name of God (vss. 5–6), warred victoriously against the saints (vs. 7), and received the worship of the pagan world (vss. 4, 8). There is little doubt that for John the beast was the Roman Empire as persecutor of the church.[8] It was that spirit of imperial power which claimed a religious sanction for its gross injustices. Yet the beast is more than the Roman Empire. John's vision grew out of the details of his own historical situation, but its complete fulfillment awaits the final denouement of human history. The beast has always been, and will be in a final intensified manifestation, the deification of secular authority.

2 The beast out of the sea combines characteristics of the four beasts of Daniel 7. The prophet saw in succession a winged lion standing upright as a man (7:4), a bear with three ribs between its teeth (7:5), a four-headed leopard with wings (7:6), and a fourth beast, terrible and strong with great iron teeth and many horns (7:7–8). In combining these beasts, which in Daniel represented four historic kingdoms hostile to the people of God (Dan 7:17, 23), John sets forth the Antichrist as the epitome of bestial opposition to the seed of the woman. Barclay writes, "For John the Roman Empire was so satanic and terrible that in itself it included all the evil terrors of the evil empires which had gone before. It was, as it were, the sum total of all evil" (II, pp. 109–10). Some writers see a special significance in each beast: the fierce cruelty of the leopard,[9] the slow, crushing power of the bear, the dreaded roar of the lion.[10] In any case the main purpose of the Seer is to describe a monster great and terrifying who utters blasphemies against God and persecutes the faithful. It is of crucial importance to note that the beast receives his power, dominion,[11] and

---

[7]Suetonius, *Dom.* 13. For the imperial inscriptions at Ephesus see Stauffer, *Christ and the Caesars,* pp. 185 ff.

[8]For a convenient presentation of the background for understanding Rev 13, cf. Barclay, "Great Themes of the New Testament: V. Rev xiii," *ET,* 70 (1958), pp. 260–64, 292–96.

[9]πάρδαλις may be the panther (only here in the NT).

[10]Hosea mentions the same three beasts when giving voice to God's opposition to wayward Israel ("So will I be to them like a lion; like a leopard I will lurk beside the way. I will fall upon them like a bear robbed of her cubs"; Hos 13:7–8).

[11]Understanding θρόνος figuratively.

authority from the dragon. The tremendous impact of the Roman Empire stemmed from its unholy alliance with Satan himself. Through it Satan would carry out his plan to devastate and devour the church.

It should be noted that the attitude toward the state in Revelation differs decidedly from that reflected in such passages as Romans 13:1-6; I Timothy 2:1-2; and I Peter 2:13-17. This is not because John differed from the other apostles regarding church and state. It is because in the developing historical situation of the first century the existing truce between church and empire had given way to conflict in which an aggressive program of emperor worship was being forced upon the populace, supported by active persecution. In the clash of loyalties between God and emperor, the Christian had no choice but to obey the One who is the source of all authority.[12] Only when the state continues to act within the limitations of its delegated authority can the believer freely submit to its regulations.

3 One of the beast's seven heads has been dealt a mortal wound (according to 13:13, by a stroke of the sword). But the beast survives the death-stroke and draws the whole world after him in amazement. Many commentators take the slaughtered head as standing for one of the Roman emperors. Caligula is a likely candidate in that he was taken with a serious illness and recovered (Suetonius, *Calig.* 14; Dio Cassius lix.8). His attempt to set up his statue in the temple could give rise to verse 6 ("He opened his mouth for blasphemies against God . . . and his tabernacle"), and the many altars erected to him throughout the empire (Josephus, *Ant.* xviii.8.1) would encourage the kind of universal worship reflected in verse 8 ("All that dwell on earth shall worship him"). Most writers, however, who take the slain head as a Roman emperor choose Nero. This tyrant, who gained the throne by the treachery of a scheming mother (banished by Caligula but brought back by her uncle, Claudius, whom she married and later poisoned), instituted in AD 64 a savage persecution of the Christian church. In order to escape the ignominious death prescribed for a public enemy, he took his own life in June of 68. So evil was he that many (especially in the eastern provinces) thought his death in a private villa outside Rome could not possibly be true. Although he was given a public funeral, the rumor persisted for a number of years that he had not died but had gone to Parthia where he remained in hiding to return some day at the head of a mighty army to regain his lost dominion. During the next two decades several pretenders arose claiming to be Nero (Tacitus, *Hist.* i.78; ii.8; Suetonius, *Nero* 57), two of whom were well received in

---

[12]For a good survey of the developing antagonism between the early church and the Roman Empire, cf. G. B. Caird's chap. on "Christ and Caesar" in *The Apostolic Age*, pp. 156-80.

Parthia. By the end of the century the belief that he was still alive had faded. It was replaced with the expectation that he would rise from the dead and return to seize power.

A basic problem with identifying the slain head as Nero (or any specific emperor) is that the text does not say that the *head* was restored. It was the *beast* who recovered from the death-stroke upon one of his heads. Later in the same chapter we read of "the *beast* who hath the stroke of the sword and lived" (13:14).[13] The interpretation of the seven heads as seven kings is a development of chapter 17 (note that in 17:19 they are also seven mountains) and does not belong to the immediate vision. Since the beast is the Roman Empire in its persecution of the church, its recovery from a mortal wound could refer to the re-establishment of order under Vespasian (AD 69–79) following the chaotic and bloody revolution which had begun less than two years before with the death of Nero and extended through the abortive reigns of Galba, Otho, and Vitellius. Or perhaps no historical allusion is intended and the purpose of the figure is to underscore the tremendous vitality of the beast. Though wounded he returns with increased might. From the beginning of history the pagan state has set itself against the people of God. From the pharaohs of Egypt to the emperors of Rome it had moved steadily forward with determined purpose to devour all who refused it homage. It had survived every assault and recovered from every deadly blow. Little wonder that in the last days the whole world will be drawn after[14] the beast in wonder and amazement. Preston and Hanson (p. 97) note that man is made to worship some absolute power and in the last analysis will give his allegiance either to the beast (whose power is that of inflicting suffering) or to the Lamb (whose power lies in accepting suffering).

4 The inhabitants of the earth worship not only the beast but the dragon as well—the one who has given his authority to the beast. Deification of secular power is in fact the worship of Satan.[15] The rhetoric of praise ascribed to the beast parodies such OT passages as Exodus 15:11 ("Who in the skies can be compared to the Lord?"). Who is like the beast

---

[13]Cf. also 13:12. The second αὐτοῦ of 13:3 would normally be αὐτῆς if it referred to μία ἐκ τῶν κεφαλῶν. Minear says it is difficult to maintain that Nero was the wounded beast because "his death did not jeopardize the power of the empire, because he died as a fugitive and enemy of the state" ("The Wounded Beast," *JBL*, 72 [1953], p. 97).

[14]Cf. I Tim 5:15, ὀπίσω τοῦ σατανᾶ; also John 12:19; Acts 5:37. Charles suggests a corruption in the Hebrew that would allow a Greek rendition which read ἰδοῦσα instead of ὀπίσω (I, p. 351). He supports the conjecture by parallels in 17:6, 8.

[15]Cullmann (*The State in the New Testament*, p. 80) writes that "the author of the Johannine Apocalypse saw with astonishing acumen that the satanic element in the Roman Empire lay in this deification" (*ie.*, emperor worship).

and who is able to war with him? The motivation for worship is not his moral greatness but the awesome power of his might. The authority he wields is the authority of Satan himself.

5 The beast is allowed to utter great blasphemies for a period of forty-two months. Once again the model is the little horn of Daniel 7 with its "mouth speaking great things" (Dan 7:8; cf. 7:20), who is to "speak words against the Most High" (Dan 7:25) and "magnify himself above every god, and . . . speak astonishing things against the God of gods" (Dan 11:36). The "great things" spoken by the beast are explained by the phrase which follows ("even blasphemies") and expanded in verse 6. In addition to a mouth, the beast is given authority. Four times in verses 5 through 7 we read the passive, "was given," emphasizing the subordinate role of the beast. Although in verses 2 and 4 it was the dragon who gave power and authority to the beast, John's readers would understand in these later verses a reference to God, the ultimate source of all power. The reign of the beast is by divine permission. He operates within the limitations determined by God. The time of his blasphemy is forty-two months, the traditional period for religious persecution (cf. comm. on 11:2). The *ASV* translation, "to continue," is weak. During the forty-two months the beast actively carries out the will of the dragon.[16]

6 The beast opens his mouth in blasphemies against God. This activity of the Antichrist is clearly portrayed in II Thessalonians 2:4: He "opposes and exalts himself against every so-called god . . . proclaiming himself to be God" (cf. *Asc. Isa.* 4:6; *Sib. Or.* 5:33–34). The blasphemy of Antiochus (Dan 7:25; 11:36) and the use of divine titles by the Roman emperors would for John identify the Antichrist as the one in whom secular authority had assumed the mantle of deity. The expression, to open the mouth, is frequently used at the beginning of a prolonged discourse (cf. Mt 5:2; Acts 8:35) and suggests that the blasphemies of the beast against God were sustained.

The relationship between the several clauses in verse 6 is variously understood. If "and" is read as the first word of the last clause,[17] there are three objects of blasphemy: the name of God, his tabernacle, and those that dwell in heaven. It is more likely that the final clause is appositional and

---

[16]ποιῆσαι is used in this sense in Dan 8:12, 24; 11:28. Sinaiticus properly interprets with ποιῆσαι ὃ θέλει. The Byzantine Text anticipates and reads πόλεμον ποιῆσαι.

[17]καί is added before τούς by **P 046*** 1 2059 *al* lat arm Ir^lat TR. Metzger says the addition appears to have been made by copyists desiring to "alleviate the strained syntax" (*TCGNT*, p. 748). **P**[47] *g* omit both τούς and σκηνοῦντας so that the final phrase reads "his tabernacle in heaven."

develops more specifically what is intended by the previous expression. To blaspheme the name of God is to speak evil of all that he is and stands for. The name sums up the person. His tabernacle is his dwelling place. In 21:3 a great voice declares, "The tabernacle of God is with men, and he shall dwell with them." Some understand the blaspheming of the temple as a reference to Caligula's attempt to set up his statue in the Holy of Holies,[18] but it is doubtful that any historical allusion is intended. In fact, the following clause speaks of those who dwell in heaven. In 7:15 God spreads his tabernacle over those who serve him day and night in his heavenly temple. Those who dwell in heaven are either angelic beings, or, possibly, the church viewed ideally as seated in heavenly places (cf. Eph 2:6; Col 3:1).

7 It is also given to the beast to make war with the saints and overcome them. The first part of verse 7[19] builds on Daniel 7:21. Swete comments that "like the... loyal defenders of Jerusalem against Antiochus, the citizens of the new Jerusalem must expect to fall before the persecuting Emperor" (p. 166). Universal authority is given to the beast. It extends over every tribe, people, tongue, and nation.[20] Although the saints are to be overcome (that is, put to death) by the beast, the real victory belongs to them. They are those who "come off victorious from the beast" (15:2). In the crucial test of faith they relinquish their lives rather than their confidence in God. This is true victory! The twice-repeated "it was given unto him" stresses the subordinate role of the beast. He is the dragon's instrument for revenge and operates at his bidding. Yet the reference goes beyond the dragon, and we are to understand that even this unholy alliance is under the control of the One in whom resides all authority and might.

8 The whole world (apart from those whose names are written in the Lamb's book of life) joins in worship of the beast. Jesus had foretold the coming of false Christs who with displays of signs and wonders would "lead astray, if possible, even the elect" (Mt 24:24). Once the Roman state had taken on a religious significance it was only natural that it should begin to demand worship. The worship of a satanically inspired perversion of secular authority is the ultimate offense against the one true God. The temptation rejected by Jesus at the outset of his public ministry (Mt 4:8–10) reappears at the end of history in its most persuasive form and gains the allegiance of all but the elect.

---

[18]Josephus, *Ant.* xviii.8.2. Charles takes the tabernacle as a reference to the Shekinah (I, p. 353), the manifested glory of God, which in Jewish thought was connected with the tabernacle (Heb., *mishkān;* Gk., σκηνή—see Barclay, II, p. 122).

[19]καὶ ἐδόθη . . . αὐτούς is omitted by P47 A C P 1* 2059s *al* sa armᵖ Ir, undoubtedly because the eye of the scribe skipped to the second καὶ ἐδόθη αὐτῷ in the same verse.

[20]καὶ λαόν is omitted by P47 1 1006 2059s *al* TR.

The *ASV* translation *"every one"* represents an unexpected change in the Greek text from the plural to the singular.[21] The shift is perhaps intended to emphasize the individual responsibility of each one who worships the beast. They are the ones whose names are not written in the book of life. The idea of a divine register is found as far back as Moses' encounter with God on Mt. Sinai (Deut 32:32–33). In the NT Paul speaks of his fellow workers as those "whose names are in the book of life" (Phil 4:3). In Revelation the designation occurs six times (3:5; 13:8; 17:8; 20:12, 15; 21:27) and refers to a register of the names of all those who belong to God. Here and in 21:27 the book of life is said to belong to the Lamb. It is through his sacrifice that life is possible (5:9–10).

The "foundation of the world" refers to the creation of the visible order. It is mentioned ten times in the NT. Jesus speaks of a kingdom prepared from the foundation of the world (Mt 25:34), and Paul of the believers' election before the foundation of the world (Eph 1:4). The problem in the immediate verse is not the meaning of the phrase but its place in the sentence. Was it the writing of believers' names or the death of the Lamb which dates from the foundation of the world? The *RSV* and many of the newer translations follow the first alternative. The faithful are guarded by their election (the writing of their names in the Lamb's book of life) from being deceived by the pretensions of the Antichrist. This is said to have taken place at the foundation of the world. Revelation 17:8, a parallel verse, would support this interpretation. However, the premise that John must be absolutely consistent in his literary expression is questionable. There is no particular reason why he should be denied the freedom to use a given phrase in several ways. It is better in this case to follow the order of the Greek syntax and read, "the Lamb that hath been slain from the foundation of the world."[22] That is, the death of Christ was a redemptive sacrifice decreed in the counsels of eternity. It is worth noting that names may be blotted out of the book of life (3:5), hence having one's name in the register at the beginning of creation would offer something less than complete security in the time of trial.

9–10 The contemporary equivalent of verse 9 would be, "Now hear this!" It occurs in each of the seven letters (2:7, 11, 17, 19; 3:6, 13, 22) and recalls the familiar expression of Jesus, "He who has ears to hear, let him hear" (Mt 11:15; cf. Mk 4:9). It alerts the reader to the importance of that which follows.

---

[21]οὖ calls for an implied ἕκαστος which distributes the collective πάντες. The plural ὧν is read by P[47] ℵ **P 046 051** 1 82 1006 1611 2059s 2329 *pl* lat TR.

[22]The other construction separates the modifier from its antecedent by twelve words.

The proverbial style of verse 10 has resulted in several scribal attempts to clarify meaning by altering the text.[23] Some manuscripts refer both couplets to the persecutors of the church by adding a verb which makes the first line read, "If any man *leads*[24] into captivity, into captivity he goes." Thus the verse would stress that the enemies of God's people would be requited for their persecution of believers in the same form they employed (captivity for captivity, sword for sword). Just how this can be called "the patience and the faith of the saints" is not clear.

Alexandrinus, a fifth-century manuscript, interprets both couplets in reference to the saints by changing the second verb to a passive infinitive and reading, "If any man is to be killed with a sword, he is to be killed with a sword."[25] This reading stresses the inevitability of persecution and death for the faithful. Charles argues that this appeal to loyal endurance suits the context and tone of the entire Apocalypse and, further, is supported by Jeremiah 15:2 and 43:11 (I, p. 355).

The *ASV* follows the text of Sinaiticus and reads, "If any man shall kill with the sword, with the sword he must be killed."[26] This corresponds to the words of Jesus in Matthew 26:52, "All who take the sword will perish by the sword." The first couplet teaches that the believer must accept what God has ordained, and the second warns against any attempt on the part of the church to defend itself by the use of force. Barclay writes, "It is an intolerable paradox to defend the gospel of the love of God by using the violence of man" (II, p. 127). This attitude of humble submission is the patience and faith of the saints. Patience is steadfast endurance in the midst of persecution, and faith is the steady trust which never wavers (cf. Gal 5:22).

5. THE BEAST FROM THE EARTH (13:11–18)

11 *And I saw another beast coming up out of the earth; and he had two horns like unto a lamb, and he spake as a dragon.*

12 *And he exerciseth all the authority of the first beast in his sight. And he maketh the earth and them that dwell therein to worship the first beast, whose death-stroke was healed.*

[23]See the apparatus in the UBS text, p. 868, and Metzger's discussion in *TCGNT,* pp. 749–50.
[24]ἀπάγει, 172 424 *pc* g vg^s,cl sy sa Ir^lat Prim; 296 TR read συνάγει.
[25]This change also requires dropping δεῖ and taking αὐτόν as a corruption of αὐτός (cf. Charles, I, pp. 355–56).
[26]ἀποκτείνει is also read by 1611* *pc*. Caird lists four persuasive reasons for accepting this text: the charge of vs. 9 is elsewhere used of the church, the threat of prison is meaningful to the prospective martyr, use of the sword echoes Jesus' words in Gethsemane, and the call for endurance and faith is directed to the church (pp. 169–70).

13 *And he doeth great signs, that he should even make fire to come down out of heaven upon the earth in the sight of men.*

14 *And he deceiveth them that dwell on the earth by reason of the signs which it was given him to do in the sight of the beast; saying to them that dwell on the earth, that they should make an image to the beast who hath the stroke of the sword and lived.*

15 *And it was given unto him to give breath to it, even to the image of the beast, that the image of the beast should both speak, and cause that as many as should not worship the image of the beast should be killed.*

16 *And he causeth all, the small and the great, and the rich and the poor, and the free and the bond, that there be given them a mark on their right hand, or upon their forehead;*

17 *and that no man should be able to buy or to sell, save he that hath the mark, even the name of the beast or the number of his name.*

18 *Here is wisdom. He that hath understanding, let him count the number of the beast; for it is the number of a man: and his number is Six hundred and sixty and six.*

11 Another beast appears in John's vision. In contrast to the first who came up out of the sea, this one arises out of the earth. Ancient tradition spoke of two primeval monsters which inhabited the ocean depths and the dry land. According to *I Enoch* 60:7–10 Leviathan (a female monster) lived "in the abysses of the ocean" and Behemoth (the male) occupied a "waste wilderness named Duidain."[27] It does not follow, however, that John is intentionally building upon the mythology of his day. He employs whatever apocalyptic imagery is appropriate for his own purposes. Some writers think that since the first beast may have been suggested by Daniel 7:3 (the four great beasts came up *from the sea*), the second beast could well have been suggested from the interpretation of this verse a bit later in the same chapter (Dan 7:17 says the beasts are kings that arise *out of the earth*). A simpler solution is that as the first beast came from across the sea, the second beast rose within Asia Minor itself. In any case, the evil triumvirate is now complete. Bruce (p. 653) notes that as Christ received authority from the Father (Mt 11:27) so Antichrist receives authority from the dragon (Rev 13:4), and as the Holy Spirit glorifies Christ (Jn 16:14) so the false prophet glorifies the Antichrist (Rev 13:12).

The beast out of the earth is a deceiver (cf. vs. 14). Elsewhere he is uniformly called the false prophet (16:13; 19:20; 20:10). His two horns like a lamb represent his attempt to convey the impression of gentle harmlessness. It recalls the warning of Jesus, "Beware of false prophets, who come

[27]See also II Esdr 6:49–52; *II Bar.* 29:4. Both monsters are referred to in Job 40:15–41:34.

258

to you in sheep's clothing, but inwardly are ravenous wolves'' (Mt 7:15). Moffatt thinks that the horns like a lamb refer to the seductive inducements (considerations of loyalty, patriotism, self-interest, etc.) held out to Christians by the beast (p. 432). It is unlikely that the two horns are intended to contrast with the two witnesses of chapter 11. Neither do they allude to the seven-horned Lamb of 5:6.[28] In the parody that runs throughout this section it is the first, not the second, beast who corresponds to the Lamb. That the beast speaks as a dragon may mean either that he speaks with the roar of a dragon (Swete, p. 169), or that, as the serpent in Eden (cf. 12:9), his speech is deceitful and beguiling.[29]

The role of the second beast is to bring men to worship the first beast. To achieve this end he is empowered to work miracles. By economic boycott and the threat of death he intends to make all men worship the image of the beast. This priestly role identifies the second beast as a religious power. In John's day the reference would be either to the local priests of the imperial cult or to the provincial council responsible for enforcing emperor worship throughout Asia.[30] In the final days of Antichrist the false prophet stands for the role of false religion in effecting the capitulation of mankind to the worship of secular power. It is the universal victory of humanism.

12 As the dragon gave his authority to the first beast (13:4), so the second beast exercises the authority of the first. He carries out the desires of the first beast as a prophet who stands in readiness before his god (cf. I Kgs 17:1). His purpose is to cause all mankind[31] to worship the beast whose death-stroke was healed. Writers who interpret the death-stroke which was healed as a reference to the Nero Redivivus legend find it necessary to point out that here and in verse 14 the beast is to be identified with the head impersonating him. It is simpler to understand that the beast himself recovered rather than one of his heads which was mortally wounded (cf. comm. on 13:3).

13 Deuteronomy 13:1 warns of the false prophet who would lead people to worship other gods by means of signs and wonders. The second beast imitates the miracles of the true prophets to deceive the people into

---

[28]This would normally call for τῷ ἀρνίῳ.

[29]Charles, although acknowledging that he can make nothing of the clause, builds a case for a corruption in the Hebrew original that yields, ''But he was a destroyer like the dragon'' (I, p. 358).

[30]Ford tentatively identifies the second beast as Flavius Josephus (pp. 227–30), noting that in Rev 13:11–18 ''the author of Revelation has depicted the monstrous behavior of Josephus and others like him who led his countrymen to submit to and honor Rome'' (p. 230).

[31]''The earth and them that dwell therein'' is a comprehensive designation for the totality of mankind.

worshipping the beast. Like Elijah he calls down fire out of heaven in the sight of all men.[32] As a false Elijah he prepares the way for a false Messiah. It was widely expected that the appearance of the Antichrist would be marked by numerous miracles. Jesus predicted the rise of false Christs who would lead astray, if possible, even the elect (Mk 13:22). Paul speaks of the lawless one "whose coming is according to the working of Satan with all power and signs and lying wonders" (II Thess 2:9, *ASV*). According to the *Ascension of Isaiah* 4:10 the Antichrist will make the sun rise at night and the moon appear at the sixth hour.[33] The second beast carries out his task of deception in fulfillment of these expectations.

14 The power of Satan to deceive (12:9; 20:3, 8) is shared by the false prophet (cf. 19:20). He is, according to Bruce, the Antichrist's Minister of Propaganda (p. 653). "Those that dwell on the earth" is a semi-technical designation for the entire body of unregenerated mankind.[34] They are deceived by[35] the miracles which the false prophet is empowered to perform in the presence of the beast. Some writers see a parody on the two witnesses who stand "before the Lord of the earth" (11:4) and devour their enemies with fire from their mouths (11:5). The second beast instructs the people to make an image of the beast who[36] survived the stroke of the sword. The translation, "who hath the stroke of the sword and *came to life*," is permissible,[37] but in view of the parallel passages (13:3, 12), which say he was *healed,* it is better to take the Greek verb in its normal sense. The image would probably be a bust or statue of the emperor rather than his image stamped on a coin.[38] According to *Ascension of Isaiah* 4:11 the Antichrist is to set up his image in every city. Only the death of Caligula prevented his intention of erecting his statue in the Jewish temple.

---

[32]I Kgs 18:38; cf. II Kgs 1:10. The sons of Zebedee requested Jesus to perform this spectacular feat in punishment upon the Samaritans who would not receive him (Lk 9:54).

[33]See also *Sib. Or.* 3:63–70 where an Antichrist figure shall even raise the dead.

[34]Cf. 6:10; 11:10; etc. In 13:8 and 17:8 they are identified as those whose names are not written in the book of life.

[35]διὰ τὰ σημεῖα: the distinction between the accusative and genitive has all but disappeared here; cf. 12:11.

[36]Sinaiticus and others (1 82 1006 1611 2059 2329 *pm* TR) read ὅ to correspond with the neuter θηρίον. Along with the Byzantine text it omits τήν before πληγήν, which makes less likely any specific reference to Nero's suicide.

[37]In its three other occurrences in Revelation the aorist of ζάω means "to come to life" (2:8; 20:4, 5). Even if that were the sense in 13:14, it could be used metaphorically of the return to health from a serious setback. It is not necessarily a reference to Domitian as Nero returned from the grave to begin again his persecution of Christians. Beckwith takes ζάω in the sense of ἀναζάω and argues that it was the miraculous revivification of the slain head which the priesthood used to urge the worship of the emperor (pp. 640–41).

[38]For εἰκών in the latter sense see Lk 20:24.

15 The second beast is given the power to animate the image of the first beast. He gives to it the breath of life,[39] and the image speaks. Belief in statues which spoke and performed miracles is widely attested in ancient literature. Simon Magus is reputed to have brought statues to life.[40] Andreas, the sixth-century commentator, reminds us that it was the age of Apollonius of Tyana, whose trickery was held to come from the powers of evil. Ventriloquism was practiced by the priests of Oriental cults, and sorcery had found a place in the official circles of Rome. Apelles of Ascalon was at home in the court of Caligula, and Apollonius was a friend of several Roman emperors. The sorcerer Elymas on the island of Cyprus sought to prevent Sergius Paulus, the proconsul, from accepting the faith as preached by Paul and Barnabas (Acts 13:6–8; see also 16:16).

The syntax of the verse suggests that the image not only spoke but also passed the death sentence upon all[41] who would not worship it. Morris suggests a change of subject so that it is the second beast who enforces worship of the image (p. 172).[42] In either case the result is the same. In the last days there is to be a great division of mankind. Some will remain true to the faith even in the face of death; others will turn in worship to the Antichrist. It is this decision which accounts for the apostasy which is to precede the return of Christ (II Thess 2:1–3). Nominal Christians do not surrender their lives for a cause in which they do not really believe. Caird's position that John is speaking of the legal status of Christians rather than their actual fate (p. 177) is strange in view of the fact that in Trajan's day failure to worship the emperor was a capital offense.[43]

16 The second beast requires all men to receive the mark of the first beast on their right hand or forehead. The coupling of opposites (small, great; rich, poor; free, bond) is a rhetorical way of stressing the totality of human society (cf. 11:18; 19:5, 18; 20:12). No one who would carry on the normal pursuits of everyday life (vs. 17) is exempt. The origin of the mark is variously explained. It could derive from the practice of

---

[39]Probably πνεῦμα ζωῆς, as in 11:11.

[40]"*Statuas moveri feci: animavi exanima*" (*Clementine Recognitions* iii.47). See Charles (I, p. 361) for further references by Theophilus and Athenagoras.

[41]Charles writes that "none can evade the inquisition and none the dread alternatives of worship or death" (I, p. 361). This theory of universal martyrdom is shown implausible by I. Howard Marshall, "Martyrdom and the Parousia in the Revelation of John" (*SE*, 4 [1968], pp. 333–39).

[42]Cf. Metzger (*TCGNT*, pp. 750–51) for the UBS committee's decision about ἵνα in the final clause.

[43]See Pliny's letter to Trajan x.96.

branding disobedient slaves[44] or soldiers defeated in battle.[45] Religious tattooing was widespread in the ancient world, and devotees of a particular god were often branded to indicate their loyal devotion.[46] Ptolemy Philopator branded Jews who submitted to registration with the ivy leaf, the mark of Dionysiac worship (III Macc 2:29). The word translated "mark" was also used for the likeness or name of the emperor on Roman coins. Caird takes this as the reason for the mark being placed on the hand as well as the forehead in the present verse (p. 173).[47] The word was also a technical designation for the seals which were attached to commercial documents and stamped with the name and date of the emperor.[48] Some writers see a reference to the Jewish custom of wearing phylacteries (little leather boxes containing portions of the law) on the left hand and on the forehead (Deut 6:8).[49] Others take the passage as an apocalyptic description of certificates issued to those who had fulfilled the ceremonial obligations of emperor worship.[50] Preston and Hanson see a reference to the X of Christ's name (in Greek) and suggest that the mark of the beast was a parody of the practice of making the sign of the cross on the forehead of the new Christian (p. 99).[51]

Whatever the background of the word, its significance in the present passage is to parody the sealing of the servants of God in chapter 7. As the elect are sealed upon their foreheads to escape the destruction about to fall upon the earth, so the followers of the beast are to escape his wrath against the church by bearing his mark. In the apocalyptic vision of John the mark is obviously visible. It symbolizes unqualified allegiance to the demands of the imperial cult. In the final days of Antichrist it will represent the ultimate test of religious loyalty. Only those who would rather die than compromise their faith will resist the mark of Antichrist.

---

[44]A runaway slave who was caught and branded was a στιγματίας (cf. the English word "stigma"). Paul referred to the wounds received in the course of his ministry as τὰ στίγματα τοῦ Ἰησοῦ (Gal 6:17).

[45]According to Plutarch (*Pericl.* 26) the Samians branded Athenian prisoners with an owl. See also Herodotus 7.233.

[46]See Lucian, *Syr. Dea* 59; Herodotus ii.113.

[47]In 13:16 and 14:9 the mark is on the brow or the hand. In 20:4 it is on both.

[48]Deissmann, *Bible Studies*, p. 242; *LAE*, p. 341.

[49]Ford notes that, ironically, the mark on the right hand and the brow would be "an obvious travesty of the practice of orthodox Judaism which required the faithful to wear phylacteries on the left hand and the head; Deut 6:8" (p. 225).

[50]Ramsay, *L7CA*, pp. 110 f.

[51]In Ezek 9:4 the mark was a Hebrew *tau*, which in Greek would be written as a cross—X, a symbol for Χριστός.

17 Not only does the mark serve to identify those who worship the beast, but[52] it allows them to engage in the simple commercial transactions of the day. An economic boycott is raised against all who refuse to fall into line. This seems to be a harassment of believers rather than the method by which they are to be put to death (vs. 15). The mark is identified as the name of the beast written in its numerical equivalent. It is not the name of the beast *or* the number of his name that is stamped on his followers. The mark *is* the number of the name.[53]

In ancient times, letters of the alphabet served as numbers. The first nine letters stood for the numbers one through nine, the next nine for the numbers ten through ninety, and so on. As there were not enough letters in the current Greek alphabet, certain obsolete letters and signs were brought into the system. Thus, every name yielded a number. To decipher a number presented a rather fascinating riddle. An often quoted graffito from Pompeii reads, "I love her whose number is 545" (Deissmann, *LAE*, p. 277). Among the Jews the practice was known as gematria. Rabbis delighted in discovering esoteric meanings in the numbers found in Scripture. For example, in Genesis 14:14 the 318 trained men who accompanied Abram to recover Lot from his captors turn out to be Eliezer, the chief servant. A striking example is found in *Sibylline Oracles* (1:324 ff) where the name of Jesus in Greek is given as 888.[54] In the following verse in Revelation we learn that the number of the beast stamped upon his followers was 666. But just who is referred to by this cryptogram is another story!

18 No verse in Revelation has received more attention than this one with its cryptic reference to the number of the beast. Although the verse opens with the declaration, "Here is wisdom," the history of interpretation demonstrates that no consensus has been reached on who or what John had in mind.[55] The man who has understanding is called upon to count up or calculate[56] the number of the beast. This is an invitation to

---

[52]If καί is read (as in **P**[47] **ℵ**c **A P** *pm* vg TR), vs. 17 is coordinate with 16b and both depend on ποιεῖ. If καί is omitted (as in **ℵ*** **C** 1611 *pc* sy Prim), the restriction against buying and selling is the specific purpose of the mark.

[53]ἥ is here roughly equivalent to τοῦτ' ἐστίν. That the scribes were puzzled by this syntax is clear from the alternatives offered: it is the mark ἥ τὸ ὄνομα τοῦ θηρίου (**P**[47] 1778 *pc* g vg[s,cl] TR), the mark τοῦ ὀνόματος τοῦ θηρίου (**C** 2028 *pc* (vg[w]) sy Ir), the mark τοῦ θηρίου ἥ τὸ ὄνομα αὐτοῦ (**ℵ** *pc*).

[54]$I = 10, H = 8, \Sigma = 200, O = 70, Y = 400, \Sigma = 200.$

[55]Cf. Barclay ("Revelation 13," *ET*, 70 [1958], pp. 295–96) and Sanders ("The Number of the Beast in Revelation 13, 18," *JBL*, 37 [1918], pp. 95–99); also Evert Bruins, "The Number of the Beast" in *Nederlands Theologisch Tijdschrift*, 23 (1969), pp. 401–7.

[56]ψηφίζω occurs only here and in Lk 14:28 in the NT. In Lk it is used in connection with counting the cost of building a tower.

work backwards from the number 666 to the name for which it is the numerical equivalent. Gematria was widely used in apocalyptic because of its symbolic and enigmatic quality. It served as a precaution against the charge of sedition.

The number of the beast is the number of a certain man. Some writers feel that the clause should be read, "for it is a human [rather than a supernatural] number." But exactly what a nonhuman number would be or why it should enter this context is not at all clear. The reference is undoubtedly to some definite historical person.

The beast's number is 666. Already by the second century the solution to this riddle had escaped so prominent a theologian as Irenaeus, a native of Asia Minor and a disciple of Polycarp. In his work, *Against Heresies* (v.30) he mentions *Euanthas* (a name no longer identifiable), *Lateinos* (the Roman Empire), and *Teitan* (the Titans of Greek mythology who rebelled against the gods). Another early conjecture was *arnoume,* a form of the Greek verb meaning "to deny." Recent suggestions are equally ingenious and similarly unconvincing. Giet finds that the initials of the Roman emperors from Julius Caesar to Vespasian add up to 666,[57] but has to omit Otho and Vitellius to make it work out. Stauffer suggests that John was counting up an abbreviated form in Greek of the full Latin title of Domitian (*Imperator Caesar Domitianus Augustus Germanicus*), which appeared in part on his coinage.[58] A rather different solution has been offered by G. A. van den Bergh van Eysinga,[59] who shows that 666 is the triangular number of 36 (1 plus 2 plus 3 etc. up to 36), and 36 is the triangular number of 8—the number of the Antichrist (cf. 17:11).

The solution most commonly accepted today is that 666 is the numerical equivalent of Nero Caesar. It is held to be supported by the variant reading 616, which also yields the name of Nero when the Latinized spelling is followed.[60] What is not generally stressed is that this solution asks us to calculate a Hebrew transliteration of the Greek form of a Latin name, and that with a defective spelling.[61] A shift to Hebrew letters is

[57]*L'Apocalypse et l'histoire,* ad loc.

[58]Stauffer, *Coniectanea Neotestamentica,* XI, pp. 237 ff. Baines writes that coins issued in AD 72 bear a legend around Vespasian's head which when placed into Hebrew would yield the sum of 666 ("The Number of the Beast in Revelation 13:18," *Heythrop Journal,* 16 [1975], pp. 195–96).

[59]For a short summary see Ruhle's article in *TDNT,* I, p. 464. The interpretation was later adopted by Lohmeyer, *Die Offenbarung des Johannes,* pp. 114 f.

[60]616 is better accounted for as a deliberate attempt to identify the beast with Caligula. His name in Greek (Γαίος Καῖσαρ) totals 616.

[61]Omitting the י from קיסר (for Καῖσαρ). This defective spelling is attested in a Qumran document dated by reference to "Nero Caesar."

unlikely in that Revelation is written in Greek and there is no indication that the riddle is to be solved by transposing it into another language. Further, the name of Nero was apparently never suggested by the ancient commentators even though his persecuting zeal made him a model of the Antichrist.

Some writers take the number more as a symbol than a cryptogram. 666 is the number which falls short of perfection in each of its digits. For Hendriksen it represents "failure upon failure upon failure" (p. 182). It is symbolic of the beast's continuing failure to accomplish his purpose. It is the trinity of imperfection. Torrance writes, "This evil trinity 666 apes the Holy Trinity 777, but always falls short and fails" (p. 86).

In view of the widely divergent and highly speculative solutions to the riddle it seems best to conclude that John intended only his intimate associates to be able to decipher the number. So successful were his precautions that even Irenaeus some one hundred years later was unable to identify the person intended. An additional 1800 years of conjecture have not brought us any closer to an answer.

CHAPTER 14

In order to keep before his readers the ultimate reward of their endurance, the author of Revelation intersperses glimpses of final blessedness among his presentations of judgment. The detailed description of the beast and the false prophet in the preceding chapter was a somber reminder of what lay in the immediate future. A note of encouragement is in order. John moves quickly beyond the storm about to break to the bright morning of eternity when the Lamb and his followers stand on the heavenly Zion with the anthem of redemption everywhere resounding like the roar of a mighty waterfall and the echo of thunder. Verses 1–5 are often referred to as in some respects the most enigmatic in the book. The major difficulty is the description of the 144,000 as "virgins" who have not "defiled themselves with women" (vs. 4). Yet even this "violent and paradoxical metaphor" (Farrer, p. 161) yields an intelligible interpretation when proper consideration is given to John's highly figurative literary style. It is worthy of note that the *NEB*, by including verse 12 with verses 9–11, presents chapter 14 as composed of seven short oracles of the end of the age (Beasley-Murray, p. 221).

6. THE REDEEMED AND THE LAMB ON MT. ZION (14:1–5)

1 *And I saw, and behold, the Lamb standing on the mount Zion, and with him a hundred and forty and four thousand, having his name, and the name of his Father, written on their foreheads.*

2 *And I heard a voice from heaven, as the voice of many waters, and as the voice of a great thunder: and the voice which I heard was as the voice of harpers harping with their harps:*

3 *and they sing as it were a new song before the throne, and before the four living creatures and the elders: and no man could learn the song save the hundred and forty and four thousand, even they that had been purchased out of the earth.*

4 *These are they that were not defiled with women; for they are virgins.*
These are *they that follow the Lamb whithersoever he goeth. These were*
purchased from among men, to be *the firstfruits unto God and unto the*
Lamb.
5 *And in their mouth was found no lie: they are without blemish.*

1 The striking quality of the vision is stressed by the opening words, "I
saw, and behold."[1] Suddenly John sees the Lamb standing on Mt. Zion,
accompanied by the 144,000 who bear his name (and the name of his
Father) on their foreheads. The scene is in obvious contrast to the beast of
chapter 13 whose followers are stamped with his mark (666) on the right
hand or forehead (vss. 16–17). The Lamb who in chapter 5 was counted
worthy to unloose the seals of the scroll of destiny, and in chapter 7 to
receive the adulation of the innumerable multitude of heaven, now stands
victorious with his followers. II Esdras has an interesting parallel to our
text in which Ezra sees upon Mt. Zion a great crowd singing hymns of
praise to the Lord. In their midst is a tall young man who places crowns on
their heads. Upon inquiry Ezra learns that it is the Son of God whom they
acknowledged in mortal life (II Esdr 2:42–47).[2]

It is fitting that the Lamb should be standing on Mt. Zion, for this
sacred place had long been associated with divine deliverance. The prophet
Joel foretold that those on Mt. Zion would escape the great and terrible day
of the Lord (Joel 2:32).[3] The mountain in John's vision, however, is not on
earth (see Ladd, pp. 189–90, for the opposite view). It is the heavenly Zion
(cf. Heb 12:22), the Jerusalem that is above (Gal 4:26). Kiddle calls it "the
celestial pattern of the once sacred site of Jerusalem" (p. 263). Some
writers take it as the earthly site of a millennial reign (Walvoord, pp.
213–14), but the entire scene is one of praise before the throne of heaven.

The identity of the 144,000 (and their relation to a group of the
same number in chapter 7) has been variously interpreted. Verse 4 seems to
set them apart as a select group of supersaints. As first-fruits they would be
consecrated to God in a special way, and as celibates they would enjoy a
privileged relationship. The absence of any article before 144,000 is argued in support of this interpretation. But, as the commentary on verses
3–5 will demonstrate in detail, they are to be taken as the entire body of the

---

[1]εἶδον καὶ ἰδού also occurs at 4:1; 6:2; 6:5; 6:8; 7:9; 14:14 (cf. 19:11)—all highly dramatic
scenes.
[2]According to II Esdr 13 the Jews expected Messiah to appear on Mt. Zion with a great
multitude (vss. 35, 39–40); cf. Mic 4:6–8; Joel 2:32; Isa 11:9–12.
[3]For Palestine as a place of refuge, see *II Bar.* 29:2; 71:1.

redeemed. In chapter 7, 144,000 were sealed against the woes that lay ahead (7:4-8). Now the same number stands secure beyond that final ordeal. The use of the number is to point out that not one has been lost. John's symbols are fluid, and there is no necessity of determining whether we are to make an exact identification between the two groups. In fact, the 144,000 of chapter 14 correspond with the innumerable multitude found in the second vision of chapter 7. Both portray the full complement of the redeemed throughout history. On their foreheads are written the name of the Lamb and the name of his Father. The contrast is more with the followers of the beast in chapter 13 than with the 144,000 who are sealed in chapter 7. Barclay lists five different things in the ancient world for which a mark could stand (ownership, loyalty, security, dependence, safety), and finds in each some truth concerning the followers of the Lamb (II, pp. 134-36). Yet in this context the mark seems primarily a symbol of basic allegiance. Those who bear the mark have committed themselves to the Lamb and to the path of self-sacrificing love. They are the overcomers upon whom the risen Christ has written his own new name (3:12).

2-3 The voice (or sound) which John hears from heaven is like the roar of a mighty cataract. Ezekiel uses the same figure for the sound of the winged cherubim in flight as they accompany the chariot throne of God (Ezek 1:24). It is like the voice of God approaching in his glory (Ezek 43:2). Apparently the Seer was greatly impressed by the voice, for he adds two other descriptive similes: it is like the sound of thunder (cf. 6:1; 19:6), and it is like the swelling refrain of an ensemble of harpists. The sound is not that of an angelic choir (as in 5:11-12 and 7:11-12), but is the anthem of redemption sung by the 144,000. They alone, having experienced deliverance, are able to sing its praise (cf. vs. 4). Many commentators see the angels teaching this new song to the redeemed, a concept which is theologically inappropriate and by no means necessitated by the text.

That the voice is actually a chorus of many voices is indicated by the plural, "they sing." Charles links this clause with the previous one, explaining that the Greek is a literal reproduction of a Hebrew idiom and should read "harpers harping . . . and singing" (II, p. 7). It is the "new song" of 5:9, but now it is sung by the very ones who have been purchased by the blood of the Lamb and made a kingdom of priests before the heavenly throne. As in so many of the "new songs" spoken of in the Psalms (96:1; 98:1; 144:9; etc.), the theme is deliverance. Only those who have paid the full price of endurance in the faith are equipped by experience to give voice to the subsequent anthem of victory. They sing before the throne of God, with the angelic orders of heaven (the living creatures and the elders) as audience. That they have been purchased[4] from the earth does not mean they were removed bodily from the earth (cf. Jn 17:15) but that they were separated from the evil ways of the world and the tyranny of its pernicious philosophies.

4 The 144,000 are now described under three figures: they are virgins who have not defiled themselves with women; they are followers of the Lamb; they are first-fruits purchased from among men. The first figure has occasioned considerable discussion. A number of commentators understand John to be describing the 144,000 as an elite group of saints who have attained the utmost in spirituality by renouncing marriage with its detracting sexual relationships.[5] They are celibates and virgins.[6] That certain segments of the early church came to exalt celibacy is perfectly true. Jesus had spoken with approval of eunuchs (Mt 19:12), and Paul wished that all men possessed the gift of continence so as to serve without hindrance the cause of Christ (I Cor 7:1; 7:32). As early as the second century, Marcion had established a church solely for celibates. Origen, the great theologian and apologist, was said to have castrated himself to insure chastity.

The major difficulty with this interpretation, however, is that it implies that the sexual relationships within marriage are defiling. This is contrary to the clear teaching of the NT. From the beginning, God made male and female for one another, and what he has joined in holy wedlock no man is to put asunder (Mt 19:4–6). I Corinthians 7 notwithstanding, Paul held marriage in such high esteem that he could use it as an illustration of the intimate relationship between Christ and his church (Eph 5:31–32). Kiddle would explain John's exalted view of celibacy as in part a recoil from the lax morality of pagan life, noting that the Seer "would have been almost more than human if his zeal had not taken him to the verge of fanaticism" (pp. 269–70). A more common tack is to suggest that this part of the verse was originally a marginal note of some monkish scribe and later copied into the text by mistake.[7] No manuscript evidence supports this conjecture.

---

[4]Cf. the use of ἀγοράζω in I Cor 6:20 (ἠγοράσθητε γὰρ τιμῆς); also I Cor 7:23; Rev 5:9.
[5]See, for example, Kiddle, who writes that "in John's opinion the married Christian is further from the godly ideal than the unmarried" (p. 268).
[6]παρθένος is occasionally used of men who have not had intercourse with women; in the apocryphal life of Aseneth (3, 6) it is so used of Joseph; also of Abel, Melchizedek, and the apostle John (cf. BAG, p. 632, for references).
[7]Charles (II, pp. 9–11) holds that the interpolation of this "monkish glosser" runs from ἀπὸ τῆς γῆς (vs. 3) through ἠγοράσθησαν (vs. 4).

Another interpretation takes the words in a more figurative sense and understands the 144,000 to be those who have kept themselves from adultery and fornication. They are virgins in the sense of having never entered into immoral relations with the other sex. Carrington thinks these verses may refer to those who have not entered into sexual rites with temple prostitutes such as those at Ephesus (pp. 337–40).[8] While chastity was a highly regarded virtue in the Christian community, it should not be elevated to the distinctive mark of the redeemed in heaven.

There is a symbolism in the description of the church as virgins which must not be overlooked. On many occasions throughout the OT, Israel is spoken of as a virgin. She is the "virgin daughter of Zion" (II Kgs 19:21; Lam 2:13), "the virgin of Israel" (Jer 18:13; Amos 5:2). When she lapsed into idolatry, she is said to have played the harlot (Jer 3:6; Hos 2:5). The figure is carried over into the NT when Paul writes to the Corinthians, "I have espoused you to one husband, that I might present you as a pure virgin to Christ" (II Cor 11:2, *ASV*). The 144,000 are here pictured as the promised bride of Christ (cf. 21:9) who, as they await the day of marriage, have kept themselves pure from all defiling relationships with the pagan world system. They have resisted the seductions of the great harlot Rome with whom the kings of the earth have committed fornication (17:2).[9] The apparent confusion of the sexes is of no moment since the entire figure is to be understood symbolically.

The redeemed are next described as those who follow the Lamb wherever he goes. Beckwith places the action in the past tense in order to correspond with the main verbs of the other two clauses and reads, "these were followers of the Lamb in all his ways."[10] They do not follow the Lamb as he strolls around heaven, but they follow his life and instructions while he was still on earth. The statement echoes the words of Jesus in such passages as Mark 8:34 ("If any man would come after me, let him deny himself and take up his cross and follow me"), Matthew 19:21, and others. While the language does not require a specific reference to martyrdom, a significant number of those who enter the final tribulation may in fact follow him to death.

If the first figure stressed the fidelity of the redeemed and the second their discipleship, the third speaks of the sacrificial offering of

---

[8] Cult prostitution was far more serious than common harlotry (*IDB*, III, p. 932).

[9] Caird arrives at much the same conclusion, but finds the source of John's imagery in the Deuteronomic regulations for holy war (Deut 20; 23:9–11). The ceremonial purity which the soldiers were required to maintain symbolized the moral purity of the redeemed in not going after the great whore of Babylon (p. 179).

[10] Beckwith proposes ἦσαν rather than εἰσίν for the missing verb (p. 652).

themselves to God. Although the Greek word translated "first-fruits" originally meant a token offering to God which released the harvest to follow for secular use, it had come to signify more often than not in the LXX no more than an offering or gift.[11] The point is that by offering themselves to God they were set free from human entanglements to belong solely to him. Purchased from among men by the blood of the Lamb (5:9),[12] they are an offering to God. A different point of view is taken by Hendriksen, who sees the 144,000 as first-fruits set apart from the world of humanity which is ripening for judgment (p. 184). Yet, if we take first-fruits in the chronological sense, we should follow through and interpret the harvest as more of the same.

5 In contrast to those who will forever be excluded from the eternal city—evil men of every sort and "every one that loveth and maketh a lie" (22:15; cf. 21:27)—it can be said of the redeemed that "in their mouth was found no lie." Unlike the pagan world which "exchanged the truth about God for a lie" (Rom 1:25), they made no compromise with the heretical claims of Antichrist. Zephaniah had prophesied that the remnant of Israel would speak no lies, neither would a deceitful tongue be found in their mouth (Zeph 3:13). Swete comments that "after purity truthfulness was perhaps the most distinctive mark of the followers of Christ" (p. 180).

The 144,000 are also without blemish.[13] When used of NT believers, the Greek word uniformly means ethically blameless.[14] Since the theme of sacrifice is present in the immediate context (cf. vs. 4c), a number of writers are of the opinion that the word should here be taken in the ritual sense of sacrificially acceptable. This is the meaning of the word when used of Christ the Paschal Lamb in I Peter 1:19 (cf. Heb 9:14).

INTERLUDE: VISIONS OF FINAL JUDGMENT
(14:6–20)

A. IMPENDING JUDGMENT ANNOUNCED (14:6–13)

6 And I saw another angel flying in mid heaven, having eternal good tidings

---

[11]Charles notes that ἀπαρχή renders ראשׁית in only nineteen of the sixty-six occurrences in the LXX (II, p. 6). א *pc t* Prim read ἀπ᾽ ἀρχῆς, "from the beginning," rather than ἀπαρχή.
[12]**046 051** 82 1611 *al* add ὑπὸ Ἰησοῦ before ἠγοράσθησαν.
[13]MSS that add γάρ after ἄμωμοι (**P**[47] **א 046** 1 2329 *al* vg[s,cl] co TR) imply that the 144,000 do not lie *because* they are without blemish.
[14]ἄμωμος: Eph 1:4; 5:27; Phil 2:15; Col 1:22; Jude 24. Rev 14:5 is a possible exception. Metzger notes that several MSS followed by TR add ἐνώπιον τοῦ θρόνου τοῦ θεοῦ after εἰσιν (*TCGNT*, p. 753).

to proclaim unto them that dwell on the earth, and unto every nation and tribe and tongue and people;

7 *and he saith with a great voice, Fear God, and give him glory; for the hour of his judgment is come: and worship him that made the heaven and the earth and sea and fountains of waters.*

8 *And another, a second angel, followed, saying, Fallen, fallen is Babylon the great, that hath made all the nations to drink of the wine of the wrath of her fornication.*

9 *And another angel, a third, followed them, saying with a great voice, If any man worshippeth the beast and his image, and receiveth a mark on his forehead, or upon his hand,*

10 *he also shall drink of the wine of the wrath of God, which is prepared unmixed in the cup of his anger; and he shall be tormented with fire and brimstone in the presence of the holy angels, and in the presence of the Lamb:*

11 *and the smoke of their torment goeth up for ever and ever; and they have no rest day and night, they that worship the beast and his image, and whoso receiveth the mark of his name.*

12 *Here is the patience of the saints, they that keep the commandments of God, and the faith of Jesus.*

13 *And I heard a voice from heaven saying, Write, Blessed are the dead who die in the Lord from henceforth: yea, saith the Spirit, that they may rest from their labors; for their works follow with them.*

6 The tableau of the Lamb and his followers standing victorious on the heavenly Zion is followed by a series of three angel proclamations (vss. 6–11). These three are interrelated and progressive. The summons to worship the Creator (vss. 6–7) leads to a prediction of the downfall of the great citadel of paganism (vs. 8) and a vivid portrayal of the torment awaiting all who worship the beast (vss. 9–11).

That the angel flying in mid-heaven is called "another angel" has no particular significance. The seventh angel of 11:15 is too far removed for an intended contrast. If the designation involves any contrast at all, it would probably be with angels in general who have appeared throughout the book to this point.[15] Like the eagle of woe in 8:13 it flies in mid-heaven to be seen and heard by all. The proclamation goes out over[16] those who dwell[17] on earth. The angel's message is called "eternal good tidings." It

---

[15]ἄλλον is omitted by P⁴⁷ ℵ* **046** 1 82 *pm* sa (for other variants see the UBS apparatus on 14:6). Bruce notes that ἄλλος in a sequence like this is used for both "one" and "another" (p. 654). It is used six times in vss. 6–17.

[16]ἐπί; not used elsewhere with εὐαγγελίζομαι.

[17]A 1 *al* read κατοικοῦντας instead of καθημένους. Charles conjectures that an early scribe may have substituted the more neutral καθημένους because κατοικοῦντας as elsewhere used by our author consistently carries a bad connotation (II, pp. 12–13).

is not the gospel of God's redeeming grace in Christ Jesus[18] but, as the following verse shows, a summons to fear, honor, and worship the Creator.[19] It is a final appeal to all men to recognize the one true God. It is an eternal gospel in that it sets forth the eternal purpose of God for man. It relates to judgment and salvation in the coming eternal age. Those that dwell on the earth are further specified as every nation, tribe, tongue, and people.[20]

7 The angel speaks with a loud voice so all can hear. The eternal gospel calls upon men to fear and honor the Creator, for the hour of judgment is at hand. God has revealed himself in nature so that men are without excuse (Rom 1:19–20). Swete notes that the basis of the appeal is pure theism: "It is an appeal to the conscience of untaught heathendom, incapable as yet of comprehending any other" (p. 182). To fear God is to reverence him; to give him glory is to pay him the respect and honor which is his due. Paul wrote of the moral retrogression of paganism which began with man's failure to glorify God (Rom 1:21). Now we hear one last call for civilization to repent and give him glory. The proclamation is couched in the language of natural theology. Men are called upon to worship the God who made the heaven, the earth, and the waters, both salt and fresh (cf. 10:6). An interesting parallel is the message of Barnabas and Paul to the multitudes at Lystra: "Turn from these vain things to a living God who made the heaven and the earth and the sea and all that is in them" (Acts 14:15).

8 A second[21] angel now appears (apparently flying in mid-heaven as the first) and announces the fall of Babylon the Great. The introduction of this symbolic reference without explanation assumes that the readers would understand the allusion. The ancient Mesopotamian city of Babylon had become the political and religious capital of a world empire, renowned for its luxury and moral corruption. Above all it was the great enemy of the people of God. For the early church the city of Rome was a contemporary Babylon.[22] The designation "Babylon the great" (used consistently throughout Rev: *eg.*, 14:8; 16:9; 17:5; 18:2, 10, 21) goes back to Daniel 4:30 and emphasizes, as Swete says, "the Nebuchadnezzar-like self-importance of the rulers of Rome rather than the actual size or true great-

---

[18]This would normally call for the article before εὐαγγέλιον.

[19]Ladd takes the eternal gospel to be the announcement of the end itself (p. 193; so also Ford, p. 236). Jeremias understands it as a special eschatological ministry of angels resulting in a widespread salvation among Gentiles (*Jesus' Promise to the Nations*, p. 22).

[20]Translating καί (after τῆς γῆς) as "even." For the four terms, see comm. on 5:9.

[21]δεύτερος is omitted by 69 *pc* vg TR. For other variations see Metzger, *TCGNT*, pp. 753–54.

[22]In *II Bar.* 11:1; 67:7 and *Sib. Or.* 5:143, 159, 434 (possibly I Pet 5:13 as well) Rome is called Babylon.

ness of the city'' (p. 183). It is a symbol for the spirit of godlessness which in every age lures men away from the worship of the Creator. It is the final manifestation of secular humanism in its attempt to destroy the remaining vestiges of true religion. Society set free from God is its own worst enemy.

The angel announces the destruction of this center of pagan power and corruption in the very words used by Isaiah when prophesying of Babylon on the Euphrates: "Fallen, fallen is Babylon" (Isa 21:9). Drawing upon Jeremiah 51:7 ("Babylon was a golden cup in the Lord's hand, making all the earth drunken; the nations drank of her wine; therefore the nations went mad"), the angel describes the doomed city as having "made all the nations to drink of the wine of the wrath of her fornication." It is the word "wrath" that makes this compound phrase difficult to interpret. Since a basic meaning of the Greek word is "passion," it could be translated, "the wine of her passionate immorality."[23] Most commentators, however, feel that the awkwardness of the phrase comes from the blending of two somewhat distinct ideas. In 17:2 we learn that the great harlot has made the kings of the earth drunk with "the wine of her fornication." This pictures Rome the prostitute seducing the world by the intoxicating influence of her corrupt practices. The other concept is that of the cup of God's wrath as divine punishment (a figure used elsewhere in Rev: 14:10; 16:19; 19:15). By joining the two symbols, the angel may be pointing out that the heady potion of Rome's seductive practices inevitably involves the wrath of God. Hanson interprets the wrath of verse 10 as the final, irrevocable judgment of God.[24] In either case, the wrath of God is falling upon the pagan city and judgment is determined.

9–10 Verses 9–11 form a counter-proclamation to that of the image in chapter 13. It was decreed that those who would not worship the image should be killed and that those without the mark of the beast should be able neither to buy nor to sell (13:15, 17). The third angel of chapter 14 pronounces a much worse fate for those who *do* worship the beast and bear his mark. They are to drink the wrath of God and endure eternal torment in fire and brimstone. This fierce warning is directed both to the pagan population (cf. vs. 6) and to those within the Christian community tempted to deny their faith in view of the coming persecution. That the warning is directed at apostate Christians as well, follows from John's added comments in verses 12 and 13, which speak of the coming trial and promised blessedness for those who die in the Lord.

---

[23]BAG, p. 366. Note, however, that they are somewhat undecided between this and a translation that takes θυμός as anger or wrath.
[24]Hanson, *The Wrath of the Lamb*, pp. 161 ff.

If any man worship[25] the beast, he shall also[26] suffer the wrath of God. This wrath is often pictured in the OT as a draught of wine (Job 21:20; Ps 75:8; Isa 51:17; Jer 25:15–38). The nations to whom the cup of God's wrath is given shall "drink and stagger . . . be drunk and vomit, fall and rise no more" (Jer 25:16, 27). God's wrath is not the outworking of impersonal laws of retribution which are built into the structure of reality, but the response of a righteous God to man's adamant refusal to accept his love. The Greek word refers to anger which is passionate and vehement.[27] The wine of God's wrath is said to be "prepared unmixed in the cup of his anger." The participle (which literally means "mixed") was used of the preparation of wine by the addition of various spices. In Psalm 75:8 the mixture is apparently poisonous. The adjective ("unmixed") refers to the practice of diluting the wine with water. When taken in a literal sense, the clause says that the wrath of God is mixed (so as to increase its strength) unmixed (not diluted with water). The participle "mixed," however, had come to mean "properly prepared" and then "poured out." The angel is saying that those who defect to emperor worship will drink the wine of God's wrath poured out in full strength, untempered by the mercy and grace of God.

The torment of those who worship the beast is to be with fire and brimstone—a figure taken from God's judgment upon Sodom and Gomorrah (Gen 19:28; cf. Lk 17:29) and used repeatedly in the final chapters of Revelation (19:20; 20:10; 21:8). That we are dealing with a rather obvious apocalyptic symbol[28] should not lead us to take it lightly. The intention of the proclamation is to startle men into the realization of the eternal conse-

---

[25]The present tense (προσκυνεῖ) may mean, "If any man *continues* to worship the beast" in spite of the call for repentance (in vs. 7).

[26]καί introduces the apodosis. Do not read, "He too [as well as Babylon] shall drink. . . ." Ford translates, "that man will drink also . . ." (p. 231). She comments, "The author probably means that one cannot drink one cup and not the other for both are linked; the consequences of drinking Babylon's cup is the inescapable necessity to receive the Lord's" (p. 237).

[27]θυμός; contrast with ὀργή (used in the following clause), which refers more to the settled feeling of righteous indignation. θυμός occurs seven times in the second half of Revelation for the "white heat of God's anger" (Swete, p. 185). Cf. William Klassen ("Vengeance in the Apocalypse of John," *CBQ*, 28 [1966], pp. 300–11) for a balanced appraisal of the wrath of God in Revelation. He rejects extreme views such as those of W. D. Davies (toward political authorities the Apocalypse discloses "an abortive hatred that can only lead, not to their redemption, but to their destruction" ["Ethics in the New Testament," *IDB*, II, p. 176]) and C. G. Jung ("a veritable orgy of hatred, wrath, vindictiveness, and blind destructive fury" [*Answer to Job*, p. 125]), and concludes that "it is doubtful that the Ap views the wrath of God any differently than do the other writers of the NT" (p. 311).

[28]Cf. *I Enoch* 91:9; 100:9; II Esdr 7:35; etc. The Qumran community expected the wicked to be judged by fire (1QS 2:2; 4:13; 1QH 17:13).

quences of denying faith in Christ and worshipping the beast. It is not the appropriate time to discuss the semantics of symbol and hyperbole! This torment takes place in the very presence of the Lamb and his holy angels. In Luke 12:9 Jesus says that those who deny him before men will be denied before the angels of God. To suffer in the presence of the hosts of heaven is not to lessen the fierceness of the judgment but to make it more grievous. Christians had borne the shame of public derision and opposition; soon their antagonists will suffer before a more august gathering. It was a common idea in Jewish apocalyptic that the suffering of the damned is increased by beholding the bliss of the righteous. II Esdras compares "the place of refreshment" with "the pit of torment" and the "Paradise of delight" with the "furnace of Gehenna," calling upon those who have been raised for judgment to look and consider whom they have denied and to view fire and torment in comparison with delight and refreshment (II Esdr 7:35–38). The book of Enoch speaks of the kings of the earth burning "as the straw in the fire . . . before the face of the holy" (*I Enoch* 48:9; also 27:2, 3; cf. *II Bar*. 30:4). In Revelation there is no suggestion that the suffering of the damned takes place in the presence of martyred believers who now rejoice to see their oppressors burning in hell. It is the holy angels,[29] and even the Lamb, who witness divine retribution upon the wicked.

11 The punishment of the damned is not a temporary measure. The smoke of their torment goes up forever and ever (cf. 20:10).[30] Without hope of acquittal, they pay the eternal price of having chosen evil over righteousness. A number of modern writers point out that the doctrine of hell is offensive to contemporary man. Glasson labels as "sub-Christian" and "impossible to reconcile with the teaching of Jesus" the idea that those who had fallen into the sin of emperor worship should be punished day and night forever (p. 86).[31] Preston and Hanson reinterpret the scene of torment as a symbolic way of portraying the suffering of men who deliberately turn away from the highest Good. Their torment consists precisely in refusing to be members of the Lamb; it is eternal in the sense that God will never violate man's personality (pp. 102–3). Yet the teaching of the NT on the eternal consequences of willfully rejecting the love of God as manifested in the death of Christ for the sin of man does not allow us to put the doctrine aside as sub-Christian or reinterpret it in such a way as to remove

---

[29] A *pc* omit ἁγίων, while **046** 82 *pm* TR add the definite article τῶν. Beasley-Murray says it is possible that "holy angels" forms a periphrasis for God (p. 226).

[30] Note the comparison with the ceaseless worship of the four living creatures in 4:8.

[31] Barclay follows the same line of thought, but counsels us not to condemn it until we have gone through the same sufferings as did the early Christians (II, p. 148).

the abrasive truth of eternal punishment. It was Jesus more than anyone else who spoke of the fires of hell. Better to enter life maimed, he said, than having two hands "to go to hell, to the unquenchable fire" (Mk 9:44). The story of the rich man tormented in the fires of hell who begged to have Lazarus dip his finger in water to cool his tongue (Lk 16:9–31) was told by Jesus. After due allowance is made for the place of symbolism in apocalyptic, what remains in these verses is still the terrifying reality of divine wrath poured out upon those who persist in following Antichrist. What the angel has proclaimed so vividly must not be undermined by euphemistic redefinition.

12 Verse 12 is a comment by the Seer appended to the angel's proclamation of divine wrath.[32] The trials and sufferings which are the lot of the faithful as a result of the enforcement of emperor worship call for steadfast endurance in obedience and faith. The demands of the imperial cult accompanied by the threat of capital punishment (13:15) would be a crucial test of the believer's loyalty. Steadfast allegiance to Christ involved the rejection of the claims of Caesar and would result in widespread martyrdom. But the price of apostasy (eternal torment, vss. 9–11) would be far greater than the temporary suffering of fidelity. The saints are described in terms of their obedience to divine revelation ("they that keep the commandments of God") and their continuing reliance on Jesus ("the faith of Jesus").[33]

13 The Seer's comment is followed by a voice from heaven which declares, Blessed are those that die in the Lord. The connection with verse 12 is clear: faithfulness to Christ issues in martyrdom, but the faithful dead are blessed in that they have entered victoriously into their rest. If verse 12 was negative encouragement, verse 13 is positive. The voice from heaven is not specifically identified, although it may be that of the Spirit. More important is the fact that a proclamation from heaven carries divine authority (cf. 10:4, 8; 11:12). The command to write emphasizes the importance of the message which follows.[34] The beatitude is the second of seven to be found in Revelation (cf. 1:3; 16:15; 19:9; 20:6; 22:7, 14). It pronounces blessed those who meet death in a state of spiritual union with Christ Jesus. They stand in sharp contrast to the apostates who have denied their faith and the pagans who have never accepted it. For the latter, death leads to

---

[32]Beasley-Murray calls vs. 12 the "punch line" for the oracle of judgment in vss. 9–11, the train of thought being, "If such be the fate of the adherents of the beast, Christ's people must at all costs continue to keep the commandments of God and the faith of Jesus" (p. 227).
[33]Ἰησοῦ is an objective genitive; cf. τὴν πίστιν μου in 2:13.
[34]γράψον is regularly used in the command to write to each of the seven churches (2:1, 8, 12, 18; 3:1, 7, 14). Cf. 19:9; 21:5 and contrast μὴ γράψῃς in 10:4.

judgment and eternal loss. This prospect of eternal blessedness is a "positive motive for heroic loyalty" (Kiddle, p. 283).

Most commentators connect "from henceforth" with the preceding clause. Those who die in the Lord from henceforth are blessed. But this seems to imply that from that point on a special blessedness is connected with the death of the faithful which sets them apart from believers who have died previously. Others connect the phrase with the following clause: "Henceforth, says the Spirit, they may rest from their labors" (*NEB*). This requires the omission of the word "yea."[35] Farrer, acknowledging the uncertainty of the text, is nevertheless sure that the meaning is "Blessed from the moment of their death" (p. 164). The apparent implication that gave rise to these alternatives, however, is more imaginary than real. To assure those facing the prospect of martyrdom that to die in the Lord is to enter into eternal blessedness is not to deny the same reward to those saints who previously died in less trying circumstances. "Henceforth" marks the transition into the more active persecution of those who hold unswervingly to their faith.

To this pronouncement of blessedness, the Spirit adds the emphatic affirmation, "Yes indeed." The blessedness consists in the cessation of all the trials and sufferings brought upon the faithful by the demands of emperor worship. The labors from which they rest are not those of normal toil, but the troubles which have arisen from their steadfastness in faith. Their supreme labor is faithfulness unto death. They are blessed because their works follow after them. God will not forget all they have endured in loyalty to the faith. Their works are acts of steadfast resistance to the demands of Antichrist. There is no need to interpret works as spiritual attitudes or inward character. Nor are we to think of them in the Jewish sense of accompanying the righteous to judgment to win for them divine approval.[36] The faithfulness of the martyrs unto death is not a legalistic work which merits eternal bliss, but a manifestation of their devotion to Christ. These works follow them in the sense that there can be no separation between what a man is and what he does.

B. HARVEST OF THE EARTH (14:14-16)

14 *And I saw, and behold, a white cloud; and on the cloud I saw one sitting like unto a son of man, having on his head a golden crown, and in his hand a sharp sickle.*

[35]This omission has the support of $\mathbf{P}^{47}$ and ℵ*. It also makes possible the conjecture of ἀπαρτί for ἀπ' ἄρτι ("Certainly, saith the Spirit, they may rest..."). Cf. Metzger (*TCGNT*, p. 754) for a discussion of the variants for ναί, λέγει.

[36]In *Pirke Aboth* 6:10 Rabbi Jose ben Kisma is quoted as saying, "In the hour of a man's death it is not silver or gold or precious stones or pearls which accompany him, but Torah and good works alone." Cf. II Esdr 7:77; *II Bar.* 14:12.

15 *And another angel came out from the temple, crying with a great voice to him that sat on the cloud, Send forth thy sickle, and reap: for the hour to reap is come; for the harvest of the earth is ripe.*

16 *And he that sat on the cloud cast his sickle upon the earth; and the earth was reaped.*

14 Two visions of judgment bring the chapter to its close. Verses 14–16 picture the advent of divine judgment in the familiar figure of a grain harvest. Verses 17–20 emphasize the violent nature of the wrath of God as the treading of a winepress into which the grape clusters of the earth have been cast.

John looks, and there appears a white cloud with "one like unto a son of man" sitting upon it. This is none other than the risen Christ (cf. 1:13). The background is Daniel 7:13-14 in which "one like unto a son of man" comes with the clouds of heaven to receive universal and everlasting dominion. The golden wreath[37] designates the Messiah as one who has conquered and thereby won the right to act in judgment. The sharp sickle is the instrument of harvest and portrays the son of man prepared to reap the harvest of earth in righteous retribution.

A few commentators identify the reaper as an angel rather than Christ. Morris argues that it would be curious for the exalted Christ to be commanded as he is in verse 15 and also unlikely that he would be ignorant of the time of the end (p. 184). But the angel is no more than a messenger from God whose purpose is not to reveal the time of the end, but to deliver the divine command to begin the harvest. Rather than taking the one "like unto a son of man" as an angel so as to have yet another series of seven (14:6, 8, 9, 15, 17, 18), the very title sets him apart from the six angels. While the designation may be used in apocalyptic as a normal reference to angelic beings, the context in Revelation indicates that he is the Messiah returning in judgment.

15 The angel that delivers the divine command to commence the harvest comes out from within the temple, that most holy place of the presence of God (cf. 7:15). Judgment upon sin is a necessary function of righteousness. He cries out in a great voice (appropriate to his role in the vision; cf. vss. 7, 9, 18) to the one sitting on the cloud that he should send forth his sickle and reap, for the hour is come, and the harvest of the earth is ripe. The command follows the language of Joel 3:13 ("Put in the sickle, for the harvest is ripe"). There is a difference of opinion about which group of people is intended by the harvest. Some understand this scene

---

[37]στέφανος χρυσοῦς; worn also by the twenty-four elders in 4:4, 10 (cf. the στέφανοι ὅμοιοι χρυσῷ worn by the demonic locusts in 9:7). The most appropriate headdress of a ruler was the διάδημα (cf. 19:12), but the two ideas of victory and royalty often merge.

(vss. 14–16) as the gathering of the righteous at the return of Christ and interpret the following verses (17–20) as the judgment of the wicked.[38] Supporting this position is the fact that in the NT the figure of the harvest is normally used of the gathering of men into the kingdom of God (Mt 9:37–38; Mk 4:29; Lk 10:2; Jn 4:35–38). The idea of an eschatological harvest, however, is not limited to the gathering of the elect. In the parable of the Wheat and Tares, it involves the gathering of the wicked for burning as well (Mt 13:30, 40–42). In the OT the harvest was a regular symbol of divine judgment (Jer 51:33; Hos 6:11; cf. II Esdr 4:35; *II Bar.* 70:2). Beckwith correctly says, "The figure is comprehensive, including in a word the whole process of the winding up of the ages, and the recompense of both the good and the bad" (p. 662). The harvest of verses 14–16 is a general picture of the coming judgment.[39]

The hour to reap is the precise moment determined by God. As in the hymn of the twenty-four elders in chapter 11 (vs. 18), the hour of judgment and reward has come. The harvest of the earth is fully ripe.

16 In an interesting display of brevity, John does no more than state that the One on the cloud casts his sickle on the earth and the earth is reaped. Details are left to the reader's imagination.

C. VINTAGE OF THE EARTH (14:17–20)

17 *And another angel came out from the temple which is in heaven, he also having a sharp sickle.*

18 *And another angel came out from the altar, he that hath power over fire; and he called with a great voice to him that had the sharp sickle, saying, Send forth thy sharp sickle, and gather the clusters of the vine of the earth; for her grapes are fully ripe.*

19 *And the angel cast his sickle into the earth, and gathered the vintage of the earth, and cast it into the winepress, the great* winepress, *of the wrath of God.*

20 *And the winepress was trodden without the city, and there came out blood from the winepress, even unto the bridles of the horses, as far as a thousand and six hundred furlongs.*

17 Verses 14–16 portrayed judgment under the general figure of the harvest. Now, by means of the more vivid figure of the vintage, John

---

[38]Beasley-Murray (p. 228) says this view is difficult to accept because (1) the two visions are rooted in the double parable of judgment in Joel 3:13, and (2) the imagery of the visions is parallel. The two harvests of II Esdr 4:28–32 are interesting but not determinative (the first harvest being of the wicked in this age and the second of the righteous in the age to come).
[39]Caird holds the harvest and vintage to be variations on a single theme, but interprets both as portraying the impending martyrdom of the elect (pp. 191–94).

stresses the violent carnage of that judgment. This is not a preview of final judgment, for that belongs to the Father (20:11–15), but of the victorious return of the Son, who smites the nations, treading "the winepress of the fierceness of the wrath of God, the Almighty" (19:11–21, esp. vs. 15).

If the harvest scene intended a separation of wheat and tares (cf. Mt 13:30) or wheat and chaff (cf. Lk 3:17), the vintage envisions nothing but unmitigated judgment. That the angel who is to reap the vintage of the earth comes out from the temple indicates that he is God's agent for this awesome event. Like the son of man, he also has a sharp sickle.[40]

18 Yet another angel (the sixth in vss. 6–20) enters John's vision, this one from the altar. As the altar is elsewhere connected with the prayers of the righteous (6:9; 8:3–5), we are probably to understand here that the prayers of the faithful play a definite part in bringing about God's judgment upon the wicked. The angel is further identified as the one having power over fire. In the developed angelology of the intertestamental period, angels are assigned to the various elements of nature. Enoch speaks of the angels of thunder, sea, hail, snow, rain, etc. (*I Enoch* 60:11–21; cf. *Jub.* 2:2). But John undoubtedly has in mind the angel of 8:3–5 who filled his censer with fire from the altar and cast it upon the earth. Fire is commonly associated with judgment in the NT (Mt 18:8; Lk 9:54; II Thess 1:7). The angel who has authority over the fire issues a command to the angel with the sharp sickle. Charles removes any apparent confusion that could arise from so many angels in these verses by removing verses 15–17 as an interpolation suggested by the poetic parallelism of Joel 3:13 (II, pp. 18–19, 21). In that case the bearer of the sharp sickle in verse 18 would be the Messiah of verse 14. Such textual surgery is not only unnecessary, but forfeits the dramatic parallelism of the two judgment scenes. The command to send forth the sharp sickle and gather the vintage follows closely the parallel command to reap the harvest of the earth. Joel 3:14 is the model for both. Like the grain which has turned golden and must be harvested immediately, the grapes are fully ripe.[41] The time for judgment is now!

19 Without delay the angel casts his sickle into the earth and gathers its vintage. We are not to think of the sickle as reaping on its own, but as active in the hand of the angel. *I Enoch* 53 speaks of "angels of punishment" who prepare the instruments which destroy the kings and mighty of the earth (vss. 3–5; cf. 56:1). The angel is God's agent to execute wrath upon the unrighteous. Those who interpret the two scenes as

---

[40]The δρέπανον was a curved blade used both for cutting grain and for pruning and cutting clusters from the vine.
[41]ξηραίνω (vs. 15) means to dry out or wither. ἀκμάζω (vs. 18) means to be at the prime; the idiom ἐπὶ ξυροῦ ἀκμῆς (on the razor's edge) meant "at the critical moment" (LSJ, p. 51).

the gathering of the elect and the judgment of the wicked usually point out that this grisly work is left to an angel rather than to the Son. Swete (p. 190) writes of the "delicate beauty" in assigning the work of death to a minister of justice, while the Savior of men appears "unto salvation" (Heb 9:28). However, in chapter 19 it is Christ himself who treads the winepress of the wrath of God, supplying the vultures with a great feast of human flesh (19:15, 17–18). John is not squeamish about the Son entering into the execution of judgment.

The vintage is now cast into the great winepress[42] of the wrath of God. In Biblical days grapes were trampled by foot in a trough which had a duct leading to a lower basin where the juice collected. The treading of grapes was a familiar figure for the execution of divine wrath upon the enemies of God. In Isaiah 63:3 God the warrior returns from Edom with his garments stained as one who has been treading in the winevat. He says, "I have trodden the winepress alone . . . I trod them in my anger and trampled them in my wrath; their lifeblood is sprinkled upon my garments" (cf. Lam 1:15; Joel 3:13; Rev 19:15). The vintage of the earth is a collective expression for all who by their obstinate refusal to embrace righteousness have made themselves the enemies of God.

20 The city outside of which the winepress was trodden is probably Jerusalem. The judgment of the nations in Joel 3:12–14 (which supplies the dual figures of harvest and vintage) takes place in the valley of Jehoshaphat, which tradition links with the Kidron valley lying between Jerusalem and the Mount of Olives. Zechariah 14:1–4 places the final battle on the outskirts of Jerusalem. *I Enoch* 53:1 speaks of judgment in a deep valley near the valley of Hinnom. Judgment "outside the city" (*RSV*) must certainly be an allusion to the One who suffered for the sins of man "outside the gate" (Heb 13:12; cf. Jn 19:20). Those who refuse the first judgment must take part in the second.

As a winepress yields the red juice of the grape, so the judgment of God issues in a blood bath which flows as deep as the bridles of the horses and extends the length and breadth of the land. Walvoord says that a flow of blood this deep seems impossible and takes it to mean a liberal splattering of blood (p. 223). This, of course, fails to grasp the hyperbolic nature of the metaphor. *I Enoch* 100:3 speaks of a carnage in which "the horse

---

[42]τὸν μέγαν stands in apposition to τὴν ληνόν. The change in gender is explained by Beckwith as due to the fact that John had in mind that which it symbolized, ὁ θυμὸς τοῦ θεοῦ (p. 664). In Gen 30:38, 41 ληνός is masculine. Sinaiticus (also 1006 *al* sy^ph TR) reads τὴν μεγάλην to correct the gender, and P^47 1611 *pc* have τοῦ μεγάλου, which may be translated, "the winepress of the great wrath of God/of the wrath of the great God." Other MSS (181 424 468 *al*) omit the adjective altogether.

shall walk up to the breast in the blood of sinners." The distance, 1600 furlongs[43] (some 184 miles), has been variously interpreted. Geographically it is the approximate length of Palestine.[44] Symbolically it squares the number four (the number of the earth: "four corners of the earth," 8:1; 20:8; "four winds of the earth," 7:1) and multiplies it by the square of ten (the number of completeness; cf. 5:11; 20:6).[45] The judgment of God, portrayed ideally as taking place outside the holy city, extends to all men everywhere who find themselves beyond the pale of divine protection.

[43]2036 *pc* read χιλίων ἑξακοσίων ἕξ; א* *pc* sy[ph] read χιλίων διακοσίων (1200), "probably because this numeral lends itself better to symbolic interpretation" (Metzger, *TCGNT*, p. 755).
[44]In the *Itinerarium* of Antonius, Palestine was said to be 1664 stadia from Tyre to El-Arish (on the borders of Egypt).
[45]1600 has also been taken as representing the whole earth or as the square of forty, the traditional number for punishment (cf. Num 14:33; Deut 25:3).

CHAPTER 15

VII. THE SEVEN LAST PLAGUES (15:1–16:21)

Chapter 15 is the shortest chapter in the book of Revelation. It opens by introducing the seven angels who later (in vss. 5–8) receive the seven bowls of divine wrath which are to be poured out upon the entire heathen world (chap. 16). Verses 2–4 picture those who have emerged victorious over the beast. They stand by the heavenly sea and sing a paean of praise to God for his great and righteous works. The seven bowls are the third series of seven in the interrelated sequence of seals, trumpets, and bowls. The divine retribution revealed by the seals and announced by the trumpets is now executed by the bowls. From a literary standpoint, the bowls seem to be the unfolding of the seventh trumpet, just as the trumpets were an expansion of the seventh seal. A caution is in order, however, against too rigid a projection of this apocalyptic device upon the one-dimensional plane of historical sequence. The visions are intended more to confront man with vivid portrayals of eschatological truth than to supply him with data for a precise chronology of the consummation.

Moffatt (p. 442) refers to the vision of judgment as a "poetic expansion of Lev xxvi.21" ("Then if you walk contrary to me, and will not hearken to me, I will bring more plagues upon you, seven-fold as many as your sins"). The seven bowls of judgment may well be the third Woe announced in 11:14.

1. PREPARATION FOR THE BOWL-PLAGUES (15:1–8)

1 *And I saw another sign in heaven, great and marvellous, seven angels having seven plagues,* which are *the last, for in them is finished the wrath of God.*

2 *And I saw as it were a sea of glass mingled with fire; and them that come*

off victorious from the beast, and from his image, and from the number of his name, standing by the sea of glass, having harps of God.

3 *And they sing the song of Moses the servant of God, and the song of the Lamb, saying,*
Great and marvellous are thy works, O Lord God, the Almighty; righteous and true are thy ways, thou King of the ages.

4 *Who shall not fear, O Lord, and glorify thy name? for thou only art holy; for all the nations shall come and worship before thee; for thy righteous acts have been made manifest.*

5 *And after these things I saw, and the temple of the tabernacle of the testimony in heaven was opened:*

6 *and there came out from the temple the seven angels that had the seven plagues, arrayed with precious stone, pure and bright, and girt about their breasts with golden girdles.*

7 *And one of the four living creatures gave unto the seven angels seven golden bowls full of the wrath of God, who liveth for ever and ever.*

8 *And the temple was filled with smoke from the glory of God, and from his power; and none was able to enter into the temple, till the seven plagues of the seven angels should be finished.*

1 John now sees another sign in heaven. In chapter 12 both the radiant woman (vs. 1) and the great red dragon (vs. 3) are called signs. They point beyond themselves and disclose the theological meaning of history. That there are seven angels having seven plagues speaks of the certainty and completeness of divine wrath against all unrighteousness. They are great and marvelous in their awe-inspiring effect upon all of nature, man, and the kingdom of Antichrist. Chapter 16, which tells the story, moves inevitably with an ever increasing crescendo from noisome and grievous sores, through water turned to blood, and scorching sun, to an earthquake so great that the entire configuration of earth is violently altered. They are the last of the plagues in that they complete[1] the warnings of God to an impenitent world. All that remains is final judgment itself. The plagues anticipate the final outpouring of divine retribution and are met with blasphemy by men whose hearts, like that of Pharaoh, are hardened against God (vs. 21). The use of Exodus typology throughout this vision is worthy of special note.[2]

---

[1] ἐν αὐταῖς ἐτελέσθη ὁ θυμὸς τοῦ θεοῦ does not mean that the plagues exhaust or bring to an end the wrath of God. The devil, the beast, the false prophet, and all whose names are not found in the book of life are yet to be thrown into the lake of fire (Rev 19:20; 20:10, 15).
[2] Caird mentions "the plagues, the crossing of the sea, the engulfing of the pursuers, the song of Moses, the giving of the law amid the smoke of Sinai, and the erection of the Tent of Testimony" (p. 197).

2 Verses 2–4 form an interlude of victory and praise that stands in sharp contrast with the narrative which follows. The exultation of the heavenly chorus is as glorious as the visitation of wrath is somber. John sees those who have emerged from their final battle with the beast standing victorious upon the crystal surface before the throne. Carrying harps of God, they join their voices in an anthem of praise celebrating the holiness of God and the righteousness of his works.

The "sea of glass" is mentioned twice in the Apocalypse. In 4:6 it is described as "like unto crystal," while in the present passage it is said to be "mingled with fire." Kiddle understands a "heavenly Red Sea" through which the martyrs have come and which is about to submerge their enemies (pp. 300–1). Others take the reference to fire as a symbol of judgment. It is not certain, however, that the mention of fire is anything more than a descriptive detail intended to heighten the splendor of the scene. While the larger context has much to say about wrath and judgment, the interlude itself (vss. 2–4) treats quite a different subject.

These who stand on[3] the crystal pavement are those who have emerged victorious[4] over the beast. They have not abandoned their faith nor succumbed to the threats of Antichrist. They are the overcomers to whom the seven letters hold out promise of eating of the tree of life (2:7), protection from the second death (2:11), hidden manna (2:17), authority over the nations (2:26), white garments (3:5), the honor of becoming a pillar in the temple of God (3:12), and the privilege of sitting with Christ on his throne (3:21). Little wonder that they break out in song!

The struggle against the beast is actually a struggle against paying homage to his image or being marked with the number of his name.[5] The two additional phrases explain and make explicit the concept of victory over the beast. The harps which the victors play are harps of God in that they belong to the celestial litany. The "pleasant harp" (Ps 81:2, *ASV*) is an appropriate instrument for songs of praise.

3 The song of the victors is a song of praise to God for his great and marvelous acts. It celebrates his righteous and redemptive activity beginning with Moses and culminating in the Lamb. We are not to understand two songs, but one. The deliverance of which Moses and the people sang in Exodus 15:1–18 prefigured the greater deliverance wrought by the

---

[3] ἐπί could be "by" (as in 3:20), but taking the sea to be a solid surface allows the more customary translation "on" (cf. 10:5, 8; 12:18).

[4] νικῶντας is an unusual construction (only here in the NT) and seems to connote deliverance from (or out of) the great ordeal of emperor worship. Bruce suggests it imitates a Hebrew construction which is translated "prevailed over" in I Sam 17:50 (p. 655).

[5] **051** 2059s *pm* add ἐκ τοῦ χαράγματος αὐτοῦ καί before ἐκ τοῦ ἀριθμοῦ.

Lamb. Although some commentators take the song of Moses as a reference to the final address of the great lawgiver recorded in Deuteronomy 32 (*eg.*, Beckwith, pp. 676–78), the many parallels between Exodus 15 and Revelation 15 argue the more widely accepted earlier song. For example, "Great and marvellous are thy works. . . . Who shall not fear, O Lord, and glorify thy name?" (Rev 15:4) echoes "Who is like thee, O Lord . . . majestic in holiness, terrible in glorious deeds, doing wonders?" (Ex 15:11). This song commemorating Israel's greatest deliverance was sung on Sabbath evenings in the synagogue service. Its imagery was stamped on the consciousness of every pious Jew.[6] The theme of victory in Exodus 15 becomes the basis for praise and adoration in the song of the victors. God is worthy of glory and honor because his great and marvelous works are true and righteous. The song does not celebrate the judgment of God upon his enemies but the righteousness of his great redemptive acts. As Moses triumphed over Pharaoh, and as the risen Lord was victor over the world (Jn 16:33), so also have the faithful maintained their fidelity against all demands of the imperial cult.

The structure of the hymn suggests that it may have been used in the liturgy of the early church. The first four lines are a classic example of synonymous parallelism:

"Great and marvellous are thy works,
O Lord God, the Almighty;
Righteous and true are thy ways,
Thou King of the ages."

Verse 4 raises the rhetorical question,

"Who shall not fear, O Lord,
and glorify thy name?"

and is followed by three causal clauses,[7]

"For thou only art holy;
For all the nations shall come and worship before thee;
For thy righteous acts have been made manifest."

Practically every phrase of the hymn comes from the rich vocabulary of the OT (Ps 11:2; 139:14; Amos 4:13, LXX; Deut 32:4; Ps 86:9; Mal 1:11; Ps 144:17, LXX; 98:2).[8]

---

[6]Moses is designated the servant of God in Ex 14:31; Josh 14:7; I Chron 6:49; Dan 9:11.
[7]Note the use of ὅτι three times.
[8]In the Nestle text (25th ed.) only ὁ θεὸς ὁ παντοκράτωρ . . . ὅτι μόνος . . . ὅτι and the final clause (ὅτι τὰ δικαιώματά σου ἐφανερώθησαν) are not in boldface. The UBS text cites Amos 3:13 and 4:13 for the first of these.

We need not limit this ascription of praise to any particular event. All God's redemptive works are great and marvelous. They are met with awe, not simply because of their magnitude, but also because of their intrinsic righteousness. They contrast with the reaction of the heathen in 13:3 who marveled after the beast.

As in the earlier song of the elders (11:17–18), God is designated the Almighty. He possesses the power to carry out whatever he determines to do. This title, which is ascribed to God nine times in the book of Revelation, is found but once in the NT outside the Apocalypse (II Cor 6:18). That God is the Almighty is supremely appropriate in the present context of ultimate victory. He is also King of the Ages.[9] His sovereignty is everlasting. Jeremiah speaks of the everlasting king at whose wrath the earth trembles, and whose indignation the nations are unable to abide (Jer 10:10). The ways of the heavenly king, says John, are absolutely just and completely in accord with truth.

4 The rhetorical question is raised, "Who shall not fear, O Lord, and glorify thy name?" Universal recognition of Jehovah as the one true God is a common expectation in the OT (cf. Phil 2:9–11). The confidence that during the messianic age the nations of the world will worship the God of Israel and glorify his name (Ps 86:9; Mal 1:11) is adapted by John as an expression of the complete sovereignty of God over all the hostile opposition of the beast and his followers in the last days. To glorify the name of God is to praise him for what he is and all he has accomplished. All shall come before God in worship because he alone is holy. Beckwith (p. 675) notes that the holiness of God refers not to his sinlessness, but to his unapproachable majesty and power (cf. Ps 99:3, 5, 9). God is to be praised by all nations because his righteous acts have been fully manifested.[10] We should probably interpret verse 4 as a metaphor of victory rather than an actual scene to be enacted at some specific time and place. A strictly literal interpretation would teach a doctrine of universal salvation unless the worship offered were in grudging recognition of his righteous acts.[11] Barclay calls the song "a lyric outburst on the greatness of God" (II, p. 157).

---

[9]The *ASV* follows the reading of **P**[47] **א*** **C** 1006 1611 *pc* vg sy sa (2), αἰώνων. Nestle (25th ed.) and UBS (3rd ed.) select ἐθνῶν (**A P 046 051** 1 82 2059s 2329 *pl g b*). The UBS designates its preference as C (a considerable degree of doubt) but prefers it on the basis that (1) αἰώνων could have been introduced by a copyist recollecting I Tim 1:17 and (2) ἐθνῶν is more in accord with the context. The reading of the TR (ἁγίων) has very slender support and arose from a confusion in Latin (Metzger, *TCGNT*, pp. 755–56).

[10]Some take δικαιώματα as judicial sentences (Charles, II, p. 36; Morris, pp. 189–90), but it is the victorious activity of God which here results in universal praise.

[11]Rist says that the line, "All nations shall come and worship thee," is thoroughly out of harmony with the idea expressed elsewhere in Rev that the nations stubbornly refuse to

5–6 After these things, that is, after the song of Moses and the Lamb sung before the throne by those who were victorious over the beast (vss. 2–4), John sees the heavenly temple open and seven angels of devastation emerge. The temple is more closely defined as "the tabernacle of the testimony,"[12] a reference to the period of Israel's sojourn in the wilderness. In this context it emphasizes that the final plagues come from the presence of God and are the expression of his unalterable opposition to sin. The ancient tabernacle was a "tent of the testimony" (Num 17:7; 18:2) because it contained the two tables of testimony brought down from Mt. Sinai by Moses (Ex 32:15; Deut 10:5).

As in verse 1, the seven angels are described as having the seven plagues, even though they do not receive the bowls of wrath until the following verse (vs. 7). That they come out of the temple points to the divine origin of their commission.[13] Their robes of linen,[14] pure and shining, denote the noble and sacred nature of their office (cf. Ezek 9:2; Dan 10:5). Golden girdles are symbolic of royal and priestly functions.

7 It is from the four living creatures that the seven angels receive the golden bowls of divine wrath. These guardians of the throne appear throughout Revelation (4:6; 5:6; 6:1; 7:11; 14:3; 15:7; 19:4) and are appropriate as intermediaries between God and the avenging angels. Each of the seven angels receives a golden bowl.[15] In 5:8 the golden bowls were full of incense representing the prayers of the saints (cf. Josephus, *Ant*. iii.143). Since the mention of the golden bowls in Revelation is limited to these two contexts, John may be calling our attention to the relationship between prayer and divine retribution. Gold does not necessarily denote the service of God. The great harlot of chapter 17 holds in her hand "a golden cup of abominations" (vs. 4).

---

repent. He offers as solutions: (1) John used a Christian hymn without changing the line on the final repentance and conversion of the heathen, (2) worship did not involve conversion but only acknowledgment of his power and might, and (3) John is not consistent here (p. 479). If in fact a problem exists, Rist's second solution would be preferable.

[12]Beckwith writes that "the sanctuary meant here is defined by the following appositional gen." (p. 678). The complete expression would be, "the temple, that is, the tent of witness."

[13]ἐκ τοῦ ναοῦ is omitted, however, by the Byzantine text.

[14]The variant λίθον is accepted by some (A C 2053 *pc* vg^w), perhaps on such grounds as (1) Ezek 28:13; (2) it is the more difficult reading; (3) a possible reference to the breastplate of the high priest. Charles suggests a mistranslation of שֵׁשׁ as λίθος instead of βύσσινος (Gen 41:42; Ex 28:39) and points to Rev 19:8, 14 for support (II, pp. 38–39). Although λίνουν (read by P⁴⁷ 046 69 *pc*) rather than λίνον is the normal designation for a garment made of flax, the latter is occasionally used (cf. BAG, p. 476, for examples). λίνον is read by P 1 *pc* vg^{s,cl} sy Prim TR.

[15]The φιάλη was a wide shallow bowl rather than a narrow-necked vial as the *ASV* translation suggests. Its contents were quickly and easily poured out.

The cups are full of the wrath of God. The vivid scene of II Thessalonians 1:7–9 is about to be expanded in detail (Rev 16). It is the wrath of a God whose existence has neither beginning nor end. He is a living God, fully able to execute punishment upon all his adversaries.

8 As the angels receive their bowls of wrath, the temple is filled with smoke, symbolizing the glory and power of God. In the OT God often revealed his presence by cloud or smoke. He descended upon Mt. Sinai, and smoke ascended as a great furnace (Ex 19:18). When the glory of God filled the tabernacle in the wilderness, a cloud rested upon it (Ex 40:34). In Isaiah's vision of the heavenly temple, the adoration of God by the seraphim was followed by smoke which filled the sanctuary (Isa 6:4). The smoke which fills the heavenly temple in Revelation indicates the presence of God in all his glory and power to actively carry out his judgment upon wickedness. Until the seven plagues are finished, no one is able to enter the temple. Once the time of final judgment has come, none can stay the hand of God. The time for intercession is past. God in his unapproachable majesty and power has declared that the end has come. No longer does he stand knocking: he enters to act in sovereign judgment.

CHAPTER 16

Chapter 16 is given over in its entirety to the carrying out of the final series of plagues (cf. 15:1). The parallels between this series of judgments and the trumpet-plagues (chaps. 8–11) are readily apparent.[1] In each series the first four plagues are visited upon the earth, sea, inland waters, and heavenly bodies respectively. The fifth involves darkness and pain (cf. 16:10 with 9:2, 5–6), and the sixth, enemy hordes from the vicinity of the Euphrates (cf. 16:12 with 9:14 ff). Both series draw heavily for their symbolism from the ten Egyptian plagues. The turning of water into blood (8:8; 16:3, 4) parallels the first Egyptian plague in which Moses struck the waters of the Nile, turning them to blood (Ex 7:20). The darkening of the sun (8:12; cf. 16:10) has as its counterpart the ninth Egyptian plague in which thick darkness prevailed over the land for three days (Ex 10:21–22). In the following discussion a number of other parallels will be mentioned.

It would be wrong, however, to imagine the Seer slavishly setting forth a standard set of plagues. Nor is he attempting a careful recapitulation of the trumpet-plagues under the new symbolism of bowls. John freely employs the vocabulary of natural disaster to describe the prophetic visions of the imminent and catastrophic denouement of human history. Overly subtle interpretations in the interest of recapitulation overlook the distinct differences between the two series. Among the more important are: (1) the trumpet-plagues are partial in their effect (one-third of the earth is burned, 8:7; one-third of the sea becomes blood, 8:8; see also 8:9–12) while the bowls are universal ("every living soul died," 16:3; "every island fled away," 16:20) and final; (2) the trumpets are to a certain extent a call to repentance while the bowls are the pouring out of divine wrath; and (3) man is affected indirectly by the first four trumpets but is directly attacked

---

[1]Dale Davis suggests a plan in which each series is primarily sequential (the fifth seal overlaps the trumpets) but all three series end simultaneously ("The Relationship Between the Seals, Trumpets, and Bowls in the Book of Revelation," *Journal of the Evangelical Theological Society,* 16 [1973], pp. 149–58).

from the outset by the bowls. It should also be noticed that the bowls are poured out in rapid succession[2] with the customary interlude between the sixth and seventh elements of the sequence missing.

2. PLAGUES POURED OUT (16:1–21)

1 *And I heard a great voice out of the temple, saying to the seven angels, Go ye, and pour out the seven bowls of the wrath of God into the earth.*

2 *And the first went, and poured out his bowl into the earth; and it became a noisome and grievous sore upon the men that had the mark of the beast, and that worshipped his image.*

3 *And the second poured out his bowl into the sea; and it became blood as of a dead man; and every living soul died, even the things that were in the sea.*

4 *And the third poured out his bowl into the rivers and the fountains of the waters; and it became blood.*

5 *And I heard the angel of the waters saying, Righteous art thou, who art and who wast, thou Holy One, because thou didst thus judge:*

6 *for they poured out the blood of saints and prophets, and blood hast thou given them to drink: they are worthy.*

7 *And I heard the altar saying, Yea, O Lord God, the Almighty, true and righteous are thy judgments.*

8 *And the fourth poured out his bowl upon the sun; and it was given unto it to scorch men with fire.*

9 *And men were scorched with great heat: and they blasphemed the name of God who hath the power over these plagues; and they repented not to give him glory.*

10 *And the fifth poured out his bowl upon the throne of the beast; and his kingdom was darkened; and they gnawed their tongues for pain,*

11 *and they blasphemed the God of heaven because of their pains and their sores; and they repented not of their works.*

12 *And the sixth poured out his bowl upon the great river, the river Euphrates; and the water thereof was dried up, that the way might be made ready for the kings that come from the sunrising.*

13 *And I saw coming out of the mouth of the dragon, and out of the mouth of the beast, and out of the mouth of the false prophet, three unclean spirits, as it were frogs:*

14 *for they are spirits of demons, working signs; which go forth unto the kings of the whole world, to gather them together unto the war of the great day of God, the Almighty.*

15 *(Behold, I come as a thief. Blessed is he that watcheth, and keepeth his garments, lest he walk naked, and they see his shame.)*

---

[2]The boils of the first plague are still active at the time of the fifth plague (vs. 11).

16 *And they gathered them together into the place which is called in Hebrew Har-Magedon.*

17 *And the seventh poured out his bowl upon the air; and there came forth a great voice out of the temple, from the throne, saying, It is done:*

18 *and there were lightnings, and voices, and thunders; and there was a great earthquake, such as was not since there were men upon the earth, so great an earthquake, so mighty.*

19 *And the great city was divided into three parts, and the cities of the nations fell: and Babylon the great was remembered in the sight of God, to give unto her the cup of the wine of the fierceness of his wrath.*

20 *And every island fled away, and the mountains were not found.*

21 *And great hail, every stone about the weight of a talent, cometh down out of heaven upon men: and men blasphemed God because of the plague of the hail; for the plague thereof is exceeding great.*

1   Isaiah tells of "a voice from the temple! The voice of the Lord, rendering recompense to his enemies!" (Isa 66:6). John also hears a great voice from out of the temple instructing the angels of recompense to pour out upon the earth the bowls of the wrath of God. The voice is probably the voice of God, for according to the previous verse (15:8) no one is allowed to enter the temple until the seven angels have completed their mission. Farrer makes the interesting suggestion that since God is named in the third person, the voice is not a personal utterance of God but a sort of thunder which expresses his mind (p. 175). In placing the adjective before the noun the Greek text stresses the impressive nature of the great voice[3] which proceeds from the heavenly sanctuary.[4] There is no necessary connection between this command and the prayers of the saints (cf. 8:3–5), although some relationship could exist.

2   The first angel is dispatched and carries out his awesome task of pouring out the wrath of God upon the followers of the beast. Lilje comments that those who once bore the mark of the beast are now visited by the "marks" of God (p. 214). The first bowl brings "loathsome and malignant ulcers" (Phillips) upon mankind. We are reminded of the sixth Egyptian plague in which sores in the form of boils and abscesses broke out upon

___

[3]μεγάλης φωνῆς; elsewhere in the chapter we find the normal Johannine order: καῦμα μέγα (vs. 9), τὸν ποταμὸν τὸν μέγαν (vs. 12); also in verses 14, 17, 18, 19, 21.

[4]42 *pc c dem* vg(2) sa read ἐκ τοῦ οὐρανοῦ (apparently because ναοῦ was taken as a contraction of οὐρανοῦ; cf. Metzger, *TCGNT*, p. 757). ἐκ τοῦ ναοῦ is omitted by **P**[47vid] **046** 82 *al*, perhaps because it seemed inappropriate for such a stern command to come "out of the temple."

men and beasts throughout the land (Ex 9:9-11).[5] Job spoke from experience of the pain and irritation of such afflictions (Job 2:7-8, 13).

3 The second angel is sent forth into the earth[6] and pours his bowl into the sea, turning it to blood. This parallels the plague of Exodus 7:20-21 in which the waters of Egypt were turned to blood. It also parallels the second trumpet in which a burning mountain fell into the sea, turning it to blood (8:8-9). Note that in all three instances it is water, one of man's basic requirements and of critical importance in the more arid regions of ancient civilization, which is affected by divine judgment. The sea becomes like the blood of a dead man—that is, coagulated and rotting. In such a state it obviously can support no life. All sea life dies.[7] Glasson observes a "grim appropriateness in this plague: those who shed Christian blood must now drink blood" (p. 92).

4 The third angel pours his bowl upon the rivers and springs, turning them to blood. In the corresponding trumpet-plague a third part of the rivers and fountains of the waters are made bitter by a great burning star which fell from heaven (8:10-11). While parallels exist between the first four trumpets and the first four bowls, it should be noticed that the latter series is not a recapitulation of the former but an intensification of divine recompense which shares its imagery. As the sea when turned to blood brought death to all living in it (vs. 3), so also do the rivers and springs spread death when turned to blood. In recounting the story of the Exodus the Psalmist says that God "turned their rivers to blood, so that they could not drink of their streams" (Ps 78:44). John draws freely from the vocabulary of judgment and adapts it appropriately to describe the final plagues.

5 The righteousness of God's action in turning water to blood is attested to by the angel of the waters (vss. 5-6). In Jewish thought the elements of nature were held to be under the jurisdiction of appropriate angels. In Revelation 7:1 we learned of angels who restrained the four winds of the earth, and in 14:18 of an angel with power over fire. *I Enoch* 66:2 tells of angels of punishment who held the subterranean waters in check. Whether such an angel is here referred to is uncertain. There is some merit in the suggestion that the "angel of the waters" is simply the angel of the previ-

---

[5] ἕλκος; the same word is found in Rev 16:2 as in Ex 9:9-11 (LXX). Deut 28:27 (LXX) speaks of God smiting the disobedient with the boil (ἕλκει) of Egypt in the seat (εἰς τὴν ἕδραν)—a case of hemorrhoids! See also Deut 28:35.

[6] ἀπῆλθεν occurs only with the first angel but is assumed with the other six.

[7] ψυχὴ ζωῆς (A C 1006 1611 *pc* sy) has occasioned several scribal alterations: P[47] ℵ P 046 051 1 2059s *pm* lat TR read ζῶσα; 2329 arm[pt] read ζώων; and the adjective is omitted in 82 *al*. The *AV* follows the reading of P[47] ℵ P 046 1 82 2329 *pl* latt TR, which omits the article τά and says that "every living soul died in the sea"—a rather different (and unacceptable) idea.

ous verse who poured out his bowl upon "the waters" (Lenski, p. 469). In any case, the lyric utterance of the angel closely resembles that of the overcomers in 15:2–4 who sang the song of Moses and the Lamb.

"Righteous art thou"	"righteous and true are they ways"
"who art and who wast"	"thou King of the ages"
"thou Holy One"	"thou only art holy"
"because thou didst thus judge"	"for thy righteous acts have been made manifest"

The judgment of God is neither vengeful nor capricious. It is an expression of his just and righteous nature. All caricatures of God which ignore his intense hatred of sin reveal more about man than about God. In a moral universe God must of necessity oppose evil. Far from undermining his righteousness, the love of God has made possible through the cross the redemption of unrighteous man. "Righteous art thou, O Lord," declared the Psalmist, "and right are thy judgments" (Ps 119:137).[8]

As in 11:17, God is addressed as the one who is and who was. In 1:4, 8 and 4:8 the title is expanded to include a future reference ("who is to come"), but in the present context this is unnecessary because the final sequence of events has already begun.[9]

6 The syntactical relationship between verses 5 and 6 is not clear. It is probably best to take verse 6 as a separate sentence which provides further evidence of the righteousness of God in carrying out his judgment by turning the waters to blood. Because they had poured out the blood of the saints, God has given them blood to drink.[10] The punishment is tailored to fit the crime. Isaiah declared that the oppressors of Israel would be fed with their own flesh and be drunk with their own blood (Isa 49:26). In Wisdom of Solomon 11:16 we read, "By what things a man sinneth, by these he is punished." That the determined action of God in righteous retribution and its resulting consequence is something more than momentary discomfort is supported by the Greek perfect tense, "and blood hast thou given them."[11] Those who have shed the blood of the faithful are said to be

---

[8]Peter Staples argues against H. D. Betz that the world of Jewish-Hellenistic syncretism is not the most plausible background for Rev 16:4–6 ("Rev. XVI 4–6 and its Vindication Formula," *NovT*, 14 [1972], pp. 280–93). Betz' article is translated in "Apocalypticism," *JTC*, 6 (1969), pp. 134–56.

[9]The *AV* incorrectly reads "and shalt be," perhaps mistaking ὅσιος for the future participle ἐσόμενος (Bruce, p. 656). ὁ ὅσιος is taken as vocative in nearly all recent translations. P⁴⁷ reads καί instead of ὁ, taking ὅσιος as an adjective parallel to δίκαιος.

[10]Some take the two ὅτι clauses as parallel or the second as an explanation of the first. The alternative tentatively accepted above understands καί in the sense of "even."

[11]δέδωκας (A C 2329). P⁴⁷ ℵ P 1 *pl* TR read ἔδωκας.

THE BOOK OF REVELATION

"worthy" of receiving blood to drink.[12] The *Twentieth Century NT* translates, "It is what they deserve." A comparison with the saints in Sardis who shall walk with Christ in white—"for they are worthy" (3:4)—is not intended. The saints and prophets are not two distinct groups but faithful believers, some of whom were leaders in the church.[13] The prophetic ministry within the early church involved not only prediction (as in Acts 11:28; 21:10-11) but also edification, exhortation, and consolation (I Cor 14:3).

7 A second voice confirms the rightness of God's retributive act. The speaking altar is obviously a personification (cf. 9:13). It represents the corporate testimony of the martyrs in 6:9 and the prayers of the saints in 8:3-5.[14] It is significant that throughout Revelation (except in 11:1) the altar is connected with judgment (6:9; 8:3-5; 9:13; 14:18; 16:7). The principles of sacrifice and judgment are inextricably interwoven. Like the angel of the waters, the voice of the altar echoes the song of Moses and the Lamb (15:3-5), whose judgments are true and righteous.[15] Both reflect OT passages such as Psalm 19:9 ("The ordinances of the Lord are true and righteous altogether"). God's acts of judging[16] are in accordance with truth and are absolutely just.

8 The fourth angel pours out his bowl upon[17] the sun, and men are scorched by its fiery heat. After the blast of the fourth trumpet, a third of the sun, moon, and stars were darkened for a third of the day and night (9:12). But now the fourth bowl is followed with scorching heat rather than a partial eclipse. Fire is commonly connected with judgment in Scripture (see Deut 28:22; I Cor 3:13; II Pet 3:7). The sovereign control of God over the entire process of retributive justice is emphasized by the fact that the power of scorching is said to be *given* to the sun.[18]

9 The intensity of the heat is re-emphasized by the expression which may be translated "scorched with a great scorching."[19] Over against

---

[12]For ἄξιος in a somewhat ironic sense see Lk 12:48 ("worthy of stripes") and Rom 1:32 ("worthy of death").
[13]This use of καί to identify a particular person or class within a larger group is clearly seen in passages such as Mk 16:7 and Acts 1:14.
[14]See comm. on 9:13.
[15]15:3 speaks of ὁδοί rather than κρίσεις and has ἀληθιναί and δίκαιαι in reverse order. Rev 19:2 corresponds to 16:7.
[16]κρίσις tends to express action, while κρίμα refers more often to a judicial verdict.
[17]Somewhat curiously the first three angels pour out their bowls *into* (εἰς, 9:2, 3, 4) and the other four *upon* (ἐπί, 9:8, 10, 12, 17). Lenski suggests that John would have us divide the plagues into groups of three and four rather than the customary four and three (p. 471).
[18]Taking ἥλιον rather than ὁ τέταρτος as the antecedent of αὐτῷ.
[19]Cognate accusative; ἐκαυματίσθησαν . . . καῦμα μέγα; cf. Mt 2:10; Lk 11:46. Cf. Lactantius, *Div. Inst.* vii.26, where it is warned that God will stop the sun for three days and the wicked will be punished by excessive heat.

this terrible plague we may compare the lot of those in heaven upon whom the sun shall strike no more, nor any heat (7:16). The heathen world does not respond to this great pain by repenting and giving glory to God, but by blaspheming his name. Following the great earthquake of 11:13 the nations were "dazzled into homage and conversion" (Kiddle, p. 320)—a temporary condition at best—but now, knowing full well that it is God himself who controls the plagues, they refuse to repent but resort to blasphemy. Like Pharaoh, their hearts have become hardened and repentance is out of the question. Caird says, "They have wholly taken on the character of the false god they serve" (p. 202).

10 When the fifth angel pours out his bowl of wrath upon the throne of the beast, a darkness settles over the kingdom and men gnaw their tongues in pain. The throne of the beast would be his authority or dominion,[20] and in John's day Rome was the geographical focus of that power. The resulting darkness is reminiscent of the ninth Egyptian plague (Ex 10:21–29). This supernatural darkness not only intensifies the distress of the previous plagues, but also adds a terror of its own. Taking the fifth bowl as in some sense an abbreviation of the first Woe, Charles (II, pp. 44–45) conjectures that the kingdom of the beast is made dark by the smoke from the pit (9:2).[21] No such explanation is necessary. The torments of darkness are vividly portrayed in Wisdom of Solomon 17. Commentators who freely interpret the images of the Apocalypse normally understand this plague in terms such as "the darkness of civil strife" (Kiddle, p. 321) or "the total eclipse of the monster's imperial power" (Caird, p. 204).[22] In any case, it causes such agony that men gnaw[23] their tongues in pain.

11 Far from repenting of their evil, the followers of the beast blaspheme God because of their pains and sores. They have become one in character with their evil master, whose most characteristic activity is to blaspheme God and his followers (13:5, 6; cf. 13:1; 17:3). The term "God of heaven" may reflect Daniel 2:44, where it is used of the One who in his sovereignty destroys the kingdoms of this world and establishes his universal reign. That men blaspheme because of their pains and their sores indicates that the discomfort of the previous plagues continues into the present. But punishment does not bring repentance. The decision to perse-

---

[20]Cf. Satan's θρόνος in 2:13 and the θρόνος which the dragon gave to the beast along with his power and great authority (13:2).

[21]Holding the darkness to be "wholly insufficient to explain the agony experienced by the adherents of the Beast," Charles infers that "after ἐσκοτωμένη several clauses have been lost" which would explain both the darkness and the sufferings of mankind (II, p. 45).

[22]Caird calls the last three plagues a "triad of political disaster"—internal anarchy, invasion, and irreparable collapse (p. 204).

[23]μασάομαι, to bite or chew; Job 30:3 speaks of men who "gnaw the dry ground" in search of food.

vere in evil has permanently precluded any possibility of a return to righteousness.

12 When the sixth bowl is poured out upon the Euphrates, the river dries up, thus opening a way for the kings from the East. There is at least a literary parallel between the sixth bowl and the sixth trumpet. When the sixth trumpet sounded, four angels bound at the Euphrates were released to lead a vast army of grotesque horses to the slaughter of one-third of mankind (9:13-19). The Euphrates marked the eastern boundary of the land given by covenant to Abraham and his seed (Gen 15:18; Deut 1:7-8; Josh 1:3-4). It also separated the Roman Empire on the east from the much feared Parthians whose expert cavalry bowmen had conquered the entire territory from the Euphrates to the Indus. It is frequently pointed out that in the OT God's great redemptive acts were often associated with the drying up of water. The Exodus (Ex 14:21) and the entrance into Canaan (Josh 3:14-17) are the two major examples.[24] In the present context it is the enemy that is allowed to advance for war by the drying up of the Euphrates.

It is unlikely that John is alluding to the famous capture of Babylon by Cyrus the Persian, but the incident is relevant. Herodotus (*Hist.* i.191) tells us that Cyrus, finding the city seemingly impregnable, temporarily diverted the Euphrates, which ran through the center of Babylon, leaving open the river bed, through which his armies entered and captured the city.

The kings from the East have been variously interpreted. Walvoord notes that as many as fifty different interpretations have been advanced (p. 236). Whatever the ultimate reference, the historical context of John's imagery favors the interpretation of the kings as Parthian rulers. The tradition that Nero, although dying by his own hand, would return from the East leading a great army of Parthian warriors is preserved in the *Sibylline Oracles* (4:115-39). Some confusion results from the fact that this tradition is partially intertwined in Revelation with an older tradition that portrayed a final assault on the people of God by the united kings of earth (Joel 3:2; Zeph 3:8). The kings of the East (vs. 12) who will lay siege to Rome (17:15-18 and chap. 18) are distinct from the kings of the whole world (vs. 14) who will wage the final war against Christ and the armies of heaven (19:11-21; note 17:12-14 as well).[25]

13 Verses 13-16 are sometimes taken as a brief interlude between the sixth and seventh bowls similar in structure to the break between the

---

[24]The closest literary parallel is Isaiah 11:15-16, where the River (Euphrates) is smitten into seven channels so men may cross dryshod and a highway leads from Assyria to Israel for the returning remnant (cf. Jer 51:36; Zech 10:11; II Esdr 13:47).

[25]The relationship between "Armageddon" and the Gog and Magog conflict at the close of the millennial period will be treated in the commentary at 20:7-10.

sixth and seventh seals (chap. 7) and the sixth and seventh trumpets (10:1–11:14). This would limit the sixth bowl to verse 12 only and thus depart from John's custom of making the fifth and sixth plagues in each series considerably longer than the first four. Verses 13–16 should be viewed as a topical expansion of verse 12. The drying up of the Euphrates may have suggested the frogs of verse 13, which in turn would remind the reader of the second Egyptian plague (Ex 8:1–15). In any case, preparation for war is the common theme.

John sees three unclean spirits coming out of the mouths of the dragon, the beast, and the false prophet. The dragon is without doubt the seven-headed dragon of chapter 12 (specifically identified as Satan in 12:9), and the beast is the beast out of the sea as described in the first ten verses of chapter 13. The false prophet (appearing by that name for the first time) is surely the beast out of the earth of 13:11–17. The unclean spirits proceed from the *mouths* of the unholy triumvirate, suggesting the persuasive and deceptive propaganda which in the last days will lead men to an unconditional commitment to the cause of evil. Swete identifies the beast as "the brute force of the World-power represented by the Roman Empire," and the false prophet as the "false spiritual power which made common cause with the temporal power in doing Satan's work" (p. 206). These historically conditioned symbols reveal eschatological truth which far transcends the limitations of their origins. In time the Roman Empire would crumble, but beyond all temporary manifestations of secular power the entire structure of human opposition to the kingdom of God will come crashing down in defeat. In the mind of the apocalyptist this will happen not by the gradual turning of men to the truth but by the dramatic and sudden return of the warrior Christ. Men duped by the subtle propaganda of secularism have cut themselves off from the source of truth and must bear the inevitable consequences.

The reference to the three spirits as frogs emphasizes their uncleanness[26] and perhaps their endless croaking. Williams takes the final phrase in an adverbial sense and supplies a verb—"Then I saw three foul spirits leap like frogs from the mouths of the dragon."

14 The first clause of verse 14 is a parenthetical remark which explains why the spirits are called unclean. "They are diabolical spirits performing wonders" (Phillips). Beckwith favors the construction which translates, "For there exist spirits of demons which work miracles," and takes the clause as explaining the power of the spirits (p. 684). In either

---

[26]Lev 11:10 classifies the frog ("anything in the seas or the rivers that has not fins and scales") as an unclean animal.

case the following clause ("which go forth") connects with "three unclean spirits" of verse 13 and completes the sentence which began "I saw."[27] John's syntax invites considerable conjecture at times. The activity of the deceptive and demonic spirits reminds us of the living spirit who through the mouth of Ahab's prophets would entice the profligate king into battle (I Kgs 22:19-23). Jesus warned that in the last days false prophets would arise and by signs and wonders would lead many astray (Mt 24:24). Paul wrote of the lawless one whose appearance would be with "signs and lying wonders" and with "evil's undiluted power to deceive" (Phillips). The unclean spirits in Revelation work their spell on world rulers rather than common men. By deceit they gather the kings of the whole world[28] for a great war against God and the hosts of heaven (explained in detail in 19:11-21). Swete writes, "There have been times when nations have been seized by a passion for war which the historian can but imperfectly explain. It is such an epoch that the Seer foresees, but one which, unlike any that has come before it, will involve the whole world in war" (p. 208). This epoch is designated "the great day[29] of God, the Almighty." It is the day when God will reckon with the ungodly nations of the world. Israel believed that in the last days her enemies would gather to war against her (Ezek 38-39; Zech 14; I Enoch 56:5-8; 90:13-19) but God would intervene and bring victory. Joel foretells a great and terrible day of Jehovah (Joel 2:11) when God will gather the nations into the valley of Jehoshaphat and execute judgment upon them (Joel 3:2). The great assize described by John goes beyond nationalistic expectations. It is nothing less than the climax of human history when, in the words of the twenty-four elders, God the Almighty takes up his great power and enters into his reign (11:17).

15 The interjection of a warning in the midst of a prophecy of final conflict is entirely appropriate. When all the forces of the beast are gathered for the last battle, the believer will enter a period of supreme crisis.[30] It is Christ himself who says, "Behold, I come as a thief."[31] We are reminded of the unexpectedness which the historical Jesus connected with his own return (Mt 24:42-44) and of Paul's statement that the day of

---

[27]Charles rejects as "wholly unsatisfactory" ἃ ἐκπορεύεται and concludes that it was changed from ἐκπορευόμενα when the marginal gloss ὡς βάτραχοι... σημεῖα was incorporated into the text (II, p. 48). P⁴⁷ ℵ* 1* al read ἐκπορεύεσθαι.

[28]ἡ οἰκουμένη ὅλη is universal in scope.

[29]1 pm sy Prim TR sharpen the reference by adding ἐκείνης after ἡμέρας.

[30]Charles, holding that the faithful have already been removed from the earth, judges vs. 15 to be an intrusion which originally belonged between 3:3a and 3b (II, p. 49). Caird objects to this kind of surgery and views it as an admission that the evidence does not support the theory (p. 208).

[31]ℵ* pc put the warning in the third person (ἔρχεται).

the Lord will come "as a thief in the night" (I Thess 5:2). The faithful are admonished to be on the alert for this great event—not taken by surprise as a soldier who, when the alarm is sounded, must run away naked[32] because he has misplaced his clothing. The kind of spiritual preparedness that Christ requires is the discernment which cuts through the deceptive propaganda of Satan and his henchmen (cf. 13:13–15). The beatitude is the third of seven scattered through the book (1:3; 14:13; 16:15; 19:9; 20:6; 22:7, 14). It promises the blessing of God for those who remain faithful in the critical hours which lie ahead.

16 Following the parenthesis of verse 15, the narrative resumes and leads directly into one of the more cryptic and difficult problems of Revelation. The kings of the world are said to be gathered into a place "which is called in Hebrew Har-Magedon." Magedon is normally connected with Megiddo, the ancient city lying on the north side of the Carmel ridge and commanding the strategic pass between the coastal plain and the valley of Esdraelon. It is one of history's famous battlefields, having witnessed major conflicts all the way "from one fought by Tuthmosis III in 1468 B.C. to that of Lord Allenby of Megiddo in 1917" (*NBD*, p. 505). "By the waters of Megiddo" Barak and Deborah defeated the chariots of Sisera (Judg 4–5; cf. 5:19). Ahaziah, wounded by the arrows of Jehu, fled to Megiddo, and died there (II Kgs 9:27). Har-Magedon would mean "the Mountain of Megiddo," but here a difficulty arises: there is no Mt. Megiddo. None of the solutions offered is especially persuasive. It is possible that Har-Magedon could be a reference to the hill country near Megiddo or perhaps a reference to Megiddo and Mt. Carmel in the same breath (Farrer, p. 178). In John's day the tell or mound upon which Megiddo was built was about seventy feet in height, hardly enough to justify the designation Mount. One frequent suggestion is that the Apocalyptist began with Ezekiel's prophecy of a great eschatological slaughter of the nations on "the mountains of Israel" (Ezek 38:8–21; 39:2, 4, 17) and then made the reference more specific by adding the name Megiddo as the place where so often in Israel's history the enemies of God were destroyed (Beckwith, p. 685). Still others interpret the term in reference to some ancient myth in which an army of demons assault the holy mountain of the gods. If one reads Armageddon (instead of Har-Magedon),

---

[32]Bruce notes that "according to the Mishnah, the captain of the temple in Jerusalem went his rounds of the precincts by night, and if a member of the temple police was caught asleep at his post, his clothes were taken off and burned, and he was sent away naked in disgrace" (p. 657). In the context of vs. 15 ἀσχημοσύνη is probably a euphemism for "private parts" (as in Ex 20:26 and Deut 23:14; cf. BAG, p. 119).

the reference could be to the city of Megiddo rather than to a mountain.[33]

Others interpret Har-Magedon without reference to Megiddo. Bruce (p. 657), following C. C. Torrey, mentions *har mō'ēd*, the mount of assembly (Isa 14:13). Or it could be a corruption in the Hebrew text for "his fruitful mountain" or the "desirable city" (*i.e.,* Jerusalem). As Rome is to be overthrown by the kings of the East (16:12; 17:16-17), so also will the kings of the whole world be destroyed in final conflict outside the city of Jerusalem (see Joel 3:2; Zech 14:2 ff). Yet another suggestion is that Megiddo could be derived from a root meaning "to cut, attack, or maraud." In this case Mt. Megiddo would mean "the marauding mountain" (a variant to Jeremiah's "destroying mountain," Jer 51:25) and indicate that John expected the battle not in northern Palestine but at Rome (Caird, p. 207; cf. Kiddle, pp. 329-31).

As in the case of the number of the beast (13:18), the cryptic nature of the reference has thus far defeated all attempts at a final answer.[34] Fortunately, geography is not the major concern. Wherever it takes place, Har-Magedon is symbolic of the final overthrow of all the forces of evil by the might and power of God. The great conflict between God and Satan, Christ and Antichrist, good and evil, which lies behind the perplexing course of history will in the end issue in a final struggle in which God will emerge victorious and take with him all who have placed their faith in him. This is Har-Magedon.

17 Several similarities exist between the last trumpet and the final bowl. Following the seventh trumpet great voices in heaven proclaimed the realization of the kingdom of God (11:15), the twenty-four elders announced the arrival of the time of judgment (11:18), the temple of God in heaven was opened (11:19), and there were lightnings, voices, thunders, an earthquake, and hail (11:19-21). Likewise the seventh bowl is followed by a great voice from the heavenly temple declaring God's purpose accomplished (16:17), judgment falls upon the entire earth (16:19-20), and there are lightnings, voices, and thunders, along with the greatest of all earthquakes and tremendous hail (16:18, 21).

The extent to which these great cataclysmic events are to be taken symbolically rather than literally will be determined by the interpreter's

---

[33]This conjecture takes עַר (transliterated ʿAρ) as the equivalent of עִיר ("city"); cf. Charles' reference, II, p. 50. Metzger notes that the usual English spelling, "Armageddon," is based on one form of the late Byzantine text; but most manuscripts give no information about the breathing (*TCGNT*, p. 757). An alternate form which drops the first syllable is Μαγεδών (82 *al c* vg(4) bo(3)) or Μαγεδδών (**046** 1611 2053 *pc* Prim). Cf. Metzger for other orthographic variations (*loc. cit.*)

[34]Jeremias has a good summary in "Har Magedon (Apc. 16:16)," *ZNW*, 31 (1932), pp. 73-77.

view of the nature of apocalyptic language. The position of this commentary is that the descriptions themselves are not John's creative attempt to portray eschatological truth in apocalyptic terminology but the faithful transmission of what he actually saw in authentic vision (1:11). That the visions draw upon John's extensive exposure to the prophetic literature of the OT as interpreted within the apocalyptic milieu of his day does not imply that their origin is best explained as the Seer's attempt to articulate in the available terminology his best thoughts about the future. Doubtless John would interpret the visions in the light of his own historical situation. Rome would be the beast, and the provincial priesthood which enforced the imperial cult would be the false prophet. What he could not know from his vantage point was that the dissolution of the Roman Empire was but a model of the ultimate collapse of all worldly opposition to the kingdom of God. The task of the contemporary interpreter is to read the symbols in the vocabulary of the first century and understand them in reference to their final and complete fulfillment.

The seventh bowl is poured out upon the air, the atmosphere which surrounds the earth.[35] A great voice from the heavenly sanctuary proclaims, "All is over!" (Moffatt). The seven plagues (15:1) have run their course, and man stands on the threshold of eternity. The voice is the voice of God. The blending of heavenly sanctuary and throne room[36] was seen in 7:15 and 8:5 as well.

18 The divine proclamation is accompanied by lightnings, voices, and thunders—the same "storm-theophany" (Moffatt, p. 449) we encountered in similar scenes in 4:5; 8:5; and 11:19. The earth is rocked with an earthquake far greater than any since man has inhabited the earth. The severity of the earthquake is emphasized by three modifying phrases, "such as was not since there were men upon the earth,[37] so great . . . so mighty." This would have a vivid impact upon people living in a century which had experienced a great number of severe quakes.

19 There is no general agreement as to the identity of the great city which is separated into three parts. Since later in the verse Babylon the Great is mentioned separately, some have taken the first city to be Jerusalem (cf. 11:8). Others, pointing to the repeated use of the designation "the great city" in chapter 18 (vss. 10, 16, 18, 19, 21), argue for Rome. Morris removes it from any geographical setting, identifying it as "civilized

---

[35]There is probably no intended reference here to the air as the abode of demons (cf. Eph 2:2).
[36]Some manuscripts read οὐρανοῦ for ναοῦ (**051*** 1 2059s *al g*); others have the longer substitution ναοῦ τοῦ οὐρανοῦ (**046** 82 *pm* TR). Sinaiticus replaces ἀπὸ τοῦ θρόνου with τοῦ θεοῦ, while 2027 *pc* add τοῦ θεοῦ after θρόνου. Apparently the scribes found some awkwardness with the concept.
[37]A free rendering of Dan 12:1?

man . . . ordering his affairs apart from God" (p. 201; cf. Kiddle, p. 332, and Bruce, p. 657, for similar interpretations). For John, at least, the allusion would be to Rome as the center of satanic power and oppression against the fledgling church. It is wrong to separate the great city from the cities of the nations as if her punishment were less severe. Nor does the subsequent reference to Babylon imply yet another city.[38] The division of the great city into three parts indicates the completeness of its destruction. That all the cities of the nations fall with Rome indicates the dominant role of the great capital in its network of imperial communications.

God remembers to give Rome "the wine-cup of his passionate wrath."[39] No longer does the goodness and forbearance of God (intended to lead men to repentance, Rom 2:4) restrain his righteous indignation against all who have by their own free will decided irrevocably for evil. If God were not to punish unrighteousness, the concept of a moral universe would have to be discarded.

20 When the sixth seal was opened, there followed a great earthquake, dramatic cosmic disturbances, and "every mountain and island were moved out of their places" (6:12–14). Likewise the great earthquake of the seventh bowl caused every island to flee away and the mountains to disappear. Some writers see in the reference to the removal of "every island" an allusion to the author's imprisonment on the island of Patmos (*eg.*, Caird, p. 209). Others find eschatological hostility toward mountains due to prophetic denunciation of high places (Kiddle, p. 335). But the references are probably general in nature and represent the devastating effects of the tremendously violent earthquake. Beasley-Murray observes that John, by means of his impressionist pictures of the last things, "depicts the unspeakable grandeur of the awe-fulness of the revelation of God's judgments and deliverances at the end of history" (p. 247). Similar indications of the end are found in the *Assumption of Moses* 10:4 and *I Enoch* 1:6. In Revelation 20:11 the earth and heaven flee away before the face of the one who sits upon the great white throne.

21 The storm of divine wrath reaches its climax with hundred-pound[40] hailstones falling from heaven upon men. In the OT God repeatedly punished the enemies of his people with hail. As the armies of the

---

[38]καί may be understood "and so" (cf. Mt 23:32; II Cor 11:9).

[39]BAG, p. 366. Cf. 19:15 ("the winepress of the fierce anger of God") and comm. on 14:8, 10. Commenting on 16:19 Lenski says that the wine is "the wrath that is hot with anger" (p. 485).

[40]The τάλαντον varied in weight among different peoples and at various times. The range seems to be from about sixty pounds to something over a hundred. Alford notes that Diodorus Siculus (xix.45) speaks of hailstones of a mina each in weight as enormous, and the talent contained sixty minae (IV, p. 704).

five kings fled before Joshua, God cast down great hailstones, killing more than died by the sword (Josh 10:11). Ezekiel prophesied against Gog a great shaking in the land with torrential rain and hailstones (Ezek 38:18–22). Hail was part of the accepted arsenal of divine retaliation.

The plague of hail produces no change in mankind. After each of the three final plagues man blasphemes God (16:9, 11, 21). Even the exceedingly great[41] hail fails to shatter their confidence in the kingship of Apollyon, the angel of the abyss (9:11), and bring them to acknowledge the sovereignty of the God of heaven. Their Faustian bargain has transformed them into blasphemers who carry out to the end the beast's hatred of God.

[41]σφόδρα; only here in Rev.

CHAPTER 17

VIII. THE FALL OF BABYLON (17:1–19:5)

Chapters 17 and 18 portray the judgment of God upon the great harlot, Rome, that citadel of pagan opposition to the cause of Christ. From a literary point of view the two chapters are quite distinct. In chapter 17, after the opening vision of the harlot seated upon the scarlet beast (vss. 1–6), the author turns to an extended interpretation of his symbols. He identifies the seven heads (vss. 9–10), the ten horns (vs. 12), the waters upon which the harlot is seated (vs. 15), and the woman herself (vs. 18). As for the beast, he is "of the seven" yet "is himself also an eighth" (vs. 11). Anticipating some bewilderment the Seer adds, "Here is a problem for a profound mind!" (Goodspeed, vs. 9). Chapter 18 is a dirge over the fallen city. Kings, merchants, and all seafaring men bewail her destruction. Echoes from the prophetic taunt songs of Isaiah, Jeremiah, and Ezekiel reverberate throughout the entire chapter.

1. THE HARLOT AND THE SCARLET BEAST (17:1–6)

1 *And there came one of the seven angels that had the seven bowls, and spake with me, saying, Come hither, I will show thee the judgment of the great harlot that sitteth upon many waters;*

2 *with whom the kings of the earth committed fornication, and they that dwell in the earth were made drunken with the wine of her fornication.*

3 *And he carried me away in the Spirit into a wilderness: and I saw a woman sitting upon a scarlet-colored beast, full of names of blasphemy, having seven heads and ten horns.*

4 *And the woman was arrayed in purple and scarlet, and decked with gold and precious stone and pearls, having in her hand a golden cup full of abominations, even the unclean things of her fornication,*

5 *and upon her forehead a name written, MYSTERY, BABYLON THE*

GREAT, THE MOTHER OF THE HARLOTS AND OF THE ABOMINA-
TIONS OF THE EARTH.
6 *And I saw the woman drunken with the blood of the saints, and with the*
blood of the martyrs of Jesus. And when I saw her, I wondered with a
great wonder.

1 The Seer is summoned to view the judgment of the harlot by one of the
seven bowl-angels. In 21:9 the same angel appears to show John the Bride,
the wife of the Lamb.[1] The connection is not accidental. When the great
harlot with all her seductive allurements is exposed and destroyed, then the
Bride of Christ will be seen in all her beauty and true worth.

In OT prophetic discourse the imagery of the harlot is commonly
used to denote religious apostasy. Isaiah laments that the once faithful
Jerusalem has become a harlot (Isa 1:21). Jeremiah speaks of Israel's
"adulteries and neighings" (elsewhere she is a wild ass in heat, Jer 2:24)
and "lewd harlotries" (Jer 13:27; cf. Jer 2:20–31; Ezek 16:15 ff; Hos 2:5).
Since the harlot of the Apocalypse is a pagan city (cf. 17:18), it is more
likely that a passage like Nahum 3:4 or Isaiah 23:16, 17 supplies the
immediate background. In the former, the harlot is Nineveh, who betrays
nations with her harlotries and her charms (cf. Rev 17:4). Isaiah pictures
Tyre as a forgotten harlot. In the context of Revelation 17 and 18 the
imagery is not that of religious profligacy but of the prostitution of all that
is right and noble for the questionable ends of power and luxury. Whether
Jezebel or Cleopatra sat for the portrait John is now painting (Caird, pp.
212–13) makes little difference.[2] The harlot is Rome.[3] Adorned in luxury
and intoxicated with the blood of the saints, she stands for a dominant
world system based on seduction for personal gain over against the righteous demands of a persecuted minority. John's images are timeless in that
they portray the essential conflicts of mankind from the beginning of time

---

[1]Note the similarities between the two passages: καὶ ἦλθεν εἷς ἐκ τῶν ἑπτὰ ἀγγέλων τῶν
ἐχόντων τὰς ἑπτὰ φιάλας ... καὶ ἐλάλησεν μετ᾽ ἐμοῦ λέγων, Δεῦρο, δείξω σοι (17:1 and
21:9); ἀπήνεγκέν με ... ἐν πνεύματι (17:3 and 21:10).
[2]J. E. Bruns holds that Valeria Messalina (wife of the emperor Claudius) was in the Seer's
mind when he described the great harlot ("The Contrasted Women of Apoc 12 and 17,"
CBQ, 26 [1964], pp. 459–63). "There can be no doubt that at this period the Roman world
recognized in one woman [Messalina] the epitome of all that was rotten and corrupt in the
empire" (p. 461; cf. the following page for quotations from Juvenal and Tacitus in support of
this position).
[3]Rist argues that the harlot is not only Rome and the empire, but *Dea Roma* (the personification of the divine state) herself, who along with the emperors and the seven-headed beast is
accorded divine worship (pp. 488–89 and throughout the exegesis of chap. 17). Ford builds a
case for Jerusalem rather than Rome as the harlot of Rev 17 (pp. 283–86).

until the end. At the close of history the great harlot stands as the final and intensified expression of worldly power. The apocalyptic proclamation that the harlot shall soon be stripped naked and be utterly destroyed (17:16) comes as a necessary and welcome reminder that God is forever sovereign and continues to occupy the throne of the universe. He will judge with equity the enemies of righteousness and will usher in the kingdom of eternal joy.

The harlot is pictured as sitting upon many waters. According to verse 15, the waters are peoples, multitudes, nations, and tongues. Since the harlot is later named Babylon the Great (17:5), it would appear that this part of the description comes from Jeremiah 51:13 where Babylon is said to dwell "by many waters." The reference to the numerous canals which distributed the waters of the Euphrates to the surrounding territory symbolizes the influence of Rome as it flows out throughout the entire world.

2 The kings of the earth who have committed fornication with the great harlot are the nations who have entered into illicit relations with Rome. They represent the apostate nations which Rome has enticed into idolatrous worship of herself and the beast. The influence of her pernicious doctrines has spread to the entire pagan population. Those who dwell on the earth are further identified in 17:8 as those "whose name hath not been written in the book of life."[4] They are portrayed as drunk with the intoxicating influence of Rome's seductive practices. In a somewhat similar way Jeremiah pictured Babylon as a golden cup in the Lord's hand whose wine the nations drank and went mad (Jer 51:7).[5]

3 The Seer is now carried away into a wilderness place to watch the coming judgment of the harlot. Four times in the Apocalypse John is said to be in the Spirit (1:10; 4:2) or carried away in the Spirit (17:3; 21:10).[6] The reference is to that state of ecstasy in which John experienced the entire visionary experience recorded in the Apocalypse. It does not necessarily point to some new state of exaltation which came over him. In this context the wilderness is not a place of divine protection and nourishment (as in 12:6, 14), but an appropriate setting for a vision of judgment. It may have been suggested by the opening statements of Isaiah's oracle against Babylon in chapter 21. In the course of Jewish history the wilderness had often been the setting for unusual and visionary experiences (Ex 3:1 ff; I Kgs 19:4 ff; Mt 4:1 ff).

As the vision begins to unfold, John sees a woman seated upon a scarlet beast. That she was earlier said to be sitting upon many waters (vs.

---

[4]Taking the ὧν clause in vs. 8 as appositional.

[5]Cf. the same imagery in Rev 14:8 and 18:3.

[6]ἐν πνεύματι refers to the Seer's ecstatic state rather than the instrumentality by which he was carried away (in which case the reference would probably be to the Holy Spirit).

1) should cause no problem. The constantly shifting scenes of apocalyptic should not be taken with a rigidity that would impose artificial conformity upon its symbols. The scarlet-colored beast is the beast that rose out of the sea in chapter 13 (vss. 1 ff). It is the great persecuting power which rules by brute force and is the supreme enemy of Christ and the church. The scarlet color does not necessarily convey an idea such as "ostentatious magnificence" (Charles, II, p. 64), nor is it symbolic of the blood of martyrs. Rather, it is primarily descriptive and heightens the terrifying appearance of the beast. Like its master, the great red dragon of chapter 12, it is terrifying to behold. Names of blasphemy cover its entire body.[7] The reference is to the blasphemous claims to deity made by Roman emperors who employed such titles as *theios* (divine), *sōtēr* (savior), and *kyrios* (Lord). The blasphemies are not so much directly spoken against God by the beast as they are implied by his self-deification. The beast (like the dragon of chap. 12) has seven heads and ten horns (cf. 13:1). John supplies his own interpretation of these later in the chapter (vss. 9–14, 16–17).

4 The woman who sits astride the scarlet beast is clothed in luxurious garments and adorned with gold and costly jewels. Purple and scarlet signify the luxury and splendor of ancient Rome. Both dyes were expensive to extract. Purple was often used for royal garments (Judg 8:26; Dan 5:7), and scarlet was a color of magnificence (cf. Nah 2:3). The costly and spectacular garb of the harlot should be contrasted with the "fine linen, bright and pure," worn by the Bride of the Lamb (Rev 19:8). The harlot is lavishly adorned with gold[8] and precious stones. In her hand she holds a golden cup which promises a heady draught of carnal satisfaction. Its contents, however, are quite otherwise. The cup is full of the abominations and[9] impurities of her fornication.[10] Moral corruption and all manner of ceremonial uncleanness are what she offers.[11]

---

[7]In Rev 13:1 the names were on his seven heads. The masculine participles γέμοντα and ἔχων (though some MSS use the neuter γέμον; cf. **046** 1 82 1006 2059s *al* TR) reflect an understanding of the beast as an intelligent being.

[8]κεχρυσωμένη χρυσίῳ does not necessarily mean that she gilded her body (Swete, p. 216). The καὶ λίθῳ τιμίῳ which follows argues for the meaning "to adorn." Cf. I Tim 2:9 where adornment with gold, pearls, and costly attire is frowned upon, and Ezek 28:13 where the king of Tyre is adorned with precious stones set in gold.

[9]καί may be taken epexegetically, in which case τὰ ἀκάθαρτα describes further the meaning of βδελυγμάτων. The accusative (τὰ ἀκάθαρτα) is to be accounted for as the object of ἔχουσα or perhaps similar to γέμοντα ὀνόματα of vs. 3.

[10]**046** 82 1611 2329 *al* g read πορνείας τῆς γῆς (‭א‬ co have αὐτῆς καὶ τῆς γῆς), probably due to the influence of vs. 2 where those who dwell on τὴν γῆν are drunken with the wine of the harlot's πορνεία.

[11]βδέλυγμα is used in the LXX of the moral and ceremonial impurity connected with idolatrous practices. The expression βδέλυγμα τῆς ἐρημώσεως in Mk 13:14 comes from Dan 12:11 where it denotes the desecration of the Jewish temple by an image or altar of Zeus (*TDNT*, I, p. 600).

5 The description of the harlot continues with special attention to the name written upon her forehead. There are seven other references in Revelation to the marking of the forehead. In 13:16, 14:9, and 20:4 the mark is the mark of the beast. Elsewhere it is the seal or name of God (7:3; 9:4; 14:1; 22:4). Placing the name upon the forehead (probably upon a headband) appears to have been a custom of Roman courtesans.[12] The *AV* includes MYSTERY as part of the inscription (following the punctuation of Tischendorf), but it is better understood as indicating that the name is to be understood in a mystical rather than literal sense. The *NEB* translates, "Written on her forehead was a name with a secret meaning." Only those to whom the meaning is revealed (vs. 7) will grasp the full significance of the title.

The harlot is Babylon the Great, that great system of godlessness which leads men away from the worship of God and to their own destruction (cf. comm. on 14:8). Specifically she is Rome, who, like Babylon of old, has gained a worldwide reputation for luxury, corruption, and power. Not content with her own evil vice, she spawns her harlotry and abominable practices throughout the world. She is the "mother of whores and of every obscenity on earth" (*NEB*). Tacitus describes Rome as the place "where all the horrible and shameful things in the world congregate and find a home."[13] Certainly Juvenal's account of the vile and debased profligacy of the Roman Empress Messalina who served incognito in the public brothels is an indication of the depths of immorality in the ancient capital (*Sat.* vi.114–32).

The woman John sees is drunk with the blood of righteous martyrs. The figure recalls OT passages such as Isaiah 49:26 where it is prophesied that the oppressors of Israel "shall be drunk with their own blood as with wine."[14] The metaphor was common among Roman writers as well.[15] It portrays the wanton slaughter of a great number of believers along with the intoxicating effect it produced upon the murderous harlot. Barclay comments that she "took a fiendish delight in hounding Christians to death" (II, p. 189). Although the Neronian persecution after the great fire of AD 64[16]

---

[12]Seneca, *Controv.* i.2; Juvenal, *Sat.* vi.123.
[13]Tacitus, *Ann.* xv.44. Seneca calls Rome "a filthy sewer" (cf. Barclay, II, p. 188). Seebass suggests that the title "mother of harlots" may reflect Cybele, the Magna Mater, worshipped in Rome with her orgiastic cult since 204 BC (*DNTT,* I, p. 142).
[14]In *I Enoch* 62:12 it is the sword of the Lord that is drunk with the blood of oppressors. Cf. Isa 34:5; 51:21.
[15]Suetonius, *Tiber.* 59; Pliny, *Hist. Nat.* xiv.28; Josephus, *Bell.* v.8.2.
[16]Tacitus tells of Nero's infamy in placing the blame for the fire upon the Christians and subjecting them to "the most exquisite tortures." They were "covered with the skins of beasts . . . torn by dogs . . . nailed to crosses . . . burned to serve as a nightly illumination" (*Ann.* xv.44).

may have been in the back of John's mind, the drunken harlot pictures the final days of persecution at the end of the age.

6 The woman is said to be drunk with the blood of saints and the blood of martyrs. The expression does not intend two groups, although it may be that the second phrase is meant to specify more closely the first and more general designation. They are saints,[17] that is, believers who have sacrificed their lives in faithful testimony to Jesus. The revolting and gory spectacle causes John to wonder ''with a great wonder.'' Upon being taken to the wilderness he had expected to see the judgment of the harlot, but up to this point she appears triumphant. Ostentatiously attired and adorned in wealth, she sits upon the scarlet beast advertising her base trade and intoxicated with the blood of her victims. The true nature of the empire is at last fully revealed.

2. INTERPRETATION OF THE HARLOT'S DESTRUCTION (17:7–18)

7 *And the angel said unto me, Wherefore didst thou wonder? I will tell thee the mystery of the woman, and of the beast that carrieth her, which hath the seven heads and the ten horns.*

8 *The beast that thou sawest was, and is not; and is about to come up out of the abyss, and to go into perdition. And they that dwell on the earth shall wonder, they whose name hath not been written in the book of life from the foundation of the world, when they behold the beast, how that he was, and is not, and shall come.*

9 *Here is the mind that hath wisdom. The seven heads are seven mountains, on which the woman sitteth:*

10 *and they are seven kings; the five are fallen, the one is, the other is not yet come; and when he cometh, he must continue a little while.*

11 *And the beast that was, and is not, is himself also an eighth, and is of the seven; and he goeth into perdition.*

12 *And the ten horns that thou sawest are ten kings, who have received no kingdom as yet; but they receive authority as kings, with the beast, for one hour.*

13 *These have one mind, and they give their power and authority unto the beast.*

14 *These shall war against the Lamb, and the Lamb shall overcome them, for he is Lord of lords, and King of kings; and they* also shall overcome *that are with him, called and chosen and faithful.*

15 *And he saith unto me, The waters which thou sawest, where the harlot sitteth, are peoples, and multitudes, and nations, and tongues.*

---

[17]Some critics discover here an earlier Jewish document referring to martyrs in the war of AD 66–70 which a Christian redactor reapplies by adding the second clause—an unlikely conjecture.

16 *And the ten horns which thou sawest, and the beast, these shall hate the harlot, and shall make her desolate and naked, and shall eat her flesh, and shall burn her utterly with fire.*

17 *For God did put in their hearts to do his mind, and to come to one mind, and to give their kingdom unto the beast, until the words of God should be accomplished.*

18 *And the woman whom thou sawest is the great city, which reigneth over the kings of the earth.*

7 The angel responds to John's amazement by offering to explain the mystery of the woman and the beast which carries her.[18] It is a single mystery which involves both figures. Neither can be understood apart from the other. While the remainder of chapter 17 is primarily concerned with the interpretation of the beast, 18:1–19:5 details the judgment of the harlot.

8 The Seer first learns from his angel-interpreter that the scarlet-colored beast "was, and is not, and is about to come up out of the abyss." This is an obvious parody of the Lamb, who was put to death yet came back to life and now is alive forevermore (1:18; 2:8).[19] The description is also an intentional antithesis to the One "who is and who was and who is to come" (1:4, 8; 4:8). In the broadest sense the beast is that satanically inspired power that, although having received the stroke of death, returns to hurl himself with renewed fury against the forces of God. It is this incredible power of resuscitation that causes those who dwell upon the earth to stand in awe. He is the beast of chapter 13 who had received a death-stroke in one of his heads and yet survived (13:3, 12, 14). Down through history he repeatedly "comes up from the abyss"[20] to harass and, if it were possible, to destroy the people of God. He is the little horn of Daniel 7 (Antiochus Epiphanes) who rises out of the fourth kingdom (the "exceeding terrible" fourth beast, Dan 7:19) to make war against the saints (Dan 7:21). He is Nero who instigates a persecution of the Christians to avert suspicion that he is responsible for the burning of Rome. The beast *was;* at the moment he *is not.* John wrote under the shadow of an impending persecution. The beast is about to come once again. This coming will be his last, for now the King of kings and Lord of lords will cast him (along with the false prophet) alive into the lake of fire. This is what it means that he goes into perdition (see vs. 11 as well).

---

[18]For a somewhat similar dialogue see 7:13–14.

[19]Farrer notes that the comparison is "between the beast as a falsification of the divine image, and the Lamb as a true offprint of it" (p. 184).

[20]Note the present tense (ἀναβαῖνον) in 11:7 as well as in the present verse (ἀναβαίνειν). Coming up from the abyss is an essential characteristic of the beast.

John understood the persecution which lay in the immediate future to be the return of the beast expressed in the ruthless tyranny of the imperial government. He had exercised a controlling influence in the successive reigns of the emperors of Rome, but in this final sortie he is to be revealed for what he really is—the very incarnation of evil in its deep-seated hatred and violent opposition to God and all that is just and good.

Those that dwell upon the earth stand in awe when they behold the beast. They are those whose names have not been written in the book of life (cf. Ps 69:28; Isa 4:3; Rev 3:5) from the foundation of the world. John is not teaching a form of determinism (according to 3:5 names may be blotted out of the book of life), but emphasizing the great distinction that exists between the followers of the Lamb and those who give their allegiance to the beast. The *RSV* is probably right in making the reappearance of the beast the cause of unregenerate man's amazement ("because"), although it is also possible that the final clauses of the verse are no more than descriptive (as in the *AV*).[21] The verb used to describe the coming of the beast is closely related to the noun[22] which regularly describes the parousia or second coming of Christ (I Cor 15:23; I Thess 2:19; I Jn 2:28; etc.).

9 In verse 8 the beast was portrayed as an evil power who had appeared throughout history and was about to put in one final appearance which would lead to his destruction. In the verses which follow (9–14) John relates this more general truth to his own historical context by providing clues for the interpretation of the beast's seven heads and identifying the ten horns as those forces which will join with the Antichrist in his last fierce assault upon the Lamb. The rather cryptic statement with which this section begins ("Here is needed the intelligence which is wisdom"; Charles, II, p. 68) may be a warning to interpret with care, or an aside to the effect that what follows "is the clue for those who can interpret it" (*NEB*). The number of the beast in 13:18 was introduced with a similar statement, but in neither case has the meaning been clear. John is saying that although the interpretation of the seven heads is not obvious, it may be understood by those who ponder the riddle with care and wisdom.[23]

The seven heads of the beast are first identified as seven mountains upon which the harlot is sitting. There is little doubt that a first-century reader would understand this reference in any way other than as a reference

---

[21]Interpretation hinges on the use of ὅτι. Erasmus has καίπερ ἐστί(ν) for καὶ παρέσται, which would add yet a further cryptic element to the description: the beast was and is not, although he is present.

[22]παρέσται, παρουσία.

[23]Moffatt translates, "Now for the interpretation of the discerning mind!" (*The NT: A New Translation*).

313

to Rome, the city built upon seven hills. Rome began as a network of seven hill settlements on the left bank of the Tiber, and was from the time of Servius Tullius (her sixth king) an *urbs septicollis*. The reference is commonplace among Roman authors.[24] Some writers point out that in OT usage the hill may be a symbol of power (cf. Dan 2:35; Jer 51:25), and interpret the seven hills as successive kingdoms or empires.[25]

Kiddle takes the number symbolically as "suggestive of the world-wide domination exercised by the Roman order of things. . . . The Beast's power is universal, stretching as far as Roman institutions" (pp. 348–49). Whatever the overtones may be, the immediate reference is to the city of Rome. In John's day Rome epitomized all the antagonism and opposition to the Christian faith. The beast is about to come from the abyss and become incarnate in this hostile world order of which the city on seven hills is the governing center.

10 But now the plot thickens. The seven heads of the beast are also seven kings, five of whom have fallen, one is, and one is yet to come. The simplest answer would be that John is locating himself within the succession of Roman emperors and pointing out that one more must rule for a short time before the final advent of the beast. The five which have fallen would be Augustus, Tiberius, Caligula, Claudius, and Nero; the one who is would be Vespasian, and Titus would be the one yet to come. This interpretation, however, has several problems. It regards Augustus as the first emperor although his predecessor, Julius Caesar, took the title *Imperator,* and was reckoned by many writers (both Roman and Jewish) as the first emperor.[26] A second problem is the omission of the three rival emperors who ruled briefly between Nero (AD 54–68) and Vespasian (AD 69–79).[27] Although Suetonius seems to dispose of them by referring to their reigns as *rebellio trium principum (Vesp.* i), Josephus, in treating the bloody period between Nero and Vespasian, names both Galba and Otho as emperors and speaks of the troubles under Vitellius before the civil war was brought to an end (*Bell.* ix.9.2). In the *Sibylline Oracles* (5:35) they are the "three kings" after Nero who "perish at each other's hands." It is

[24]Vergil, *Aen.* vi.782; Martial iv.64; Cicero, *Att.* vi.5; and many others.

[25]Seiss, *The Apocalypse,* pp. 391–94; Ladd, pp. 227–29.

[26]Suetonius, *Vesp.* i; Josephus, *Ant.* xviii.2.2; *Sib. Or.* 5:12 (in cryptic form). It is commonly pointed out that other writers consider the empire to have begun with Augustus (*eg.,* Tacitus, *Ann.* i.1; *Hist.* i.1). In any case, the evidence is divided and provides no firm basis for omitting Caesar.

[27]Galba assumed power in June of 68 but was murdered seven months later. Otho, who followed, committed suicide in April of 69, and Vitellius was killed before the end of the same year.

therefore not at all certain that these three emperors should be passed over so lightly.

By starting with Augustus and skipping the three pretenders, we would arrive at Vespasian as the king who is, that is, the ruler in power at the time of the writing of the book. Yet the evidence is fairly conclusive that the book of Revelation was written at a considerably later period, during the reign of Domitian (AD 81–96). Different answers are offered for this anachronism. One frequent suggestion is that John incorporates an earlier oracle from the time of Vespasian (Charles, II, p. 69). Another is that John placed himself back in time and after the manner of apocalyptists wrote history in the guise of prophecy. These and others lack persuasion.[28] The text is quite clear: king number six is ruling at the time of John's writing. However one tries to calculate the seven kings as Roman emperors, he encounters difficulties which cast considerable doubt on the entire approach.

A different approach is to take the seven kings as a succession of secular empires. Alford, for instance, lists Egypt, Nineveh, Babylon, Persia, and Greece as the five that have fallen; Rome is the present kingdom; and the one to come is the Christian empire beginning with Constantine (IV, pp. 710–11). Hendriksen has a slightly different listing and makes the seventh a "collective title for all antichristian governments between the fall of Rome and the final empire of antichrist" (p. 204; cf. also Ladd, p. 229). The basic problem is that the Greek word under consideration is everywhere throughout the NT translated "king," not "kingdom."[29]

Perhaps the most satisfactory explanation of the seven kings is that the number seven is primarily symbolic and stands for the power of the Roman Empire as a historic whole.[30] John is not interested in a careful tabulation of the past but is declaring the nearness of the end by the commonly accepted use of a numerical scheme. For John seven is the number of completeness. Five kings have fallen, one is, and the last one remains for only a short time. In other apocalyptic writings the number of ages or world periods conforms to different numerical schemes. In II Esdras 14:11 history is divided into twelve parts, of which 9½ (or 10½)

[28]By starting with Caligula who first provoked a crisis over emperor worship and by ignoring the three short reigns, it is possible to arrive at Domitian as the sixth ruler. By counting only those emperors who had been apotheosized by the senate, Rist also arrives at Domitian as the ruling emperor (p. 495).

[29]It is βασιλεύς, not βασιλεία. The argument for kingdoms is usually built upon Dan 7:17, where the four beasts are said to be four kings although they do in fact stand for four kingdoms. Note, however, that the LXX and Theodotion have βασιλεῖαι for מַלְכִין.

[30]For an excellent excursus leading to this conclusion, see Beckwith, pp. 704–8.

have already passed.[31] In the *Apocalypse of Weeks,* Enoch divides history into ten periods, seven of which are already past (*I Enoch* 93), and three yet future which lead to eternal judgment (*I Enoch* 91:12–17). The single purpose of the apocalyptists in all such number schemes is to declare the imminent end of the age. In Revelation the seven kings represent the entire period of Roman domination regardless of the exact number of emperors. The important point is that the end is drawing near. Caird writes, "The one point John wishes to emphasize is that the imperial line has only a short time to run before the emergence of a new monstrous Nero, an eighth who is one of the seven" (p. 219).

11 John now arrives at the heart of the riddle. The beast himself is an eighth king who is at the same time one of the seven. If the seven kings were specific Roman emperors, then the most likely candidate for number eight would be Domitian. This would identify the beast as the emperor reigning at the time John receives his vision. Yet three times in the chapter we are told that the beast *is not* (19:8 [twice], 11). At the time of writing, the beast has not yet ascended from the abyss (19:8). He is an eighth in the sense that he is distinct from the other seven. He is Antichrist, not simply another Roman emperor. He is not a human ruler through whom the power of evil finds expression—he is that evil power itself. He belongs to the cosmic struggle between God and Satan which lies behind the scenes of human history. Yet he will appear on the stage of history as a man. He is of the seven—not *one* of the seven—[32] in that he plays the same sort of role as his earthly predecessors. He himself, however, belongs to another sphere of reality. His period of hegemony is the great tribulation preceding the return of the Messiah.

This interpretation requires no reliance upon the Nero Redivivus myth (cf. comm. on 13:3), although its existence would aid in the understanding of John's prophecy of Antichrist. Nero, the epitome of evil and the abuse of power, *was* (he lived and ruled) and *is not* (that is, he is now dead). Yet (according to the myth) he will *return to life* and once again seize power. Commentators who understand the eighth king as Domitian stress that early writers recognized a resemblance between Nero and Domitian.[33] But since all the beast's heads were part of the same imperial system through which the evil intent of Antichrist found expression, we would of course expect the two prominent persecutors to be comparable.

---

[31]Cf. *II Bar.* 56–74 for the interpretation of the vision of the black and bright waters which symbolize the span of time between Adam and the coming of Messiah.

[32]This would normally call for εἷς ἐκ τῶν ἑπτά.

[33]Eusebius, *Hist. Eccl.* iii.20; Tertullian, *Apol.* v; Juvenal iv.37f.; Martial xi.33.

A somewhat different approach is set forth by Zahn and followed more recently by Ladd (pp. 228–31). The beast is Antichrist in but two of his heads (successive worldly kingdoms at enmity with God). He was embodied in Antiochus Epiphanes, he does not now exist in the same malevolent form, but will in the future arise from the abyss in the person of the eschatological Antichrist. It is questionable, however, that the essentially Gentile church in Asia Minor at the end of the first century would place into such an exclusive category a Syrian ruler who, more than 250 years before, had persecuted the Jews in Palestine. Certainly the terrors of the Neronian persecution in AD 64, which only a few years before had set the stage for Roman opposition to the Christian faith, would be a more likely historical expression of Antichrist.

12–13　The ten horns are said by the angel-interpreter to be ten kings who as yet have not received their royal power.[34] When they do receive authority they will turn it over to the beast and join him in war against the Lamb. The ten kings are not the ten emperors of Rome because, unlike the Roman emperor, these have received no kingdom as yet. Nor are they the kings of the earth who in 18:9 mourn the fall of Babylon. Many writers identify them as Parthian satraps coming from the east in a massive invasion under the leadership of a revived Nero. This would fit the context of the following paragraph in which the ten kings and the beast destroy the harlot city Rome (19:16–18). Still others take them to be the governors of senatorial provinces who held office for one year. Whatever the immediate historical allusion, the complete fulfillment of the imagery awaits the final curtain of the human drama. Beckwith correctly identifies the ten kings as "purely eschatological figures representing the totality of the powers of all nations on the earth which are to be made subservient to Antichrist" (p. 700). The number ten is symbolic and indicates completeness. It does not point to ten specific kings nor to ten European kingdoms of a revived Roman empire.

All the forces which join with Antichrist rule but a short period.[35] With one mind they turn over their power and authority to the beast. Swete interprets this to mean that the beast can count not only on the actual military power of the kings, but on the moral force which belongs to their position as well (p. 223). They are "willing collaborators" (Morris, p. 212), who share the same hostility to Christ and his followers.

14　Verse 14 passes on quickly to the final conflict between Antichrist and the Messiah (19:11–21). It is a promise of victory for the Lamb in

---

[34]Cf. Lk 19:12 for this use of βασιλεία.
[35]The judgment of Babylon comes in "one hour" (Rev 18:10, 17, 19).

the battle of Armageddon. The Lamb shall overcome his adversaries, for he is "Lord of lords and King of kings." These well-known phrases emphasizing the sovereignty of God go back to Deuteronomy 10:17 where the Lord God is named the God of gods and Lord of lords (cf. Ps 136:2, 3; Dan 2:47; II Macc 13:4). In *I Enoch* 9:4 the Most High is named "Lord of lords, God of gods, King of kings, and God of the ages."[36] The beast will be overcome because he has met the One to whom all others will ultimately be subordinate. The armies of heaven share his victory as well (cf. Rev 19:14). Those that overcome will exercise the authority of the Lamb over the nations of the earth and will rule them with a rod of iron (Rev 2:26–27). The concept of the righteous taking part in the destruction of the wicked is a standard apocalyptic theme. In *I Enoch* 98:12 the unrighteous are warned that they are to be delivered into the hands of the righteous, who will cut off their necks without mercy (cf. *I Enoch* 38:5; 91:12; 96:1). The specific role of those who accompany the Lamb in battle is not discussed. They are simply identified as called, chosen, and faithful. Moffatt (p. 454) notes that success depends not only upon their divine election but also upon their corresponding loyalty (Rev 13:8; 12:11).

15 The angel continues his interpretation (cf. vss. 8 and 12) by identifying the waters upon which the harlot sits as peoples, multitudes, nations, and tongues. This fourfold grouping stresses universality.[37] The imagery of the waters comes from Jeremiah 51:13 where Babylon is pictured as dwelling by many waters,[38] a reference to the Euphrates and its system of waterways in and around the city. For John the symbol serves to emphasize the vastness of the power of Rome, the capital city of the entire Mediterranean civilization. Kiddle brings up a small difficulty by noting that John did not tell us that in his vision he *saw* any waters. He suggests that to "see" a vision is to arrive at an inspired conviction, which may then be clothed in familiar apocalyptic terms (pp. 356–57). It is perhaps simpler to assume that John's account of the experience is less complete than the actual vision. It is the position of this commentary that John received his revelation through visions (Rev 1:11, 18) rather than prophetic insight which he then translated into apocalyptic narrative.

16 John now describes the fate of the harlot in phrases reminiscent of Ezekiel's vivid allegory of Oholibah (Ezek 23:11–35), who doted

---

[36]Cf. *I Enoch* 63:4; 84:2; I Tim 6:15; Rev 1:5; 19:16.

[37]See comm. on 5:9. It is used both of the church (5:9; 7:9) and the heathen world (10:11; 11:9; 13:7; 14:6; 17:15: the alteration of one member in 10:11 and 17:15 is inconsequential).

[38]Invasions by foreign powers are spoken of under the figure of floods (Isa 8:7; Jer 47:2) but are not the point here. Nor is any "impious parody" of the Lord who "sits enthroned over the flood" (Ps 29:10) intended (as suggested by Alford, IV, p. 712).

on the Assyrians (23:12), was defiled by the Babylonians (23:17), and played the harlot in the land of Egypt (23:19). The beast and the ten kings turn in hatred upon the harlot ("they shall deal with you in hatred," Ezek 23:29), make her desolate ("strip off your clothes and take away your fine jewels," Ezek 23:26) and naked ("leave you naked and bare," Ezek 23:29), eat her flesh ("cut off your nose and your ears," Ezek 23:25), and burn her utterly with fire ("your survivors shall be devoured by fire," Ezek 23:25). This turning of the beast upon the woman who sits upon him speaks of "a terrible and mysterious law of political history, according to which every revolutionary power contains within itself the seed of self-destruction" (Lilje, p. 229). It describes the self-destroying power of evil. Morris notes that the wicked are not a happy band of brothers, but precisely because they are wicked they give way to jealousy and hatred, so that "at the climax their mutual hatreds will result in mutual destruction" (p. 213).[39]

The woman who was once arrayed in purple and scarlet and adorned with jewelry (Rev 17:4) is now stripped bare. The eating of her flesh[40] suggests wild beasts tearing at the body of their prey and portrays the fierceness with which the harlot is attacked by her assailants. One is reminded of the bloody scene when Jezebel, who was thrown from the window and trampled by the horses, was then eaten by the dogs except for skull, feet, and palms of hands (I Kgs 9:30–37).[41] Finally, the harlot is burned with fire. Leviticus teaches that if the daughter of any priest plays the harlot, she is to be burned with fire (Lev 21:9). So also is the man who takes a wife and her mother also—the three shall be burned with fire (Lev 20:14). Farrer ties together the three clauses which describe their punishment by commenting that as a harlot she is exposed, as a victim of the lion-jawed beast her flesh is devoured, and as a city she is burned down (pp. 186–87).

17 The angel explains that it was God who brought about the slaughter of the harlot by putting it into the hearts of the ten kings to do his will. They were of one mind[42] in relinquishing their sovereignty to the beast and joining in his assault upon the harlot (vs. 17) and in his final campaign against the Lamb (vss. 13–14). This verse denies the existence of any ultimate dualism in the world. In the final analysis the powers of evil

---

[39]The concept of internecine warfare as God's method of destroying his enemies is seen in such OT passages as Ezek 38:21; Hag 2:22; Zech 14:13.

[40]The plural σάρκας refers to portions of flesh.

[41]Cf. Jer 10:25; Mic 3:3; Zeph 3:3 for similar uses of the figures.

[42]Charles brackets καὶ ποιῆσαι μίαν γνώμην as an early gloss from vs. 13 (II, p. 73), but there is no reason why their common agreement cannot be understood as part of his will. God's will is their unanimous decision to give their kingdom to the beast.

serve the purposes of God. The coalition between the beast and his allies will continue until the words of God—the prophecies leading up to the overthrow of Antichrist—are fulfilled.

18 For the fourth time in this chapter the angel identifies and interprets a figure in the vision.[43] The woman is the great city which rules over the kings of the earth. For John, the city is Rome. She is the wicked seducer whose pernicious influence has permeated the whole of the Mediterranean world. Yet Babylon the Great, source of universal harlotry and abomination (vs. 5), is more than first-century Rome. Every great center of power which has prostituted its wealth and influence restores to life the spirit of ancient Babylon. John's words extend beyond his immediate setting in history and sketch the portrait of an eschatological Babylon, which will provide the social, religious, and political base for the last attempt of Antichrist to establish his kingdom.

---

[43]Note the recurring ὁ/ἃ/ἣν εἶδες in vss. 8, 12, 16, and 18.

CHAPTER 18

In chapter 18 John lays before us a detailed account of the destruction of Rome, that center of power, luxury, and fierce antagonism against the Christian faith. Drawing heavily upon prophetic oracles and taunt songs of Jewish scripture, the Apocalyptist composes an extended dirge over the accursed city. A number of critical scholars assume that some sort of Jewish source lies behind this section. Moffatt, for instance, conjectures a Jewish Vespasianic source which "breathed the indignant spirit of a Jewish apocalyptist against the proud empire which had won a temporary triumph over the city and people of God" and was taken over by John for the purpose of making Rome responsible for the persecution of Christians (p. 455).[1] The idea of a non-Christian source is strengthened by what appears to be an antagonism against Rome so violent as to be inconsistent with teaching elsewhere in the NT concerning the state (*eg.,* Rom 13:1–7). But the author of Revelation is not at this point discussing how believers are to live under normal circumstances within the state. He is portraying in a prophetic manner the ultimate collapse of a monstrous antichristian world order determined to defeat the purpose of God in history. It is not personal vindictiveness but loyalty to God and his great redemptive purpose that moves the Seer to deliver a prophetic oracle in the accepted literary genre of his predecessors. Squeamishness about his rhetoric results more from a misunderstanding of the literary nature of the prophetic taunt song than from any supposedly sub-Christian ethic being expressed.

The argument against the idea of a specific source adapted by the Seer rests mainly upon John's regular practice of drawing freely upon the words and phrases of Jewish literature. Elaborate attempts to discover an earlier source (such as that by Charles, who finds a Vespasianic source written soon after the destruction of the temple, apparently in Hebrew but

---

[1]Vss. 20 and 24 are taken as Christian editorial insertions. The special source theory is based on the large number of rare words in the chap. and differences of outlook which are held to exist. See the summary of criticism of chap. 18 in Beckwith, pp. 722–25.

found by John in Greek translation; II, pp. 87–95) are unnecessary and detract from the accomplishment of the author himself. John is more original than some of his interpreters would allow him to be.

3. BABYLON DECLARED DESOLATE (18:1–8)

1 *After these things I saw another angel coming down out of heaven, having great authority; and the earth was lightened with his glory.*

2 *And he cried with a mighty voice, saying, Fallen, fallen is Babylon the great, and is become a habitation of demons, and a hold of every unclean spirit, and a hold of every unclean and hateful bird.*

3 *For by the wine of the wrath of her fornication all the nations are fallen; and the kings of the earth committed fornication with her, and the merchants of the earth waxed rich by the power of her wantonness.*

4 *And I heard another voice from heaven, saying, Come forth, my people, out of her, that ye have no fellowship with her sins, and that ye receive not of her plagues:*

5 *for her sins have reached even unto heaven, and God hath remembered her iniquities.*

6 *Render unto her even as she rendered, and double* unto her *the double according to her works: in the cup which she mingled, mingle unto her double.*

7 *How much soever she glorified herself, and waxed wanton, so much give her of torment and mourning: for she saith in her heart, I sit a queen, and am no widow, and shall in no wise see mourning.*

8 *Therefore in one day shall her plagues come, death, and mourning, and famine; and she shall be utterly burned with fire; for strong is the Lord God who judged her.*

1 In verses 1–3 an angel descends from heaven to announce the fate of Rome. The messenger is not the interpreting angel of the previous chapter (see vss. 1, 7, etc.) but another angel. The designation serves only to distinguish between the two and carries no further significance.[2] The angel comes from the presence of God, empowered with great authority and reflecting the radiance and glory of God. Swete aptly comments, "So recently has he come from the Presence that in passing he flings a broad belt of light across the dark Earth" (p. 226). One is reminded of the return of the glory of God to the temple through the east gate as described in Ezekiel 43:1–5. Elsewhere in Scripture God is pictured as dwelling in

---

[2]Cf. 7:2; 8:3; 10:1; 14:6, 8 (where the angel proclaims the same basic message as in vss. 2–3 of the present chap.), 9, 15, 17, 18; 18:1.

unapproachable light (I Tim 6:16) and as covering himself with light as a garment (Ps 104:2). Little wonder that those who come from his presence are marked by a lingering radiance (Ex 34:29-35). The authority of the angel should be understood in terms of the power required to proclaim to all the complete destruction of Rome.[3]

2 The declaration of the angelic herald is like that of Isaiah 21:9 when news of the capture of Babylon by Cyrus reaches the children of Israel—"Fallen, fallen is Babylon; and all the images of her gods he has shattered to the ground."[4]

Babylon has always been symbolic of opposition to the advance of the kingdom of God. As it fell in times past, so also will it be destroyed in the future. The past tense denotes the certainty of future fulfillment. It is the prophetic way of declaring that the great purpose of God in triumphing over evil is a *fait accompli*.

The once-proud city of Babylon is to lie utterly desolate. It is to become the haunt of demonic spirits and all kinds of unclean creatures. For background we should turn to Isaiah's oracle against ancient Babylon. There we find that Babylon once fallen will never again be inhabited except by wild beasts and howling creatures (Isa 13:20-21). Satyrs (demonic creatures having the appearance of hairy goats) will dance among the ruins to the howling of hyenas and jackals (Isa 13:21-22).[5] There is some question about the meaning of the word twice translated "hold" in verse 2 as well as the relationship between the parallel clauses.[6] The structure of the verse would suggest that the word is roughly parallel to "habitation." Demons dwell among the ruins of Babylon, as do unclean spirits and animals. It is not a place of detention[7] but a place where they dwell undisturbed. In any case, it is a prophetic picture of absolute desolation where the proud achievements of man become the demonic haunts of unclean and horrible creatures.

---

[3]ἐξουσία is used in the sense of capability in Rev 9:3, 10, 19 as well. Note reference to his "mighty voice" in vs. 2.

[4]The LXX uses the perfect, πέπτωκε, rather than the aorist, ἔπεσεν, as in Rev; cf. Jer 51:33.

[5]The same creatures are found in the judgment pronounced upon Edom in Isa 34, with the night hag (perhaps a reference to the Assyrian female storm god Lilitu; Heb., לִילִית), hawk, porcupine, owl, and raven added. Deut 14:12-18 identifies the raven, ostrich, hawk, and owl as unclean birds.

[6]The *AV, ASV,* and *RSV,* following the important witnesses ℵ 2053 2080 *al* vg, omit καὶ φυλακὴ παντὸς θηρίου ἀκαθάρτου. The UBS text includes it in brackets (following A 1611 2329 *al g* (sa)) since each of the three elements involves an allusion to Isa 13:21; 34:11 and probably belonged to the original text of Rev (Metzger, *TCGNT*, pp. 758-59).

[7]The primary meaning of φυλακή is "prison," although Swete points out that in Hab 2:1 (cf. *I Bar.* 3:34) it may designate a watchtower (p. 227). The picture would be one of evil spirits perched in a tower like vultures waiting for their prey.

3 Verse 3 supplies the reason for the fall of Rome. It is because she has made the nations drink[8] of the wine of her fornication.[9] Fornication is a well-known figure in the OT for apostasy from God (Hos 4:10; Jer 3:2). It is used here to denote the unclean and illicit relationships between the capital of the empire and all the nations of the earth. In the last days it will be epitomized by worship of the beast. The merchants of the earth have profited from their economic alliances with Rome. They have become rich through the power of excessive luxury. The wantonness[10] of Rome is spoken of as an actual power which has made the merchants of the earth rich.

4 John hears another voice from heaven, addressing itself first to the people of God (vss. 4-5) and then to those who execute his wrath (vss. 6 ff). The voice is probably that of an angel who speaks on behalf of God. Although the reference to believers as "my people" would seem to designate God as speaker, the following verse indicates otherwise by placing God in the third person. The people of God are called upon to come out of the doomed city. Prophets of former days had issued similar warnings. "Depart, depart, go out thence, touch no unclean thing," cried Isaiah (52:11). "Go out of the midst of her, my people!" echoed Jeremiah (51:45).[11] The call to separation has marked the elect throughout the history of God's redemptive activity. The Jewish race had its origin with God's command to Abram, "Go from your country . . . to the land that I will show you" (Gen 12:1). "What partnership have righteousness and iniquity?" asks Paul (II Cor 6:14). The summons in Revelation 18:4 suggests a literal flight from the doomed city (as Christian Jews fled to Pella at the fall of Jerusalem), but when projected on the larger screen of the consummation it becomes a call to the last generation of believers for "spiritual withdrawal from Vanity Fair" (Kiddle, p. 364). The persecuted church has always faced the temptation to compromise with worldliness and thus ease the tension of living in a hostile environment. Separation is the order of the day: sometimes physical, always ideological. Augustine

---

[8]Reading πεπότικεν (94 *pc* sy^ph), the form which occurs without variants in the parallel passage, 14:8. The choice of πέπτωκαν (**A C** *pc* co) or πεπτώκασιν (**א 046** 82 1006 *al*) seems to say that Babylon fell because the nations have fallen.

[9]See comm. on 14:8 for this phrase. The five alternatives listed in Nestle (25th ed.) indicate how difficult the phrase was to early copyists. Cf. Jer 25:15-17, 27 for a similar mingling of the two ideas of drunkenness and divine judgment. Cf. also Jer 51:7; Rev 17:2.

[10]στρῆνος occurs only here in the NT. Beckwith notes that, along with the verb form στρηνιάω (Rev 18:7, 9 only), it contains the idea of "excessive luxury and self-indulgence with accompanying arrogance and wanton exercise of strength" (p. 713).

[11]Cf. also Isa 48:20; Jer 50:8; 51:6, 9. Cf. *II Bar.* 2:1.

interpreted the section spiritually, commenting, "We must renounce our rights as citizens of this world, and flee unto God on the wings of faith" (*De Civ. Dei* xviii.18).

Two reasons are given for separation from the city: so as not to have fellowship with her sins and so as not to receive her plagues. To share in her wickedness is to reap her recompense. The most common NT designation for a believer ("saint") means to be set apart to God for a holy purpose.

5 Plagues are about to come upon the city because her sins have accumulated[12] to such an extent that they extend up into heaven so that God has not forgotten them. If the verse builds on Jeremiah 51:9 ("for her judgment has reached up to heaven"), the figure would be less vivid. God remembers the iniquities of Babylon and will make her drink the cup of his wrath (cf. 16:19).

6 The voice from heaven continues to speak, but now addresses itself to undesignated agents of divine vengeance.[13] Attempts to soften the passage out of consideration for the character of God (as well as the credibility of the Seer) misunderstand the eschatological wrath of a righteous deity.[14] Babylon has shed the blood of prophets and saints (vs. 24) and is about to receive in kind the reward for her cruelty. Not divine revenge but just requital is the issue. The martyrs of chapter 6 need not wait any longer for the sovereign God, holy and true (6:10), to avenge the death of all whose faith has conquered the sword.

Beckwith notes that "double *unto her* the double" is a "conventional expression for *full requital*" (p. 715; cf. Jer 16:18; 17:18). Other commentators, however, think that the verse calls not for *lex talionis* but for a more severe punishment—one which corresponds to Babylon's enlightenment (cf. Morris, p. 217). The parallel structure of the first two clauses and the demand for equal payment in the following verse favor the first interpretation. John follows the prophetic tradition—"Requite her according to her deeds, do to her according to all that she has done" (Jer 50:29). In the very cup from which she made the nations drink the intoxicating brew of her immorality (Rev 14:8), she must now drink the wrath of God (cf. *II Bar.* 13:8).

---

[12]κολλάω in this context suggests the joining of sins one to another until the pile reaches to heaven. Holtzmann conjectures the gluing together of leaves in a scroll upon which the sins of Rome are recorded. If unrolled it would reach to heaven (cited in Moffatt, p. 457).

[13]1 2059s *pm* it vg[s,cl] arm TR add ὑμῖν after ἀπέδωκεν, which would make those addressed in vss. 6 and 7 the people of God to whom the previous vss. (4 and 5) were directed.

[14]Preston and Hanson write, "Zeal for the vindication of God's righteousness and O.T. prophecy have run away with John here" (p. 117).

7 The division between verses 7 and 8 obscures the poetic structure of the section. There should be a full stop after "torment and mourning" in verse 7. The following clause ("for she saith in her heart") begins a new sentence which runs through verse 8.[15]

The voice from heaven continues by declaring that the misery which is about to fall upon Babylon is to be in exact proportion to the self-glorification and luxurious life style she has chosen. Like the daughters of Zion who "walk with outstretched necks, glancing wantonly with their eyes" (Isa 3:16-17), the harlot Babylon is also to be smitten by the Lord. The Greek idea of *hybris* (an arrogant self-assertiveness which insults and abuses others)[16] is an attitude uniformly decried in Scripture. "A man's pride will bring him low," reads Proverbs 29:23. "Everyone who exalts himself will be humbled" is the NT counterpart (Lk 14:11). The humbling of Babylon will involve torment and grief.

With arrogant pride Rome sees herself as mistress of the world beyond any possibility of personal loss or sorrow. The rhetoric of her monologue is modeled after Isaiah 47:7-8 where Babylon, the lover of pleasures, says in her heart, "I am, and there is no one besides me; I shall not sit as a widow or know the loss of children." Rome's assertion that she is no widow is not a retort against the suggestion that she is without lovers, but indicates that she has not experienced the debilitating effects of war and loss of life. Her men are victorious: they have not died on the fields of battle. There is no mourning in her streets. Caird (p. 223) remarks of the proud city that "her fault is not mere arrogance, but an unquestioning faith in her own inexhaustible resources, unaccompanied by any sense of a deeper lack (cf. iii.17)."

8 Because of her arrogant self-confidence, her plagues will come suddenly[17] upon her and she will be utterly devastated by the fire of divine judgment. Belshazzar, his court and his concubines, drinking wine from the sacred vessels of the temple, suddenly saw their fate being written on the wall of the palace by the fingers of a man's hand (Dan 5). Rome, drunk with the blood of martyrs (17:6; 18:24), will suddenly meet a like disaster. The three plagues which come are death, mourning, and famine. Charles rearranges the plagues and corrects a conjectured corruption in the Semitic original. He finds an allusion to the approach of the Parthians under Nero

---

[15]διὰ τοῦτο (vs. 8) is stylistic and refers back to all that follows ὅτι in the preceding verse. The *RSV* (but not the *AV* or *ASV*) follows this syntactical arrangement.

[16]The verb form ὑβρίζω, when used of over-fed horses, meant "to neigh, snort, or prance" (LSJ, p. 1841).

[17]ἐν μιᾷ ἡμέρᾳ does not designate a span of time, but like μιᾷ ὥρᾳ in vss. 10, 16, and 19 it is a symbolic term for suddenness. Some MSS (69 *pc m* Cypr Prim) have ὥρα in 18:8. Cf. Isa 47:9.

which would cut off food supplies (famine), lead to pestilence (death), and prepare for destruction (mourning) by fire.[18] It is much more the style of the Seer to join together words and phrases for their rhetorical impact than for some carefully designed schema which organizes the future. Judgment by fire is a common Biblical concept. In one chapter in Jeremiah Babylon is pictured as a burnt mountain (51:25) whose dwellings (vs. 30), bulwarks (vs. 32), and high gates (vs. 58) are all to be burned with fire. Fire will test the work of each man on the day of the Lord (I Cor 3:13). In ancient times the smoke of a burning city signaled its collapse. Once under way, nothing could prevent the spread of its hungry flames until the city was left in smoldering ruins. In the case of Rome it is the Lord[19] God in his strength who will bring about judgment by fire.

4. LAMENT OF KINGS, MERCHANTS, AND SEAMEN (18:9–20)

9 *And the kings of the earth, who committed fornication and lived wantonly with her, shall weep and wail over her, when they look upon the smoke of her burning,*

10 *standing afar off for the fear of her torment, saying, Woe, woe, the great city, Babylon, the strong city! for in one hour is thy judgment come.*

11 *And the merchants of the earth weep and mourn over her, for no man buyeth their merchandise any more;*

12 *merchandise of gold, and silver, and precious stone, and pearls, and fine linen, and purple, and silk, and scarlet; and all thyine wood, and every vessel of ivory, and every vessel made of most precious wood, and of brass, and iron, and marble;*

13 *and cinnamon, and spice, and incense, and ointment, and frankincense, and wine, and oil, and fine flour, and wheat, and cattle, and sheep; and* merchandise *of horses and chariots and slaves; and souls of men.*

14 *And the fruits which thy soul lusted after are gone from thee, and all things that were dainty and sumptuous are perished from thee, and* men *shall find them no more at all.*

15 *The merchants of these things, who were made rich by her, shall stand afar off for the fear of her torment, weeping and mourning;*

16 *saying, Woe, woe, the great city, she that was arrayed in fine linen and purple and scarlet, and decked with gold and precious stone and pearl!*

17 *for in one hour so great riches is made desolate. And every shipmaster,*

---

[18]Charles (II, p. 100) takes θάνατος to mean pestilence (as in Rev 6:8) and conjectures that אבל (πένθος) was corrupt for חֶבֶל. The "natural order" of the plagues would otherwise be λιμός, θάνατος, πένθος.

[19]κύριος is omitted by **A** 1006 *pc* vg, perhaps because of the preceding ἰσχυρός. Cf. Metzger (*TCGNT*, p. 760) for other variants.

and every one that saileth any whither, and mariners, and as many as gain their living by sea, stood afar off,

18 *and cried out as they looked upon the smoke of her burning, saying, What city is like the great city?*

19 *And they cast dust on their heads, and cried, weeping and mourning, saying, Woe, woe, the great city, wherein all that had their ships in the sea were made rich by reason of her costliness! for in one hour is she made desolate.*

20 *Rejoice over her, thou heaven, and ye saints, and ye apostles, and ye prophets; for God hath judged your judgment on her.*

9-10 Verses 9-19 consist of three dirges raised over the fallen city of Babylon. They are chanted by the kings of the earth who have shared in her wantonness (vss. 9-10), the merchants of the earth who have grown rich by supplying her insatiable appetite for luxury (vss. 11-17), and the entire maritime trade which had prospered in delivering her desires (vss. 17-19). The section is modeled after Ezekiel's lamentation over Tyre (chap. 27). Fifteen of the twenty-nine commodities listed in Revelation 18:12-13 are also found in Ezekiel 27:12-22. The same three groups of mourners are all referred to in the Ezekiel passage, although their reactions to the fall of the cities differ somewhat—the mariners wail (vss. 29-30), the kings are afraid (vs. 35), and the merchants hiss (vs. 35).

The first lament is that of the kings of the earth. These are not the kings of 17:16 who turn upon Rome to bring her down to destruction, but the governing heads of all nations who have entered into questionable trade with the commercial center of the ancient world. They represent "the bankruptcy of an arrogant existence which believed that it was 'secure' because it was living in a perverted political order" (Lilje, p. 235). They have committed fornication (entered into illicit relations; cf. 17:2) with the harlot and lived voluptuously[20] with her. Now their fortunes have changed, and they weep and wail[21] as the rising smoke announces her destruction by fire. Like the princes of the sea who "clothed themselves with trembling" at the fall of Tyre (Ezek 26:16-18), the world leaders lament the unexpected disaster which falls upon Rome. The imagery of fire is prominent in the description of the eschatological collapse of the world order—epitomized in John's day by Rome (17:16; 18:8, 17; 19:3; cf. Isa 34:10;

---

[20]στρηνιάω may mean to live sensually (cf. BAG, p. 779).

[21]κλαίω is used of any loud expression of pain or sorrow; hence, to sob openly (cf. the less vivid δακρύω, to shed tears). In the middle voice, κόπτω (to cut) is used of beating one's breast as an act of mourning. In vss. 11, 15, and 19 πενθέω replaces κόπτομαι.

Ezek 28:18). Peter speaks of the coming day of God when the heavens will be kindled and the elements will melt with fire (II Pet 3:12).

The kings of the earth do not rush to the rescue of their paramour but "stand at a distance, horrified at her torture" (*TCNT*). They are astounded that judgment could fall so suddenly ("in one hour") upon a city as great and strong as Rome. Caird observes that "the one hour of persecution [17:12–14] is balanced by the one hour of retribution" (p. 226). Both the English word "woe" and its Greek equivalent (pronounced *ouai*) have a desolate and mournful sound. The city that seemed so strong has fallen. Those who admired the accomplishments of strength are amazed that the most powerful city in existence lies smoldering in the ashes of destruction.

11 In verses 11–17 the dirge is taken up by the merchants of the earth. They weep and mourn, not out of sympathy for a proud city now brought low, but because with its collapse they have been deprived of their major source of financial gain. There is no longer anyone to buy their merchandise. The tremendous volume of this trade may be inferred from contemporary writers such as Pliny and Aristides.[22] The excessive luxury of Rome and its passion for the extravagant are discussed at length by Barclay (II, pp. 200–13). At one of Nero's banquets the Egyptian roses alone cost nearly $100,000. Vitellius had a penchant for delicacies like peacocks' brains and nightingales' tongues. In his reign of less than one year he spent $20,000,000, mostly on food. One Roman, after squandering an immense fortune, committed suicide because he could not live on the pittance which remained—about $300,000. In the Talmud it is written, "Ten measures of wealth came down into the world: Rome received nine, and all the world one" (*Kidd.* 49). Small wonder that the suppliers of such gross extravagance mourned the passing of their market!

12–13 We are now presented with a list of imports brought from all over the world into Ostia, the port of Rome. The inventory is quite similar to the one found in Ezekiel 27 where Tyre is the chief maritime capital in a former period of splendor. The twenty-nine items fall into six groups of four to six each:[23] (1) precious metals and gems, (2) fabrics for expensive clothing, (3) ornamental pieces, (4) aromatic substances, (5) foodstuffs, and (6) animals and men. The purpose of the long list is to impress the reader with the tremendous flow of trade which poured into Rome, enabling her to live luxuriously as the mistress of the world. Not

---

[22]Pliny, *Hist. Nat.* vi.26; Aristides, *In Rom.* 200.
[23]Beckwith makes seven groups by adding the choice fruits of vs. 14 (p. 716). Ladd arrives at seven by placing slaves in a separate group (p. 240). The number of items in each group seems to be determined to a large extent by rhetorical considerations.

every item requires discussion. Barclay reports that at this time there was in Rome a passion for silver dishes (II, pp. 205 ff). Women would bathe only in silver tubs. Even generals on the field insisted upon dining on silver dishes. Gems and pearls were greatly prized. Julius Caesar gave Servilia a single pearl costing more than $18,000. Purple was imported primarily from Phoenicia where the expensive dye was extracted a drop at a time from a shellfish called the murex. Silk came from the distant land of China and was extremely expensive. Yet it was imported in such quantities that Josephus reports how the triumphant army appeared before Vespasian and Titus arrayed in silken garments (*Bell*. vii.5.4).

Thyine wood was an expensive dark wood imported from North Africa and used for costly furniture and inlay work. Its unusual ornamental veining resembled at times the eyes of the peacock's tail or the stripes or spots of wild animals (Martial, xiv.85; Pliny, *Hist. Nat*. xiii.96). Seneca is reported to have had three hundred tables of citrus wood[24] with ivory feet. The change in the Greek text from genitives to accusatives is stylistic.[25] The wood and various kinds of vessels are a further expansion of the merchandise of verse 11 which no one any longer will buy. Wealthy Romans ate from ivory plates. Ornaments of precious wood,[26] brass, iron, and marble decorated the homes of the rich. Cinnamon was an aromatic spice imported from South China. The harlot in Proverbs 7:17 perfumed her bed with myrrh, aloes, and cinnamon (cf. Cant 4:14). The word translated "spice"[27] is an Eastern perfume used to scent the hair. Incense was burned for its fragrant odor. The ointment was myrrh, used medicinally and as a perfume. Wheat was imported mainly from Egypt. The word translated "cattle"[28] means a beast of burden. The chariot[29] was a four-wheeled carriage in which the Roman aristocracy rode. The word translated "slaves" is literally "bodies."[30] This is a vivid commentary on the social conditions of the day. Slave traders regarded their human cargo as so much merchandise to be auctioned off to the highest bidder. It is estimated that

[24]Thyine wood was from the tree which in Latin was called citrinus.

[25]After eight genitives modifying γόμον the text turns to accusatives until it arrives at ἵππων in vs. 13. The last item, ψυχάς, is once again accusative.

[26]A 1006 *pc* vg read λίθου for ξύλου.

[27]ἄμωμον; omitted by **046** 1 82 1006 2059s *pm dem* vg[cl] TR. The Byzantine text also omits οἶνον.

[28]In Lk 10:34 the good Samaritan places the wounded man on his own κτῆνος to take him to the inn. Paul rides from Jerusalem to Caesarea on a κτῆνος (Acts 23:24).

[29]ῥέδη only here in the NT. The word entered Greek by way of Latin authors (cf. BAG, p. 742).

[30]σώματα. A slave merchant was called σωματέμπορος. In Gen 36:6 Esau left Canaan with his wives, sons, daughters, and all the σώματα τοῦ οἴκου αὐτοῦ—his slaves (cf. Tob 10:10; Bel 32; II Macc 8:11).

there were as many as 60,000,000 slaves in the Roman Empire. The final item on the list, "souls of men," is an old Hebrew phrase which, according to Swete, means little more than human livestock.[31] Most commentators take the expression in apposition to slaves and translate the connective "even." Bengel suggests the *bodies* are slaves used for carrying goods and the *souls of men* are slaves considered as merchandise (II, p. 916).[32]

14 Charles removes verse 14 to a place after verse 21, holding that it forms the opening stanza of the Seer's dirge over Rome (II, p. 108).[33] It is hardly necessary to carry out such relocations since the fruits which Rome lusted after are certainly those which have just been listed in detail in the two previous verses. The concluding clause, "men shall find them no more at all," brackets the list along with the earlier statement, "no man buyeth their merchandise any more" (vs. 11). The change to second person ("thy soul") is typical of the Seer's freedom of expression. The dainty things probably refer to exotic foods, and the sumptuous things to expensive clothing and decorative objects.[34]

15–17a The merchants' dirge resumes following the parenthetical listing of imports to Rome. They had profited richly from their lively trade with the great capital of the world-empire. Now, like the kings of the earth (vs. 10) they take their stand at a safe distance to weep and mourn. Their lament is like that of the kings, but the changes in phraseology are instructive. To the kings, Rome was "the strong city" (vs. 10); to the merchants she was "lavishly arrayed and adorned with costly ornaments" (cf. 17:4). Each group sees her fall in terms of its own interests. The merchants mourn because so suddenly ("in one hour") her great riches have been laid desolate.

17b–18 The dirge is now continued by a third group, those involved in and connected with the shipping industry. The shipmaster was the steersman or pilot rather than the owner of the ship.[35] The mariners were the rank-and-file seamen.[36] "Every one that saileth any whither" is an awkward phrase but probably refers simply to passengers. One conjec-

---

[31]בְּנֶפֶשׁ אָדָם; Ezek 27:13; Num 31:35; I Chron 5:21 (Swete, p. 235).

[32]This distinction has the advantage of linking σωμάτων with the genitives which precede it and allowing the awkward shift to the accusative ψυχάς.

[33]For Charles' reconstruction of vss. 21–24 (which also includes vss. 14 and 20) see II, pp. 92–93.

[34]Note the poetic quality of πάντα τὰ λιπαρὰ καὶ τὰ λαμπρά.

[35]κυβερνήτης rather than ναύκληρος; cf. Acts 27:11 where both words are used. Cf. the Latin *gubernare*, to guide.

[36]ναῦται; cf. Acts 27:27, 30. Ezek 27:27–29 designates the πρωρεύς (the lookout man who stood at the ship's head to give signals to the pilot), the ἐπιβάτης (the soldier on board), and the κωπηλάτης (the rower).

ture substitutes "upon the sea" for "any whither,"[37] but this is a bit repetitive. "Those who gain their living by the sea" may refer to all those who earn their living in connection with the maritime industry (cf. Ps 107:23) or, if the phrase is taken more literally ("as many as work the sea"), it could refer to such trades as fishing or pearl diving (Lenski, p. 527). Like the others, they too stand afar off (vss. 10, 15). As they watch the smoke rise from the burning ruins, they cry out in amazement, "What city is like the great city?" The same note of astonishment is heard in the lament over Tyre: "Who was ever destroyed like Tyre?" (Ezek 27:32).

19 Again we hear the mournful lament, "Woe, woe, the great city" (cf. vss. 10, 16). The phrase "by reason of her costliness" is taken by Beckwith to mean that the sea-going merchants and maritime personnel were made rich "through the greatness of her costly trade" (p. 718). Charles judges the text corrupt and restores the last line to read, "For in one hour are her precious things laid waste" (II, pp. 106-7).[38] The laments are accompanied by casting dust on the head, another act of sorrow also found in the Tyre lament (Ezek 27:30).

20 The sudden change from an extended lament (vss. 9-19) to a call for rejoicing (vs. 20) is in perfect keeping with the free style of the Apocalypse. Some writers feel that verse 20 is a call to the church to rejoice over the suffering of the unrighteous. The call, however, is first of all addressed to heaven. If we interpret the verse in light of its parallel in 12:12, then the saints, apostles, and prophets[39] would be "you that dwell therein." It is the church glorified, not believers on earth, who are invited to rejoice. The specific reason offered for their rejoicing is variously understood. In an excellent discussion, Caird posits a forensic setting in which Babylon is found guilty of perjury and God requires from her the penalty she has exacted from her victims. He translates, "God has imposed on her the sentence she passed on you" (pp. 228-30). This interpretation comports well with an earlier verse in the chapter, "Render to her as she herself has rendered" (vs. 6). The church victorious is to rejoice that God the righteous judge has turned back the evidence laid against believers and in turn has served to bring judgment upon the accuser himself.

---

[37]469 582 2076* 2254 cop^bo read πόντον for τόπον. Metzger (*TCGNT*, p. 761) lists five additional readings. The UBS text reads ὁ ἐπὶ τόπον πλέων, "he who sails for [any] part," but evaluates the reading as "C" (considerable doubt).

[38]ἐκ τῆς τιμιότητος becomes ἡ τιμιότης and in parallel with the corresponding clauses in vss. 10 and 16 serves as the subject for ἠρημώθη in vs. 19.

[39]There is no necessity of careful delineation between the three groups. Some texts (**C 051** 1 2059s 2329 *al* it vg^s,cl arm TR), by omitting the second καὶ οἱ, read οἱ ἅγιοι ἀπόστολοι. Note also that all three may be vocative as well as nominative.

5. BABYLON DESTROYED (18:21–24)

21 *And a strong angel took up a stone as it were a great millstone and cast it into the sea, saying, Thus with a mighty fall shall Babylon, the great city, be cast down, and shall be found no more at all.*

22 *And the voice of harpers and minstrels and flute-players and trumpeters shall be heard no more at all in thee; and no craftsman, of whatsoever craft, shall be found any more at all in thee; and the voice of a mill shall be heard no more at all in thee;*

23 *and the light of a lamp shall shine no more at all in thee; and the voice of the bridegroom and of the bride shall be heard no more at all in thee: for thy merchants were the princes of the earth; for with thy sorcery were all the nations deceived.*

24 *And in her was found the blood of prophets and of saints, and of all that have been slain upon the earth.*

21 In verses 9–19 we saw how Rome's political and commercial allies were affected by her fall. In the verses which follow we view her collapse from within. The arts, crafts, commerce, and customs of the great city have all been permanently silenced. Six times in verses 21–23 the phrase "no more at all"[40] tolls the collapse of the city. The paragraph consists of a doom song introduced by symbolic action. It recalls an event in the days of Jeremiah when Seraiah the quartermaster was to go to Babylon and read a prophetic oracle against the proud city, bind a stone to it, and cast it into the Euphrates saying, "Thus shall Babylon sink, to rise no more" (Jer 51:59–64; cf. Neh 9:11; *Sib. Or.* 5:155–61). In Revelation a strong angel takes a great boulder and hurls it into the sea, declaring that thus shall Babylon be cast down and disappear forever. Twice before we have encountered a strong angel. In 5:2 he was the guardian of the great scroll. In 10:1 a strong angel arrived from heaven with the little scroll. Caird joins these three references and suggests that the appearance of a third marks the consummation of the contents of both scrolls (pp. 230–31). The stone this "apocalyptic Paul Bunyan" (Blaney, p. 498) hurls into the sea is like a great millstone[41] in size. As it plunges to the depths of the sea, the angel interprets the action as symbolizing the disappearance of Rome. The word translated "with a mighty fall" appears in its cognate verb form in Mark 5:13 to describe the herd of swine that rushed down the steep bank into the

---

[40]The double negative οὐ μή with the aorist subjunctive expresses emphatic denial for the future (see Moule, *Idiom Book*, p. 156). The addition of ἔτι in each case strengthens the negative affirmation.

[41]The μύλινος μέγας is to be compared with the μύλος ὀνικός (the donkey millstone, that is, the one turned by donkey power) of Mk 9:42. Sinaiticus reads λίθον (a second time) instead of μύλινον; other texts read μυλικόν (**C**) or μύλον (**P 046** 1 *pl* TR).

sea, and in Acts 19:29 of the crowd of people who rushed into the great theater in Ephesus. The great millstone does not fall but is violently hurled into the sea. This stresses how suddenly and spectacularly the judgment of God will be executed not only upon an ancient city but ultimately upon the entire antichristian world in its opposition to God.

22 Silence reigns in the fallen city. Where once the streets were filled with the sounds of harp and voice,[42] flute and trumpet, now an eerie silence has taken over. Isaiah describes the coming universal judgment as a time when "the mirth of the timbrels is stilled, the noise of the jubilant has ceased" (Isa 24:8; cf. Ezek 26:13). In Isaiah 5:12 the harp and flute are associated with carousing, and in II Samuel 6:5 David and the house of Israel make merry before the Lord with harps, lyres, and various percussion instruments. Flutes were used both at festivals (Isa 30:29) and funerals (Mt 9:23). Trumpets served for games and in the theater (Juvenal vi.249).

Not only has music ceased, but the sounds of craftsmen plying their trade as well. The entire economy has abruptly ceased. The sound of the mill is heard no more.[43] Jeremiah describes the years of Israel's exile as a time when God will banish from them "the voice of mirth and the voice of gladness, the voice of the bridegroom and the voice of the bride, the grinding of the millstones and the light of the lamp" (Jer 25:10). The parallels in these two passages are not accidental. John writes out of an extensive acquaintance with the prophetic literature of his Jewish predecessors.

23 The absence of all light adds to the desolation of the fallen city. It is not known whether or not Rome had street lights, but everyone had at one time or another watched the wealthy as they were escorted home from festivals by a large entourage of slaves carrying torches. The busy city was accustomed to lights which burned by night as craftsmen worked long hours to fill their orders. But now the blackness of night blankets the deserted and lonely metropolis. Weddings are a thing of the past. The merry sounds of bridal festivities have been forever silenced.

The exact connection between the two final clauses of verse 23 is not readily apparent.[44] It is clear, however, that both supply reasons for the judgment which has fallen on Babylon. First, Rome's merchants[45] had become the princes of the earth—a title scarcely able to conceal consid-

---

[42]μουσικός means skilled in music. In the present context the noun form refers either to instrumentalists or vocalists (Swete, p. 239). Charles translates "singers" (II, pp. 109–10).
[43]Without the grinding of grain there would be little to sustain normal life in antiquity.
[44]Swete favors taking the second ὅτι clause as explaining the first (pp. 240–41), while Beckwith holds them to be coordinate (p. 719).
[45]ἔμπορος is from πόρος, a journey; thus οἱ ἔμποροι may well be those merchants who dealt in foreign imports and exports.

erable arrogance. Through their places of business had passed into the capital city enormous cargoes of extravagant and luxurious goods from around the world. The merchants' personal fortunes had grown alongside the insatiable appetites of their patrons. Wealth had made them "the great ones" (literal translation of the Greek).[46]

A second reason for judgment was the deception of the nations, which Rome had achieved by means of her sorcery. It is unlikely that we are intended to understand this as the actual practice of magic for the benefit of commerce, although the black arts were widely known in Rome (cf. *Sib. Or.* 5:165). It is intended to be taken in the broader sense of that art of deception by which Rome had bewitched the nations into a false sense of security, leading them to believe that she was in fact the eternal city (Caird, p. 231).

24 A third reason for judgment is added—the blood of Christian martyrs which ran red in the streets of Rome. In fact, Rome's guilt extends to all who have been slain upon the earth because she is the reigning sovereign of the entire world. Wherever life has been sacrificed, the responsibility lies at her door. In Semitic thought the blood of innocent victims cries out for vengeance. Cain learned that the blood of his murdered brother Abel cried out to God from the ground (Gen 4:10; cf. II Macc 8:3–4). The martyrs under the altar in chapter 6 demanded to know how long it would be until their blood will be avenged (Rev 6:10). The prophets and saints are not to be taken as two distinct groups: the first is a special class within the second.[47] The massacre under Nero in AD 64 as well as current troubles under Domitian would supply a realistic background for this stark reminder of imperial brutality.

---

[46]οἱ μεγιστᾶνες. The ἔμποροι of Tyre were called ἔνδοξοι ἄρχοντες τῆς γῆς (Isa 23:8).
[47]In Rev 16:6 the order is reversed. Cf. 17:6 and 19:2.

CHAPTER 19

6. HYMN OF VINDICATION (19:1–5)

1 *After these things I heard as it were a great voice of a great multitude in heaven, saying,*
   Hallelujah; Salvation, and glory, and power, belong to our God:
2 *for true and righteous are his judgments; for he hath judged the great harlot, her that corrupted the earth with her fornication, and he hath avenged the blood of his servants at her hand.*
3 *And a second time they say, Hallelujah. And her smoke goeth up for ever and ever.*
4 *And the four and twenty elders and the four living creatures fell down and worshipped God that sitteth on the throne, saying, Amen; Hallelujah.*
5 *And a voice came forth from the throne, saying,*
   Give praise to our God, all ye his servants, ye that fear him, the small and the great.

1 In response to the admonition of 18:20, "Rejoice over her, thou heaven," comes the "Hallelujah Chorus" of 19:1–2. The first five verses of chapter 19 constitute a fitting climax for the lengthy section on the fall of Rome which began at 17:1.[1] The heavenly jubilation breaks out in marked contrast to the solemn dirges of the kings, merchants, and seafarers whose economic empires collapsed with the devastation of the imperial capital. The series of three laments is followed by the adulation and worship of a new grouping of three: the heavenly multitude (vss. 1–3), the twenty-four elders and four living creatures (vs. 4), and a voice from the throne (vs. 5).

The great multitude in heaven praises God for judging the harlot and avenging the blood of the martyrs. Many writers understand this multitude to be an angelic host; others believe it to be made up of the faithful

---

[1]Continuity with the preceding paragraph is stressed by those MSS which add καί as the first word in vs. 1 (**051** 1 2059s *pm* TR).

dead. The specific mention of salvation (as in 7:10) and the concern for avenging the blood of the martyrs (as in 6:10) make it more likely that they are the church triumphant of 7:9-10, 13-17.[2] The word "Hallelujah" occurs only in this passage in the NT (vss. 1, 3, 4, 6). It is derived from two Hebrew words (*halal* and *Jah*), and means "Praise Yahweh." Swete observes that the transliteration into Greek must have been used by Hellenistic Jews prior to the Christian era and was taken over from the Hellenistic synagogue by the apostolic church.[3] The Hebrew form introduces a number of Psalms (106, 111-13, 117, 135, 146-50), and is regularly translated "Praise the Lord." Salvation, glory, and power belong to God. Salvation is more than personal deliverance. In this context it refers to the safeguarding of God's entire redemptive program. Glory and power refer to the majesty and might revealed in effecting a deliverance of such scope.

2 The outburst of praise rests upon the fact that the judgments of God—specifically, his judgment of the great harlot[4]—are true and righteous. The same two attributes are ascribed to God by the victors in 15:3 and by the voice of the altar in 16:7. Following the sounding of the seventh trumpet, it was announced that the time of judgment had arrived (11:18). With the fall of Babylon that judgment is under way. Once again we hear the grounds on which the judgment of the harlot is based: she has corrupted the earth with her fornication and has murdered the servants of God (cf. 18:23-24). Constant reference to her corrupting influence upon the kings of the earth (14:8; 17:2; 18:3) stresses the extent of her guilt. Her fornication is her seductive and unholy alliances with the entire civilized world. By the utter destruction of Babylon God has avenged the blood of his servants at her hand.[5] Early in the history of Israel God was portrayed as one who avenges the blood of his servants and takes vengeance on his adversaries (Deut 32:43).

3 Once again the heavenly multitude lifts its voice in praise to God. The second "Hallelujah" is not simple repetition but a sort of

---

[2]The angels in 5:12 and 7:12 sing of power, riches (thanksgiving in 7:12 replaces riches in 5:12), wisdom, might, honor, glory, and blessing, but not of salvation. Blaney (p. 499) interprets the great multitude more inclusively as "the accumulated celestial personnel of 7:9-12." In 4:11 the twenty-four elders sing a similar song, but there the praise is based on God's creative activity rather than his role as judge.

[3]Swete, p. 242. Note the occurrence of "Hallelujah" in Tob 13:18 (usually dated about 200 BC).

[4]The second ὅτι clause does not justify the first ὅτι clause—the righteousness of divine judgment needs no justification or human approval—but is parallel to it and supplies a specific example of the more general truth.

[5]ἐκ χειρὸς αὐτῆς here means "upon her." Cf. the parallel in the LXX of IV Kgs 9:7, which Moffatt says represents the Hebrew idiom meaning "to exact punishment from a murderer" (p. 462).

"heavenly encore"[6] which heightens measurably the dramatic quality of the scene. If the second "and" in verse 3 is a Hebraism which introduces a circumstantial clause and not a mere conjunction (Charles, II, p. 120), then the clause which follows supplies the reason for that praise. The multitude praises God because the destruction of the wicked city is absolutely final. The smoke of her burning rises for ever and ever.[7] John's readers would perhaps recall the oracle of Isaiah against Edom in which the enemy's land is to burn night and day and "its smoke shall go up for ever" (Isa 34:8–10; cf. Rev 14:11).

4 In 5:6–10, when the Lamb took the scroll from the right hand of God, the four living creatures and the twenty-four elders fell down before him and sang of his worthiness to open the seals. Once again they join in the same act of worship, this time honoring God for his righteous judgment.[8] This is their last appearance in the book of Revelation. Their words, "Amen; Hallelujah," echo the close of the doxology which marked the end of Book IV of the Psalter (Ps 106:48).

5 A voice is heard from the throne calling upon all the servants of God to praise him. The voice is probably that of one of the heavenly beings who surround the throne. It is not the voice of God; nor is it the voice of the Lamb, who would have said "my God" rather than "our God" (cf. 3:12; Jn 20:17). The servants of God are not a limited and select group such as the glorified martyrs, but, as the two following phrases indicate, the entire group of faithful believers.[9] "Ye that fear him, the small and the great" (cf. Ps 115:13) are believers on earth from every socio-economic level, and represent every stage of spiritual maturity.

IX. THE FINAL VICTORY (19:6–20:15)

1. MARRIAGE OF THE LAMB ANNOUNCED (19:6–10)

6 *And I heard as it were the voice of a great multitude, and as the voice of many waters, and as the voice of mighty thunders, saying,*

[6]Robertson, *Word Pictures,* VI, pp. 447–48. He also notes that εἴρηκαν is not aoristic perfect for "they say" but a dramatic perfect (as in 5:7) which describes a fact in an unusually vivid manner (Dana and Mantey, *Grammar,* p. 204).

[7]On the basis that the earth on which Rome is situated is soon to disappear (cf. 20:11; 21:1), Rist warns that the prediction about smoke rising forever and ever "should not be taken too literally" (p. 506).

[8]Prostrating oneself before God is more often connected with the twenty-four elders than with the four living creatures (4:10; 5:14; 11:16: both may take part along with the angels in 7:11).

[9]If καί is read before οἱ φοβούμενοι (as in A **046 051** 1 1006 1611 2059s 2329 *pl* bo TR), it should be translated as "even." The servants are those that fear God, καί is omitted by ℵ C P. See Metzger, *TCGNT,* pp. 761–62.

Hallelujah: for the Lord our God, the Almighty, reigneth.

7 Let us rejoice and be exceeding glad, and let us give the glory unto him: for the marriage of the Lamb is come, and his wife hath made herself ready.

8 And it was given unto her that she should array herself in fine linen, bright and pure: for the fine linen is the righteous acts of the saints.

9 And he saith unto me, Write, Blessed are they that are bidden to the marriage supper of the Lamb. And he saith unto me, These are true words of God.

10 And I fell down before his feet to worship him. And he saith unto me, See thou do it not: I am a fellow-servant with thee and with thy brethren that hold the testimony of Jesus: worship God: for the testimony of Jesus is the spirit of prophecy.

6 In verses 1–3 a heavenly multitude praised God for his judgment of the harlot (previously described in chaps. 17 and 18). In verses 6–8 they rejoice that the marriage of the Lamb is at hand. This change of perspective suggests a new division in the narrative. The sound that John hears is like the sound of a great throng of people, the roar of a mighty cataract, and a great peal of thunder. Such drama is appropriate for the announcement that God has at last established his universal reign on earth.[10] While the universal and timeless sovereignty of God is assumed in Judaeo-Christian thought, it can be said to be established on earth in a special eschatological sense when the powers of evil are destroyed and the kingdom of God becomes a visible reality (cf. 11:15).[11] In the historical context of a proud and powerful Roman Empire, for John to call God "the Almighty" is an act of extreme confidence. Domitian had conferred upon himself the title "Our Lord and God" (Suetonius, *Dom.* 13). Literally the word means one who holds all things in his control. Nine times in Revelation the Seer uses it of God, while only once is it found elsewhere in the NT. The multitude declares that this all-powerful being who has entered into his reign is a personal God—he is the Lord *our*[12] God.

7 The heavenly multitude continues its song of praise with the exhortation, "Let us rejoice and be exceeding glad." The only other place in the NT where these two verbs are used together is Matthew 5:12 where the cause for rejoicing is given as the greatness of the heavenly reward awaiting those who were reviled and persecuted for the cause of Christ.

---

[10]For similar phrases see Ezek 1:24; 43:2; Dan 10:6; Rev 1:15.

[11]ἐβασίλευσεν is an inceptive aorist, "has taken up his reign." Against most commentators Lenski takes the aorist as historical and constative, looking back over all past history and seeing how the Lord God has ever reigned (p. 540).

[12]Some manuscripts (A 1 1006 *at t* co TR) omit ἡμῶν, perhaps because it is not found in the other instances of κύριος ὁ θεὸς ὁ παντοκράτωρ in Rev (1:8; 4:8; 11:17; 15:3; 16:7; 21:22). It may have been felt inappropriate with the title as well (Metzger, *TCGNT*, p. 762).

That reward is now pictured as a great wedding feast in which the Lamb and his bride celebrate their union. The metaphor of marriage as expressing the relationship between God and his people has its roots in the prophetic literature of the OT. To Israel God said, "I will betroth you to me for ever" (Hos 2:19). Israel in exile is comforted by the remembrance that the Lord of hosts is her husband and will bring her back (Isa 54:5-7). This same symbolism runs throughout the NT. Matthew 22:2 ff compares the kingdom of heaven to a king who gave a marriage feast for his son. Paul portrays the relationship of Christ and his church in terms of the intimacy of marriage (Eph 5:32).

In Biblical times a marriage involved two major events, the betrothal and the wedding. These were normally separated by a period of time during which the two individuals were considered husband and wife[13] and as such were under the obligations of faithfulness. The wedding began with a procession to the bride's house, which was followed by a return to the house of the groom for the marriage feast. By analogy, the church, espoused to Christ by faith, now awaits the parousia when the heavenly groom will come for his bride and return to heaven for the marriage feast which lasts throughout eternity. John is not saying that the eternal festivities have in fact arrived, but is speaking proleptically of that period of blessedness which follows the millennium (cf. the declaration in 14:8 with the actual fall of Babylon in chaps. 17 and 18).

8 The bride is attired in fine linen, bright and pure. In contrast, the harlot was arrayed in purple and scarlet, adorned with gold, jewels, and pearls (17:4). The following clause explains that the fine linen is the righteous acts of the saints. The plural ("acts") may indicate that the bride's garment is woven of the innumerable acts of faithful obedience by those who endure to the end. This does not deny the Pauline doctrine of justification based on the righteous obedience of Christ (Rom 5:18-19), but suggests that a transformed life is the proper response to the call of the heavenly bridegroom. Note that it was *given* to her to array herself in righteous acts: believers are created for divinely prepared good works (Eph 2:10). Swete writes, "Corporately the whole Church is seen to be attired in the dazzling whiteness of their collective purity" (p. 247).

9 We now arrive at the fourth of the seven beatitudes in the Apocalypse (1:3; 14:13; 16:15; 19:9; 20:6; 22:7, 14). The speaker is probably the interpreting angel of chapter 17, although, as the following verse indicates, John apparently mistakes him for the Lord (elsewhere he never falls before the feet of an angel). The Seer is told to write of the blessedness

---

[13]Note ἡ γυνὴ αὐτοῦ; cf. Mt 1:18-20.

of those who are called to the marriage supper of the Lamb. Although the feast is nowhere described, we should understand that the time of blessedness it portrays is presented under different symbolism in the last two chapters of the book. This great feast is prefigured in Isaiah 24:6–8 where the Lord prepares on Mt. Zion a great banquet, removes the reproach of his people, and "swallow[s] up death for ever." The concept of a sacred meal shared by Israel and the Messiah is common in Jewish thought. *III Enoch* 48:10 places this banquet in Jerusalem. The idea is found in apocalyptic settings as well. According to the *Apocalypse of Elijah* the righteous are to feast with the Messiah during the forty-year *interregnum* between this age and the age to come. In Luke 13:29 Jesus speaks of those from all points of the compass who will come and sit at table in the kingdom of God. Later in his ministry he foretells a day when he will drink the fruit of the vine anew with his disciples in the kingdom of his Father (Mt 26:29). Such promises cause the believer to anticipate with joy the great messianic banquet which will celebrate the long-awaited marriage of the Lamb and his bride the church. Note that in verses 7–9 the church is pictured both as the bride and as the guests who are invited to the wedding. Far from constituting a contradiction, this sort of freedom is a normal characteristic of apocalyptic writing.

At the end of the beatitude the angel adds, "These are the true words of God."[14] This authentication should probably not be limited to the beatitude itself but refer as well to the song of the heavenly multitude (vss. 6–8), and even to all that the angel has explained beginning in chapter 17.

10 Apparently John mistakes the speaker to be the Lord, for he falls at his feet to worship. The suggestion that he is acting out a charade in order to discourage some tendency toward angel worship which may have lingered among the churches of Asia Minor (Col 2:18) is improbable. It is difficult to imagine the Seer waiting for an opportunity to prostrate himself before an angel in order to teach his readers that God alone is worthy of worship. John is brought up sharply with the command, Don't do that.[15] One recalls Peter's words to Cornelius who had fallen at his feet, "Stand up: I too am a man" (Acts 10:25).[16] Such an act of worship is inappropriate because the angel is simply a fellow servant with John and his brethren. Since both Christians and angels are servants of the same Lord (cf. Mt 18:28–33 with Heb 1:7, 14), it follows that they are fellow servants with

---

[14]If οἱ is added before ἀληθινοί (as in A *pc*), the clause would read, "These true words are of God."

[15]ὅρα μή understands a following ποιήσῃς.

[16]Cf. Josh 5:14; Judg 13:20; *Asc. Isa.* 7:21–8:5.

one another.[17] The brethren are those who hold "the testimony of Jesus." As in the three previous occurrences of this phrase (1:2, 9; 12:17), the "testimony of Jesus" is the witness which was borne by Jesus (subjective genitive). By his life and death Jesus has demonstrated to his followers what it means to bear a faithful witness (1:5; 3:14) to the message revealed by God.

The last clause of the verse ("for the testimony of Jesus is the spirit of prophecy") has been variously interpreted. In this instance the testimony of Jesus is often taken as an objective genitive so that the clause would mean that the testimony about Jesus is the common substance of all prophecy (Erdman, p. 148), or that the true spirit of prophecy always manifests itself in bearing witness to Jesus (Morris, p. 228). It seems better, however, to retain the subjective genitive (as earlier in the same vs.) and interpret the saying to mean that the message attested by Jesus is the essence of prophetic proclamation.[18] It is for this reason that man is to worship God, the giver of revelation, and not the angel, who is merely the interpreter of visions. This approach makes it unnecessary to consider the explanatory sentence as a gloss added by someone who had 22:8 ff in mind (as suggested by Beckwith, pp. 730, 742) or (following the punctuation in the *RSV*) as John's explanation of why the angel should not be worshipped.

2. WARRIOR-MESSIAH APPEARS (19:11–16)

11 *And I saw the heaven opened; and behold, a white horse, and he that sat thereon called Faithful and True; and in righteousness he doth judge and make war.*

12 *And his eyes* are *a flame of fire, and upon his head* are *many diadems; and he hath a name written which no one knoweth but he himself.*

13 *And he* is *arrayed in a garment sprinkled with blood: and his name is called The Word of God.*

14 *And the armies which are in heaven followed him upon white horses, clothed in fine linen, white* and *pure.*

15 *And out of his mouth proceedeth a sharp sword, that with it he should smite the nations: and he shall rule them with a rod of iron: and he treadeth the winepress of the fierceness of the wrath of God, the Almighty.*

16 *And he hath on his garment and on his thigh a name written, KING OF KINGS, AND LORD OF LORDS.*

---

[17]In line with her thesis that Rev 12–22 was probably written by a disciple of John the Baptist (pp. 3, 28–37), "fellow servant" is said by Prof. Ford to suggest a circle of prophets around the Baptist (p. 312).

[18]Ford writes that "Rev 19:10d is a succinct reference to the return of prophecy as a sign of the New Covenant with Jesus as Lord" ("'For the Testimony of Jesus is the Spirit of Prophecy' [Rev 19:10]," *Irish Theological Journal*, 42 [1975], p. 291).

11 Almost without warning heaven opens. There appears a white horse whose rider is to wage a holy war and bring to a close the present age. The imagery used to depict this great event reflects the Jewish tradition of a warrior Messiah more than the NT teaching of the second advent of Christ. Beckwith notes that among the Hebrew prophets it was Jehovah himself who as a warrior was to come forth to establish his kingdom over rival nations in the last days, and that as the figure of the Messiah became more distinct in Jewish expectation, it is he who emerged as the great defender of God's cause in the final conflict (pp. 730–31). In *II Baruch* 72 it is the Messiah who summons the nations, sparing some and slaying others. The Jewish dream of a conquering Messiah is clearly advanced in the *Psalms of Solomon* 17:23–27, a passage closely related to the present text.[19] This representation of the Messiah is not at variance with NT teaching. In II Thessalonians 1:7–8 Paul teaches that the Lord Jesus will be revealed from heaven in flaming fire to inflict vengeance upon the wicked. In Matthew 25:41 Jesus commands the cursed to depart into eternal fire prepared for the devil and his angels. Whatever difference of emphasis may exist between the appearance of a warring Messiah and the return of Christ as generally depicted in the NT can be accounted for on the basis of two complementary (not antithetical) themes—messianic judgment upon the wicked and the fulfillment and vindication of the Christian hope. Both themes are found in II Thessalonians 1:9–10 where Paul speaks of Christ inflicting vengeance upon the wicked at his return as well as being glorified in those who believe. After noting that the idea of Christ pictured as a warrior going forth to battle "comes perilously near to being irreconcilable with the Christian concept of God," Schlatter goes on to say that the metaphor is then transformed from one of battle into one of judgment. "God triumphantly clears the battle field and swallows up his enemies in death."[20]

In 4:1 a door opened into heaven. Later (11:19; 15:5) the heavenly sanctuary itself was opened for further revelations. Now the heavens themselves open (cf. Ezek 1:1; *II Bar.* 22:1; Mt 3:16; Jn 1:51) to reveal the conquering Messiah and his armies returning from heaven to war against the beast, the false prophet, and the nations of the world who flock after them. Like the first of the four horsemen of chapter 6 the rider is mounted upon a white horse, a symbol of victorious conquest. He is called "Faithful and True,"[21] and in righteousness he judges and makes war. The righteous-

---

[19]It reads in part, "With a rod of iron he shall break in pieces all their substance. He shall destroy the godless nations with the word of his mouth." Cf. *Test. Dan* 5:13; *Sib. Or.* 5:108–10; *II Bar.* 39:7–40:4.

[20]*The Church in the NT Period*, p. 283.

[21]The placement of καλούμενος after πιστός (ℵ), before πιστός (**046** 82 1006 1611 2329 *pm* vg sy Ir Or TR), or its omission (**A P 051** 1 2059s *al*), makes little difference unless one

ness of divine judgment is a prominent theme throughout Revelation. In 16:5–7 the angel of the water proclaimed, "Just art thou in these thy judgments," and the altar responded, "Yea, Lord God the Almighty, true and just are thy ways." The great multitude in 19:2 praised God, "for true and righteous are his judgments." There is no doubt in the Seer's mind that the righteous retribution about to be enacted upon the beast and his followers is perfectly compatible with truth and justice. Centuries before, the Psalmist had sung of the coming of the Lord when he would judge the world with righteousness and the peoples with his truth (Ps 96:13). If "Faithful and True" is understood as a title,[22] it is the first of four ascribed to Christ in the immediate paragraph. He also has a secret name (vs. 12), is called "The Word of God" (vs. 13), and on his garment displays the title "KING OF KINGS, AND LORD OF LORDS" (vs. 16). In 3:14 Christ was called the faithful and true witness. Ladd notes that the two words are practically synonymous in that the Hebrew idea of truth was reliability rather than correspondence to reality as in Greek thought (p. 253).[23] God is faithful to his promises and will in due time vindicate the faith of all who place their confidence in him.

12 The first thing that John records about the Rider of the white horse is that his eyes are a flame of fire.[24] Nothing can be hidden from the penetrating gaze of Messiah. Upon his head are many diadems. Here is an obvious contrast to the seven diadems of the dragon (12:3) and the ten diadems of the beast out of the sea (13:1). Many crowns indicate unlimited sovereignty.[25] As King of kings all authority is his. The entire description is obviously symbolic and should not be visualized in any concrete way. The Rider also bears a name which only he knows. Some find here a reference to the sacred tetragrammaton, *YHWH*, a name too holy to pronounce so that the vowels of another name for God (*Adonai*) are read with the consonants of the holy name, with the resulting combination usually represented (in English) as Jehovah. Farrer thinks that the name is mentioned after reference to the diadems because the high priests wore the

---

assumes that its inclusion suggests that the rider was merely *called* "Faithful and True," highly improbable in a context such as this! Metzger holds that the reading of Sinaiticus best explains the others, although the UBS text follows the Byzantine text, placing καλούμενος between brackets to indicate some uncertainty (*TCGNT*, pp. 762–63).

[22]Moffatt says the two words are a description of the Messiah's character and function, rather than a title (p. 467). He translates, "His rider is faithful and true" (*The NT: A New Translation*).

[23]In Jer 10:10 the "God of truth" is the God who can be trusted to keep his covenant.

[24]A 1006 *al* lat sy sa TR read ὡς before φλόξ, undoubtedly due to the influence of 1:14 and 2:18. The UBS text places it in brackets.

[25]The two crowns which Ptolemy wore symbolized his kingship over Egypt and Asia (I Macc 11:13).

tetragrammaton on a gold plate upon the forehead (p. 198). Others hold the name to be "the name which is above every name" ("the Lord," Phil 2:9–11) given to Christ in fulfillment of his messianic ministry. Rist tentatively concludes that the secret name is "Jesus" and discerns martyrological overtones (p. 513). Lilje suggests that it may be the name inscribed upon the Rider's thigh in verse 16, which was not legible at first because of the radiance of the vision (p. 244). The most common interpretation is that it is a secret name whose meaning is veiled from all created beings. It expresses the mystery of his person. There will always remain a mystery about Christ which finite minds will never fully grasp. There exists an ancient idea that to know the name of a god or demon is to possess certain powers over him. This could account for the refusal of the divine visitors in Genesis 32:29 and Judges 13:18 to identify themselves (cf. *I Enoch* 69:14; *Asc. Isa.* 9:5). It is highly questionable that the returning Messiah would share such a reluctance.

13 The garment which the Rider wears has been dipped[26] in blood. The figure draws heavily upon the poem of vengeance in Isaiah 63:1–6. In answer to the prophet's inquiry, "Why is thy apparel red, and thy garments like his that treads in the winepress?" God replied, "I trod them in my anger and trampled them in my wrath; their lifeblood is sprinkled upon my garments." The blood which stains the garment of the conquering Messiah is not his own (as in 1:5; 5:9; 7:14; 12:11), but the blood of the enemy shed in conflict. The Palestinian *Targum* on Genesis 49:11 reads in part, "How beauteous is the King Messiah! Binding his loins and going forth to war against them that hate him, he will slay kings with princes, and make the rivers red with the blood of their slain. . . . His garments will be dipped in blood and he himself like the juice of the winepress" (cf. Rev 14:14–20). The argument that the blood cannot be the blood of battle because the conflict has not yet been joined misunderstands the nature of apocalyptic writing.[27] The blood-stained garments of the Messiah symbolize his victory in the coming conflict.

The name of the warrior is "The Word of God." Here is a striking link with the prologue of the Fourth Gospel where the pre-existent Son is the Word (Jn 1:1) who in God's time became incarnate and dwelt among men (Jn 1:14). As the title is used in Revelation, however, it emphasizes not so much the self-revelation of God as it does the authoritative declaration by which the nations of the world are destroyed. In Hebrew thought a

---

[26] βεβαμμένον has stronger manuscript support (**A 046** 1 82 2059s *pl* TR) and can account for the variants better than any of the six forms of ῥαίνω or ῥαντίζω listed in the UBS apparatus.
[27] Charles says the blood is that of the Parthian kings already destroyed (II, p. 133), while Caird takes it as "the indelible traces of the death of his followers" (p. 243).

word is not a lifeless sound but an active agent that achieves the intention of the one who speaks (Gen 1:3, 7, 9, etc.). The Word of God is God fulfilling his divine purpose. This idea finds expression in Hebrews 4:12, "The Word of God is living and active, sharper than any two-edged sword." The same concept is found in the Wisdom of Solomon in connection with the death of the firstborn in Egypt: "Thy all-powerful word leaped from heaven, from the royal throne, into the midst of the land that was doomed, a stern warrior carrying the sharp sword of thy authentic command" (19:15–16). The Messiah as avenging warrior is appropriately named the Word (the powerful and active utterance) of God.

14 The conquering Messiah commands a heavenly army clothed in fine linen and mounted, like their leader, on white horses. Normally, one would think of a heavenly army as composed of angels (cf. Mt 26:53; *II Enoch* 17; Zech 14:5), but the parallel in Revelation 17:14 in which those who battle on the Lamb's side are designated "called and chosen and faithful" would indicate that the martyrs (those who have remained faithful unto death) should be included as well. Apparently, the armies take no part in the actual battle, although later (in vs. 19) the armies of Antichrist make war "against him that sat upon the horse and against his army."[28] It is the sword of the Messiah that smites the enemy (vss. 15, 21), and his garment alone is dipped in blood. The "fine linen, white and pure," in which the armies are clothed, speaks of the righteousness of divine retaliation.

15 The activity of the warrior Messiah is portrayed by three figures taken from the OT. First, he is said to smite the nations with a sharp sword proceeding from his mouth. In Isaiah 11:4 we find that the messianic king will "smite the earth with the rod of his mouth" (cf. *Ps. Sol.* 17:39; *I Enoch* 62:2). The sharp sword symbolizes the lethal power of his word of judgment. We are not to envision a literal sword but a death-dealing pronouncement which goes forth like a sharp blade from the lips of Christ. In the initial vision of Revelation the Lord is pictured with a sharp two-edged[29] sword issuing from his mouth (1:16; 2:12) with which he will wage war against the Nicolaitans (2:16). The same general figure is seen in II Thessalonians 2:8 where the Lord Jesus is to slay the lawless one with "the breath of his mouth." Swete says that the figure represents the smiting of nations "not by judgements only, but by the forces which reduce them to obedience of faith"—hence the expansion of Christianity and ultimately the conversion of the world still being worked out in our time (p.

---

[28]Beasley-Murray calls the armies "angelic attendants" who do not engage in mortal combat but accompany the Lord in his parousia to witness their Commander exercise authority in judgment (p. 281).

[29]The δίστομος of 1:16 and 2:12 is added here by **046** 82 2028 2329 *pm* vg^{s,cl} sy.

254). Yet the war is eschatological and results in massive slaughter (vs. 21). Ladd's counsel is apropos, "The radical spiritualization of this concept which sees a conflict of human ideologies in human history and the triumph of Christianity does not accord with the nature of apocalyptic thought" (p. 256).

The second figure is that of ruling with a rod of iron. In Psalm 2 the Lord tells his anointed, "I will make the nations your heritage. . . . You shall break them with a rod of iron." To rule with a rod of iron means to destroy[30] rather than to govern in a stern fashion. The shepherd not only leads his flock to pasture but defends the sheep from marauding beasts. His rod is a weapon of retaliation. The Messiah's rod is a rod of iron; that is, it is strong and unyielding in its mission of judgment.

The third figure is that of treading the winepress (cf. comm. on 14:19–20). Once again we meet the stern reality of the "fierce anger of God" (Weymouth). The two nouns translated "wrath" or "anger"[31] are found thirteen times in chapters 6 through 19. Any view of God which eliminates judgment and his hatred of sin in the interest of an emasculated doctrine of sentimental affection finds no support in the strong and virile realism of the Apocalypse.

16 On the garment of the Rider where it falls across his thigh (a most prominent place for one mounted on a horse) is inscribed the name "KING OF KINGS, AND LORD OF LORDS."[32] This name emphasizes the universal sovereignty of the warrior Christ in his eschatological triumph over all the enemies of God. The title, as it occurs here and elsewhere in Scripture (Rev 17:14; I Tim 6:15; Dan 2:47), goes back to Moses' declaration to Israel, "The Lord your God is God of gods and Lord of lords" (Deut 10:17; cf. *I Enoch* 9:4). He will smite the nations, break them with a rod of iron, and tread the winepress of his fierce wrath because all power is his and all the nations are subject to the might of his righteous retribution.

Commentators differ on the exact location of the inscription. If written in two places (as the *ASV* suggests) it could be inscribed on the girdle (or hilt of the sword) as well as on the outer garment. If "and on his thigh" means "that is, on his thigh,"[33] then it could refer to the place where the sword would customarily hang.[34] The simplest explanation is

[30] ποιμαίνω in Rev 7:17 has the sense of gentle care, but elsewhere in Rev (2:27; 12:5; 19:15) it connotes punishment.
[31] θυμός, ὀργή; see note on 14:10. Hahn notes that "this thought of the future wrath of God is unfolded on a massive scale in Rev." (*DNTT*, I, p. 111).
[32] Patrick Skehan computes the dual name to add up to 777 when placed into Aramaic ("King of Kings, Lord of Lords (Apoc. 19:16)," *CBQ*, 10 [1948], p. 398).
[33] Taking καί exegetically, a common interpretation.
[34] Charles lists several instances of names and inscriptions on the thighs of statues (II, p. 137).

347

that the name was written on that part of the garment which fell open across the thigh.

3. ANTICHRIST AND ALLIES DESTROYED (19:17–21)

17 *And I saw an angel standing in the sun; and he cried with a loud voice, saying to all the birds that fly in mid heaven,* Come *and* be gathered together unto the great supper of God;

18 *that ye may eat the flesh of kings, and the flesh of captains, and the flesh of mighty men, and the flesh of horses and of them that sit thereon, and the flesh of all men, both free and bond, and small and great.*

19 *And I saw the beast, and the kings of the earth, and their armies, gathered together to make war against him that sat upon the horse, and against his army.*

20 *And the beast was taken, and with him the false prophet that wrought the signs in his sight, wherewith he deceived them that had received the mark of the beast and them that worshipped his image: they two were cast alive into the lake of fire that burneth with brimstone:*

21 *and the rest were killed with the sword of him that sat upon the horse,* even the sword *which came forth out of his mouth; and all the birds were filled with their flesh.*

17–18 The heavens have opened, revealing the Messiah and his armies about to engage in final conflict. Now, as if to heighten still further the suspense of this dramatic moment, John interposes yet another brief vision (vss. 17–18). An angel appears in the sun, a position of splendor appropriate to a herald of victory. From this vantage point he will be able to deliver effectively his message to the birds that circle in mid-heaven. His message is, Come to the great supper of God and gorge on the flesh of the fallen! Barclay calls this a "bloodthirsty picture . . . far more in line with Old Testament apocalyptic expectations than with the gospel of Jesus Christ" (II, p. 237). That it draws upon OT apocalyptic is obvious. It is a free interpretation of Ezekiel's oracle against Gog, which reads in part, "Speak to the birds of every sort and to all the beasts of the field, 'Assemble . . . to the sacrificial feast which I am preparing for you. . . . You shall eat the flesh of the mighty, and drink the blood of the princes of the earth" (Ezek 39:17–20). It is not true, however, that with the coming of the gospel age the God of the OT decided to prove to men that he really was a gentleman after all and so dispensed with any further recourse to judgment. The good news is that man need not bear the just punishment due his

---

Bruce (p. 661) refers to a conjecture that (assuming a Semitic original) *regel* (leg) has replaced an original *degel* (banner).

sin but that Another has paid the price on his behalf. Only when man refuses forgiveness must he bear the penalty for his wickedness.

The supper of God presents a grim contrast to the marriage feast of the Lamb. It is the supper of God in the sense that God will provide it. The ranks of the enemy are composed not only of kings and captains, but of all men, free and bond, small and great. Beasley-Murray correctly observes that "all men" here indicates "all kinds of men" (p. 283). In the final conflict no preference will be given to rank or station. The bodies will lie on the field of battle to be devoured by birds of prey. To remain unburied for the pleasure of the predators was considered by the ancients to be an ignominious fate. The scene is one of universal dishonor and destruction.

19 John now sees the beast and his[35] armies arrayed against the Messiah and his army. The battle of Armageddon has arrived. Earlier we learned that demonic spirits went forth from the mouth of the beast and the false prophet to assemble the kings of the whole world for battle on the great day of God the Almighty (16:13–14): "They gathered them together into the place which is called in Hebrew Har-Magedon" (16:16). The scene is eschatological in an absolute sense. The Seer is not describing the gradual conquest of evil in the spiritual struggles of the faithful, but a great historic event which brings to an end the Antichrist and his forces and ushers in the long-awaited era of righteousness. History may offer examples of the triumph of right over wrong, but far from exhausting the truth of Revelation, they merely prefigure the actual consummation with its end to wickedness and beginning of universal peace.

20 Interestingly enough there is no description of the actual warfare. This should remind the reader that the Apocalypse is dominated by metaphor and symbol. While the events portrayed in apocalyptic language are to be taken with all seriousness, they are not to be taken literalistically. Armageddon portrays the eschatological defeat of Antichrist (an event which takes place in time and brings to a close this age as we know it) but does not require that we accept in a literal fashion the specific imagery with which the event is described.

The beast and false prophet are seized[36] and cast alive into the lake of fire. The beast is the personification of secular power in its opposition to the church. The false prophet represents the role of false religion in persuading man to worship the antichristian power (cf. comm. on 13:1, 11). The false prophet is again described in terms of his two characteristic

[35]The armies of the kings of the earth are in fact the armies of the beast. A*pc* sa have αὐτοῦ for αὐτῶν after στρατεύματος.

[36]πιάζω rather regularly means "to lay hold of with hostile intent"; cf. Jn 7:30, 32; Acts 12:4; *Ecclus.* 23:21.

functions: he deceives men by working great signs (cf. 13:13–15), and he brands with the mark of the beast all but those who are willing to die for their faith (cf. 13:16–17).

The beast and false prophet are destined to be cast alive into the lake of fire. This designation for the place of final torment occurs only in Revelation, although the idea of punishment by fire is prominent in the extra-Biblical Jewish writings. *I Enoch* 54:1 speaks of the place of judgment as "a deep valley with burning fire," and in *II Enoch* 10 it is described as a place of terror with all manner of tortures including a fiery river.[37] Although the actual word Gehenna is not used in Revelation, this is what John refers to as the lake of fire. Gehenna (an abbreviation for "valley of the son of Hinnom") was the name given to the valley lying to the south and west of Jerusalem (the modern *Wadi er Rababi*). As the site of a cultic shrine where human sacrifices were offered (II Kgs 16:3; 23:10; Jer 7:31), it acquired an unholy reputation. Because of prophetic denunciation of this place of terrible wickedness (Jer 7:32; 19:6), it came to be equated with the hell of final judgment in apocalyptic literature. In NT times Gehenna was a place of fire and the abode of the wicked dead (Mt 5:22; Mk 9:43).[38]

In the Revelation passage the lake of fire is said to burn with brimstone, a yellow, sulphurous substance which burns readily in air. It is found in a natural state in volcanic areas such as the valley of the Dead Sea (cf. Gen 19:24; Ezek 38:22). A lake of burning brimstone would not only be intensely hot, but malodorous and fetid as well. It is an appropriate place for all that is sinful and wicked in the world. The Antichrist and the false prophet are its first inhabitants. Later the devil (20:10), Death and Hades (20:14), and all evil men (21:8) will join them in this place of ceaseless torment.

21 The armies of Antichrist are killed by the sword which proceeds from the mouth of Messiah. While this is obviously not to be understood as a literal sword, neither is it to be taken as a metaphor for the gospel message. The scene is one of judgment, and the sword is the proclamation of divine retribution that slays all who have in the final alignment of loyalties arrayed themselves against God and the forces of righteousness. The supper of God is ready, and the vultures gorge themselves on the flesh of the wicked.

---

[37] Cf. II Esdr 7:36; *I Enoch* 27:2; 48:9; 90:26 f; 103:8; *As. Mos.* 10:10; *II Bar.* 59:10.
[38] The NT distinguishes sharply between ᾅδης (the temporary abode of the ungodly in the period between death and resurrection) and γέεννα (the place of eternal punishment following the last judgment). See Jeremias, γέεννα, *TDNT*, I, pp. 657–58.

CHAPTER 20

Judging from the amount of attention given by many writers to the first ten verses of chapter 20, one would judge it to be the single most important segment of the book of Revelation. The tendency of many interpreters at this point is to become apologists for a particular view of the millennium. Without denying the significance of this important passage, it should not be elevated above such basic themes as the return of Christ, the final judgment and removal of all wickedness, and the splendor of the eternal state. A careful reading of the millennial passage (vss. 1–10) will show that it is perhaps limited to the resurrected martyrs alone, and that it contains no specific indication that their reign with Christ takes place on earth or that it necessarily follows the second advent. This commentary understands the millennium portrayed as an earthly reign which follows the second coming of Christ, although the text itself does not rule out alternate explanations.[1]

4. SATAN BOUND (20:1–3)

1 *And I saw an angel coming down out of heaven, having the key of the abyss and a great chain in his hand.*

2 *And he laid hold on the dragon, the old serpent, which is the Devil and Satan, and bound him for a thousand years,*

3 *and cast him into the abyss, and shut* it, *and sealed* it *over him, that he should deceive the nations no more, until the thousand years should be finished: after this he must be loosed for a little time.*

1 The angel that descends from heaven has in his hand a key to the abyss and a great chain. The angel is probably the one who in chapter 9 released the demonic locusts by opening the shaft leading to the abyss. The abyss

---

[1]Because elsewhere in Rev there is no indication of an intermediate reign, Schnackenburg thinks that 20:1–6 may be an interpretive doublet of 19:11–21 (*God's Rule and Kingdom*, pp. 339–47).

was thought of as a vast subterranean cavern[2] which served as a place of confinement for disobedient spirits awaiting judgment (Jude 6; *Jub.* 5:6; Lk 8:31). In *I Enoch* 88:1 a fallen angel is bound hand and foot and cast into an abyss that is "narrow and deep, and horrible and dark." In (or upon, *ASV* margin) the hand of the angel is a great chain[3] with which he is about to bind Satan. There is no specific indication in verse 1 to determine when this event takes place, although it should be noted that the recurring "and I saw"[4] of 19:11, 17, 19; 20:1, 4, 12; and 21:1 appears to establish a sequence of visions which carries through from the appearance of the Rider on the white horse (19:11) to the establishment of the new heaven and new earth (21:1 ff). The interpretation that discovers recapitulation for the segment 20:1–6 must at least bear the burden of proof.

2–3 The angel seizes[5] the dragon, binds him (with the chain), and casts him into the abyss. There he remains for a thousand years, unable to carry on his practice of deceiving the nations. At the close of the thousand years he is to be loosed for a little time (this brief period is described in 20:7–10). In verse 2 all four titles by which Satan is designated in Revelation are brought together. He is the dragon defeated in heavenly combat by Michael (12:7–8), the serpent who tried to sweep away the messianic community with a flood (12:15), and the devil who knows that his time is short (12:12).

What the binding of Satan entails depends upon whether the passage is taken as descriptive of the present age or of a period which will follow the second advent. Representative of the first point of view, Hendriksen holds that in the period between the two comings of Christ the devil's influence is curtailed so that he is unable to prevent the extension of the church by means of an active missionary program (p. 226). In support he lists a number of verses in which the binding, casting out, or falling of Satan is associated in some way with the first coming of Christ (Mt 12:29; Lk 19:17–18; Jn 12:31; Col 2:15). Walvoord, on the other hand, says that the intention of the passage is not to represent Satan as merely restricted but as rendered completely inactive during the thousand-year millennial period following the second advent (p. 291). In support of his position Walvoord cites a number of NT passages which show Satan as extremely active in the present age (Lk 22:3; Acts 5:3; II Cor 4:3–4; 11:14; Eph 2:2; I Thess 2:18;

---

[2] ἄβυσσος was originally an adjective meaning "bottomless" or "unfathomed."

[3] Probably to bind the hands: ἅλυσις in Mk 5:4 is coupled with πέδη, "fetter" (cognate with πούς, ποδός, foot), and in Acts 12:7 the ἁλύσεις fall off Peter's *hands*. Perhaps some sort of handcuffs is intended.

[4] καὶ εἶδον.

[5] κρατέω (from κράτος, strength, power) has the basic idea of exercise of power. In Mt 26:50 it means "to take into custody."

II Tim 2:26; and especially I Pet 5:18, "Your adversary the devil prowls around like a roaring lion, seeking someone to devour"). The answer to the problem obviously does not lie in one's ability to support his interpretation by collecting verses from other contexts in Scripture. Careful attention needs to be given to the text of Revelation itself. All the text actually says is that during a period designated as a thousand years Satan is to be bound and cast into the abyss, which is then shut and sealed. The purpose of the confinement is not punishment. It is to prevent him from deceiving the nations.[6] The elaborate measures taken to insure his custody are most easily understood as implying the complete cessation of his influence on earth (rather than a curbing of his activities). The abyss is sealed (cf. Dan 6:17; Mt 27:66) as a special precaution against escape. Satan's imprisonment is to last a thousand years. Some understand this period as a literal one thousand years, while others take it to indicate a lengthy period of undetermined duration. The latter interpretation cites in support such verses as Psalm 50:10 which speaks metaphorically of cattle on a thousand hills, and II Peter 3:8 with its equation of one day and a thousand years. Nothing in the immediate context favors either interpretation. It is the larger concern to find a consistent millennial position which leads each exegete to commit himself on the meaning of the thousand years.[7]

In chapter 19 the kings of the earth and their armies were slain by the sword of Messiah (19:19–21). Yet now in chapter 20 the nations are pictured as still in existence. Moffatt notes that "such discrepancies were inevitable in the dovetailing of disparate conceptions" (p. 471), but adds that the reference in 20:3 is probably to those outlying nations on the fringe of the empire who had not shared in the campaign of the Antichrist. Caird, on the other hand, says that the battle of chapter 19 is the smashing of the political power which, undergirded by idolatrous religion and materialistic seduction, organized the nations in resistance to the sovereignty of God (p. 252). It is probably best to understand the nations of 20:3 as the remnant from nations who opposed Messiah rather than as select nations here and there who never entered the final battle. In either case, however, they are no longer under the seductive influence of Satan. No longer are they deceived into giving to the emperor the worship which belongs to God

---

[6]Ostella argues that discontinuance of deception in Rev 20:3 is a critically decisive exegetical point and "ultimately demands the conclusion that the millennium involves an extension of redemptive history subsequent to the parousia" ("The Significance of Deception in Revelation 20:3," WTJ, 37 [1974–5], pp. 236–38).
[7]Summers says the number does not represent a period of time at all but should be understood as a way of saying that the devil will be completely restrained (p. 204). Love says that Satan is bound whenever believers surrender their lives to Christ, and the end of the thousand years is the sphere outside the utterly surrendered life (p. 116).

alone. Looking ahead to the close of the thousand-year period, John adds that for a little while Satan must be released again. It is futile to speculate just why there needs to be yet another conflict. Satan will gather a following from around the earth and march on the beloved city. He is to be devoured by fire from heaven and cast finally into the lake of fire. Apparently a thousand years of confinement does not alter Satan's plans, nor does a thousand years of freedom from the influence of wickedness change man's basic tendency to rebel against his creator.

5. MILLENNIAL REIGN (20:4–6)

4 *And I saw thrones, and they sat upon them, and judgment was given unto them: and I saw the souls of them that had been beheaded for the testimony of Jesus, and for the word of God, and such as worshipped not the beast, neither his image, and received not the mark upon their forehead and upon their hand; and they lived, and reigned with Christ a thousand years.*

5 *The rest of the dead lived not until the thousand years should be finished. This is the first resurrection.*

6 *Blessed and holy is he that hath part in the first resurrection: over these the second death hath no power; but they shall be priests of God and of Christ, and shall reign with him a thousand years.*

4 John now sees thrones and the faithful martyrs who gave their lives rather than worship the beast or receive his mark. All we know for sure about the occupants of the thrones is that judgment is given to them. It is not likely that this judgment relates to the question of who is worthy to be resurrected and share in the millennial reign with Christ. The judgment appears to be connected in some way with the vindication of the martyrs and their right to assume the empire of the defeated powers of wickedness. Daniel's vision of the four beasts, their judgment and the passing of the kingdom to the saints of the Most High, is undoubtedly the background for much of John's presentation. In Daniel, one like a son of man receives everlasting dominion from the Ancient of Days (Dan 7:13–14). The interpretation is then supplied, which is that with the coming of the Ancient of Days judgment is given for[8] the saints of the Most High and they receive the kingdom (Dan 7:22).

The problem of naming the martyrs as those who sit upon the thrones is that they are not mentioned until later in the verse. Charles says that the one way to "restore sanity to the text" is to connect the opening

---

[8]The Aramaic text reads לְקַדִּישֵׁי (LXX, ἁγίοις), which could mean "to the saints" (cf. לְהּ in Dan 7:14 and לְעַם in Dan 7:27 where ל indicates the indirect object rather than signifying "on behalf of").

words, "and I saw," with "souls of them that had been beheaded" and move the intervening words to a position after "upon their hand" (II, pp. 182–83).[9] Others hold the occupants of the thrones to include apostles (who in Mt 19:28 are promised that they will sit on twelve thrones judging the twelve tribes of Israel), saints (who in I Cor 6:2–3 are reminded that they will judge both the world and angels), and all who remain faithful in the final trial (Rev 3:21). Since the text remains silent about the occupants of the thrones, it may be wise not to go beyond suggesting that they may be a heavenly court (as in Dan 7:26) that will assist in judgment. One possibility is that mention of the martyrs in verse 4 leads away from the original theme of judgment, which is then picked up again in verse 11.

In addition to thrones John sees the souls of those who had been martyred for faithfulness in bearing the testimony of Jesus[10] and the word of God. These are the souls under the altar in 6:9 and all who are to meet a similar fate until the time of their vindication (6:11). They are called souls because at this point they are still awaiting the resurrection. That they are said to have been beheaded does not restrict the group to those martyrs who had met death in this specific fashion.[11] It is representative of all who gave their lives in faithfulness to their commitment to Christ.

There is a question as to whether one or two groups of believers are mentioned in verse 4b–c. A straightforward reading of the English text seems to suggest two. Barclay speaks of those who were actually martyred and "those who suffered everything short of death for their loyalty to Jesus Christ" (II, p. 246).[12] Yet in 13:15 John had written that "as many as should not worship the image of the beast should be killed." Consistency would suggest that in the final conflict there are none who resist the Antichrist without paying for their stand with their life. The relative pronoun translated "such as"[13] may indicate a fuller definition of the group just mentioned. They are those of chapter 13 who refused to worship the

---

[9]Supply καὶ εἶδον before θρόνους. Charles' view is that John died after finishing 1–20:3 and the remainder of the book was put together from documents he left by a faithful but unintelligent disciple (II, p. 147). Gaechter studies the thesis with care and concludes that the editor did not grasp the original sequence because John gave him no written documents and he had to rely wholly upon his memory ("The Original Sequence of Apocalypse 20–22," *Theological Studies,* 10 [1949], pp. 485–521).

[10]Taking τὴν μαρτυρίαν Ἰησοῦ as a subjective genitive (as in 1:2, 9; 12:17; 19:10).

[11]The verb πελεκίζω occurs only here in the NT. It is derived from πέλεκυς, a double-edged axe, which was the instrument of execution in republican Rome (Diodorus Siculus xix.101; Josephus, *Ant.* xiv.7.4).

[12]Swete calls the second group confessors and others who remained faithful in persecution (p. 262).

[13]ὅστις often introduces a relative clause which emphasizes a characteristic quality of its antecedent; cf. Mt 7:15, προσέχετε ἀπὸ τῶν ψευδοπροφητῶν οἵτινες ἔρχονται πρὸς ὑμᾶς ἐν ἐνδύμασι προβάτων; Rom 1:25; Acts 10:47. In this case καί would serve as an explicative ("namely"); cf. Mt 8:33; I Cor 15:38.

beast (13:12) or to receive his mark (13:16) and consequently paid for their loyalty by death (13:15).

These martyrs are said to live and reign with Christ for a thousand years. How one interprets this simple statement reveals his position on the millennial question. Ladd (p. 265) correctly observes that the crux of the entire exegetical problem is the meaning of "they came to life again" (ASV, "they lived"). Apart from the immediate context (vss. 4–5) where it is used twice and in reference to two distinct groups, the verb is found in Revelation in but two other places: in 2:8 of Christ who "died and came to life" (RSV) and in 13:14 of the beast who was wounded by the sword "and yet lived" (RSV). There is no basis for the claim that if the author of Revelation had wished to speak of an actual physical resurrection he would have used some other verb since there is no Greek verb which exclusively means "to raise from the dead."[14] The verb he did use also occurs in such passages as Matthew 9:18 where the ruler of the synagogue tells Jesus that his daughter has just died but that if he will lay his hand on her "she will be restored to life" (TCNT), and in Romans 14:9 of the bodily resurrection of Christ ("For to this end Christ died and lived again").

The strong presumption is that the verb in verse 5 should be taken in the same sense as it is in verse 6. In the second case the statement, "The rest of the dead lived not until the thousand years should be finished," certainly refers to a bodily resurrection at the close of the millennial period. If "they lived" in verse 4 means a spiritual resurrection to new life in Christ, then we are faced with the problem of discovering within the context some persuasive reason to interpret the same verb differently within one concise unit. No such reason can be found. Alford's much-quoted remark is worth repeating: "If, in a passage where *two resurrections* are mentioned . . . the first resurrection may be understood to mean *spiritual* rising with Christ, while the second means *literal* rising from the grave;—then there is an end of all significance in language, and Scripture is wiped out as a definite testimony to anything" (IV, p. 732).

The length of the martyrs' reign is a thousand years. It is this number which gives rise to the term millennium (from the Latin *mille*, thousand, and *annus*, year). Only in Revelation 20:1–10 do we find any

---

[14]Note that ἀνίστημι (used quite regularly in the gospels for bodily resurrection; Mt 20:19; Mk 12:25; Lk 12:46; etc.) can also mean "to erect, cause to be born, stand up, appear, get ready" (BAG, p. 69). ἐγείρω may mean "to wake, lift up, restore, bring into being, appear" as well as "to raise from the dead" (BAG, pp. 213–14). ἀναζάω is found only twice in the NT (and not at all in the post-apostolic fathers or the Apologists): in Lk 15:24 of the return of the prodigal son, and in Rom 7:9 of sin springing to life at the coming of the commandment. ζάω, on the other hand, is found more than 140 times in the NT scattered through a wide range of contexts, each of which determines its specific meaning in that instance.

NT teaching about the millennium.[15] The origin of the idea seems to stem from the eschatological expectations of late apocalyptic Judaism. In earlier times the Jews pictured a messianic kingdom which would last on the present earth forever (Isa 11:10–16; 65:20–25; Dan 7:14, 27). Under the influence of dualism there developed from about 100 BC onward an increasing pessimism about this earth as a proper place for such a glorious period. Beckwith thinks that the idea of a partial and temporary realization of God's kingdom prior to its complete establishment arose in an effort to mediate between the earlier eschatological hope of an earthly kingdom in Palestine ruled by Jehovah himself, and a later conception of a transcendental and universal kingdom for risen saints in a renewed heaven and earth (p. 735).[16] Charles says that the millennium is really "a late and attenuated form of the old Jewish expectation of an eternal Messianic Kingdom on the present earth" (II, p. 142).

Jewish speculation as to the length of this temporary reign ranges from forty to 7,000 years.[17] In Enoch's *Apocalypse of Weeks* human history takes place in seven weeks, followed by the messianic kingdom established in the eighth and lasting through the tenth week (*I Enoch* 93; 91:12–17). In II Esdras 7:28 it is definitely set at four hundred years. Some argued from the week of creation and the thousand-years-equals-one-day idea reflected in Psalm 90:4 (cf. II Pet 3:8) that after 6,000 years of world history there would be a thousand-year cosmic sabbath corresponding to the seventh day of creation in which God rested from his work (*Barn.* xv). In *Slavonic Enoch* the world is to last seven days of one thousand years each, followed by an eighth day with time divisions (*II Enoch* 32:2–33:2).[18] It comes as no surprise, therefore, that the reign of the martyrs sketched in Revelation (preceding judgment and the eternal state) should last one thousand years. Nor is there any particular reason to suppose that in the mind of John the one thousand years represented a period

---

[15]The attempt to attribute to Paul a belief in the millennium on the basis of I Cor 15:20–28 is unconvincing. See Beckwith (pp. 98–100) for an excellent treatment of this claim. He concludes that although millenniums may be conceived to intervene between steps in the progress of the kingdom toward completion, in Paul's view what lies ahead is simply the absolute triumph of the kingdom and the inheritance which awaits the Christian.

[16]Ford says that "in earlier writings Israel contemplated a new historical and national era, but eventually developed a more transcendental hope which included the concept of new heavens and a new earth.... It was, perhaps, in order to harmonize these divergent views that the belief in an interim messianic period arose" (p. 352).

[17]For a summary of rabbinic views on the duration of the messianic age see Strack-Billerbeck, III, pp. 823–27.

[18]See Beasley-Murray (pp. 288–89) for further references illustrating the wide variation of belief concerning the ultimate future which existed in contemporary Jewish and Christian literature; also Ford, pp. 352–54.

of time of some other duration. Many of the earliest church fathers were millenarians. Toward the middle of the second century Justin Martyr said that properly instructed Christians were assured of a resurrection of the dead to be followed by a thousand years in Jerusalem (*Dial.* 80). Irenaeus, in the last of the same century, believed in an earthly millennium during which the saints and martyrs would be rewarded (*Adv. Haer.* v.32). Unfortunately, many chiliasts allowed their imaginations to run riot and read into the thousand-year period all manner of materialistic and sensuous extremes. Papias records as the words of Jesus an extravagant portrayal of the fertility of the earth in which each grape would yield twenty-five measures of wine and every grain of wheat 10,000 pounds of flour.[19] Eusebius records that the heretic Cerinthus taught an earthly kingdom of sensual pleasure ("the gratification of appetite and lust; *ie.,* in eating, drinking, and marrying") to follow the resurrection (*Hist. Eccl.* iii.38). He also refers to Nepos, an Egyptian bishop who "supposed that there would be a certain millennium of sensual luxury on this earth" (*Hist. Eccl.* vii.24).

These extremes led later scholars to condemn the materialistic chiliasm which had taken root in the church. In the third century Origen rebuked those who looked forward to bodily pleasure and luxury in the millennium (*De Princ.* ii.11.2–3). It was Augustine, however, who about the beginning of the fifth century made the first serious effort to interpret Revelation 20 in a non-millenarian fashion. He held that the thousand-year period was to be taken as the interval between the first advent and the final conflict. The binding of Satan during this period was accomplished by Christ during his earthly ministry. The first resurrection was the spiritual birth of believers (*De Civ. Dei* xx.7 ff). This same embarrassment over the chiliasm of sectarians carried over into the theology of the Reformers. Lilje notes that "the modern rejection of chiliasm is usually based on dogmatic considerations, not on biblical exegesis" (p. 252). Beckwith adds that the fundamental fault of those who interpret this passage in a nonliteral fashion is "that they mistake the nature of apocalyptic prophecy, and read into the vision of our Apocalyptist here a meaning of which he gives no intimation and which is at variance with his language. Apocalyptic prophecy is not allegory.... Nor can the age-long struggle of the Church militant... answer to the picture of the millennial reign of the risen martyrs" (p. 738).[20]

---

[19]See Irenaeus, *Adv. Haer.* v.33.3; Eusebius, *Hist. Eccl.* iii.39. The quotation is given in Barclay, II, p. 243 as well. It is paralleled in *II Bar.* 29:5–8 and in the rabbinical tradition.
[20]For a convenient summary of the two millennial interpretations (literal and allegorical) see Erdman, pp. 154–62.

A question normally raised by non-millenarians is, What is the purpose of the thousand-year reign? The usual answer is that it is the vindication within history of the cause of Christ. With the establishment of the kingdom of God upon earth, there is tangible and convincing proof of the victory of righteousness over evil. There is another response, however, that is more specific and grows out of the text itself. Noting that the millennial reign with Christ is probably to be limited to the martyrs who gave their lives rather than submit to the blasphemous demands of emperor worship, it understands the thousand-year reign as a special reward to the martyrs of chapter 6. These were told to wait under the altar until their number would be complete and then their blood would be avenged upon those who dwell upon the earth (6:9–11). The millennium is not, for John, the messianic age foretold by the prophets of the OT, but a special reward for those who have paid with their lives the price of faithful opposition to the idolatrous claims of Antichrist.

This leads to a further question, Are we to think of this millennial reign as an actual period of political and social history which is to follow the return of Christ? Beckwith argues that when we distinguish the essential truth of prophecy from the form in which it is communicated (this being determined by the historical circumstances and dominant religious conceptions of the day), we will cease to find in Revelation 20 the prediction of an *eschatological* era. The essential truth of the passage is that the martyr's steadfastness will win for him the highest life in union with God and Christ. It is a commentary on the Lord's saying in Matthew 10:39, "He that loses his life for my sake will find it."[21] This does not mean that the author composed an allegory to communicate to his readers certain abstract truths. He worked within the necessary limitations of his own historical perspective and wrote for his own day. His understanding reflects the immediacy of the culture in which he lived and worked. Beckwith states his confident belief in the final realization of the divine ideal revealed, but does not look for anything like a literal fulfillment of the predictions shaped by the conditions of a transient period of history (p. 301). Some will disagree with the distinction between form and content, but others will find in this approach a reasonable answer to some of the more perplexing aspects of predictive prophecy. In short, John taught a literal millennium, but its essential meaning may be realized in something other than a temporal fulfillment.

---

[21]Beckwith, pp. 736–38; for the underlying argument see the earlier section entitled "Permanent and Transitory Elements in the Apocalypse Distinguished," pp. 291–310.

5 The rest of the dead who lived not until the close of the thousand years would be all the faithful except the martyrs, plus the entire body of unbelievers. Only if the martyrs of the first resurrection are taken as symbolic of the church universal would the second resurrection be limited to the ungodly. The first sentence in verse 5 is a parenthetical statement which anticipates the activity depicted in verses 11 and following.[22] The second sentence of the verse, "This is the first resurrection," continues the thought of verse 4 and refers to the resurrection of the martyrs.

6 Those who participate in the first resurrection are pronounced blessed and holy. The basis for their blessedness is threefold: they are not subject to the second death, they shall be priests of God and Christ, and they shall reign with him a thousand years. The second death is defined in 20:14 and 21:8 as being cast into the lake that burns with fire and brimstone. It is to share the eternal fate of the devil, the beast, and the false prophet (19:20; 20:10, 14–15), which is to endure torment day and night for ever and ever (20:10). Farrer notes that while the first resurrection is selective[23] and the second absolutely universal, the first death is virtually universal (some will be alive at the parousia) and the second is selective (p. 206). At Sinai God promised the Israelites that if they would obey his voice and keep his commandments they would be to him a kingdom of priests and a holy nation (Ex 19:6). The faithful, by remaining true to Christ in the final trial by Antichrist, are thus priests[24] of God and Christ. As a royal priesthood (cf. I Pet 2:5, 9; Rev 1:6; 5:10) they reign with him a thousand years.

6. SATAN DESTROYED (20:7–10)

7 *And when the thousand years are finished, Satan shall be loosed out of his prison,*

8 *and shall come forth to deceive the nations which are in the four corners of the earth, Gog and Magog, to gather them together to the war: the number of whom is as the sand of the sea.*

---

[22]It is omitted by ℵ 82 *al* sy.

[23]Ford suggests that it is probably best to understand "first resurrection" in the sense of "the first group to enjoy resurrection" (p. 350). Meredith Kline argues from the use of *prōtos* that the first resurrection is the death of the Christian ("The First Resurrection," *WTJ*, 37 [1974–5], pp. 366–75). Norman Shepherd takes the first resurrection as the resurrection of Christ ("The Resurrections of Revelation 20," *WTJ*, 37 [1974–5], pp. 34–43). James Hughes claims there is no mention in Rev 20:4–6 of a bodily resurrection, let alone two bodily resurrections ("Revelation 20:4–6 and the Question of the Millennium," *WTJ*, 35 [1972–3], pp. 281–302).

[24]One Latin word for priest is *pontifex*, bridge builder. The role of the priest is to establish a bridge between God and man.

9 *And they went up over the breadth of the earth, and compassed the camp of the saints about, and the beloved city: and fire came down out of heaven, and devoured them.*

10 *And the devil that deceived them was cast into the lake of fire and brimstone, where are also the beast and the false prophet; and they shall be tormented day and night for ever and ever.*

7 The next four verses (7–10) portray the release of Satan from his thousand-year imprisonment, the gathering of the nations for a final assault on the people of God, the fire from heaven which devours the enemy, and Satan's final destiny in the lake of fire. Ezekiel had described an attack upon Israel in the last days in which the aggressors would be completely defeated after a cataclysmic battle (Ezek 38–39). This eschatological warfare against Israel became one of the standard ideas in Jewish teaching about the last days. The *Sibylline Oracles* 3:662–701 is a good example. We are told that "fiery swords" (673) shall fall from heaven upon the "undisciplined empty-minded people" (670) who have surrounded Jerusalem. God is to judge "with war and sword and with fire and cataclysms of rain" (689–690).[25] It is worth noting that in Ezekiel and Revelation the assault *follows* the period of the messianic kingdom. In Ezekiel 36–37 Israel is restored to the land; then comes the warfare in chapters 38 and 39. This is followed by a portrayal of the eternal state under the figure of a rebuilt temple in the New Jerusalem (chaps. 40–48).

The release of Satan was anticipated in verse 3. Perhaps the most reasonable explanation for this rather unusual parole is to make plain that neither the designs of Satan nor the waywardness of the human heart will be altered by the mere passing of time. Once loosed from prison, Satan picks up where he left off and men rally to his cause. Reference to the Babylonian legend of Tiamat (the chaos-monster) who is released at the end of time and once again defeated by Marduk (the god of light; cf. Glasson, p. 112) is an interesting parallel but adds little to our understanding of the Apocalypse. The verb translated "finished" carries the idea of bringing to an appointed end or goal.[26]

8 Both Satan and the false prophet are portrayed in Revelation as deceivers (12:9; 20:3; 13:14; 19:20). It comes as no surprise that upon Satan's release from the abyss he returns to his nefarious activity. It is probable that the second infinitive clause in verse 8 builds upon the first (rather than being parallel),[27] so that the verse says that Satan shall come

---

[25]See also Dan 11; Zech 14; Isa 66:15–23; II Esdr 13:5 ff.

[26]τελέω. Note that the Byzantine text reads μετά for ὅταν τελεσθῇ, which tends to present the χίλια ἔτη as a more definite period of time.

[27]MSS which add καί before συναγαγεῖν (ℵ 051 2059s *al g* vg) understand a parallel syntax.

forth to deceive the nations *for the purpose* of gathering them together to war. The nations which fall prey to Satan's propaganda are said to be in "the four corners of the earth." This figure of speech is not intended to stress some ancient cosmology but to emphasize universality (cf. Isa 11:12; Ezek 7:2; Rev 7:1). The nations are further identified as Gog and Magog. In Genesis 10:2 Magog is listed as one of the sons of Japheth. In Ezekiel 38:2 Gog is the chief prince of Meshech and Tubal,[28] who leads the invasion against Israel. Magog, according to Ezekiel 38:9, is a territory located in "the uttermost parts of the north." In Revelation, however, both Gog and Magog are symbolic figures representing the nations of the world which band together for a final assault upon God and his people. No specific geographical designations are intended. They are simply hostile nations from all across the world.

Kuhn notes that apart from two "fruitless references" in the *Sibylline Oracles,* Gog and Magog are not mentioned in the apocalyptic and pseudepigraphal literature. On the other hand, the war of Gog and Magog is a constituent part of the apocalyptic thinking of the rabbis. Kuhn concludes that the Apocalypse is closer to the more scriptural apocalyptic of the rabbis than to the noncanonical writings (*TDNT,* I, p. 791). The assault itself may be modeled on the invasion of the Scythians into Asia in 630 BC.[29] According to Caird not only are the names Gog and Magog mythical, but the entire account should be interpreted as such. "The myth of Gog," he writes, "enshrines a deep insight into the resilience of evil." It is the "mythical equivalent of the Pauline doctrine of justification by faith alone" (p. 257). While these insights are no doubt true, and may well be illustrated in the Gog and Magog account, it would be questionable to reduce all events to the nonhistorical truths of which they are an expression. The war itself should be distinguished from that in 17:14 and 19:19 in that it follows the thousand-year reign.

9 The nations which have been gathered by Satan surround the millennial capital and are devoured by fire from heaven. II Esdras, a contemporary Jewish apocalypse, contains a vision which is remarkably parallel. An innumerable multitude of men gather to make war on the Man from the sea. Although seized with fear they dare to fight, but are burned to ashes by a fiery stream which suddenly flows from the mouth of Messiah (II Esdr 13:1-12).

---

[28]Meshech and Tubal are not the original forms of Moscow and Tobolsk! (They are the Hebrew names of the East Anatolian groups known to classical historians as the Moschi and the Tibareni.)

[29]Josephus identifies Magog with the Scythians (*Ant.* i.6.1).

The phrase "the breadth of the earth" is not clear, but in this context it seems to refer metaphorically to a great plain sufficiently large to accommodate the multitude of assailants determined to bring down the citadel of the saints. In Habakkuk 1:6 the same expression is used in connection with the Chaldeans, "that bitter and hasty nation, who march through the breadth of the earth." The camp of the saints is to be understood in the OT sense of the Israelite encampments during their wilderness wanderings (Ex 14:19 f; Num 2:2 ff; Deut 23:14). It is a reminder that while on earth the people of God will always be pilgrims in a foreign land. The camp of the saints is also the beloved city. Morris says that the expression signifies man who has willingly placed himself under the dominion of God (p. 239).[30] The fire that comes down out of heaven[31] is reminiscent of the account in II Kings 1 in which Elijah twice calls down fire from heaven which consumes groups of fifty soldiers with their captains. This incident had apparently impressed the brothers James and John, who during the days of Jesus' earthly ministry wanted to call down fire upon an unreceptive Samaritan village (Lk 9:51–54). The judgment of fire upon Gog (Ezek 38:22) and Magog (Ezek 39:6) is also in mind.

10 The devil does not share the same fate as those he has led to the final assault. They are devoured by fire from heaven, but he is cast into the lake of fire and brimstone. In the preceding chapter the beast and false prophet were cast into the lake of fire (19:20). They are now joined by the arch culprit, the devil himself. Following the great white throne judgment, Death, Hades, and all whose names are not found in the book of life are to be cast into the same fiery grave (20:14–15; cf. 14:10). The torment of the unholy trinity continues unceasingly, "day and night for ever and ever." Ladd interprets this figure as describing in picturesque language a "real fact in the spiritual world: the final and everlasting destruction of the forces of evil which have plagued men since the garden of Eden" (pp. 270–71).

7. FINAL JUDGMENT (20:11–15)

11 *And I saw a great white throne, and him that sat upon it, from whose face the earth and the heaven fled away; and there was found no place for them.*

12 *And I saw the dead, the great and the small, standing before the throne;*

---

[30]Bruce says it is not a walled city but "a community of the true Israel" (p. 662).

[31]The UBS text lists seven variant readings for ἐκ τοῦ οὐρανοῦ involving changes in the preposition and/or addition of (or change to) θεοῦ. The reading of A *pc* Prim is favored but labelled "C" (considerable degree of doubt).

and books were opened: and another book was opened, which is the book of life: and the dead were judged out of the things which were written in the books, according to their works.

13 *And the sea gave up the dead that were in it; and death and Hades gave up the dead that were in them: and they were judged every man according to their works.*

14 *And death and Hades were cast into the lake of fire. This is the second death, even the lake of fire.*

15 *And if any was not found written in the book of life, he was cast into the lake of fire.*

11 We now come to the scene of final judgment. John sees a great white throne and One who sits upon it. A somewhat similar portrayal is found in Daniel 7 where the Ancient of Days takes his seat upon a throne of fiery flames to execute judgment upon the kingdoms of this world. In Revelation the throne is great in size and white or shining[32] in appearance. Its size conveys the grandeur of its authority, and its appearance reflects the presence of the glory of God.

There is some question about the identity of the One who sits upon the throne. The NT teaches generally that judgment has been committed to the Son. John 5:22 specifically says, "The Father judges no one, but has given all judgment to the Son" (cf. II Cor 5:10; II Tim 4:1). Similarly, in *I Enoch,* eschatological judgment is the function of the Messiah ("On that day Mine Elect One shall sit on the throne of glory and shall try their works," 45:3; cf. 51:3; 55:4; 61:8). Yet in the present passage it is apparently God the Father who is judge. Elsewhere in Revelation the One seated upon the throne is the Father (4:2, 9; 5:1, 7, 13; 6:16; 7:10, 15; 19:4; 21:5). It is more natural in the present context to see the Father rather than the Son in the role of judge.[33] The ease with which the NT speaks of the judgment seat of Christ (II Cor 5:10) and the judgment seat of God (Rom 14:10) implies a unity which makes unnecessary any quibbling over exact assignment of functions. In his gospel John records the statement of Jesus, "I and the Father are one" (Jn 10:20).

Earth and heaven flee away before the awesome grandeur of God seated upon the throne of judgment. This action may be only poetic imagery expressing the fear of the corruptible in the presence of God, although it may be understood more literally as the dissolution of the universe as we

---

[32] λευκός may mean "bright, gleaming" (see Mt 17:2). *I Enoch* 18:8 says that a certain mountain "reached to heaven like the throne of God, of alabaster" (a fine-textured stone, white and translucent).

[33] II Esdr expresses the traditional view of Judaism that God alone will bring about the consummation (6:1–10; 7:33 ff).

know it in preparation for the new heaven and new earth which will shortly appear (21:1).[34] Isaiah 51:6 spoke of a time when the heavens would vanish like a garment. Jesus contrasted the permanency of his words to the transitoriness of heaven and earth (Mt 24:35). Peter indicates that it is by fire that the heaven and earth are to be dissolved (II Pet 3:10–12). Some feel that we are dealing with two variant traditions concerning the end of the physical universe. Whether it simply passes away or is melted by fire is of minor import. The central truth is that God is in charge and will execute a just sentence upon all that has fallen under the control of evil. In its flight from the presence of God no place is found for the terrified universe. One is reminded of the Psalmist's query, "Whither shall I go from thy Spirit? Or whither shall I flee from thy presence?" (Ps 139:7). There is no place, for God is everywhere.

12 Before the great white throne stand the dead, both great and small. These are the "rest of the dead" who were resurrected at the close of the thousand-year period (vs. 5). If the first resurrection is limited to actual martyrs, then the judgment of verses 11–15 involves both believer and impenitent. If the second resurrection is of the wicked only, then the judgment is of those who will in fact be consigned to the lake of fire. Reference to the book of life as part of the final testimony suggests a general judgment of all mankind (excluding the martyrs who had already entered into their reward). There is no significance in the change from "small and great" (11:18; 13:16; 19:5, 18) to "great and small" in verse 12. The point is that no one is so important as to be immune from judgment and no one is so unimportant as to make judgment inappropriate.

The great white throne judgment is not arbitrary but based upon the evidence written by the life of every man.[35] Books are opened, and the dead are judged on the basis of their works as recorded therein. The teaching of judgment by works runs throughout both the OT and the NT. Psalm 62:12 gives expression to the commonly accepted principle that God requites a man according to his work. In Jeremiah 17:10 God says, "I the Lord search the mind and try the heart to give to every man according to his ways, according to the fruit of his doings." The same principle is taught in the NT. Paul writes that God "will render to every man according to his works" (Rom 2:6), and Peter reminds his readers that God "judges each

---

[34]Beasley-Murray says that the language here (and in 6:1 ff—which is parallel if one subscribes to a view of recapitulation) does not imply the destruction of the physical universe but belongs to the traditional language of cosmic signs, and is here employed to identify the parousia and expose the terror of messianic judgments (pp. 300–1).

[35]Hough notes that literature treats fully the motif of character becoming destiny and cites Dante's *Divine Comedy* in which "men are seen permanently fastened to the central meaning which they have given to their lives" (*IB*, IV, p. 525).

one impartially according to his deeds" (I Pet 1:17). The issue is not salvation by works but works as the irrefutable evidence of a man's actual relationship with God. Man is saved by faith, but faith is inevitably revealed by the works it produces.

In addition to the record of men's deeds[36] there is another book to be opened, the book of life. The idea of a divine register is an ancient one. Isaiah speaks of those who had been recorded for life in Jerusalem (Isa 4:3). Many years before, Moses had pleaded with God to blot him out of his book (a register of those included within the theocratic community) rather than to withhold forgiveness from those who had sinned (cf. Dan 12:1; Mal 3:6; Rev 3:5; 17:8; 21:27). The relationship between the record of men's deeds and the book of life is not clear. Farrer (p. 210) suggests that those whose names are missing from the citizen-list have access to the "books of deeds" as a last assessment of their claim to remain. The list in its final or revised state would then admit to the New Jerusalem immediately descending from heaven (21:2). In any case, judgment proceeds on the evidence supplied both by the record of deeds and the book of life. This seems to support a general judgment rather than one restricted to the wicked dead.

13 It is a bit pedantic to argue that verse 13 is out of sequence since resurrection (vs. 13) must precede judgment (vs. 12). John mentions the sea, death, and Hades all giving up their dead to indicate and emphasize the universal scope of judgment. The sea is specifically mentioned to show that no one—not even those whose bodies had gone unburied because lost at sea—[37] would escape resurrection and judgment.[38] In 6:8 Death and Hades appeared as the rider of the pale horse and his inseparable companion. In 1:18 they designate the regions of the underworld whose keys are in the possession of the glorified Christ. Here (20:13) they appear as the realm of the dead, and in the following verse they personify all that remains of the effects of wickedness in the world. In Acts 2:27, 31 Hades denotes the place of all souls during the intermediate state, but elsewhere (such as in Lk 16:23) it is the abode of the unrighteous dead. This dual concept of Hades existed within later Judaism and carried over into NT thought (Jeremias, *TDNT*, I, pp. 146–49). Thus nothing definitive can be

[36]In Dan 7:10 the judgment of the court apparently rests upon the evidence of books which were opened. *I Enoch* 90:20; *II Bar.* 24:1; and II Esdr 6:20 all speak of books in which the deeds of men are recorded for judgment.
[37]*I Enoch* 61:5 speaks of the elect "who have been devoured by the fish of the sea."
[38]Charles holds that an original τὰ ταμεῖα was deliberately changed into ἡ θάλασσα in order to introduce the idea of a physical resurrection. The earlier text taught a resurrection of persons, not dead bodies (II, p. 196). Kiddle calls this emendation "both arbitrary and illogical" (p. 407).

determined from the term itself about the nature of those resurrected. A general resurrection of all except martyrs seems most plausible.

14–15   Death and Hades are now cast into the lake of fire[39] where the beast, the false prophet (19:10), and the devil (20:10) are already in torment. In I Corinthians 15:26 death is the last enemy to be destroyed (cf. I Cor 15:54–55). Coupled with Hades (that "grim receptacle of death's prey"; Moffatt, p. 477), it symbolizes the effects of sin and wickedness that entered the world through the sin of the first man (Rom 5:12). In a great psalm of thanksgiving the prophet Isaiah declares that God "will swallow up death for ever" (Isa 25:8). The last vestige of sin's unlawful hegemony is cast into the lake of fire. The lake of fire indicates not only the stern punishment awaiting the enemies of righteousness but also their full and final defeat. It is the second death, that is, the destiny of those whose temporary resurrection results only in a return to death and its punishment. Alford writes, "As there is a second and higher life, so there is also a second and deeper death. And as after that life there is no more death (ch. xxi. 4), so after that death there is no more life" (pp. 735–36).

In Matthew 25:41 Jesus indicated that the eternal fire was prepared for the devil and his angels. In the final judgment all whose names do not appear in the book of life will share their fate. The grim simplicity of the narrative stands in contrast with the lurid descriptions found in Jewish apocalypticism. In *I Enoch* 48:9 the wicked are given over into the hands of the elect in whose presence they burn like straw in the fire and sink like lead in water. Later in *I Enoch* the apostates burn in a fiery abyss in full view of Jerusalem (90:26).

---

[39]Beasley-Murray says that the lake of fire does not signify annihilation, but "torturous existence in the society of evil in opposition to life in the society of God" (p. 304). Although this statement would seem to indicate a concurrence with the conviction of some exegetes (such as Rissi, *Time and History*, pp. 123 ff, and *The Future of the World*, pp. 36 ff, 67 ff) that John anticipated that those who had rejected the rule of God would ultimately make it into the New Jerusalem, he adds, "Candour compels us to state that John has given no clear indication of any such teaching" (*loc. cit.*).

CHAPTER 21

X. THE NEW HEAVEN AND THE NEW EARTH (21:1–22:5)

In the closing chapters of Isaiah God promised that he would "create new heavens and a new earth" (Isa 65:17) which would remain before him forever (Isa 66:22). The fulfillment of this promise begins to unfold in John's vision of the New Jerusalem coming down out of heaven to take its place upon a renewed earth. It comprises the last major unit of the Apocalypse (21:1–22:5). Ladd emphasizes that Biblical thought—in contrast to Greek dualism in which salvation consists of the flight of the soul from the earthly and transitory to the spiritual and eternal—"always places man on a redeemed earth, not in a heavenly realm removed from earthly existence" (p. 275; cf. Glasson, p. 115).

1. THE NEW CREATION (21:1–8)

1 *And I saw a new heaven and a new earth: for the first heaven and the first earth are passed away; and the sea is no more.*

2 *And I saw the holy city, new Jerusalem, coming down out of heaven from God, made ready as a bride adorned for her husband.*

3 *And I heard a great voice out of the throne saying, Behold, the tabernacle of God is with men, and he shall dwell with them, and they shall be his peoples, and God himself shall be with them,* and be *their God:*

4 *and he shall wipe away every tear from their eyes; and death shall be no more; neither shall there be mourning, nor crying, nor pain, any more: the first things are passed away.*

5 *And he that sitteth on the throne said, Behold, I make all things new. And he saith, Write: for these words are faithful and true.*

6 *And he said unto me, They are come to pass. I am the Alpha and the Omega, the beginning and the end. I will give unto him that is athirst of the fountain of the water of life freely.*

7 *He that overcometh shall inherit these things; and I will be his God, and he shall be my son.*

8 *But for the fearful, and unbelieving, and abominable, and murderers, and fornicators, and sorcerers, and idolaters, and all liars, their part shall be in the lake that burneth with fire and brimstone; which is the second death.*

1 In John's vision the first heaven and earth are replaced by a new heaven and a new earth. The renovation of the old order is a concept which belongs to the common stock of apocalyptic tradition. In *I Enoch* 45:4–5 the heaven and earth are to be transformed as a place for the elect (72:1; 91:16). II Esdras 7:75 speaks of a future time when God shall "renew the creation" (cf. *II Bar.* 32:6). In II Peter 3:10–13 we learn that following a great conflagration in which the heavens are to be dissolved and the earth is to melt with fire, there will be new heavens and a new earth in which righteousness will dwell. Interpreters understand these figures with varying degrees of literalness. Paul spoke of the whole creation groaning in travail while it waits with eager longing its emancipation from decay (Rom 8:19–22). Probably the new order of things is not to be thought of primarily as a physical transformation.[1] The entire presentation stretches the limits of human vocabulary and thought to emphasize the glorious reality of God dwelling among his people. As the new covenant is superior to and replaces the old (Heb 8:7–13), so the new heaven and earth provide a setting for the new and eternal state.[2]

In the new earth there is to be no more sea. Various explanations are offered to account for this omission. The suggestion that it reflects the dread of the sea which was felt by ancient peoples[3] is not especially persuasive. To discover a mythological connection with the Babylonian legend of Tiamat, the ancient dragon of chaos who struggles with Marduk, the god of order, is to read too much into what could be at best only a passing reference. Swete is closer to the truth when he says that the sea disappears because "in the mind of the writer it is associated with ideas

---

[1] Commentators often discuss whether the new order of things is to be a renovation of the old or a distinctly new creation. Neither the language employed nor rabbinic commentary on relevant passages such as Isa 65:17 ff will supply a definite answer. Beasley-Murray writes, "We cannot be sure how he viewed the new heaven and new earth, but the context of this statement suggests that his real concern is not with physical geography, but to describe a context of life for God's people which accords with the great and glorious purpose God has in mind for them" (p. 308).

[2] Swete notes that here καινός, as the opposite of παλαιός, "suggests fresh life rising from the decay and wreck of the old world" (p. 275). This is the παλιγγενεσία, the new world, of which Jesus speaks in Mt 19:28.

[3] Egyptians apparently regarded the sea, not as a part of nature, but as alien and hostile (see Plutarch, *De Isid.* 7 f, 32).

which are at variance with the character of the New Creation'' (p. 275). Isaiah compares the wicked to the tossing sea which cannot rest, whose waters toss up mire and dirt (Isa 57:20). It was out of the sea that the beast who blasphemed God and made war on the saints had arisen (Rev 13:1, 6–7). According to the *Assumption of Moses,* when God shall appear in the last days to punish the Gentiles, ''The sea shall retire into the abyss'' (10:6).[4]

2 John's vision includes not only a new heaven and earth but a New Jerusalem as well. The concept of a New Jerusalem unveiled at the advent of the Messiah is common in Jewish apocalyptic. Apparently, the earliest reference is that in the *Testament of Dan* (late second century BC) which pictures the New Jerusalem as a place in which the saints rejoice and enjoy the glory of God forever (5:12). *II Baruch* 32:2–4 says that it is to be ''renewed in glory, and perfected for evermore.'' The New Jerusalem is more than the old rebuilt. When ''the city that now is invisible [shall] appear'' (II Esdr 7:26), it will be constructed according to a heavenly pattern (II Esdr 10:49).[5] In the NT it is ''the Jerusalem above'' (Gal 4:26) whose ''builder and maker is God'' (Heb 11:10; cf. 12:22; 13:14; Phil 3:20). Those who remain faithful in the church in Philadelphia are to be inscribed with the name of ''the new Jerusalem which comes down from my God out of heaven'' (Rev 3:12).

Some difference of opinion exists as to whether the New Jerusalem in John's vision should be taken as an actual city[6] or as a symbol of the church in its perfected and eternal state.[7] The vision itself takes the form of a magnificent city descending from heaven. It symbolizes the eternal felicity of all who follow the Lamb. Kiddle writes that the heart of the symbol is a community of men: ''It is a city which is a family. The ideal of perfect community, unrealizable on earth because of the curse of sin which vitiated the first creation, is now embodied in the redeemed from all nations'' (pp. 415–16). Hunter writes, ''The consummation of the Christian hope is supremely social. It is no 'flight of the alone to the Alone' but life in the redeemed community of heaven.''[8] The holy city (cf. Isa 52:1; Mt 4:5) is

---

[4]In the *Sibylline Oracles* (5:158–59) a great star falls from heaven and burns up the deep sea. Elsewhere in apocalyptic literature the waters dry up at the judgment (*Test. Levi* 4:1; cf. *Sib. Or.* 5:447).

[5]Cf. *II Bar.* 4:2–6; II Esdr 13:36; *I Enoch* 90:28–29.

[6]For example, Walvoord, p. 313. Ladd makes it the dwelling place of departed saints between death and resurrection which in the consummation descends from heaven to settle permanently in the new earth (p. 276).

[7]For example, Lilje (p. 259), who takes it as the church universal, the Biblical counterpart of the political unity of the Roman Empire.

[8]*Probing the New Testament,* p. 156.

of heavenly origin. It comes down from[9] God, that is to say, the church is not a voluntary organization created by man but a fellowship initiated and given by God (cf. Mt 16:18).

Mention should be made of Charles' rather extensive rearrangement of the text of chapters 20–22. In a section entitled "XX.4–XXII. The Text Incoherent and Self-Contradictory as it Stands" (II, pp. 144–54), Charles conjectures that John died when he had completed his text up through 20:3. The remaining materials were for the most part ready in a series of independent documents which a faithful but unintelligent disciple placed in the order he thought to be correct. In reality the material contains two distinct and separate visions of two different heavenly cities. The first is the millennial capital of the Messiah's kingdom (21:9–22:2, 14–15, 17), which should have followed immediately after 20:3. The second (21:1–4c; 22:3–5) is an eternal city. Few commentators have followed Charles' reconstruction, although Preston and Hanson hold that "some such theory becomes almost essential" (p. 129).[10]

The New Jerusalem descends from heaven adorned as a bride for her husband. The adornment is given in detail in verses 11–21. In 19:7 the people of God were presented as a bride; here the same figure is used of the place of their abode, the heavenly Jerusalem. The contrast between the earthly city as harlot and the heavenly city as bride is obvious. Beasley-Murray notes that "Revelation as a whole may be characterized as *A Tale of Two Cities*, with the sub-title, *The Harlot and the Bride*" (p. 315).

3 A great voice is heard out of the throne,[11] announcing the fulfillment of a basic theme that runs throughout the OT. It is clearly stated in the Holiness Code of Leviticus 26, "I will make my abode with you . . . and will be your God, and you shall be my people" (Lev 26:11–12; cf. Jer 31:33; Ezek 37:27; Zech 8:8). The voice from heaven declares that the tabernacle of God is with men and that he shall dwell with them. The Greek word for tabernacle (*skēnē*) is closely related to the Hebrew *Shekinah*,[12] which was used to denote the presence and glory of God. In the wilderness wanderings the tabernacle or tent was a symbol of the abiding presence of God in the midst of his people. In the Fourth Gospel, John writes that the Word became flesh and *tabernacled (eskēnōsen)* among men so that they

---

[9]Note: it is ἐκ τοῦ οὐρανοῦ and ἀπὸ τοῦ θεοῦ.

[10]On pp. 129–33 Preston and Hanson argue that the millennial city is a picture of the church militant as she should be, and the eternal city is a picture of the church as she will be when time and space are no more.

[11]A number of MSS (**P 046 051** 82 1006 1611 2059s 2329 *pl g* sy TR) read οὐρανοῦ, an assimilation to ἐκ τοῦ οὐρανοῦ of vs. 2.

[12]Although they belong to unrelated linguistic families, the consonants are the same, and σκηνή often translates the Hebrew מִשְׁכָּן in the LXX.

beheld his glory, glory as of the only Son from the Father (Jn 1:14). When the Seer writes that the tabernacle of God is with men, he is saying that God in his glorious presence has come to dwell with man. The metaphor does not suggest a temporary dwelling. From this point on God remains with his people throughout eternity.

It is interesting that most recent translations have the plural, peoples ("they shall be his peoples"), rather than the singular, people.[13] Apparently, John modified the traditional concept (Jer 7:23; 30:22; Hos 2:23) and substituted a reference to the many peoples of redeemed humanity. Jesus had spoken of "other sheep, that are not of this fold" which must become part of the one flock (Jn 10:16). It is with the redeemed peoples of all races and nationalities that God will dwell in glory. God himself will be with them, and he will be their God.[14] Erdman writes, "It is the presence of God, and fellowship with him, which forms the essential feature of the age to come" (p. 167).

4 John now describes the benefits that come to God's people when he takes up his eternal abode in their midst. Abolished forever are the debilitating effects of sin. Sorrow, death, mourning, and pain are all part of the "first things" which are now past and gone. They belong to a previous order which has now become history. Eternal blessedness is couched in negation because the new and glorious order is more easily pictured in terms of what it replaces than by an attempt to describe what is largely inconceivable in our present state.

In Isaiah's portrayal of Zion restored, the ransomed of the Lord return "with singing; everlasting joy shall be upon their heads; they shall obtain joy and gladness, and sorrow and sighing shall flee away" (Isa 35:10; cf. 65:19). John employs much the same language in writing of the final restoration—God "shall wipe away every tear from their eyes," and there shall be no more death, mourning, crying, or pain (cf. Rev 7:16–17). The tears are not tears of remorse shed in heaven for failures on earth, but tears of suffering shed on earth as a result of faithfulness to Christ (Walvoord, p. 315). Death had entered the world as a consequence of man's sin (Gen 3; Rom 5:12), and man not only became subject to death (Heb 9:27) but also was enslaved by the fear of death (Heb 2:15). In an eschatological section of the Isaiah Apocalypse God is said to "swallow up death for

---

[13]Metzger confesses it is extremely difficult to decide between λαοί and λαός. Chiefly on the basis of slightly superior manuscript evidence (א A 1 2059s 2329 *pm* Ir TR), the committee preferred λαοί (*TCGNT,* p. 765).

[14]The *ASV* follows those MSS which add θεὸς αὐτῶν (P 051 1006 [1611] 1854 2060 *al* vg sy Ir TR) or αὐτῶν θεός (A 2329 *pc*) and translates "and be their God." The UBS text follows A (αὐτῶν θεός) but encloses the words within square brackets and indicates that a very high degree of doubt exists.

ever'' (Isa 25:8). Paul echoes the theme in his triumphant announcement, "Death is swallowed up in victory" (I Cor 15:54). Now at last prophetic declaration receives its fulfillment, and death exists no longer.[15] With the extinction of death, grief and affliction disappear as well. The old order [16] marred by sin and its accompanying distress gives way to the new and perfect order of eternal blessedness.[17]

5 The silence of God in Revelation[18] is broken by his declaration, "Behold, I make all things new." The throne upon which God sits (cf. 4:2, 9; 5:1, 7; 6:16; 7:10, 15; 19:14) symbolizes his sovereignty and majesty. It is from this position of awesome power that he announces his intention of creating the new order. The renovation of the universe was a familiar concept in apocalyptic literature. *Jubilees* 1:29 spoke of a "new creation when the heavens and the earth shall be renewed" (cf. *I Enoch* 91:16; *II Bar*. 57:2; 44:12; II Esdr 7:75; etc.). Through the prophet Isaiah God had promised, "For behold, I create new heavens and a new earth; and the former things shall not be remembered or come into mind" (Isa 65:17). The transformation which Paul saw taking place in the lives of believers (II Cor 3:18; 4:16–18; 5:16–17) will have its counterpart on a cosmic scale when a totally new order will replace the old order marred by sin.

Most commentators hold that the command to write comes from an angel, as in 14:13 and 19:9. The interpretation is based primarily on the changes of verb tense in verses 5 and 6 ("said . . . saith . . . said"). Since the first and third utterances are from God, why would the second be altered if the speaker remained the same? There is no particular reason, however, why the second verb should not be altered for stylistic reasons and God be the one who speaks throughout. In 1:19 the glorified Christ had also instructed John to write. The content of what he is to write is contained in the vision of eternal blessedness given in verses 1–5. He is to write it because[19] the revelation is reliable and genuine.

6 The descent of the New Jerusalem and all the attendant bless-

---

[15]For the contemporary view of Jewish apocalypticism about the coming destruction of death see *II Enoch* 65:10; II Esdr 8:53; *II Bar*. 21:23.

[16]τὰ πρῶτα. Metzger calls attention to the absurd reading of the original version of Sinaiticus (τὰ πρόβατα) as "an example of what nonsense scribes can produce" (*TCGNT*, p. 766, n. 1). The final clause of vs. 4 is made causal by the MSS which read ὅτι before τὰ πρῶτα. The evidence for omission is strong (**A P 051** 1006 1611 2329 *al*), but both Nestle (25th ed.) and the UBS text include it (see Metzger, *loc. cit.*).

[17]Cf. Isa 42:9; II Cor 5:17 for changes which prefigure this final and glorious transformation.

[18]God had spoken in 1:8 and probably in 16:1, 17 as well. Farrer holds that 21:5 is not an utterance by God which John actually heard, but a report of what God had formerly said (pp. 212–13).

[19]ὅτι does not introduce the following clause (as direct discourse) but supplies the reason why John is to write as directed.

ings may now be considered as having taken place.[20] God says, "They are come to pass" (*AV*, "It is done"). There is no uncertainty about the eternal felicity of those who hold fast in the trial of faith because from God's vantage point the future is determined. He is not subject to the vagrancies of time because time itself is encompassed by his eternal nature. He is the Alpha and the Omega (the first and last letters of the Greek alphabet), the beginning and the end (cf. 1:8; 22:13 and Isa 44:6; 48:12). That God is the beginning refers not only to the fact that he was first in point of time (cf Jn 1:1, *NEB*, "When all things began, the Word already was"), but also that he is the source and origin of all things. He is the end in the sense that he constitutes their goal or aim (as in I Tim 1:5; Rom 10:4). As such he gives "the water of life freely" to all who thirst. Scripture often employs the figure of thirst to depict the desire of the soul for God. "As a hart longs for flowing streams, so longs my soul for thee, O God," sang the Psalmist (Ps 42:1; cf. 36:9; 63:1; Isa 55:1). God is a fountain of living water (Jer 2:13; cf. Ps 36:9) that assuages thirst and wells up into eternal life (Jn 4:14). In the arid climate of Palestine a spring of cool water would be a vivid symbol of refreshment and satisfaction.

7 It is the overcomer who is to inherit these blessings of the eternal state. In the letters to the seven churches we learned that the overcomer will eat of the tree of life (2:7), not be hurt by the second death (2:11), be given hidden manna and a white stone (2:17), receive power over the nations (2:26), not have his name blotted from the book of life (3:5), be a pillar in the temple of God (3:12), and sit with Christ on his throne (3:21). All this is the inheritance of those who remain constant in their faith during the period of final testing.

With Abraham God established a covenant "to be God to you and to your descendants after you" (Gen 17:7). To David he promised, concerning Solomon, "I will be his father, and he shall be my son" (II Sam 7:14). This age-old covenant is fulfilled to all who are Abraham's heirs by faith (Gal 3:29). God declares that it is the overcomer who shall be his son and to whom he will be God. Those who deny Christ and are enticed by the allurements of the harlot to follow the beast have no inheritance in the family of God. The thirst for God mentioned in verse 6 is satisfied only by the reality of divine sonship. Caird writes that before John "attempts to summon up the full resources of language to depict what is beyond language and thought, he leaves us with the first indelible impression that heaven is belonging to the family of God" (p. 267).

---

[20]Hence the perfect, γέγοναν : "they are come to pass."

8 In contrast to the overcomers are all those who have cowered in the face of persecution and joined the company of the reprobate. Leading the retreat are the cowardly,[21] who in the last resort choose personal safety over faithfulness to Christ. They are the rootless ones of the Parable of the Sower who "when tribulation or persecution arises on account of the word, immediately [fall] away" (Mt 13:21). It is not a natural timidity that makes them what they are, but a lack of genuine commitment which provides the incentive for continuing in spite of persecution. They choose to forget the admonition of Jesus that "whoever would save his life will lose it" (Mk 8:35). The unbelieving are not the secular pagan world (as in I Cor 6:6; 7:12 ff; 10:27; 14:22 ff) but believers who have denied their faith under pressure. In fact, all eight classes of people mentioned in the verse may refer to professing believers who have apostatized (although after the second or third class they apply to pagans as well). Kiddle says, "To swerve into disloyalty through cowardice or lack of trust was . . . to align oneself for ever with the enemies of God" (p. 422). The "abominable" are those who have joined in the detestable and unholy ritual of emperor worship. They are successors to the idolatrous Israelites who "consecrated themselves to Baal, and became detestable[22] like the thing they loved" (Hos 9:10; cf. Ex 5:21; Titus 1:16; Rev 17:4 ff). They have become defiled by the impurities of the imperial cult. "Murderers" may refer to those committing acts of homicide under the tyranny of the beast (13:15). "Fornicators"[23] are those who practice sexual immorality, and "sorcerers" are those involved with magic arts (cf. Acts 19:19). "Idolaters" are mentioned because the practice had become the major vice of paganism. The inclusion of "liars" is appropriate in view of John's emphasis on truth (cf. I Jn 2:21–22; 3:19; 4:6). Throughout Revelation deviation from truth has been stigmatized (2:2; 3:9; 14:5; 21:27; 22:15). The lot of all apostates and pagans is to be cast into the lake that burns with fire and brimstone (cf. 20:15).

2. THE NEW JERUSALEM (21:9–22:5)

> 9 *And there came one of the seven angels who had the seven bowls, who were laden with the seven last plagues; and he spake with me, saying, Come hither, I will show thee the bride, the wife of the Lamb.*

---

[21]The *ASV* translation, "fearful," for δειλός is insufficiently specific. The "cowardly" are those who "fear the threats of the beast more than they trust the love of Christ" (Beasley-Murray, p. 314).

[22]ἐβδελυγμένοι, LXX.

[23]In earlier writers πόρνος designated a male prostitute (BAG cite Aristophanes and Xenophon, both fourth century BC; p. 700), but the word had developed a more general meaning by NT times.

10 *And he carried me away in the Spirit to a mountain great and high, and showed me the holy city Jerusalem, coming down out of heaven from God,*

11 *having the glory of God: her light was like unto a stone most precious, as it were a jasper stone, clear as crystal:*

12 *having a wall great and high; having twelve gates, and at the gates twelve angels; and names written thereon, which are* the names *of the twelve tribes of the children of Israel:*

13 *on the east were three gates; and on the north three gates; and on the south three gates; and on the west three gates.*

14 *And the wall of the city had twelve foundations, and on them twelve names of the twelve apostles of the Lamb.*

15 *And he that spake with me had for a measure a golden reed to measure the city, and the gates thereof, and the wall thereof.*

16 *And the city lieth foursquare, and the length thereof is as great as the breadth: and he measured the city with the reed, twelve thousand furlongs: the length and the breadth and the height thereof are equal.*

17 *And he measured the wall thereof, a hundred and forty and four cubits,* according to *the measure of a man, that is, of an angel.*

18 *And the building of the wall thereof was jasper: and the city was pure gold, like unto pure glass.*

19 *The foundations of the wall of the city were adorned with all manner of precious stones. The first foundation was jasper; the second, sapphire; the third, chalcedony; the fourth, emerald;*

20 *the fifth, sardonyx; the sixth, sardius; the seventh, chrysolite; the eighth, beryl; the ninth, topaz; the tenth, chrysoprase; the eleventh, jacinth; the twelfth, amethyst.*

21 *And the twelve gates were twelve pearls; each one of the several gates was of one pearl: and the street of the city was pure gold, as it were transparent glass.*

22 *And I saw no temple therein: for the Lord God the Almighty, and the Lamb, are the temple thereof.*

23 *And the city hath no need of the sun, neither of the moon, to shine upon it: for the glory of God did lighten it, and the lamp thereof* is *the Lamb.*

24 *And the nations shall walk amidst the light thereof: and the kings of the earth bring their glory into it.*

25 *And the gates thereof shall in no wise be shut by day (for there shall be no night there):*

26 *and they shall bring the glory and the honor of the nations into it:*

27 *and there shall in no wise enter into it anything unclean, or he that maketh an abomination and a lie: but only they that are written in the Lamb's book of life.*

1 *And he showed me a river of water of life, bright as crystal, proceeding out of the throne of God and of the Lamb,*

2 *in the midst of the street thereof. And on this side of the river and on that*

was the tree of life, bearing twelve manner of *fruits, yielding its fruit every month: and the leaves of the tree were for the healing of the nations.*

3 *And there shall be no curse any more: and the throne of God and of the Lamb shall be therein: and his servants shall serve him;*

4 *and they shall see his face; and his name* shall be *on their foreheads.*

5 *And there shall be night no more; and they need no light of lamp, neither light of sun; for the Lord God shall give them light: and they shall reign for ever and ever.*

9 One of the seven angels who carried out the seven last plagues (chap. 16) now commands[24] the Seer to come and see the bride, the wife of the Lamb. The angel is undoubtedly the one who in 17:1 summoned John to witness the judgment of the great harlot. This seems to be the purpose of the identical introductions.[25] It also draws attention to the contrast between the great harlot (the wicked city Babylon) and the bride of the Lamb (the holy city Jerusalem). One is of the earth, symbolizing the unbridled passion and evil of man, and the other descends from heaven, the epitome of all that is pure and beautiful. It is perhaps overly subtle to find in the different messages delivered by the angel an indication that God's servants do not choose their roles but without question fulfill their mission whether it involves doom or bliss (so Barclay, II, pp. 266–67). Likewise it is a bit pedantic to balk at the designation of God's people as both bride and wife of the Lamb.[26] As bride the church is pure and lovely, and as wife she enjoys the intimacy of the Lamb. To question whether or not the marriage has taken place at this point is to miss the significance of the metaphors.[27] As we approach the close of the Apocalypse, the figure of the Lamb becomes increasingly prominent. In the next twenty-two verses he is mentioned seven times.

10 Verses 10–14 in the Greek text comprise one compound sentence which describes the New Jerusalem coming down from heaven. In a vision the angel transports John to a great, high mountain to watch the descent. The mountain is neither a literal mountain nor merely a symbol of that "elevation of spirit . . . necessary for the one who would see the

---

[24] δεῦρο is an adverb commonly used as an imperative (cf. Mt 19:21; Jn 11:43; Acts 7:3).
[25] The only difference in the first twenty words is the insertion of an explanatory clause in 21:9 (τῶν γεμόντων . . . ἐσχάτων). The antecedent of γεμόντων is probably φιάλας (1 1006 *al* TR read γεμούσας) rather than ἀγγέλων, although this appears to be a grammatical error. According to Beckwith the error results from the prominence of τῶν ἑπτὰ . . . ἐχόντων (p. 756).
[26] See the critical apparatus in Nestle for variations in the dual designation.
[27] For that matter, γυνή may refer to any adult female (Mt 9:20; I Tim 2:11) and in some contexts may mean bride (Gen 29:21, LXX; Mt 1:20).

heavenly vision" (Swete, p. 284). It is an essential part of the visionary experience. It is an appropriate vantage point from which to view the descent of the eternal order. The idea of spiritual exaltation has already been emphasized by the expression "in the Spirit" (cf. 1:10; 4:2; 17:3). The mountain "existed" in John's vision of eternal realities. When taken into the wilderness in the Spirit John had seen the wicked Babylon (17:3), but it is from a high mountain that he views the New Jerusalem. In Jewish thought mountains have always played a significant role. Moses' historical encounter with God on Mt. Sinai marked the origin of the Jewish nation (Ex 19 ff). Ezekiel's great vision of the restored temple and land was given to him "upon a very high mountain" (Ezek 40:1–2). Enoch portrays one of seven magnificent mountains excelling the others in height and beauty as the throne of God (*I Enoch* 24–25).

The holy city descending from God out of heaven should be understood as a "real event" within the visionary experience. That in 21:2 there is a similar reference does not mean that there are two descents. The expression is more than a convenient metaphor for God's continuing entrance into our earthly existence. The descent is an announcement in visionary terms of a future event which will usher in the eternal state. That the city comes down from God means that the eternal blessedness is not an achievement of man but a gift from God.

11 As the holy city descends from heaven, it glitters with a shimmering radiance[28] which manifests the presence and glory of God. It is the eternal fulfillment of God's promise to captive Israel that in the restoration the glory of the Lord will be upon them and he will be their everlasting light (Isa 60:1, 2, 19). In apocalyptic literature the glory of God is a designation of his presence (Ezek 43:5). The radiance of the city is likened to a glittering gem. "Clear as crystal" is a somewhat unfortunate translation because it suggests transparency. In antiquity the designation jasper was used for any opaque precious stone. The point of comparison is the brilliance and sparkle[29] of the gem. The reference could be to the diamond.

12–13 The city is surrounded by a great wall with twelve gates,[30] which are guarded by twelve angels. On the gates are inscribed the names of the twelve tribes of Israel. The mention of a wall is not to suggest the

---

[28] φωστήρ properly means "a light-giving body," but may also indicate "splendor or radiance." In the NT it is found elsewhere only in Phil 2:15.

[29] BAG ask if perhaps the older meaning of κρύσταλλος, "ice," is not to be preferred. A precious stone would shimmer like a sheet of ice (p. 455).

[30] πυλών properly denotes a gateway and should be distinguished from the actual gate (ἡ πυλή) (Jeremias in *TDNT*, VI, p. 921). Since names cannot be inscribed upon an opening, the designation here refers either to the gate itself or the tower which rises above the city wall over the gateway.

necessity of security precautions in the eternal state. Nor does it imply that Christians are a people set apart (although in one important sense this is certainly true; cf. Titus 2:14). The wall is simply part of the description of an ideal city as conceived by ancient peoples accustomed to the security of strong outer walls.[31]

The twelve gates are distributed three on each side of the city. In Ezekiel 48:30–34 the twelve gates of the New Jerusalem are named after the twelve tribes of Israel.[32] Through these gates the tribes go out to their allotted land. In John's vision the gates which bear the names of the twelve tribes are entrances for all the peoples of the earth whose names are written in the Lamb's book of life (Rev 21:24–27). Twelve gates symbolize abundant entrance. Reference to twelve tribes emphasizes the continuity of the NT church with God's people of OT times. John chooses to list the sides of the city in the order of east, north, south, west (vs. 13), although Ezekiel, who seems to be his model, places north before east.[33] Caird suggests that John chooses "the most erratic" order to discourage any interest his readers might have in the "zodiacal cycle" (p. 272).[34] The twelve angels are celestial gatekeepers and may reflect the Isaianic picture of watchmen upon the walls of Jerusalem (Isa 62:6). They belong to the concept of an ideal city.

14 The wall of the city, evenly divided by twelve gates, rests on twelve foundations upon which are inscribed the names of the twelve apostles of the Lamb. "Twelve apostles" is obviously a corporate reference to the disciple group without specific attention to Judas.[35] In Ephesians 2:20 Paul teaches that the household of God is built upon the foundation of the apostles and prophets. The church in a historical sense rests upon the apostles and prophets, that is, upon the faith and labors of those who first proclaimed the gospel message. The juxtaposition of the twelve tribes and the twelve apostles shows the unity of ancient Israel and the NT church.

15 Verses 15–17 describe the measuring of the heavenly city. In chapter 11 it was John who was told to measure the temple of God, its altar, and those that worship there (11:1). The holy city, however, is to be measured by the angel (cf. 21:9), who appropriately uses a reed or staff of

---

[31]For the wall as a metaphor of security see Isa 26:1; Zech 2:5.

[32]Levi is assigned a gate, and Ephraim and Manasseh are combined in Joseph.

[33]In the directions for encampment the order is east, south, west, north (Num 2). John's order follows that of the measuring of the temple area in Ezek 42:16–20.

[34]A 1 *pc* change the order of νότου and δυσμῶν, which would reverse the entire direction of the zodiac (E N W S).

[35]In I Cor 15:5 the twelve are only eleven. Cf. Jn 20:24.

gold.[36] The reed was a measure slightly more than ten feet in length. This part of the vision may have been suggested by the elaborate measuring described in Ezekiel 40–41 (cf. Zech 2:1–5). The measuring in chapter 11 was to insure protection; here it serves to portray the enormous size and perfect symmetry of the eternal dwelling place of the faithful.[37]

16 The city that appears to John is said to be foursquare. This could mean that it was laid out in a square pattern,[38] but more likely it refers to a three-dimensional form—a cube whose length, breadth, and height are all equal. Not only are the terms in which the city is described most naturally interpreted as a cube, but the Greek word itself is used of huge rocks in the shape of a cube and of stones appropriate for building blocks.[39] Some have imagined the city to be in the form of a pyramid[40]— this would allow the river of life to flow down from the throne of God— but all such concrete visualizations obscure the symbolic meaning of the cube-shaped city. This particular shape would immediately remind the Jewish reader of the inner sanctuary of the temple (a perfect cube, each dimension being twenty cubits; I Kgs 6:20), the place of divine presence. A city foursquare would be the place where God has taken up residence with his people.

The angel measured the city with his golden reed and found it to be 12,000 furlongs.[41] Some writers take this distance to be the circumference of the entire city rather than the length of a given side. This attempt to reduce the size of the city forgets that the numbers are symbolic. Farrer notes that a cube has twelve edges, so that when the city is measured 12,000 furlongs along each edge the sum would be 144,000, the sacred number of God's Israel (p. 217). Others understand the 12,000 as symbolizing immensity and perfection. Twelve times the cube of ten stands for the perfect total of God's people (Morris, p. 250). In rabbinic writing the size of the restored Jerusalem is often mentioned. One source says that it will reach the gates of Damascus and will cover as much ground as the whole of Israel. Another source sets its height at twelve miles (cf. Charles, II, p. 164; Swete, p. 289). In the *Sibylline Oracles* (5:247–51) a great ring is to be built around the city, reaching as far as Joppa. The best interpreta-

---

[36]Cf. the golden crowns of 4:4, the golden incense bowls of 5:8, the golden altar of 9:13, etc.

[37]It is not immediately apparent why the Byzantine text omits καὶ τὸ τεῖχος αὐτῆς, especially since the wall is in fact measured in vs. 17.

[38]Like Babylon (Herodotus i.178), Nineveh (Diodorus Siculus i.3), Nicaea (Strabo xii.4.7), and other ancient cities; note that 2329 omits καὶ τὸ ὕψος.

[39]Cf. BAG, τετράγωνος, p. 821.

[40]William Hoste, *The Visions of John the Divine*, p. 178; Lilje, p. 267.

[41]A στάδιον is about 607 English feet; thus the city would be about 1400 miles in each direction.

tion of the measuring of the city is that of Beckwith, who says that the apocalyptist is "struggling to express by symbols the vastness, the perfect symmetry, and the splendor of the new Jerusalem" (p. 760).

17   When the angel measures the wall, it is found to be 144 cubits. It is not clear whether this measurement is to be taken as the height or the thickness of the wall. In either case the wall would be hopelessly out of proportion for a city some fourteen miles high! The significance of the measurement lies in the fact that it is a multiple of twelve and has to do with the people of God in their eternal sanctuary. The Seer notes that the 144 cubits are calculated by the normal measurements of man (a cubit being roughly the length of a man's forearm), and then quickly adds that it makes no difference that the measuring is being carried out by an angel. In either case a cubit is a cubit.[42]

18   The exact meaning of "the building of the wall" is not clear. The word translated "building," when taken in a literal sense, indicates "the act of building into."[43] Because the first of the city's twelve foundations is made of jasper (vs. 19), it would be well to understand this ·earlier reference to jasper as indicating some sort of inlay of precious stone rather than solid jasper as a building material. In either case it is the splendor and worth of the wall that is so graphically reported. But it may be more. In Revelation 4:3 the One upon the throne appears like jasper. Earlier in chapter 21 the holy city aglow with the glory of God emits the radiance of precious jasper (vs. 11). Thus it is called to our attention that even the wall of the city speaks of the glorious presence of God.

The city itself is said to be of pure gold. While no allusion is necessarily required, it may be that in the back of John's mind is the memory of Herod's temple whose golden front reflected the first rays of the morning sun so brilliantly that those who looked upon it had to turn away their eyes from its "fiery splendour" (Josephus, *Bell.* v.5.6). The gold of the heavenly city is like unto pure glass. This is normally taken to mean that it had a transparent quality. The complete absence of any impurity in the gold is comparable to the lack of any trace of opaqueness in rare crystal glass. In verse 21 the gold is compared to transparent glass rather than pure glass. Walvoord writes that "the constant mention of transparency indicates that the city is designed to transmit the glory of God in the form of light without hindrance" (p. 325).

19–20   In verse 14 we learned that the wall of the city had twelve foundations bearing the names of the twelve apostles. The foundations are

---

[42]*TCNT* translates "as men measure, that is as the angel measured."
[43]ἐνδώμησις is from ἐν and δωμάω.

now further described as adorned with precious stones, a different gem for each foundation. It is not clear whether the foundations are to be understood as the segments between the twelve gates (21:12) or as layers built upon each other and extending all around the four sides of the city. The twelve stones correspond generally to the twelve gems set into the breastplate of the high priest.[44]

In a fairly extended discussion Charles suggests that when the stones are placed around a square in the order given in 21:13 (E N S W) and compared with the twelve signs of the zodiac, it will be seen that the order will be the exact reverse of the actual path of the sun through the signs (II, pp. 165–69).[45] He concludes that the author was familiar with current astrological thought, and that by reversing the order he intended to stress that the holy city has nothing to do with ethnic speculations regarding the city of the gods (II, p. 168). Morris says that by this means John expresses the idea that in the end God reverses human judgment (p. 252). Another approach is that of Farrer, who observes that all but three of the stones end with "s" sounds and these three end with "n" and divide the list into four parts. He holds that John did no more than "give a euphonious list in some general correspondence with the Exodus catalogue" (p. 219). The privileges reserved for the high priest alone under the old covenant are now freely given to the entire people of God.

In ancient times, as today, precious stones were desirable for their beauty and scarcity. The various stones mentioned in the Bible are hard to identify with any exactness because of the many different species and colors as well as the lack of a standard terminology. Jasper was a translucent rock crystal green in color. Sapphire was a deep blue stone with spangles of iron pyrite (the modern lapis lazuli). Chalcedony is usually taken as a green silicate of copper found near Chalcedon in Asia Minor. The emerald was another green stone. The sardonyx was a layered stone of red (sard) and white (onyx). It was prized for use in making cameos. The sardius was a blood-red stone and commonly used for engraving. Chrysolite may have been a yellow topaz or golden jasper. The beryl was a green stone, and the

[44]John's list omits four included in the LXX (Ex 28:17-20)—ἄνθραξ, λιγύριον, ἀχάτης, and ὀνύχιον—and includes four additional stones—χαλκηδών, σαρδόνυξ, χρυσόπρασος, and ὑάκινθος. Part of this difference may be accounted for by the uncertainties of translation. The order in the two lists is totally distinct.

[45]The identification of the stones with the signs of the zodiac on Egyptian and Arabian monuments is furnished by Kircher, *Oedipus Aegyptiacus* II.ii.177 ff. Both Philo and Josephus interpret the stones on the high priest's breastplate in this way (*De Monar.* ii.5; *Ant.* iii.7.7). Glasson says that he has been in touch with several Egyptologists and no one is aware of any zodiac/jewel scheme such as Kircher set forth ("The Order of Jewels in Revelation XI. 19-20: A Theory Eliminated," *JTS*, n.s. 26 [1975], pp. 95-100). His own position is that if Rev was written in exile, then the gems and their order would have been based on the Seer's memory (p. 100).

topaz a greenish gold or yellow. The jacinth was bluish-purple and similar to the modern sapphire. The amethyst was a purple quartz, so called because it was regarded as an antidote for drunkenness.[46]

The overall picture is of a city of brilliant gold surrounded by a wall inlaid with jasper and resting upon twelve foundations adorned with precious gems of every color and hue. The city is magnificent beyond description. As the eternal dwelling place of God and his people, it is described in language which continually attempts to break free from its own limitations in order to do justice to the reality it so imperfectly describes.

21 Two descriptive touches remain. First, each of the twelve gates consists of a single pearl. A rabbinic prophecy promises that God will set up in the gateways of Jerusalem gems and pearls thirty cubits by thirty in which he will hollow out openings ten cubits wide and twenty cubits high (*Baba Batra* 75a; *Sanh.* 100a). Along with gold and expensive clothing the pearl was a mark of affluence (I Tim 2:9). Jesus spoke of a pearl so valuable that the merchant sold all he possessed in order to purchase it (Mt 13:45–46). The spectacle of a pearl large enough to serve as a city gate boggles the mind. Secondly, the street (or streets)[47] of the city was made of gold so pure that it seemed to be transparent as glass. Like the priests of the OT (I Kgs 6:30) who ministered in the temple, the servants of God walk upon gold.

22 In the heavenly city there is no temple. At this point John demonstrates his independence from the prophet Ezekiel whose imagery plays a prominent role in the Seer's vision. Ezekiel spent seven chapters describing the restored temple and its ordinances (Ezek 40–46). For John there is no temple because symbol has given way to reality. The temple is replaced by "the Lord God Almighty,[48] and the Lamb." Jesus told the woman at the well that the day would come when worship of God would no longer be geographically circumscribed (Jn 4:21). Paul later declared that the believing congregation was in fact the temple of the living God (II Cor 6:16). The final state toward which this points is eternity itself, where the presence of God the Father and the Lamb permeates and sanctifies all that the heavenly Jerusalem symbolizes. It is unimportant that in 7:15 it was said that the tribulation martyrs serve God day and night "within the temple." The purpose of the statement is not to describe the architecture of

---

[46]From ἀ-μεθύω. For further material on all these stones see Marshall's article in *NBD*, pp. 631–34; also Una Jart, "The Precious Stones in the Revelation of St. John xxi.18–21," *Studia Theologica*, 24 (1970), pp. 150–81.

[47]πλατεῖα is an adjective and understands ὁδός. It probably refers to the one broad street characteristic of Oriental cities. Since the entire city was pure gold (21:18), all the streets would be of gold. There is no necessity of taking the singular, πλατεῖα, as generic.

[48]This title is used liturgically in 4:8 by the living creatures, in 11:17 by the twenty-four elders, in 15:3 by the martyrs, in 16:7 by the altar, and in 19:6 by the great multitude.

heaven but to speak meaningfully to a people for whom the temple was supremely the place of God's presence.

23 The heavenly city has no need of sun or moon to shine because it is illuminated by the glory of God. Isaiah had pictured the glorious restoration of Jerusalem in much the same terms (Isa 60:19–20). John is not supplying his readers with information about future astrological changes but setting forth by means of accepted apocalyptic imagery the splendor which will radiate from the presence of God and the Lamb. In his gospel John used language in much the same way. He called Jesus the "true light which enlightens every man" (Jn 1:9) and the "light of the world" (Jn 8:12; cf. 3:19; 12:35). The metaphor is not uncommon in apocalyptic language (II Esdr 7:39–42).

24 The nations are said to walk by the light of God's glory, and the kings of the earth bring their glory into the city. Isaiah 60 serves as a model. The glory of the Lord is seen upon Jerusalem, and nations and kings are attracted to its brightness (Isa 60:1–3). The wealth of the nations comes back to Zion as her sons and daughters return from afar (Isa 60:4–5; also vss. 6, 9, 11, 13, 17).

The problem raised by verses 24–26 (along with 22:2 and 22:15) is the presence of Gentiles outside the heavenly Jerusalem following the final judgment, the overthrow of evil, and the restoration of a new heaven and earth. Just who are these referred to in such a manner?

Beckwith notes that many critics (*eg.*, Vischer, Pfleiderer, J. Weiss, and others) regard the paragraph 21:9–22:5 as a slightly changed Jewish document which retains mention of the heathen who remain on earth as the subjects of God's people in the messianic kingdom (p. 769; also pp. 51 ff). He argues against the position, noting that a borrower who needed to make at least eight additions to give it a Christian tone would hardly have failed to remove the reference to the heathen. A second solution is to interpret the nations as redeemed peoples. Lenski calls them the glorified saints mentioned in 5:9 and 7:9 (p. 644), and Kiddle says that they are the redeemed who belong spiritually but not racially to the twelve tribes (p. 439).[49] But in our metaphor the redeemed live *within* the city.

Barclay is representative of another point of view which sees in these verses a picture of universal salvation (II, pp. 276–78). After gathering together a goodly list of prophetic promises that all nations shall come to God, he concludes that John was "foretelling the consummation of a hope which was always in the hearts of the greatest of his countrymen" (p. 279). Caird agrees. God is not content to save a few martyrs and let the rest

---

[49]Walvoord finds here references to a body of saved Gentiles distinct from the church (p. 327). Note that the *AV* (following TR) has without any substantial support (variants are not even suggested in Kilpatrick, Nestle, or UBS) added "of them which are saved" after "nations."

of mankind perish along with all of human culture. He writes, "Nowhere in the New Testament do we find a more eloquent statement than this of the all-embracing scope of Christ's redemptive work" (p. 280).[50] This interpretation, while possessing a great deal of rhetorical persuasiveness, reads far too much theology into incidental references which are more easily explained in another way. Beckwith is undoubtedly right in saying that John has taken over verbally from the prophets language and figures of speech which presuppose the continuance of Gentile peoples on the earth after the establishment of the eschatological era (pp. 769–70). Glasson puts it this way, "The prophets were thinking mainly of a future under the historical conditions of our present life. John makes use of their sublime visions, lifting them on to the eternal plane; and at times he retains words not entirely appropriate to this new setting" (p. 120). This is certainly the answer to the presence of nations "outside the new Jerusalem" throughout eternity. The imagery of the Apocalypse must of necessity be concrete and spatial, but its significance is inevitably spiritual.

25–26 The gates of the New Jerusalem stand open because with the demise of evil security measures are no longer necessary. John's parenthetical remark about the absence of night explains why only day is mentioned in the preceding clause. Day extends indefinitely without interruption because darkness never comes. Thus there is no need of closing gates. One is reminded of the Isaianic declaration concerning the restored Jerusalem, "Your gates shall be open continually" (Isa 60:11). Through these open gates the kings of the earth bring the glory and honor of the nations. The reference is to the choicest of earthly treasures. Once again we are to think of the imagery, not in a literal sense, but in its symbolic significance.

27 Those who enter the city are not the wicked and defiant but those whose names have been written in the Lamb's book of life. In the imagery of this paragraph the people with free access to the city are one with those who dwell within it. The earlier prophetic reference to Gentiles has in John's reinterpretation been redirected to refer to the entire body of the people of God. The sanctity of God's city was proclaimed by the prophets (Isa 52:1; Ezek 44:9) and echoed by the writers of the NT (I Cor 6:9–10; II Pet 3:13).[51]

---

[50]Rist holds that both in Jewish messianism and apocalypticism it was often held that in time Gentiles would convert to Judaism. There existed, however, an opposing concept more characteristic of apocalyptic literature, that the wicked would be punished forever. Rist accounts for this "glaring inconsistency" by conjecturing that John, in using Isa 60:3, 11, "failed to modify them to suit his own severe and unrelenting views concerning the fate of the nations" (pp. 539–40).

[51]For the Lamb's book of life, see comm. at 13:8. Note also Ex 32:32–33; Ps 69:28; Dan 12:1; Phil 4:3.

CHAPTER 22

The description of the New Jerusalem which began at 21:9 continues on through the fifth verse of chapter 22. Throughout this section John employs the imagery of a magnificent city to describe the people of God in the glorious and eternal age to come.

1 The angel shows John a sparkling river which flows crystal clear from the heavenly throne. The background seems to be Ezekiel's vision of the sacred river (47:1–12) which flowed from under the threshold of the temple eastward past the altar and ultimately into the Dead Sea where it healed the water of its saltiness so that many fish could again live in it.[1] Elsewhere in Revelation we read of "fountains of waters of life" (7:17; cf. 21:6 and 22:17) as a significant part of the blessings of the eternal state. Some writers find in the imagery of flowing water a reference to the Holy Spirit (Swete, p. 298). Others find the promise of immortality (Ladd, p. 286) or a reference to the abundant life which God now gives to his people (Barclay, II, p. 283). Obviously, all this is true, but the central affirmation of the verse is that in the eternal state the faithful will live at the source of the life-giving stream which proceeds from the very presence of God. In the hot and arid climate of Palestine this figure would hold special appeal.

"Bright as crystal" describes the river as a sparkling rush of pure water. Its source is the throne of God and of the Lamb. In 7:15 and 12:5 we read only of the throne of God. This place of honor is now shared with the Lamb, whose sacrificial death has made him worthy of heavenly praise (cf. 5:9–15).

2 The crystal river is bordered on either side by the tree of life, which bears fruit continually throughout the year and whose leaves bring healing to the nations. The exact placement of river, street, and trees is less

---

[1]Cf. Zech 14:8 for somewhat the same idea; also Joel 3:18 where a fountain in the house of Jehovah is to water the valley of Shittim.

than clear. If the initial phrase ("in the midst of the street thereof") goes with the preceding verse, then the river would flow down the center of a wide avenue.[2] If it is taken with what follows, then the street and river probably run side by side, with the trees in between. Other possibilities have been suggested,[3] but the specific geographical layout is of no particular importance in understanding the symbolism of the verse.

The imagery has a double source. In the early chapters of Genesis we read that if Adam had eaten of the tree of life he would have received immortality (Gen 2:9; 3:22).[4] In Ezekiel there is the picture of healing water flowing from the temple to form a river along whose banks are trees which each month bring forth new fruit and whose leaves are for healing (Ezek 47:12). The tree of life was a regular feature in Jewish portrayals of Paradise (cf. II Esdr 8:52; *II Enoch* 8:3–4). To eat of its fruit would be to live forever. In John's vision the tree "produced twelve kinds of fruit, yielding a fresh crop month by month" (Weymouth). Both the abundance and variety of fruit are being emphasized. God's provision is ever new and always more than adequate.

Not only does the tree provide fruit to be eaten, but its leaves are therapeutic and bring about healing. But why would healing be required in the eternal city? Although John speaks of "the healing of the nations," we are not to infer that nations will continue to exist outside the New Jerusalem. As in 21:24 ff, imagery borrowed from the present state of affairs is carried over into the description of the eternal state. The glory of the age to come is necessarily portrayed by means of imagery belonging to the present age. The healing leaves indicate the complete absence of physical and spiritual want. The life to come will be a life of abundance and perfection.

3–4 Perhaps the greatest of all eternity's blessings is reflected in the one phrase, "and they shall see his face." Moses, the great lawgiver of the old dispensation, was not allowed to see the face of God because God had declared, "Man shall not see me and live" (Ex 33:20; cf. 33:23 where Moses is allowed to see only the back of God). In the ancient world criminals were banished from the presence of the king and not allowed to

---

[2]*ASV, RSV, NEB* ("down the middle of the city's street"). The TR separates vss. 1 and 2 with a full stop after 'Αρνίου.

[3]Cf. Caird, p. 280; Walvoord, pp. 329–30; Lenski, p. 650; Beasley-Murray mentions (without necessarily approving) a tree in the middle of the street situated at a point where the river diverged into two branches (p. 331).

[4]Most commentators mention that apocalyptic thought tends to unite the end of history with its beginning. Rist observes that we are not surprised to find predictions of a reconstituted Garden of Eden in apocalyptic speculation: "Apocalypticism in positing a new age frequently taught that it would reproduce the newly created beginnings of the first" (p. 541).

look upon his face (Esth 7:8; cf. II Sam 14:24). Jesus taught that only the pure in heart shall see God (Mt 5:8), and John in his first epistle speaks of the great transformation to take place at the return of Christ when "we shall be like him, for we shall see him as he is" (I Jn 3:2).

On the foreheads of God's servants will be stamped the name of God.[5] His name stands for his character. The faces of those who have experienced the beatific vision will reflect the unmistakable likeness of their heavenly Father. The process of transformation now under way in the life of the believer (II Cor 3:18) will be brought to completion when the church enters its ultimate and ideal state. As the followers of the beast bore his mark upon their foreheads (Rev 13:16), so will the faithful bear the name of God upon theirs (cf. Rev 3:12). The metaphor stresses ownership and likeness.

5 The disappearance of night and the lack of any need for the light of the sun is modeled on Isaiah's description of that time in Zion's future when the light of the sun and the moon is to be replaced by the everlasting light of the glory of God (Isa 60:19–20; cf. Rev 21:23). As Zechariah prophesied, the age to come will not be divided between day and night but will be one continuous day (Zech 14:7). In the New Jerusalem God is ever present, and his glory makes unnecessary all other sources of light. Charles takes the clause "God shall give them light" as a Hebraism which would be rendered, "The Lord God shall cause His face to shine upon them" (II, p. 211). The face which the saints behold (vs. 4) will shine upon them in eternal benediction (vs. 5). In contrast to the martyrs of 20:4, 6, inhabitants of the New Jerusalem are to reign for ever and ever (cf. Dan 7:18, 27 and Rev 5:10).

XI. EPILOGUE (22:6–21)

6 *And he said unto me, These words are faithful and true: and the Lord, the God of the spirits of the prophets, sent his angel to show unto his servants the things which must shortly come to pass.*

7 *And behold, I come quickly. Blessed is he that keepeth the words of the prophecy of this book.*

8 *And I John am he that heard and saw these things. And when I heard and*

---

[5]Some have suggested as a background for the metaphor Ex 28:36–38, which says that Aaron wore upon his forehead a golden plate inscribed with the phrase "HOLY TO JEHOVAH." In this case the thrust of the metaphor would be "entire consecration to the service of God" (Swete, p. 301).

saw, I fell down to worship before the feet of the angel that showed me these things.

9 *And he saith unto me, See thou do it not: I am a fellow-servant with thee and with thy brethren the prophets, and with them that keep the words of this book: worship God.*

10 *And he saith unto me, Seal not up the words of the prophecy of this book; for the time is at hand.*

11 *He that is unrighteous, let him do unrighteousness still: and he that is filthy, let him be made filthy still: and he that is righteous, let him do righteousness still: and he that is holy, let him be made holy still.*

12 *Behold, I come quickly; and my reward is with me, to render to each man according as his work is.*

13 *I am the Alpha and the Omega, the first and the last, the beginning and the end.*

14 *Blessed are they that wash their robes, that they may have the right to come to the tree of life, and may enter in by the gates into the city.*

15 *Without are the dogs, and the sorcerers, and the fornicators, and the murderers, and the idolaters, and every one that loveth and maketh a lie.*

16 *I Jesus have sent mine angel to testify unto you these things for the churches. I am the root and the offspring of David, the bright, the morning star.*

17 *And the Spirit and the bride say, Come. And he that heareth, let him say, Come. And he that is athirst, let him come: he that will, let him take the water of life freely.*

18 *I testify unto every man that heareth the words of the prophecy of this book, If any man shall add unto them, God shall add unto him the plagues which are written in this book:*

19 *and if any man shall take away from the words of the book of this prophecy, God shall take away his part from the tree of life, and out of the holy city, which are written in this book.*

20 *He who testifieth these things saith, Yea: I come quickly. Amen: come, Lord Jesus.*

21 *The grace of the Lord Jesus be with the saints. Amen.*

6 Verses 6–21 of chapter 22 form the Epilogue of the book of Revelation. This section consists of a number of rather loosely related utterances which are difficult to assign with any certainty to specific speakers. Kiddle appropriately notes that the difficulty of identifying speakers is only superficial because ultimately we hear the voice of Christ, whether echoed by the angel or recorded by the prophet (p. 447). It is unnecessary to account for the disjointed nature of the Epilogue by conjecturing that John left only a rough draft that needed additional rewriting and a final edit. The material itself has determined the form it has taken. Although falling into a number of short sections, it sets forth but two major themes: the authenticity of the book as a divine revelation, and the imminence of the end.

The similarities between the Prologue and Epilogue of Revelation have often been noted. The book is a genuine prophecy (1:3; 22:6, 9–10, 18–19) by a duly commissioned prophet (1:1, 9–10; 22:8–10) to be read in the churches (1:3, 11; 22:18) for the encouragement of the faithful (1:3; 22:7, 12, 14). These and other similarities support the view that the Prologue may have been the last part of the book to be written and thus reflects the influence of the Epilogue.[6]

The speaker is apparently the angel of the preceding paragraph who showed to John the eternal city with its crystal river and life-giving tree. He now attests the genuineness of the entire revelation. The words which relate the visions of things to come are faithful and true. They are worthy of belief because they correspond to reality.

As in the Prologue, it is an angelic intermediary who is sent to show to God's servants "the things which must shortly come to pass" (cf. Rev 1:1). It is through the servant John that the message then goes out to the members of the churches—the servants of 22:6 (cf. vs. 16). The source of the revelation is the Lord, who is further described as "the God of the spirits of the prophets." The plural ("spirits") would indicate that the reference is not to the Holy Spirit. The spirits of the prophets are the "natural faculties of the prophets, raised and quickened by the Holy Spirit" (Swete, p. 303). It is unnecessary to decide between OT or NT prophets because in either case the same prophetic function is being carried out. All true prophecy originates with God and comes through men moved by the Holy Spirit (II Pet 1:21).

The nearness of the consummation, as reflected by the clause "which must shortly come to pass," is not a problem peculiar to Revelation. Paul, as well, writes that the time is short and that men should adjust their manner of life accordingly (I Cor 7:29–31). In one of his earliest letters the apostle includes himself with those who are to be alive when Jesus returns (I Thess 4:15). One way to solve the problem of this as-yet-unfulfilled expectation is to hold that God is more concerned with the fulfillment of his redemptive purposes than he is with satisfying our ideas of appropriate timing. All the issues which find their complete fulfillment in that point in time yet future when history will verge into eternity, are also being fulfilled in the ever advancing present. The end and the beginning are but two perspectives on the same great adventure. The final overthrow of evil was determined from the beginning and has been in force

[6]See Beckwith, pp. 771–72, for a further development of this point of view.

ever since the defeat of Satan by the sacrificial death of Christ and his triumphal resurrection.

7 The words "Behold, I come quickly" are those of the risen Lord.[7] The coming of Christ is to be "without delay" or "in a short time."[8] It is best to take the utterance at face value and accept the difficulty of a foreshortened perspective on the time of the end rather than to reinterpret it in the sense that Jesus "comes" in the crises of life and especially at the death of every man. Revelation has enough riddles without our adding more. Matthew 24:42-44 counsels every generation to be on the alert for the return of the Son of man. An infallible timetable would do away with that attitude of urgent expectation which has been the hallmark of the church through the centuries.

We come now to the next to the last of the seven beatitudes in the Apocalypse (1:3; 13:13; etc.). It is pronounced upon those who stand fast in the great persecution about to break upon the church. They are those who keep the prophetic injunctions of the book. Note again the insistence of the author that his visions of the end constitute genuine prophecy. Under the impulse of the Holy Spirit he has faithfully recorded what God has revealed concerning the end of all things.

8 John now attests that he has actually heard and seen all the things which are recorded in the book. His literary product is not the result of any flight of imagination. Then, curiously—since in Revelation 19:10 he was corrected by the angel for the same ill-advised act—he falls before the angel to worship him for his role as revealer and interpreter.[9] It is the vision of the New Jerusalem which is primarily in view, although the response of the Seer comes as the culmination of the entire series of revelations.

9 John is stopped from carrying out his intention when the angel explains that he himself is a fellow servant with John, the other prophets, and those who keep the words of the book.[10] Charles cites a number of passages to show that the worship of angels, although prohibited, did exist among the Jews before the Christian era (II, pp. 224-25). This tendency seems to have made some inroads into the Christian community (cf. Col

---

[7] καί requires some continuity with what precedes, in this case an angelic announcement. Perhaps the words of Christ come through the mouth of the angel. The *RSV* connects 7a with 6 and then opens a new paragraph.

[8] ταχύ used as an adverb may mean "quickly" in the sense of "at a rapid rate," although this usage does not fit the context of the five occurrences of ἔρχομαι ταχύ in Rev (2:16; 3:11; 22:7, 12, 20). Cf. BAG, pp. 814-15.

[9] Cf. the response of Cornelius to Peter, the messenger of God in Acts 10:25-26.

[10] 1 2059s *al* omit καί after προφητῶν, which further identifies the prophets as those who obey the revelation. 2020 *pc* vg^(s,cl) Prim add προφητείας after λόγους.

2:18; Justin Martyr, *Apol.* 1:6), although it was strongly resisted. Since angels are fellow servants with the redeemed, they may be esteemed for their contribution but are not in any way to be worshipped. This honor is reserved for God alone.

10 The speaker in verses 10 and 11 is probably the angel, but it matters little because behind all the instruction and admonition of the Epilogue lies the will of the risen Christ.

In the first chapter of Daniel the prophet is told to "shut up the words, and seal the book, until the time of the end" (Dan 12:4). Considerable time is to elapse before the fulfillment of all that Daniel has predicted.[11] Not so in the Apocalypse. The crisis is imminent and John is *not* to seal up the prophecy of the book. Since "the time is at hand," the message of judgment and hope is to be proclaimed among the churches. This raises once again the problem of a postponed consummation. In view of the fact that nearly two millennia have passed since the announcement that the time was at hand, some have concluded that John was simply wrong in his eschatological expectation. Writers with a higher view of the reliability of Scripture usually take the phrase in a less than literal way. Bruce writes that the end is always near in the sense that each successive Christian generation may be the last.[12] For Walvoord it is the return of Christ at the rapture which makes the end always impending during the church age (p. 334). One of the more helpful suggestions is made by Ladd, who holds that the Apocalypse has a twofold perspective: it is primarily concerned with the struggle between Christ and Antichrist which comes to a climax at the end of the age, but this struggle also existed between church and state in the first century and has surfaced in history whenever the state has made totalitarian demands (pp. 291–92). Thus the time has always been at hand. The tension of imminence is endemic to that span of redemptive history lying between the cross and the parousia.

11 From the perspective of the Seer the end is so close that there is no longer time to alter the character and habits of men. Those who are unrighteous will continue in unrighteousness and those who are morally unclean[13] will continue in their ways. Hendriksen refers to the "let of withdrawal" rather than the "let of positive exhortation" (pp. 251–52), but this nomenclature could hardly be applied to the two remaining clauses, which use the same imperative with reference to the righteous and the holy. The major thrust of the verse is that since the end time is now at hand men

---

[11]Cf. *I Enoch* 1:2 in which the knowledge revealed by God was not for his generation but "for a remote one which is to come"; also *II Enoch* 33:9–11.

[12]"In the Christian doctrine of the Last Things, however, the imminence of the end is moral rather than chronological" (F. F. Bruce, p. 665).

[13]ῥυπαρός literally means "filthy," but is used here in the sense of morally defiled.

are certain to reap the consequences of the kinds of lives they have led. The time arrives when change is impossible because character has already been determined by a lifetime of habitual action. The arrival of the end forecloses any possibility of alteration. "The deliberate choice of each man has fixed his unalterable fate" (Erdman, p. 178).

12 Christ announces that he is coming without delay and brings with him a reward which each man is to receive according to his work. The distribution of rewards on the basis of works is taught throughout Scripture. Jeremiah 17:10 is representative: "I the Lord search the mind and try the heart, to give to every man according to his ways, according to the fruit of his doings." Paul teaches that God "will render to every man according to his works" (Rom 2:6), and Peter declares that God "judges each one impartially according to his deeds" (I Pet 1:17).[14] The reward will be spiritual blessedness to the righteous but judgment for those who are evil. It is the quality of a man's life which provides the ultimate indication of what he really believes.

13 In 1:8 and 21:6 it was God who identified himself as the Alpha and the Omega. The risen Christ now applies the title to himself. Its meaning is essentially the same as that of the two following designations—"the first and the last, the beginning and the end"—the first of which Christ has already applied to himself in 1:17 and 2:8. The names set him apart from the entire created order. He is unlimited in any temporal sense, and in that all things are found both in the Father and in the Son the attributes of the former belong to the latter as well. Charles notes that the last of the three phrases is an abbreviated form of an ancient Orphic saying first recorded in Plato (*Leg.* iv.7) and well known in the first-century Palestinian world (II, p. 220).

14 A blessing is pronounced upon those who wash their robes, that is, those who remain undefiled by their steadfast refusal to comply with the demands of the beast. In 7:14 the great multitude around the heavenly throne clothed in white robes are "they who have come out of the great tribulation: they have washed their robes and made them white in the blood of the Lamb." It is instructive to note that in Revelation 7:14 the verb "washed" is aorist, denoting an action belonging to a specific point in time, while in the verse under consideration the participle "they that wash" is present tense, suggesting continual action.[15] One is reminded of Jesus' injunction to Peter, "He who has bathed does not need to wash,

---

[14]Cf. also Prov 24:12; Isa 59:18; II Cor 11:15; II Tim 4:14; Rev 2:23; 18:6; 20:13.

[15]ἔπλυναν, 7:14; οἱ πλύνοντες, 22:14. **046** 1 82 1611 2059s 2329 *pl g* sy bo Tert Cypr TR read ποιοῦντες τὰς ἐντολὰς αὐτοῦ, an understandable variant but undoubtedly a scribal emendation (Metzger, *TCGNT*, pp. 767–68). The author uses τηρεῖν with ἐντολή in its two occurrences, 12:17; 14:12.

except for his feet" (Jn 13:10). Caird writes that "those who wash their robes" are "those who face martyrdom in the confidence that the Cross is the sign of God's victory over evil without and evil within" (p. 285).

Those with white robes are blessed in that they have the right to come to the tree of life. Eternal life is the reward of faithfulness in the face of tribulation. To "enter by the gates into the city" is another way of portraying the same condition of eternal blessedness. The city represents the eternal dwelling place of God and redeemed humanity; the tree of life is a symbol of immortality.

15 The text now describes those who have no right to the tree of life and may not enter the heavenly Jerusalem. Five of the six designations are also found in the slightly longer list in 21:8 of those whose lot is the lake which burns with fire and brimstone.[16] The verse does not intend to teach that in the eternal state all manner of wicked men will be living just outside[17] the heavenly city. It simply describes the future with the imagery of the present. The contrast is between the blessedness of the faithful and the fate of the wicked.

John describes six (or perhaps seven, depending upon how one views the two kinds of liars) types of evildoers who are excluded from the city. The term "dog" is used in Scripture for various kinds of impure and malicious persons. In Deuteronomy 23:17–18 the term designates a male cult prostitute.[18] In the Jewish culture of first-century Palestine it was used in reference to the heathen (Mt 15:22 ff), and in Philippians 3:2 Paul turns the tables and applies it to the Judaizers. Sorcerers, fornicators, murderers, idolaters, and all liars are to be excluded along with the dogs. To love and do lies is to be totally devoid of truthfulness. These have become like their leader, Satan, "the deceiver of the whole world" (Rev 12:9; also 13:13–15; 16:14).

16 The angel who has guided John through the various visions of the book is now authenticated by Jesus himself. It is to the angel of Christ[19] that the revelation has been delegated. The plural "you" indicates that it was intended for others besides John. It stresses that the revelation is not a private affair but for the entire church.

Jesus identifies himself as "the root and the offspring of David." He is the fulfillment of the Isaianic promise that the Messiah shall come

---

[16]Cf. the kinds of people who will not inherit the kingdom of God according to I Cor 6:9–10, and the shorter, more general list in Rev 21:27 of those to be excluded.

[17]Moffatt supplies an imperative and translates, "Begone, you dogs..." (Kiddle, p. 453).

[18]Charles says that according to an inscription in the temple of Astarte at Larnaka "dog" was the technical term for a קָדֵשׁ or male prostitute (II, p. 178).

[19]In 1:1 the revelation is διὰ τοῦ ἀγγέλου αὐτοῦ, and in 22:16 Jesus calls the angel τὸν ἄγγελόν μου.

forth as "a shoot from the stump of Jesse" (Isa 11:1, 10; cf. Rom 1:3). In the throne-room vision of Revelation 5 he was "the Lion of the tribe of Judah, the Root of David" (vs. 5). Jesus also calls himself "the bright and morning star." In the fourth oracle of Balaam the prophet declares that "a star shall come forth out of Jacob" (Num 24:17). While the immediate reference is to David, in the passage under consideration it is transferred to David's greater son. Bruce writes that "in the Qumran texts Num 24:17 is a recurring *testimonium* of the messianic warrior of the endtime" (p. 666). The star was a familar symbol in Jewish writings for the expected Davidic king (*Test. Levi* 18:3; *Test. Judah* 24:1). The morning star is a promise that the long night of tribulation is all but over and that the new eschatological day is about to dawn.

17 Verse 17 consists of four invitations. It is possible to take the first two as requests directed to Christ for his return and the second two as invitations to the world to come and take of the water of life. It is more likely, as Ladd indicates, that the first half of the verse should be interpreted by the second, and the entire invitation as addressed to the world (p. 294). The Spirit is the Holy Spirit,[20] and the bride is the church (21:2, 9). It is the testimony of the church empowered by the Holy Spirit that constitutes the great evangelizing force of this age.

Those who hear and accept repeat the invitation to others who thirst for the water of life. Whoever will may take of this life-giving water without charge. Isaiah had issued a similar call—"Ho, everyone who thirsts, come to the waters . . . come, buy wine and milk without money and without price" (Isa 55:1; cf. Jn 7:37). The threefold use of the present imperative ("come/let him come") serves to extend the invitation until that very moment when history will pass irrevocably into eternity and any further opportunity for decision will be past.

18–19 The book draws to a close with a severe warning against adding to or taking away from its prophetic message. It is addressed not to future scribes who might be tempted to tamper with the text (nor to textual critics who must decide between shorter and longer variants!) but to "every man that heareth," that is, to members of the seven churches of Asia where the book was to be read aloud. The warning is against willful distortion of the message. It is not unlike Paul's stern words in Galatians 1:6, 7 to those who would pervert the gospel.

Warnings of this nature were not uncommon. In Deuteronomy 4:2 Moses tells the Israelites, "You shall not add to the word which I com-

---

[20]Kiddle, however, takes the spirit as a collective reference to the prophets, personifying the gift which distinguishes them from their fellows (p. 456).

mand you, nor take from it." When the translation of the Septuagint was completed, it was ordered that they "pronounce a curse in accordance with their custom upon anyone who should make any alteration either by adding or changing in any way whatever any of the words which had been written or making any omission" (*Letter of Aristeas* 310–11).[21] Moffatt notes that the warning is a "stereotyped and vehement form of claiming a canonicity equal to that of the O.T." (p. 492). The solemnity of the injunction suggests that the speaker is Christ himself.

Note again that the book is considered a prophecy. Apocalyptic imagery is pressed into the service of NT prophecy. Charles takes 18b–19 as a later interpolation on the basis that (1) the passage presupposes a considerable lapse of time before the second advent, (2) the style is not John's, and (3) the penalty is temporal rather than eternal (II, pp. 222–23). None of these arguments is convincing. The message could easily have been altered (in theory) by the first person to hear the book. It is best to take the passage in a straightforward manner as a severe warning to the hearers not to distort the basic message revealed through John. To lose one's part in the tree of life and the holy city is an awesome punishment. Commentators who hold that this verse does not teach that a man can lose his salvation interpret it to mean that it is a very serious matter indeed to tamper with the word of God (cf. Ladd, pp. 295–96; Walvoord, p. 338).

20 The verse opens with the testimony of Christ that his coming will be without delay,[22] and closes with the Seer's response which echoes the church's longing for that great day. "Come, Lord Jesus" is the equivalent of the transliterated Aramaic in I Corinthians 16:22, *maranatha*.[23] At the very close of the book is the confession that the answers to the problems of life do not lie in man's ability to create a better world but in the return of the One whose sovereign power controls the course of human affairs. "Christianity is not a faith which bids us look for a gradual upward march of man till he reaches an ideal state of civilisation" (Preston and Hanson, p. 145). Redemptive history remains incomplete until Christ returns. It is for the final act in the great drama of redemption that the church awaits with longing.

21 For an apocalypse to end with a benediction is unusual. Its presence may be accounted for by the fact that since it began as an epistle

---

[21]Cf. *I Enoch* 104:10; Eusebius, *Hist. Eccl.* v.20.2.

[22]Only in Mt 28:8 does ταχύ mean "quickly" in the sense of "at a rapid rate" (and even there it may indicate that the departure was immediate rather than calling attention to the rate). Elsewhere it means "at once" or "in a short time" (Mk 5:25; Lk 15:22; and the five Rev passages in which it is used of the coming of Christ: 2:16; 3:11; 22:7, 12, 20).

[23]Cf. *Didache* 10:6, μαϱὰν ἀθά.

(1:4 ff), it would be appropriate to close with a benediction (cf. I Cor 16:23; Eph 6:24; etc.). The benediction is pronounced upon all who have listened to the book as it was read aloud in the churches of Asia. The final "Amen" (*AV, ASV, RSV*) is probably a scribal addition (in view of the weakness of manuscript evidence supporting its inclusion).[24]

---

[24]It is found in ℵ **046** 82 1611 2329 *pl* vg sy sa TR. It is omitted in the text of the UBS as well as the 25th ed. of the Nestle-Aland text. See Metzger, *TCGNT*, pp. 768-69, for this and two additional textual problems in the final verse of Rev. Metzger rejects the addition of Χριστοῦ after Ἰησοῦ and reads the shorter μετὰ πάντων rather than any of the other six alternatives listed.

(1:4 ff), it would be appropriate to close with a benediction (cf. I Cor 16:23; Eph 6:24; etc.). The benediction is pronounced upon all who have listened to the book as it was read aloud in the churches of Asia. The final "Amen" (*AV, ASV, RSV*) is probably a scribal addition (in view of the weakness of manuscript evidence supporting its inclusion).[24]

[24]It is found in ℵ **046** 82 1611 2329 *pl* vg sy sa TR. It is omitted in the text of the UBS as well as the 25th ed. of the Nestle-Aland text. See Metzger, *TCGNT*, pp. 768–69, for this and two additional textual problems in the final verse of Rev. Metzger rejects the addition of Χριστοῦ after ᾽Ιησοῦ and reads the shorter μετὰ πάντων rather than any of the other six alternatives listed.

INDEX OF SUBJECTS

INDEX OF AUTHORS

INDEX OF SCRIPTURE REFERENCES

419

INDEX OF EXTRABIBLICAL LITERATURE